CRITICAL SURVEY
OF
SHORT FICTION

CRITICAL SURVEY
OF
SHORT FICTION

Essays
407–817

2

Edited by
FRANK N. MAGILL

Academic Director
WALTON BEACHAM

SALEM PRESS
Englewood Cliffs, N. J.

LIBRARY OF CONGRESS CATALOG CARD NUMBER: 81-51697

Complete Set: ISBN 0-89356-210-7
Volume 2:   ISBN 0-89356-212-2

PRINTED IN THE UNITED STATES OF AMERICA

LIST OF ESSAYS IN VOLUME 2

CRITICAL SURVEY
OF
SHORT FICTION

THE ARABIAN NIGHTS' ENTERTAINMENTS

Alf Layla Wa Layla, "the book of a thousand nights and a night," often called *The Arabian Nights' Entertainments*, is a collection of some 260 stories set in the famous frame tale of Shahrazad (commonly Scheherazade. All proper names in the work are variously transliterated.) Since these stories were collected while they remained current in a continuing tradition of professional storytelling, the book exists in several forms. Only about half the stories associated with *The Arabian Nights' Entertainments* are found in all its versions, and even particular tales are extant in substantially different forms. The textual history is thus extremely complicated. Although manuscripts, particularly partial ones, abound, complete editions of the work were printed only in the nineteenth century, long after the tales became popular in Europe. These rely primarily on the so-called "Egyptian Recension," an eighteenth century compilation. William Macnaghten's Second Calcutta Edition (1839-1842) is, for the present, the standard edition.

The collection reached essentially its present shape by about 1500, but there are several phases in its evolution. The names in the frame story are Persian, and the tenth century historian el Mesoudi discusses a lost Persian collection, *Hazar Afsanah*, framed by the Shahrazad story and translated into Arabic probably during the ninth century. This is the first distinct stratum. Many of the oldest stories—most of those told in the first forty-five nights, and such others as "The Ebony Horse" and "The Queen of the Serpents"—are also Persian in origin, although they have been more or less extensively adjusted to Arabic manners and settings. In this stratum, however, there are traces of remote Indian origins; for example, the device of having characters make a point by telling stories, which appears in the frame, in the group called "The Malice of Women," and elsewhere. For that matter, the beast fables generally used in these instances also come from India.

The second stratum originates in Baghdad during the tenth through twelfth centuries, at the height of the Abbasid period (750-1258). Many historical and legendary tales enter at this point, most notably those involving Harun al-Rashid, the greatest caliph of this golden age of Islam. The third stratum is Egyptian, from the Mameluke period (1250-1517) in Cairo. These are largely tales of city life which take their place in the work between the thirteenth and fifteenth centuries.

The range of *The Arabian Nights' Entertainments* is considerable. It includes "The History of King Omar," a vast romance of nearly four hundred pages, almost an eighth of the whole book, as well as several sets of related tales that were originally independent collections; for example, the twenty-seven stories of "The Malice of Women," the eighteen of "King Jelyaad of Hind and His Vizier," and, of course, the seven voyages of Sindbad. At the other extreme, however, are many tales only a page or two long, and in between

there are love stories, moral fables, fairy tales, saints' lives, historical anecdotes, satirical sketches, realistic depictions of daily life, and picaresque tales
of rogues and opportunists (such as "Aladdin"). The air is thick with supernatural beings—jinns, marids, ifrits—and people of every station have access
to an armory of herbs, potions, and instruments of magic, yet all is circum-
scribed by the trenchant monotheism of Islam. Similarly, the teeming local
color of *The Arabian Nights' Entertainments*, represented not only by exotic
creatures real and imagined, but also by the human denizens of metropolitan
Cairo and Baghdad, is shaped by the elegant formal inventiveness of the
narrative. One of the glories of the work is the faith it projects in unities that
dwarf all diversity: the formal control of prodigal narrative impulses and the
complicity of all conflicting powers in one Power and of all conflicting wills
in the one will of Allah.

The only piece of Arabic literature generally known in the West, much
more familiar here than the Koran itself, *The Arabian Nights' Entertainments*
is paradoxically considered subliterary in the Arab world. Classical Arabic
literature is formal, courtly, and complex, while these tales have the humblest
of origins in the motifs and stories of the *rawis*, the professional storytellers
still a part of Muslim society from West Africa to Pakistan. The style of the
tales is often extempore, marked by the rhetorical devices of the oral performer (including improvised effusions in verse), and the language is for the
most part a colloquial, chiefly Egyptian, Arabic.

The Arabian Nights' Entertainments became part of Western literature when
from 1704 to 1717 Antoine Galland published the twelve volumes of what
Burton called his "brilliant paraphrase," *Les mille et une nuit: contes Arabes.*
Galland presented a popular version of tales he had virtually stumbled upon.
He excised sexuality, violence, and historical anecdote to suit European tastes;
since he lacked an ending for the frame story, he invented one. In the Age
of Reason, however, his tales captured the imagination of Europe, and soon
the demand was so great that when Galland produced translations too slowly
his publisher filled out volumes with completely unrelated tales to get them
into print. The vogue for "Oriental" and "Turkish" romances continued into
the nineteenth century, producing such masterpieces as Voltaire's *Zadig*
(1747), Samuel Johnson's *Rasselas* (1759), and William Beckford's *Vathek*
(1782), as well as a great deal of woefully inferior material. The impact of
Galland's book is still apparent in the Orientalism of the Romantic poets, and
even today the most familiar of the tales are those presented by Galland. The
famous story "Ali Baba and the Forty Thieves," for example, is not actually
in any collection of *The Arabian Nights' Entertainments*. Galland heard it,
along with "Aladdin" and several others, from a Syrian scholar who visited
Paris in 1709. When Burton felt the need to include it at least in a supple-
mentary volume of his own collection, in spite of the absence of a manuscript,
what he printed was a friend's English translation of an Urdu translation of

Galland's French.

Hack translations of Galland's book into English appeared at once, but the first English translation directly from Arabic was that of Edward Lane (1838-1841). This translation is incomplete and bowdlerized; as Burton put it, "at once turgid and emasculated." The first complete English translation is John Payne's (1882-1884), including four times the material in Galland. The best-known translation is that of Richard Burton (1885), which relies heavily on the work of his friend Payne, often reproducing it verbatim, but adding extensive "anthropological" notes.

The frame story of *The Arabian Nights' Entertainments* is more complex than most readers remember. Shazaman, King of Samarcand, returns home unexpectedly to find his beloved wife sleeping with a black slave. He kills them both and leaves to visit his elder brother Shahryar, king of "the Islands of India and China." Shazaman remains despondent until the discovery that his brother's wife is also dallying with the slaves somewhat relieves him. The two brothers then go off to ease their common grief by finding someone similarly betrayed. At the seashore they come upon a huge jinn who keeps a woman locked in a chest with seven locks. As soon as the jinn dozes off, however, she forces both kings to sleep with her, and, demanding a ring from each of them as a token, she adds them to a necklace of 570 rings from their predecessors. Their search for a fellow sufferer thus ended, the kings return to the palace, where Shahryar has his wife and concubines killed. To avoid further betrayal, he swears to take a virgin to his bed every night and in the morning put her to death. Shazaman swears the same oath and returns to Samarcand. Shahryar's vizier faithfully provides virgins until the country's supply is all but exhausted. Then his eldest daughter, Shahrazad, proposes to offer herself to the king in the hope of somehow ending the slaughter. Father and daughter debate the wisdom of this through several beast fables, but she is resolved. She goes to the king, but at a crucial moment he allows her sister Dunyazad to stay with them until the dawn. Dunyazad asks (it is prearranged between them), "O my sister, tell one of your stories," and the King, "being wakeful," agrees. Then, for one thousand nights, she tells tales, leaving them unfinished at dawn so that the king puts off her death day by day to hear the sequel. On the last night she presents the three children she has borne, and pleads for her life for their sake. Shahryar replies weeping, "I pardoned you long ago," and the two brothers marry the two sisters in a festive wedding.

In a collection gathered over centuries, not every tale will bear expressive relation to the frame story, and reading deep in *The Arabian Nights' Entertainments* the frame is often forgotten, but many tales seem to have been included because of some link with the situation of Shahrazad, and this is especially true of both the opening stories (among the oldest in the collection) and of the concluding story, one of the last additions.

Shahrazad begins her narration with "The Merchant and the Jinni." The very first event sets the moral atmosphere of the whole work: a merchant on the road is munching a date. When he throws away the pit, a jinn appears explaining that since the pit struck dead the jinn's son, who was walking invisibly down the road, the merchant must die. The merchant is given a year to set his affairs in order. At the end of that time he returns to the spot and, while awaiting death, meets three old men who ask his story. The jinn returns with drawn sword, and the three strike a bargain with him: each of them will tell a story of his own, and for each that the jinn approves, he will remit a third of the merchant's blood. Shahrazad's first dawn comes at the crisis of the first old man's tale, as he tells how he was about to sacrifice a calf, not recognizing it as his own enchanted son. He is, of course, telling this to a jinn about to sacrifice a merchant for inadvertently killing his son, and Shahrazad in turn is telling it to the king who threatens her with imminent death because of the behavior of his former wife.

Next night it is learned that the calf was spared, and the jinn agrees the tale is wonderful. Shahrazad then goes on to the second and third old men's stories. The second too is judged wonderful, but the third is ingeniously devised. It is in fact rather dull, but it is also dangerously close to Shahryar's own experience: the teller returns from a journey to find his wife in bed with a black slave, and this wife manages to turn her husband into a dog before he can react. He is at once restored, she is punished, and the story ends lamely. Dawn comes when the story has been finished, but the jinn has not yet judged it—a moment of considerable suspense if the story is intentionally weak. Next night, however, the jinn is satisfied and the merchant is freed. "But," says Shahrazad, "this is not more wonderful than the story of the fisherman," and Shahryar like the jinn takes the bait: "What story is that?"

There follows the famous story of the fisherman who is threatened with death by a jinn not for harming him, but for releasing him from bondage in a vase. Thus at the third dawn Shahrazad leaves another character under the shadow of death. Later the fisherman tricks the jinn back into the vase, and after a few tense moments the two are reconciled. So far the story resembles those of the preceding nights, but it becomes much more complex. When the encounter seems to have been resolved by the modest reward of a few fish, the tale turns mysteriously magical. The fish are the enchanted inhabitants of a city under a spell, at the center of which is a young prince turned half to stone by an unfaithful wife (yet another man in a worse position than Shahryar), who can be freed only by the king guided to the place by the fisherman and his own curiosity.

Fictive resolutions and the dawns that threaten Shahrazad's life never coincide. The closure of art is always counterpointed to the closure of life. These stories are told in the conviction that the act of telling can defeat death, that reality can eventually be changed by fictions. This conviction is the keynote of the final story of the collection, the late Egyptian tale of "Maaruf the Cobbler."

Maaruf is a Cairene with a terrible shrew of a wife. Fleeing her, he meets a sympathetic jinn who carries him to a remote city. Here he finds a boyhood friend who advises that if he pretends he has a caravan on the way, merchants will extend credit so he can start a business, make his fortune, and soon pay them back. Yet for Maaruf the phrase "as soon as my caravan arrives" becomes a magic spell. He soon seems to believe in his own wealth, and he borrows endlessly only to spend extravagantly. On the strength of lies and luck he marries the princess, but just as he is about to be exposed at last, an act of gratuitous kindness to a peasant leads him to a powerful jinn who, of course, provides not only the fabled caravan but an endless source of wealth as well. There are further vicissitudes. A scheming vizier, so frequent in the collection, obtains the ring that controls the jinn; but he is defeated, and Maaruf and his father-in-law are rescued by the princess who believed in him, lied for him, and eventually gave him an heir. The attractive and shrewd figure of the princess seems drawn for Shahryar's eyes, being in a sense a portrait of the wife Shahrazad proposes to be. This point is emphasized by the final twist of the story. The king and the princess die, leaving Maaruf and his son. Suddenly his old wife from Cairo appears, brought by the same jinn who had rescued Maaruf from her years before. He takes pity on her, but she becomes jealous, and as she tries one night to steal the ring of power, she is killed by the young son of Maaruf. This story, which among other things depicts the incorrigible wickedness of a first wife and the redeeming goodness of a second and ends asserting the value of an heir, is followed not by another tale, but by the presentation of the heirs Shahrazad has borne, and by her acceptance as wife to Shahryar. Just as the early stories make constant reference back to the frame, so the very last uses related motifs to conclude the whole collection and anticipate the resolution of the frame.

Apart from the very shortest, most of the tales in *The Arabian Nights' Entertainments* impress the reader with their unmatched inventiveness and corresponding asymmetry. Almost as a rule the reader is led from episode to episode by trapdoors, shipwrecks, and unexpected jinns. In contrast to European fairy tales, in these stories winning the hand of the princess is rarely the end of one's troubles. False and deceptive resolutions abound, as in "The Fisherman and the Jinni," and this rhetorical trait is characteristic of an oral milieu: a listener never knows how much longer a story is; he must wait and see. This rambling, discursive manner is epitomized in the voyages of Sindbad. Sindbad the poor porter stops to grumble in front of the house of a rich merchant, Sindbad the sailor, who invites him in and in effect justifies his wealth by narrating the ordeal of his voyages. The adventures are harrowing and delightful, and the narrative seems unsophisticated.

Although the seven voyages are all different, full of sensational but familiar

material from medieval travel books, a subtle order is evident, as Gebhardt
has demonstrated. While there are significant variations, each voyage begins
with a calamity leading to an adventure followed by an account of some oddity
or marvel, and each story ends with Sindbad's uneventful return from the
scene of the adventure. The grouping of the voyages is also highly symmet-
rical: the central voyage includes three adventures, while the second, third,
fifth, and sixth contain two each, and the first and last only one. All this is
framed in a story about the reconciliation of two men who share one name
but radically different fates. This denouement is one of the collection's countless expressions of the deep fatalism of Islam (the word means "submission").
In this world any date pit may kill a jinn, any beast may be an enchanted
relative, and at every turn one's luck may change utterly. Stories such as
Sindbad's literally figure forth this sense of the world by underpinning a
freewheeling narrative with discreet but rigorous structures. This combination
of ebullient invention with self-consciously complex form is apparent in a
number of the very best stories, of which "The Tale of the Hunchback" can
serve as an example.

The story begins as farce. While drinking with a tailor, the King's hunchbacked jester chokes on a fishbone and dies. Frightened, the tailor leaves the
body at the doorstep of a Jewish doctor, who trips over it, and so thinks he
has killed him. The doctor passes the corpse to a steward, and he to the
King's broker, a Christian, who is arrested for the crime. Next day, the order
is reversed: each of the four is about to be hanged when his predecessor
confesses. When the tailor finally stands in the noose, the execution is interrupted by a message from the King, who wants to know what happened to
his jester.

The scene shifts to the audience hall where everything is repeated to the
King. He marvels at the story and orders it written down in letters of gold.
This apparent conclusion is only the beginning, however; nine-tenths of the
story remain to be told. For the King says, "Has anyone heard a more marvelous story?" Each of the accused then tells of meeting a man crippled in
some way, who told the story of his injury. The first three do not impress the
King, so the tailor, who started the affair, now seems destined to end it. He
tells of meeting a lame young man at breakfast on the day of the hunchback's
death. The story would resemble the previous three, except that it includes
a secondary character, the supposed cause of the lameness (as the tailor is
the supposed cause of the hunchback's death). This is a barber also in at-
tendance at the breakfast, so garrulous and meddlesome (according to the
lame man) that he causes nothing but disaster. The lame man, refusing to
stay in the same room with his nemesis, departs. Had the story ended there,
it might not have satisfied the King either, but the tailor goes on to recount
the barber's defense. He asserts that in fact he is known as the Silent One,
and illustrates with a bizarre story of how his extreme discretion nearly caused

his death. This story leads to six others, about how each of his brothers was mutilated in some way because they were not as circumspect as he. The breakfasters respond to the long saga of the Silent One by locking him up. The King finds all this more marvelous than the adventure of the hunchback, and to satisfy his curiosity, he sends for the barber. He appears, everything we have heard is repeated to him, and he is ordered to tell some stories of his own. Instead, he reaches down, pulls the bone out of the hunchback's throat, and the man revives. The King finds this most marvelous of all, and concludes the story by distributing honors to all involved.

Like Shahrazad, the four accused of murder are trying to circumvent death by telling stories to a curious monarch; but here storytelling not only puts off death, it actually overcomes it when, thanks to the tailor's explosion of narrative, the hunchback is restored to life. Amid all the talk is the silent figure of the corpse, a suspended dissonance awaiting resolution that keeps the story moving past several deceptive cadences. The motif of mutilation that occurs in all eleven inserted stories not only unifies the group, but also keeps us conscious of the hunchback's haunting presence—actually an absence. The corpse also embodies a challenge: the accused must tell something more marvelous than this reality. Only the tailor's story meets this challenge, and it does so, ironically, because it is so complex. Throughout *The Arabian Nights' Entertainments*, the strongest illusion of reality is created by highly formal means, just as by the formal rules of perspective a line drawing can depict a solid object. Further, the tailor's story will turn out to transform the reality in which it is told, because it introduces into that reality a new element, the barber.

This is the hero of the story, a main character who emerges from the heart of the narrative, from Shahrazad's story of the recorded account of the tailor's story of the lame man's story. The first portrait of him is satirical and lifelike, but it has the special vividness of fiction, not life. When he later appears as an actual person, he has a much more commanding presence, but decidedly less literary "color." Although he is the only whole, unmutilated man in the inserted stories, the various accounts of his character are never finally reconciled. He proves he is the Silent One by a narrative that rather proves he is a great talker, yet he concludes the affair of the hunchback by cutting through all talk. Furthermore, although he resolves the story at a single stroke, he himself remains irresolvably ambiguous.

The barber is one of the relatively few individualized characters in *The Arabian Nights' Entertainments*; another is the most important of the many "curious king" figures, the historical Harun al-Rashid, caliph of Baghdad (786-809) at its height and contemporary of Charlemagne. He appears in some fifty of the tales, not necessarily as a hero, but as a presiding spirit, much like King Arthur in the tales of European chivalry that *The Arabian Nights' Entertainments* often resemble. His nature is established in stories such as "The Mock Caliph" and "The Awakened Sleeper" (which recalls Calderón's *Life Is a Dream*, 1635): he is a jaded insomniac, and several stories exploit his legendary habit of wandering in disguise through the Baghdad night, seeking diversion. With his appetite for experience and also for stories which make available the experience of others, he is the chief of many covert images of Shahryar, the sleepless, insatiable listener. In this regard he is balanced by Sindbad, the chief avatar of Shahrazad, the exuberant teller.

It is of course the relation between these two that in some sense generates the whole work. The tales themselves are the charms and beguilements by which Shahrazad manages a seduction at once leisurely and desperate. One of the products of her success is our most extensive demonstration that every story has designs on its audience. Another, which exists not so much in the book as in the imagination of its readers, is the image of an oddly perfect marriage: in a darkened room, a disembodied female voice inexhaustibly creates a world for an invisible and endlessly receptive male presence. These two types, one who will tell stories even in the face of death and one who will drop all business to pursue a wonder, wander through *The Arabian Nights' Entertainments* in a variety of forms, seeking each other out. They come to rest in Shahryar and Shahrazad.

Bibliography
Barth, John. "Dunyazadiad," in *Chimera*.
Burton, Richard. "Terminal Essay," in *The Book of the Thousand Nights and a Night*.
Gerhardt, Mia. *The Art of Storytelling: A Literary Study of The Thousand and One Nights*.

Laurence A. Breiner

THE HASIDIC TALE

The Hasidic tale was very much in vogue in American short fiction in the 1960's. Its holistic world view and its sense of the presence of God in all things, of the sanctity of the commonplace, strongly appealed to that generation. Martin Buber's smooth translations did much to popularize Hasidism, and Gershom Scholem's monumental studies of mysticism showed that the Zohar, the Book of Splendor, was a text as profound as the Torah and the Talmud. Elie Wiesel drew standing-room-only crowds with his lectures on the Hasidic masters, while the fascination of Isaac Bashevis Singer's cabalistic fictions renewed interest in the world view that informed them. When S. Y. Agnon became the first Jewish Nobel laureate, the magic inherent in the Hasidic tale was once more confirmed. It was noted that the stance of Agnon's persona is that of a zaddik (a righteous one, a rebbe) addressing his disciples. Norman Mailer and Meyer Levin were both attracted to the genre; Woody Allen wrote parodies of it; Saul Bellow and Philip Roth each composed one version of it; Harold Bloom has derived a critical terminology based on Lurianic cabala; and Franz Kafka and Isaac Leib Peretz retold many Hasidic tales.

Cabala

The literal meaning of "cabala" is "tradition." The term itself illustrates the paradoxical nature of Jewish mysticism, which claims that the most personal intuition of God's immediacy is also traditional wisdom. It is a paradox that the secrets of the hidden are considered public doctrine. What is unique about the Cabalists is their attitude toward language: words were the sacred instruments by which the world was created, and each letter had a magic potency. The ultimate revelation is The Name which brought the universe into being when It was uttered.

Although Cabalists studied the same texts as other Jews, they apprehended them differently; they read the Torah symbolically. The commandments were not outmoded ordinances which had to be modified by disputation in order to apply to their lives, but mystery rites, sacraments. The rabbinic mind regarded Law as signs whose referents had altered. The cabalistic mind did not see Halaka as signifying anything, but as manifesting the ineffable; the Infinite become finite. Every "mitzvah" (following of the commandments) thus became an act of cosmic importance which influenced the dynamics of the universe. Thus, the importance of cabalism for fiction was that it glorified language, gave man heroic stature, thought in symbols, and fused all these aspects into a coherent myth.

Hasidism in Medieval Germany (1150-1250)

Legends about the Kalonymos dynasty appear in the *Book of the Pious* (Sefer Hasidim) and in the *Book of Stories* (1602, Maaseh Buch). The Kalonymos family had lived since the ninth century, in the Rhineland, where they attained such stature that the Duke of Regensburg and the Bishop of Salzburg were numbered among their friends. Ashkenazic Hasidism was founded by Rabbi Samuel of Mainz, his son, Rabbi Judah ben Samuel (who died in Regensburg in 1217), and his disciple, Rabbi Eleazar ben Judah of Worms (who died about 1230).

The German Hasidim valued piety above intellectuality, praising asceticism, martyrdom, and extreme altruism. They believed that "the fear of God leads to the flame of love for God," and their visionary experiences were often described in erotic terms, using sexual metaphors for spiritual states. They codified an elaborate penitential system through which restitution could be made for every sort of transgression. These self-imposed punishments were often extravagantly painful and humiliating; they are called "tortures as bitter as death" in the *Book of the Pious*, where it is related that martyrs plunged naked into the snow or exposed their bodies to stinging bees to purge the world through their suffering. One Hasid immersed his feet in a bucket of water in winter until they froze. When his pupil asked him why he did this, he answered, "the truly just man must suffer to assume the sins of his generation." Another Hasid lay on the prayer house steps so that everyone entering had to tread on him.

The harsh Teutonic retributive justice found in the tales of the *Book of the Pious* persists in the German folktales collected by the Grimm brothers seven centuries later, many of which they found in this thirteenth century anthology. Here Rabbi Eleazar compiled fairy tales, occult miracles, superstitions, folklore about ghosts and witches, demonology, incantations, and formulas for protective amulets, as well as visionary prayers. Here also is the oldest recipe for creating a golem, a creature who could be animated by the secret Name and who crumbled back to dust when the Name was withdrawn. This legend has exerted a peculiar fascination on later writers, and a vast body of literature has accumulated about the man-made monster. Some recent versions of the legend are by Isaac Leib Peretz, Ira Levin, and Joanne Greenberg, and a whole book of golden legends was collected by Chayim Block in 1925.

Of importance to modern criticism is the approach toward texts taken by the German Hasidim. They regarded the texts as ciphers which could be decoded by a variety of techniques, so they devised the systems of Gematria, Notarikon, and Temurah. Gematria consists of calculating the numerical value of a word (which is easy to do in Hebrew, since the letters of the Hebrew alphabet double as numbers), connecting these with other words of the same arithmetical value, and then seeking correspondences or hidden significances. For example, Rabbi Eleazar entitled his mystical book *Sefer Raziel* (published in 1701) because the sum of the title equals the sum of his name in gematria. Notarikon is a mode of deciphering the meaning of a word by considering each letter to be the abbreviation for a sentence. Temurah is the interchange of letters according to a system of rules—in other words, a cryptography.

The Hasidim's approach helped prepare the way for twentieth century structuralism, fathered by Claude Levi-Strauss (the grandson of a rabbi) and developed by many Jewish linguists who share this notion that the hidden meaning of a text can be revealed by systematically decoding it according to a set of rules. Harold Bloom, for example, has mastered all the Jewish mystical documents and derived from them a mode of interpreting Romantic poetry, with which those documents have so many affinities.

In 1187, the Crusaders stormed into Mainz, massacring Jews. In the *Book of the Pious*, Rabbi Eleazar tells how his wife and three children were slaughtered and how afterward he became an extreme ascetic whose fasts and self-inflicted sufferings resulted in visions. Many of the wonder tales he relates about his master, Judah the Pious, have analogues in the stories about Saint Francis, who was his exact contemporary. Interestingly, modern writer Bernard Malamud's diction, themes, and characters are derived largely from the *Book of the Pious*; his novel *The Assistant* (1957) contains many parallels to the St. Francis stories, and his stories often valorize suffering. In a deliberately idiomatic diction Malamud in *The Assistant* relates the conversion to goodness of a common man who has undergone moral torment; in fact, all of Malamud's Jews suffer to expiate the sins of others. From his stories one could derive a casuistry of penitential acts as extreme as those in the *Book of the Pious*.

One of the stories in the *Book of the Pious* which could be an ancestor of the Malamudian moral fable is about a poor man who longed for a fiddle. He finds a piece of wood in a cemetery and carves himself a violin. The plank had been the top of a coffin, and the ghost whose grave he has robbed haunts him. He becomes desperately ill, and his agony is not relieved until he returns what he has stolen. His intense fear is the prelude to his redemption. The same is also true for Malamud's characters, in whom the undercurrent of terror stimulates the love of God.

Malamud's suffering Jews are typically tailors, cobblers, or grocery store owners, barely making a living. These poor laborers exemplify the "lamed vovnik" tradition. The legend of the thirty-six just men upon whose goodness the continuance of the world depends derives from the *Book of the Pious*. Its tales are about humble workingmen, unlearned but devout, whose goodness is not recognized in this world, but is rewarded in the next. One such story is about an ignorant cowherd. Since he was unversed in the liturgy, the only form of prayer he had was one he invented. He used to praise God by assuring Him that he would gladly herd His cows for Him. A learned rabbi, overhearing this improvisation, was shocked by such irreverence and shamed him into employing more appropriate formulas. The cowherd, being simple-minded, could not remember all those complicated words, so out of embarrassment, he stopped praying at all. God reproached the rabbi for having silenced a saint, telling him that the cowherd was a lamed vovnik who had an assured place reserved for him in the world to come.

Peretz, who in nineteenth century Poland was trying to educate the common laborers to a sense of their innate dignity, seized on this story mode. He retold tales of anonymous saints to instill a feeling of inner worth in the Jewish proletariat. "Bontsha the Silent" is about an illiterate porter, whipped, cheated, starved, spat upon, and eventually run over, whose uncomplaining goodness gave him access to the Heavenly Throne. "Jochanan, the Water-carrier" is another analogue. The poor man, unable to study himself, honored scholarship by bringing water to the yeshiva students as they sat bent over the Talmud. Without status on earth, he was greeted in heaven as a lamed vov. In this century, the French novelist André Schwarz-bart structured *The Last of the Just* (1961) on the legend, which originated in Ashkenazic Hasidism, that it is the suffering of thirty-six anonymous saints which permits the world to endure.

The Hasidic tale, which began in eleventh century Germany, was continued first in Palestine, then in Eastern Europe. The stories of Isaac Luria differed from those of Judah the Pious because they were infused with the Zohar. With the expulsion of the Jews from Spain in 1492, the study of cabalism moved to Safed. A change of emphasis resulted: the Zohar was concerned with the creation of the world, not with its end. The Lurianic mysticism stressed the apocalyptic end and was concerned with messianism and the final redemption.

As all these elements coalesced later in Eastern Europe, Hasidism again assumed a different character. The Palestinian version had been aristocratic; Polish Hasidism returned to the democratic ethos, which valorized the common man. It was a pietistic movement which began in the last half of the eighteenth century; it stressed humility and selflessness, and taught that God's presence permeated and sustained all matter. Its precepts were Kavana (concentration upon God); Devekut (communion with God); and Hitlahavut (enthusiastic, fervent worship). The founder of this movement was Rabbi Israel ben Eliezer (1700-1770), called the Ba'al Shem-Tov (Master of the Divine Name). At his death, the movement was organized by his disciple, Rabbi Dov Ber (d. 1772), who was called the Great Maggid of Mezhirich. Many dynastic courts were established by other followers, and in each of these the telling of stories assumed a religiously sanctioned status.

In 1970, the legends about the founder of Hasidism were translated and edited by Dan Ben-Amos and Jerome R. Mintz in their book *In Praise of the Ba'al Shem Tov*. The plots all have the same structure, beginning with a problem, which can be a misfortune, a dilemma, or a riddle that various people attempt to solve. Physicians, scholars, or miracle workers are summoned, and then when all attempts have failed, the Ba'al Shem-Tov resolves the difficulty. The stories end with his having won new disciples by his demonstration of his powers.

Little is known about Ba'al Shem-Tov's life except that he was orphaned early, lived in the Carpathian Mountains, had no formal education, and supported himself by a variety of rude trades. He wandered from village to village, healing the sick, exorcising dybbuks (dead souls inhabiting the bodies of the living), inscribing amulets, lifting the curse of barrenness, treating with herbs and incantations, and predicting the future. When he was thirty six, Rabbi Israel ben Eliezer revealed himself as a zaddik (charismatic leader) and, gathering his disciples around him, he began to preach by means of stories. None of these parables and legends were written down in his lifetime. Not until fifty-four years after his death were they printed by his scribe, Rabbi Dov Ber, in Kopys, Poland. All the signs of oral transmission remain: the diction is colloquial; there are frequent pronoun shifts in person and number; and there are innumerable repetitions, such as people resort to in speech.

The Zohar

The Zohar has proved to be a powerful armature for fiction. It supplies the author with a myth which is cosmogony, psychology, and theology fused into striking images. It enables the writer to depict the consequences of his characters' behavior in terms of their effect upon the universe and upon God Himself. Each word and act occurs on a cosmic stage. Since all of creation emanated from the Divine Substance with which it is still infused, everything in the world is holy.

The Zohar's psychology is based on binary oppositions. Its philosophy consists of warring contraries, of two opposed and contradictory notions, called logical paradoxes, and it is on the continued tension between conflicting forces that the continuance of the cosmos depends. Since the Zoharic system is composed of irreconcilable opposites in all its parts, even its linguistic surface reflects this duality. Its chief rhetorical device is the oxymoron, a figure of speech in which one part contradicts the other.

The Zohar, composed in Spain about 1270, pretends to be the work of a second century sage, Rabbi Simeon ben Yohai. Its very narrative structure is paradoxical. It was actually written by a thirteenth century Spanish mystic, Moses de Leon, who poses as a wanderer in Palestine discoursing with his son, Eleazar, and his disciples. It is a sort of pseudepigraphic novel which weaves together stories and monologues. The pseudo-Aramaic in which it is composed betrays, through its syntax and diction, its own later composition. The scenery, which conforms to no real Palestinian landscape, shows that the author had read about but had never visited the Holy Land himself. He learned the geography he described, as he did the language in which it was couched, by studying medieval manuscripts, whose errors he has faithfully transcribed.

Thus the Zohar is paradoxically both second century and thirteenth century at once, just as it is paradoxically neither. Its surface structure conforms to the philosophical paradoxes in the deep structure. The world is pictured as emerging from nothingness. The Hebrew word for nothing, "ain," has the same consonants as the word for "I." Since Hebrew is written without vowels, these, then, are equivalent. The Nothingness, the divine substance without attributes, assumed Being, revealing Itself through its own creation. This paradox can only be expressed dialectically. The beginning of creation was "a dark flame" (oxymoron) which sprang forth out of the mysterious recesses of the Infinite Nothing (oxymoron). The colorless flame was radiantly colored (oxymoron). The paradox that an invisible force manifests itself as the visible creation which then becomes His essence or "ani" means that by "ain" (Nothing) saying "ani" (I am) the world was created. The Sefiroth (emanations) which issued from the Divine Substance are graduated into ten stages of revelation. Sometimes these are pictured as a tree of life, sometimes as a primordial being, Admon Kadmon, whose left side is feminine and whose right side is masculine. This is the ultimate oxymoron, male and female conjoined.

The dynamics of the universe depend upon balance being sustained. The forces of evil and darkness pull against the forces of goodness and light. As long as the tensions between wrath and love, between rigor and mercy sustain their opposition, life continues. If, however, the left side exerts a stronger pull, death results. Men, through their prayers and good deeds, can exert an influence on this flow of energies; they can recharge the depleted Sefiroth on the right side so that the flow of holiness is restored by their devotions. The supreme religious obligation thus becomes "devekut" (adhesion to God): if men fail in their concentration on God, the equilibrium of the Sephirot might be disrupted, causing disorder and even chaos to ensue in the world.

Several scholarly book-length attempts have been made to show the affinities between the Freudian drives and the flux of discharges in the Sephirotic system. There are certainly parallels between Freud's Thanatos and Eros and the death and life impulses of the Zohar, and the oceanic feelings Sigmund Freud posits are like the concept in the Zohar that all men yearn for that mystical oneness with creation which they knew before birth. The Zohar says that each soul had a heavenly preexistence as pure radiance. This fraction of divine light is incarnated and sent to earth, longing always for the effulgence from which it descended, and to which at death it will return if it has not been stained by sin, in which case it must be purged. To cleanse itself it is condemned to rebirth. The Zohar's psychology is as paradoxical as the other aspects of the Zohar: death is seen as a reward and birth as a punishment. The mystical return to God reverses the process by which man emanated from God. This echoes the diastole-systole of the universe.

Lurianic Mysticism
Around the charismatic figure of Isaac Luria (1534-1572) grew the school

of Cabalists in sixteenth century Safed, which has remained a center of mysticism in present-day Israel. His disciple, Hayyim Vital, wrote down the miracles he performed in *Tales in Praise of the Ari* (1629). At his birth, which had been predicted by Elijah (in Jewish tradition the annunciation is typically made to the father in the synagogue), the entire house was filled with light. He was still very young when his father died, so he was sent to Cairo to be brought up by his uncle, whose daughter he married when he was fifteen. He distinguished himself in mastering the sacred texts when he was still a child and in becoming an "elui," a sage, at an early age. There are legends of wonders he performed on behalf of the poor and the barren and legends of visions in which he encounters the Shekina, or converses with dead philosophers. He had the gift of invoking the secret names of God in order to right injustices.

What is particularly interesting about this hagiography is that it supplies the structure which is repeated in all later wonder tales; the same attributes and miracles attributed to Isaac Luria are told of Rabbi Nahman of Bratslav and of the Ba'al Shem-Tov. In each case, the annunciation to the father while at prayer is made by Elijah, who also appears at the circumcision where the prophet serves as godfather. This revelation is always followed by descriptions of prodigious learning mastered at an early age: the young boy comprehends the Bible, the Commentaries, and the Talmud and illuminates disciples with his wisdom. He then receives the gift of exorcising dybbuks, healing the sick, making fruitful the barren, and ascending to heaven to intercede for the unfortunate.

The historic process is not determined by an interplay of economic and political forces; it is seen as an expression of the will of God. The tales all share the view that events are caused by God's intervention in history. The Jewish people are seen as beloved children enduring chastisement from a heavenly father, and enduring communal punishment for failure to obey the commandments. It is their obligation to fulfill meticulously God's will as it has been recorded in the sacred texts in order to move the world toward its messianic end. Every aspect of life is governed by the 613 commandments in the Old Testament, of which there are 365 prohibitions and 248 positive precepts. Because everything in the universe has been designed as a series of intricate correspondences, there are 365 days of the solar year, and 248 bones and 365 sinews in the human body, which the Lurianic Cabala says is equal to the divisions in the human soul.

Because the microcosm mirrors the macrocosm in its minutest detail, the slightest deviation from ritual or the most fleetingly entertained doubt can infect the entire cosmos, can delay the coming of the Messiah and the salvation of the world. The scrupulous performance of the commandments purifies not only the body, but also the soul, and even the universe, since all are intimately related. Life becomes a continual struggle to purify oneself and to lift up the sparks of goodness in others. The consequences to fiction of such a holistic world view is to endow it with tremendous coherence; the early stories of S. Y. Agnon, for example, are illuminated by this harmonious ordering of all levels of being. The characters interpret their experiences as a direct expression of God's will, so that every mundane event has supernal resonances. All orders of being, human, natural, and divine, are interfused and coextensive. Agnon's later stories depict the chaos that ensues when this order is subverted.

The stories of Isaac Bashevis Singer, whose father, Rabbi Menachem Mendel, was a Hasidic zaddik, are also set in this milieu. The lapsed Hasidim in Singer's tales can be purged only in Gehenna or by being punished with reincarnation. Their bodies, contaminated by their misdeeds or by the evil inclinations festering in their minds, must be cleansed, either by undergoing rebirth or by enduring hellfire; otherwise, the entire dynamics of the universe will be adversely affected. For example, "The Slaughterer" and "Blood" both deal with butchers maddened by their own bestiality. Their murder of animals causes them to see the whole world as a fallen place. An analogue to these tales is ascribed to the Belzer rebbe who said that howling dogs were the reincarnations of ritual slaughterers who had declared in previous lives that treyfe (unclean) meat had been kosher. This kind of vision Singer shares with Franz Kafka, who was also a vegetarian.

The devils in Singer's stories, who release men's covert fantasies and urge them to act out their suppressed desires, are the visible and articulate counterpart of an invisible and silent deity. The demonic, which is manifest, challenges the divine, which is hidden, to exert itself. By depicting the satanic excesses which result from flaunting discipline, Singer lures his readers to respect its constraints and shows how the smallest deviation from the law leads inevitably to greater crimes. This is not, as his critics allege, for the sake of sensationalism, but rather for the sake of harnessing the "yetzer hara" (the evil impulse), which, once yielded to, soon assumes mastery. "Short Friday" depicts the cabalistic ideal. In it the devotional and the sexual fuse into a mystical ecstasy as the elderly couple simultaneously die and are translated into saints. Such a miracle story depends upon a belief in a universe whose parts are interrelated, whose mysterious workings can be interpreted, and which, though intense discipline, can even be controlled. The author of fiction who can lay claim to such a coherent cosmos can avail himself of extraordinary powers.

Lurianic cabalism explained evil in a way that seems strikingly modern. It is this theodicy that enables Singer to construct fictions that seem psychologically sound by avoiding the splitting into good and bad which leads to sentimental fictions or to didacticism. According to the Lurianic cosmogony, good and evil have been mixed together since the creation of the world. This creation myth, called "tzim-tzum," says that the divine substance was coextensive with all creation. In order to make space for the universe, it had to withdraw itself momentarily; and from that shudder of withdrawal, that contraction of the primordial demiurge, a vacuum resulted. In that space, from which the divine essence was absent, the cosmos was created. The divine essence then emanated itself into forms which were unable to contain its radiance. They shattered and these broken shards and vessels, the "klippot" or shells, were gathered up and reshaped. Now, however, the divine sparks were mixed with impurities. The good and evil were so intermingled that it becomes a lifelong task to redeem the divine sparks from their fallen condition. It is the purpose of existence to uplift all life from its klippot and restore its radiant oneness. No one is exempt because the salvation of the world depends upon each individual's redeeming the sparks in all things.

This explanation of the existence of evil enabled Elie Wiesel to bear witness to the Holocaust. Himself the scion of a Hasidic dynasty, he continues to transmit the tales that were told to him. In his "Afterword" to *Souls on Fire* (1972), he notes that the faithful transmission of the tales is more important to the Hasidic storyteller than innovation; the tale must be given just as it had been received. The verb "limsor," which means "to transmit," is the root of the noun "masora," which means "tradition." By transmitting the stories of the Ba'al Shem-Tov, "inside the ghetto walls, inside the death camps, in the shadow of the executioner, they celebrated life."

Jerome R. Mintz in *Legends of the Hasidim* (1968) describes the multiplication of dynastic courts such as Ger in Poland; Lubavitch, Karlin-Stolen, and Rizhyn in Russia; Belz in Galicia; and Sziget in Hungary. Each was a self-sufficient community with its own artisans, storekeepers, and ritual slaughterers whose center was the "besmedresh" (the house of study and prayer). Each court had a corpus of oral tradition testifying to the powers of its leader. These religiously sanctioned tales were carried with the group when it was dispersed by Nazism. Some Hasidim settled in Montreal, London, Chicago, and Philadelphia, but most went to Israel or to Brooklyn. The Satmar and Klausenberg Hasidim moved to Williamsburg, the Lubavitch and the Bobover to Crown Heights, and the Stoliner to Boro Park. In 1954, a group of Hasidim purchased 130 acres in suburban New York to establish the community of New Square. Philip Roth's great story "Eli, the Fanatic" was inspired by this event, as was Cynthia Ozick's powerful novella "Bloodshed," about a community of Holocaust survivors.

Each Hasidic group has its own rebbe except the Bratslaver, who are called "The Dead Hasidim" because they worship the memory of Rabbi Nahman of Bratslav, the great-grandson of the Ba'al Shem-Tov, after whose death in 1810 no man was deemed worthy enough to be his successor. He had said "My light will glow till the days of the Messiah," and his followers interpreted this literally. In the Mea Shearim quarter of Jerusalem, the Bratslaver Hasidim meet daily to reread and discuss the thirteen short stories of Nahman, whose intricately carved black wooden chair was broken into pieces and smuggled across the Russian border to be reassembled in Israel. Nahman's tales are regarded as holy revelation and are read as a form of worship.

In all of these Hasidic sects, the storyteller is accorded a special status since he preserves the history of the court and transmits the wisdom of its rebbe. Furthermore, since the theater and secular books are banned, storytelling is the primary source of entertainment; and since the graphic arts are forbidden as idolatrous, according to the prohibition against graven images, the telling of stories is the single sanctioned creative expression in the culture. Storytelling is also the most important instrument of social control, since it is used to induct the young into the communal value system; it initiates them into acceptable modes of behavior by making the consequences of wrong conduct explicit. The smallest deviation from the commandments is always harshly punished in the stories, so that the children listening learn that misfortunes follow transgressions. Scrupulous adherence to the commandments is rewarded, so that the children learn to emulate the model of virtue presented to them. In addition to transmitting history and ethics, the tales, having a psychological dimension, often have curative powers. The telling of stories about the miraculous healing of others sometimes results in the healing of someone similarly afflicted. Since they tell of sufferings alleviated through prayer and charity, the stories affirm adaptive responses, mitigate anxiety, and assume a kind of magical potency.

Storytelling is an established part of the sabbath ritual. Traditionally there are four communal meals, and at the third, "Seudah Shelishit," and the fourth, "Melaveh Malkeh," tales are told. At the third, at dusk after afternoon prayer, the rebbe teaches his listening disciples by means of extended metaphors, parables, or exemplary tales. His Hasidim stand in a hushed circle straining to memorize his proverbs, allusions, and illustrations so that they can discuss them later. Since writing is forbidden, concentration is intense so that the quiet words will not be lost.

At the fourth meal, stories of Hasidic saints and sages are told. Particularly on the "yahrzeit" (the anniversary of the death) of a famous rebbe, the miracles he performed are recounted; this practice is thought to elevate his soul another degree in heaven. The rebbe leads in the storytelling, often followed by an honored elder or a learned visitor. The language is always direct and the diction simple. There is commentary, explication of the deeper meanings, and conversational byplay linking the narrations. Each story is authenticated by citing the name of the original teller and including the testimony of witnesses to its veracity. Not only wonder tales but also humorous anecdotes, jokes, and numskull stories are related. As a unique form of preserving social cohesion, the Hasidic tale continues today to perform the same functions as it did in the days of the Ba'al Shem-Tov, preserving law, ritual, social structure, and daily life through orally transmitted narratives.

Ruth Rosenberg

FORMS OF SHORT FICTION
IN THE EARLY MIDDLE AGES

The early Middle Ages (for the purposes of this discussion, c. 476-1050) represent a time of transition and readjustment from the declining Roman, classical era to a culture that more and more clearly defined itself as a new age in the West (medieval scholars considered themselves modern men). This period saw the gradual development of the romance languages from Vulgar Latin and, especially as social conditions stabilized in the late eighth and early ninth centuries, the development of an increasingly varied body of literary work.

It is only fair and necessary to assume literary continuity in this transitional time. The great Latin writers, Ovid for example, were recopied as well as imitated, and Latin versions of the fables of Aesop continued to be produced and read. There was, of course, a considerable body of oral fiction, but this study will be confined to such exemplars of short fiction that have survived in written form. It will be necessary, especially for the early centuries of the period, to abstract our exemplars from works that are not fictional per se. Many of the writings of the late classical and early Christian periods were grammatical or historical, and early Christian writings were primarily dogmatic treatises. Furthermore, the Church Fathers tended to distrust pagan literature even when their own writings betrayed their classical educations in every sentence, as an examination of the works of St. Jerome or St. Augustine easily shows. Later, although the Church was responsible for the suppression of a great deal of pagan literature, notably the Germanic heroic works, remnants of which survive in Old Icelandic (Old Norse) versions, the accommodation of the literary impulse to the Christian ethos would produce a significant body of hagiographical literature and, in the later Middle Ages, the various romance cycles in which the didactic element does not overwhelm real literary merit.

The *Etymologies* (622-623) of Isidore, Bishop of Seville, provides us a contemporary definition of story (*fabula*): story does not speak of things done (*res factae*) but of things created in speech (*res fictae de loquendo*). The emphasis in this study will be on the latter point, "things created," because even in historical or quasihistorical works, authors such as Pope St. Gregory the Great or Bishop Gregory of Tours would break the flow of their narratives to develop or expand upon a striking episode, making of it more a vignette than a mere recital of details. What one finds, in other words, are coherence of focus and intensity of presentation that make of such an episode a totality of intrinsic narrative interest. One looks for fictive *form* and not necessarily fictive *content*. The writer imposes his creative skill upon the incidents, factual or not, so that they become almost independent of the historical, narrative matrix in which they are found.

These early works of "short fiction" should possess as well the sharp, intense focus of the lyric or the *lai* as opposed to the broader scope and grander scale of the epic or extended romance. Most of the works considered in this study will range from 250 to 500 words, but length is less of a concern than focus, scale, or ambiance: *Beowulf* (early eighth century?) is not lengthy, but it fits the definition of epic very obviously when compared to the unity of conflict to be found in the late ninth century *Waltharius* or the Irish tale *The Exile of the Sons of Uisliu*, also written in the ninth century. These two works are better termed heroic lays or tales than epics. Other generic categories of short fiction include the vignette or anecdote, both of which tend not to be found independently from some larger narrative framework; the saint's life or miracle tale whether in verse or prose; and, at the end of our time period, the romantic tale, even when it still possesses a strong heroic or mythic content.

The period under discussion extends from A.D. 476, the date of the deposition of the last Roman emperor in the West, to c. 1050, a time when it was manifest that political and economical stability, along with an influx of new knowledge and the rise of the great cathedral schools, had led to the beginnings of the high Middle Ages. As Chart I (see page 436) indicates, the historical events relevant for this study go back to 375, the death of Ermanaric, the Ostrogothic emperor whose deeds, filtered through the lost chronicle of Cassiodorus and its condensation written by Jordanes, figure in the Old Icelandic *Hamðismal* (tenth century, the *Poem of Hamðir*). A similar process occurred with the stories of Attila the Hun and Theodoric the Ostrogoth as history was transmuted into heroic legends that spread from their places of origin near Rome or the Rhine as far west as Iceland.

As important to this study as historical personages are events marking the development of European national units, such as the Treaty of Verdun (843) that created France and Germany, and of the major European languages, such as The Strasbourg Oaths (842), which testify to the necessity of using both Old French and the Germanic dialects so that all witnesses of the proceedings might understand the oaths of peace between Charles the Bald and Louis the German. A history of literary development in the early Middle Ages is also a history of the development of the major European languages as tools of creative expression as well as of day-to-day communication. Indeed, for some time, many of the works to be discussed in this study were analyzed chiefly as linguistic monuments rather than as literary exemplars. Twentieth century studies, however, have repeatedly established their literary merits.

The chronological arrangement of Chart II (see page 437) illustrates the increasing variety of forms in the literature of the early Middle Ages as well as the linguistic variety that characterizes the latter part of the period. The apparent consistency of literary forms of the pre-Carolingian period is somewhat misleading since the vignettes and anecdotes found in the various works differ widely in content and in presentation. Consider, for example, the Munderic episode in Gregory of Tours's *History of the Franks* (III, 14; c. 575-594) and one of the dialogues from the first book of the *Dialogues* (c. 593) of Gregory the Great.

The story of Munderic is actually an episode in the reign of Thierry I (511-534), son of Clovis (466?-511). Munderic, a relative of Thierry I, revolts against his king, claiming that his blood makes him equally entitled to the throne. He gains followers and is besieged by Thierry I. His defense is strong enough that Thierry I resorts to guile, luring Munderic from his stronghold with false pledges of good faith and having him executed once he is vulnerable.

This episode has multiple functions in Gregory's narrative: it is one of the historical events he is bound to include in his work, but it is also one of a series of episodes portraying the ruthlessness and administrative ingenuity of Thierry I. Although Gregory deplores Thierry I's tactics, this attitude is mixed with some admiration for Thierry I's strength of character. Furthermore, the Munderic episode offers an opportunity for Gregory to exercise his skill as a storyteller. The events are not complicated, but the episode stands out because of Gregory's use of two motifs—good faith and bad faith—that are intensified by repetition. Munderic is a traitor, but he has a loyal following; Thierry I, the rightful ruler, does not hesitate to use deceit, and his envoy, Aregyselus, is able to persuade the strangely guileless Munderic that Thierry I will honor the oath sworn on the altar in his name. Aregyselus promptly betrays Munderic to Thierry I's forces and Munderic, finally aware of treachery, kills the messenger and dies, honorably defending himself. With no real description of his personality, one still can perceive a rather simple, straightforward man who is destroyed as much by his ambition as by the machinations of his opponent. The techniques of fiction, especially the coherence provided by the emphasis of two major motifs, elevate the episode from a mere sequence of events to the status of story.

The anecdotes of Gregory the Great are more easily identified as fiction because the narrator himself describes them as tales he has heard from others and will now relate to his interlocutor, Peter. One such story, found in Book I, 3 of the *Dialogues*, is a conventional exemplum describing the powers of a holy man and the chastising of a thief. The latter has stolen vegetables from the monastery garden, so the prior commands a snake to guard the path. The thief, startled by the snake, tries to escape but finds himself entangled in the fence, hanging head downward. The prior dismisses the snake with a blessing and rebukes the thief, giving him the vegetables he had tried to steal.

Many scholars have commented on the naïveté Gregory shows toward these stories. He relates tale after tale, seeming to give critical acceptance to even the most preposterous. This may be, but Gregory saw as a function of the anecdote or exemplum the edification through pleasure of the least sophisticated of his audience. What appears to be naïveté, a quality one can ascribe to a politician and religious leader such as Gregory only with difficulty, is actually an absence of ironic overtones. The snake obeys a command made in the name of Christ; this is simply one of the conventions of the miracle tale. The miracle is the focus and *raison d'être* of the story and is the one element that cannot be called into question if the tale is to succeed.

The anecdotes and miracle stories told by Bede the Venerable in his *Ecclesiastical History of the English People* (731) are of a more sober variety than those of Gregory the Great. They are generally biographical, such as the story of Caedmon, and the focus of the miracles is on personal help—healing or the conferring of some special gift such as Caedmon's gift of song. A good example of Bede's narrative skill is his description of Caedmon's painful reluctance even to remain in the hall when others were drinking and singing lest he be required to sing; this realistic touch heightens the effect of the miraculous bestowal of musical talent. Likewise, Bede's usual narrative restraint enhances the effect of such stories as one comes upon them as gems in a plainer matrix.

Bede and Gregory have in common their use of hagiography as the controlling convention for the stories they incorporate into their works. With Paul the Deacon, readers return to the more secular, heroic cast of story that was observed in the work of Gregory of Tours. One much-praised episode, the story of Alboin, was reworked in various versions as late as the Elizabethan period. Alboin's career is developed at length in the first two books of Paul's *History of the Lombards* (after 787), but it is the story of his winning his weapons and a man's place in his society that deserves critical consideration. Alboin must receive his weapons from the king of a foreign nation, and the king he chooses, Turisind, is the father of a man Alboin has just killed. Turisind, mindful of the oath of peace extended to all guests, restrains his men, gives Alboin his weapons, and allows him to depart unharmed. It is the tension between Alboin's audacity and Turisind's honorable restraint that gives the episode its power. Paul allows the story to stand on its own merits, which are considerable, but in other instances such as the story of Lamisso (I, 15) he feels free to comment if the details of the story strain the readers' credulity too much His doubts and disclaimers appear as storyteller's asides which do not hamper the progress of the narrative; the asides do not prevent him from giving all of the details of the story, however improbable.

To suggest that the most prominent literary monuments of the sixth through the eighth centuries were, for the most part, Latin secular histories that incorporated short tales rather misrepresents the fictive activity of that period. Much has been lost, for example, of stories in Old High German. It is also safe to assume oral versions for the stories that have been dated as eighth century or later. When stories are connected, however tenuously, with historical events, one can assume that some version of those events entered the storyteller's realm soon afterwards. One of the best sets of examples involves the heroic tales concerning the Huns, the Burgundians, and the Goths; there is enough of the historical to tempt scholars to link each character with a historical personage and enough events that are patently contrary to established fact that one is forced to see the storyteller's hand and judgment at work.

The first example of the evolution of story from history concerns the death of the Ostrogothic ruler, Ermanaric, in 376, an event attested by a contemporary historian Ammianus Marcellinus and in the later histories of Jordanes and thus presumably in the lost history of Cassiodorus. Ermanaric had executed Sunnilda, the wife of a treacherous member of his following, having her torn apart or trampled by wild horses. Her brothers attempted to avenge her death but succeeded only in wounding Ermanaric so that he was permanently incapacitated. Later, this story becomes linked with the legends of the Nibelungs and the Völsungs and forms the background for the Old Icelandic *Hamðismal*. Gudrun, a well-known figure in the Nibelung and Völsung legends, urges her sons, Hamðir and Sọrli, to avenge the death of Svanhildr, their sister. As in the earlier account, the death of the sister is not part of the action of the story proper, but forms a powerful motivation for her brothers. The *Hamðismal* departs from its sources in the introduction of Erpr, an illegitimate half-brother, killed by Hamðir and Sọrli when he offers, with taunting speeches, to accompany them. The brothers succeed in mutilating Iọrmunrekkr (Ermanaric) but they are destroyed by his men, realizing too late that, if they had allowed Erpr to assist them, they would have killed Iọrmunrekkr and survived the encounter. The focus of the lay has shifted from simple revenge to a tragedy of hubris and folly as the brothers' wrongful violence against Erpr destroys them. The *Hamðismal*, an excellent example of the stark narrative of the lays in the collection known as the *Poetic Edda*, is brief and tightly constructed, with no word or incident that is irrelevant to the plot. The author has as well a gift for understatement, especially in Sọrli's rebuke to Hamðir: "You'd have had a brave heart [Erpr's], Hamðir/if you'd had a wise one:/a man lacks much/when he lacks a brain" (*Hamðismal*, stz. 27).

Ermanaric figures in several heroic tales such as the *Völsunga Saga* (c. 1200), the Old English *Widsið* (seventh century?), and the Old Icelandic Ϝ*idreks saga* (seventh century?). He is usually depicted in negative situations, although some versions of the Ermanaric stories show some sympathy for his plight. The Ϝ*idreks saga* links him, in a totally nonhistorical fashion, with another figure of history and legend, Theodoric the Ostrogoth, who was known in legend as Dietrich von Bern (Dietrich of Verona) and as Ϝidrek. Theodoric's literary development is much more involved than that of Ermanaric; his fame as a conqueror and a ruler made him the focus of many legends. One of the earliest tales in which he figures, albeit not as a character, is one of the best, the fragmentary *Hildebrandslied* (c. 800), the only extant example of Old High German heroic tale.

Hildebrand, returning to Italy with Dietrich from exile, is confronted by the army of his enemy, Odoaker (Odovacar). The conflict is to be decided by a duel, and Hildebrand's opponent is his own son, Hadubrand, who had been a very young child when his father was exiled. Hildebrand identifies himself, but Hadubrand, convinced that Hildebrand had died long before, refuses to believe him. Hadubrand insists on fighting, even when his father begs him to reconsider. The poem breaks off but the outcome is certain to be tragic: either the father will kill the son as in the case of Rustum and Sohrab, or the son will kill the father as Oedipus does Laius. In fewer than seventy lines, however, the poet has presented an episode that is powerful and deeply moving—almost a drama since much of the poem is in dialogue. The two characters reveal their personalities in their speeches. Hadubrand is all adolescent pride and truculence; Hildebrand is desperate as he realizes the futility of his pleading, seeing that his paternal affection must yield before the demands of his honor as a warrior.

Although events in the *Hildebrandslied* can be located in the historical context of Theodoric's conflict with Odovacar, the poet has chosen the father-son conflict as the focus of his work and has even altered historical fact for the sake of his story. Theodoric defeated Odovacar; the latter did not drive him out of his kingdom. This nonhistorical detail is a kind of "name-dropping," a storyteller's device to attract and hold the attention of his hearers as he proceeds to tell a story of his own making. Furthermore, the motif of exile works well for the conflict in the *Hildebrandslied* and, in fact, becomes a part of the Theodoric legend. Theodoric's and Hildebrand's exile also allow the poet to allude to another character, Attila the Hun, with whom they presumably resided for a time.

The impact of Attila on Western civilization is undeniable, and the legends of the races he encountered attest to his impact on their fiction as well. The "Scourge of God" was also the benevolent patron of Walther in the ninth century *Waltharius* and received positive treatment as Etzel in the thirteen century *The Nibelungenlied* (c. 1200). The negative portraits of Attila are to be found in the Old Icelandic tales of the Nibelungs and the Völsungs such as the *Atlakviða* (the *Lay of Atli*, ninth century?). Later medieval stories would link him with the other legendary figures from the time of the migrations, making him the contemporary not only of Theodoric, born twenty years after his death, but also of Ermanaric, who lived and died long before Attila's time. These complexities are of less importance than the tales themselves, two of which, the *Waltharius* and the *Atlakviða*, will be discussed here.

The *Waltharius* contains the stuff of epic. Attila has taken hostages from three of the kingdoms he has encountered: Walther, a prince of Aquitaine, Hildegund, a Burgundian princess, and Hagen, a Frankish nobleman. The *Waltharius*, however, is not the story of war but of the ingenuity and martial prowess of Walther himself as he extricates himself from various dilemmas.

Moreover, Walther is not an Odysseus; his struggles are with men, not with gods. He wishes only to free himself and Hildegund, his beloved, from the benevolent captivity of Attila, who considers him one of his best warriors. The lovers escape when Attila and his men are all intoxicated after a feast given by Walther. They reach the kingdom of the Franks only to be attacked by Gunther, the Frankish king who covets the treasure Walther has brought from his Hunnish captivity. Among Gunther's men is Hagen, who had escaped earlier from Attila. Hagen is forced by his allegiance to Gunther to join him in a two-against-one combat with Walther, who before this was his friend, but he rationalizes his acquiescence to Gunther's demand by means of the vengeance he must seek for a nephew killed by Walther during the battle. All three fighters survive the conflict, although Walther loses his right hand, Gunther loses a leg, and Hagen loses one eye; at the end, Walther mocks Hagen for joining Gunther against him.

The poet uses all the techniques of the epic—scholars have suggested the influence of Vergil's *Aeneid* (c. 29-19 B.C.)—while maintaining his focus on personal conflicts, especially that between Walther and Hagen. In this, the poet of the *Waltharius* resembles the poet of the *Hildebrandslied*. The great events and personages of the migrations and the fall of the Roman Empire are simply contest and background for the central conflicts of the tales. The *Hildebrandslied* and the *Waltharius* are heroic lays that achieve narrative power by concentrated focus on potentially tragic confrontations.

In the *Atlakviða*, Attila is given the negative role which is more familiar to most readers. Gunther and Hagen appear as the brothers of Gudrun, the wife of Atli (Attila). Atli has persuaded the brothers to come to his court, and, once they are there, he tortures them to force from them the location of the great treasure of the Nibelungs. Hǫgni (Hagen) is killed and Gunther eventually dies in a pit of snakes. Gudrun takes vengeance in Aeschylean fashion; she kills her sons by Atli and serves him their flesh. She then sets fire to the hall and all perish. The *Atlakviða* is as terse and stark as the other example of the Eddic lay, the *Hamðismal*. The poet attends to the basic matter of the conflicts—Atli's avarice, the heroic resistance of the brothers, and the total vengeance of Gudrun.

The tales of the Goths, the Burgundians, and the Huns are primarily interesting because of their literary style, which combines narrative simplicity with compelling, dramatic situations that in and of themselves serve the purposes of characterization. The other aspect of their importance involves the way in which important figures and events of history find their way into fictional narrative, a process much more complex than this study can indicate, but one which demonstrates the interaction between fact, tradition, and the creative impulse.

History and fable (or story) come together also in one of the major Old English heroic works, the *Battle of Maldon* (c. tenth century). The poem has been much admired for the clarity with which it illustrates both the glory and the tragedy of the heroic ethos in confrontation with the reality of war. Byrthnoth, the leader of an English troop, permits an invading party of Norwegians to cross, at low tide, a causeway that at any other time would be impassable. His heroic and hubristic generosity dooms him and his men in the subsequent battle. They die to a man, one of the last survivors rendering in epigrammatic fashion the code by and for which they lived and died: "Heart must be braver, courage the bolder/Mood the stouter as our strength grows less!"

The *Battle of Maldon* exists for us without the opening lines, but the point at which the story begins is nevertheless lyrical in force: a young knight frees his falcon and this, the poet says, is a sign that he will not fail his leader; the poem maintains this elegiac note throughout. Scholars have established nearly all of the details concerning the historicity of the battle, but it is the work of the poet—his skill in depicting Byrthnoth's *ofermoδ*, hubris, and the dogged courage of his men—that makes the *Battle of Maldon* unequaled in tragic impact within its scope except by the *Hildebrandslied*.

An earlier passage in this study mentioned the accommodations that Christian literary sensibilities made to some of the modes of secular literature. The various hagiographical stories of the early Middle Ages are a good index to this accommodation. One might argue that the tales of saints and martyrs are not, strictly speaking, fiction, yet their narrative form quickly becomes standardized—miraculous birth, early piety, many miracles, much self-denial, fortitude under oppression, and painful martyrdom or blissful death—and, of greater significance, these tales participate in one of the major fictional modes, that of romance. No matter how gruesome the details of a martyrdom might be, the tale has, in the Christian context, the requisite "happy ending" of romance. The saint's life or miracle is yet another aspect of the wish-fulfillment that underlies the mode of romance.

One must make distinctions among the various forms of medieval hagiography. The Old English *Andreas* (eighth century?) or the *Elene* (750-785), or the Irish *Voyage of St. Brendan* (ninth century, written in Latin), are quite different from such Old French works as the *Cantilena of St. Eulalia* (c. 880) sequence or the *Life of St. Alexis* (1040). The Old English tales have a strong heroic element and have a wider scope of action than the Old French tales. The *Voyage of St. Brendan* takes the form of a quest and has been linked with the Old Irish voyage tales (*Imramma*) such as the *Voyage of Bran* (seventh century) or the *Voyage of Maeldune* (seventh-ninth century). It is as much a tale of the wonders witnessed by St. Brendan and his companions as it is the story of a holy ascetic.

The *Voyage of St. Brendan* relates the quest of the abbot St. Brendan and several of his monks for a fabled "Promised Land of the Saints," an earthly Paradise. The journey is a series of encounters with strange creatures and enchanted places, but it is also a spiritual journey. Some scholars have argued that the various islands or sailing conditions, such as the Coagulated Sea (the Sargasso?), can be identified and that the *Voyage of St. Brendan* suggests actual journeys perhaps even to the Americas. This hint of possible veracity accounts in part for the popularity of the work all through the medieval period, but its popularity resulted as well from the writer's descriptions of the beautiful and the strange; from the way in which monastic spirituality is unified with the quest for marvels (centuries before the Old French *Quest of the Holy Grail*, 1225-1230); and from the person of St. Brendan himself. His calm faith sustains his monks through all of their fantastic adventures, and even the presence of a sea monster, the leviathan Jasconius, does not disrupt the tranquil tone of the work.

In contrast to the *Voyage of St. Brendan*, the spirituality and piety of the *Andreas* and the *Elene* seem more vigorous and active. Andreas (the apostle Andrew) must rescue his fellow-apostle Matthias from a race of cannibals. The poem graphically describes the torments suffered by Andreas once he rescues both Matthias and the youth of the cannibal race chosen to die in Matthias' stead. Among the best passages of the poem are those that describe Andreas' sea journeys with a mysterious boatman who catechizes him on matters of faith and who is, as Andreas slowly realizes, Christ himself. Andreas' role as deliverer and missionary crystallizes in the image of the water from the rock, a flood Andreas invokes to destroy his enemies. He relents so much as to pray for the resurrection of the youths of the cannibals, and, having converted them to Christianity, he departs. For all his passivity, Andreas is a fighter, a thane of Christ, and a Moses-figure. He is timid when first confronted with his task, but the dominant impression left by this heroic miracle tale is the forceful personality of its protagonist.

The same evaluation applies to Cynewulf's *Elene*, the story of the recovery of the True Cross by St. Helena, mother of the emperor Constantine. Confronted by the obstinacy of the elders of Jerusalem, she incarcerates a wise man who is known to hold the key to the mystery of the rebel teacher executed in that city. The wise man, named, oddly enough, Judas, yields before Elene's harshness and reveals not only the identity of the rebel, but also the place of His crucifixion. Only one of the crosses found there can resurrect a dead youth, and Elene claims it as the long-sought relic. Judas converts to the Christian faith and receives the name Cyriacus, and Elene returns to her son in a triumph of healing miracles.

The *Elene* and the *Andreas* have been described here as heroic miracle tales because they emphasize the power of their protagonists (and their protagonists' Patron). Andreas, although broken by torture, can nevertheless invoke an enemy-destroying miracle, and Elene uses the power of her imperial rank, usually a negative element, in the service of the Faith. Indeed, the *Elene*, from its first episode, the triumph granted Constantine by the sign of the Cross, deals with the *power* of the new Faith. This emphasis on militant Christianity is in marked contrast to the hagiographic narratives of the *Cantilena of St. Eulalia* and the *Life of St. Alexis*.

The *Cantilena of St. Eulalia* is the first literary monument of the French language. In addition to its linguistic significance it also attests to the adaptation of the liturgical sequence (an extended embellishment of a line of text) to the uses of lyric poetry. The poem is very brief and tells the story of Eulalia's martyrdom in the simplest manner. Eulalia, a young Christian noblewoman, refuses to give up her faith; brought before Maximian, she persists in her resistance and is given over to be burned. When the flames do not harm her, Maximian orders her beheaded. Her soul flies to heaven in the form of a dove.

For all its brevity, the *Cantilena of St. Eulalia* presents a complete dramatic action that builds in intensity from Eulalia's resistance through the torturing and martyrdom, and is resolved in her soul's flight. As stated above, this tale differs from the Old English tales here described in its emphasis not on Eulalia's active power but on her endurance and her helplessness to resist, physically at least, her tormentors. Also, the focus of the tale is on the personal rather than the social effects of the miracles.

The *Life of St. Alexis*, another early French monument, deals again with the struggles of an individual. Alexis, a wealthy young man, decides on his wedding night to reject all—wife, riches, and family—to devote himself to prayer and self-denial. After a lengthy self-exile, he returns to his home and lives, unrecognized by his family, as a poor holy-man under the staircase of his former home. His family only learns of his true identity by means of a letter that they find after his death. The poem ends proclaiming Alexis' joy in Heaven where he is reunited with his maiden bride. The *Life of St. Alexis* follows the conventions of the flight-from-the-world, which is one of the many varieties of saints' lives. Its compact narrative and careful handling of rhythm and assonance show the French language in the process of becoming one of the major literary languages of the West.

The saints' lives have been described as participating formally in the mode of romance in a period in which, for the most part, heroic tales dominated. The great age of medieval romance would begin in the early decades of the twelfth century, but as early as the ninth century and possibly even earlier, there were Celtic precursors to many of the major romances. The Irish *Exile of the Sons of Uisliu* has been linked with the development of the Tristan legend, and the *Wooing of Etain* (ninth century), also Irish, with the legend of Lancelot and Guinevere at least insofar as the abductions of Guinevere are concerned.

The *Exile of the Sons of Uisliu*, sometimes called the story of Deirdre, describes the fate of those sons of Uisliu who accompany Noisiu, their brother, into exile after he elopes with Deirdre, who has been promised to Conchobar, king of Ulster. The outcome is tragic for both lovers: Noisiu is treacherously slain, and Deirdre, who sings two poignant laments for her lover, later commits suicide rather than be given to one she despises. One can see the details that later became part of the Tristan story—the illicit love affair, the lovers' flight, and their tragic demise—but the work has its own inherent interest. One sympathizes with Deirdre, fated from before her birth to cause dissension among men, when she chooses Noisiu in defiance of the arrangement that makes her the property of the aging Conchobar. Likewise, Noisiu draws the reader's sympathy as he is taunted by Deirdre into accepting her, an act that seals his fate.

The *Wooing of Etain* is the story of how King Eochaid Airem wins Etain, a princess of the fairy-folk, loses her to her former mate who is also of Faery because of a rash boon, and regains her by besieging the fairy-mounds and eventually succeeding in the trials set before him there. This tale reappears in many guises, not only in the *Lancelot* (after 1164) of Chrétien de Troyes but also in *Pwyll, Prince of Dyred*, one of the tales included in *The Mabinogion*, a group of Welsh tales dating from the very end of the period under discussion here. Like the *Exile of the Sons of Uisliu*, the *Wooing of Etain* is important as a good piece of fiction in its own right, from the lavish description of Etain with which it begins to the moment of surprise when Etain is magically abducted despite the hapless Eochaid's attempts to guard her.

In bringing together an extended discussion of the forms of short fiction in the Middle Ages, a danger exists of oversimplification or of a too-pat schematic view of diverse developments. The period of the early Middle Ages was an unsettled time. Necessary social and economic adjustments to the collapse of Roman domination in the West threatened the preservation of the classical tradition of education. The number of surviving works of fiction seems small beside the compendia of rhetorical, historical, or doctrinal works, but at no time did the art of fiction lapse, certainly not as far as oral transmission and development was concerned, as the complicated history of the Goths, Burgundians, and their heroes clearly shows. Often, however, "story" was put to work in sermons or in histories without losing the essential crafted nature that sets a work of fiction apart from mere sequential reportage. Many of the independent stories never ceased to engage their audiences, and storytellers adapted them by retelling or forging ever more complex combinations of the tales, some with the range and scope, for example, of the Theodoric stories. Although many of the gems of early medieval fiction remain buried in little-read histories or in collections primarily of interest to scholars, others, some of which have been discussed here, are now receiving the scholarly and critical attention they have deserved as literary works.

CHART I

Historical		Literary	
375	Death of Ermanaric	520	Cassiodorus' *History of the Goths* (lost)
435	Defeat of Gundaharius by the Huns	c. 591	Gregory of Tours's *History of the Franks*
451	Defeat of Attila by the Burgundians	c. 550	Jordanes' *Getica* (abbreviated version of Cassiodorus' work)
453	Death of Attila		
476	Odovacar king in Italy (deposition of the last Roman ruler)	593	Gregory the Great's *Dialogues*
		622-623	Isidore of Seville's *Etymologies*
493	Theodoric the Ostrogoth conquers Italy	731	Bede's *Ecclesiastical History of the English People*
		750-785	Cynewulf; *Elene Andreas*
		eighth century	
		after 787	Paul the Deacon's *History of the Lombards*
768-814	Reign of Charlemagne	c. 800	The *Hildebrandslied*
842	The Strasbourg Oaths	ninth century	Irish tales: *Exile of the Sons of Uisliu; Wooing of Etain*
843	The Treaty of Verdun		

c. 850-890?	The Waltharius
c. 880	The Cantilena of St. Eulalia
ninth and tenth centuries	Icelandic tales: Atlakviða; Hamðismal
tenth century	Welsh tales: The Mabinogion
1040	The Life of St. Alexis
987	Hugh Capet crowned
991	The Battle of Maldon (poem composed soon afterwards)

CHART II

Author	Work	Date	Language	Form
PRE-CAROLINGIAN c. 500-750				
Cassiodorus	History of the Goths (lost)	520	Latin	History/Vignettes
Jordanes	Getica	c. 550	Latin	History/Vignettes
Gregory of Tours	History of the Franks	c. 575-594	Latin	History/Vignettes
Gregory the Great	Dialogues	593	Latin	History/Vignettes
Bede	Ecclesiastical History	731	Latin	History/Vignettes
Paul the Deacon	History of the Lombards	after 787	Latin	History/Vignettes
CAROLINGIAN AND ANGLO-SAXON c. 750-1000				
Cynewulf	Elene	750-785	Old English	Heroic miracle-tale

Andreas	eighth century	Old English	Heroic miracle-tale
Hildebrandslied	c. 800	Old High German	Heroic verse-narrative
Waltharius	late ninth century	Latin	Heroic verse-narrative
Cantilena of St. Eulalia	c. 880	Old French	Verse hagiography
Battle of Maldon	early tenth century	Old English	Heroic verse-narrative
Life of St. Alexis	mid-tenth century	Old French	Verse hagiography

CELTIC AND ICELANDIC c. 800-1050

Voyage of St. Brendan	ninth century	Latin	*Prose hagiography*
Exile of the Sons of Uisliu and Wooing of Etain	ninth century	Old Irish	Heroic/romantic prose narrative
Atlakviða; Hamðismal	ninth/tenth centuries?	Old Icelandic	Heroic verse-narrative
The Mabinogion	tenth century?	Welsh	Heroic/romantic prose-narrative

Bibliography
Auerback, Erich. *Literary Language and Its Public in Late Latin Antiquity and in the Middle Ages.*
Curtius, Ernst R. *European Literature and the Latin Middle Ages.*
Ker, W. P. *Epic and Romance: Essays in Medieval Literature.*
Laistner, Max L. W. *Thought and Letters in Western Europe, A.D. 500-900.*
Previté-Orton, Charles W. *The Shorter Cambridge Medieval History.*
Southern, Richard W. *The Making of the Middle Ages.*

Amelia A. Rutledge

THE ROMANCE FORM IN THE LATE MIDDLE AGES

The Middle Ages witnessed the flowering of one of the most important predecessors of the modern short story, the romance. By the late Middle Ages, this genre had become an extremely popular literary form. During the genre's inception in the eleventh century, the term "romance" referred exclusively to a composition written in French—a "Romance" language. During the literary history of the Middle Ages, however, the term came to denote a fictional narrative of a particular type: the romance focused upon love and/or adventure, but it relied on conventional plots to achieve this focus; it was daringly unrealistic in conception and frequently employed remote settings, but nonetheless strove for psychological realism; and it contained characters who were usually stylized but, by being types, were universal and therefore readily and uniquely understandable.

Although this sort of literature assumed a generic identity and acquired a defined form during the Middle Ages, it had its roots in much earlier tradition. Classical epics such as the *Odyssey* (c. 800 B. C.) and the *Aeneid* (c. 29-19 B. C.); sagas such as *The Nibelungenlied* (c. 1200); *chansons de geste* such as *The Song of Roland* (c. 1100); and the early chronicle accounts of Arthur all contain the elements of love, mystery, adventure, and psychology that have now come to be associated with romance. These earlier works, however, differ from romance in being consciously nationalistic and either historical or pseudohistorical, whereas romance, even while striving for verisimilitude, is nonetheless consciously and deliberately fictional.

During the Middle Ages the romance became a distinct literary type in part because writers wished to free themselves from the restrictions of the epic form and in part because the developing interest in new themes and ideas required new modes of expression. The treatment accorded the story of Arthur, surely one of the most famous figures in English literature, well exemplifies the change in literary expression from epic to romance. Whereas the earliest accounts in which Arthur appears portray him as a historical hero who comes to assume national importance, by the time of the Middle Ages he has been transformed by courtly writers from a historical and national hero to a hero of romance. Apparently the first historian to mention Arthur is Nennius, whose ninth century *Historia Britonum*, a redaction of previous chronicles from the seventh and eighth centuries, describes Arthur as "the leader of battles" who slaughters many pagans, and notes Arthur's use of Mary's image to assist him in combat; Arthur is said to have singlehandedly slain 960 men in one day. A similar but much briefer account of Arthur's prowess in battle is found in the *Annales Cambriae*, the tenth century work of a Welsh writer who states that Arthur, having carried the cross of Christ on his shoulders for three days and three nights, was victorious in the Battle of Badon. Around 1125, William of Malmesbury, in his *Gesta Regum Anglo-*

rum (*Acts of the Kings*), attests Arthur's historicity while he simultaneously acknowledges that mythmaking concerning Arthur is taking place; he differentiates between the Arthur of truthful histories and the Arthur of false myths produced by the Bretons. In fact, the Arthurian legend expanded greatly during this time, both in England and on the Continent; with every crossing of the English Channel the legend accumulated more and more material, so that the actual historicity of Arthur became increasingly difficult to verify.

These historical and pseudohistorical accounts provided the basis for the more deliberately imaginative Arthurian writings, which are the major sources of contemporary Arthurian legendry and which begin to appear in the twelfth century. In that century there is a shift from treatment of Arthur as a historical figure to treatment of him as a figure of mythic proportion. Geoffrey of Monmouth's *Historia Regum Britanniae* (*History of the Kings of Britain*), written around 1136, consciously builds upon the scant writings of Nennius to create a national hero for England; to do this Geoffrey added to Arthur's primary historical characterization as a fighter and a leader of warriors the coloration of chivalry, thus combining in his work, and in the figure of Arthur, both epic and courtly traditions. Geoffrey adds to the legend the descent of Arthur from Aeneas of Troy, the begetting of Arthur by Uther Pendragon, the figures of Merlin and Mordred, and the courtly entourage which was necessary in order to reshape Arthur from a local chieftain into a great king. Indications of courtliness are displayed in the notions that a woman could be an incentive for the knight to excel and that the knight's bravery and nobility could be an incentive for the woman to be pure.

This transformation of the Arthurian story from epic to romance was continued in Wace's *Roman de Brut* of 1155; Wace adds to the written legend the tradition of the Round Table, dramatizes the Arthurian story through the addition of dialogue and action, and portrays Arthur as more courtly and less barbaric, as possessing other than martial attributes and abilities. Layamon's *Brut*, written around 1200, makes further additions to the legend of an extraordinary and supernatural nature, such as the fays who nurture the infant Arthur and the mysterious ladies who take Arthur away to Avalon. As other writers drew upon and developed the Arthurian material, the story of Arthur, the national hero, eventually became merely a backdrop, or a departure point, for stories which focused on such corollary themes as the quest for the Holy Grail and on such other knights as Perceval, Lancelot, and Gawain. By the time *Sir Gawain and the Green Knight* was written late in the fourteenth century, Arthur had been completely transformed from the epic hero he had been at his inception to the chivalric hero of romance.

This transformation of Arthurian material represents only one reflection of that radical shift in literary interest from epic to romance which occurred in the Middle Ages. Prior to this time literary expression had taken the epic form of such works as the *Iliad* (c. Sixth Century B. C.), the *Aeneid, Beowulf*

(c. 1000), and *The Song of Roland*, works which had a national character and which presented a hero who represented national ideals and virtues. By the time of the twelfth century, however, it became evident that national traditions were no longer so clearly separate and distinct, that cultural interpenetration was causing traditions to blend, and in consequence that themes and ideas, and modes of expressing those themes and ideas, were held in common by writers of many nations.

In addition to the diminishing nationalism in literary themes, other trends also contributed to the maturing of the romance form in the Middle Ages. The genre's development was significantly aided by the infusion of material from classical sources, particularly such Latin works as Ovid's *Metamorphoses* (before A. D. 8) and *Ars Amatoria* (*Art of Love*, before A. D. 8), and of Celtic materials, many of which may have provided substance for the Arthurian legend. An additional influencing factor was the formation of a new perspective on women; in the Middle Ages women came to assume a position of greater importance in society than they had previously enjoyed, in part because of the popularity of the cult of the Virgin, which venerated Mary and through her all womankind, and in part because of the dissemination of chivalric and courtly ideals which similarly respected and exalted women. Although debate continues as to whether or not a "system" of courtly love was recognized as such in the Middle Ages, we do know for certain that courtly attitudes existed, that people aspired to courtly ideals, and that those courtly attitudes and ideals influenced people's conduct. In conjunction with, and perhaps as a result of, the cult of the Virgin, the courtly mystique elevated women to positions of morally and spiritually superior beings who could inspire admirers to transcend human limitations and rise to new heights of nobility; courtly love made a religion of male devotion to his lady, and courtly idealism demanded a high degree of civilized and sophisticated behavior in its adherents.

Medieval romance, then, can be seen to differ from epic—a term which includes saga and *chanson de geste*—in content, in form of presentation, and in emphasis. Whereas the epic usually concerns a serious subject of national importance and a warrior-hero whose actions have national implications, the romance often has a weak and insignificant plot which concerns a matter of personal importance, such as a love affair and its attendant problems or a chivalric adventure; the plot of the epic serves to reveal the hero's character and to establish his national importance, while the plot of the romance serves to reveal motivation, to delineate psychological processes and responses, and to explore intellectual and emotional dilemmas. Although many romances deal with the four "matters" of Rome, France, Britain, and England, which would lead one to believe they were historical in nature, their purpose was nonetheless primarily entertainment, and they often contained elements of the mysterious and the supernatural. Further contrasting the epic, which is usually sharply focused and unified, the romance is often of much looser structure; the plot is often episodic, and the episodes are both undeveloped and yet usually embellished by picturesque and detailed descriptions. Moreover, whereas the epic usually focuses on the character of the hero, the romance often relies upon stylized types or faintly drawn characterization, focusing instead on the hero's generally exaggerated adventures, which often lack real purpose. The romance hero fights for the sake of fighting, while the epic hero ordinarily fights only for a highly significant or exalted purpose. Finally, while the epic very often is tragic, ending with the hero's death, the romance frequently has a happy ending.

The courtly idealism so characteristic of the romance form during the Middle Ages first appeared in members of the French aristocracy and in the poetry of the Troubadours and Trouvères. From France the courtly ideal spread to England, advanced in part by the enormously influential work of Andreas Capellanus. A chaplain to the French court, Capellanus, in the latter quarter of the twelfth century, codified the system of courtly love in his work *De Arte Honeste Amandi* (*The Art of Courtly Love*). The work's first two books define love, establish its rules, and detail the appropriate conduct for its devotees, while the third book, curiously, serves as a retraction which seems to contradict everything said before. The first two books, emphasizing the ennobling nature of passionate love, explain the incompatibility of love and marriage; in fact, Capellanus states that love has no place in marriage since love requires secrecy, jealousy, apprehension, and difficulty in attainment. Marriage is not, however, an excuse for not loving, but of course the beloved must be someone other than one's spouse. Capellanus also states that the lover's whole mind is on the beloved and, in consequence, the lover will suffer greatly, will exhibit paleness, and will experience sleeplessness, heart palpitations, and loss of appetite.

The influence of this codification of courtly love on medieval romance, on the later romance tradition, and indeed on Western society, is immeasurable, since the work of Capellanus is both descriptive in recording existing attitudes and prescriptive in establishing those attitudes as the ideal. The emotional concept which we now call "romantic love" is thus "born" during the Middle Ages, when love was separated from marriage; marriage, after all, was based on such things as property and politics and was therefore practical and mundane, whereas courtly love, as depicted by Capellanus, is spiritual and passionate. Thus, in its establishment of love as an ennobling social influence, in its systemization of the rules for the conduct of love, and in its development of the notion of feminine worth, the work of Capellanus influenced to a very great extent both literature and society. Many of the deepest patterns of behavior which today govern relations between the sexes have their genesis in the code which Capellanus describes.

If Capellanus provided a formulization of the rules of courtly behavior, two other French poets of the latter part of the twelfth century, Marie de France and Chrétien de Troyes, provided extremely influential artistic celebrations of the courtly system. The approximately fifteen extant lais which are attributed to Marie are all short, simple, and direct, and were probably intended to be sung to harp accompaniment; emphasizing love rather than warfare, the poems reflect courtly sentiment in their focus upon courtesy, chivalry, and loyalty in love. Typical of Marie's themes and treatments is the lai of "Lanval." In disfavor with his king, Lanval one day rides into the country; lying down to rest, he is approached by two beautiful maidens who take him to their lady in a nearby pavilion. The lady, obviously a supernatural being, gives Lanval her love and a bottomless purse but warns him that if he speaks of her to anyone he will never see her again. When Guinevere accuses Lanval of being false to his lord, of having secret sins, and of despising women, he defends himself by stating indignantly that in fact he has a lover and that the lowliest of her servants excels Queen Guinevere in every way. Denounced by Guinevere to Arthur, Lanval is directed to produce his lady and prove his statement but he is, of course, unable to summon her. Saved from prison only by the surety of his friends, he is about to be sentenced to exile when a procession of beautiful maidens arrives, the last of whom is Lanval's mistress. When Arthur agrees that she is indeed more beautiful than the queen, Lanval's supernatural lover takes him away with her to Avalon.

Marie claimed that her intent in her work was merely to turn traditional tales into romance, and clearly she uses in her lais many conventional topoi: the woman scorned motif draws upon the theme of Potiphar's wife; the idea of the supernatural lover comes either from Celtic fairy lore or from the classical myth of Cupid and Psyche; and the bottomless purse and the outcast who becomes favored above all are elements common in folktale. Marie has, however, imbued these thematic strands with the coloration of courtly love, so that the lai serves as an exemplum illustrating one of the courtly love tenets—the necessity of keeping love secret.

Chrétien de Troyes, also writing in the last half of the twelfth century, produced several romances for the French court. Of those five extant, the unfinished *Perceval* (c. 1180) is notable as a spiritual romance concerning the quest for the Holy Grail which was used by Wolfram von Eschenbach for his romance *Parzival* (c. 1200), and which inspired as well a number of later romances concerning the Grail legend; this romance overtly links chivalry and religion in the romance form. Chrétien's *Lancelot* (after 1164) is significant for its development of the ideas that love between a husband and wife is impossible and that love requires an absolute and unhesitating devotion. Although Chrétien undoubtedly received the material for this romance from Marie de France, his emphasis on psychological analysis, and his examination of the parameters of human commitment to a code of conduct, make his treatment of the material unique. In the course of the romance Lancelot sets out to rescue the queen who, as a result of Arthur's rash promise, has been taken captive. Having been unhorsed by the captor, Lancelot is walking disconsolately behind a cart when the driver tells him to get in if he wishes to learn about the queen. Although Lancelot's love for Guinevere is great, his pride and his dismay at having to ride in so unknightly a fashion cause him to take two more steps behind the cart before getting into it. After this act, although he triumphantly passes a number of tests of his devotion to his queen which require him, among other things, to resist a seduction attempt, to crawl painfully over a bridge made of swords, to fight backwards so as to keep his eyes fixed on the tower where his lady watches, and to play the coward in a tournament, Lancelot is nevertheless treated disdainfully by the queen because of the incompleteness of his devotion, indicated by those two additional steps which he had taken behind the cart before climbing in. This romance clearly demonstrates the absolute necessity of total commitment to the loved one.

In the twelfth century, then, and beginning with such writers as Chrétien de Troyes and Marie de France, the romance tradition began to flower. Writers at that time, engaged in freeing themselves from the limiting confines of the epic tradition, were exploring new ways of expressing new ideas and themes. Many of these new ideas and themes concerned the four "matters" we have come to associate with romance: the matter of France, which focuses upon the adventures of Charlemagne and his peers; the matter of Rome, which consists of romances based upon classical material, whether legendary or historical; the matter of Britain, which concerns stories from Arthurian legend; and the matter of England, which treats native English heroes or heroes whose lives and adventures in some way concerned England.

Those romances concerned with the matter of France—the Charlemagne romances—are closest in kind to the epic form. They concern themselves less with love and psychology and more with warfare and heroism. Just as the matter of Britain romances derive ultimately from the epic treatment of Arthur, the Charlemagne romances have as their ultimate source *The Song of Roland*, the Old French epic detailing Roland's heroism, Oliver's wisdom, Ganelon's treachery, and Archbishop Turpin's bravery and piety. The Charlemagne romances (fourteenth century) fall roughly into two groups; one group, concerning the story of Otuel, contains such romances as *Otuel*, *The Sege of Melayne*, and *Roland and Vernagu*, while the other group, concerned with the story of Ferumbras, contains such romances as *The Sowdone of Babylone* and *Sir Ferumbras*. *Otuel*, the earliest Charlemagne romance in English, is a tale which contrasts the original Old French epic in diminishing the stature of Roland in order to elevate that of the hero Otuel. After detailing Otuel's conversion to Christianity in the midst of his combat with Roland, who had killed Otuel's uncle Vernagu, the romance describes Otuel's performance as a Christian knight in battles against the Saracens. *The Sege of*

Melayne, another romance in the Otuel group, is notable for its depiction of Archbishop Turpin as a heroic figure in battle and for its presentation of religious visions and miracles. *Roland and Vernagu* makes use of the Latin legend that Charlemagne went to the Holy Land and received there such relics as St. Simeon's arm, Mary's smock, and the crown of thorns; the romance also tells of the invasion of Spain and of Roland's battle with Vernagu. Unfinished, the romance was perhaps intended as an introduction to *Otuel*. The Charlemagne romances, in their treatment of the religious conflict between Christians and infidels, are in some ways akin to Arthurian romances concerned with the Grail theme, in that in both sorts of romances religious faith provides a significant motivating force.

In the second group of romances, which concern the Ferumbras theme, *The Sowdone of Babylone* tells of Laban, Sultan of Babylon, and his twenty-foot-tall son Ferumbras who sack Rome and, having obtained the relics of the Passion—the cross, the crown of thorns, and the Crucifixion nails—remove them to Spain. When Charlemagne's army comes to recover the relics, many adventures ensue. Oliver meets Ferumbras in single combat, conquers him, and converts him, after which Ferumbras fights with the Christians against the Saracens. This romance has a noteworthy love story which concerns Floripas, the Sultan's daughter, who falls in love with Guy of Burgundy, one of Charlemagne's knights. Her ingenuity and determination, which are inspired by her love, are ultimately significant in the victory of Charlemagne's forces and the rescue of the relics; consequently, after being baptized, she is married to her lover. A number of the incidents in the second part of this romance form the substance of another romance titled *Sir Ferumbras* which is consciously and carefully crafted and which is perhaps therefore one of the best of the English Charlemagne romances.

Although medieval romances concerned with the matter of Rome had as possible subjects the adventures of Alexander the Great, the Trojan War, the siege of Thebes, and the adventures of Aeneas, stories of Alexander and of Troy seem to have been the most popular. *Kyng Alisaunder* (fourteenth century), the best of the Alexander romances, first tells of Alexander's begetting through the magical powers of the Egyptian king Nectanebus, who contrives to mate with Olympias, the wife of Philip of Macedon, and thereby fathers Alexander. The romance also details Alexander's rise to power and his various military accomplishments, particularly his wars with Darius, King of Persia. The second part of the romance, treating Alexander's conquest of India and the many adventures he experienced in the Far Eastern countries, relies heavily on the excitement of the unknown and the distant in its description of mythical beasts and other wondrous sights.

The Alexander romances, although concerned with a historical figure, had little basis in history, as did the romances based upon the Troy theme. Since Homer was unknown to Western Europe in the medieval period, Troy romances were based not upon the *Iliad*, but upon two later accounts of the Trojan siege by Dictys Cretensis and by Dares Phrygius, whose works concern the story of Jason and the Argonauts in their quest for the Golden Fleece, the siege of Troy, and the Greeks' return home. Among the Troy romances which make use of these accounts is *The Gest Historiale of the Destruction of Troy* (thirteenth century) which details Jason's adventures; the history of Troy; the kidnaping of Helen; the story of Cassandra; the Greeks' preparation for the journey and the journey itself; the siege, the battle, and the destruction of Troy; the departure of Aeneas; and the return adventures of Ulysses. Other romances on the Troy theme include the *Laud Troy-book*, which selectively treats the material of the *Gest Historiale*; John Lydgate's *The Hystorye, sege and dystruccyon of Troye* (c. 1412-1420); and, of course, Geoffrey Chaucer's poem *Troilus and Criseyde* (1601-1602), which is considered by many to be among the finest executions of this theme. Chaucer uses the Trojan War, however, merely as a backdrop for an examination of chivalric love and the complex psychologies of his two main characters; his concern is with human love, human relations, and human idealism, and the student of romance could do no better than to study Chaucer's poem in order to obtain a thorough understanding of the genre of romance.

One of the most popular of the four matters was the Arthurian theme, the matter of Britain, which was treated extensively by writers in England and on the Continent. As time passed, and as more and more material accrued to the legend of Arthur, several other personages came in their own right to be the focus of romances; Gawain, Tristan, Lancelot, Galahad, and Perceval are all the subject of stories in which Arthur is only a minor or a corollary figure. Sir Thomas Malory, one of the most influential writers of Arthurian material, pulled together for his *Le Morte d'Arthur* (1485) much of the legendary and many of the romances into a more or less unified whole; although Malory's work is certainly a redaction of earlier writings, it is much more than that, in large part because of Malory's reshaping of the material into a body of writing which has coherence and purpose. Many later treatments of the story of Arthur are based upon Malory's work. The enduring popularity of the Arthurian theme is evident in such twentieth century works as Thomas Berger's *Arthur Rex* (1979), Richard Monaco's *Parzival: Or, a Knight's Tale* (1977), T. H. White's *The Once and Future King* (1958) and *The Book of Merlyn* (1977), and the several treatments of the theme by Mary Stewart.

The romances said to concern the matter of England for the most part differ in some important ways from the other medieval romances here discussed; they are often much less courtly and less sophisticated than the other romances, and they advance and support humble and simple virtues rather than the aristocratic virtues of chivalry and the courtly life. The inherited material of these romances, whether of native or foreign origin, having been adapted to the lower-class taste, is consequently often spare and realistic, with little of descriptive set pieces and other courtly elements. Action is preferred to introspection and analysis, and the poems are usually vigorous and balladlike in their concision.

Among these romances concerning the matter of England are *King Horn* (c. 1250), which uses the exile and return theme; *Bevis of Hampton* (1622), which begins with a variation on the Hamlet theme; *The Tale of Gamelyn* (c. 1350), from which Shakespeare drew for *As You Like It* (1599-1600); and *William of Palerne* (early fourteenth century), which uses the popular were-wolf theme. Perhaps most reflective, however, of the spirit and the values of England's peasantry and its growing middle class is *Havelok the Dane* (c. 1350), a romance concerning a hero who is wrongly excluded from his kingdom in Denmark by an untrustworthy guardian. When the poor fisherman who reared Havelok can no longer support him, Havelok obtains work as a kitchen-helper, soon earning renown locally for his ability to putt the stone; while such activities seem the very antithesis of courtly endeavor, they are nonetheless solidly representative of middle-class virtues. In time Havelok marries an orphaned English princess, Goldeboru, who, like Havelok, was betrayed by a guardian; when one night Goldeboru sees a luminous mark on Havelok's shoulder which indicates his royalty, she is overjoyed. After re-turning to Denmark and claiming his throne, Havelok conquers England and rewards all who have treated him well. The emphasis throughout the poem is on adventure, justice, and homely but traditional virtues, an emphasis which clearly distinguishes this romance, and the other romances on the matter of England, from those romances of the period which emphasize courtliness.

In sum, then, medieval romances can be seen to encompass a wide variety of subjects and to represent various cultural attitudes. In the medieval age the form drew upon a broad spectrum of sources, including history, legendry, folktale, saint's life, exemplum, fairy lore, and classical materials. After its beginning in the twelfth century, the romance was widely adapted throughout the next three centuries by writers of many countries whose works cross-influenced one another to the extent that establishing direct lines of descent for particular themes or subjects is generally impossible. The pervasiveness of those ideas in later fiction results in part from the genre's use of themes which transcend temporal limitations; the motifs of the wicked guardian, the disinherited hero, the scorned admirer, the wronged lover, and the love-triangle, which are found in such abundance in medieval romances, continue to inform later works of short and long fiction. The medieval romance, like myth and folktale, thus draws on archetypal situations and figures for the presentation of its themes, but at the same time it satisfies the reader's desire for the unusual, the strange, and the alien.

Romance also transcends time in its presentation of the idealized world; the impulse to depict such a world, seen continually in medieval romances, persists in contemporary fiction. Similarly, the medieval romance's insistence on seeing women as admirable creatures and as sources of inspiration enabled the genre to posit the validity of love as a motive for and a cause of nobility, an idea which continues to govern much twentieth century writing. Clearly, the importance of medieval romance in contributing form, material, and attitude to the development of modern prose fiction can hardly be over-estimated; the romance provided a broad imaginative scope while it simultaneously bequeathed a legacy of rich material for plot and characterization.

In the late seventeenth and early eighteenth centuries the romance as a literary form declined in popularity, making way for neoclassical forms. In the late eighteenth century the Gothic romance became popular, but this was a variation on the traditional romance form which relied heavily on sensational material and the evocation of emotions heightened to a painful degree. In the nineteenth century romance ceased to be primarily a generic distinction and became instead an attribute, or a characteristic, or an attitude, which was frequently juxtaposed to realism; whereas realism meant the objective literary consideration of ordinary people in ordinary situations, romance came to mean the subjective literary consideration of the unusual. Nathaniel Hawthorne, in his "Preface" to *The House of the Seven Gables* (1851) illustrates this perception of the genre as he states that romance implies for the author a latitude in content and expression which permits the manipulation of the atmosphere and the delicate and judicious inclusion of the marvelous.

In the twentieth century, romance has undergone yet further alterations. When hearing the term now, one usually thinks either of "confessional" love stories found in pulp magazines or of popular love stories in novel form, of the sort sold in dime stores. The *form* of romance has clearly deteriorated from that of the Middle Ages, but the *characteristics* of romance are deeply ingrained in our literary heritage. Any literature which is other than firmly realistic, which strives for psychological analysis, which establishes a world as it ought to be rather than as it is, which sees love as a motive force for nobility, or which is imaginative in simultaneously portraying an unreal world with unreal characters who nonetheless reveal human truths, owes its very essence to the romance tradition.

Evelyn Newlyn

THE ROGUE IN SIXTEENTH CENTURY LITERATURE

The roots of rogue literature in sixteenth century Western Europe reach to the wellsprings of comic irony. The rogue embodies irony; he is the radical element that undermines dull predictability. Conventional as a literary type, he is always the upsetter of conventions in the fictive worlds through which he bustles. Although he devastates complacency and defies circumspection, he remains comic, never so endangering our sense of order that we wish his overthrow. The rogue is a satirist, a practical joker, perhaps a thief from the rich, a confidence man among the pompously wise; if he takes a life—and this is rare—it is of one whose evil far surpasses his own. The rogue represents energy, variety; he opposes routine, complacent institutions, strict laws, etiquette, and such stifling emotions as timidity and fear of public opinion. Because the rogue knows no place in established society, he is protean in manner and appearance, and often, though not always, literally placeless— a traveler.

The rogue spirit in literature is embodied in as ancient a story as Genesis, particularly in the figure of Jacob, the second son who outwits and escapes his older brother, then outwits, robs, and flees his miserly master. Among the Greeks, Odysseus excels in roguery: spy, intriguer, thief, lover, storyteller, beggar, soldier, Odysseus coolly fills whatever role serves his turn. Like Jacob, he is a darling of the divine, an affirmation of godly freedom from restraint by human laws or customs. Because all literary rogues partake of this semidivine character, with their incredible self-confidence, intuitiveness, and willingness to take risks, they have continued to capture the imagination.

In addition to these qualities of character which distinguish rogue literature from all other forms of satire and from literary realism, rogue literature is often called realistic for its notable faithfulness to vernacular speech, its details of life among all classes, and its scrutiny of manners and morals. Whether one calls its protagonists heroes or antiheroes, however, rogue literature is primarily one of larger-than-life personalities, and is therefore romantic. Among the more recent predecessors of the sixteenth century rogues are the wily slaves of Roman comedy, direct ancestors of the clown Harlequin and the scoundrel Brighella in the *commedia dell'arte* of Italy and France, and the roguish servants in William Shakespeare's and Ben Jonson's plays of the 1590's. Prose predecessors include the first-class German rogue Tyll Eulenspiegel of the late Middle Ages and the witty intriguers in the French *fabliaux* of the thirteenth century, which inspired Geoffrey Chaucer's tales of the Reeve, Miller, Friar, and Summoner. Folktales about such spirits as Oberon and Robin Goodfellow are also firmly in the rogue tradition which influenced sixteenth century writings.

Among philosophical influences, commentators point to Desiderius Erasmus' *Praise of Folly* (1511), with its condemnation of worldly wisdom and institutions based on Paul's conception of the Christian as the truly wise man judged a fool by men (I Corinthians 3:18-19). Whether or not we accept the specific influence of Erasmus on *Lazarillo de Tormes* (1553) or Robert Greene's Ned Browne, certainly the idea of the wise fool and the foolish wise man inspires all rogue literature. The rogue's peculiar charm is that he defines his goals in worldly, not spiritual, terms, so that his poverty-born insight into men and mores is always in danger of subversion by his own bitterness and greed. The rogue is both wise man and fool; rogue literature challenges the reader to distinguish the wisdom from the folly.

In the anonymous *Lazarillo de Tormes* and Mateo Alemán's *Guzmán de Alfarache* (1599), Spain produced the Continent's most fully developed rogue writings of the century, works which launched a form that flourished in Spain for the next half century and which reached across Europe and to England via translation. Coming at the close of the century, *Guzmán de Alfarache*, several hundred pages of picaresque autobiography, cynically exposes the shams and atrocities of Church, Court, and marketplace, as experienced by the title character, a poor boy who rises to wealth through crime, falls, rises again, and finally learns wisdom and repentance aboard a galley as a slave. In many ways a vicious work, *Guzmán de Alfarache* eventuates in the relative serenity of the protagonist's spiritual awakening. As *Guzmán de Alfarache* explores a man's journey through self-delusion to a clearer vision of the good, it anticipates *Don Quixote de la Mancha* (1605, 1615).

It might be said that *Guzmán de Alfarache* could not have been written if *Lazarillo de Tormes* had not preceded it. Concise, gracefully written, satiric yet charitable in tone, this small book won immediate popularity in Spain and condemnation by the Church; within twenty years it had been translated into several other languages, including English. Without purporting to do so, it provided a fresh alternative to the well-worn chivalric romance. Although as romantic as any tale of knight-errantry, this tale told by the humble Lazaro strikes the modern reader (and no doubt struck the sixteenth century reader as well) with its details of place and manner in the Spain of its time. The portraits of Lazaro's masters, in particular the blind man, the priest, the squire, and the pardoner, are drawn precisely; we are convinced of the actuality of these very men, even as we understand their functioning as representatives of several classes of Spanish society. Lazaro's self-portrait is the most convincing. He describes so minutely, confesses his faults so honestly, accepts his sufferings so humbly that we do not doubt that we are being addressed by the same man who has lived these adventures. We do not question, as we read, how the illiterate son of illiterate parents can so casually allude to the classics during his discourse; we merely enjoy his erudition, his practiced blending of formal address with the minutiae of the streets. Yet herein lies the romantic illusion of the story, and perhaps the essence of its charm: *Lazarillo de Tormes* simultaneously allows the reader to rub elbows with the oppressed, but always persevering, child of poverty, *and* to be comforted that his life of pain does not lead to early death or to a career of evil, but, rather, to mental peace and the material affirmation of his clever tactics of survival.

The plot is briefly outlined. Lazaro's father, a poor miller given to "bleeding" sacks of grain, dies in battle in the service of his lord. Burdened with a young son, Lazaro's mother becomes a washerwoman in Salamanca. After building temporary prosperity on the thefts of food by her blackamoor lover, Lazaro's mother is reduced to beggary when the lover is caught. No longer able to support her son, she gives him as servant to a blind beggar, who starves Lazaro, then beats him for stealing some of his food and wine. When Lazaro eventually learns more tricks than his master can better, he escapes to the village of Maqueda, where he comes into the service of a priest. This new master teaches him that life can always get worse, for "compared with this master, the blind man was an Alexander the Great, in spite of his being, as I have said, miserliness personified." Still, his greater need teaches him greater wiles, which keep him alive ultimately to be turned out when the priest discovers his trickery. Lazaro's third master, a well-dressed young squire, gives him no food at all because he has none himself. Miraculously unembittered by his sufferings, Lazaro stays with this new master and even shares with him the food he himself begs. Having survived the unsurvivable in his youth and now confident of his talents, Lazaro views the starving, pompous squire philosophically:

> How secret are thy works, Oh Lord, which the people know not! Who would not be deceived by that goodly presence and that respectable cape and coat? Oh Lord, how many of that kind must thou have scattered about the world, who suffer for the sake of their faded honor what they would not suffer for thee!

Of the several masters who succeed the squire, only one, an indulgence-peddling pardoner, is given more than a page, and his work is described only to expose his trickery of credulous congregations. Social satire is the sole intent of these brief chapters. Lazaro's travels end when he lands a "government job" in Toledo: that of town crier. Now he is not only well-fed, well-clothed, and well-housed, but he shares his lot with a wife, who serves an archpriest. That Lazaro is certainly above putting public opinion before prosperity and companionship is shown by his ignoring the common gossip that his wife is the priest's mistress; he defends her vociferously to all comers. "For I will swear by the consecrated Host that no better woman lives within the gates of Toledo. . . . In this way they say nothing to me and I have peace in my home." Lazaro concludes that he has arrived "at the zenith of all good fortune."

Although throughout the narrative *Lazarillo de Tormes* attacks the cruelty, deceit, and obsessiveness of the greedy in all walks of life, the work ultimately applauds Lazaro's opportunism, tempered as it is by generosity. The tale proclaims that to gather wealth by starving others is evil, but that to starve is an evil far greater.

None of the English rogue writings of the sixteenth century so well wins the reader's sympathy for the rogue protagonist as does *Lazarillo de Tormes*, primarily because the English rogues are generally hard-bitten characters, more sinning than sinned against. Moreover, most of the pamphlets are written from the point of view of the merchant class out to protect its goods against thieves, feigning beggars, and confidence men ("connycatchers"). Only Thomas Nash's *The Unfortunate Traveller* (1594), Luke Hutton's *The Black Dog of Newgate* (1596), and Robert Greene's *A Disputation Between a He-Connycatcher and a She-Connycatcher* (1592) and *The Black Book's Messenger* (1592) present rogue autobiography; none offers so simplehearted a protagonist as Lazaro.

The earlier decades of the century produced works which show us the rogue's world from the burgher's point of view. Robert Copland's verse dialogue, *The Highway to the Spital-House* (1535-1536), describes the tricks of all manner of beggars and vagabonds; it bids its readers to "eschew vice" lest they, as have so many, wind up at the poorhouse door. Presented totally from the solid citizen's viewpoint, it charms only in the array of clever schemes it exposes. While it preaches charity to the poor, it implies that a beggar's plea is not to be believed. *A Manifest Detection of Dice-Play* (1552), possibly by Gilbert Walker, authoritatively details the "naughty practices" of cheating dice-players, card sharpers, and prostitutes. A dialogue between an elderly courtier and a young gentleman new to the Court, the work is less a warning against vice than a consumer's guide for detecting rigged games and faulty virgins.

John Awdeley's *The Fraternity of Vagabonds* (c. 1561) follows Copland's focus on vagabondage and his caveat against credulity toward beggars. Awdeley, however, presents more rogue cant than Copland had and speaks of the shifting crew as of a society with clearly defined trades. Awdeley is far surpassed in this mystification of the rogue by Thomas Harman, whose *A Caveat for Common Cursetors, Vulgarly Called Vagabonds* (1566) not only describes the practices of such people of the road as the upright men, rufflers, and priggers of prancers, but also goes on to delineate ranks in the roguish hierarchy; he even names more than a hundred living vagabonds. Harman purports to be a country justice, fearlessly exposing this "uncomely company." We credit his authority because of his intimate command of rogue argot and his vivid conversations with particular vagabonds, more authentic than anything in earlier rogue literature and surely more realistic than the erudite speech of Lazaro. Still, Harman's condemnatory viewpoint precludes our empathy with the rogues themselves.

With Robert Greene's "connycatching" pamphlets of 1591-1592, rogue literature is brought into the service of a satiric point of view broader and less self-righteous than that of any other work of the century. In six small books published in the last eighteen months of his life, the versatile Greene moves from a Harmanlike, Walkerlike exposé of London card sharps (*A Notable Discovery of Cozenage*, 1591) through vivid "jests" depicting the tricks of London merchants (*The Second Part of Connycatching* and *The Third and Last Part of Connycatching*, 1592) to diverse forms of rogue autobiography (*The Defence of Connycatching*, 1592; *A Disputation Between a He-Connycatcher and a She-Connycatcher*; and *The Black Book's Messenger*). All of Greene's works, particularly the latter, are suffused with a comic warmth reminiscent of Chaucer's *fabliaux* and *Lazarillo de Tormes*, but missing in the ungenerous work of Copland and his followers. Only the Falstaff of *Henry IV, Part I* is as smilingly portrayed in the 1590's; twenty years after Greene, Shakespeare's Autolycus and Jonson's tricksters in *The Alchemist* (1610) and *Bartholomew Fair* (1614) again rogue it mirthfully.

In both these plays and in Greene's stories, the high spirits are largely a function of the rhetorical virtuosity of the rogues. Greene's characters are never at a loss for the appropriate word: they shift manner and vocabulary to suit each new "conny," they successfully feign knowledge of places they have never been and of people they have never met, and they spellbind with words while their hands lighten pockets.

In structure and tone Greene's series combines the bourgeois moralism of the vagabond tracts with the Christian humanism exemplified in such jest collections as *The Marvelous Adventures and Rare Conceits of Master Tyll Howleglas* (c. 1548) and *Tarltons News out of Purgatory* (c. 1590). Greene has it both ways: throughout the series he purports to be the scourge of all connycatchers, crossbiters, nips, foists, and whores, while admonishing his readers to "laugh and learn" as thieves gull greedy merchants and prostitutes outwit lusting lawyers. In the series a panorama emerges of an entire society swept up in foolish schemes to win easy money or easy sex. Greene even brings himself into the ship of fools via the one pseudonymous work, *The Defence of Connycatching*, supposedly written by "Cuthbert Connycatcher, Licentiate in Whittington College" and self-admitted card sharp. "Cuthbert" accurately accuses Greene of having sold his play *The History of Orlando Furioso* (1594) to two different acting companies. "Was not this plain connycatching, Master R. G.?" he asks. Yet there is no rancor in Cuthbert's claim. To him, Greene's is another victimless crime, since the actors would have short-changed the playwright had he not gulled them. Most of the jests of Greene's later pamphlets fit this pattern of thief versus thief; if the narrative at all urges us to take sides it is always with the sleight-of-hand artists—the nips and foists—against their affluent connies, who have most likely prospered through shady dealings, although remaining pure in the public eye. Moral outrage is shown only toward those connycatchers who prey on the relatively innocent, especially women, with the loss of livelihood or reputation. With self-righteous glee, Cuthbert tells how a poor country wife takes revenge on a land swindler, and how a group of women "pay" the polygamist who had wedded them all.

The works which follow Greene's emulate his use of the rogue's point of view and his exposure of crimes by the "decent" citizen. *The Black Dog of Newgate*, ostensibly by Luke Hutton, a real thief actually executed, details the evils of bribe-taking prison officials. *Greene's News Both from Heaven and Hell* (1594) presents Robert Greene, returned from the grave as a Puckish spirit, describing how he now thwarts swindles by erstwhile connycatchers. John Dickenson's *Greene's Ghost Haunting Connycatchers* (1602) works the same vein.

The most important of the post-Greene works, Thomas Nash's *The Unfortunate Traveller*, adopts the rogue narrator and the satire of the citizenry; but Nash's protagonist, Jack Wilton, surpasses Greene's clever rhetoricians in verbal fireworks, while his satire, fierce and blindingly vivid, tears away at grotesque villainies—massacres, gluttonies, sexual perversions—scrupulously avoided, or at least less bloodily rendered, by earlier writers. Nash sends Wilton across Europe from one scrape to another. In his travels, set in the 1530's, Wilton moves from poverty to wealth and back again; he meets and anatomizes most of the famous people of the time.

Nash's work creates in prose the hellish atmosphere that characterizes the Italianate revenge tragedies of the Jacobean years, such as *The Duchess of Malfi* (c. 1613), *The Changeling* (1622), and so forth—works dominated by villains, not rogues. Only Wilton's Lazaroian knack for dodging certain death and moving on to the next adventure preserves the romantic illusion of the protean fellow blessed by the gods. Yet Wilton is a rare survivor in a maelstrom of the ravished, the mangled, and the mad.

In Spain, rogue literature flourished until the middle of the seventeenth century, with Francisco de Quevedo y Villegas' *The Life and Adventures of Don Pédro the Sharper* (*La vida del Buscón*, 1626) the most respected work of this period. In England, the rogue genre faded after 1625, Thomas Dekker's *The Belman of London* (1608) and *Lanthorne and Candlelight* (1608) being the most notable pieces of the Jacobean years. Rogue fiction, especially Greene's and Dekker's (derived in large part from Greene's) established a taste for middle-class London comedy that was fed by the plays of Ben Jonson, Thomas Middleton, Philip Massinger, and Richard Brome before the close of the theaters in 1642. With the Restoration, London satiric comedy was kept alive, in various new guises, by dramatists, verse satirists, and journalists, until Daniel Defoe, John Gay (*The Beggars' Opera*, 1728), and, later, Henry Fielding and Tobias Smollett made the rogue live again.

Bibliography

Bjornson, Richard. *The Picaresque Hero in European Fiction.*
Chandler, Frank W. *The Literature of Roguery.*
Flores, Angel. *Masterpieces of the Spanish Golden Age.*
Judges, A. V., ed. *The Elizabethan Underworld.*
McPeek, J. A. S. *The Black Book of Knaves and Unthrifts.*
Miller, Stuart. *The Picaresque Novel.*
Parker, Alexander. *Literature and the Delinquent.*
Whitbourn, Christine J., ed. *Knaves and Swindlers.*

Christopher J. Thaiss

THE EUROPEAN SENSIBILITY IN SHORT FICTION

The sensibility of a writer is the force that nurtures his imagination and sparks his intellect to master existential experiences and give them artistic expression. His characteristic response to a given environment and personal fate is the effluence of his unique sensibility which endeavors to find its bearings in time and space. The literary expression of this endeavor is fundamentally subjective even though it may be clad in traditional forms with well-wrought definitions and contours.

The European writers of the nineteenth and twentieth centuries have been caught up in the converging fields of force of history, society, and individual crisis. The exterior boundaries of their world have long been defined and the spirit of exploration and adventure relegated to the spiritual and imaginary spheres. This inner expanse is for Blaise Pascal a frightening eternal silence. To the modern writer this terrifying silence has become a constant companion. The old world seems the worse for too much well-documented investigation and sagacious study and has lost its magic. Furthermore, the future of mankind appears bleak and promises little else but destruction and despair. Thus, the contemporary artist is driven more and more to focus on the inner expanse and to probe in its sequestered nooks and ill-lighted corners for the meaning of life.

In this essay, some of the ways in which history, society, and the inner expanse reflected upon the creative sensibility of European writers of short fiction in the course of the nineteenth and twentieth centuries will be traced.

The early nineteenth century was dominated by the Romantic Movement, one of the most vital and formative periods within the entire history of European literature. Germinal in the *Sturm und Drang* of eighteenth century Germany, the main political and social forces determining this movement were the French Revolution and the Industrial Revolution which began in the mid-eighteenth century in England and led to the awakening of a new social conscience. The fundamental ideals of Romanticism, however, sprang from literary and philosophical sources, and the German Romantic school of thought became the chief vehicle through which the movement swept across Europe, affecting the literary expressions of all nations and leaving its vestige in literary conditions and tendencies of the twentieth century.

Self-knowledge was the fundamental creed of Romantic thought. The individual and his condition in this world became the center of interest. Partly as a reaction to the rationalism of the previous century with its emphasis upon the intellect, the Romantics sought the verities of existence in individual experiences in the context of nature and primitive emotions. The ancient concept of the poet as "vates"—a visionary whose power lies in inspirations—was revived, and he claimed a central role as legislator of mankind answerable only to himself and the ultimate truth. The language of the heart replaced classical models of speech in literary works, and the idiom of the peasants and the simple folk, which appeared to be its purest expression unadulterated by formal education, was coveted.

The Romantic Movement was originally intracultural. Writers and thinkers not only sought self-knowledge as individuals, but also, by turning backward in time and delving into the history of their people and the lore of its past, they hoped to comprehend their national individuality and give its specific culture a valid form of expression. Of all fictional forms, the novel lent itself most naturally to this aim, and the great works of epic prose from Russia, England, Germany, and France are no doubt the finest contribution of the nineteenth century to world literature. A whole new genre of historical fiction came into being wherein facts borrowed from history were masterfully blended with the inventions of a fertile imagination. Sir Walter Scott (1771-1832), the creator of this genre of writing, became immensely popular in England and on the Continent. This form of fiction was to be carried on in England with much success by William Makepeace Thackeray and in France by Alfred de Vigny and Victor Hugo, and to this day its practitioners such as Sergeann Golon reach a vast reading public regardless of the literary value of their prolificacy.

Historical documents of all kinds were collected with great enthusiasm. In the wake of the concurrent surge of nationalism all over Europe, historiographers compiled many tomes of facts and fates of their peoples. Folk songs and popular prose romances, ballads and poems, and legends and fairy tales were eagerly collected everywhere, and many motifs and themes, discovered in this search for national idiosyncrasy, were finding their way into creative writing. The collection of German folk songs known as *Des Knaben Wunderhorn* (compiled by Achim von Arnim and Clemens Brentano from 1805 to 1808) was probably the most characteristic and most widely influential product of these endeavors. In those countries where a literary consciousness of their particular cultural heritage had first to be kindled, traditional and fictional elements were undistinguishably entwined, so that the authenticity of such accumulations of folklore gave rise to much dispute. Many writings which were passed as Gaelic, Breton, or other literary heritage were fictionalized life stories of their collectors touched up with the *fantastique* or mysterious for additional effect. Still, this collecting zeal brought to light many valuable poems and prose pieces and deeply influenced the subsequent developments both of prose and poetry.

Writers from countries with a great living literary tradition rediscovered epic forms of prose which had fallen into neglect during the two preceding centuries. Such vaguely defined short prose forms as the anecdote, the fable, the sketch, and the short novel appealed to the Romantics because they had preserved a certain natural freshness while having been left by the wayside of the main literary currents of the classical period. In the hands of the

Romantics these short fictional forms were infused with new life and luminosity. They seemed most yielding to the theme of the individual at odds with circumstance when seeking fulfillment of his nature against ethical, political, or social imperatives and strokes of fate, a theme cherished by many a Romantic author. Also, they offered the writer a great measure of freedom by their lack of formal rigidity. By abandoning the classical precepts of form, epic prose opened to innovation and experimentation with various techniques, from which arose the grave danger of overwriting and shapelessness. For the novel, however, the fruition of this newfound liberty of expression became a basic component of its overwhelming prestige in the European literature of the nineteenth century. In short prose the very nature of its succinctness demanded a high degree of condensation of subject matter and adornment and a strict economy with regard to form in order to put across successfully the desired effect. Furthermore, the impact of the circumstances in which the story was told upon its form was of prime importance for the atmosphere created within the narrative. In many cases the narrative framework was as essential to the success of the story as its plot.

To tell a tale has been man's favorite pastime since the day he could assemble an audience. With his story he communicated to his fellow beings experiences and reflections and conveyed his hopes, fears, and desires. His first and central aim, however, was to entertain his listeners. The tales recounted at courts, around the camp fires, or in the marketplaces usually recreated a well-known occurrence of the past. As the past came alive again in the words of the narrator, he conjured up the illusion of a continuity in time. Through such stories the old generation spoke to the young and handed down tradition. The shared treasure of tales represented a set of social values and a concept of cultural unity. The retelling of familiar plots time and again and the artistic talents of the narrators gradually furnished such stories with hyperbolic motifs and cryptic symbols no longer immediately comprehensible. These manifold aspects of tale telling fascinated the Romantic mind.

The short story emerged as a separate literary genre almost simultaneously in France, Russia, and Germany, at the same time as in the United States, and almost at once rose to a degree of artistic perfection which seemed hard to equal. Questions of form and technique were a fundamental concern for the writer of short stories from the start, mainly because the borderlines of numerous other forms of short prose were ill-defined and intentionally kept fluid, while wielding a strong influence on the newly created genre. In France, Prosper Mérimée (1803-1870) presented masterful stories charged with emotion and violent passions, told in what appears to be almost inhuman detachment, which won him the honor of being appointed "académicien." The widely popular tales filled with nostalgic fantasy and picturesque detail created by Alphonse Daudet (1840-1897) reflect almost the whole spectrum of ideals and techniques of the period. Guy de Maupassant (1850-1893), considered the greatest among the many French storywriters, captured with marvelously contrived design such revealing moments in the lives of middle-class citizens as laid bare the innocence and corruption of human nature; what he told in easy-flowing prose from a strictly objective viewpoint were basically anecdotes of intensely vivid effect.

Short prose became popular in Russia through the fables of Ivan Krylov (1769-1844), who borrowed liberally from many sources including Aesop and Jean de La Fontaine. All the names of Russia's golden age of creative prose appear in the body of short fiction, and each author left his indelible stamp thereon. Nicolai Gogol (1809-1852), Ivan Turgenev (1818-1883), and Anton Chekhov (1860-1904) exerted foremost influence upon the genre of the short story. Gogol excelled in the impressionist technique, artfully blending fact and fantasy into a poetic web, and his story *The Overcoat* (1842) was possibly the most influential narrative of the first half of the century in Russia. The liberal-minded Turgenev studiously avoided everything artificial in plot and style, and by capturing the qualities of places and people, transcended the topical problems. The true master of the objective story was Anton Chekhov. He was less interested in constructing a well-plotted narrative than in sounding out the depths of human characterization for which his training as a physician had sharpened his ear, and in describing what he found with compassion and subtle humor and no trace of moralizing intent.

The early German Romantics cultivated an original romance form of short fiction, the *Novelle*, which had made its appearance in German literature in imitation of the most famous set of stories in Europe, *The Decameron* (1353) by Giovanni Boccaccio. Even the name given to this form of prose was an import into the German language. It had gained recognition as a literary genre in the course of the eighteenth century. Simplicity of structure and the restriction of the scope of the plot to a single occurrence rather than allowing for a development of action set it apart from the novel. The early *Novellen* maintained a narrative framework similar to the Italian original through which the narrator addressed a specific audience, and social entertainment remained its chief purport. In some cases even the escapist motif was adapted to the new plot. In *The Decameron*, it is the plague of 1348 that drives the Florentines away from the chaos ravaging their city to pass the time of waiting in pleasant and profitable disport. In Johann Wolfgang von Goethe's *Unterhaltungen deutscher Ausgewanderter* (1795) the danger of invading armies makes the aristocrats flee from their castles on the Rhine to amuse themselves with what is essentially gossip raised to the dignity of literature, until it is safe for them to return to their ordinary lives again. In the framework of his cycle of seven *Novellen* entitled *Das Sinngedicht* (1881), Gottfried Keller sends out a young man to experience life so that he may return with maturity and understanding. The German *Novellen*, however, often became freighted with a moralizing intention totally alien to the Italian source. Thereby, the center of gravity shifted away from the event itself toward its inner significance. In the narrative to which Goethe gave the title "Novelle" (1828), the ethical significance of the occurrence related is developed to the furthest degree compatible with the fictional form. (See E. K. Bennett's *A History of the German Novelle*, 1961, second edition revised and continued by H. M. Waidson.) The concentration upon a single event and its effects upon a person or group naturally gave it such great importance as to make it the turning point from which the narrative moved in an unexpected direction and often came to an altogether surprising conclusion. Like the peripeteia in drama this striking "twist in the story" engendered a momentum of tension and a swiftness of denouement. (See Ludwig Tieck in volume forty of *Gesammelte Werke*, 1829.)

The German Romantics gradually discarded the idea of social entertainment and focused their interest on the individual and his relationship to fate. The extraordinary twist of the narrative came more and more frequently in the guise of incomprehensible and irrational forces from the universe which assaulted the individual self-determination and led to the dissolution of ethical responsibility. Below the surface of the conscious self-governing will in man, there appeared a core akin to the irresponsible powers of nature which distinguished the Romantic human being fundamentally from the rational creatures of the classical age. The partly metaphysical and partly psychological *Novellen* by Heinrich von Kleist (1777-1811) were born out of the anguish and solitude of the soul fallen prey to such mysterious and mostly sinister forces of a chaotic world.

The *Novelle* is in its essence a literary development of the anecdote, and the insistence upon introducing *aliquid novi* reveals a certain kinship with the fairy tale. Folktale and fairy tale elements and a wealth of arabesque embroidery were woven into the Romantic *Novellen* to create delightful lyrical moods of exquisite charm in the masterpieces by Clemens Brentano, Achim von Arnim, and Josef von Eichendorff, to mention but a few. The writer of genius who gave European currency to the specifically German renascence of wonder, however, was E. T. A. Hoffmann (1776-1822).

In his Preface to a collection of his works published in 1829, the influential theorist on short forms of fiction, Ludwig Tieck, allowed for a development of the form in almost any direction. In order to create a specific mood, for the most part mysterious or lugubrious, the author was at liberty to pursue any chain of consequences as long as it was in keeping with his characters and circumstances. Tieck himself was best known for his creation of the awesome atmosphere of sylvan solitude in the story of his invention which he called *Der blonde Eckbert* (1797). In many stories a concrete object was chosen to introduce a specific mood and was endowed with symbolic implications. Annette von Droste-Hülshoff named the ominously symbolical tree already in the title of her narrative "Die Judenbuche" (1842), whereas Theodor Storm crystallized the implications underlying his *Novelle*, "Immensee"

(1850), in the image of a frail waterlily.

In due course, the fervor of Romantic sensibility diminished; it had abstracted from reality an illusory world suffused with emotions so intense and postulated a predominance of the imagination so absolute, as could but lead to total dissolution, thus destroying itself by the dream. By the end of the 1830's, transcendental ideas began to lose ground to a new poetic realism that sought to bring ideals and reality back into harmony. Writers began increasingly to free themselves from the bondage of tradition and speculation and turned to contemporary conditions reflecting the fundamental changes in the social order brought about by years of revolutionary strife. Although a number of authors continued celebrating the recent and distant past with much success, many others turned to their own environment for inspiration, studied the demands of everyday existence, eyed critically the contemporary society's negative aspects as revealed in actual conditions, manners, and events, and consciously circumvented the vagueries of mysticism and boundless fantasies. They concentrated on subjects they could, through familiarity, accurately describe and looked for positive values in reality.

The newfound objectivity in fiction readily adopted some properties of popular journalism, and writers drew much of their inspiration and originality from their native rural or provincial regions. Dialects, details of the toils and hardship of the frugal existence of peasants and artisans in surroundings barely in touch with civilization, and rugged rustic types became the subject matter of reginal tales, whereas the confines of provincialism and philistine quaintness made admirable themes for longer prose forms. Realist writing with a regionalist flavor attracted writers for several different reasons. Some returned to their native soil to seek revival for the creative sensibility both in the domain of the senses and in the domain of the spirit, thus following the train of thought of Jean-Jacques Rousseau; others hoped to restore their souls in bounteous nature and the peasant world which they believed to be sound and firmly rooted in its environment and which would thus soothe the confusion in their hearts and minds; yet another group merely satisfied their taste for pastoral idylls and put local color and idealized rusticality to use for stylistic effects. The most interesting regionalist efforts, however, were the attempts at self-realization undertaken by authors within the realm of their own native region.

Within the literature in the German tongue, the farming communities of Austria, Switzerland, and various German provinces acquired a new thematic emphasis, counterbalancing the inevitable industrialization and its adverse effects. Descriptions of landscape and local customs made a realistic setting for tales from small villages and isolated farms. Many of these narratives followed in the tradition of amusing anecdotes with an edifying bent which filled the almanacs for farmers and uneducated readers in a similar social milieu, for which *Schatzkästlein des Rheinischen Hausfreundes* (1811), composed by Johann Peter Hebel (1760-1826), is perhaps the best-known example. Unlike the gracefully unrealistic idylls about the life of the peasantry which had delighted readers in the eighteenth century, writers now told of a whole new, self-contained world, with laws and customs all its own, which reached back into the Middle Ages and which had lost none of its rigidity when it became the object of nineteenth century literature. The prose both long and short by Jeremias Gotthelf (1797-1854) dealt with the peasant world in Switzerland. Although it was controversial from its very first appearance, his prose remains the most interesting example of this type of regional writing, for these humorously realistic narratives in their entirety acquire the depth and grandeur of a myth that, like an erratic block, stands apart in the prose of the mid-nineteenth century. Other typical examples of the literary exploitation of the writer's homeland are the stories about the lonely folk from the backwoods of Styria by Peter Rosegger (1843-1918) to whom he had devoted his life as a teacher. (See *Als ich noch der Waldbauernbub war*, 1916, selected from his autobiographical writings.) The sequence of tales from the hamlets of the Black Forest, *Schwarzwälder Dorfgeschichten*, published from 1843 onwards and narrated by Berthold Auerbach (1812-1882), is of a more sentimental tone and features the contrast between peasant tradition and ethical ideals. Theodor Storm's (1817-1888) prose tales, *Sommergeschichten* (1851), bear the stamp of his native Schleswig-Holstein and tell of life's ephemerality in a delicately lyrical style. There is much common sense and understanding for life's little matters in Otto Ludwig's (1813-1865) portrayals of homeliness and comfort in village life in Thuringia, *Die Heiteretei und ihr Widerspiel* (1857), whereas Adalbert Stifter (1805-1868), in his *Studien* (1844-1850) and *Bunte Steine* (1853) depicted everyday events in the Bohemian forest heightened with emotional significance to show that exemplary life true to nature should come about from gentleness of character, humane action, and the admiration of beauty.

Regional authenticity and local color naturally called for the use of dialect and vernacular prose. The revival of nationalism all over Europe had inspired a new interest in indigenous forms of language and had spurred the zeal of lexicographers and grammarians. In Spain, for example, the *Grammar and Apology of the Catalan Language* (1814) was the forerunner of an actual literary and linguistic renaissance in Catalonia. In countries where the native language had been superseded by an official foreign idiom, the nationalist movement restored the indigenous tongue to literary currency. This was the case for several small ethnic groups in Eastern Europe, where Slowenians, Croatians, Galicians, and Czechs had suffered under the centralizing tendencies of the Habsburgs. In Finland, writing in the native tongue only came about when Finnish was given parity with Swedish as a national language in 1863.

The background for a vast number of popular realistic stories were big cities such as Madrid, Stockholm, and St. Petersburg. The tone in these descriptions of urban conditions and mores reaches from humor, irony, and satire to bitter criticism of social injustice and human depravity, as exemplified by Ramón de Mesonero Romanos' *Escenas matritenses* (1842); August Blanche's *Bilder ur verkligheten* (1860); and Fyodor Dostoevski's *Poor Folk* (1846). The most influential social stratum in nineteenth century Europe was the opulent bourgeoisie. It lacked the extravagant flourish and heroic grandeur which had marked the courts and cultured milieux of previous epochs. It upheld ideals of moderation and self-restraint rooted in the desire to maintain emotional balance and economic stability. This closed, middle-class world, however, tended to slip all too readily into facile complacency and cruel self-indulgence within a highly restrictive decorum. Delicate shades of sentiment displaced the devouring Romantic passions, and the nature whose beauty was much adored lost its demonic threat which had fascinated the Romantic mind. Man was expected to resign to his fate and to accept the shortcomings of the situation into which he happened to be thrust.

Only the novel could successfully cope with the many facets of urban bourgeoisie. The huge monographs on middle-class conditions in France in the 1820's meticulously compiled by Honoré de Balzac (1799-1850) are not only epic masterpieces but also have great documentary value. His realistic descriptions of streets and houses, clothes and furnishings, economic ramifications and family relationships, and details on business transactions in those days form the background whereupon the protagonists fight for economic prestige and political power; they not only make fascinating reading but also expose the banality of bourgeois existence in all its cynicism and wretchedness. There is a strong undercurrent of pessimism in his version of the human comedy as in the other magnificent tableau of nineteenth century Parisian society with the telling title *Les Misérables* (1862) by Victor Hugo. The realistic picture of provincial life in those days drawn in lucid prose by Gustave Flaubert (1821-1880) did much to exorcise the century's complacent bourgeois sentimentality. Truly satisfactory short prose narratives on the bourgeois theme were not abundant, and the *Novellen* by Theodor Fontane (1819-1898) mixing idyllicism and milieu were probably the most effective.

In the second half of the century the scope of the narratives narrowed down more and more to a naturalistic study of the individual in hostile surroundings and the clash of personal freedom with the codes of society. The former idealistic conceptions of man were gradually discarded, and down-to-earth portrayals of specimens of urban or rural characters accomplished either in a tone of benevolent humor or with heartfelt compassion took their place.

The unforgettable characters in the vast panoramas of contemporary city life in Victorian England created by Charles Dickens (1812-1870), the most widely read writer of the middle decades of the century, were such ordinary men, women, and children. His irresistible pathos born out of profound sympathy for all the wronged and humbled of life and his inexhaustible humor laid bare the ills of atheist industrialism, and his essentially conservative instinct for democratic justice scourged Victorian orthodoxy. Dickens started out as a parliamentary reporter and contributed articles to several magazines. His first literary achievement of any note was *Sketches by Boz* (1836); the *Pickwick Papers*, begun in April, 1836, and appearing in monthly installments, made him the most popular writer of his day. Like Sir Walter Scott, Dickens wrote for the purpose of entertaining his readers and studiously avoided all that he deemed unpopular with the reading public. Although his fiction is by no means faultless, either in composition or in style, and despite the fact that he lacks the power of restraint essential to the purest works of art, his stories and novels have lost none of their great appeal to this day.

Characters of moral uprightness, sensual richness, and great independence of spirit peopled the cycles of short prose by Gottfried Keller (1819-1890). His stories were firmly ingrained in the traditions and institutions of Allemanic Switzerland and the author's love for his country permeated his work. This prose captivated through a singular inner luminosity devoid of all false sentiment; exuberant humor, occasionally coupled with pungent social criticism, alternated with passages touchingly lyrical and expressions of sound self-assurance, as exemplified in *Züricher Novellen* (1878) and *Sieben Legenden* (1872).

European writing in the last decades of the nineteenth century emphasized individualistic expression in keeping with an intense awareness of social injustice and an active reforming zeal stemming from the teachings of Herbert Spencer and John Stuart Mill. Naturalist prose seemed mesmerized by the lurid sides of industrialism that led to an extreme exploitation of body and soul and fostered the decay of human values. Man's brief span on this earth was conceived as being determined solely by race, milieu, and time, and was stripped of all transcendental meaning. The deployment of free will was felt to be inconsequential. Creatures huddled in overcrowded urban areas out of touch with the soil could no longer form any meaningful relationships and forfeited all sense of belonging. Loneliness in the crowd and lack of orientation were shown to lead to a slackening of vitality and a dangerous disregard for the value of the individual existence. Positivist thinking accepted only natural sciences and sociology as true sciences. The politics widened the gulf between "to have and to have not." The art of psychological dissection perfected by Dostoevski, who regarded himself as the writer of the proletariat, became vastly influential, as did the scientifically exact prose style of Émile Zola.

Friedrich Nietzsche postulated that the value of man's culture determined the order of merit among men. The judgment of artistic merit became wellnigh impossible without universally accepted standards by which to proceed. Daring effects in style and subject matter and momentary whims of the reading public more and more frequently constituted the transient appeal of literary works and built reputations the lasting value of which seemed more than questionable. French symbolist writers saw themselves as heirs to a dying culture and their keynotes of decadence and despondence added to the *fin-de-siècle* pessimism. The dilemma spurred the activity of literary critics to search for new criteria of evaluation and modes of interpretation.

The cataclysm of World War I was the overt transition from a relatively stable era to a new age of uncertainty and unrest. Doubts as to the psychological stability of the individual personality and a fundamental questioning of all philosophical and religious solutions offered for the problems of mankind added to the urgency of an impending crisis. The inner expanse attracted the creative writer with magic lure. In the wake of Friedrich Nietzsche and Sigmund Freud, the realms of the unconscious and the irrational were explored, not as in previous centuries in the universal context of nature, society, and fate, but as individual case studies. Man as an intellectual being, the working of the mind, and linguistic creativity as a conscious act continuously to be refined and clarified, fascinated the great prose writers Marcel Proust, James Joyce, Hermann Broch, and many others. Language, both in poetry and prose, became detached from ordinary usage and significance and was lifted into hermeneutic spheres.

Cumulative pressures from the technological developments accelerated by World War II added to the dissolution of cultural identity and intensified the general feeling of being at sea in fluctuating, perilous circumstances. The creative mind took flight from the vicissitudes of reality into a realm where it could formulate its own truths, values, and aesthetic ideals. Experimental writing, formal dissolution, stylistic refractions, the interior monologue, several intermingling layers of meaning, and *tours de force* of language became the elements out of which such realms were built, thus making literary works ever more complex, eclectic, and restricted in their appeal. Traditional concepts of motivation and verisimilitude were thrown overboard; and last, the justification of fiction as such came to be questioned when stipulations were made that all literature should become "inspired journalism," as in the case of Jean-Paul Sartre. Short prose forms could not cope with these trends. Whereas poetry and the drama dominated the first decades of the century, long forms of prose took over as the preferred medium for literary expression in the course of time, as the spirit of experimentation gradually obliterated all definable contours between literary genres.

Nevertheless, short prose prospered the world over during the first half of the twentieth century, but on a quite different plane. As standards of education improved among the masses, a vast new reading public came into being. Periodicals and magazines of the most varied kinds created a great demand for short pieces to be consumed in one sitting, and publishing houses were avid for fiction for easy reading with a thrilling plot, protagonists that fulfilled the dreams and wishes of the man in the street, and little or no moral or philosophical probing. Writers everywhere were eager to comply, and many hundreds of excellent short stories were published. The genre, which at the beginning of the century had flourished chiefly under the influence of British and American authors, shed its ties with any particular school of writing or country. Influences from all over the world inundated the literary scene in Europe, and the influx of ideas and manners from America despoiled much of its writing of its specifically European characteristics. Curiosity about far-away lands which had become known through imperialism whetted the taste of the reading public for tales with an exotic touch, as told by Rudyard Kipling, Joseph Conrad, and Graham Greene. Technology and electronics had made the world grow smaller, as it were, and differences of culture and heritage ceased to be a barrier for communication. Worldwide conflicts and problems not only ngendered clashes of opinion but also created the need for mutual understanding. Travelogues and entertaining sketches of customs and beliefs elsewhere became all the more popular as international tourism expanded. The fate of the "little man" interested the ordinary reader more than did heroes with inhuman ideals, and short stories frequently became the means of expression for "submerged population groups." (See Frank O'Connor's *The Lonely Voice*, 1963.)

As familiarity with the form increased, the short story underwent significant changes. The unique and overwhelming occurrence central to the form throughout the nineteenth century fell out of favor with authors of the twentieth century, who were wont to trace subtle emotions and unspectacular reactions of the soul rather than to display physical actions. Since the plot and dramatic evolution were no longer central concerns to the writer, formal presentation became decisive. Sometimes it is merely an archetypal model or a *leitmotif* which holds a narrative together, but many a reader has been baffled by stories in which nothing seems to happen.

The communications media have been influential in a very questionable way in the last few decades. On the one hand, they have helped to create something resembling an international popular culture, but, on the other hand, the visual and aural impact of electronics has threatened the supremacy of the written word. Mass media demand no active participation on the part of the audience. Escapist fiction cannot compete with the thrills and vivid suspense in motion pictures and on television. Furthermore, glib commercialism and hermeneutic writing from within an "ivory tower" have alienated large portions of the reading public. The writer's concern with his own mission has become a fundamental problem. To quote J. M. Cohen in his *A History of Western Literature* (1956), he sees himself as

the superfluous man, the artist misunderstood, the unhappy lover, the Hamlet figure paralysed by his own sensitiveness.

Paul Heyse, James Joyce, Thomas Mann, and many others have drawn "a portrait of the artist." He is driven further and further into the silence of the inner expanse lest he is willing to compete with the jarring cacophonies and glaring flickering lights in the wasteland of the electronic age. *The Voices of Silence* (1951, *Les Voix du Silence*) is the title André Malraux chose for his history and philosophy of world art, the expression of man's sensibility and its will to live.

Bibliography

Baldensperger, Fernand and Werner P. Friederich. *Bibliography of Comparative Literature*.

Brett-Fames, Antony. *The Triple Stream: Four Centuries of English, French, and German Literature*.

Brooks, Cleanth and Robert Penn Warren. *Understanding Fiction*.

Cazamian, Louis F. *A History of French Literature*.

Croce, Benedetto. *European Literature in the Nineteenth Century*.

Encyclopedia Britannica. 1977 edition.

Kayser, Wolfgang. *Das sprachliche Kunstuerk*.

Lukacs, Georg. *Studies in European Realism*.

Petsch, Robert. *Wesen und Formen der Erjãhlkunst*.

Waterhouse, Gilbert and H. M. Waidson. *A Short History of German Literature*.

Marie-Antoinette Manz-Kunz

THE GOTHIC INFLUENCE ON SHORT FICTION

When short fiction came into its own as a genre in the nineteenth century, owed some of its essential features to the development of Gothic fiction. he Gothic authors had found techniques for evoking dream states and night-1ares, which the short fiction writers of the nineteenth century used to full ffect in their tales of terror and their mystery and ghost stories. Above all, iothic authors had developed means of creating suspense, which is so nec-ssary for the sustained effects of short fiction, in general, as well as for horror :ories.

Many romances, from the earliest Greek to those of the late seventeenth nd early eighteenth centuries, were short works, as, of course, were the tories of *The Decameron* (1353) and *The Arabian Nights' Entertainments The Thousand and One Nights*, 1450). The early Gothic writers found some f their techniques and devices in them: characters which, because they were ot strongly individualized, could serve symbolic purposes; indirect narration 1 the form of a story told by a character within the work which created a ense of a closed world; and the fragment as a genre, such as Henry Neville's *he Isle of Pines* (1668), which could be used to give a sense of remoteness. ven these they put to new uses, and their works were highly innovative xpressions of the ideas of their time.

By the time the first Gothic novel—Horace Walpole's *The Castle of Otranto* 1764)—came into being, the romances, already despised as a form of prose ction, had been superseded by the social novel as it became established as respectable literary genre. By its very nature, with the reflection of the real orld of every day as its purpose, the social novel tended to be long, indeed, ery long, and often rambling. Yet it was Samuel Richardson, the "father" f the social novel, who supplied Gothic authors with a prime means of reating suspense. In transforming the epistolary form, which had been a taple of many of the short romances of the late seventeenth and early eigh-eenth centuries, he discovered that it lent itself to a very special effect—the etter-writer could be supposed to be ignorant of the future, of the outcome f his (or more usually her) own story. This he called "writing to the moment," r, to use a term then unheard of, what we would call "suspense." Although Richardson probably holds the record among novelists for long-windedness, he method is one that may keep the reader on the edge of his chair, wondering what is going to happen next."

This method was the literary discovery that made the middle-aged Rich-rdson a sudden and dramatic success. As long as the audience for literature vas a leisured and highly educated élite, it simply had not been an accepted >art of a writer's duty to keep his reader reading. Once the novel-reading >ublic began to grow, however, the need for suspense appeared and, whatever

prose genre they chose, the nineteenth century writers paid heed to th
requirement.

The first Gothic novels had altogether different reasons for creating su
pense. Like the Sentimental novels of the time, they aimed to approach th
reader through his feelings before his reason, to teach him the moral lesso
which the work of literature sought to convey by causing him to share th
characters' feelings and experiences. A product of the movement of Sens
bility, or Sentimentalism, which dominated the second half of the eighteent
century, the Sentimental novels appealed to the reader's pity and compassior
while Gothic tales sought to fill him with that "pleasing terror" which evoke
a sense of the sublime. In both cases, the purpose was to appeal to the reader
moral sense, through his feelings, and, while the Sentimental novels presente
scenes of pathos, the Gothic tales needed suspense to produce their effect
of terror.

The sublime was the favorite aesthetic concept of late eighteenth centur
authors. Its effect was to draw the reader (or the observer, if the sublim
object were a natural one) out of himself, to enrapture him in order to arous
"sympathy," feelings correlative to those of the characters about whom h
was reading. Sublime objects ranged from craggy mountains and vast seas t
Gothic cathedrals and ominous-looking villains. Their common denominato
was a vastness which conveyed a sense of limitlessness, of infinity, filling th
reader or observer with awe and fear. According to the theory of the sublime
however, the "terror" he experienced was pleasing to him only because h
knew himself to be safe. To teeter on the edge of a real cliff would be
terrifying experience which, to the eighteenth century mind, could have n
pleasure in it at all; to see such a cliff while knowing oneself to be safe fron
falling, or to watch in one's mind the heroine of a Gothic tale faced by
threatening and beetle-browed villain, would fill one with a sympathetic terro
which is pleasurable.

At first, there was no thought that spine-tingling tales were simply enjoyabl
reading. Eighteenth century critics, such as Edmund Burke (in his *A Philo
sophical Enquiry into the Origin of Ideas of the Sublime and Beautiful*, 1757)
John Aikin and his sister Anna Barbauld in their essays (*Miscellaneous Piece
in Prose*, 1773, 1775, 1792), Clara Reeve, herself a Gothic novelist (in *Th
Progress of Romance*, 1785), and poet James Beattie, in his essays (*Disser
tations Moral and Critical*, 1783), all discuss the possible reasons why anyon
would seek to experience a disagreeable feeling such as fear. Their answe
is that the sublime ravishes the soul, drawing the reader out of himself s
that he sympathizes with, or, as we would say, identifies with the characters
and this is a pleasurable experience.

For the Sentimentalists, with their ideally virtuous characters, the purpos
of evoking sympathy is clear, but we need to look a little closer to understan
the aim of the Gothic authors. The Benevolist movement, so widespread i

the eighteenth century, posited a belief in man's potential for good. (The movement and its connection with Sentimentalism is explained in Louis I. Bredvold's *The Natural History of Sensibility*, 1962.) Fallen though man is, the Benevolists believed, he is not inevitably and irrevocably depraved. He is endowed with his nature by God, as a feeling as well as a reasoning being. If he lives in conformity with that nature, he will be in harmony within himself and with the natural order, which is God's order. This harmony in man is virtue, and since it is inner harmony, it is also happiness. Conversely, evil is an inner disharmony, and the wicked are unhappy because they are torn by inner conflict. This—evil as disharmony, as a psychic conflict in man's nature— was the subject that the first Gothic novelists set out to explore, drawing their readers after them into remote lands and far-off times and terrifying them with supernatural occurrences, so that they might experience, through the pity and terror aroused in them, the very nature of evil as a psychological force.

The works produced by this movement were not necessarily short; indeed, as yet, the short story as a self-conscious genre had not come into being. When nineteenth century authors started to write short stories, however, one of their reasons for doing so was the suitability of short forms for raising the hair on the back of the reader's neck. Among the early works of Gothic fiction, the very first, Walpole's *The Castle of Otranto*, is very short, as is William Beckford's *Vathek* (1786). This tale, which revives *The Arabian Nights' Entertainments* and uses the grotesque to chill the reader's soul with horror, also fills him with terror and pity. These—the emotions aroused by tragedy and evoking the sublime—are experienced as the central character, the Caliph Vathek, and his beloved Princess Nouronihar find themselves trapped in the Halls of Eblis (the Moslem Satan), there to wander for all eternity among the damned, their hearts aflame in their chests.

These two short works contrast with the lengthy tales of terror of Matthew ("Monk") Lewis, nicknamed for his novel *The Monk* (1795), and of Mrs. Ann Radcliffe, who wrote *The Mysteries of Udolpho* (1794), *The Italian* (1797), and others. Long Gothic novels continued to appear in the nineteenth century from the pens of authors such as Robert Maturin, whose most famous work is *Melmoth the Wanderer* (1820). Nevertheless, short fiction became a prime vehicle for exploring the psychology of evil, and techniques developed with that purpose in mind were quickly adapted to the purposes of the well-wrought short tale in general.

Even in the eighteenth century, the fear had arisen that, by presenting the reader with a sublimely evil character, the author would defeat his own didactic purposes. James Beattie suggested that Richardson's villain, Lovelace, in *Clarissa* (1747-1748), and even John Milton's Satan in *Paradise Lost* (1667) might be a corrupting influence, simply because they were drawn with sufficient skill to evoke the "pleasing terror" of the sublime.

It was soon clear that he was right, and nineteenth century writers found themselves free to use Gothic devices to explore man's evil nature without the eighteenth century's rather narrow concern for didacticism. Their freer attitude also led them to combine the grotesque with the sublime, to produce the ultimate in chilling tales. The eighteenth century, and Mrs. Radcliffe in particular, had carefully differentiated the two, believing that the terror evoked by the sublime was soul-expanding and so both didactically useful and pleasurable, whereas the horror which the grotesque produced filled the reader with soul-shrinking horror (Ann Radcliffe, "On the Supernatural in Poetry," 1826).

Beckford, as we have seen, had already combined the two. Undoubtedly, his Byronic sense of damnation, derived like Byron's from a Calvinistic upbringing, made him an early precursor of Romantic fascination with the dark side of man's soul. Matthew Lewis, writing ten years later than Beckford, shows the same propensity and, indeed, a friend of Lord George Byron and Sir Walter Scott, he may be numbered among the Romantics. It was not really until the late 1830's and the 1840's, however, that the Gothic heritage burst forth in short fiction, in the tales of Edgar Allan Poe and Nathaniel Hawthorne.

By their time there was a large middle-class reading public whose members often lacked the classical education and erudition of the audience for whom earlier authors had written. It was a public that was hungry for prose fiction and that had an appetite for suspense; that demanded that literature be absorbing, exciting, enthralling; and that wished to be entertained at least as much as, if not more than, it hoped to be enlightened. The Victorian writers obliged with the great age of the novel, borrowing from the Gothic authors many of their suspense-creating devices. Even the largest of the great realistic novels was, as often as not, divided into chapters, each a masterpiece of suspense in itself, so that, when published serially a chapter at a time, the readers would await eagerly and remember to buy each succeeding installment. Thus, even long novels were first read in short sections, and, at the same time, the short story itself came into its day.

It was not, however, only because it had devised means for creating suspense that the Gothic tale exerted an influence on nineteenth century fiction, especially short fiction. The Victorian age had also inherited from the eighteenth century its interest in psychology. Every major eighteenth century philosopher was concerned with discovering the nature of man and exploring the labyrinth of his mind. By the nineteenth century, this interest had spread to the general public and had become more individualized. Not only man in general, but the particular personality and development of an individual was set forth, at first in Jane Austen's novels, and then in the *Bildungsroman*, of which Charles Dickens' *David Copperfield* (1849-1850) is an example. The multifarious interplay of individuals in society and history was treated by author after author—Charles Dickens, William Makepeace Thackeray, George Eliot, Honoré de Balzac, Gustave Flaubert, Guy de Maupassant, Fyodor Dostoevski, Leo Tolstoy, and Ivan Turgenev, to name but a few.

Although at least Dickens, Balzac, and Dostoevski include Gothic elements in their novels, the strongest influence of the Gothic appears when the author is striving to portray the psychology of human evil in general, and, for this purpose, short fiction is ideal. It can put less emphasis on the detail of individual characters; it lends itself to fantasy; and it can sustain from beginning to end a breathless atmosphere of terror. Above all, it can plunge the reader into a dream-state, and when the dream is a nightmare, it is peopled with the weird and dreadful monsters of Gothic fiction. From America, England, and the European Continent there poured a stream of tales peopled with the figures of Gothic fiction and using Gothic devices of structure and characterization and its special form of symbolism. Wherever they appear, the ultimate purpose of the author turns out to be the same exploration of psychic evil.

In the short fiction of the nineteenth and twentieth centuries, Gothic features of structure, theme, and imagery recur again and again: narrative structures creating a closed world; the Faust theme and a related use of the witch-figure; monsters and ghosts; and double figures, mirrors, and other reflecting devices. All these are closely associated with the imagery and atmosphere of dreams and nightmares.

Because Gothic literature is an exploration of the mind and is particularly concerned with evil and guilt, its figures and settings have much in common with those which we see in dreams. The villain is no ordinary wicked man but a monster of psychic conflict; the heroine is an embodiment of the good. Houses and castles are structural forms of their owners' personalities; the storms that break over them express thunderous rage and the lightning flashes of violence. The eerie shapes of monsters and supernatural figures are embodiments of guilt and reflections of the evil self.

No master of the weird and awful has ever exceeded Edgar Allan Poe in his ability to create such a dream world in his stories. Undoubtedly because he, like Hawthorne, consciously used dream material to delineate the mind, he saw and developed possibilities of short forms for creating sustained suspense.

One prime means of giving the reader a sense that he is entering a strange world, closed off from the everyday and the ordinary—the dream world of the mind—is indirect narration. Poe uses it in his sustained nightmare account of the complete disintegration of a personality in "The Fall of the House of Usher." The story is told to us by a friend of Roderick Usher's, a minor character who rides into the remote world of the story. This is the same technique that is used by Clara Reeve in *The Old English Baron* (1777). That remote world is, in fact, Roderick's mind, and the house is explicitly identified with him. The only other being in the doomed house is Roderick's sister, his twin, with whom he is obsessed. She drifts into sight, pale and silent, only once. When she dies, Roderick and the narrator bury her with mad, nightmarish logic. Roderick has said that he dare not bury her in the graveyard for fear she is only in a trance; yet they nail her in her coffin, despite the lifelike flush on her cheeks, and close her up in a copper-lined vault with a heavy door, deep beneath the house. After an interval of oppressive days, a storm, which is the mental storm of Roderick's breakdown, breaks over the house. The wraithlike figure of Madeline appears in a white, blood-stained robe, and brother and sister collapse together. As the narrator leaves the house, it also collapses as the villain's castle had fallen in ruins around him in Walpole's *The Castle of Otranto*.

The suggestive power that gives such a story the atmosphere of a nightmare lies in its features, which are clearly symbolic but, at the same time, refuse to yield neat and tidy meanings. Roderick lives in terror, able to express his unknown fears only in his strange art—but fears of what? Fratricide? Incest? Incest real or only desired? The suggestion of incest is clearly there, but the very vagueness of it leaves our awareness all the more strongly focused on the overwhelming sense of guilt that brings about Roderick's collapse.

In short pieces, "The Masque of the Red Death," "The Oval Portrait," and "Ligeia," Poe uses a device related to the indirect narration of "The Fall of the House of Usher" to enhance the ambiguous, dreamlike atmosphere that resists simplistic interpretation. Here, it is a character within the story that constructs a closed world, intensifying the reader's sense of a secret and terrible guilt. In "The Masque of the Red Death," Prince Prospero decorates the rooms of his palace and closes it off to all but a chosen few, shutting himself and them away from the "plague," but among the dancers at the masquerade appears death himself.

The emphasis here on the decoration of the rooms, each in a different color and lighted by the eerie light of braziers flaming behind colored glass, brings us to another central and complex Gothic theme: the conflict of art and life, the black arts of witchcraft, and the Faustian theme of the scientist who ventures into realms forbidden to all but God Himself.

In "The Oval Portrait," the narrator, enclosed within the velvet curtains of a four-poster bed, reads the story of the chamber in which he lies, the story of an artist so wedded to his art that, as he captures the perfect likeness of his young wife on his canvas, the life drains from her and she dies.

It is tempting to interpret "Ligeia" in the light of this other story. Here the dream atmosphere is established by the narrator's strange, amnesiac statement that he cannot remember where or when he met Ligeia, his first wife, nor what was the name of the ancient family from which she came. Imbued with the wisdom of the ages, he tells us, she resisted death by the sheer force of will, and then, when finally overcome by it, returned in spirit to drain the life from his second wife, the Lady Rowena. Yet it is the narrator himself who has decorated and closed off from all outside help the tomblike room in which Rowena lies, and as he watches solicitously by her beside, it is his hand that holds the cup into which drops of poison mysteriously fall and from which she drinks. It is a confused story, the opium-eating narrator tells us, in which Ligeia may be a dream figure of the intellectual pursuits to which he was "wedded" before he married Rowena, who may herself be a "real-life" figure within his dream. Whether the fantasy is within the narrator's mind, or the narrator is a figure on the same level of reality as the two female figures in Poe's fantasy, the association of Ligeia with the wisdom of the ages and her supernatural power to overcome death give her a witchlike quality.

The association of knowledge with the occult is a major theme in Beckford's *Vathek*, in which the Caliph's mother Carathis is a witch, and she, the Caliph, and Nouronihar are damned because of their pursuit of forbidden knowledge. This theme appears repeatedly in nineteenth century Gothic works, the prime example being Mary Shelley's *Frankenstein* (1818). It is a theme Hawthorne weaves into many of his works, in none more strikingly than "The Birthmark" and "Rappaccini's Daughter."

In "Rappaccini's Daughter," as in *Frankenstein*, there are two scientists. Rappaccini is, to all appearances, evil, while Baglioni is an honest man. By his evil arts Rappaccini has grown within his enclosed garden flowers of great beauty which exhale deadly poisons. Also in the garden, and as beautiful and deadly as they, is his daughter Beatrice. When the hero, Giovanni, influenced by the good Baglioni, seeks to rescue her with an antidote, he kills her in the attempt, and, thus, we do not know whether Rappaccini is a magician conjuring pure evil, or creating beauty at the price of evil, or creating beauty of which the seductiveness seems evil, indeed, poisonous, to more mundane minds.

The ambiguity of Hawthorne's "The Birthmark" lies in our not knowing whether the scientist, Aylmer, is truly a genius or merely thinks he is. Like Poe's narrator in "Ligeia," he encloses his beautiful and virtuous wife in a room from which the world is entirely shut out and proceeds to try to remove her only visible imperfection, a birthmark on her cheek, shaped like a tiny hand. He fails, killing her in the process. A further ambivalence appears in this story in the figure of Aylmer's assistant, a dark creature of the earth, who tends the furnace and appears almost witless. Yet it is he, not Aylmer, who laughs at the notion that a human being can be rendered perfect.

The dilemma presented in "Rappaccini's Daughter" and "The Birthmark" we find again in Anton Chekhov's "The Black Monk," a tale very different from his usual, gently satiric stories of Russian life. Here, echoing the incestuous theme that appears in *The Castle of Otranto* as well as "The Fall of the House of Usher," we have a young man, a student, who marries a girl, Tanya, with whom he has grown up and whose father has been like a father to him.

Their home is a cultivated garden that the father can entrust to him alone. When he immerses himself in his studies, however, represented by the Black Monk, an apparition appearing in the uncultivated countryside, he suffers greatly and is deemed mad; when Tanya persuades him to undergo a cure, life becomes unbearable to him and he dies. Once again, we do not know whether he was a genius when mad or a madman who thought he was a genius. Once again, good and evil have become inextricably intertwined as the loved one is killed by the attempt of the lover to save him.

In these three stories, the scientists, Aylmer and Rappaccini, and the student, Kovrin, are associated with the occult and the supernatural. Thus, "modern" nineteenth century scientists are equated with the magicians of olden times, and thence with witches. At the same time, Rappaccini's daughter, being poisonous, is for all her beauty a monstrous figure, as is Aylmer's ugly assistant, and the Black Monk is an apparition. All three stories take us back to the ghosts of Matthew Lewis and Ann Radcliffe, to Frankenstein and his monster, and forward to many another creatures from the abyss.

The cat in Poe's "The Black Cat" is no ordinary domestic animal, but a haunting demon which haunts increasingly as the narrator sinks deeper into evil and guilt. Poe's "Hop-Frog" has as a central figure a stunted dwarf, who, himself apelike, dresses his tormentors up as orangutangs before immolating them in a fiery death. The cruelty of his revenge is in perfect consonance with the cruelty with which they have treated him. Thus, it makes him just such a monster as they are. Both cat and dwarf do more than symbolize guilt; they also personify in an external form the inner evil of their persecutors, as Frankenstein's monster embodies his evil.

These monsters, then, are reflecting devices. In one form or another, we find such devices in every Gothic tale. As projections of inner evil, they not only have a close correspondence to the symbols of real dreams, but they are also reflections of the evil self. When such a monster is a transmogrification it becomes even more disturbing. The vampire is such a phenomenon, and probably the most ambiguous of all monsters. Although it is the victims of vampires who themselves become vampires, and therefore it is true that every vampire was once an ordinary human being, it is also true that once the transformation has taken place, then the ordinary human being who appears to others is the false front concealing what is now the true being, the vampire. John Polidori's Lord Ruthven in "The Vampyre" (1819) is a seducing society-man in London who, in Greece, becomes a destroying vampire. Even this very simple story associates the vampire with sexuality. In more subtle vampire tales, the association is a complex development of sexual themes that appear throughout Gothic literature as frequently as the Faust motif: seduction, rape, and incest are there from the very beginnings of the genre in the eighteenth century. The fact that the vampire is a form-changing monster adds to this theme, for it may appear in its human form and of the opposite or the same sex as its victim. In Sheridan Le Fanu's "Carmilla," the victim is an innocent young girl. The vampire, Carmilla, appears as a young woman who addresses her in such strangely seductve tones that she wonders if Carmilla is a man in disguise. As a vampire, however, Carmilla becomes a formless dark mass which slithers over her, blanketing her young body as she lies sleeping, and draining the blood from her neck. The very confusion of sexes and the un-awareness of the young victim introduce a theme of awakening sexuality of which Bram Stoker was to make full use in *Dracula* (1897).

The monster thus becomes a projection and a reflection, not only of evil, but of the sexual self. Vampire stories are especially ambiguous because of the ambivalence of attitudes toward sexuality. Le Fanu's ghosts with their malignant stares are, like the ghosts from the earliest Gothic works onward, embodiments of the reproachful conscience, and, as such, they reflect in form the entire person of the victim of the conscience-stricken characters to whom they appear. In Nikolai Gogol's famous story *The Overcoat* (1842), for example, the ghost of the harmless little clerk, which comes back to haunt his erstwhile superior, is the figure of the clerk himself.

Gothic works are also positively cluttered with works of art which have similar reflecting qualities—portraits and statues abound, as do mirrors. Here again, Hawthorne refines the device in "The Man of Adamant" (1837) and in "Ethan Brand." In the one, the central character is himself petrified, turned into his own statue. In the other, Ethan Brand's heart is turned to stone, to pure marble, shining among the flames of the kiln he used to tend. In both cases, human stoniness becomes literally stone, a reflection of the spiritual state of the characters.

There is, however, still a stranger reflecting device—the double. We have seen that, from the beginning, Gothic literature portrays the villain as inev-itably in conflict with himself, torn between his God-endowed nature and that part of it which is twisted into evil. The ambivalence and ambiguity of the nineteenth century stories faced the author with the need to portray the central Gothic figure not as a roaring villain but as a man in tragic conflict. Hence is developed the projection of the evil into a monster, and hence appears the more subtle figure of the double. The torn and terrified protag-onist is faced with his own exact likeness, indeed, with himself.

Here, too, Poe is a forerunner. The central character of his "William Wilson," in his progressive decline into wickedness, finds himself faced with himself at recurring intervals; but this second self is merely his conscience, just as the double that Spencer Brydon meets in Henry James's much later story, "The Jolly Corner," is merely the self he might have been. Dostoevski uses doubles figures in many forms, and in *The Double* (1846) makes the two identical figures the manifestation of a split personality—a timid copy-clerk, Golyadkin, and the terrible double who does all the things the clerk would like, but does not dare, to do. In Joseph Conrad's "The Secret Sharer," too, the "sharer" is the captain's other self, but here he is the man who stands in an ordinary relationship to society, and is now in flight from it because he has killed a man. The Captain is that same man as head of a ship, the sole figure responsible for the lives, safety, and management of a miniature society. The conflict here becomes one of duty and responsibility, and compassion, albeit an ambiguous compassion for his own sinful self.

The double is, of course, a living, mobile mirror image. Dostoevski's tormented clerk sometimes finds that the figure of his double is, after all, his own reflection in a mirror. William Wilson, in Poe's story, also finds himself face to face with his double, then thinks it is his own reflection at which he is looking in a mirror, then finds it is the double after all, and kills him; that is, he kills his own conscience.

In 1891, Oscar Wilde raised this device to consummate perfection in *The Picture of Dorian Gray*. As with so many of his precursors among the characters of Gothic fiction, Dorian's perfect innocence is externalized in his perfect beauty. That beauty is caught in the portrait of him painted by Basil, the observing eye in the story. Here, as in Poe's "The Oval Portrait," the very soul of the sitter is caught in the perfect likeness; but Dorian does not die. Instead, he embarks on a life of depravity, each act of which mars the beauty, not of his face, but of the portrait's. When, finally, he can bear the sight of it no longer and rends the portrait with a knife, it is he who is found dead, with the knife in his heart, his face seamed with the marks of depravity, and the portrait once more shining forth in the perfection of its beauty.

Wilde's tale is highly moralistic, yet it nevertheless uses the Gothic devices to point up the psychological understanding of the connection between suicide and murder. It shows how far forward the nineteenth century had carried the eighteenth century investigations of human psychology. *The Picture of Dorian Gray* appeared chronologically between two works which show this advance even more clearly: Robert Louis Stevenson's *Dr. Jekyll and Mr. Hyde* (1886) and Henry James's *The Turn of the Screw* (1898). Together these works show three aspects of the trend toward a conscious, scientific understanding of man's psychological makeup, which was to burst upon the world with the works of Sigmund Freud, a contemporary of Stevenson, Wilde, and James. By the end of the nineteenth century, the eighteenth century Benevolist concept of man as essentially good and, consequently, as in conflict with himself when he turns evil, was no longer a dominant notion. Mankind, however, was still seen as potentially healthy (a concept not so different from the harmony of the Benevolists), and his antisocial behavior as a distortion of that potential, for the more scientific psychology became, the more it tended to see environment as the determining factor. It thus developed a concept of the personality in conflict not as evil, but as sick, and the harmonious personality, as healthy, or "normal."

It is the corrupt upper-class society of London from which Dorian learns his depravity. Yet, it is the respectable, middle-class painter Basil who has captured Dorian's soul with his art and so made his descent into depravity possible. Consequently, the question of moral responsibility in *The Picture of Dorian Gray* is confused and confusing, and Dorian's depravity is hateful to him. In a somewhat similar way, Robert Louis Stevenson's *Dr. Jekyll and Mr. Hyde* at first seems to be reviving the old notion of man as inevitably depraved, as a seething mass of animal passions which must be controlled by the reason. Here too, however, the ambiguity of the presentation shows Stevenson's thought to be no more than throwback.

His scientist, Jekyll—successor to Frankenstein, Rappaccini, Aylmer, and others—is a resentfully respectable Victorian doctor who releases his own animal self, Mr. Hyde, to roam the streets of London, committing atrocious deeds. Dr. Jekyll never comes face to face with this double, for it is himself in a more frightening sense than the earlier forms of this literary device. When Hyde is loose, there is no Jekyll. When Jekyll has him under control then he, Jekyll, is, in fact, both Jekyll and Hyde. There is a Hyde without Jekyll, but no Jekyll without Hyde. Worse still, the more often he lets Hyde out, the more difficult it becomes to suppress him again. It is clear that we are approaching the Freudian view of life, a view in which Jekyll's losing struggle with Hyde can almost be seen as the battle between id and superego. Our sense of the story's "scientific" view is enhanced by the method of multiple, cumulative narration, which Wilkie Collins, a master of the long tale of terror, had developed, but which Clara Reeve had also used in *The Old English Baron*.

A more objecive view still appears in Henry James's *The Turn of the Screw*. Here, within the entirely closed world of the house and grounds of Bly, we find two children, apparently as innocent as they are beautiful; a faithful retainer (also a standard fixture of the Gothic convention); a young governess; and two ghosts. Again the story is told by indirect narration, and has basically the same narrative structure as *Frankenstein*. The account is a manuscript, read long after the events, and written by the governess who lived through them but was far from understanding them.

The house at Bly is a prison (as so many buildings in Mrs. Ann Radcliffe's Gothic novels are), in which the governess would like, if she could, to keep the children forever young and innocent, in an eternal childhood, like Beckford's Gulchenrouz in *Vathek*. The ghosts are enigmatically presented. To the governess they are demons from hell, returned to corrupt the children; to the children they are friends, if they see them at all (we have only the governess' hysterical word for it); to the housekeeper they are illusions; to the reader they are figures like those in Poe's stories, full of a not-quite-graspable symbolic meaning. In this tale, once again, the effort of the self-avowed "good" character (the governess) to save the children arouses fear and revulsion for her in the little girl and results in the death of the boy, Miles. In this, James's story resembles "The Black Monk" and "Rappaccini's Daughter."

Although it is deliberately ambiguous, like these early tales, James has, nevertheless, introduced a new element. The ambiguity and uncertainty of the tale lies in the reader's uncertainty about the governess' perception of the events, while, at the same time, she is the very center of those events. As a result, the nature of the doubt with which we are left has changed. The question is no longer one of whether the narrator is mad, or whether art and science are blasphemous continuations of the ancient black arts. The question now is whether the governess is battling heroically against evil sexuality, or whether, herself inhibited and frustrated, she fears and sees as evil the inevitable development of the children toward adult sexuality.

To argue whether *The Picture of Dorian Gray*, *Dr. Jekyll and Mr. Hyde*, and *The Turn of the Screw* are short novels or substantial novellas, or even long short stories, seems pointless, but their particular effects could certainly not have been achieved in an extended form. A full-length novel could not have sustained the governess' hysterical tone, so important to our final assessment of the meaning of *The Turn of the Screw*, nor could it have kept the ghosts and the children alike enigmatic enough to convey the sense of ambiguity that forces us toward that assessment. Similarly, only in a short work could Dr. Jekyll's house and laboratory maintain their respective symbolic correspondences to his respectable outer self and the monster within him. Also Hyde's rampages, the singular effect he has on all who see him, and the symbolic functions of the streets and fogs of London could not have withstood the techniques of longer fictional forms. *The Picture of Dorian Gray* still less could have succeeded in a substantial narrative. Its almost allegorical pattern demands a short, lean treatment.

Furthermore, these three seminal works of the last decade of the nineteenth century set the stage for twentieth century developments in short fiction. For those living in this century, the findings of Freud and his successors have become a part of everyday life, and the line between Gothic and social novel has become blurred. We find Gothic devices reappearing, however, particularly in short fiction, and, as well, a new burst of Gothic techniques which create the necessary suspense of the well-wrought tale.

In the short stories of W. Somerset Maugham, H. H. Munro (Saki), and Graham Greene, the mysterious East, werewolves and other monsters, ghosts and supernatural happenings combine to create tales of terror. Our world grants this terror an entertainment value in its own right that would have puzzled and nonplused the eighteenth century inventors of the devices used.

At the same time, we find Gothic conventions integrated into twentieth century works of short fiction with otherwise quite realistic settings. Again, a short form is necessary to these works. To maintain the balance between the supernatural effects, almost always used to convey psychological meaning, and everyday life, compression and imagery must be used to juxtapose the fantastic and the realistic without their clashing and destroying each other.

D. H. Lawrence in "The Rocking-Horse Winner" evokes the supernatural to express the driving force of a son's unconscious oedipal need to replace an inadequate father. In "Sorrow Acre," Isak Dinesen goes back to the eighteenth century for the setting of a tale of an old woman's superhuman feat of endurance, performed to save her son, and ending in her death. Here, as in "The Fall of the House of Usher," house and owner (the old lord) are one, and the characters are caught in a myth of nobility and the continuity of the bloodline. Like Manfred in *The Castle of Otranto* and Heathcliff in Emily Brontë's *Wuthering Heights* (1847), the father is doomed to watch his sickly son die before he can continue the line. Like Manfred again, he marries his son's betrothed in his obsession with ensuring the direct succession. Eudora Welty conjures up the atmosphere and features of a fairy tale to follow a young girl's passage through puberty to sexual maturity in *The Robber Bridegroom*. Pär Lagerkvist sets *The Dwarf* (1944) in historical times and leans toward allegory in a story of a prince's dwarf who is free and favored when the prince goes to war and locked in a deep dungeon when he is conducting a policy of peace and general benevolence. In "Tree of Night," Truman Capote turns the story of two sharpers on a train, who steal a college girl's purse, into a Gothic nightmare. He thus conveys the psychological sense of robbery as an assault, which, in truth, arouses so many paranoid feelings in our crime-ridden cities.

The examples of such twentieth century uses of Gothic devices in short fiction are myriad, and sometimes an example of a short work appears which may be called "pure Gothic," even though it is not fantasy. Carson McCullers' "The Ballad of the Sad Café" is a tale which brings, through the story of a small Southern town, a revelation of the nature of human love; the tyrannous need to love and be loved; and the cruel patterns of rejection, loneliness, and self-isolation. It is a perfect piece of short Gothic fiction. The reader enters the isolated world of the small town with the narrator. The café of the title is equated with the changing states of its owner—the open center of the town's social world when she can love, a gray, shuttered, lonely shell when she is locked up in self-isolation. The characters, a giant, mannish woman and a dwarfed, hunchbacked, womanish man, manifest in their physical appearance the psychological states they represent, as all the gigantic villains, monsters, and gentle heroines among their predecessors had done.

From the late eighteenth century to the present day, the themes of guilt, sexual repression, madness, and man's prideful defiance of God have found expression in Gothic devices used in works of all lengths. Yet undeniably, the short forms of fiction lend themselves particularly well to the suspenseful, ambiguous, anomalous nature of Gothic literature. By the same token, the master writers of the short forms of fiction have repeatedly used Gothic techniques to create tales of pure terror, as well as for the technical purpose of creating the suspense that rivets the reader's attention, making the value of shortness, whatever the work's particular purpose, felt and appreciated.

Bibliography
Birkhead, Edith. *The Tale of Terror*.
Foster, James R. *History of the Pre-Romantic Novel in England*.
Hume, Robert D. "Gothic versus Romantic: A Revaluation of the Gothic Novel," in *PMLA*.
MacAndrew, Elizabeth. *The Gothic Tradition in Fiction*.
Nelson, Lowry, Jr. "Night Thoughts on the Gothic Novel," in *Yale Review*.
Railo, Eino. *The Haunted Castle*.
Summers, Montague. *The Gothic Quest*.
Thompson, G. R., ed. *The Gothic Imagination: Essays in Dark Romanticism*.
Varma, Devendra P. *The Gothic Flame*.

Elizabeth MacAndrew

BRITISH SHORT FICTION IN THE SIXTEENTH AND SEVENTEENTH CENTURIES

Modern scholars have disagreed sharply over whether Renaissance prose fiction can best be seen as taking tentative steps toward the eighteenth century novel or whether it marks the end of a medieval tradition. As with most academic debates, both approaches are useful and depend on the critic's perspective. In fact, in some limited but important ways, the state of prose fiction between the first use of movable type in England (1485) and the last decades of the seventeenth century is comparable to that in our own time. It was an era of deep-rooted sociocultural change: a traditional mode of literature was slowly dying or being adapted to an apparently less discriminating audience; also, a bewildering variety of literary experiments, many of which were uncertain or outright failures, was accompanied by an uncertainty about the conventions and the value of prose fiction. To read the works of George Gascoigne, Thomas Deloney, or Aphra Behn is certainly to have received notions about the nature of prose fiction radically challenged. Yet a useful comparison of their strangeness to the modern reader can be made to the reader's increasing familiarity with the postmodern experiments in fiction of today. There is also the awareness that although the world they describe is, largely, one that is now lost, they do nevertheless articulate important aspects of modern cultural heritage and so of modern self-understanding.

The period marked by the English revolution, the Restoration, and the Settlement of 1688 makes one of the vital watersheds in our history, and its effects can be sensed in the age's prose fiction. By the late seventeenth century, many of the European literary fashions which England had belatedly adapted were taking root, and as socioeconomic balance shifted radically, so a new form of prose fiction developed. Historical changes of such magnitude, however, rarely occur overnight, and the whole era, in particular between 1570 and 1640 when the period's social, intellectual, and cultural turmoil was at its most concentrated, provides anticipations and experiments of enormous interest. In any period of unusual turbulence, writers and texts tell the reader more than they know, and the role of the critic is more than usually that of deconstructing the obvious surface referentiality of texts, as the reader searches for evidence for deeper implicit, but eventually enormously important, changes in a society's culture.

So far as "short" fiction is concerned, the Renaissance, unlike later centuries, had no coherent theory of prose fiction in general, let alone for distinguishing between shorter and longer forms. The period inherited a huge variety of shorter forms from its past—jests, anecdotes, fables, exampla, romances, *fabliaux*, homilies, folktales, *récits*, *novelle*—but few writers seem to have given conscious attention to questions of length. Instead, they seem to have been anxious to justify the art of fiction-making itself—"poetry" was their usual term—alongside other human activities. Much Renaissance fiction is uneasily claimed to be "history" and contains elaborate justifications of the teller's veracity. Although George Gascoigne and John Barth are worlds apart in sophistication of technique, both show a self-conscious uneasiness about their craft that points not merely to the uncertain quality of fiction but, beyond, to the nature of their societies. If one looks to France, Italy, or Spain, one finds evidence for a more self-conscious concern with shorter as opposed to longer forms of fiction and, indeed, in France between about 1560 and 1600 and again between 1660 and 1700, various short forms dominated fashions in prose fiction. In England, however, no such self-consciousness seemed to have existed, and in order to get an adequate sense of what forms of short fiction did exist, it will be necessary to stretch and at some points to ignore the limits of the topic.

Notwithstanding uncertainty over the nature of prose fiction (and this is not simply an English phenomenon), an increasing amount was written and published as the new technology of moving type coincided with the expansion of the reading public. Among the earliest books printed by William Caxton and Wynkyn de Worde were editions of medieval romances, and by 1600, approximately one-quarter of the books printed in England were prose fiction. The expansion of a literate, book-buying class was a complex business, and one of its most relevant aspects was the growing fear observable among the dominant and educated classes that the more the reading public grew, the more literary standards and—by association—social and political order, would be threatened. Authors who preferred the traditional role of court entertainer slowly adapted to the new commercial market, often with some reluctance, as new economic relationships developed between authors, entrepreneurs, and readers that would eventually radically transform the nature and status of the craft. Whereas Sir Philip Sidney's primary audience was his sister, his family, and his friends, and John Lyly saw his fiction as a means of social advancement, Robert Greene, Thomas Nash, Deloney, and, by the mid-seventeenth century, most writers of fiction had abandoned the traditional role. While still archaically addressing their readers in continual parentheses as "gentles" and "fayre ladies" in approved courtly manner, writers increasingly found themselves related commercially to their audiences and usually conceived their role as purveying and reinforcing what they saw as their audience's normative values. Any emergent values or techniques observed, in hindsight, in Nash, Deloney, or Behn are expressed indirectly in their works.

The major emergent literary form in the period was, of course, the drama of the public theater. Like prose fiction, the drama went through a period of uncertainty and experimentation and had to reconcile a long tradition of communal entertainment with new intellectual pretensions and the new demands of the marketplace. A brief comparison is instructive. While the best of Elizabethan prose fiction is manifestly the expression of the same energies that produced the Elizabethan drama, it is striking that while in the theater an art form developed which expressed the energies of the period in a remarkable fusion of popular entertainment and philosophical and psychological profundity, fiction-writing remained a minor and peripheral form. One cannot simply say that the energies that later ages gave to the novel and short story were directed into the drama: the theater seems uniquely equipped to explore the bewildering variety of problems the age felt within experience of contingency and change. The role-playing of the theater, its inherent relativism, its juxtapositions of opposing philosophies and moods, and its fierce demands on emotional involvement, all seem, in hindsight, to have captured the needs and confusions of the age—better, perhaps, than the age itself knew.

The theater had, as well, the advantage of developing subtle forms of independence of court values (although not of court patronage or censorship). By making the fascination of human actions its central interest, it opened the possibilities for audiences to contemplate themselves, their society, their world. More than any other literary or art form, the drama articulated the age's struggle to free itself from archaic and residual intellectual, social, and political forces and to release the emergent drives of a new world. Readers look back to *Hamlet* (1600-1601), *Doctor Faustus* (1588), *The White Devil* (1612), and *The Tempest* (1611) as embodiments of energies and insights that were—and often despite the immediately succeeding age—to come through as forming and directing subsequent history. By contrast, the greatest work of prose fiction in the age, Sidney's *Arcadia* (1590), looks back nostalgically to an earlier world of order and stasis. What seemed to Sidney's contemporaries to be the shoring up of standards was eventually to be seen as retrogressive and nostalgic, and so far as prose fiction is concerned, the real growing points—for the eighteenth century novel and beyond—were peripheral and obscure parts of Renaissance culture.

Having identified somewhat the place of prose fiction in the sociocultural dynamic of the age, it is now appropriate to examine specifically the characteristics of short prose fiction. Notwithstanding the difficulty of defining "short" forms for the period, there are a variety of interesting works and points of potential growth for later ages. First to be dealt with will be those forms of fiction to which Renaissance authorities would have given greatest approval, those directly associated with the aesthetic demands of the court—adaptations of medieval romances, translations, and imitations of Continental modes (especially the *novella*, the *conte*, and the various picaresque forms). Second, the counterdominant forms of prose fiction which, explicitly or not, modified or challenged the dominance of the court will be covered. These included the middle-class adaptation and eventual transformation of romance, fiction which bore the marked impact of Protestantism, and the various forms of short fiction that emerged from sociopolitical realities on the periphery of or outside the dominant culture. These forms—folk stories, anecdotes, jests, tales of ordinary and seemingly trivial experience—however excluded by the hegemonous forms, nevertheless constitute a crucial part of the cultural life of England and point beyond to the life and literature of later periods.

During the sixteenth century, literature and the arts generally became increasingly subject to the control and values of the age's dominant institution, the court. As the Tudor state took a more confident shape, it systematically—although on a European scale, belatedly—attempted to use the arts as an instrument in its policy of centralization and control. Epic and lyric poetry and the masque particularly felt its pressure, and the development of these modes especially show the power of the court over its subjects. The most important works of prose fiction in the European Renaissance—those by François Rabelais, Miguel de Cervantes Saavedra, and Sidney—all articulate directly or in reaction the new buoyancy and aggressiveness of the Renaissance court. Most writers of any kind were either courtiers or financially dependent on court patronage; until late in the sixteenth century, most conceived of themselves as court entertainers. As the court hegemony broke down over the succeeding century, writers were forced to find alternative social roles and audiences and to change their modes of writing to express the new social realities.

The dominance of the court in the Tudor period meant that the works written or translated were heavily influenced by court taste. The majority of early works of prose fiction drew on traditional medieval chivalric material—stories of romantic love, Arthurian adventures, and the like. Even as early as 1500, their values were fast becoming archaic so far as actual social practices are concerned, but their increasingly escapist aura continued to appeal to readers for the next two centuries by means of an intriguing mixture of nostalgia and practicality. Their settings, characters, and actions are essentially escapist—enchanted islands, captured ladies, gallant knights, monsters, miracles, coincidences—but they are invariably heavily moralistic.

Indeed, it is one of the strengths of the late Elizabethan flowering of prose fiction that even the most tedious and confused tale can suddenly break into an earnest moral argument between the author and his readers. Prompted by marginal notes and directly addressed by the author (who in the most unpredictable and seemingly postmodernist manner can drop his seeming objectivity at any moment), one may be asked to enter an intense moral debate. Walter R. Davis has argued that central to Elizabethan romance is an attempt to test traditional moral and intellectual beliefs, embodied in the romance world of pure, idealized motives opposed to reminders of a harsher reality in which the readers uncomfortably lived. He points further to the higher interest in ideas in English romances than in their European counterparts; one witnesses the earnest adaptation to pragmatic ends of a set of values essentially idealistic, escapist, and archaic.

In most cases, however—the earliest signs of a countermovement are not found before the works of Deloney in the 1590's—the reified values of the romances are the traditional chivalric ones, and any real possibility of debate, like that afforded by the drama—*Hamlet, Troilus and Cressida* (1601-1602), *The White Devil*, say—is lost. Nevertheless, an aristocratic reader of the typical romance tale in 1590 makes a fascinating case history: surrounded by the uneasiness of a world increasingly threatened by strange new sociocultural forces, he turned to prose fiction as he turned to Edmund Spenser's *The Faerie Queene* (1590-1596) or, a decade after, to the Jacobean court masque, for the reassurance of values and habits long archaic and unlike the reality outside his chamber. Perhaps a few miles away, however, in a dank public theater, a new play about a German necromancer was alluring or disturbing audiences from very different social groups with the thrill of blasphemy, ambition, and the possibility (reassuringly, to most of the audience, unsuccessful) of avoiding a just damnation.

When turning to the examples of short prose fiction from which the Renaissance reader had to choose (especially those few occasions when writers seemed more conscious writing "short" forms), one discovers that the prose fiction of the English Renaissance was, as in so many other fields, dominated by Continental models. Most important for the period's short fiction was the Italian *novella*, best exemplified by Giovanni Boccaccio in the fourteenth century, a form able to use a variety of serious, romantic, and satiric elements within a framework of transmitting a sense of vivid, immediate life from teller to hearer. Various *novelle* by Boccaccio himself were translated or imitated and published in sixteenth century England, including, quite early, the anonymous, lively *Frederyke of Jennen* (1509), derived through various intermediaries from Boccaccio's *The Decameron* (1353) II.ix. Later in the period, many of the 214 *novelle* by Matteo Bandello, richly melodramatic stories of love and violence, were translated or imitated. In 1567, William Painter published *The Palace of Pleasure*, taken from François de Belleforest's French version of Bandello. Subtitled "tragicall Novells and dolorous Histories," Painter's work was described rather disapprovingly by the humanist educator, Roger Ascham, in *The Scholemaster* (1570) as "fond books, of late translated out of Italian into English, sold in every shop in London." Painter includes more than one hundred short tales, including the contemporary story of the Duchess of Amalfi (later adapted by John Webster), all combining rich melodrama and dogged, simplistic moralization. Painter offers them as demonstrations that the world is "a stage and theatre" providing "diversitie of matter pleasant and plausible" as well as being "for example and imitation good and commendable." Titillating scandal exists side by side with moral lectures—a typical combination in the English collections of *novelle*.

A similar combination, even more diverse in its elements, is Geoffrey Fenton's adaptions of Belleforest and Bandello in his *Certain Tragicall Dis-*

courses (1567), thirteen short tales, mainly about the evils of lust, combining prurient details and long moralizing harangues on the inevitability of divine punishment. George Pettie's *A Petite Palace of Pettie His Pleasure* (1576) also adapts twelve *novelle*, but their direct brevity is swamped, again, by coy moralizing and also—a new element which shows how the form was being adapted to genteel courtly taste—by a self-consciously elegant prose style, heavy-handed allegory, stylized debates, stolid abstractions, and sly asides to members of the courtly audience. Despite the sycophantic tone, however, Pettie's work does show a strong sense of its audience, as does Barnaby Rich's *His Farewell to Militarie Profession* (1581), eight stories adapted from various *novelle* and addressed to the "righte courteous Gentlewoman" of the court with the usual mixture of titillation and moral commonplaces. All these examples of framed *novelle* and others—Edmund Tilney's *Flower of Friendship* (1568) or George Whetstone's *An Heptameron of Civill Discourses* (1582)—seem unaware that the *novella*'s power lies precisely in its brevity and directness; they aspire to longer, leisurely, more courtly forms of prose fiction. It was left to later dramatists such as William Shakespeare and Webster to use the concentration of the *novella* in a different medium.

Similarly, sophisticated in its handling of a short form—and providing an instinctive contrast with England—is the tradition in France. Until the reign of François I, France, like England, remained dominated by Italian or Spanish models. From the 1530's, however, and as part of the sudden rebirth of secular and religious literature associated with the Pléiade and the court *salons*, there grew up an impressive tradition of prose fiction. Its longer forms were dominated by Rabelais, its shorter forms (the *conte*, *novelle*, or *récit*) by Marguerite de Navarre in the *L'Heptaméron* (1558) and in her circle, including Bonaventure Des Périers, Henri Estienne, and Belleforest. The vogue for short fiction, either as part of a collection told by a variety of *dévisants*, or storytellers, who frequently offered diverse interpretations of similar situations and so involved the readers in a moral debate, or else in separate unlinked examples, resulted in great advances in the art of short fiction. One can see a dramatic thematic widening, an unprecedented sophistication of style and technique, and an important contribution to the expressive powers of French prose. By the end of the century, short fiction in France was not merely highly popular but had become a major literary form in a way that English prose fiction did not until the eighteenth century. English writers adapted material from the French collections of stories, but seemed to learn little about the sophisticated possibilities of the form.

The third major source—and, again, it provides a contrast with English fiction writers—is Spain. As in Italy and France, the Iberian peninsula developed a varied tradition of fiction, seen at its greatest in Cervantes' *Don Quixote de la Mancha* (1605-1615; English translation 1612, 1620). Sentimental novels, pastoral romances, picaresque tales, and rogue fiction, are all evidence of vigorous interest in shorter forms of fiction in Spain and Portugal. David Rowland translated the *Lazarillo de Tormes* (1554) in 1576, "strange and mery reports, very recreative and pleasant," and James Mabbe in 1622 *The Rogue* or *The Life and Adventures of Guzmán de Alfarache*, (1599, 1604), thus bringing two notable examples of the picaresque into English. Margaret Tyler's *The Mirror of Princely Deeds* (1578) and Anthony Munday's *Palmerin of England* (1581) and many others adapted the rambling, idealized adventure-romance. These chivalric works—which Cervantes attempts to "demolish" for their "ill-founded structure" and absurdities—were enormously popular in England, but as long works, they need not detain us, except to underline how the English taste turned inevitably to such leisured, essentially escapist, fiction.

One further foreign influence, although one hardly contemporary with Sidney, Lyly, and their fellows, should be mentioned. English writers were usually aware that their literary inheritance included a number of distinctive stories written in pre-Christian Greece. Usually referred to as "the Greek romances," these included Heliodorus' *Aethiopica*, Longus' short tale *Daphnis and Chloë*, and Achilles Tatius' *Clitophon and Leucippe*, all of which were translated into English in the 1560-1590 period. All are elaborate in incident, intricate in plot, held together by a graceful, sensual melancholy, and stressing the fickleness of human affairs. Greene's prose romances and Shakespeare's dramatic romances are among English works which show a careful study of their attractive atmosphere and incident-packed plots.

Between about 1570 and 1610, then, occurred what can justly be seen as a most interesting flowering of prose fiction. A great variety of short and long fiction—much derived from Italian, Spanish, and French sources—was translated, adapted, or imitated. Medieval romances, English and Continental alike, were revived in prose versions; the new writers of the Elizabethan younger generation—Gascoigne, Sidney, Greene, Thomas Lodge, Nash, Deloney, Emmanuel Forde—produced a variety of native examples. Although it is, once again, difficult to sort out distinctively "short" forms—and in some cases impossible if one wishes to get a rounded picture—one can nevertheless note some of the most important trends and illustrate them largely from short examples. Interestingly, one of the best pieces of prose fiction in English was written early in the period and is sufficiently contracted—about 32,000 words long—to almost qualify as "short" fiction. It is the court poet-translator George Gascoigne's *The Novel of Master F. J.*, first published in 1573 and ostensibly set in some unnamed Northern castle, and then republished in 1575, somewhat rewritten, retitled, and set in a typical Italianate court, accompanied by a denial that the early version had been, as had been alleged, a *roman à clef*. The work appeared as part of a miscellany of court entertainments by Gascoigne entitled *A Hundred Sundrie Flowres Bound Up in One Small Poesie* and included poems and translations, all "gathered partely . . . in the fyne outlandish Gardins of Euripides, Ovid, Petrarcke, Ariosto, and others: and partly by invention, out of our own fruitful Orchardes in Englande." *The Novel of Master F. J.* itself is described as "a pleasant discourse of the adventures of master F. J. conteyning excellent letters, sonnets, Lays, Ballets, Rondlets, Verlays and verses."

Alongside most other examples of prose fiction, short or long, between 1500 and 1700, *The Novel of Master F. J.* is an unusually coherent and skillful piece of fiction. Put in a European perspective, it appears as a typical product of a sophisticated court society, an antiromantic *novella*. It depicts the affair between a young man, saturated with the rhetoric of courtly love, learning something of his own naïveté and the archaic nature of his ideals, and a highly manipulative young married woman. *Amour courtoise* was, by the 1570's, long dead in practice, except in the archaic rituals revived in the Elizabethan court; Gascoigne's tale is an amusing scrutiny of its irrelevance to the actual experience of human love—as opposed to its value for social allegiance to the Queen. Within a very limited sphere, Gascoigne is doing for the courtly tale, and the ethos behind it, what Cervantes was to do for longer chivalric romances.

During the late 1570's and 1580's, there was a concentrated attempt, largely initiated by Sir Philip Sidney and his circle, to bring about a renaissance of English letters. Sidney's own *Astrophel and Stella* (1591), *The Defence of Poesie* (1595), his sister's *Psalms*, and Spenser's *The Faerie Queene* are all parts of this movement. In prose fiction he also led the way with the age's most important prose work, *The Countesse of Pembroke's Arcadia* (written 1579-1580; revised c. 1582-1584, first published 1590 under the title *Arcadia*). Sidney's work epitomizes the dominance of the court over Elizabethan culture but, interestingly, it also betrays something of the intellectual and sociocultural strains that were to challenge the hegemony of the court over the next fifty years. Unlike most other prose fiction of the period, the *Arcadia* presents a complex and challenging model for aristocratic living, for action in and comprehension of the world. The debate Sidney takes us into may, finally, be settled by archaic and regressive ideas, but it is infinitely more complex and disturbing than any other work of prose fiction, and far more interesting. Motivation and moral insight are rooted in actual cultural and intellectual values. Technically, too, Sidney's work is far in advance of any other work of prose fiction, short or long, before the eighteenth century. While the *Arcadia*'s plot is appropriately elaborate (especially in the revised new *Arcadia*), it is nevertheless unified by a coherent and subtle vision, all the more interesting because one senses that, like Spenser, Sidney increasingly felt the pressure to explore and question the values of his class and age. It is arguable, indeed, that the new *Arcadia*, like *The Faerie Queene*, is an unfinishable work, its elaborate display and complexity an epitome of its author's uneasiness before the questions his work raised for him and his society, and one that he sensed would never be settled within his lifetime.

Sidney's work was the most admired piece of prose fiction in English before Samuel Richardson's *Pamela* (1740). It was imitated, completed, translated, summarized, and, in part, dramatized; it increasingly became regarded as a storehouse of lost moral wisdom. The *Arcadia* was a mine of plots and situations for dramatists and for later writers of prose fiction; only the collections by Pettie, Painter, and their like were used so much by the following century's writers. The most popular tale within the complex fabric of Sidney's work was that of Argalus and Parthenia, which was probably at least as familiar to English readers as the story of Romeo and Juliet and which inspired poems, plays, and a variety of cheap chapbook condensations or summaries of the *Arcadia*. Some versions, late in the seventeenth century, add characters such as a villainous mother and a tricky maid and vastly increase the melodramatic violence and suspense. None of the imitations, short or long, approach the intellectual richness or formal mastery of Sidney's work. Indeed, so great was the power of Sidney, as an ideal even more than as a person, that the *Arcadia* might well be seen as hindering developments in prose fiction over the next century or so.

The other major writer of the 1570's and 1580's who, although not strictly a writer of "short" fiction, nevertheless deserves mention is John Lyly. His works, *Euphues, the Anatomy of Wit* (1579) and *Euphues and His England* (1580), provide excellent examples of the pressure of the court upon the role of the fiction writing and the style and scope of his work. Whereas by his position as an aristocrat, Sidney had both the freedom and security to challenge or at least severely qualify court values, Lyly was an eagerly aspiring court-follower, anxious for preferment and happy to write according to court taste. *Euphues, the Anatomy of Wit* is court fiction *par excellence*, a courtly game designed primarily to provide stylish entertainment with a minimum of intellectual substance. Although occasionally ironical in intent, Lyly is concerned less with the substance of ideas than with their manipulation as part of a demonstration of wit and sophisticated cleverness. His audience is almost exclusively the ladies and gentlemen of the court, and his intention is to flatter, titillate, and reassure; what moral insights he offers are incidental to the use of stylistic devices as witty display. Yet beneath the glittering surface of Lyly's prose there can be clearly sensed the unresisted pressure of the court: contrary ideas are balanced to "prove" that moderation and judicious reasoning coincide with the commonplaces of the Elizabethan regime. Commonplace didacticism is presented, through the formal and mellifluous structure of the prose, as universal truth. In other words, Lyly is not simply offering his elegant style for admiration: he is asserting against the chaos of the world outside the mannered beauty of the court the order of the courtly ideal. His style creates an emblem of harmony, a sense of formalized security, completely controlled so that the harsher realities of the outside world cannot invade.

The constant use of superlatives—"the sweetest wine turneth to the sharpest vinegar"—has often been commented upon for its formal beauty, but it is more than decorative: it is a device designed to suggest that the whole possible range of experience has been considered and, through art, is being controlled and ruled. Lyly's style is thus a flattering mirror of the court, and the readers of his books are invited to enter and take their places in that world. Almost as much space is given to such invitations, flattering the reader, as to dialogue: "Euphues had rather lye shut in a Ladyes casket, than open in a Schollar's studie" is Lyly's own gloss on his work.

Sidney and Lyly epitomize different aspects of the court aesthetic's hold over prose fiction—although, of course, it was not only over prose fiction, nor was it simply an aesthetic. Hardly any prose fiction, short or long, during the 1580's or early 1590's escaped their influence. Euphuism gave writers such as Greene, Lodge, Brian Melbancke, and William Warner an elegant mode of presenting characters and ideas as part of a tapestry of stylistic effects; Sidney gave his followers an emphasis on moral seriousness and, interacting with the influence of Greek romance and Spanish chivalric romances, an emphasis on the unpredictability and the infinite complexity of human events.

It is with Lodge and Greene that we can see the romance tradition being adapted to shorter fictional forms. Although Stephen Gosson's *The Ephemerides of Phialo* (1579), Anthony Munday's *Zelauto* (1580), and Brian Melbancke's *Philotimus* (1583) are all medium-length adaptations of Lyly's mode, with exemplary dialogues and debates and a self-conscious elegance of style, Greene and Lodge provide us with the best evidence for the popularity and the adaptability of the court-dominated forms. Lodge is the more influenced by Sidney. In *Rosalynde* (1590), for example, the major source for Shakespeare's *As You Like It* (1599-1600), the typical (although not exclusively) Arcadian motif of the contrast between court and country is used to test charmingly the ideals of conduct and style on which the court prided itself. *A Margarite of America* (1595) is similarly Sidneian in its mellifluous pastoral atmosphere and delicate moral touches. Between 1579 and 1592, Greene (who was probably the best-selling short-fiction writer of the whole period, with some seventy editions of his romances published before 1640), published about thirty pieces of fiction and, in fact, derived much of his income from what he termed his "trifling Pamphlets . . . and vaine fantasies." He continually adjusted his work to prevailing fashion, writing Euphuistic fiction (*Mamilius*, 1583), love-tales, low-life and criminal stories, moral *exempla*—*The Myrrour of Modesty* (1584) shows that "the graie heades of dooting adulterers shall not go with peace into the grave"—and adventure stories. Of his shorter works, *Pandosto, the Triumph of Time* (1588) is an especially interesting use of the Greek romance tradition. Used by Shakespeare for the main source of the plot of *The Winter's Tale* (1610-1611), it is a tale of lost love, unpredictable fortune, and unexpected joy and sorrow all designed to stress the illogicality and unpredictability of fortune, but unlike Shakespeare's play, revealing, in Walter Davis' words, an "almost cynical or Calvinistic assumption of the inconsequentiality of human purposes." Another example of Greene's adaptability in a brief form is *A Quip for an Upstart Courtier* (1592), a calculated criticism of the waste and self-deception of pretentious gentility, written from the conservative viewpoint of a cautious bourgeois. The ethos of this and of his lively "conny-catching" rogue-fiction pamphlets, which display something of the vigorous anarchy of the low-life and the criminal subculture of London, show the gradual adaptation of the romance to a wider audience and, eventually, to anticourt sentiments. As Davis comments, Greene "began his career as the staunchest of the young Euphuists, but by the end of it he had neglected everything Lyly stood for." As such he epitomizes the revolution that was coming over much of the literature of the age by the time of his death in 1592.

Before looking in some detail at the distinctive features of the short fiction of the 1590's, it is perhaps important to sense something of an overview of the courtly fiction that dominated the 1570's, 1580's and early 1590's, and which in increasingly adapted forms continued to be overwhelmingly popular through the seventeenth century. As can be seen from looking at its two dominant writers, Sidney and Lyly, courtly fiction is essentially conservative in intellectual outlook: originating in the values of the court, it harks nostalgically back to a world of order, harmony, and mystery. Essentially escapist in its values, it therefore tends to avoid or else to romanticize the pressures and contradictions of material life. Its characters are abstractions and types. Its settings are exotic and romantic, its plots episodic, coincidental, melodramatic, and unsurprising in their continual unexpectedness. Its style, if rarely as explicitly as in Lyly, tends to reinforce the ethos of nostalgia. It is rhetorically heightened, static and emblematic, and self-conscious in its use of rhetoric and ornament to convey the experience of participation in a ritual of comfort and wish fulfillment. In its origins, courtly fiction grew from a tradition of oral entertainment, its tellers subservient (although aspiring) members of the court whose values it espoused. Its narrative techniques go back to those courtly origins. They still show marks of the storyteller, the court entertainer, conscious always of the audience before him and of the roles he must therefore play. Although there is no clear break with the writers of the 1590's, readers do start to become aware of new forces threatening and disconcerting the dominance of the court. Even Lyly betrays something of an unease before a crucial transition that had, in fact, been under way since the invention of printing: the creation of a larger, more impersonal, and more diverse audience created by the printing press. This was a literate although not necessarily a learned audience eager for entertainment and the reinforcement of its own very different and rapidly changing values and experiences.

In many areas of literature, the 1590's saw disturbing formal and thematic developments—in satire, in a pared-down rhetoric in both poetry and prose, in the public theater, in the influx of new ideas, and in the virtual invention of new literary forms. So far as prose fiction is concerned, the developments have often been described as the surfacing of a new strain of realism, anticipating, clumsily, developments in the eighteenth century novel. The confusions and the achievements of the 1590's deserve better than that. They are both important crystallizations of the enthusiasms and anxieties of their time and indicative of wider and more long-term cultural changes. Erich Auerbach's observation that "courtly culture was decidedly unfavorable to the development of a literary art which should apprehend reality in its full breadth and depth" has real point here. It is seen, very clearly, the ways in which the public theater of Shakespeare's time responded to and in part created the tastes and self-consciousness of a new audience, and how its new modes of perceiving reality were in part dependent on its growing independence and rejection of the values of the court—paradoxically even while it was ostensibly responsible to and dependent on the court. Only spasmodically does one see such possibilities develop in prose fiction.

The 1590's show some of the few signs. The later works of Greene, written just before his death in 1592, show him turning to the raw energies of contemporary London life for the material of fiction, and the possibilities of a new, disturbing realism can be seen in another transitional writer, Thomas Nash. Like Greene, Nash adapted his considerable talents to both traditional courtly tastes and to a new, wider, less discriminating audience. He attacked the "idle pens," "fantasticall dreams," and "worne out impressions of the feyned no where acts" of the chivalric romances and saw his *The Unfortunate Traveller: Or, The Life of Jack Wilton* (1594) as written in a "cleane different vaine." Using an impressive range of satire, parody, burlesque, and realistic observation, Nash's work is a picaresque biography of one Jack Wilton, an adventurer who observes warfare, travel, and various aspects of contemporary life. Nash's plot is unsophisticatedly episodic, and the straightforwardness of his hero, a roguish outsider able to inhabit a variety of recognizable milieux, affords him an unusual degree of realistic observation. *The Unfortunate Traveller* is a typical 1590's work, akin to experiments in poetry and drama, mixing the characteristics of a variety of traditional literary modes, held together by the restless persona of its author, and betraying signs of emergent cultural experiences straining at the restrictions of older artistic forms.

Some of Nash's other works, including *Nashe's Lenten Stuffe* (1599) and *Have with You to Saffron Walden* (1596), are on the boundary (not easy to draw in the 1590's) between fiction and disputation. In these two works, he fictionalizes his enemy Gabriel Harvey, pouring scorn on his learning and affectations and complaining that true learning and wit go unrewarded. In his complaint, one senses less the iconoclast than the aspiring court entertainer, harking back to older, more traditional ways, idealized in *Pierce Penniless* (1592) by the Sidneys. He bewails that a gentleman like himself should have to make himself "a gazing stock and a publique spectacle to all the world for nothing." Like many of his generation—restless, ambitious, Inns of Court or University men—Nash is self-indulgent, insecure, and despite his astringent style, still seeing his fiction as a means to preferment in a world where advancement seems increasingly denied. While he has the true performer's delight in rhetoric and a vivid sense of his audience—"Readers, be merry; for in me there shall want nothing I can doo to make you merry" he cries in *The Unfortunate Traveller*—his qualities of realistic observation and pointed commentary remain incidental to his residual conception of the role of fiction, and they point forward to later developments despite his own intentions.

Nash, Greene, and Lodge all show signs of a vital transition in the nature and function of prose fiction. Even in the *Arcadia*, in so many pivotal ways the age's most significant work, there are signs of the incipient breakdown, even at its apparent height, of the cultural hegemony of the court. Any culture contains, as has been shown, residual elements of an earlier phase of society—frequently embodied in the dominant and therefore more conservative tastes of society—and emergent cultural values and experiences, which often appear unbeknown to authors and which the modern reader identifies as culturally significant. The confusion and experimentation of the 1590's is not unique to prose fiction writers, but in their searches for social and literary identity one can certainly sense something of the age's most important cultural shifts.

Raymond Williams, commenting on the *Arcadia*, points to the irony that the work which gave its name to a central facet of the English pastoral tradition should have been written on a real country estate whose wealth had been created by upsetting traditional bonds between men and their land, and then ruthlessly exploiting the enclosures thus acquired. Sidney certainly seems unaware of the irony, and the reader may notice, perhaps a little uncomfortably, that he seems supremely indifferent to the pressures of the real-life values or problems of tenants, peasants, or any class below the level of his admirable, if erring, heroes and heroines. What, as was seen with Greene and Nash, the 1590's bring is a gradual transformation of the forms and function of traditional fiction by an audience and an incipient structure of values, beliefs, and habits that would eventually transform not only prose fiction but also the sociocultural fabric of England. It is therefore fascinating to see the court romance invaded and subverted increasingly in the years following the 1590's. What are usually termed "bourgeois romances" can be seen as early as the 1580's. At first they are simply adaptations of the traditional fantastic adventures, except that their heroes are not aristocratic but middle-class knights errant. In works such as Lodge's *The Life and Death of William Longbeard* (1593), Henry Roberts' *Pheander the Mayden Knight* (1595), and Richard Johnson's *The Most Pleasant History of Tom a Lincolne*

(1607), the quests of the heroes are to protect values that express the world not of Arcadia but of Southwark or Eastcheap.

The bourgeois romances are cautious and decorous to the point of incongruity, however, calling into question their courtly antecedents by implication only and explicitly intent on appealing still to the values of "the gentleman reader," although the term is taking on a meaning far broader than Baldassare Castiglione, Sidney, or even Nash would have approved. The most successful writers of this form of fiction are Emmanuel Forde and Thomas Deloney, whose works, like Gascoigne's or Greene's, are somewhat awkwardly located between "long" and "short." Forde's enormously popular *The Most Pleasant History of Ornatus and Artesia* (1595?) and *Parismus* (1598-1599) are works of moderate length which add to an explicitly although romanticized bourgeois setting an interest in the motivation of humble people exploited by over-bearing aristocrats. Deloney was almost as popular a writer and even more interesting in his mixture of realism and traditional romance. In 1596 he was accused of "bringing in" the Queen to one of his works, "to speak with her people in dialogue in very fond and undecent sort," which would never have done for Sidney (or Spenser). His heroes typically rise from being lowly apprentices or servants to becoming wealthy clothiers or Members of Parliament. His settings are still idealized, but are recognizably related to England rather than Arcadia and are peopled with a variety of merchants, shoemakers, citizens, and goodwives, whose natural loyalties are more patriotic, Deloney constantly asserts, than those of the aristocracy. In *Thomas of Reading* (c. 1600) after an especially jovial interview with the King, Hodgekins the clothiers' spokesman "affirmed on his faith that he had rather speak to the king's majesty than to many justices of peace." With such a revolution in the content of his work, Deloney is, however, disappointingly traditional, even archaic, in the structure and mode of his fiction. His work is still chivalric romance, adapted for a new class anxious to see its newfound respectability and power idealized in the way its superiors continued, more uneasily, to idealize theirs.

One can, however, find fiction (and significantly, specifically short fiction) that escapes the dominance of the residual court modes if one looks even further from Whitehall than Hodgekins and his like afford. The recovery of popular, especially lower-class, literature in the period is beset with extraordinary difficulties. Much, if not most, has been lost simply because it was not or could not be written down and printed; much that has survived in print has been laundered for a more genteel audience. From various written sources, often very indirect ones, however—commonplace books, letters, and the like, as well as some printed sources—one can piece together a vivid tradition of folk and popular art that never escaped the force of the dominant sociocultural pressures, but which nevertheless constituted a rich tradition in its own right and which surfaced, increasingly, in the seventeenth century in the Commonwealth and in works such as John Bunyan's *The Pilgrim's Progress*

(1678). Difficult as it may be to pin down a visible tradition of folk stories actually published in the period, one can nevertheless from indirect sources (letters, brief mentions in plays, and other works) see how the stories of traditional folk heroes, such as Robin Hood, served as outlets for the frustrations and ambitions of the underprivileged and unlettered.

Indeed, perhaps the most pervasive form of short fiction, written or oral, in the period is the short, homely anecdote or tale. Hundreds of examples are found, often tucked away in other literary forms (in Shakespeare's *Henry IV*, 1597-1598, for example) or assembled in the enormously popular collections of jest-books. Jest-books were accumulations of varying length of tales and jokes, most centered on a clinching or witty *riposte* designed to provoke laughter or admiration (or a free drink); the tales used a variety of typical characters—faithless wives, capacious clergy, corrupt lawyers—that simultaneously drew on traditional wisdom and sharp observation. A typical example is the anonymous *The Sackful of News* (1558), a collection of twenty-two miscellaneous jests, some with dialogue, some with brief, pithy morals, but all meant for entertainment. Some of the jests are developed into short capsule-biographies and become picaresque tales of a rogue or practical joker whose exploits demand the reader's sympathy. Examples include George Peele's *Merry Conceited Jests of George Peele* (1607), *Dobson's Dire Bobbes* (1607), and *Long Meg of Westminster* (published 1620, probably written thirty or more years earlier). The atmosphere is usually colloquial and vulgar, and the basic narrative structure is episodic, with a rapid focus on a succession of individual incidents.

Anecdotes, jest-books, and jest-biographies all bring us much closer to the world that court romances were deliberately written to exclude and control. They constitute an undercurrent of short fiction that, while surfacing as much indirectly in other forms of literature as in their own right, nevertheless constitute a genuine alternative to the dominant cultural forms. The sources of energy in key works of the age—again, Bunyan provides an important example—coincide with and reinforce the tradition the reader must next consider. That tradition, Protestantism, on the surface seems antithetical to the dominant characteristics of prose (or any) fiction, and it is usually ignored in histories of the prose fiction of the period. This neglect is unfortunate, since in many ways Protestantism constituted the most important forward-looking movement of the whole age.

Except for occasional references, one group of Renaissance writings neglected as examples of prose fiction are the popular theological tracts. Many, admittedly, are among the most memorably unreadable works ever written—with exceptions such as John Foxe's *The Book of Martyrs* (1563), which is a masterwork of propaganda, of religious devotion, and, it might be suggested, of fiction. At its greatest moments—in the account of the deaths of Latimer and Ridley, for example—Foxe sets the reader down as an eyewitness (even ear- and nostril-witnesses) to events purportedly historical, revealing the details of which only the victims themselves could have been aware. Facts are redoubled, hearsay becomes fact, rumor is given tongue, and Foxe's rhetoric above all else directs his readers to participate in the revulsion against the persecutions of Bloody Mary.

In short, Foxe, self-consciously or otherwise, takes over the rhetorical duplicity and inherent depravity that pious Protestants mistrusted in literature, art, and above all prose fiction. During the 1570's, indeed, as the new movement in prose fiction gathered impetus, Protestant moralists shifted their traditional attacks on medieval verse romances to the new prose examples. Ascham, no extremist, regretted that the Bible was banished from the court and "Morte Arthure received into the Princes Chamber." Philip Stubbes, Gosson, and Perkins described the prose romances as "idle tales," "dreams merely to amuse the idle," "bookes of love, all idle discourses and histories," "nothing else but enticements and baites unto manifold sinnes." In the 1630's, the sophisticated Nicholas Ferrar spoke for a century of Protestant condemnation when he stated that romances and tales could not be allowed "to passe for good examples of vertue among Christians." Protestant theologians such as William Prynne in the 1630's or John Milton a decade later saw prose fiction as "profane discourses," or "baits for sin and corruption."

Behind such condemnations lies a suspicion of the autonomy of the human imagination, expressed in Saint Augustine's oft-cited definition of a tale or fable as "a lie, made for delectation sake." Yet, although Protestants attacked their society's increasing tolerance of books "whose impure Filth and vain Fabulosity, the light of God hath abolished utterly," as one Puritan pamphleteer put it, there is nevertheless a sense of the gradual fusion of fiction writer and theologian in a traditon of popular theological pamphlets heavily influenced by Foxe. Of course, as C. S. Lewis noted, while most of the attacks on prose fiction were by Protestants, so were most of the defenses. Sidney's *Arcadia* was praised by such stern moralists as his friend Fulke Greville for its moral seriousness, and it has been made apparent how consistently English readers and writers alike were most comfortable when their fiction was reassuringly moralized. In Europe, the Council of Trent was attempting to create a religious literature to replace the secular forms that dominated genteel and popular taste, and its influence can be seen in both the devotional lyric and in a fashion for explicitly Christian romances. The movement is especially associated with Jean Pierre Camus, Bishop of Bellay, whose *Dorothée* (1621) and *Palombe* (1624) are examples of the genre. Each is a Christianized pastoral romance designed to teach, respectively, the purity of marriage and the duties of parents. The typical romance features that have been observed are all present—dreamlike atmosphere, idealized characters, complicated plots—all held together by an explicitly theological drive.

Even more interesting are works that, while explicitly rejecting any fictional status, nevertheless show the marked influence of fictional techniques. Thomas Beard's *The Theatre of Gods Judgements* (1596, and many subsequent editions) is a case in point. Beard's aim is to survey the whole course of human history to demonstrate the inevitability of God's revenging judgments over a world which is "nothing else but an ocean full of hideous monsters or a thicke forest full of theeves and robbers." Apart from its highly colorful interpretation of God's nature, Beard's work is distinctive for its reliance on an endless succession of anecdotes, tales, and gossip—in short, on a variety of short fictions. Beard's style has the dash and crudity of Greene's conny-catching pamphlets and the vividness of Nashe or Bandello: of the eighty-seven chapters in his first edition, eighteen are concerned with lust, whore-dom, and uncleanness, twelve with the crimes of great men, and eleven with murder. Even within chapters dealing with offenses against less spectacular commandments—such as blasphemy (4), false witness (3), idolatry (3), and perjury (2)—his examples are chosen for their lurid powers of persuasion. Many of his examples are taken from Foxe and significantly elaborated by techniques which are drawn from the sources in popular culture which pro-vided the strength of the best Elizabethan fiction. Yet another unusual hybrid is John Reynolds' *The Triumphs of God's Revenge, against Murther* (1621), in which quite explicitly the enemy is not merely sin but fiction. Reynolds attacks the popularity of the amorous romance which, he says, panders to mankind's bare appetites by their "Perfuming, Powdering, Croping, Paynting, Amarous kisses, Sweet Smyles, Suggered speeches, Wanton embracings, and lascivious dalliance."

When one thinks of the importance of prose fiction in succeeding centuries, one might well look back to Beard and Reynolds (or to Bunyan's self-chas-tisement for reading lewd romances) as misguided opinions bypassed by his-tory. Paradoxically, however, it was the Puritan dynamic, with its emphasis on self-understanding and the conscience of the individual before God, which came through into the eighteenth century to provide the intense moral con-cerns of Daniel Defoe, Richardson, and others. Protestant books of devotion and moral treatises turned inevitably to fictional portraits to exemplify worthy behavior. The classical genre of the character-book was revived and infused with a distinctive moralistic caste and again stressed not idealized characters in unrealistic settings, but the temptations and contingencies of the world and the correct inner attitudes to cultivate. In short, the intense moral seriousness of the Protestant dynamic started, through the seventeenth century, to con-stitute a genuine countercultural movement which radically transformed the whole tone of English (and, by the 1620's, North American) life. Part of that transformation is the effect not only on forms of popular literature, but also on the creation of a sensibility which would look to fiction with a new con-centration on realistic motivation, recognizable settings, verisimilitude of characterization, and intense and complex moral dilemmas. Protestant polemics against fiction may have, in the period, distorted or helped prevent the maturing of an audience for prose fiction, but ultimately it provided crucial elements to make it possible.

The best short fiction in the sixteenth and seventeenth centuries, then, was written in this period of transition, between about 1570 and 1620, when it looked as if the tradition established by Sidney, Gascoigne, Lyly, Lodge, Greene, and Nash and then modified by Deloney and Forde might produce a flowering in fiction akin to that in France, Italy, or Spain. This did not happen, however. R. A. Day has described the period between the death of Elizabeth and the early eighteenth century as a "wasteland" so far as fiction is concerned. It is a pardonable exaggeration. Continental fiction continued to dominate, especially the Spanish picaresque such as the old *La Celestina* (1499), which was first translated into English in 1631, and the long French heroic romance such as Honoré d'Urfé's *L'Astrée* (1607-1627), which was imitated in England in the 1640's and 1650's. Of the shorter works, Cervantes' *Exemplary Novels* (1613), one of the landmarks in the development of the European short story, was translated by James Mabbe but was not widely influential in England. Mabbe, in fact, translated only the romantic, melodramatic stories, not the more important and forward-looking low-life examples. Of the native works, the most popular were reprints of Sidney, Forde, Johnson, Munday, and Deloney. Overall, the fiction of the whole century presents a depressing picture.

Nevertheless, one can certainly pick out both interesting trends and a variety of fictional forms. Of the shorter kinds of fiction—tales of sentiment and love, collections of *novelle* in the manner of Boccaccio (who was first translated in 1620), didactic and exemplary fiction, jest-books, cautionary tales—all continued to be published. By and large, however, C. C. Mish's summary is an apt one: the course of short fiction during the years 1600-1660 was a "downward decline; the bright promise went down in sterile entertainment and preciousness." While (as Mish and others have shown) it is possible to put together an anthology of entertaining pieces from the period, most of the work is derivative, nostalgic, uncertain in style, and vitiated by inconsistency of technique and uncertainty of aim. The best continues to be translation—from the French, Italian, or Classical sources which continued to dominate European taste in fiction—or short, popular tales and anecdotes in the jest-book or jest-biography tradition such as Hugh Peters' *The Tales and Jests of Hugh Peters* (1660) and Nathaniel Crouch's *English Jests Refined* (1687), or picaresque fiction such as the anonymous *Murther upon Murther* (1684), *Sir John* (c.1700), and *Bateman's Tragedy* (c.1700). It is in the later seventeenth century, in fact, that the folklore and folktales of which there was only spasmodic evidence a century before start to surface in published works. Stories of Robin Hood, Fortunatus and his Magic Purse, and the like were clearly the main fictional diet of the lower classes, and had been for centuries. Only gradually were they becoming part of the mainstream of English culture. Other fiction remained firmly in the tradition of improbable, elaborate romance, often with exotic settings expressing the public's interest in newly discovered or fashionable parts of the world such as America, Turkey, or Surinam.

Major historical transitions do not occur overnight, and although in post-Restoration England there is little to change the picture of what short fiction was written there, nevertheless from the 1680's on there are signs of a new impetus in prose fiction that would lead to the re-creation of the genre as central to English culture during the following two hundred years. One sign is the indirect but crucial impact of the Protestant emphasis on soberly meeting and contemplating oneself as an individual and learning what it was, in this world, that might make for one's salvation. Indicative of this new importance of self-analysis was the gradual rise of epistolary fiction, stories in the form of letters, which was eventually to lead to Richardson's *Pamela*. In the seventeenth century, epistolary fiction was typically focused on the personal lives of wellborn or respectable women, and, while hardly (to modern taste) penetrating beneath the genteel surfaces, in retrospect these attempts represent an enormous breakthrough towards psychological realism. Telling a story in letters, as in the anonymous *Lettres portugaises* (France, 1669, translated as *Five Love-Letters from a Nun to a Cavalier* in 1678), allows the reader to focus on and partly inhabit the self-consciousness of the narrator. Gradually prose-fiction writers were discovering what the dramatists had almost a century before—the need to let the reader participate in the making of the work's meanings. Another important change was the growing insistence, already anticipated by Nash or Deloney, on a degree of external verisimilitude in fiction. Details of setting became more functional, characters were introduced as part of the ongoing plot, motivation was more carefully linked by logic and circumstance, and speeches became more colloquial.

Particularly in France, there was a rapid growth in the variety and sophistication of short fiction. The long romance, *le roman de longue haleine*, gradually became less important in France and a variety of shorter, more realistic forms, became more dominant. The crucial difference between the earlier tales of Bandello, Cynthius, or Marguerite de Navarre and those of Madame de Lafayette (*La Princesse de Montpensier*, 1662, or *La Princesse de Clèves*, 1678) and others is precisely the movement towards some degree of *vraisemblance* in setting and, especially, in psychology. In England the development was slower, but a growing verisimilitude of setting at least appears in some of the tales of roguery such as John Davies' *Scarron's Novels* (1665), translated and adapted from the diverse short pieces in Paul Scarron's *Roman comique* (1651, *Comic Novel*).

In the various kinds of fiction written after the Restoration, too, a new solution slowly developed for a problem that had clearly worried Elizabethan prose fictionists—the role of the narrator within the work. In collections such as Boccaccio's, Cynthius', or Painter's, there is usually a close relationship maintained between the narrator and the author in the introductory or "frame" material that links the individual tales together. At other times, as in Gascoigne or Sidney, the narrator will directly address his reader, at times be seemingly omnipotent, and at other times be disarmingly frank about his ignorance of his characters' motives, actions, or origins. In short, there is a shifting and often arbitrary relationship between the different narrative voices of the work; there is a characteristic opaqueness which continued into the eighteenth century in Laurence Sterne and which, interestingly, has reappeared today in such fictionists as John Barth, Robert Coover, Raymond Federman, and Ronald Sukenick.

Gradually, however, especially after the Restoration, one can sense in fiction, first in France and then in England, the rise of fictional illusionism. The question of the author's access to the states of mind of his characters, especially if they were portrayed as historically real, which by the time of Jane Austen or William Makepeace Thackeray or Henry James was seen as jejune, was for Madame de Scudéry or Aphra Behn a most awkward one. The diverse solutions—the claims of having seen letters, read diaries, spoken to the persons involved—seem naïve to later eyes, but the questions being asked gradually produced the belief in the illusionism of fiction, the omnipotence of the narrator, and the self-contained autonomy of the world of the novel or tale. Without such developments, the so-called "realistic" novel of later centuries would not have been possible.

Of all the shorter fiction written in England after the Restoration, the most significant, and still readable, is that by the woman dramatist-novelist Aphra Behn, who wrote a dozen or so pieces of short fiction. Most are interesting mixtures of traditional romance with a few rather genteel hints of the new realism. Her stories are melodramatic, generalized, and elevated, but nevertheless—as in *The Perjur'd Beauty* (1688), *The History of the Nun* (1689), or the longer (posthumously published in 1688) *The Fair Jilt* and *Oroonoko*—reach unusual levels of intensity. *The Perjur'd Beauty* compresses into twenty-one pages the complicated love affairs of five men and women, including one, the beautiful and unpredictable Ardelia, who falls in love with three men, causing the death of all three men, the sister of one, and her own. Superficial, exploitative, and psychologically improbable, the work nevertheless has some energy and concentration that make it more approachable than the longer works of the period such as the Earl of Orrery's labored *Parthenissa* (1654-1669), which drags its reader lugubriously through six volumes nostalgically looking back to the world of Sidney's *Arcadia*.

In 1692, near enough to the end of this study's period to constitute a landmark, an indication at least of slowly changing tastes and of the deeper sociocultural currents beneath, William Congreve published his *Incognita*.

Written when Congreve was twenty-two, the work—a charming, well-plotted, amusing Scarronian tale, a not altogether unsympathetic attack on the romance tradition—contains a preface which was to set out many of the issues for prose fiction in the next decades. He comments on the incredibility of the romance tradition: romances, he argues, are "generally composed of the Constant Loves and invincible Courages of Hero's, Heroins . . . where loftly Language, miraculous Coningencies and impossible Performances, elevate and surprise the Reader into a giddy Delight." Novels, by contrast, "are of a more familiar nature; come near us . . . with . . . Events but not such as a wholly unusual or unprecedented." Congreve's terminology was not new— Jean Regnault de Segrais in 1656 had distinguished the *nouvelle* from the *roman* by its greater *vraisemblance*—but in England, Congreve's explicit statement marks an important turning point in the development of fiction, as he bids farewell to the archaic world of romance and looks to the already emergent modes of short and long fiction that were to dominate the next century.

Looking back over this survey of short prose fiction between the impact of printing in the late fifteenth and the late seventeenth centuries, one can see that the changes in literary taste are inevitably the expressions of complex but definable structures of idea and feeling in the life of the whole society. In England the period was one of political and social energies for radical change, concentrated, thwarted, and then overwhelmed by forces closely tied to the new dominance of entrepreneurial capitalism. At the beginning of this period, the sociocultural power was slowly slipping from the older feudal aristocracy to classes more in harmony with the new forces of secularism, industrialism, and dominance over the world, nature, and one another. The cultural development of England between 1500 and 1700 is too complex to summarize thus, but one can see how the fiction of the period responds to and articulates such pressures—the slow replacement of an increasingly archaic mode of romance narrative, the slow growth of a confident new illusionism ("realism" is far too question-begging a term), an uncertainty not merely about the mode of fiction but about the very place of fiction in such a society, the spasmodic surfacing of repressed cultural modes of living in folktale, jest, or other popular forms—through the otherwise dominant cultural forms. Such changes can be discussed in literary terms, but they are not simply literary changes. In particular, this is the case with the so-called growth of realism. The triumph of realistic prose narrative in the eighteenth century is the triumph of a way of seeing the world, which provides an illusion that chosen events are linked causally, that details can be selected from human events and be perceived as inevitable, given, and irreducible. Realism, however, like the social system that it expresses, stresses the product and its consumption by the reader, not the production. Just as capitalist society represses the mode of production of any article and stresses the product's marketable value, so realism (produced, in fact, by a certain use of language) stresses only the final illusion of reality and the harmonious final effect on the reader-consumer. The writer's concern throughout this period with the place of the narrator in his text reflects more than a technical problem; in the eighteenth century, both Jonathan Swift and Laurence Sterne mercilessly satirize the notions that language is simply instrumental and reading is simply consumption. They look back, angrily or whimsically, to the earlier period when the writer-narrator was on more arbitrary but nevertheless intimate terms with his reader, and the writer did not feel obliged to believe that language was identical with the real world. The gradual triumph of the illusion of realism is undoubtedly the single most important development in this period—which, as we have seen, does contain (despite many modern scholars' opinions) a goodly variety of amusing, interesting fiction—but its triumph is not simply a passing fashion. Realism, with all its apparent naturalness, is the exact, and in many ways limited and limiting, articulation of the dynamic of a new age. In England (in America, a very different pattern was starting to emerge triumphantly) readers must wait another two hundred years for an equivalent literary change—and for the complex cultural changes intertwining with and expressed by it.

Bibliography

Baker, Ernest A. *The History of the English Novel.*

Davis, Walter R. *Idea and Act in Elizabethan Fiction.*

Mish, Charles C. *English Prose Fiction, 1600-1700: A Chronological Checklist.*

——————— . "English Short Fiction in the Seventeenth Century," in *Studies in Short Fiction*, VI, 1968-69.

O'Dell, Sterg. *A Chronological Checklist of Prose Fiction in English, Printed in England and Other Countries, 1475-1640.*

Patchell, Mary. *The Palmerin Romances in Elizabethan Prose Fiction.*

Rodax, Yvonne. *The Real and the Ideal in the Novella of Italy, France, and England.*

Schlauch, Margaret. *Antecedents of the English Novel, 1400-1600* (from Chaucer to Deloney).

——————— . "English Short Fiction in the 15th and 16th Centuries," in *Studies in Short Fiction*, III, 1965.

Gary F. Waller

BRITISH SHORT FICTION IN THE EIGHTEENTH CENTURY

The outline of short fiction in England in the eighteenth century must begin with some notice of The Glorious Revolution, for England's eighteenth century really begins not in 1700 with the death of John Dryden but in 1688 with the triumph of King William. The new age which followed was much affected by the political and social changes wrought by the arrival of William and Mary, and the literature reflected the new order of society. The new bourgeois class in power demanded and got what might be called a more businesslike literature, a literature not merely realistic (eschewing the aristocratic romances that began to decline as early as 1600 and the escapism of seventeenth century stories) but partaking of all the virtues of the new governing class, especially stressing seriousness, usefulness, social responsibility, and thrift. This change led to new self-images for writers, and unabashed didacticism and concern with the generality, and the "short take" episode in longer fiction as well as "wit" in verse which impressed as much by its concision and point as by its profundity and elegance. There is a hint of the poet as manufacturer and distributor, rather than as maker and expresser, in Alexander Pope's reference to "what oft was thought, but ne'er so well exprest."

It was hoped that the new age would be an Augustan Age, referring to the emperor who was said to have found Rome made of brick and left it made of marble. It was to be an Age of Reason, an Age of Sense, a Neoclassical Age. The commonsense approach of philosopher John Locke (1632-1704) was seen in his *Essay Concerning Human Understanding* (1690), *Thoughts on Education* (1693), *Toleration* (1689-1692 and a posthumous fragment), and the *Reasonableness of Christianity* (1695), in addition to his epoch-making *Treatises on Government* (1689). The commonsense approach was also seen in the works of Anthony Ashley Cooper, third Earl of Shaftesbury (1671-1713), whom Locke served as physician and as tutor; and it was seen in the works of writers opposed to Locke's views (such as Bernard Mandeville, 1670-1733, author of *The Fable of the Bees*, 1723). It permeated literature in general, as Alexander Pope's *Essay on Man* (1733) followed Shaftesbury's philosophy, and other writers echoed Mandeville's paradoxes and satiric approach.

It was also an Age of Satire, and once again philosophers of skepticism argued that concepts of reality affected literature. Prominent among these were Thomas Hobbes (1588-1679), author of what has been described as the "greatest, perhaps the sole, masterpiece of political philosophy in the English language," *Leviathan* (1651), which presented a concept of human character that was to shape characterization and point of view in fiction thereafter; Bishop George Berkeley (1685-1753), whose phenomenalism, *esse est percepi*, was much to alter views of nature and to affect later writers, pro or con; and David Hume (1711-1776), author of the brilliant works *Human Understanding* (1748) and *Natural Religion* (1779, posthumously published). These three philosophers, one English, one Irish, and one Scottish, can serve as significant examples of the way thought molded literature in an age when literature conceived of itself more as expression than as self-expression and was, to an extent surprising to moderns in a post-Romantic era and an age of literary individualists, "seraphically free/From taint of personality."

The eighteenth century authors with their cool common sense and hot satirical prodding tended to use fiction to make generalizations, another difference between them and many modern writers of fiction. "The business of a poet," proclaimed Dr. Johnson, speaking of all makers, in verse or prose, "is to examine, not the individual, but the species; to remark general properties and large appearances." Modern writers tend to seek unique characters and unusual situations. Johnson would fault them for a desire to "number the streaks of the tulip" and accuse them of indulging in "the minuter discriminations, which one may have remarked, and another neglected" instead of scoring intellectual and social points regarding those "characteristics which are alike obvious to vigilance and carelessness." In a nutshell, the eighteenth century author strove not to be more sensitive or more inventive than the average man but to say something more cogently, lucidly, and memorably. No eighteenth century English writer of fiction requires the sort of critical interpretation that is lavished on Franz Kafka or his successors; this may, in part, explain why eighteenth century writers have not received the academic attention and shrewd *explication de texte* which modern writers enjoy (or are subjected to). Clarity was an eighteenth century virtue in fiction; today it is almost derided as "lack of complexity." It was an age of Habbakuk's "he who runs may read."

With the beginning of the eighteenth century, the first daily newspaper appeared; it was soon followed by others and by a number of literary and popular periodicals. In journalistic reports (both accurate and imaginative) and in essays and sketches, a new kind of short fiction was created. Form and restraint were married to smoothness and elegance. Whereas the Restoration had to some extent made poetry pedestrian and prosaic, the eighteenth century gradually developed a familiar and evocative prose.

William Congreve (1670-1729), the greatest of those whom Lord Macaulay attacked in *The Comic Dramatists of the Restoration* (1853), developed for his devastatingly witty plays (such as *The Way of the World*, 1700) a dazzling repartee which is only partly achieved in his immature novelette *Incognita: Or, Love and Duty Reconciled* (1692). The bantering tone and apparently effortless narrative techniques continued into the 1700's in the work of other writers and was fortified by the demands of magazines dealing in entertaining essays. Insofar as *Incognita* partakes of some of the characteristics of the romance tradition, however, it was an end rather than a beginning—despite the fact that what was to come afterwards was in some degree predicted and fashioned by the remarks on fiction that served as a Preface to *Incognita*, an artistic statement at least as important for fiction in the succeeding decades as *Discourse upon Comedy* (1702) by George Farquhar (c. 1677-1707) was for the English drama. As a Neoclassic Age, the eighteenth century was always seeking rules, new or old.

Some of the eighteenth century's rules in England were derived from foreign sources. Italy's influence on English fiction was greatest, perhaps, in such masters as Giovanni Boccaccio (1313-1375) and Matteo Bandello (1480-1561), but even in the seventeenth and eighteenth centuries, Italy's fiction was not without models for British writers. Spain's greatest influence, strongly felt in the picaresque novel of the eighteenth century, was *Don Quixote de la Mancha* (1605, 1615); however, the satiric thrust of José Francisco Isla (1703-1781)— expelled from Spain with the Jesuits in 1767 and resident thereafter in Italy— appealed to the English, even though (directed as it was against Spanish preachers, especially friars, and not against the more international targets of Miguel de Cervantes Saavedra, romances, and so on) it was far less well-known and less applicable to English needs. Later in the century, Johann Wolfgang von Goethe's novels of Werther (*The Sorrows of Young Werther*, 1774) and Wilhelm Meister (*Wilhelm Meister's Apprenticeship*, 1795-1796) were published and inevitably attracted some attention, but not nearly as much as later works (such as the continuation, *Wilhelm Meister's Travels*, 1821-1829) which were central to German, and to some extent British, Romanticism. Rather, eighteenth century influence may be said to have traveled in the other direction, for the most part: Daniel Defoe's *Robinson Crusoe* (1719) produced German imitations, just as Spanish picaresque romances accounted for *Simplicissimus the Vagabond* (1669) of Hans Jacob Christoffel von Grimmelshausen (1622-1676).

In France, the connections established in the previous century by such works as the *Comic Novel* (1651) of Paul Scarron (1610-1660) and the *La Princesse de Montpensier* (1662) and *La Princesse de Clèves* (1678) by Marie-Madeleine Pioche de La Vergne, Contesse de La Fayette (1634-1693), were strengthened appreciably by eighteenth century authors. These included Alain René Le Sage (1668-1747), who wrote not only novels such as *Gil Blas* (1715, 1724, 1735) but also short pieces such as the *Mélange amusant* (1743); Pierre Carlet de Chamblain de Marivaux (1688-1763), whose precious, overwrought style in *Marianne* of 1731 through 1741 and other romances had a baleful influence on English as well as French letters; François-Marie Arouet (Voltaire, 1694-1778), a genius among whose works *Candide* (1759) is but one gem; and the Abbé Antoine-François Prévost [d'Exiles] (1697-1763), still remembered for such operatic characters as Manon Lescaut and Carmen.

France and other countries continued throughout the century to collect and translate into more accessible languages old stories and folktales which helped to remind English writers of the heritage and the long-established techniques of short fiction. With the period beginning in 1697, there appeared the *Mother*

Goose Tales, the famous fairy tales of Charles Perrault (1628-1703), and throughout the eighteenth century English and Continental collectors and scholars made available to writers and readers everything from European folktales to ancient stories from the Orient. Nothing was without its appropriate effect on the literature of the time. In the absence of important influences on fiction that were to come after the birth of Alexander Sergeyevich Pushkin (1799-1837) in Russia and the birth of a new Realism in France, these old works, often presented in fashionable new guises, were to exert a considerable, if temporary, force on short fiction.

These brief references to foreign influences are not to suggest that English fiction of the period was entirely derivative. The fact is that the eighteenth century saw the rise and triumph of the English novel, producing some of the greatest masters of fiction and exerting a deep influence on Europe. As Sir Edmund Gosse writes in his *History of Eighteenth Century Literature 1660-1780* (1896):

> Yet far more important than any foreign influence from English verse was the stimulus given abroad by the English novel. Here again it was a Frenchman, Lesage, who first started the modernisation of the Spanish story of adventure, and so prepared the way for Fielding and Smollett; while another, Marivaux, may possibly have had some slight effect on the manner of Richardson. But the French critics immediately received the first great English novels with enthusiasm, and acknowledged them to be, in almost every respect, far superior to their own. This admiration for *Tom Jones* and *Clarissa* being admitted, it is strange that Crébillon, rather than Richardson or Fielding, continued to be imitated in France almost to the end of the century; but the influence of the English novel abroad, although suffused, was manifested in many ways before the age of Rousseau, and is to be considered as perhaps the most vivid which our purely eighteenth-century literature exercised on the continent of Europe.

Gosse, by the way, is discussing not Prosper Jolyot de Crébillon (1674-1762) the dramatist but his son the novelist, Claude Prosper Jolyot de Crébillon (1707-1777), whose *"conte moral"* of *The Sofa* (1745) was so immoral (or indecent) that he was banished from Paris for years.

The career of Daniel Defoe (1660-1731) illustrates the journalist-turned-novelist and the close connection in his period between periodicals and prose fiction. Sir Roger L'Estrange (1616-1704) was not only the founder of *The Observator* (1681-1687), a precursor of Defoe's *The Review* (1704-1713) and his *Mercurius Politicus* (1716-1720), but also the author of *The Fables of Aesop* (1692) and *Fables and Stories Moralized* (1699). It should not be forgotten that Defoe's "A True Relation of the Apparition of One Mrs. Veal" (1705) is a very early milestone in the English short story that was the product of a kind of reporting, or that Defoe's *Robinson Crusoe* was first printed in *The London Post*, one of many newspapers and journals for which this prolific writer wrote copiously and well. Perhaps Defoe writes a trifle too copiously for the short story limitations, but his mastery of the pseudohistorical narrative

(*A Journal of the Plague Year*, 1722; *Roxana*, 1724; *Memoirs of a Cavalier*, 1720; and so forth), his eye for "the speaking sight" and convincing detail, his ability to make fact sound like fiction and fiction sound like fact, and his translation of the tradesman's ethic into highly salable and yet durable fiction—and all this made him a tremendous force in shaping all subsequent storytelling. It is unfortunate that *The Fortunes and Misfortunes of the Famous Moll Flanders* (1722) and *Roxana: Or, The Fortunate Mistress* did not convince more writers of fiction, short and long, of the power of minute observation and vivid expression; that would have mightily assisted the development of the short story. What was not of such help was Defoe's tendency to moralize and to manipulate so that the whores and rakes repented at last and lived happily ever after. Following this pattern, the short story for a long while was to be a vehicle for the Protestant Ethic.

When, very long after, the reaction came, it was equally extreme: today, short-story writers often seem disinclined to point any moral at all or indeed to conclude their stories: they discard their final pages and their final responsibility. Defoe may have been weak on the larger archetectonics and sketchy in characterization of his low-life and adventurous people, but he was always aware of his social obligations as a writer.

Eighteenth century writers in the religious vein of John Bunyan (1628-1688) carried on Defoe's traditions. Bunyan's methods of allegorical storytelling in *The Pilgrim's Progress* (1678 and 1684) were to have their echoes in eighteenth century preaching and in the short stories of Nathaniel Hawthorne, Jorge Luis Borges, and many others. As with the *exempla* in medieval sermons, the effects of preaching on narrative are likely to be underestimated in this century when churchgoing is not the major activity it was in the eighteenth century. The fact that Jonathan Swift (1667-1745) was a clergyman explains more about *Gulliver's Travels* (1726) and similar works than this age of equal anger but more unbelief appreciates. It is also significant that Sir Richard Steele (1672-1729) numbered among his major works a manual of ethics, *The Christian Hero* (1701), and that his colleague Joseph Addison (1672-1719) was the son of a Wiltshire clergyman and the poet of "The Spacious Firmament on High" (1712).

In periodicals such as Steele's *The Guardian* (a daily begun in 1713) and especially Steele and Addison's *The Tatler* (1709-1710) and *The Spectator* (1711-1712) which preceded it, old traditions of storytelling were combined with those of the essays of Sir Francis Bacon and Michel de Montaigne and the character writers of the previous century such as Bishop Hall, Sir Thomas Overbury, and John Earle to produce what are probably best described as sketches rather than short stories but which have their place in the development of the short-story genre. They were dedicated to the new morality and designed "to enliven morality with wit, and to temper wit with morality." "The Vision of Mirza" can be described as a sort of allegorical short story, and some of the adventures of Sir Roger de Coverley and his crew qualify as short fiction rather than as essays. They were all designed to mock foolishness gently and to recommend virtue entertainingly; and they had an influence on the *Fables* (1727, Second Series 1738) of poet and playwright John Gay (1685-1732) and *The History of Rasselas, Prince of Abyssinia* (1759), by Dr. Samuel Johnson (1709-1784), a work which is interesting to compare with Voltaire's *Candide* and which, although stronger in philosophy than in incident, is important to the history of shorter fiction.

Samuel Johnson's life and circumstances—he is said to have written *The History of Rasselas, Prince of Abyssinia* in a few days to pay the expenses of his mother's funeral—go some distance toward explaining his fiction. Other connections between life and literature are to be found in the biographical works of the previous century, such as the *Brief Lives* (1813) of John Aubrey (1626-1697); the lives of Oxford graduates in *Athenae Oxonienses* (1691-1692) by Anthony à Wood (1632-1695); the *Lives* (1640-1678) by Izaak Walton (1593-1683); and the biographies of their husbands by Lucy Hutchinson (1620-1675) and Margaret Cavendish, Duchess of Newcastle (c. 1624-1674). To this add character sketches and descriptions of incidents in the magnificent histories of the seventeenth century of which the *History of the Rebellion and the Civil Wars in England* (published 1702-1704) by Edward Hyde, Earl of Clarendon (1609-1674) is a prime example.

In the eighteenth century the histories of Scotland, America, and other places were written with a sharp eye for detail and a mastery of incident by William Robertson (1721-1793), and "the triumph of barbarism and religion" was to have its superb chronicle in the magisterial *The History of the Decline and Fall of the Roman Empire* (in six parts, completed 1788) by Edward Gibbon (1737-1794). These and other histories obliquely contributed a great deal to the understanding of the manipulation of narrative and thus to the development of the short story. Many histories contain within them what might well be extracted and presented as short stories more or less based upon fact. Also contributing to the short story were jests, anecdotes, and a number of other kinds of fiction and semifiction which tend to be ignored by historians of narrative art.

There are likewise what might be regarded as separate short stories embedded in the epistolary novels of Samuel Richardson (1689-1761) and in the picaresque novels of other greats of the eighteenth century novel: Henry Fielding (1707-1754), Tobias Smollett (1721-1771), and Laurence Sterne (1713-1768). More neglected by historians of fiction are the education novels of the end of the century, including Henry Brooke's *The Fool of Quality* (1765-1770), Thomas Day's *Sandford and Merton* (1783-1789), and Elizabeth [Simpson] Inchbald's *A Simple Story* (1791). One hopes that a positive result of the current agitation for recognition of women's rights now and women's accomplishments in the past will be a deeper study and fairer evaluation of the contribution of Inchbald and a great number of women who wrote fiction in the eighteenth century. Women's writing was practically a cottage industry even though it was not yet ready to gain for its workers the increasing public attention that greeted, in the next century, such women as the Brontë sisters, Mary Wollstonecraft Shelley, Elizabeth Gaskell, George Eliot, and, most of all, Jane Austen.

Among writers of the Gothic tradition launched by *The Castle of Otranto* (1764, by Horace Walpole, Earl of Orford, 1717-1797), the name of Ann [Ward] Radcliffe (1764-1823, author of *The Italian*, 1797, and the better-known but lesser novel *The Mysteries of Udolpho*, 1794) ranks high. Deserving equal praise is Maria Edgeworth (1767-1849), who worked in the tradition of the education novel (*Practical Education*, 1798) before producing her principal works in the nineteenth century (*Castle Rackrent*, 1800; *The Absentee*, 1812; and *Ormond*, 1817). She must also be noted as the author of a number of short pieces. So must Mary Shelley's father, William Godwin (1756-1836), author of the great early novel of detective fiction and social justice, *The Adventures of Caleb Williams: Or, Things as They Are*, (1794); Thomas Holcroft (1745-1809), author of dozens of plays, including the pioneering melodrama *A Tale of Mystery* (1802) and the immensely popular *The Road to Ruin* (1792), as well as novels of political purpose in the style of Godwin, such as *Hugh Trevor*, (1794); and rich amateurs of eccentric tastes such as William Beckford (1759-1844), author of sketches of Europe and *Vathek*, an Oriental romance first written in French and published abroad in 1786. Along with them must be included the writers of all sorts of much inferior work: trashy romantic stories of the sort that occupied Richard Sheridan's Lydia Languish, true-crime and other persistent departments of the short and simple entertainments of the poor, and children's stories of all kinds. All of them had some effect upon the development of the short story which, by the end of the eighteenth century, had passed from the traditional stories of the folk to the kind of embryonic modern short story such as that of a soldier which we find in Oliver Goldsmith (1728-1774) and the verse stories of William Blake (1757-1827) and Robert Burns (1759-1796).

The short story as we know it today did not begin to take its recognizable shape until after the eighteenth century, and yet we need to understand how narrative developed between the so-called Glorious Revolution and the Industrial Revolution. Whether in the work of well-known writers or in the chapbooks of anonymous Grub Street hacks or whether in fables or fairy stories or magazines and periodicals, the unquenchable desire to hear a story was catered to by both "serious" writers and commercial publishers, who offered the full range from a book to a ballad.

With the nineteenth century, the magazine market exploded and suddenly there was an audience for everything from the penny dreadful to the work of great novelists. The audience to some extent was always there, and in the eighteenth century it had its suppliers of both artistic and historical importance.

Leonard R. N. Ashley

BRITISH SHORT FICTION
IN THE NINETEENTH AND TWENTIETH CENTURIES

The masters of the English novel in the eighteenth century created an avid reading public for fiction of all sorts, and with the beginning of the nineteenth century the market expanded in many areas, including that of the more sensational tales of terror and mystery derived from the Gothic tradition. These tales were successfully launched by Horace Walpole with *The Castle of Otranto* (1764), so cleverly exploited in the long romances of Mrs. Ann Radcliffe, whose *The Mysteries of Udolpho* of 1794 is still read. Radcliffe taught writers of shorter fiction how to build up terrific climaxes and how to explain away all the mystery at the end. From dramatists of the theatrical *frisson*—such as Thomas Holcroft (1745-1809), author of the milestone *A Tale of Mystery* (1802) for the stage and also translator of *Tales of the Castle* (1784)—and from the weird horror of the novel *Ambrosio: Or, The Monk* (1796) by Matthew Gregory ("Monk") Lewis (1775-1818), writers learned new techniques of fiction. These techniques were to stand them in good stead when the detective story—strongly foreshadowed in William Godwin's revolutionary novel *The Adventures of Caleb Williams: Or, Things as They Are* (1794) and definitely established by Wilkie Collins in such masterpieces as *The Woman in White* (1860) and *The Moonstone* (1868)—came into its own.

The supernatural proved a strong suit of Irish writers of about this time. Oscar Wilde's ancestor, Charles Robert Maturin (1782-1824), created in *Melmoth the Wanderer* (1820) a gripping story of a man who sold his soul for prolonged life. It is, in the style of the period, a somewhat rambling and verbose story, but as George Saintsbury says, it is "marvellously involved with tales within tales"; from these examples, writers of briefer pieces picked up many ideas. Another striking Irish success—this one a descendant of Richard Brinsley Sheridan—was Joseph Sheridan Le Fanu (1814-1873), author of the horrific novel *Uncle Silas* (1864) and of shorter pieces of which his vampire story "Carmilla" is probably the most famous. The echoes are heard later in such British writers as Charles Dickens and Montague Rhodes James and such American ones as Charles Brockden Brown and Edgar Allan Poe. These men are in the same long tradition, one that ranges from the preciously exotic (such as William Beckford's *Vathek*, 1786) through *Varney the Vampire* (1972) and other attempts at making the reader's flesh crawl to the modern ghoulish magazines and comics, and Rod Serling and Alfred Hitchcock television stories of strange and sensational goings-on.

The necessity in the horror tale for creating really vivid situations and the pressure on the author not to sustain the tension too long lest the effect evaporate, both contributed mightily to certain details of short-story creation. When long novels were the fashion, in the age before other entertainments competed for leisure time, the brief episodes were woven into a tapestry of intrigue and mystery. In later times, when a story readable in a single sitting was demanded, one basic incident could be isolated and exploited for all it might hold.

Other Irish writers of the early nineteenth century specialized in sketches and tales. Samuel Lover (1797-1868) is today sadly undervalued for his stories; better remembered, although not well-known by any means, is Crofton Croker (1798-1854), who published his *Fairy Legends and Traditions of the South of Ireland* anonymously in 1825. He was followed by such retellers of old Irish stories as Patrick Kennedy (1801-1873), author of *Legendary Fictions of the Irish Celts* (1866). Bringing to the modern world the ancient tales of Ireland's greatness, these served as inspiration for many artists, from novelist William Carleton (1794-1869), ballad collector Sir Charles Gavan Duffy, poet and poetry collector James Clarence Mangan (*Poets and Poetry of Munster*, 1849, and *Romances and Ballads of Ireland*, 1850), and folktale and verse collector Dr. Douglas Hyde (later President of The Irish Free State). Hyde's work inspired William Butler Yeats, Lady Gregory (whose plays are very similar to short stories), and others to launch the Celtic Renaissance and to found the Irish National Theater.

In the old tradition of Irish tale-spinning were playwright John Millington Synge (1871-1909); George Moore (1852-1933), author of *A Story-Teller's Holiday* (1918) and *The Untilled Field* (1903), with which critic Vivian Mercer says "the modern Irish short story begins"; and many other Irish writers in a genre that, according to Mercer, "has stayed closer to its folk roots than any other national or ethnic school of fiction except the Jewish." Most recently the Irish writers have striven to escape the bardic for the personal voice of Frank O'Connor and Mary Lavin or the artistic profundities of James Joyce and Samuel Beckett. Other Irish writers of the short story who must be mentioned are Lord Dunsany, Seán O'Faoláin, Somerville and Ross (actually Edith O. Somerville and Violet Florence Martin), Liam O'Flaherty, James Plunkett, Bryan MacMahon, Padráic O'Conaire, Seumas O'Kelly, James Stephens, Brendan Behan, and Lynn Doyle, who illustrate the scope and variety of Irish short fiction.

In other countries, too, the influence of folktales—greatly increased by the collections of the Brothers Grimm in Germany and Peter Christen Asbjørnsen in Norway, and the work of such writers as Hans Christian Andersen, E. T. A. Hoffmann, Sholom Aleichem, and many others—was long felt in the development of short fiction and can still be seen in works as different as those of Isaac Bashevis Singer, Jorge Luis Borges, and the anonymous tales collected in such books as Tristram Potter Coffin and Henning Cohen's *Folklore: From the Working Folk of America* (1972) and *Folklore in America* (1970), to name but two anthologies in a vast library of material. The short story has in the last century or so changed radically from the comic sketches of Charles Dickens (*Sketches by Boz*, 1836; and *Pickwick Papers*, 1836-1837) to the odd stories of "tough guys" around Warsaw in the work of Marek Nowakowski (b. 1935), the Yoruba tales of Amos Tutuola (b. 1920), the nightmares of Julio Cortázar (b. 1914), the satirical jibes of Klaus Röehler (b. 1929), the work of the "decadent" writer Mikhail Zoshchenko (1895-1958), the surrealistic stories of Tomasso Landolfi (b. 1908), and those of Americans John Barth, Donald Barthelme, and Richard Brautigan, to mention but a few names of short-story writers of distinction. The folktale's emphasis on brevity and point, however, lies at the heart of all storytelling, even in the work of very modern writers such as Franz Kafka, Albert Camus, Alberto Moravia, Pär Lagerkvist, Yukio Mishima, Grace Paley, and Joyce Carol Oates. Much has changed since George Eliot's "Mr. Gilfil's Love Story" in *Scenes of Clerical Life* (1858), or Elizabeth Gaskell's work (1810-1865), or the tales and fantasies of Robert Louis Stevenson (1850-1894), or the medieval and Greek verse tales in *The Earthly Paradise* (1868-1870) of William Morris (1834-1896). It is the basic elements of fiction, however, which are seen at their most basic in the folktale, that have been embroidered by writers as diverse as Joseph Conrad (1857-1924), H. G. Wells (1866-1946), John Galsworthy (1867-1933), D. H. Lawrence (1885-1930), Virginia Woolf (1882-1941), and their twentieth century successors in Britain.

Other important names in British fiction of the last part of the nineteenth century and the early part of the twentieth century are W. W. Jacobs (1863-1943, whose story "The Monkey's Paw" is enough to keep his name alive), C. E. Montague (1867-1928), Algernon Blackwood (1869-1952, a master of the macabre), T. F. Powys (1875-1953, brother of the novelists John Cowper and Llewelyn Powys), P. G. Wodehouse (1881-1971), Wyndham Lewis (1884-1957), and E. M. Delafield (1890-1943). These authors were all novelists as well as short-story writers. In addition, there were many others who wrote short stories as well as biography, criticism, and travel books. One example is Richard Garnett (1835-1906), author of a collection of short stories, *The Twilight of the Gods* (1888). We must pause in this rush of names, however, to dwell a little on some of the major figures.

Walter Pater (1839-1894) produced in his fiction what Ian Fletcher calls "transposed and distanced autobiography"; and although the novel *Marius the Epicurean* (1885) is his best work in this line, his story "The Child in the House" is an evocative and sensitive re-creation of the experience of a twelve-year-old boy. Max Beerbohm (1872-1956) is another writer of high polish; the satire so prominent in his novel *Zuleika Dobson* (1911) creeps into his short stories as well. M. R. James (1862-1936) was a master of the ghost story in the tradition of Arthur Machen (1863-1947), but surpassed Machen with such thrilling tales as "Casting the Runes" and "The Mezzotint."

Hubert Crackanthorpe (1870-1896) was closely connected with *The Yellow Book* and the "decadence" of the 1890's and brought into English literature a modified version of the French realism of Émile Zola and Guy de Maupassant. He also, says Wendell Harris, transmuted "scenic description into the natural symbolism which Conrad was shortly to develop into so effective a literary device." "Lisa-la-Folle" (from his *Sentimental Studies and a Set of Village Tales*, 1895, the year of his mysterious disappearance in France) demonstrates that between his first collection of stories, *Wreckage* (1893), and his last only two years later he had made great strides in the short story.

George Gissing (1857-1903) also died in France, but not before he had come to America, sold short stories in Chicago, and established a reputation for a quiet realism in such stories as those collected in *The House of Cobwebs and Other Stories* (1906) and *Stories and Sketches* (1938). Gissing's first success was with novels about the degradation that accompanies dire poverty (*Demos*, 1886, and *Thyrza*, 1887), and poverty was also the theme of Arthur Morrison's best work: novels such as *A Child of the Jago* (1896) and *The Hole in the Wall* (1902) and short stories such as those in *Tales of Mean Streets* (1894), his first book. Morrison (1863-1945) also wrote stories collected as *Divers Vanities* (1905) and *Green Ginger* (1909) and excellent detective stories about Martin Hewitt, the subject of several books. V. S. Pritchett gives Morrison high praise, justifiably, in *The Living Novel and Later Appreciations* (1946); and he is hailed in histories of the detective story such as H. Douglas Thomson's *Masters of Mystery* (1931) and Howard Haycraft's *Murder for Pleasure* (1941). He is, as a recent anthology stresses, one of the contemporaries of Arthur Conan Doyle.

Israel Zangwill (1864-1926) published both essays (*Dreamers of the Ghetto*, 1898) and stories (*The King of the Schnorrers*, 1893, a novel composed of linked short stories). He wrote *Ghetto Tragedies* (1893) and *Ghetto Comedies* (1907) and other fiction and even plays and historical works, but his short story "A Rose of the Ghetto" is the work for which he is probably best remembered; Edgar Bernstein called him "the Jewish Dickens."

H. H. Munro (1870-1916) is known by his pen name, that of the cupbearer of *The Rubáiyát of Omar Khayyám* (1859), "Saki." He ended a brilliant career by getting shot at Beaumont-Hamel in World War I. His short stories all have a wry humor which works better in the smaller compass of a story than in his novels *The Unbearable Bassington* (1912) and *When William Came* (1913). His collections include the books about Reginald (1904 and 1910), *The Chronicles of Clovis* (1911), and *Beasts and Super-Beasts* (1914). Perhaps his two best stories are "The Open Window" and "Shredni Vashtar," but his many fans might argue over "Tobermory," the story of an embarrassing talking cat, or the one about why Lady Anne was so reticent, or the one about an odd method of educating children.

There is a charming humor also in Ernest Bramah (1869-1942), who gave up farming (*English Farming and Why I Turned It In*, 1894) for literature. He created Kai Lung, a Chinese philosopher (*The Wallet of Kai Lung*, 1900; *Kai Lung's Golden Hours*, 1922; *Kai Lung Unrolls His Mat*, 1928; *Kai Lung*

Beneath the Mulberry Tree, 1940) who tells marvelous tales which seldom permit the chill light of reality to fall on the garden of beatitudes. He also created the blind detective, Max Carrados (*Max Carrados*, 1914; *The Eyes of Max Carrados*, 1923; *Max Carrados Mysteries*, 1927). He spent some time in China and much time in England, and he uses both backgrounds with great skill as a point of departure in stories.

Arthur Symons (1865-1945) was a poet much influenced by the French symbolists (he introduced Paul Verlaine, Arthur Rimbaud, and Charles Baudelaire to English readers) and a critic famed for *The Symbolist Movement in Literature* (1899) as well as works on Walter Pater, Thomas Hardy, Oscar Wilde, Robert Browning, the Romantics, and the Elizabethans. He is not so limp and enervated a personality as Ernest Dowson (1867-1900), another figure of the "decadence" whose stories tend to focus on a rather energetic, if often disturbed state of mind—natural material, perhaps, for a man who suffered a mental breakdown, spent some time in asylums, and wrote *Confessions: A Study in Pathology* (1930).

Having mentioned ten representative minor masters of the British short story of the period under discussion, we must now turn to writers of major importance. A major influence during this period was Robert Louis Stevenson, for whom the short story was an occupation, not a sideline. Even his *Dr. Jekyll and Mr. Hyde* (1886) is really an attenuated short story. In his anthology of *Great English Short Stories* (1957), Christopher Isherwood (b. 1904, author of the *Berlin Stories* which reached a very wide audience through John Van Druten's play *I Am a Camera*, 1952, and the musical theater and film versions, *Cabaret*) does not include Stevenson. He does make room for Ethel Colburn Mayne who in *The Yellow Book* wrote "daintily breathless tales" in which a "neo-Jamesian kind of dialogue . . . resembled championship tennis"; later she left Ireland and wrote in London, with "delicacy of perception" and "robust and sometimes quite unladylike wit," stories such as those in *Inner Circle* (1925). Also significant are Robert Graves (b. 1895, best known as a major poet and the popular novelist of *I, Claudius*, 1934, and *Claudius the God*, 1934; represented by "The Shout," a tale of "the neurasthenic verge of nightmare" in World War I) and William Plomer (b. 1903 in the Transvaal and author of stories collected in *I Speak of Africa*, 1928, and *The Child of Queen Victoria*, 1933, among others). Clearly Stevenson with the fantastic stories of *The New Arabian Nights* (1882) excels these notable writers and earns the title "great." His study of evil and the corrosive power of guilt, "Markheim," which was published in *The Merry Men and Other Tales and Fables* (1887), may be too explicit in its moral point to look modern but is so concentrated and haunting in its effect that it must be ranked with the work of Poe, which it strangely resembles. "A Lodging for the Night," in which the poet François Villon bursts in upon the Seigneur de Brisetout and offers him insolence in exchange for protection from the police, is more subtle and more modern in feeling; indeed, T. O. Beachcroft writes: "The confrontation of this frozen-up young intellectual beatnik with the dignified old gentleman is curiously up-to-date." The Samoans of his last retreat called Stevenson Tusitala (Teller of Tales), and in a certain kind of romantic story he is (as Desmond McCarthy said) "a little master."

Rudyard Kipling (1865-1936) was probably the most popular author in English in the years between Stevenson's death and World War I. From *Plain Tales from the Hills* (1888) and longer stories in the *Pioneer* of Allahabad (in which he published "The Man Who Would Be King") to the year 1907, in which he became the first Englishman ever to win the Nobel Prize for Literature, and beyond (in years saddened by the death of his only son in World War I), Kipling's stories grew in power and suggestiveness. H. G. Wells believed that Kipling's best story was "The Man Who Would Be King"; however, "They" seems a better choice for it has a resonance that more than compensates for the exotic adventure in the startling tale of the British *raj*, and it sidesteps the current prejudice against Kipling's Tory views and concept of the "white man's burden" in a now defunct empire. There is a kind of supernatural revelation of Masonic mysticism in "The Man Who Would Be King," but in "They" the paranormal is less tangible but more pervasive, more disturbing, less theatrical.

Oscar Wilde (1856-1900), author of *The Happy Prince and Other Tales* (1888) and *Lord Arthur Savile's Crimes and Other Stories* (1891), is rather heavy on morality for a writer who asserted that books are, simply, either well-written or badly written, and that art for art's sake and morality does not come into it. "The Birthday of the Infanta" (from *A House of Pomegranates*, 1891), which substitutes sentiment (or sentimentality) for morality, exhibits great skill. Still, F. L. Lucas is perhaps correct when he observes that Wilde, with Meredith and Shaw, would have shone brighter if he had "struggled less to be brilliant."

Henry James (1843-1916) was born in New York but became a British subject, with the Order of Merit. His being out of place (socially, sexually, geographically) contributed to his sensitivity, and that sensitivity demanded a circumspect and circumlocutory style that has both its merits and its deficiencies: it can achieve wonders and it can decline into self-parody. Philip Guedalla aptly summarized the whole career of "The Master" as falling neatly into three periods: James the First, James the Second, and The Old Pretender. Of the famous Jamesian style, David Garnett remarked that "it seems improbable that his movements have any connection with the job you hope he has in mind, but he always comes back with the bird in his mouth." This is true for more or less direct stories such as "The Real Thing" and for more complex ones such as "The Jolly Corner" and *The Turn of the Screw* (1898). James's large number of short stories are all of what (to use a phrase that supplied a title for one of his later works) we might call "the better sort," and some of them are masterpieces. Seán O'Faoláin says James "*tells* too much, i.e., has almost no power of indirect suggestion," but most critics would disagree. He tells all the truth—sometimes perhaps more than even he realizes—but he tells it *slant*. If he has not been an even greater influence on modern letters than he wanted to be, it is only because he is so difficult to emulate.

Writers such as Arnold Bennett (1867-1931) and A. E. Coppard (1878-1957) are worthy of note. Coppard's *Adam and Eve and Pinch Me* (1921) is a classic. Also notable is "The Hammer of God" by G. K. Chesterton (1874-1936), whose concern with the paradox and the orthodox has put him (perhaps temporarily) out of fashion but whose skill as a storyteller is undeniable. Two of the detective stories of Father Brown, "The Man in the Passage" and "The Blue Cross," are representative of Chesterton's permanence. S. S. Van Dine wrote that "Father Brown is concerned with the moral, or religious aspect, rather than with the legal status of the criminals he runs to earth," which gives Chesterton's stories of him "an interesting distinction" and a high place in detective fiction. Sin is a more important subject than crime.

Joseph Conrad, one of the greatest masters of the short story in any language, was a Pole who late in life became a naturalized British subject and a prominent English author. (English was his third language, but he published nothing in Polish or French.) He developed new forms of narration to suit his shy and retiring yet probing and adventurous spirit and to contain the moral and psychological ambiguities of his ideas and insights, some of which have (to quote from a letter of Conrad's about the first draft of *The Rescue*, 1920) "the bluish tenuity of dry wood smoke . . . lost in the words as the smoke is lost in the air." His penchant for indirect narration has not been very widely adopted in the modern short story, but the stories of heroism and moral choice in such collections as *Tales of Unrest* (1898) and *Youth* (1902) set a standard for subsequent craftsmen. Conrad will be remembered for *Heart of Darkness* (1902), "Youth," "Typhoon," and "The Secret Sharer." He pieced together the "destructive element" of reality and conjured up vivid backgrounds for his stories, always striving to make the reader *believe*, or at least attain what Samuel Taylor Coleridge described as "the willing suspension of disbelief." His task (and his achievement) was, as he explained in the Preface to *The Nigger of the "Narcissus"* (1897), "by the power of the written word to make you hear, to make you feel—it is, before all, to make you see."

This approach is antithetical to fiction which draws too much attention to the photography or back projections of reality—the work of writers in American fiction as different as Henry Miller, John P. Marquand, John Steinbeck, John O'Hara, James T. Farrell, Saul Bellow, and Piri Thomas—and to fiction which draws too much attention to the writer himself through mannerism—Ernest Hemingway, Dashiell Hammett, Gertrude Stein, Thomas Wolfe, William Faulkner, Norman Mailer, Philip Roth, and Peter De Vries. Although

Conrad's art has proved inspirational, American writers have not followed his lead; and, to the limited extent that a few British writers have done so, there persists in Britain a certain level of attainment in a certain kind of Conradian fiction that American writers have not achieved. American writers have been more attracted to challenging the leaders in the area of impressionism and the stream of consciousness, the purview of Marcel Proust, Virginia Woolf, Katherine Mansfield, and James Joyce, who have influenced many American authors from Hemingway and Faulkner to John Dos Passos and James T. Farrell.

D. H. Lawrence, writing about "phallic consciousness" and mother-son relationships (among other very American concerns), was easier for American writers to copy. Anyone who made sex "valid and precious" and who preached that "Man wants his physical fulfillment first and foremost" was certain of an interested audience. That he was occasionally a clumsy and incoherent writer did not much trouble American critics, and in Britain he had fewer followers than in America. On both sides of the Atlantic he may have been most influential with a story of fantasy, "The Rocking-Horse Winner," which Laurence Perrine suggests can be "like an observation balloon" and "provide a vantage point from which we may view the world." It is an admonitory tale which demands that at the start we grant that a little child (Paul, and "Paul" means "little") can ride his rocking horse into the future and that an old house can "whisper." What all this can *signify* holds immense appeal for American writing with what St. Paul might call its "tinkling symbols"; in the age of Freudian psychology it was irresistible. Lawrence's emphasis on the primacy of sex and the inconsistency of human beings has been carried too far by inferior writers, and he can be accused of having fathered (or rather having been the grandfather of) a tremendous amount of bad writing as well as some new directions in the short story.

Katherine Mansfield (1888-1923) began writing short stories in her native New Zealand. Her first collection, *In a German Pension*, established her as a formidable writer in 1911. Unlike Lawrence and others who were most successful or best known in the field of the novel, her sensitivity and insight, her ability to get to the heart of the matter, made her exclusively a writer of short fiction. She plays tricks with point of view, has dazzling insight into character, and jumps into her story, substituting perception for exposition. Donald Heiney and Lenthiel H. Downs in their survey of contemporary British literature comment on her effect on younger writers: "The influence has been especially notable in the 'woman's magazine' short story in America, where a large proportion of stories read like parodies of her work." Her best stories are probably those which gave their titles to her collections *Bliss and Other Stories* (1920) and *The Garden Party and Other Stories* (1922). The contents of *The Dove's Nest and Other Stories* (1923), however, published in the year she died of tuberculosis, prove that her talent never waned; and since her death her reputation and influence have grown yearly.

E. M. Forster (1879-1970) was an important novelist (*A Room with a View*, 1908; *Howard's End*, 1910; *A Passage to India*, 1924) and critic of the novel (*Aspects of the Novel*, 1927) who must also be mentioned among short-story masters. His work is marked by the psychological element which has been one of the hallmarks of twentieth century fiction, and in this department of "the invisible life" he ranks very high in the post-Jamesian period. "The Celestial Omnibus" is about a little boy who lives "at Agathox Lodge, 28, Buckingham Park Road, Surbiton" and who encounters a signpost standing almost opposite that reads "To Heaven." The story is a discussion of the world of culture and includes a Mr. Bons (*snob* spelled backwards); it equates the boy's purity of imagination with literature and elevates both over the patent snobbery and pseudoculture of Mr. Bons. Forster's work is a corrective to fantasy that has become either more fuzzy and incredible than it ever was in the work of Maurice Maeterlinck or overwhelmed by technological implications. There may be, as A. W. Ward alleges, a "thin, dry atmosphere" in Forster's work, but his characters do breathe; however fantastic he gets, however "overstrung, emotionally and intellectually" his characters become, they do connect with reality in a subtle and meaningful way. When this works, it can be illuminating. Forster's reputation, the more remarkable because it rested upon a comparatively small *oeuvre*, did much to push the modern short story away from the realism that Sir Paul Harvey defines as "truth to the observed facts of life (especially when they are gloomy)." In this regard, Forster influenced another "novelists' novelist," Ivy Compton-Burnett (1892-1969), who was (as Arnold Bennett instantly saw on the publication of *Brothers and Sisters*, 1929) "incontestably true to life" and yet probed deeply beneath what Eugene O'Neill identified as "the banality of surfaces."

If Forster's stress on truth rather than fact was unusual for his time, so were the satire and sagacity of Aldous Huxley (1894-1963), who is important in the development of the twentieth century British short story even though his stories are difficult to read, demanding much intellectuality and knowledge of period. More readable by all was W. Somerset Maugham (1874-1965), a writer of many talents who, after a number of very important novels such as *Of Human Bondage* (1915) and *The Moon and Sixpence* (1919) and a fairly brief and exceptionally brilliant career as a dramatist (*The Circle*, 1921, and *Our Betters*, 1923), concentrated more and more on his stories, which, like most of his work, were immensely popular with all but the critics. When he was at his best, his short stories—although they are much out of favor with those who regard anything the public can and will read and understand as *ipso facto* shallow—are direct, spare, witty, wise, and unforgettable. He did not preach; he practiced. Millions read his tales or saw them on the screen in *Quartet* (1949), *Trio* (1950), and *Encore* (1951), where the public also enjoyed cinematic treatments of *The Razor's Edge* (1944) and "Rain." The cinema still awaits adequate treatment of *Ashenden* (1928), the novel based on his espionage experiences; *Cakes and Ale* (1930), his favorite among his books; and *The Trembling of a Leaf* (1921), the story of "the tragic flaw of unhealthy aestheticism."

More fashionable but equally understandable is Frank O'Connor (1903-1966), who always has a tale to tell as he fixes us with his glittering eye for detail. His subject matter is often less theatrical than that of Maugham, but he approaches it with the same calculation and determination to tell a clear tale as effectively as possible. Whereas Maugham may gravitate to farce, O'Connor uses a wry Irish irony. One finds that in attempting to recount one of his stories a certain *something* is lacking. "One thing you will notice," said Maugham of his own stories, "is that you can tell it over the dinner table or in a ship's smoking room, and hold the attention of listeners"; but when one recounts an O'Connor story some small but essential feelings, rather than facts, seem to be unaccountably missing. What is missing, of course, is the teller, his stance, his tricks, and his tone.

In *Swans on an Autumn River* (1966) Sylvia Townsend Warner (1893-1979), author of the novel *Mr. Fortune's Maggot* (1927) and the sophisticated fantasy "The Phoenix," writes busy little stories with a sting in the tail. The wry twist at the end of the tale, popularized by O. Henry in America and continued to our day in the work of such writers of note as John Collier ("The Chaser" being a famous example), became "old hat" in the days of *The New Yorker* or "walk-away" ending; however, it has always been effective when properly prepared for and tastefully done.

Mary Lavin (b. 1912 in East Walpole, Massachusetts, of Irish parents and now a longtime resident in Dublin) published her first short-story collection, *Tales from Bective Bridge*, in 1942 (with a prefatory note by Lord Dunsany); it has been followed by better and better work, both short pieces such as "Brigid" (*Selected Stories*, 1959) and longer ones such as "The Great Wave" (*The Great Wave and Other Stories*, 1961). Frank O'Connor found her more fascinating than any of the other Irish writers of his generation because "more than any of them, her work reveals the fact that she has not said all she has to say."

Christopher Isherwood has already been noted in passing. He can be represented by the original version of "I Am Waiting" (not the one as altered for publication in *The New Yorker* in 1939), a story of psychic phenomena which was taken as being the same sort of doctored documentation, fictionalized experience, as the famous stories of Berlin (where Isherwood lived from 1929 to 1933). He has been an American citizen since 1946 but remains at least as typically English in his reaction to the world around him as he was when a student in Hitler's Germany. What he discovered about the techniques of fictionalizing autobiography or basing stories more or less on fact has not been lost on such writers as Truman Capote.

The surfaces of the stories and novels of Graham Greene (b. 1904) are exciting—some are confessedly mere "entertainments." Many readers have enjoyed *Brighton Rock* (1938) or even *The Heart of the Matter* (1948) or a story such as "The Destructors" and other stories from *Twenty-One Stories* (1954) plus pieces from *May We Borrow Your Husband?* (1967) and *A Sense of Reality* (1963) without worrying about the "extra-literary purposes" of "the saving need for a Sense of Sin" and Catholic apologetics. They have even romped through *The Power and the Glory* (1940), *A Burnt-Out Case* (1961), *The Quiet American* (1955), and *The Comedians* (1966) without getting "bogged down in theology." Laurence Perrine says of "The Destructors," for example, that "on the surface this is a story of action, suspense, and adventure. At a deeper level it is about delinquency, war, and human nature." When Sir Carol Reed made a film of the story "The Basement Room," he just scrapped the ending to make *The Fallen Idol* a hit movie—a hit almost as "big" as Greene's *The Third Man* (1950), which was written with the screen in mind. In all, fourteen Greene novels have been filmed, but only a very few of his stories. Perhaps they are at once too small in action and too big in thought for the medium.

Elizabeth Bowen (1899-1973) showed great short-story talent as early as *Encounters* (1923) and then turned to novels, of which *The Death of the Heart* (1938) and *The Heat of the Day* (1949) brought the most acclaim. She never abandoned the short story, however, and reached exceptional heights in *Joining Charles* (1929), *The Cat Jumps and Other Stories* (1934), *Look at All Those Roses* (1941), and *A Day in the Dark and Other Stories* (1965), among other collections. Bowen's fiction may lack the scope of her contemporary Graham Greene's—she has always been a novelist of the mannered, moneyed upper middle class, Britain's gentry—but it is at least as sensitive and often exquisitely penetrating.

Angus Wilson (b. 1913) began writing suddenly in 1946 as a "hobby," turning out one completed short story every weekend. He was so successful that he quit his job as a librarian and became a major British novelist in the great tradition of Dickens. Among his novels are *Hemlock and After* (1952), *Anglo-Saxon Attitudes* (1956), *The Middle Age of Mrs. Eliot* (1958), *The Late Call* (1964), and *As If by Magic* (1973). He has also produced a wide variety of other works, from *For Whom the Cloche Tolls* (1953), "a scrapbook of The 'Twenties,'" to a play (*The Mulberry Bush*, 1955), to a critical study (*Émile Zola*, 1952), a critical autobiographical study (*The Wild Garden*, 1963), and *The World of Charles Dickens* (1970), as well as such publications one might expect of a professor of English. Above all he is one of the best short-story writers anywhere—"mercilessly accurate and never dull," testifies Poet Laureate Sir John Betjeman—and from the start (*Wrong Set*, 1949; *Such Darling Dodos*, 1950; *A Bit Off the Map*, 1957) his eye and his tongue have been sharp and malicious. Moreover, there is probably no one except perhaps

Anthony Burgess with so infallible an ear for the eccentricities of speech who gets right to the point, and the jugular.

Dylan Thomas (1914-1953), although most famous as a poet, also wrote a fine collection of short stories about his childhood, *Portrait of the Artist as a Young Dog* (1940). These stories—"A Story," "A Child's Christmas in Wales," and the others—are prose poems, or poetic prose, and their language sometimes seems self-indulgent. V. S. Pritchett (b. 1900) has been writing truly distinguished short fiction (among other things) for nearly half a century, ever since *The Spanish Virgin and Other Stories* (1930). *The Sailor, Sense of Humour, and Other Stories* (1956) and his latest book, *On the Edge of the Cliff and Other Stories* (1979), are vivid proof of his remarkable development. In our post-Chekhovian period, Pritchett is the best short-story writer alive when it comes to the sensitive use of everyday material. William Sansom's "The Vertical Ladder," "The Wall," and "Among the Dahlias" are worthy of note. Sansom (1912-1976) was, Elizabeth Bowen said, "a short storyist by birth, education and destiny," and "The Vertical Ladder" is connected to his assertion that "The Blitz [in World War II] taught me to write seriously." His first collection of stories was *Fireman Flower and Other Stories* (1944).

Mention should be made of the genres in which Sir Arthur Conan Doyle (1859-1930) and H. G. Wells worked, for theirs are among the very special achievements of the British short story. The scope and flavor of British short fiction of the Victorian period include memorable tales of melodrama and mystery. A list might appear as follows: Scott's "The Tapestried Chamber" with its uneasy night in an old castle; Mary Shelley's "The Parvenue" (lacking the electricity that brought *Frankenstein* (1818), or Frankenstein's monster, to life, but typical of its time); Elizabeth Gaskell's "The Half-Brothers" ("The Grey Woman" looking too dated now and "Cousin Phyllis" too long); Dickens' "Hunted Down" (although as Angus Wilson frankly says: "in general Dickens' genius was not suited to short stories," and this example tends to confirm the fact); Wilkie Collins' "A Traveller's Story of a Terribly Strange Bed"; Walter Pater's "The Child in the House" (which, as has been noted, is something between autobiographical essay and fictional portrait); Thomas Hardy's "The Three Strangers" (although his great novels and poems tend to put his first-rate short stories into second place); Stevenson's "Markheim," Wilde's "The Birthday of the Infanta," and Conrad's "An Outpost of Progress." Then comes the Sherlock Holmes story, followed by George Moore's "Home Sickness" (showing "the strength of his style before it degenerated from consciously artistic to unconsciously mannered"), M. R. James's "Casting the Runes," Arthur Morrison's "That Brute Simmons," Israel Zangwill's "A Rose of the Ghetto," Wells's "Lord of the Dynamos," Hubert Crackanthorp's "Lisa-la-Folle," and Max Beerbohm's *The Happy Hypocrite* (1900). Simply listing names and titles serves little purpose except to review this special category (or categories) of the British short story with great economy and to recognize a few authors otherwise excluded.

If Kafka can be said to have invented a certain kind of nightmare fiction (now copied from China to Brazil), and Theodore Dreiser, Sinclair Lewis, Frank Norris, and other Americans to have developed a particular kind of realism, and *The New Yorker* a hard-to-define but instantly recognizable kind of American story, it can be said that the British have excelled in the horror and mystery lines. True, Americans from Poe to Dashiell Hammett and Raymond Chandler have contributed to what one critic called "pre-eminently the literature of the sick-room and the railway carriage" but what others might describe as the last infirmity of noble minds, the leisure reading of high-powered intellectuals. The French have Émile Gaboriau and Georges Simenon and a long tradition of *romans policiers*. Other nations have made their contributions, but somehow the British have had an effect far beyond their numbers. Their upper-class detectives (Lord Peter, The Saint, and the rest) seem to outrank Sam Spade and Travis McGee. What creations can stand up against Sherlock Holmes, Miss Marple, Hercule Poirot, Father Brown, and the rest "made in Britain"?

The detective story has been mocked (Mark Twain's *The Stolen White Elephant*, 1882; Stephen Leacock's "Murder at $2.50 a Crime," James Thurber's "The Macbeth Murder Mystery"), mugged (Edmund Wilson's "Who Cares Who Killed Roger Ackroyd?," one devastating example), and hotly defended (G. K. Chesterton's "A Defense of Detective Stories," W. H. Auden's "The Guilty Vicarage," Dorothy L. Sayers in her Introduction to *The Omnibus of Crime*, 1928). Many of the authors mentioned in this survey of the short story have also written first-rate detective fiction, among them Dickens, Arthur Morrison (creator of the detective Martin Hewitt), Henry James ("The Tree of Knowledge"), Elizabeth Bowen ("The Demon Lover"), and Lord Dunsany ("Two Bottles of Relish"), to name a few. So hungry has the public been for the Sherlock Holmes stories Sir Arthur Conan Doyle did not get around to writing that his son Adrian was compelled to supply *Exploits of Sherlock Holmes* (1954, in collaboration with the American John Dickson Carr), all in the overstuffed prose of *The Strand* magazine stories. Detective fiction has been written under famous pseudonyms by such literary notables as Nicholas Blake, Edmund Crispin, Lynn Brock, Michael Innes, and Ian Fleming; and we have already mentioned Wilkie Collins and Ernest Bramah. Even Arnold Bennett, Israel Zangwill, Aldous Huxley, W. Somerset Maugham, A. A. Milne, J. B. Priestley, and Ronald A. Knox have tried their hands at detective stories. Abroad there were Richter Frich with his detective Asbjørn Krag in Norway, Balduin Groller in Austria with his Detektiv Dagobert, and Émile Gaboriau in France with his M. Lecoq and Père Tabaret; for detective fiction has been truly an international industry in the last hundred years. A "spinoff" has been the secret-service (E. Phillips Oppenheim) or spy (John Le Carré) story or novel, although Chesterton said one should not "mar the pure and lovely outlines of a classical murder or burglary by wreathing it round and round with the dirty and dingy red tape of international diplomacy." The new spy story, however, increasingly tends toward the sense of sin emphasized in the works of Chesterton and Greene (whose latest film treatment boldly retains the downbeat ending of one of his most disillusioned short stories).

It may be foolhardy to name the "best" writers of detective fiction and their best works, but Marjorie Allingham, Agatha Christie, P. D. James, Ngaio Marsh, Dorothy L. Sayers, and Josephine Tey are names enough to refute Marjorie Nicholson's argument that women cannot write good detective fiction. As for the men, the top British authors in the development of the form are E. C. Bentley, Nicholas Blake, Ernest Bramah, John Buchan (Lord Tweedsmuir), G. K. Chesterton, Freeman Wills Crofts, Arthur Conan Doyle, R. Austin Freedman, E. W. Hornung, A. E. W. Mason, Henry Wade, Michael Innes, and Raymond Postgate. Some of these writers are the authors of classic short stories of detection, but many detective-fiction writers naturally seek the freedom offered by the novel's length to develop their complicated plots, even if the plots do tend often to be episodic, like those of Edgar Wallace, for example.

The two gentlemen who used to write as "Ellery Queen" remarked:

> Considering the virulence of the literary bug and its affinity for all manner of hosts, the first century since Poe has produced a remarkably small number of books of detective short stories. . . . Even detective story writers must live, and such books do not sell. . . . If the number of books of detective short stories of all types is surprisingly small . . . [there are] only 347 known titles [of the "pure" detection type] . . . 56 are the work of only 5 authors.

The British predominate in that group, and among the best individual stories are "The Giaconda Smile" (Aldous Huxley), "Murder" (Arnold Bennett), "Hunted Down" (Charles Dickens), "The Man Who Liked Dickens" (Evelyn Waugh), and "The Grey Ones" (J. B. Priestley), calling into question Dorothy L. Sayers' dictum that the detective story "does not, and by hypothesis never can, attain the loftiest level of literary achievement." Also interesting were the more or less fictionalized memoirs of nineteenth century British detectives such as "Waters" and true crime stories such as those written to the delight of Henry James and subsequent generations by William N. Roughead (1870-1952), a Scottish lawyer ("Writer to The Signet" of the courts of Scotland). These, as well as the work of eminent novelists who also attempted the shorter format, significantly influenced the detective short story and contributed to this British specialty, discussing what a character in "The Adventure of the Speckled Band" called "the manifold wickedness of the human heart."

In comparison with the detective novel, the detective short story is a poor relation. V. S. Pritchett once wrote that "poor relation" is exactly what the short story was once thought to be:

> It was the chapter left over, the anecdote to be tossed off in a spare moment. Even in the hands of genius, like those of Maupassant and Chekhov, the short story was thought to be the *pis aller* of writers who would have written novels if they had only known how. . . . We now think differently: the originating genius of Poe in America, of these French and Russian writers and (very late) of Kipling in Britain, has turned out to be decisive and, in this century, writers have had the excitement of a new, intensely individual prose art at their disposal.

It is the important British contribution to that art that has been outlined here, the "lonely voice," as Frank O'Connor called it, that has the immediacy of journalism, the compression of poetry. A short story, like a poem, offers "a clarification of life—not necessarily a great clarification, such as sects and cults are founded on," notes Robert Frost, just "a momentary stay against confusion." The English as a group may not be especially suited to the demands of writing short stories. As W. Somerset Maugham wrote:

> The English, as their novels show, are inclined to diffuseness. They have never been much interested in form. Succinctness goes against their grain. But the short story demands form. It demands succinctness. Diffuseness kills it. It depends on construction. It does not admit of loose ends. It must be complete in itself.

Maugham, however—and Kipling, whom Maugham was here praising—and many other British writers (as well as those in the British tradition, in Canada, or in Australia) have overcome that difficulty and created a superb tradition in which, without doubt, British writers of the future will strive and seek and find continued success.

Leonard R. N. Ashley

AMERICAN SHORT FICTION
IN THE NINETEENTH AND TWENTIETH CENTURIES

It may seem strange to begin a brief survey of the American short story with a discussion of the influence of the Germans, but our English heritage through the early days of the American colonies led chiefly to serious theological and historical writing, not to fiction. There was some anecdote in history and diaries, but mere entertainment was missing; and when novels did begin to appear (William Hill Brown, 1765-1793, author of *The Power of Sympathy*, 1789, is credited by Milton Ellis as being "the author of the first American novel"), they were heavily didactic, although Hugh Henry Brackenridge (born in Scotland in 1748, lived in America 1753-1816) in his *Modern Chivalry* (1792-1815) used satire as a pedagogical device, as had Benjamin Franklin and other American writers.

The first American professional writer was Charles Brockden Brown (1771-1810), and it was with him that the German influence was first felt. Inevitably, Brown copied English novels, especially the epistolary devices of Samuel Richardson (*Pamela*, 1740, and *Clarissa*, 1747-1748) and the combination of sensationalism and social theory of William Godwin (*Caleb Williams*, 1794). Yet Brown's *Wieland* (1798) with its Carwin (a ventriloquist who pretends to be the voice of God) and *Edgar Huntly* (1799) with its "memoirs of a sleep-walker and its characters who go up in spontaneous combustion or come down with the plague in Philadelphia," mark Brown as in the German tradition of the novelle with its emphasis on the "unheard-of event."

Early American fiction was less influenced by the efflorescence of the novel in Britain in the eighteenth century (when giants such as Richardson, Henry Fielding, Laurence Sterne, and Tobias Smollett were building on the earlier masters such as Daniel Defoe) than by the German Romantics. It is true that it was an Englishman (Horace Walpole, 1717-1797, Earl of Orford) who launched the vogue of the Gothic romance with "A Gothic Tale," *The Castle of Otranto* (1764), but the Americans picked up the germ largely through his imitators, importantly E. T. A. Hoffmann (1776-1822), whose *Fantastiestücken* (1814-1815, *Fantastic Tales*) are not so well known today in America (except for the three that Jacques Offenbach used for the opera *Tales of Hoffmann* in 1880) but once were seminal.

Very early, the Germans categorized and legislated for the novella: Johann Wolfgang von Goethe reflected and fostered pedantic criticism of the form with the didactic framework of his *Unterhaltungen deutscher Ausgewanderter* (1795, *Conversations of German Emigrés*), stories which reflected the sentiment he had picked up from Oliver Goldsmith's *The Vicar of Wakefield* (1766) but more especially the Romanticism of Johann Gottfried Herder (1744-1803), a collector and translator of Oriental, mythological, and other tales and folk poetry (*Volkslieder*, 1778-1779). The *Professorenroman* may or may not have accounted for the remarkable success of the Germans in novelle; the list since Goethe includes Heinrich von Kleist, Ludwig Tieck, Adalbert Stifter, Gottfried Keller, Conrad Meyer, Wilhelm Raabe, Gerhart Hauptmann, Arthur Schnitzler, Hermann Hesse, Thomas Mann, Franz Kafka, and many other writers of international fame. Johann Klein has distinguished with meticulous scholarship the tale and the fairy tale, the sketch and the anecdote, and the novella and the short story, but clearly the novella is (with other narrative forms) a mixture of old and new.

What was new in the novella as the Germans dictated its form, and what connects it to our consideration of the short story, was its emphasis on economy—it must concentrate on a single event and on important turning points; it must present rather than expatiate upon character; it must be spare. That economy was even more important than the concentration on the supernatural or the astounding.

Brown's novels tended to be more in the English form; they were diffuse, although the subject matter or tone might be German. He paused to lecture on women's rights, deism, and morality (continuing the puritanical and polemical tradition). Russell B. Nye in *American Literary History 1607-1830* (1970) rightly accuses Brown of never being able to concentrate his talents: "He scattered his energies into a dozen fields and was so anxious to get on to the next project that he published four novels in less than a year and three more within the next two." Recalling *Wieland* and *Ormond* (1799), a pale imitation of *Caleb Williams*, one remembers extremely vivid individual episodes, images, and moments. It was in these electrifying episodes that Brown was at his best, and it was in creating transitions that he was at his weakest. The big moments of his novels are German Expressionist; the rest is filler, fiddling, or philosophizing. In a way, sensational short stories are embedded in the text.

With Washington Irving (1783-1859), the German influence increased and the short pieces came into their own. Irving's sense of humor often defused (but never diffused) his Gothic stories, which remained simple borrowed plots decorated with details which most often, although not infallibly, supported the main scheme. He moralized, but he stuck to the point. He was ready to borrow from the folk tales of Germany but also from American sources, and, although he was a somewhat clumsy writer, he became "The Father of American Letters" because he created "Rip Van Winkle" and other important stories. "If the tales I have furnished should prove to be bad," he said in his Preface to "strange stories by a nervous gentleman" called *Tales of a Traveller* (1824), "they will at least be found to be short." In "The Legend of Sleepy Hollow" (in *The Sketch Book of Geoffrey Crayon, Gent.*, 1819-1820), "The Stout Gentleman" (in *Bracebridge Hall*, 1822), "The Adventure of the German Student" (in *Tales of a Traveller*), and other stories and sketches "by Diedrich Knickerbocker," Irving borrowed from Europe, made the material his property, and went as a sort of literary ambassador back to Europe with the news that America was inventing a new fiction of its own.

His companion on *Salmagundi* (1807-1808) was James Kirke Paulding (1778-1860), whose *The Old Continental* (1846) was an excellent novel surpassing *The Spy* (1821), the book with which James Fenimore Cooper (1789-1851) launched his immense success as a popular novelist. Through the techniques and success of their longer popular works, writers who were not in the magazine market influenced the development of short fiction. Along with his less-idealized Indians in *The Yemassee* (1835), William Gilmore Simms (1806-1870) created lower-class characters who were far more interesting, deftly drawn, and convincing than his aristocrats; in so doing, he initiated a trend in Southern fiction. Novelist Richard Henry Dana, Jr. (1815-1882), by introducing propaganda into *Two Years Before the Mast* (1840), demonstrated the use of fiction for social causes, later to be seen both in short stories as well as in the "book that started the great war," *Uncle Tom's Cabin: Or, Life Among the Lowly*. That novel, although published serially between June of 1851 and April of 1852, was no more a collection of short stories than, say, the Charles Dickens novels published in parts. Note, however, that the practice of periodical publication did inevitably put an emphasis on modules, on "cliff-hanging" conclusions skillfully approached, and on other techniques of interest to writers of fiction complete in one episode. In addition to Harriet Beecher Stowe, another important woman author was Louisa May Alcott (1832-1888), who began as a writer of short stories and then drew on her own experiences to write *Little Women* (1868) and *Hospital Sketches* (1863). Also making use of autobiographical material was Thomas Bailey Aldrich (1836-1907), who wrote *The Story of a Bad Boy* (1870) and contributed to the development of the detective story with *The Stillwater Tragedy* (1880). For a long time his "Marjorie Daw" was considered a masterpiece of the American short story or novelette. Perhaps William Dean Howells' *A Chance Acquaintance* and Charles Dudley Warner and Mark Twain's *The Gilded Age*, both published in the same year (1873) as "Marjorie Daw," look much fresher; and of course *The Adventures of Tom Sawyer* (1876) and Henry James's *Roderick Hudson* (1876), only a few years younger, are very much alive now.

A certain kind of "genteel" style hampered some American short fiction for a long, long time; even the "vulgarity" of Edgar Allan Poe (as Huxley called it) was preferable, or the vivid if not always grammatical writing of Cooper and other gifted but not well-educated writers. The "Genteel Tradition" did, however, produce some excellent narrative (as well as lyrical) poets—Henry Wadsworth Longfellow, for one—and a master of both the novel *and* the short story, Nathaniel Hawthorne. Born in 1804 Hawthorne fit comfortably into the German tradition, for the "daytime nightmares" of the Gothic bore close connection to the inner life of this pale flower (as he thought of himself), nurtured too much in the shade, haunted by Calvinism if not ghosts, introspective, gloomy, and suffering from both classic Teutonic plagues: *Weltschmerz* and *Angst*.

Hawthorne was haunted not merely by the German Gothic romances but by the English Gothic novel and by the native American books by Increase Mather on *Illustrious Providences* (1684), his son Cotton Mather's *Magnalia Christi Americana* (1702), and other superstitious reports of the "wonders of the invisible world," as well as by the history of the witchcraft trials in which Hawthorne's own ancestors were involved. It is worth noting the title of his first important publication (if one does not count *Fanshawe*, 1828), *Twice-Told Tales* (1837). Arlin Turner has traced "Young Goodman Brown," for example, back to Cotton Mather's *Wonders of the Invisible World*, 1693 (although it can be found in Miguel de Cervantes Saavedra as well), and the Gothic tradition hovers over all. To use the title of one of his own works, Hawthorne had a "Haunted Mind." His stories not only have the "bi-lateral structure" (objective/subjective) demanded in the German novelle; but they are also bicultural, in the sense that they are an American reinterpretation of the German tradition.

During Hawthorne's earliest period, the magazine was flourishing in America, offering a market which modern writers of short fiction would envy. He published in *The Token* and *New England Magazine*, among others; and there were periodicals, "keepsakes," gift books, and miscellanies. The market helped form authors' products, even in the case of a dedicated artist and withdrawn individual such as Hawthorne. From the earliest stories of the periodicals (reprinted in *Twice-Told Tales*, which explains the title), Hawthorne concentrated on the Puritan tradition of sin and guilt, on the dangers and ambiguities of intellectual pride and righteousness, and on weaknesses and wounds. His best stories are all in this vein: witness "The Minister's Black Veil" in *Twice-Told Tales*, "Young Goodman Brown" and "Rappaccini's Daughter" in *Mosses from an Old Manse* (1846), and "Ethan Brand" in *The Snow Image and Other Twice-Told Tales* (1851).

His more penetrating mind enabled Hawthorne to dwell on the moral significance of his stories, whether in short pieces or in novels such as *The Scarlet Letter* (1850), *The House of the Seven Gables* (1851), *The Blithedale Romance* (1852), and *The Marble Faun* (1860). Hawthorne also wrote delightful children's works such as *Biographical Tales for Children* (1842) and *Tanglewood Tales* (1853); he was thus an early master in a department of fiction much neglected by critics, but one in which American authors of the twentieth century, at least, are absolutely preeminent.

Hawthorne came to prominence in the mid-nineteenth century just as another great American short-story writer passed from the scene. That theatrical character, the son of itinerant actors, was Edgar Allan Poe (1809-1849). With him, the American short story reached world importance. Poe exploited his early life, in a tradition that was to be much honored by later American writers, for the details and background of stories such as "William Wilson" (a description of a boy at school in England, published 1839), "The Gold Bug" (which won a prize in *Dollar Magazine*, 1843), and "The Balloon Hoax" (published as a supposed news story in the New York *Sun*, 1844). His youth was wild, and, after failing to graduate from either the University of Virginia or West Point, he published poems in New York and magazine stories in Baltimore (1831-1835). The practice of periodicals awarding prizes for stories helped him to make a little money and to attract attention: his "MS. Found in a Bottle" won a prize in 1833, which led to a job on the *Southern Literary Messenger*. In that magazine, he published several good short stories before he lost the job and moved to New York, where he did odd journalistic jobs. Next, in Philadelphia, he became coeditor of *Burton's Gentleman's Magazine* and published "The Fall of the House of Usher." While an editor of *Graham's Magazine* (1841-1842), Poe wrote "The Murders in the Rue Morgue," "The Masque of the Red Death," "The Imp of the Perverse," and other stories, plus the important essay on "The Philosophy of Composition."

In New York, Poe published "The Mystery of Marie Rogêt," based on a real case in New York but set in Paris and involving the amateur detective C. Auguste Dupin. Dupin was introduced in Poe's epoch-making first tale of "ratiocination," the detective masterpiece "The Murders in the Rue Morgue," in which M. Dupin discovered that the murders were committed by an orangutan which had escaped from a sailor's keeping. This is, therefore, not only the first detective story of the modern genre but also the only one in which the murderer winds up not in jail but in a zoo. (Later murders were to be committed with a snake in "The Speckled Band," a cat with poisoned claws, a horse, and so on, as writers tried to become more and more baffling and dramatic.) Poe, himself often accused of plagiarism, was much stolen from; for example, a story such as "The Purloined Letter" with its amateur sleuth has been written over and over through the decades, although it is difficult for the literary historian to determine whether Émile Gaboriau was stealing from Poe or whether both were stealing from the *Mémoires* (1828) of François-Eugène Vidocq (1775-1857), a French criminal who eventually became the head of the *Brigade de Sureté* in Paris and amazed everyone with the speed with which he solved crimes until it was discovered (1825) that he was personally engineering many of the burglaries he so ingeniously solved. If Poe's detective stories seem alarmingly theatrical today, one must remember that nineteenth century police work did have its very lurid aspects.

After 1844, in New York, lurid elements appeared increasingly in Poe's work and his life. Poe was employed on several periodicals, published "The Raven" and other poems, and wrote the macabre and death-obsessed stories which have done the most to keep his fame alive: "The Pit and the Pendulum," "The Premature Burial," and "The Tell-Tale Heart." James Russell Lowell's estimate of him as "three-fifths genius and two-fifths sheer fudge" must be mostly drawn from a reading of erratic horror tales such as "The Black Cat" and others which appeared in *Tales* (1845). "Ligeia" is perhaps Poe's most undervalued story and "The Cask of Amontillado" his most overpraised. The prose poems such as "The Domain of Arnheim" were less successful, while the overlong "The Gold Bug" was very popular. On the whole, Poe was too concerned with the abnormal, and his autodidactic elaborate style is annoying, but in these respects as well as in the powerful concentration of his horror stories and the ingenuity of his "tales of ratiocination" he has bequeathed an important legacy to the American short story.

All literature reflects the locale in which it is written; but in the middle of the nineteenth century in America many writers placed an especially strong emphasis on setting, and a whole school of "local colorists" emerged, giving the American short story a flavor of its own. Bret Harte (1836-1902) was one of these; "The Luck of Roaring Camp," "The Outcasts of Poker Flat," "Tennessee's Partner," and other stories spread his fame from the *Overland Monthly* on the West Coast overland to the East Coast. The same artistic mixture of fact and fancy, reality and interpretation was also to be found in the nineteenth century in other countries. Ivan Sergeevich Turgenev (1818-1883), for example, whose Russian works in translation became exceedingly popular in America in approximately the same period as Bret Harte's success, also used colorful, real people and incidents as a point of departure to give the surface of his work the appearance of reality (although after his departure from Russia his tales often took on a melancholy overcast, and elements of the supernatural crept in). Turgenev was much influenced by and had a profound influence upon French literature and, through it, on British and American short stories.

In America, the local color of Prosper Mérimée and others (such as Guy de Maupassant and Victor Hugo) was combined with backwoods taletelling and wild exaggeration by Mark Twain (1835-1910) to create "The Celebrated Jumping Frog of Calaveras County." Local-color techniques were also employed in the "fireside stories" of Harriet Beecher Stowe; in the pictures of rural Maine in Sarah Orne Jewett's *The Country of the Pointed Firs* (1896); and in the dialect tales of New England in the work of Mary Eleanor Wilkins Freeman. In New Orleans there were the Creole and Cajun stories of Kate Chopin (1851-1904) in *Bayou Folk* (1894) and *A Night in Acadie* (1897). For the West and the Midwest there were the stories of Willa Cather (1873-1947), whose "Paul's Case" must be one of the most admired of all American short stories. In Virginia there was Thomas Nelson Page (1853-1922), author of *In Ole Virginia* (1887). In Georgia there was Joel Chandler Harris (1848-1908), creator of the immortal Uncle Remus. In Kentucky there was John Fox, Jr. (1863-1919), best known for the sentimentalities of novels such as *The Trail of the Lonesome Pine* (1908), but also the author of important if stereotyped novelettes of the Cumberland Mountains. In Tennessee there was Charles

Egbert Craddock (Mary Noailles Murfree, 1850-1922), who combined romantic plots with realistic backgrounds in Tennessee and even contrived to
write about the Cherokee Indians of the Southwest. In Vermont, Rowland
Evans Robinson (1833-1900) wrote stories about French-Canadians and English farmers, starting with *Forest and Stream Fables* (1886) and ending with
the posthumous *Out of Bondage and Other Stories* (1905). In the Midwest
there were especially good writers such as Hamlin Garland (1860-1940), who
wrote of "prairie folks" and the Middle Border in *Main-Travelled Roads*
(1891) and *Other Main-Travelled Roads* (1910). There was also Zona Gale
(1874-1938), who won the Pulitzer Prize for her novel of the Middle West,
Miss Lulu Bett (1920), but who was at her best in her short stories, such as
those in *Friendship Village* (1908).

Of all the local colorists, George Washington Cable (1844-1925) was one
of the most significant. He wrote for *Scribner's* and *Appleton's* in the 1870's
and in the 1880's published *The Grandissimes* and the novelette *Madame
Delphine*. His stories in *Old Creole Days* (1879) are superior as a whole to
most of the local-color collections previously mentioned. His sketches are
weak in incident but redolent of New Orleans life. "E. Junius" (Adrien Emmanuel Rouquette) attacked the accuracy of Cable's portraits of Creoles in
A Critical Dialogue Between Aboo and Caboo (1880); but whether *Old Creole
Days* is an accurate picture is beside the point—it *is* great local-color literature.
Likewise, photographic accuracy would not give the same effect as "The
Screamers" (LeRoi Jones) or "The Man Who Went to Chicago" (Richard
Wright) or "World Full of Great Cities" (Joseph Heller). Local color is an
aid, not an aim, and when the world of Ring Lardner or Flannery O'Connor
or some other author who seems perfectly to capture time and place is pre-
sented, it is that world which will be preserved in people's minds. The real
New Orleans for most Americans is the one captured in Cable's books.

America was not really like what one read even in the "veritist" writers.
Even the little town of Sherwood Anderson's *Winesburg, Ohio* (1919) existed
mostly in his reactions to reality, and the Dust Bowl in John Steinbeck's *The
Grapes of Wrath* (1939) and short stories of a similar type was based on reality
but bent to suit the author's purpose. The search for realism in American
fiction which followed the French example—called for in William Dean Howells' *Criticism and Fiction* (1891) and later, inspired by political rather than
aesthetic demands for "socially significant" art—produced only a slightly more
credible posturing in the "hard-boiled" mannerism of Dashiell Hammett
(1894-1961) in the detective story and Ernest Hemingway (1899-1961) in the
"art" story. James T. Farrell's Chicago and John Updike's suburbia are works
of imagination. When the reader is presented with an author such as John
O'Hara who does magically capture the minutest details of how people live,
they tend to dismiss him as shallow. Americans are more impressed with
"social significance" (a hold-over of the Great Depression), with those who

grapple with large moral issues (Herman Melville, William Faulkner), or with case histories of the paranormal, the paranoid, and the pathological, psychology having become for many American writers what theology was for the Age of Faith.

Much work of local or national importance in the later nineteenth century and the early years of this century was overshadowed by that of Henry James, Stephen Crane, and Ambrose Bierce, among others whose reputation spread to Europe. Here in America, good, if largely forgotten, work was being written by local colorists more minor than those already listed. In the West and Midwest were the journalistic writers for the newspapers of the boom towns and such wry reporters of life in the prairie towns and farms as Joseph Kirkland (1830-1894), Alice French (1850-1934), and E. W. Howe (1853-1937), inspirer of Sherwood Anderson and Sinclair Lewis. In the East were Edward Everett Hale (1822-1909, whose "My Double and How He Undid Me" is uncharacteristic but unforgettable); Mary Catherwood (1847-1902); and William Dean Howells (1837-1920), who wrote tales of the occult in *Questionable Shapes* (1903), children's tales in *Christmas Every Day* (1893), and sketches in *A Day's Pleasure* (1898), and notable short stories which are now seldom read.

Other writers of (or in) the South included James Lane Allen (1849-1925), author of *The Alabaster Box* (1923), Grace Elizabeth King (1851-1932), author of *Tales of a Time and Place* (1892), and Mark Twain, whose "The Man That Corrupted Hadleyburg" touches themes of decadence and corruption that were to become common in the literature of the area in this century. Constance Fenimore Woolson (1840-1894), practically unknown today even to American Literature majors and professors, was a pioneer realist and the first local colorist of all. Born in New Hampshire, the grandniece of James Fenimore Cooper, she defies Faulkner's statement (made by a character in one of his famous novels) that an outsider cannot understand the South.

Woolson's first local-color stories were of an Ohio childhood. In *Castle Nowhere* (1875), she presented "Lake Country Sketches" of the French settlers around the Great Lakes. In the 1870's, she lived in Florida and the Carolinas and wrote about the people there in stories published in Northern magazines and collected as *Rodman the Keeper: Southern Sketches* (1880). Then, like Henry James (who highly commended her work), she went abroad. There she wrote five novels and two posthumously published collections of "Italian Sketches," *The Front Yard* (1895) and *Dorothy* (1896), chiefly about Americans in Italy. No one interested in the American short story ought to ignore such finely crafted works as "Jeanette" and "Wilhelmina" in *Castle Nowhere*; the title story and "In Cotton Country" in *Rodman the Keeper*; the title story and "The Street of the Hyacinth" in *The Front Yard*; and the title story and "A Transplanted Boy" in *Dorothy*. Her short stories were far superior to the novels she published in *Harper's*, and they represent a neglected milestone in American short fiction.

Not neglected by any means is Stephen Crane (1871-1900), famous for the magnificent *The Red Badge of Courage* (1895). His Civil War stories (*The Little Regiment*, 1896) do not approach *The Red Badge of Courage*, although they sometimes are vaguely reminiscent of episodes in the life of Henry Fleming. His best stories are in *The Open Boat* (1898) and *The Monster and Other Stories* ("The Blue Hotel") of the next year. *Whilomville Stories* (1900), which includes "The Angel Child," "Showin' Off," and other tales of childhood in a small New York town, represents a distinct falling off. *Whilomville Stories* has been pushed aside, although it still has some good stories in it, while even *Maggie: A Girl of the Streets*, Crane's first novel published at his own expense (under the name "Johnston Smith") and found unsalable in 1893 is now praised for the grim realism that once damned it. The last sentence of Crane's "The Bride Comes to Yellow Sky" is: "His feet made funnel-shaped tracks in the heavy sand." Crane's footsteps in the short story were followed by many subsequent writers: his handling of point of view, for example, was instructive.

Ambrose Bierce (1842-1914?), like Crane, wrote journalism and some first-rate, sardonic stories, although he was decidedly not (as Percival Pollard argued in 1909) "the one commanding figure in our time." His newspaper bits were followed in 1891 by *Tales of Soldiers and Civilians*, among which "Chickamauga," "One of the Missing," and "An Occurrence at Owl Creek Bridge" are famous. The two dozen stories in *Can Such Things Be?* (1893) are less impressive. His work, without much exaggeration, can be said to summarize the major trends noted in the American short story of the nineteenth century: German and Gothic influences (Irving, Hawthorne, Poe); French influences (especially Maupassant) on style and form; growing native strength and regional and local-color stories, with some infusion of history, folklore, and tall-tales; and connections between writers and magazine markets, journalism and art.

At about the beginning of the twentieth century, the romantic imagination of Hawthorne was still to be seen in writers such as Edward Bellamy (1850-1898), now known for the Utopian romance *Looking Backward: 2000-1887* (1888), but also the author of *The Blindman's World and Other Stories* (1898). The Gothic tradition lived on in writers such as F. Marion Crawford (1854-1909), who thought "the moral lesson is a mistake," avoided social commitment in his many novels, and wrote electrifying ghost stories such as "The Upper Berth" in *Wandering Ghosts* (1911). Humor was mixed with mystery in "The Lady or the Tiger?" and in the practically annual collections of short stories by Frank R. Stockton (1834-1902).

Frank Norris (1870-1902), author of The Epic of Wheat Trilogy (only *The Octopus*, 1901, and *The Pit*, 1903, were completed) and stories published in *The Smart Set* and other magazines (collected in *The Third Circle*, 1909), carried on the realist traditions of Émile Zola, which triumphed in Theodore Dreiser's *Sister Carrie* (1900), which Norris persuaded a publisher to print. Local color reached out to include Alaska in the stories of Jack London (1876-1916), such as "To Build a Fire" and *Love of Life* (1906). Local color was also utilized in proletarian propaganda, not only in novels (*Martin Eden*, 1909, *The Iron Heel*, 1907, *The Valley of The Moon*, 1913) but also in stories such as "South of the Slot" (published first in *Saturday Evening Post*, long an excellent market for American short stories, and much later in *The Strength of the Strong*, 1914).

Dialect humor, a nineteenth century American specialty, culminated in Finley Peter Dunne (1867-1936), creator of the Irish philosopher Mr. Dooley (*Mr. Dooley in Peace and in War* and *Mr. Dooley in the Hearts of His Countrymen*, both 1898). The pieces in these works were more nearly essays than stories, but they had some effect on dialect stories to follow, not only on ethnic storytellers (such as Jewish writers Arthur Kober, Leonard Q. Ross, and Sam Levenson), but also on writers whose appeal depends partly on a keen ear for lower-class American speech. These include such writers as Will Rogers, George Ade with his *Fables in Slang* (1899), the incomparable Ring Lardner, S. J. Perelman of *The New Yorker* and surrealistic satire, Damon Runyon, whose stories inspired the musical *Guys and Dolls* in 1950, and others who connected the crude folk humor and the satire of "Artemus Ward," "Josh Billings," "Petroleum V. Naseby," and others in the nineteenth century with the social criticism of American writers after World War I.

Humor, or at least a critical attitude toward American life after World War I, was to be used by authors of novels and important short stories, writers such as Gertrude Atherton (1857-1948), Owen Wister (1860-1938), Booth Tarkington (1869-1946), Gertrude Stein (1874-1946), Dorothy Canfield Fisher (1879-1958), James Branch Cabell (1879-1958), Ernest Poole (1880-1950), Elizabeth Madox Roberts (1886-1941), Wilbur Daniel Steele, Edna Ferber, Christopher Morley, Ruth Suckow, Glenway Wescott, Oliver La Farge, Erskine Caldwell, John O'Hara, William Saroyan, and Walter Van Tilburg Clark. Their works and those of many other writers are well represented in such standard anthologies of the short story as Ronald V. Cassill's *Norton Anthology of Short Fiction* (1977), R. F. Dietrich and Roger H. Sundell's *The Art of Fiction* (1967), James H. Pickering's *Fiction 100* (1974), and Virgil Scott and David Madden's *Studies in the Short Story* (1968). A comparison of these anthologies with those of the last few decades will illustrate not only the major trends and individual achievements but also the rise and fall of literary reputations, since the attempt in all such anthologies is to illustrate "representative" short fiction.

One important writer of the American short story, now much out of fashion but deserving tribute, is William Sydney Porter, who adopted the pseudonym O. Henry. O. Henry (1862-1910) lived roughly between the birth dates of

Gertrude Atherton and Walter Van Tilburg Clark. He was born in the same year as Edith Wharton and the publication of *Artemus Ward* and died about the time of the birth of James Agee, Richard Wright, and Eudora Welty. At his peak, he turned out popular stories at the rate of one a week; and once he started to collect his stories (*Cabbages and Kings*, 1904), the books came out with amazing rapidity and success. *The Four Million* (1906), *Heart of the West* (1907), *The Trimmed Lamp* (1907), *The Gentle Grafter* (1908), *The Voice of the City* (1908), *Options* (1909), *Roads of Destiny* (1909), *Whirligigs* (1910), and *Strictly Business* (1910) were all in print by 1910; and after he died, collections continued to appear, including *Sixes and Sevens* (1911), *Rolling Stones* (1912), and *Waifs and Strays* (1917). Titles such as *Whirligigs* suggest his view of life; *The Four Million*, a response to society's estimate that New York contained only four hundred people socially prominent or worthy of attention, and *The Voice of the City* (New York) represent his interests.

O. Henry was both quintessentially American and derivative. Nicholaus Mills's *American and English Fiction in the Nineteenth Century: An Antigenre Critique and Comparison* (1973) stresses that our fiction and the British were more alike than dissimilar; O. Henry was the inheritor not only of British influences but also of the German tradition discussed in connection with such early writers as Irving and Hawthorne, as well as with Maupassant and the French tradition. Today Kenneth Tynan argues that "modern readers care only for long-distance, marathon writing," but O. Henry lived in a time when the brief, journalistic piece was at its height of popularity. He was pithy and witty, ingenious in plotting (although he relied too much on circumstance), to the point, and able to give his short stories of simple working stiffs a neat twist at the end. He established an enviable popular reputation with ironic stories such as "A Municipal Report," "The Gift of the Magi," "The Last Leaf," "The Furnished Room," "An Unfinished Story," "Mammon and the Archer," "The Ransom of Red Chief," and "A Retrieved Reformation." *Respice finem* was his motto, his formula. Poe had suggested that a story must be written backwards, with a concentration on one, preconceived effect; O. Henry also wrote backwards, with the last line in mind.

The surprise ending is seen today in many forms, from the startling detective story to the horror story. The trick wore thin after O. Henry, however, which explains both his notable absence from modern anthologies, and also, perhaps, the proliferation of *The New Yorker* stories in which it looks as if the last page or two of the story failed to reach the printer. O. Henry is responsible for both the trick ending and the reaction against it and has therefore been a considerable force for good or ill in American fiction. His avoidance of sex also set a fashion, for a time, and his rather vulgar mixture of the colloquial and the overblown can almost be said to be the native language of cheap fiction. The trick ending, however, was his trademark and his legacy.

O. Henry, like many American authors to follow, concentrated on the urban lower and middle classes. It is often said that until very recently important minorities received no adequate attention in American letters, but the fact is that the most neglected minority has been (partly because of the social origins of our leading writers) the upper class. Ellen Glasgow, Louis Auchincloss, and a few others have written about aristocrats in decline or in power, but O. Henry's near contemporary Edith Wharton (1862-1937) is quite unusual in writing about the aristocracy from the inside (F. Scott Fitzgerald wrote from the outside, with a nose pressed up against the glass and awed by the idea that the "rich are different from other people"). Wharton, author of superb tragic novels such as *The House of Mirth* (1905) and *Ethan Frome* (1911), cast a shrewd eye on a much-neglected section of American society in many of her brilliant short stories in *The Greater Inclination* (1899), *Crucial Instances* (1901), *The Descent of Man* (1904), *Xingu* (1916), and other collections; she also wrote the cerebral *Tales of Men and Ghosts* (1910) and *Ghosts* (1937).

Wharton's characters, like many of Henry James's, according to *The Literary History of the United States* (1974), belonged to "a group where worth as human beings had little relevance to the importance of their behavior as individuals conditioned by a uniform environment"; and they "spoke her language, and belonged to an environment where no lack of refinement in the art of mere living prevented the free play of the subtler emotions or suppressed the adventures and obscured the rebuffs of the intellect." More simply, her stories dealt subtly with not only the supernatural and the limited lives of the New York middle class, but also with the morals and manners of the "old guard" who were being replaced by the robber barons of commerce and the struggling bourgeoisie. Her studies are precise, honest, and knowledgeable examinations of what people think and do in sometimes extraordinary situations, not plots devised to show "what the situation would be likely to make of" the characters, and the characters are often drawn from a set higher than those discussed in the pages of middle-class publications such as *The New Yorker* with its stories by James Thurber, E. B. White, Dorothy Parker, Sally Benson, John Cheever, John O'Hara, Kay Boyle, Marjorie Kinnan Rawlings, Robert M. Coates, Hortense Calisher, Mary McCarthy, and others. No better American story involving psychology and class can be found than Wharton's "Roman Fever." Wharton represented in some ways the end of an era. The 1880 to 1914 period saw the growth of American realism, and after the Great War the realists and the naturalists (urban and rural, revolutionary and regionalist) became firmly entrenched until the romantic reaction and the new psychology emerged.

Theodore Dreiser (1871-1945), said Sherwood Anderson, personified "something gray and bleak and hurtful," and Dreiser was a relentless and often clumsy realist, getting his powerful stories down somehow, influencing many other American writers: as Anderson said, "making a path" with "heavy brutal feet." His short stories sometimes achieve equally massive effects without the awkwardness and with force more under control.

Dreiser was one of the giants of the Naturalism Movement in American literature. His amorphous and often awkward novels, including *Sister Carrie*, *The Genius* (1915), *An American Tragedy* (1925), and the Yerkes trilogy, are the basis of his fame; his short stories, however, ought not to be ignored. Some are included in *Theodore Dreiser*, an anthology of 1962, with an Introduction by James T. Farrell (to whom H. L. Mencken once wrote: "Dreiser, without doubt, is one of the worst writers seen on earth. Nevertheless, he has something that is hard to match. . . .").

Jack London was more interesting as a personality than as a writer and his adventures were more colorful than the books (such as *Martin Eden*) in which he presented them as fiction. He was praised for his leftist views and still remains popular in the U.S.S.R., and in America he was one of the models for the "on the road" writers. In his best stories he presents a simple picture of man against nature, as in "To Light a Fire"; but when he makes men act like animals and animals like men (as in *The Call of the Wild*, 1903), he sometimes violates modern taste.

With *Winesburg, Ohio* an important new writer appeared on the American scene: Sherwood Anderson (1876-1941). *Dark Laughter* (1925) brought him to the attention of the readers of best sellers; but Anderson was also admired by serious readers in stories such as those which comprised Winesburg's history, describing the personal drives of ambitious and imaginative characters and the restrictions of provincial life. His autobiography, *A Story Teller's Story* (1924), is part fiction and his fiction is partly based on fact: in many cases the immediacy and insight in an Anderson story arise from the fact that it is the author himself who wants "to know why" or who is reflecting on life's promises and disappointments. Two of his most important stories have given their titles to collections: *The Triumph of the Egg* (1921) and *Death in the Woods* (1933). In the tales in these classic collections the author is never far from his creations.

Late in life Anderson looked back on himself and other writers of his period who rebelled against "babbitry" and narrow-mindedness; and he described himself, Sinclair Lewis, and others as "a little band of soldiers who were going to free life." What they wanted most was sexual freedom:

> We wanted the flesh back in our literature, wanted directly in our literature the fact of men and women in bed together, babies being born. We wanted the terrible importance of the flesh in human relations also revealed again.

Today, Anderson's work, like D. H. Lawrence's, might seem somewhat old-fashioned if it were not for the fact that his stories have more universal appeal than antiprovincial propaganda, more timeless technique than outdated application. Their humanity takes them out of any dated struggle and makes them true representatives of classic American literature.

Susan Glaspell (1882-1948) worked on Des Moines newspapers (the *News* and the *Capital*), and after observing a murder trial created the fine short story called "A Jury of Her Peers," which also became a one-act play, *Trifles* (1916). With Wythe Williams (born in 1881), author of "Splendid with Swords" (a prize-winning O. Henry story of 1925), she has slipped into obscurity, despite some recent efforts by the women's movement to revive her reputation.

Ring Lardner (1885-1933) wrote about baseball players with the same force that Anderson brought to horsemen; and in *What Of It?* (1925), *The Love Nest* (1926), *Round Up* (1929), and *First and Last* (1934), he fulfilled the promise of his early collection *How to Write Short Stories* (1924). With savage wit he showed what H. L. Mencken dubbed the *booboisie* in all their tawdry commonplaceness. "The Golden Honeymoon" is typical of his malicious observation. "Haircut" appears in many anthologies as a masterpiece of storytelling technique.

Wilbur Daniel Steele (1886-1970) began as a writer with what he called a "pretty awful" story sold to a magazine aptly named *Success*. Soon thereafter, "White Horse Winter" was published in the *Atlantic Monthly* and by the 1920's, Steele was being called the best writer of short stories in America. He won many prizes, and "How Beautiful with Shoes" (one of the *Best American Short Stories 1933*) is still regarded as a masterpiece, although his fame has declined since he published his *Best Stories* (1946).

P. G. Wodehouse was born in 1881 and died on Long Island in 1975; he had continued writing about the Edwardian period of his native England until the end of his life. His career started with a very successful first novel, *The Pothunters* (1902), and he achieved international status with the creation of Jeeves the butler, Bertie Wooster, the members of The Drones, Mr. Mulliner, Psmith, and other comic characters. After innumerable plays and more than sixty novels (including *Very Good, Jeeves*, 1958, *Blanding's Castle*, 1957, and *Money in the Bank*, 1942), P. G. Wodehouse became the *doyen* of comic writers. Such tales as "Jeeves and the Song of Songs" and "The Ordeal of Osbert Mulliner" are deathless, and his deft manipulation of incident and the clever combination of antique rhetoric with modern slang gave the funny story a new structure and a language all its own. Faint echoes are to be heard in writers right through the years from George Ade to Peter De Vries.

The work of Ruth Suckow (1892-1960) was first published in *The Midland* and *The Smart Set* (edited by H. L. Mencken and George Jean Nathan); Suckow went on to bring to the whole country the tales of her German background and Iowa upbringing in such volumes of stories and sketches as *Iowa Interiors* (1926), *Children and Older People* (1931), and *Some Others and Myself* (1952). She has a masterful sense of place, and her plots are intriguing puzzles presented at a swift pace which charitably covers a multitude of weaknesses in the author's style.

James Thurber (1894-1961) as cartoonist, essayist, and short-story writer draws on the antics of men, women, and dogs for his comedy. Such disconcerting topics as the war between the sexes provide the basis for humor, but underneath the gaiety is a current of pathos which gives a ridiculous event (the night the bed fell) or person (such as an aunt who suspected that electricity was leaking out of an empty light socket) or animal (such as the dog that bit people) something more than mere hilarity. His short stories for *The New Yorker* often look deceptively simple, but they are the product of the most thoughtful American humorist since Twain, making the scintillating parody of S. J. Perelman, Woody Allen, and others look superficial.

Katherine Anne Porter (1890-1980), educated at several convent schools, began to publish short stories in *Century Magazine*, edited by Carl Van Doren. With *Flowering Judas and Other Stories* (1930) the qualities which have won her both literary prizes and a wide popular readership became inescapably apparent and her reputation was increased by the appearance of *Noon Wine* (1937), *Pale Horse, Pale Rider* (1939), and *The Leaning Tower* (1944), among other works.

Starting late to publish her stories and destroying many which did not please her, Porter distanced herself from other American writers by her self-criticism and high standards as well as her self-realization and consistent quality. Her long residence in Mexico produced far less material—although material of a far better sort—than might have been the case with other writers. Moreover, whatever her locales, however colorful, she managed to get beneath the surface to deeper significances. It was particularly disappointing, therefore, to discover that her novel *Ship of Fools* (1962), on which she had worked for more than twenty years, was not the masterpiece that many had expected. The author tried, like her character Granny Weatherall, to "spread out the plan of life and tuck in the edges orderly," but there was "something not given back."

More recently, Corinne Jacker, one of whose earliest dramas was a version of Porter's famous "Pale Horse, Pale Rider" for the stage, adapted "The Jilting of Granny Weatherall" for television's series *The American Short Story*, saying: "To me it's less important that people run out and read 'The Jilting of Granny Weatherall' than that, hopefully, we've shown them the world as Katherine Anne Porter saw it."

Dorothy Parker (1893-1967) had, as Ogden Nash wrote, "an eye for people, an ear for language, and a feeling for the little things of life that are so immense a part of the process of living." Her acid wit and sarcastic one-liners have done something to preserve her reputation, as have (to a lesser extent) her short stories, which range from monologues ("A Telephone Call" and "You Were Perfectly Fine") to reporting of the Jazz babies ("Big Blonde").

Stretched to fill a television drama, "Big Blonde" became far too fragile and transparent; as a short story it has power. With Frederick B. Shroyer, Parker in 1965 edited a thematic anthology which identified a good short story as "both a window into a segment of the human experience and an interpretive record of it by one who has either lived it himself or who has somehow understood and experienced it vicariously."

Dashiell Hammett created hard-boiled detective fiction by drawing on his experiences as a Pinkerton man and his knowledge of American underworld lingo. Sam Spade and the Thin Man became classics heroes, and *The Maltese Falcon* (1930), as novel and film, is the object of a cult. As a writer of pop fiction of the *Black Mask* pulp magazine variety, Hammett (with Raymond Chandler and others) destroyed the Sherlock Holmes tradition; they managed (as Chandler said) "to get murder away from the upper classes, the weekend houseparty, and the vicar's rose garden, and back to the people who were really good at it." With Ned Beaumont in *The Glass Key* (1931), Hammett told his story through a racketeer's bodyguard; elsewhere, he called his detective Sam Spade "a hard, shifty fellow." Hammett's major contribution to American short fiction was his terse, tough-guy style, picked up by Ross Macdonald, John D. MacDonald, and other writers, including Ernest Hemingway.

The new interest in popular culture has provided many books one can consult on the detective story and studies of masters of detective fiction of all kinds, from Rex Stout and Erle Stanley Gardner and "Ellery Queen" to the latest purveyors of violence and experts on police procedures. The readers of detective stories, both novels and short stories, are far more varied (and so, therefore, is the product itself) than was admitted by W. H. Auden when he wrote: "The typical detective story addict is a doctor or a clergyman or scientist or artist, *i.e.*, a fairly successful professional man with intellectual interests and well-read in his own field, who would never stomach the *Saturday Evening Post* or *True Confessions* or movie magazines or comics. . . ." Today detective fiction in its manifold variety appeals to all levels of the reading public and ranges from theological speculations to pure trash. Some of our very best writers grace the genre and some of our worst disgrace it.

Caroline Gordon (1895-1981) edited with Allen Tate an important anthology of the short story, *The House of Fiction* (1950); and she has published, in addition to criticism and more than half a dozen thoughtful novels, a number of short stories of merit collected in *The Forest of the South* (1945) and *Old Red and Other Stories* (1963). "Old Red," which won second prize in the O. Henry Memorial competition of 1934, is probably her best story; Cleanth Brooks and Robert Penn Warren dissect it in *Understanding Fiction* (1943).

Stephen Vincent Benét (1898-1943) is remembered most for the Pulitzer Prize-winning poems *John Brown's Body* (1928) and *Western Star* (1943), which won for him the Pulitzer Prize posthumously in 1944; but his short stories include *The Devil and Daniel Webster*, 1937, (which has by now been adapted to nearly every media) and "By the Waters of Babylon," an uneven but frightening story of a great city destroyed and life clinging on amid the Dead Places, a story now more chilling, some fifty years later, in the nuclear age.

Ernest Hemingway was one of the giants of American literature. His work reflects his Michigan boyhood; his necessity as a reporter for the *Kansas City Star* to write clearly and concisely; his service in World War I, in which he was severely wounded, and as a European correspondent for the *Toronto Star*; his expatriate years in Paris; his pleasure found in hunting, fishing, drinking, and watching bullfights; and his personal problems. Some of his earliest work was in the short form (*Three Stories & Ten Poems* of 1923 and *In Our Time* of 1924), and he became a master of the short story. His best work—*The Sun Also Rises* (1926) and *A Farewell to Arms* (1929)—belongs to the 1920's; but in the 1930's he continued to publish important fiction and nonfiction (*To Have and Have Not*, 1937, *Death in the Afternoon*, 1932, and *The Green Hills of Africa*, 1935); in the 1940's such work as *For Whom the Bell Tolls*; and in the 1950's *The Old Man and the Sea* (1952). He was awarded the Nobel Prize for Literature in 1954 for his "mastery of the art of modern narration."

Hemingway very early declared his independence from Sherwood Anderson (another journalist) by parodying him in *The Torrents of Spring* (1926) and soon perfected his tough-guy style, which influenced a generation of American writers. Its grace under pressure informs Hemingway's best stories, which include "Big Two-Hearted River," "The Killers," "A Clean, Well-Lighted Place," "The Short Happy Life of Francis Macomber," and "The Snows of Kilimanjaro." His last works (including *Across the River and into the Trees*, 1950, and *Islands in the Stream*, 1971) were not worthy of the author of the great novels and his best stories.

E. B. White was born in 1899 and ever retained some gentlemanly charm which looked old-fashioned even in *The New Yorker*, where he published humorous essays and short stories. His particular charm was also evident in such children's books as *Charlotte's Web* (1952). White's delightful *The Second Tree from the Corner* (1954) provides a close look at some of his essays, reports, poems, and stories, and earns him mention in any survey of the American short story; the work is at once influential and inimitable, for it is all style—and "the style is the man himself."

Two Southern writers who greatly influenced the development of fiction were Thomas Wolfe and William Faulkner. Although Wolfe (1900-1938) was better suited to the sprawling novel (*Look Homeward, Angel* of 1929 and *Of Time and the River* of 1935 are titanic) than to short fiction, some of his short stories (such as "Only the Dead Know Brooklyn") are excellent. William Faulkner (1897-1962) was capable of both the grand design and the small masterpiece. Like Hemingway, he was an impressionist saluted for his "realism."

That Americans too much ignore Canadian writers is illustrated by the case of Morley Callaghan (1903-   ), a Canadian who has been seriously engaged in writing since 1926. His short stories are collected in volumes such as *A Native Argosy* (1929) and *Now That April's Here* (1936), and his finely crafted novels deserve attention. Those who do not know the inspired nonsense of Stephen Leacock or the charming stories of French Canada by Gabrielle Roy, Thomas Costain, and others (not to say the older work of such excellent writers as Marjorie Pickthall and Thomas Chandler Haliburton) should begin immediately with an introductory sampling such as Alec Lucas' *Great Canadian Short Stories* (1971). Although some Canadian writers were born elsewhere (such as Leacock, Frederick Philip Grove, Ethel Wilson, Malcolm Lowry) and others emigrated (such as Anne Hébert, Mordecai Richler, Brian Moore, and Mavis Gallant), Canadian short fiction has been able to develop and maintain a character all its own. Critics are now beginning to discover just how distinguished that literature is.

The city has played an increasingly dominant role in American culture and American literature, providing the setting for everything from the optimistic novels of Horatio Alger to the despairing cries of the poets of the slums. Some of the best American short stories and some of our most characteristic reporting, from Thomas Wolfe's "Only the Dead Know Brooklyn" to Clark Whelton's "Papo and the Hydrant," have questioned the lives of "that vast army of workers, held captive by poverty" in urban slums and have wondered, with Jacob Riis, "what will the harvest be?"

James T. Farrell (1904-1979) has written several hundred good short stories about the poor and middle-class Catholic dwellers of Chicago's South Side, which is also the setting of his Studs Lonigan trilogy (1932-1935), the Danny O'Neill series (1936-1953), and other novels. He has had many imitators, although the more modern trend is to emphasize the spiritual desert of the megalopolis, as in the short stories of James Purdy (1923-   ) and others. Yet public taste may return to the reportorial approach of Farrell rather than the impressionism of more recent writers. Farrell, Hemingway, Anderson, and others brought reporting sensibilities to short fiction, and now reporting is getting closer to art. Reporters write "stories," and whereas short fiction used to feed the film mills, now jazzed-up news stories (the reporter entering into the "story" more since Hunter S. Thompson, Tom Wolfe, and others have revitalized journalism and reporters on the beat have given pride of place to "feature writers on assignment") become motion pictures. Think of a *New York Magazine* "story" on a Brooklyn disco (*Saturday Night Fever*) or an *Esquire* article on the "urban cowboy," just to mention two John Travolta films. Many short-fiction writers have gravitated to feature writing, script "development," and television "software."

Isaac Bashevis Singer (1904-   ), a native of Poland, wrote in Yiddish of Jewish life in the *shtetl* in his novels and in the short stories collected in *Gimpel the Fool* (1957), *Short Friday* (1964), and other books. As the numerous translations of his work testify, however, Singer is an international author. Alfred Kazin and Ben Siegel are among the Jewish critics who have carefully explicated his works, but Singer's little tales are fraught with meaning that Jew and non-Jew alike can appreciate.

Robert Penn Warren (1905-   ) was once described as the "pentathlon champion" of American literature: short-story writer, novelist, poet, biographer, critic. He won Pulitzer prizes for fiction and poetry (*All the King's Men*, 1946, and *Promises*, 1957), collaborated with Cleanth Brooks on the milestone textbooks *Understanding Fiction* and *Understanding Poetry* (1938), and generally achieved distinction in all branches of letters. A good introduction to his work, collected in *The Circus in the Attic and Other Stories* (1947) and elsewhere, is the brief masterpiece "Blackberry Winter," found in many anthologies. The typical American theme of the adolescent's initiation into the realities of adult life, search for identity, and pain of self-discovery has seldom been essayed with such delicacy and point. It deserves to rank with Hawthorne's "My Kinsman, Major Molineux," Cather's "Paul's Case," Anderson's "I'm a Fool," Conrad Aiken's "Silent Snow, Secret Snow," and the other classic stories about the journey toward self-realization of the sensitive young man.

Another academic writer is Lionel Trilling (1905-   ). Although Trilling is most famous for his work in literary criticism, such short stories as "The Other Margaret" and "Of This Time, Of That Place" are memorable. Mark Schorer (1908-   ) has found time in a busy scholarly career to publish short stories in the *Hudson Review*, *Kenyon Review*, and elsewhere. "In Populous City Pent" is a fair example of the skill which has earned him a number of prizes. Thirty-two of his stories are collected in *The State of Mind* (1947). Another writer and teacher in California is Wallace Stegner (1909-   ). His first novel, *Remembering Laughter* (1937), launched a career full of prizes, some of which have been awarded for short stories; the best stories may be found in collections such as *The Women on the Wall* (1950) and *The City of the Living* (1956). He has contributed to American literature also by his continued and sincere interest in budding writers in creative writing courses, and the fact that today many thousands of such hopefuls are busy in college seminars and workshops is in no small measure due to the success of Stegner and other dedicated teachers.

Collections by John O'Hara (1905-1970) include *The Doctor's Son* (1935), *Files on Parade* (1939), *Pipe Night* (1945), and *Hellbox* (1947). If (as he told Robert Van Gelder in an interview) his writings, such as *Appointment in Samarra* (1934), *A Rage to Live* (1949), and *Ten North Frederick* (1955), went directly from the typewriter to the printer, they must be the most facile and accurate first drafts in the history of American letters.

William Saroyan (1908-   ) came into the literary spotlight in 1934 with the publication of *The Daring Young Man on the Flying Trapeze* in *Story*, a magazine that consistently introduced and nurtured new talents and to which the American short story owes a great debt of gratitude. Saroyan increased his reputation with plays that, for a time, caused him to be hailed as a great new talent for the American theater. On both the stage and in fiction, unfortunately, his early promise was unfulfilled, but he contributed a number of fine stories to our literature and encouraged other writers to emulate (not always with equal success) his insouciant and innovative approach to short fiction.

To appreciate the distance and direction of the development of the American short story, one should look at the year 1909. In that year Sarah Orne Jewett, the New England regionalist who dealt in little things, first as impressions and sketches in *Deephaven* (1877), *Country By-ways* (1881), and *Old Friends and New* (1879) and then in a novel, *The Country of the Pointed Firs*, died; and in that same year, two writers who might be called regionalists, and who can be compared to and contrasted with Jewett, were born: Walter Van Tilburg Clark and Eudora Welty.

Walter Van Tilburg Clark (1909-1971) attained fame with his first novel to reach print, *The Ox-Bow Incident* (1940), probably best recalled as a classic of the American cinema. He never equaled this success in his later work, but his stories collected in *The Watchful Gods and Other Stories* (1950) show his manifold talents in the realm of short fiction. Eudora Welty (1909-   ) was awarded the Pulitzer Prize for one of her novels (*The Optimist's Daughter*, 1972), but she has made her place as one of the most distinguished of modern American writers largely through her short stories, the first of which were collected in *A Curtain of Green* (1941). In reviewing her *Collected Stories*, which covers the period 1936 to 1980, *The New York Times* critic Anatole Broyard found that they ranged "from the heavy-handed genre story to the weightless, unclassifiable kind that *The New Yorker* has made famous," and, although he ventured the opinion that recently this most famous resident of Jackson, Mississippi, has been substituting "a much-elaborated technique" for some of her earlier power, he was obliged to call this collection of stories "a national monument."

Welty's world is full of odd people: a self-centered and nasty woman who explains "Why I Live at the P.O.," a petrified man, an undaunted black woman of almost superhuman proportions, an old couple who set fire to their own kitchen table in fruitless protest against the hard life they lead. The grotesqueries that have decorated modern Southern writing, however, are in Welty's unforgettable stories capable of making readers not mere gawkers at a sideshow but amazed spectators at the wonders of the world of men; evident in her most extraordinary characters is something that makes one sense more deeply the fact that all are members of a "mystical body." Welty startles, amuses, and explains, and most of all she writes stories which are, to use the words of Robert Frost, "a clarification of life—not necessarily a great clarification, such as sects and cults are founded on, but . . . a momentary stay against confusion."

Paul Bowles (1910-   ) has written operas, music for Tennessee Williams' *The Glass Menagerie* (1945) and *Sweet Bird of Youth* (1959), and music for ballets and films, as well as novels and short stories. Of the latter, one of the best is "The Scorpion," from *The Delicate Prey and Other Stories* (1950), dedicated to his mother, who "first read me the stories of Poe." It is spare, strong, and staccato in dialogue. Herbert Barrows in *Reading the Short Story* (1959) stated that Bowles was among the most "original and consistent" writers who had achieved prominence since World War II and that he achieved his effects of horror "by a more direct exploitation of actuality than we find in Poe" by throwing his protagonists, Americans in Morocco or Mexico, for the most part, into alien and hostile environments where "America's codes of behavior" and the protagonist's idea of himself "have no meaning or validity whatever."

Wright Morris (1910-   ) was born in Nebraska but has long been associated, as a teacher and a writer, with San Francisco. His novel *Love Among the Cannibals* (1957) is superior to his *The Field of Vision* (which won the National Book Award the previous year), and his too-neglected short stories are sometimes even better.

Hortense Calisher (1911-   ) achieved critical acclaim with her first collection of short stories, *In the Absence of Angels* (1951), and has since suffered from too close an identification with the "walk-away ending" of *The New Yorker* type of story. This reputation persists despite her *Tale for the Mirror* (1962), which showed she belonged to no particular school but that of the meticulous writer. Her stories about "private tragedies, of loneliness and the dissolution of marriage" are her best.

Irwin Shaw (1913-   ) followed the success of his propagandistic play *Bury the Dead* (1936) with a number of stories in *The New Yorker* and elsewhere. Such stories as "The Girls in Their Summer Dresses" are still found in textbook anthologies, but their slick style and tendency to flirt with moral problems, then not know what to do with them, do not work as well in short stories as they do in best-selling novels. *Sailor off The Bremen* (1939) is one of several collections of Shaw's stories, most of which are inferior to the work of other novelists who also have essayed the short-story form, such as Kay Boyle (*Thirty Stories*, 1946), Ronald V. Cassill (*The Happy Marriage*, 1966), George P. Elliott (*Among the Dangs*, 1961), William Kotzwinkle (Elephant Bangs Train, 1974), Tillie Olsen (*Tell Me a Riddle*, 1961), and Jean Stafford (*Collected Stories*, 1969), for example.

Although there are many writers who are essentially novelists for whom short stories are a sideline, in this age in which short-story writing more resembles poetry than it used to do (once long narrative poems went out of style), one must say something of the prose of poets. Delmore Schwartz (1913-1966) can stand for a number of leading American poets whose ability to find *le mot juste*, as Gustave Flaubert called it, sparks their ventures into short fiction. His stories are to be found in *The World Is a Wedding* (1948) and *Successful Love* (1961). "In Dreams Begin Responsibilities" is a classic discussion of the things that mean "too much." Like the young and innocent girl determined to perfect a graceful dive in Herbert Gold's story "Susanna at the Beach," poets ignore the "oily, brackish, waste-ridden water" and the "veiny old men" and devote themselves to the artistic gesture which is at once a test and a triumph.

One example of a prolific writer remembered for a single story is Frank Rooney (1913-   ), whose "Cyclists' Raid" in *Harper's* in 1951 epitomized the problem of people who found their peaceful world a sudden nightmare and discovered that, as Pogo said in the cartoon, "the enemy is us." Rooney, like Russell Maloney (who wrote "Inflexible Logic," about the chimps let loose on typewriters who began to produce masterpieces of literature in defiance of the odds), seems to be able to tell a story that is remembered in all its details by people who cannot recall the author's name or perhaps have not even read the story but have simply heard it as an anecdote from someone else.

Whereas tall tales and morbid imaginings gave rise to many short stories in the last century, in our time reportorial "photography" and the presentation of sensational events of real life are the seeds of much modern fiction. Something, however, must be done to enrich reality. Bernard Malamud (born in 1914), with an "idiots first" attitude, does just that. As Malamud said in an interview with Haskel Frankel, "As a writer I want uncertainty. It's part of life. I want something the reader is uncertain about. It is this uncertainty that produces drama. Keep the reader surprised." What the reader is never uncertain about in *The Magic Barrel* (1958) and other stories by Malamud is his dedication to humanistic values and his unswerving loyalty to the idea of human potential.

The search for identity, always a principal theme in American fiction, is interestingly pursued by the introspective and yet confused protagonists of Saul Bellow (1915-   ). Born in Canada but identified since 1924 with Chicago, Bellow is the laureate of the *Luftmensch*, a historian of the process of becoming, a painter of the "queerness of existence," a guide for the perplexed. Daniel Stern in *Commentary* (October 24, 1975) identified Bellow's enduring themes as

the exhaustion of the Western mind and its received ideas . . . the difficulty of the ethical and imaginative life in America . . . the maniacal distractions among which people of good will and good minds must live . . . the Yeatsian paradox of aging and dying in the midst of heedless enthusiasm,

and these themes inform his well-crafted stories quite as much as they do such novels as *The Dangling Man* (1944), *The Victim* (1947), *Herzog* (1964), *Henderson the Rain King* (1959), *Seize the Day* (1956), and *The Adventures of Augie March* (1953). "Vividness is what [novelists] desire most," Bellow has written, "and so they must value human existence," and in his short and longer fiction there is always not only a penetrating intellectuality but also abundant detail derived from close observation. Novels such as *Mr. Sammler's Planet* (1970) and *Humboldt's Gift* (1975) helped to win Bellow the Nobel Prize for Literature (1976), and it is to be hoped that his fame will eventually direct more attention to his shorter fiction.

Elizabeth Hardwick (1916-   ), wife of poet Robert Lowell, published important stories in *Sewanee Review*, *Partisan Review*, and *The New Yorker* and won inclusion several times in *O. Henry* and *Best American Short Story* collections. "What We Have Missed" is typical of her work. She is one of the writers (prized by academics) whose work has not received wide public recognition.

One way to attract attention is to have some connection with the better-publicized media (such as the theater) and the better-attended media (such as the cinema). Carson McCullers (1917-1967) did that. McCullers, like Flannery O'Connor and Tennessee Williams, dealt best with misfits and the maimed, in a well-established tradition of Southern literature. Her resonating novels (*The Heart Is a Lonely Hunter*, 1940, *Reflections in a Golden Eye*, 1941, and *The Member of the Wedding*, 1946) always lose something of their evocative power on the screen; her work is equally disappointing when adapted for the stage (*The Member of the Wedding*, *The Ballad of the Sad Café*, 1951), although it is still effective in many ways. McCullers was most successful in stories which play upon the imagination and create theme out of character, as do "The Ballad of the Sad Café" and "Madame Zilensky and the King of Finland."

J. F. Powers (1917-   ) achieved fame in 1943 with "Lions, Harts, Leaping Does." Powers wrote about what he knew, drawing upon his Catholic background for his portraits of priests, which are marked by their honesty and affection. He also wrote very meticulously and produced a relatively small volume of work.

Peter Taylor (1917-   ) specializes in a subtle mixture of comedy, disorder, and despair; he writes about things fading and falling apart. His *Collected Stories* (1970) contains dazzling gems of sensitive narration and wry understanding such as "The Fancy Woman," "What Do You Hear From 'Em?," "Venus, Cupid, Folly and Time," and "Miss Leonora When Last Seen." Now John Barth and Thomas Pynchon are taking the modern story in directions dictated by still another apprehension of the absurdity of life, writing with less realism and less plot, but Taylor's stories will never go out of fashion any more than mature nostalgia or adolescent expectation ever will. As long as tradition interacts with the tensions of the present, Taylor's work will survive.

J. D. Salinger (1919-   ) became famous with the publication of *The Catcher in the Rye* (1951), immediately recognized as an American classic. His short stories, many written for *The New Yorker*, have also gained him a devoted following, and inclusion of one of his pieces is almost compulsory in textbook anthologies.

Russian-born Isaac Asimov (1920-   ) has lived in the United States since the age of three and has been important in science fiction since the age of nineteen. Although he writes far too much and attempts vast projects such as the saga based on Edward Gibbon's *The History of the Decline and Fall of the Roman Empire* (1776-1788), most of his products are well-made. *The Best of Isaac Asimov* (1974) contains some very good stories.

The subject of the American contribution within the short-story genre to the lively art of science fiction is too complex to cover here. It should simply be noted that while *The New Yorker* prints more than one hundred stories of its kind each year, there are hundreds of science-fiction stories published in a wide variety of places. The American science-fiction tradition goes back to Poe's *The Narrative of Arthur Gordon Pym* (1838) and to magazines such as *Black Cat, Argosy, Popular Magazine, Amazing Stories, Weird Tales*, and *Astounding Science Fiction*, all concerned not only with the fantastic but also with what Asimov has called "literature which is concerned with the impact of scientific advance upon human beings." These led to *Fantasy and Science Fiction* and *Galaxy* (appearing at the height of activity in the genre in the 1950's), to Arthur C. Clarke, Rod Serling, Frederick Pohl, Ray Bradbury, and to many lesser lights.

Dozens of science-fiction collections are published each year. Fewer, but perhaps more significant, are the stories of another sort written by women today. For example, Grace Paley (1922-   ) has been highly successful with the economic short story. The title of her 1959 collection, *The Little Disturbances of Man*, reveals her usual subject matter, which was given wider implications in *Enormous Changes at the Last Minute*, a 1974 collection cut down to size by the author with a sly deliberation and a comic sense of proportion.

Mavis Gallant (1922-   ), born in Montreal, Quebec, shares Grace Paley's precision but tends to tackle larger topics, such as people from other cultures addressing themselves to European attitudes. Her work has been influential both in *The New Yorker* and elsewhere in American and Canadian letters and in France, where she has lived a good part of her life. Her stories appear in collections of *The Other Paris* (1956) and *My Heart Is Broken* (1964).

A comparable talent is Maureen Patricia Daly (1921-   ), born in Ireland but long a resident of the United States, where she worked for the *Ladies'*

Home Journal. Her work has not been as popular as Sally Benson's stories in *The New Yorker*, but she represents an advance over the Ruth Suckow stories in the *Smart Set*, Dorothy Canfield Fisher's *Made-to-Order Stories*, and other work from women who have found time in literary careers of various sorts to write some notable short fiction.

Shirley Ann Grau (1929-   ) was born in New Orleans; she published in *The New Yorker* and *New World Writing* (an annual remarkable for discovering new talents) before *The Black Prince and Other Stories* (1955) made her reputation with a story she had written while a graduate student at Tulane. As a teacher of writing she has influenced many young writers, and her own reputation as a writer grows with every novel and short story.

Other women who now combine effective teaching with memorable writing (as did Kay Boyle and many others before them) are Joyce Carol Oates and Anne Beattie. Joyce Carol Oates (1938-   ) born in Lockport, New York, has taught in Canada and elsewhere and has, since the 1960's, poured forth a continuous stream of fiction, winning the National Book Award for *them* (1969) and plaudits for other novels and for stories collected in half a dozen or more volumes. *Marriages and Infidelities* (1972) is as good an introduction as any to her sensitivity to characters of all sorts and to her amazing ability to contrive a new means of telling a story with almost every attempt.

Ann Beattie (1947-   ) has taught both the history and the craft of fiction and has published *Distortions* (1976) and other stories, as well as longer fiction, always to great acclaim.

Shirley Jackson (1919-1965), who taught at Bennington College (as did her husband, critic Stanley Edgar Hyman), may be said to represent the older school of women teachers and practitioners of creative writing, those who entered a predominately male field and competed with men on their own terms. Jackson, for example, was a brilliant exponent of the old-fashioned Gothic horror tale as modified by Alfred Hitchcock in the cinema and a host of writers of thrillers (cinematic in conception, often intended from the first to be "sold to the movies") since. Her technique was to detail frightening developments in an apparently innocuous, even disarmingly ordinary, setting. "The Lottery" is a prime example.

Oates, Beattie, and a number of up-and-coming new talents, however, make it clear that women do not have to write like men to succeed and that the short story can be enlarged in its scope and deepened in its psychological penetration by the sensibility of women writers who see the world from a particular perspective. These writers need no tokenism or "affirmative action" to gain them a place in the first rank.

One woman who has made herself an undisputed place in a field usually an almost completely male preserve is Ursula K. Le Guin (1929-   ), born in Berkeley, California. She is among the best of modern writers of those strange "maps of hell" and satiric or prophetic commentaries on the present disguised as fantasies or prophecies of the future. Her trilogy *A Wizard of Earthsea* (1968), *The Tombs of Atuan* (1971), and *The Farthest Shore* (1972), and other novels are better known, perhaps, but her shorter fiction (such as *Orsinian Tales*, 1976) shows great inventiveness. She is something of a popular culture cult figure today.

How much an American woman can accomplish without gaining the recognition that comes to starlets and sportswomen can be illustrated in 1980 by the case of Kay Boyle, whose twenty-ninth book, *Fifty Stories*, was noted in *The New York Times* as "unaffectedly true to the author's time, place and situation" and yet received less public acclaim than Ann Beattie's *Falling in Place* (a novel that caused critics to term her "prodigiously gifted," a talent to watch), Stephen Dixon's *14 Stories* ("Henry Miller brought up-to-date"), Benedict Kiely's novella and seventeen stories called *The State of Ireland*, Richard Stern's third collection of perky *Packages*, the "short takes" woven into the novel *Ray* by the clever Barry Hannah (another writer to bet on), and *World's End and Other Stories* by Paul Theroux, to mention just some of the other serious work of the same year—and not to mention the huge works of a "commercial" sort that dominated the best-seller lists for the most part. 1980 was the year of Eudora Welty's *Collected Stories* as well, but Boyle's career deserves acclaim even if not such ringing bravos as Welty earned and received.

John Cheever (1922-   ) as a commentator on the decay of urban life and the increasing dislocation and alienation of people in modern society is best known through his novels, the very first of which, *The Wapshot Chronicle* (1957), won the National Book Award. As William Peden has pointed out, however, Cheever "is essentially a writer of short stories. More than a hundred of his stories have appeared in American magazines, many of them in *The New Yorker*." The fact that the novels are more famous than the stories is due more to the nature of American reading habits and the preferences of critics for larger works than to the nature of Cheever's art.

The Way Some People Live, the title of his collection of stories published in 1943, is always his subject in his often satiric examination of urban and suburban dissatisfactions and defeats, and many of his stories treat matters that are most effectively handled in the narrower and more trenchant short form: his collection of 1961 is called *Some People, Places, and Things That Will Not Appear in My Next Novel*. Startling effects such as he produces in *The Enormous Radio* (1953), for example, are not attainable in enormous novels, proving that short stories are not mere sketches or scraps of longer works but a necessary and powerful contribution to literature in their own way and in their own right. *The New York Times* wrote of his immense ability to explain why "proper suburbanites fall in love with baby sitters, commit ghastly improprieties while roaring drunk and carry out useless acts of rebellion against entrenched respectability" and yet could not complain that these "vast forces of unreason" were slighted in the brief compass of stories, for what the *Oakland* [California] *Tribune* identified as "the secret and obscene drives which motivate human beings dragging them toward unknown ends" were wholly captured in the economically presented people, places, and things that need not appear in any long-winded novel.

Truman Capote (1924-   ) burst on the scene as an *enfant terrible* of literature in his teens with "The Walls Are Cold" (*Decade*, 1944), "Miriam" (*Mademoiselle*, 1945), "Tree of Night" (*Harper's Bazaar*, 1945), and "Jug of Silver" (*Mademoiselle*, 1945). He still recalls being dizzy with excitement at three acceptances in one day. With the appearance of his first novel, *Other Voices, Other Rooms* (1948), he became a celebrity and went on to build an international reputation in fields as diverse as gossip and the nonfiction novel (*In Cold Blood*, 1966). Capote is a very sensitive and meticulous writer (he writes several drafts in pencil before going to the typewriter); his cold eye and his warm heart create complex and haunting fictions and often hilariously memorable characters, part reportage and part whimsy, in such a work as *Breakfast at Tiffany's* (1958). His short stories display a pyrotechnical virtuosity and a sympathy for some of the most outrageous characters in modern fiction. His evocative and often lapidary style is especially effective in quick but detailed portraits.

In Capote's writing, the grotesques so common in Southern literature take on both comic and complex dimensions. The complaint that his characters are too extraordinary, his approach trivial, and his topics mere gossip is not borne out in a study of his work; and one thing is certain: there are few writers today in any genre, big or small, who are more serious (or, for that matter, more ambitious or talented) than Capote.

Black American fiction is inevitably influenced by the context of white society, but it has some roots in factual narrative (such as the slave narratives, many of which were reprinted as a result of renewed interest in the 1970's) and folktales (such as those collected in the South and in Michigan and reprinted from his earlier work by Richard M. Dorson in *American Negro Folktales*, 1967), in sermons, polemics, and orations. Sterling Brown's *The Negro in American Fiction* (1938) helps to explain the "sudden" emergence of writers such as Jean Toomer (1894-1967), Charles Waddell Chesnutt, Paul Laurence Dunbar, Frances Ellen Harper, and the important figures of the Harlem Renaissance: Langston Hughes, Arna Bontemps, Countee Cullen, James Weldon Johnson, Claude McKay, and others, who (although poetry and the novel and to some extent drama were their main interests) also wrote some notable short stories.

Toomer's *Cane* (1923) was "a mosaic of encounters linked by lyric poems," a sort of initiation novel composed, among other elements, of short stories. After *Cane*, Toomer wrote more novels, poetry, and short stories, but editors would not touch his work, even when he denied his black ancestry. His economy ("outlines reduced to essences") and folk basis, however, were to have repercussions in black fiction thereafter. Toomer died in obscurity near Philadelphia in 1967.

Much more successful was Langston Hughes (1902-1967), who died in the same year after having published poetry (from *The Weary Blues* of 1926 to *The Panther and the Lash*, 1967), novels (such as *Tambourines to Glory*, 1958), plays (including one adapted from *Tambourines to Glory*), autobiography, important anthologies of black literature (including *The Best Short Stories by Negro Writers*, 1967), short-story collections of his own work (*The Ways of White Folks*, 1934; *Laughing to Keep from Crying*, 1952; *Something in Common and Other Stories*, 1963), and sketches and tales of Simple (see *The Best of Simple*, 1961). Vachel Lindsay "discovered" Hughes as a poet— while working as a busboy in a Washington restaurant Hughes put some poems by Lindsay's plate—but many short-story writers discovered the techniques he employed to translate folk material and dialect into humor and social comment. With Bontemps he edited *The Book of Negro Folklore* (1958). His treatment of urban life was more or less echoed by many other black writers, among them Ann Petry (1912-   ), whose "Like a Winding Sheet" was voted the best American short story in 1946, Paule Marshall (born in 1929), author of the collection *Soul Clap Hands and Sing* (1961), and Maya Angelou (1928-   ), best-known for her autobiographical works (*I Know Why the Caged Bird Sings*, 1970, and *Gather Together in My Name*, 1974) and poetry, who is the author of a neglected collection of stories entitled *All Day Long* (1974). In addition to these women writers, there are many neglected men in the genre, from John Frederick Matheus of West Virginia (born in 1887), whose short stories were collected in 1974, to Henry Dumas (1935-1968), author of *Ark of Bones and Other Stories* (1974). There are also a number of black writers of juvenile stories and of many other varieties in the genre of the short story.

Probably the most successful of black writers in the first half of this century was Richard Wright (1908-1960). He began with short stories (*Uncle Tom's Children*, 1938) but gained national and international fame as a novelist: *Native Son* (1940, adapted for the stage with Paul Green), *The Outsider* (1953), *The Long Dream* (1958), and *Savage Holiday* (1954). He died after sixteen years of self-imposed exile in Paris, but he still remains an important force in American writing and has been hailed as "the most representative voice of America and of oppressed people anywhere in the world." Unfortunately for readers of the short story, his stories (which include *Eight Men*, 1961) lack the full force of his novels and his classic autobiography, *Black Boy* (1945).

Perhaps the three modern black writers in the short-story genre most requiring discussion are Ralph Ellison, James Baldwin, and LeRoi Jones.

Ralph Ellison (1914-   ) won the National Book Award in 1952 with the novel *Invisible Man*, later voted by *Book Week* experts the most significant

American novel of the years 1945 to 1965. His essays in *Shadow and Act* (1964), while not so important, have been collected, but not his excellent short stories, which include the much-anthologized "Battle Royal" (really an excerpt from *Invisible Man*), "A Coupla Scalped Indians," "Flying Home," and the "grimly negative" story called "King of the Bingo Game." Ellison chose the "path of individualism instead of racial unity" and was criticized by fellow blacks for "writing white instead of righting wrongs." His "Mister Toussan," however, was dismissed as "marred by the smudge of left-wing politics," and "Flying Home" was said to be politically incorrect because it stressed the powerlessness of the black. Ellison's best short fiction transcends political questions and belongs to the tradition of American literature, not to the polemics of any period.

James Baldwin (1924-   ) was born a few years after the publication of Fenton Johnson's *Tales of Darkest America* and three years before such black short-story writers as William Melvin Kelley (*Dancers on the Shore*, 1964) and Hoyt W. Fuller. He grew up in a more radical world than Ellison and has always had a love-hate relationship with the United States, far more so than most other black writers. As novelist, essayist, prophet, and poet he has undertaken to "vomit the anguish up," if not always sincerely or successfully. He is the author of *Go Tell It on the Mountain* (a milestone in black novels, 1953), *Giovanni's Room* (one of the earliest important homosexual novels, 1956), and many other works, including *Nobody Knows My Name* (1961), *Another Country* (1962), *The Fire Next Time* (1963), *Tell Me How Long the Train's Been Gone* (1968), *The Amen Corner* (1968), *Blues for Mister Charlie* (1964), and *Notes of a Native Son* (1955). The short stories in *Going to Meet the Man* (1965) deserve the sort of recognition that has greeted his essays such as "Stranger in the Village," and to some extent they carry the message of that essay: that the world is white no longer and never will be white again. It is for their manner even more than their message, however, that the stories will last.

Perhaps less significant as literature than as social protest are the stories (and the rest of the work) of LeRoi Jones (1934-   ), poet, secessionist, playwright (*Dutchman* and *The Slave*, 1964, *Slave Ship*, 1967, *Black Quartet*, 1970), theorist on black arts (*Blues People*, 1963, *Black Magic*, 1970), political and religious leader (as Amiri, sometimes Ameer, Baraka), and fiction writer (*The System of Dante's Hell*, 1965). Henry S. Resnik in *Saturday Review* greeted his *Tales* (1967) as heralding "one of the boldest and most vital of contemporary American authors," but these "racial nightmares" are more to be noted as activist than as aesthetic achievements.

The very titles of anthologies from the days of the blacks (*The Best Short Stories by Negro Writers*, edited by Langston Hughes, and *American Negro Short Stories*, edited by John Henrik Clarke, both in the mid-1960's) to those of the Afro-Americans (the *Black Voices* anthologies by Abraham Chapman in 1968 and *Black Literature in America*, 1971, by Houston A. Baker, Jr., and *Black American Literature*, 1971, by Ruth Miller, and beyond) indicate the movement of society and document the involvement (or lack of it) by writers of the short story. The same is true of other minorities, Jews (*Great Jewish Short Stories*, 1963, edited by Saul Bellow is one collection), Chicanos and Hispanics (both of whom await really good collections), Vietnam veterans (*Free Fire Zone*, 1973, collects some excellent work), workers (*On the Job*, 1977, edited by William O'Rourke is important), homosexuals (Seymour Kleinberg's *The Other Persuasion*, 1977, is but one collection of stories by and about homosexual men and women in what is now a burgeoning field), and so on. All reflect and to some extent fuel the consciousness-raising and emergence of vocal elements in our increasingly pluralistic American society, whether the writers come out of their ivory towers of literature into the streets of protest literature or not. Those who collect and examine the fiction of the 1970's and the 1980's and beyond will more likely deal in "yes" and "no" than in "what" and "wherefore" and increasingly will have to take minorities into consideration.

This might be as good a place as any to mention that the short story and tale have flourished in many regions of this vast country and that a number of anthologies can serve as a good introduction to regional fiction past and present. The South, for example, is represented in older collections such as Edwin Anderson Alderman and Joel Chandler Harris' fifteen-volume *Library of Southern Literature*, 1907, and in more recent ones such as Henning Cohen and William B. Dillingham's *Humor of the Old Southwest*, 1964. Southern humor, to name one sparkling specialty, is covered in studies such as those by Walter Blair, T. C. Halliburton, Arthur Palmer Hudson, Kenneth S. Lynn, Montrose J. Moses, Constance Rourke, and others. Some well-known writers (such as William Faulkner, Richard Wright, Flannery O'Connor, Ralph Ellison, and Eudora Welty) and some lesser-known ones of merit (such as Caroline Gordon, Peter Taylor, Ernest J. Gaines, George Garrett, Diane Oliver, and others) appear in Allen F. Stein and Thomas N. Walters' anthology *The Southern Experience in Literature* (1971), and this is just one collection chosen almost at random; there are many more. It is remarkable how many Southerners appear in the annual collections of best stories by Martha Foley (drawn from *Atlantic Monthly* and other mass-circulation magazines as well as from *Hudson Review*, *Kenyon Review*, and other "little magazines") and in the representative anthologies of modern American fiction produced for the college textbook market. Unfortunately, many of the most promising writers are known almost exclusively in these circles; many regional writers are more or less unappreciated and unknown in the very areas from which they come (or in which they still live) and of which they write. Unless and until these writers of short fiction move into more visible markets and publish novels or write screenplays or otherwise come to the attention of national audiences, they tend to reach only a specialized audience. Everywhere in the country, short stories are slighted in favor of what the public thinks of as "bigger and better" genres.

The American love of things large is accompanied by a fascination with things small, such as the self. The preoccupation with identity and the *Bildungsroman* of the intellectual (schooling, marriage, the writer's life) inform *Letting Go* (1962) by Philip Roth (1933-   ) and many of the stories in *Goodbye, Columbus* (1959) and his later work. The same satirical outlook that might be called "wry on the rocks" that one finds in *Portnoy's Complaint* (1969), *Our Gang* (1971), *My Life as a Man* (1974), and *The Professor of Desire* (1977) is also present in the work of other writers about the Jewish experience in America such as Leonard Q. Ross (creator of *H*Y*M*A*N K*A*P*L*A*N*) and those included in Saul Bellow's anthology, *Great Jewish Short Stories*, and other collections.

Many Jewish stories concern the search for identity of displaced or outside-the-mainstream people or the attempts of minorities to preserve their culture and values in a foreign environment. This is not solely a Jewish concern, however, as can be illustrated by the stories of *The American's Search for Identity*, a college reader of 1972 edited by James E. Brogan, or *The American Disinherited* (1970), edited by Abe C. Ravitz and including a number of stories of "Greenhorn and Bottom Dog," "Down and Out," and "Beat and Cool," by authors both famous and somewhat lesser known (among the latter are Clarence Darrow, Bruno Lessing, Ben Hecht, Albert Halper, John Fante, William Eastlake, John Figueroa, Alfredo Otero y Herrera, and LeRoi Jones). The early 1970's saw many of these texts prepared for classrooms in which students were seeking Relevance and an opportunity to discuss not so much the technique of the short story but the circumstances of their own lives. Myron Simon's *Ethnic Writers in America* (1972) was typical. In the 1980's the pendulum began to swing back to basics; yet since there are few things in America more basic than the social problems that such stories address, one can confidently expect more stories about the search for identity and religious and ethnic diversity to be written and read.

A luminous example of a Catholic writer in the Southern tradition is Flannery O'Connor (1925-1964). Born in Georgia, O'Connor adopted most of her material from her region. After a Master's degree in the creative writing program at Iowa, which has produced many American writers of distinction, she held two Kenyon Fellowships and, a decade out of college, won the O. Henry Award and a grant from the National Institute of Arts and Letters (both in 1957). She later won a number of other prizes and fellowships and yet was by no means the academics' darling: her stories gained her a wide and understanding public. What explains O'Connor's unparalleled success with her material is a dramatic power William Goyen characterizes as "percussive and stabbing" and a "brutal irony," what *Time* has called "slam-bang humor and a style of writing as balefully direct as a death sentence." Her characters are unforgettable, her points inescapable, and her genius, in the end, indefinable: she was simply one of the greatest modern short-story writers of this or any other country.

James Leo Herlihy (1927-   ) is one of many short-story writers whose excellent short fiction has gained them less attention than it deserves, and certainly less attention than their novels, plays, and films. The novel *All Fall Down* (1960) was greeted by Tennessee Williams as the work of "the most important new writer since [Carson] McCullers" and reached the large audience of the cinema in 1962. Herlihy's Broadway hit *Blue Denim* (1957, retitled *Blue Jeans*) became a motion picture in 1959, and his work has otherwise brought him to wide public attention, and yet the stories in *The Sleep of Baby Filbertson and Other Stories* (1959, containing short fiction which had previously appeared in *Partisan Review*, *Eve*, and *Discovery*) effectively summarize most of what he has to communicate.

In the same way that James Gould Cozzens (author of the Pulitzer Prize-winning novel *Guard of Honor*, 1948, and the dazzlingly successful best-seller *By Love Possessed*, 1957) displays in the stories of his *Children and Others* (1964) talents and insights often unmatched in his Book of the Month Club selections, so Herlihy sometimes shows in his stories that "edge of iron that Steinbeck lost and [William] Saroyan never had," as Nelson Algren put it, "a real indignation at humiliation of human spirit" that may have been somewhat blunted even in the notable film version of Herlihy's *Midnight Cowboy* (1965).

John Updike (1932-   ) was graduated from Harvard in 1954 and worked only very briefly for *The New Yorker* (1955-1957) before retiring from New York to Ipswich, Massachusetts, to be a full-time writer of charming children's stories (with Warren Chappell and alone), verse (including *Telephone Poles* of 1963 and *Tossing and Turning* of 1977), unimportant plays, and very important fiction. Best known for novels such as *The Poorhouse Fair* (1959), *Rabbit, Run* (1960) and *Rabbit Redux* (1971), *Couples* (1968), *Marry Me* (1976), and *The Coup* (1978), this sensitive and sophisticated writer is probably at his best in the short stories collected in such volumes as *Pigeon Feathers* (1962), *The Music School* (1966), *Museums and Women* (1972), and *Picked-up Pieces* (1975).

Like the frustrated teacher in *The Centaur* (1963), the modern descendant of Chiron the Centaur (who tried to teach ancient Greeks the wisdom of the priests and their oracles), Updike is a moralist much concerned with message, even if he is often to be identified with the protagonist of the more recent novel, *Marry Me*, who laments that one must contend with "the twilight of the old morality, and there's just enough to torment us, and not enough to hold us in." Joyce B. Markle in her study (1973) of the themes of Updike's novels identifies his people as *Fighters and Lovers*. It is from his characters, from an amalgam of detail and doubt, of a lively sense of the surface of life and a disturbing reflection on the fragility and yet specialness of life's sensitive survivors, that Updike's meticulous, highly crafted short fictions are made. They are written in a prose that *Saturday Review* rightly called "beautiful and fresh, and the tone is that of reason, with a wry sense of humor and a head-shaking sense of wonder. . . ."

Donald Barthelme (1931-   ) was born in Philadelphia and reared in Texas. While working as a journalist he began writing "fragmentary fantasies" for *The New Yorker*, and his pieces were collected in books whose titles suggest Barthelme's humor and concerns: *Come Back, Dr. Caligari* (1964), *Unspeakable Practices, Unnatural Acts* (1968), and *City Life* (1970). Humor is but one aspect of Barthelme's language play, a brilliant manipulation of "found objects" of language (cliché, jargon, and the rest) and original ideas. "Fragments are the only forms I trust," he states. The mosaic, like much other modern art, has often baffled the uninitiated and brought Barthelme a reputation for difficulty that keeps many who could enjoy the shimmering surfaces of his work and recognize, at least, bright shards of pop culture, from giving him the attention he deserves.

Fiction such as the stories in *Sadness* (1972) and the novel *The Dead Father* (1975) make, as Jonathan Baumbach has written, order out of arbitrary selection, unity out of fragments, and "wit out of banality." It is perhaps best approached with Baumbach's caveats:

> Don't look for symbols or meanings. Expect nothing but what you get. Don't worry about understanding everything. Or anything. Don't try to translate into other language. These stories resist paraphrase. They are exactly what they seem.

One can understand how the average reader and the traditional critic might rebel against, respectively, so much freedom and so much limitation; but for the brave and the open-minded, Barthelme's stories offer many rewards. The reader may find real entertainment, and the critic may for a while stop worrying about the points being scored and watch the game not with dogmatism but with delectation.

There are short-story authors writing now, of course, who were born after the mid-1930's, and it would be evasive to conclude this survey of recent American short fiction without making room for at least a paragraph on those among them whose performances in the short-story mode make them artists to watch. These include Walter Abish, whose cleverness in *Alphabetical Africa* (1974) has been echoed in the story-story collections published by New Directions; Jonathan Baumbach and the others in Fiction Collective; Thomas C. Boyle of *Iowa Review*; Russell Edson, who has published a half dozen striking collections of prose poetry which could be classed with short stories; and Barry Hannah, whose recent novel *Ray* includes brief scenes which will undoubtedly draw new attention to his stories in *Airships* (1979). In addition, there is Tim O'Brian and others who will be assuming the places in anthologies vacated by Wilbur Daniel Steele, Robert M. Coates, Nancy Hale, James Agee, Shirley Jackson, Tillie Olsen, and other noted writers of the past; Jayne Ann Phillips (*Black Tickets*, 1979), Alice Walker, and other black women writers; Roger Skillings, whom critic Lou Asekoff has labeled "Protestant fatalist"; Richard Stern delivering thoughtful "packages"; and Joy Williams and William S. Wilson, III, who publish in *Partisan Review* and *Paris Review* and similar prestigious magazines that are breathing new life into a whole school of short fiction.

As for new directions in short fiction, Donald Hall's rubrics for "Contemporary Fiction" in *To Read Literature* (1981) indicate where "the action" is chiefly going to be: fantasy and absurdity (he includes Max Apple's "The Oranging of America"), the comic story (he includes Woody Allen's "The Whore of Mensa"), and science fiction (he includes Stanislaw Lem's "How Erg the Self-Inducting Slew a Paleface." Computer and other sciences will play an increasingly important part in the increasingly elitist business of writing for readers (as opposed to consumers of images), and escapism and amusement are going to grow ever more common (in uncommon forms) as the short story and all writing (except writing for the movies and television) takes, like the hero of Robert Musil's *The Man Without Qualities* (1953), "a permanent vacation from ordinary institutionalized life." With any luck, short fiction, freed from historic responsibilities as other forms of communications take over, will become irresponsible and undisciplined and encourage genius more than talent. Now fantasy, comedy, and science fiction, along with less imaginative and corrective and prophetic kinds of writing, may be freed to emerge wilder and wiser than before.

Edward J. O'Brien (whose annual collections of *Best Stories* from 1915 to 1940 presented a number of new writers of importance, and not only those who attained popular acclaim in *Saturday Evening Post* and similar markets) wrote of *The Advance of the American Short Story* (1923) but also decried the genre as catering to the American taste for immediate results. It certainly cannot be argued that writers who choose the short-story form are trying to take the easy way to art or to an audience; the modern novel demands far less technique per thousand dollars earned and commands more attention from reviewers and more loyalty from readers. There are scholarly reviews of the short story (such as *Studies in Short Fiction*) but academics are much more impressed by longer essays on longer fiction than insightful brief analyses of short stories.

When Americans say they "read a lot," they generally mean nonfiction (which has a certain "legitimacy" because it deals with facts) or long novels (some of which most recently are barely disguised fact or deliberate "nonfiction novels" or treatments in which fact and fiction are mixed). The American short story gains its practitioners even less attention than is garnered by poets (many of whom are not read at all, or are admired for their unreadability), and every year seems to see a shrinking market for brief fiction for the page (as opposed to episodes for the television screen). *Saturday Evening Post*, *Collier's*, and other mass markets are gone and the "little magazine" markets are comparatively small, while excellent new stories do tend to get lost among the other features of magazines such as *Esquire* and *Playboy*.

Some years it seems that there are more novels published than short stories. Sometimes it seems that (as Jorge Luis Borges predicted in a story) "English, French, and mere Spanish will disappear from this planet," but although literature may be threatened by film and video-disc and other modern marvels, the short story will survive. Whatever happens to the modern world and its technological triumphs, tales will always be told, if not written down and published. The short story is as old as the first yarns told around the campfire and as basic to humankind as fire itself.

Leonard R. N. Ashley

AMERICAN FANTASY SHORT FICTION

The relationship between fantasy writing and short fiction is an intricate one, and the development of modern fantasy writing could not have been achieved without the genre of short fiction to create in. As the Greek myth concerning the great God of Nature, Pan, was replaced by the development of the Roman myth concerning Bacchus, so in turn both were incorporated, redefined, and developed into the Christian concept of Satan during the Middle Ages; one implication led to another until only a thin but traceable line between the three remained. So it has been with fantasy writing, and short fiction as well, as something simple and straightforward in approach evolves into something complex and not so straightforward. Or, in a much broader sense, what were once humankind's gods become in turn the most complex demons imaginable. As society becomes more complex, its writings become more complex and more fantastical; so do its perversions and joys.

As a creative genre, American fantasy short fiction came into its own internationally by way of the imaginative writings of Edgar Allan Poe, Lafcadio Hearn, and H. P. Lovecraft, and reached the complex level we have today in the writings of Clark Ashton Smith, Ray Bradbury, Robert Bloch, and Fritz Leiber, Jr.—to mention but a few outstanding American authors who have taken short fiction to a higher, more imaginative level of development.

Many critics have said that short fiction would not have developed without the innovations of fantasy, and many other critics have said that fantasy writing would not have developed without the advance and acceptance of short fiction written by such American masters as Poe, Nathaniel Hawthorne, Ernest Hemingway, William Faulkner, Flannery O'Connor, and Paul Bowles. Such an argument, however, is irrelevant, since both fantasy writing and short fiction developed side by side and prospered because there was a demand and need for them in a hurried, technological world where there is little time to enjoy reading.

Fantasy short fiction has a definite escapist appeal, for it can lift the reader out of an ordinary existence and transport him to a strange world that offers various levels of interpretation; it has many facets, most of them subtle and hidden. Fantasy writing can take an ordinary situation and make it strange, or with equal ease, it can take a highly strange situation and make it appear normal and ordinary. It can be humorous, childish, whimsical, wry, satirical, psychologically insightful, horrifying, mysterious, or terrifying.

In our time, there has been a tremendous growth in fantasy short fiction, and, as our life-styles become more traumatic and complex, so will our need for the kind of relief and solace found in fantasy. There is only a thin line between short fiction and fantasy short fiction, and often the line cannot be seen at all; one can read the story as straightforward fiction or as fantasy depending on one's approach. What distinguishes fantasy short fiction from short fiction is its approach and its use of imaginative words that change the reality of the situation for the reader. A writer can change a reflective image in the reader's mind by these two methods, taking the reader out of the ordinary into the extraordinary. In addition to imaginative word-handling and approach, the two keys that distinguish fantasy writing from other writing, there is a final ingredient that ties the two together and makes fantasy such a unique, magical genre: emphasis on the strange.

It would be impossible to list all of the many gifted American authors writing fantasy short fiction today, but there are some who can be mentioned briefly, and through them we can see, understand, and appreciate the fascination for fantasy writing.

Fredric Brown (1906-1972) wrote hundreds of short-fantasy pieces during his lifetime, among them such classics as "Nasty," "Abominable," and "Paradox Lost." In the story "Nasty," one is confronted with an ordinary situation of an aging but powerful man seeking to regain his youth and sexual vigor. He prays to the Devil, who appears, listens to him, and decides to grant the wish. The Devil is not nicknamed "Nasty" for nothing, however; he grants the wish in the form of swimming trunks which the man must wear. The man slips into the swim trunks and becomes young, handsome, and virile once again; he goes to the pool, selects the most beautiful woman available, and retires to his penthouse bedroom for the night. The story concludes with the distraught man sitting on his bed beside a sleeping, naked woman; he is crying. He realizes that to remove his unusual swim trunks would be to revert once again to what he originally was.

In "Abominable" a man pursues a beautiful actress lost in the Himalayas. He is captured by creatures known as the yeti, also called abominable snowmen. By a simple method of transference, he is changed into one of them, never again to return to the world of beautiful human women. He becomes a mate for a very hairy yeti. Life for him has suddenly become abominable. In the complex "Paradox Lost," a young man named Shorty McCabe meets himself going, coming, and progressing down a time continuum without fully realizing the irony of having been present. Such stories as these have secured for Fredric Brown a special place in the genre of fantasy short short fiction. Some of his creations are less than a page in length, and each one carries a searing, biting point. During his lifetime he wrote twenty-eight novels, numerous television scripts, and more than seven hundred short stories.

Ray Bradbury (1920-   ) is a master of fantasy whose work often contains subtle psychological meanings, as seen in "The Veldt," and "A Medicine for Melancholy." "Small Assassin" tells the story of a young mother who almost dies in childbirth, and who fears that her baby is something other than what it appears to be. By the end of the story, the baby has successfully eliminated its parents. The Doctor alone, having realized the truth, stands at the foot of the stairs and faces the decision of destroying this creature; but the question remains: does he, too, fall victim to the small assassin?

The haunting theme of loneliness is explored in "The Fog Horn," a story involving two men on a lonely outpost that warns ships offshore to be wary of the rocks. A prehistoric beast from the ocean depths is awakened by the mournful sound of the foghorn, and believing it to be its lost mate, seeks it out. The beast seeks love and solace, only to be cheated; it destroys the foghorn and returns alone to die in the dark depths. There is a touch of melancholy and sadness to Bradbury's fantasy; it is very tangible and real.

Many writers have attempted interpretations of Lewis Carroll's *Alice's Adventures in Wonderland* (1865), but few have approached the work as uniquely as Henry Kuttner (1914-1958) does in "Mimsy Were the Borogoves." Two children discover the key to Carroll's book, finding it a complex set of magical formulae and mathematics that only the imagination of a child can comprehend. To understand them, one must believe and accept innocently and without question. The story ends as the two children perform the ritual to the bafflement of adults and disappear into the happy, mystical land of Alice.

Writing in the vein of psychological fantasy, Fritz Leiber, Jr. (1910-   ) explores the technological horrors that await mankind in such classics as "The Hound" and "Smoke Ghost." In the same vein are David H. Keller's (1880-1966) "The Worm" and the terrifying tale "The Thing in the Cellar." In the story, a young boy is afraid to go down into the cellar of his home. The parents know there is nothing down there, and so does the reader, for the writer has given us every detail of what lies below: nothing, absolutely nothing. Yet the boy's terror is genuine. The boy is finally forced into the cellar for a brief time to erase his fears. Later, when the parents open the cellar door to let him out, they discover a horribly mutilated thing—a thing that was once young their son, now dead and disfigured almost beyond recognition.

For sheer terror in fantasy, there is little to surpass Frank Belknap Long's "A Visitor from Egypt" and "The Hounds of Tinaldos." In "The Hounds of Tinaldos," a man discovers that the only way to prevent the entry of invisible demons into his world is to live in a perfectly round room without angles; he discovers too late that one corner is not circular, and the demons gain entry and shred him alive. "A Visitor from Egypt" is about a reincarnated Egyptian god in human form who seeks to destroy a priceless find in a museum and succeeds. Long also has a keen sense of humor, as evidenced in his fine tale, "Fisherman's Luck," an involved piece about a fisherman who unknowingly goes fishing with Apollo's Staff and catches many strange things from the River of Time.

Robert Bloch (1917-   ) presents us with a quaint tale called "Sweets to the Sweet" about a little girl detested by her father, who often beats her and calls her a mean, nasty little witch. The girl is lonely and has only her dolls and books for company. The father falls ill, and his brother comes to help him. There have been growing rumors concerning the powers of this unusual little girl. The brother sees she is cuddling a doll, and to his horror finds that it is formed in the image of the girl's father. He questions the girl; she replies it is only a candy doll, a sweet to eat. She squeezes the doll; immediately, her father screams from the bedroom. The brother realizes what the doll is and attempts to grab it; the little girl avoids him with ease, smiles from a safe distance, then bites off the head of the doll and eats it. There is a bloodcurdling, strangled scream from the father and then silence: a simple case of sweets for the sweet. Bloch has written so many brilliant fantasy stories that it would be difficult to say which is his best; among the finest are "The Eyes of the Mummy," "The Secret of Sebek," "The Seal of the Satyr," "Yours Truly, Jack the Ripper," "The Learning Maze," "Beetles," "The Movie People," "The Hell Bound Train," "The Man Who Collected Poe," and "Catnip."

Fantasy short fiction also shows the influence of classical myths. This trait is particularly true of some of the stories of Paul Bowles (1910-   ), Clark Ashton Smith (1893-1961), and Harry Brewster. Harry Brewster concentrates on the motif of the Greek myths in such stories as "Saint Philomean," "Sappho's Leap," "The Aesthete and the Sibyl," and the enchanting story called "Where the Trout Sing." Paul Bowles employs myths, and often creates his own in such unusual pieces as "The Scorpion," "Allal," and "The Circular Valley." One of the most important American fantasy writers is Clark Ashton Smith, and it would require a book to discuss not only his influence on fantasy short fiction but also his techniques. An artist as well as a writer, Smith was almost wholly self-educated. Among his many books, the following are collections of fantasy short fiction with which every reader wishing to appreciate the scope of fantasy writing should be familiar: *Out of Space and Time* (1942), *The Abominations of Yondo* (1960), *Lost Worlds* (1944), *The Black Abbot of Puthuun* (1948), and *Genius Loci, and Other Tales* (1948).

These are but a few of the important fantasy short-fiction writers; there are many, many more. The effect of fantasy short fiction on American literature continues to grow and to be felt. As we continue to become more complex creatures, our fiction will become more complex, and so will our fantasies. Fantasy short fiction provides an escape route for the reader into the magical world of the extraordinary—a place where the imagination can transcend all boundaries.

H. L. Prosser

AMERICAN INDIAN SHORT FICTION

For those Americans whose literary sensibilities were formed during the 1930's when Hal Borland wrote "Beaver" and "A Mule from Californy," or during the 1940's when Dorothy Johnson, a Montana college professor, wrote "Flame on the Frontier" and "A Man Called Horse" (the latter becoming the basis for an enormously popular and controversial motion picture starring Richard Harris), or for those Americans who read stories during the 1950's when Ernest Hemingway wrote "Indian Camp" and "The Indians Moved Away," it perhaps seems odd to think of the American Indian short story as a piece of fiction written *by* an Indian, not *about* Indians. Admittedly, it takes a vast change of perspective on the part of American readers to turn their attentions away from those wondrous storytellers of the past, those "image makers" who told stories about Indians, the inheritors of James Fenimore Cooper, Bret Harte, and Zane Gray, to mention only a few precursors. Indeed, the new perspective which encompasses the body of short stories written *by* Indians, those of the new breed of storytellers, themselves the inheritors of long-standing traditions in oral literatures and languages, is one which has come into significance only recently. It is important, then, to attempt to give form and structure to this new tradition which has roots in the archaic past but came to fruition only in this century.

The stories which first appeared in this century are rather easy for re-searchers to trace. Although barely perceptible when viewed in the broader context of the development of the short story as a genre—that is, the tradition of Herman Melville and Edgar Allan Poe—the publishing of the Indian short story was begun by such stalwarts as *Harper's Monthly*, *The Ladies' Home Journal*, *Sunset*, and *Craftsman*, all pioneers in the magazine publishing world. It was in the pages of these magazines that the initial discovery of the American Indian writer of the short story was noted.

It can be said, perhaps, that such magazines as these discovered the works of a Santee Sioux (Dakota) named Charles A. Eastman and made them accessible to the American public, some of them published under his Indian name, Ohiyesa. In 1904, coincidentally the same year that Teddy Roosevelt opened up thousands of acres of Indian Reservation land to white settlement, *Harper's Monthly* published Eastman's "The Gray Chieftain" and *The Ladies' Home Journal* published "War Maiden of the Sioux." Some time later, *Sunset* published "The Singing Spirit," and in 1912, *Craftsman* published "The Song of the Birch Canoe," all of them stories which interested the American public because they investigated the cultural experiences of the full-blooded Sioux, Eastman, and his people. Eastman was to become the first American Indian physician, another achievement which indicated his outstanding capabilities; and, although he did not continue to become the William Carlos Williams of the Indian world, his achievement as a writer was, perhaps, no less remarkable.

About the same time that these small magazines were publishing Eastman's work, other fictional work written by American Indians began to appear in the form of collections and novels: a Dakota woman named Zitkala-Sä published *Old Indian Tales* (1901), and Hum-ishu-ma (Mourning Dove), a woman of the northwest Okanagan tribe, wrote a novel called *The Half Blood* (1933), thus helping to popularize the theme of the conflict of Indian-White loyalties. After that, several ethnographic biographies, studies of Indian personages by white scholars, appeared. Subsequently, scholarly research into the oral storytelling tradition of the tribes became an activity which non-Indians pursued with great vigor, and some research of significant quality was done by Indians themselves. One of the scholarly works by an Indian deserves mention; namely, *Dakota Texts* (1932), done by the Dakota woman scholar Ella Deloria, who became renowned for her remarkable translations and generic classifications of Dakota storytelling tradition. In addition, Deloria published a personal account called *Speaking Of Indians* (1944), which is a rare work done by an Indian scholar of the 1930's.

While much of what was published in popular magazines during the early years of the century seemed to emphasize a realistic approach to native life and experience, it also reflected an interest and an effort on the part of publishers to contribute to the public understanding about the ordinarily isolated groups of Americans called Indians who were set apart on Indian Reservations as early as the mid-1800's. Although it is not the object of short-story readers and researchers to either condone or condemn the process of isolation of Indian populations—and there are many who suggest that it is this isolation which ultimately preserved Indian culture and life and today accounts for its survival—it is the exploration of this condition which is pervasively evident in contemporary Indian writing and which is, inadvertently, commented upon by the Irish short-story writer Frank O'Connor in his perceptive volume *The Lonely Voice* (1963). O'Connor says:

> I am strongly suggesting that we can see in the short story an attitude of mind that is attracted by submerged population groups, whatever these may be at any given time . . . tramps, artists, lonely idealists, politicians, and spoiled priests.

O'Connor might have included, of course, the various ethnic and racial groups which have been in America a part of those submerged populations. Such a theory, interestingly enough, might account for the beginnings of the Indian short story at the turn of the century, and it quite probably accounts for the current excitement in the development of the contemporary Indian short story as witnessed through various collections such as *The Man to Send Rain Clouds* (1974), edited by Kenneth Rosen; *The Remembered Earth* (1979), edited by Geary Hobson; *American Indian Literature* (1979), edited by Alan R. Velie; and *The Third Woman* (1980), edited by Dexter Fisher.

As we look back at those early Indian writers of the 1900's, we see them quite literally translating, recording, and presenting marvelous tableaux which required little of the kind of creativity that is expected of the genre today. That is not to say that creativity is not necessary to translation, nor is it to suggest that this early work should be dismissed as unimportant. Quite the contrary, the early writers and their works provide a "literary" tradition for those scholars and readers who assume that literacy and a written syllabary are the basis for tradition. In addition, these early works suggest a continuity which is invaluable to the understanding of storytelling as a process rather than an end.

The stages of that process, while not easily traced, seem to suggest the growth of English language acquisition on the part of American Indian creators of literature, and it is in this capacity that the early American short-story writer such as Eastman stands out as a significant figure. He has made particular experience accessible in a new and different language and has paved the way for contemporary writers such as Leslie Silko, Simon Ortiz, Gray Cohoe, and others to utilize the creative force of ancient belief, ritual, myth, and experience in ways which are peculiar to the short story as it has become more identifiable as a genre. Even though these writers are utilizing the English language as the medium of communication rather than the native languages which traditionally possess myth and experience, they are, to the perceptive reader of their stories, writing about what may be called an "Indian past" in a particularly intimate way.

To suggest that this transition and process was accomplished with ease is probably to distort the truth, for there is a long drought between Eastman's work and the work of Simon Ortiz and those writers of the late 1960's who began to publish in small literary magazines such as *South Dakota Review* and *Sun Tracks*. Further evidence of the difficulty involved is described by the Sioux writer Vine Deloria, Jr., in the Preface of *Wa-Kon-Tah* (1974), a collection of poetry edited by Dodge and McCullough:

> Indian poetry, like Indian art, has struggled to emerge from the stereotypes imposed on it by non-Indians who wished to see the simple and childish recitations and drawings of a creature not yet civilized but containing that possibility.

This statement can be made just as emphatically about the Indian short story. For the Indian storyteller, if he is thought of at all, is ordinarily believed to be aged, wrinkled, and extinct. He is pictured sitting at the campfire in the evening, speaking in cryptic tones of esoteric or simple things, depending upon one's bias, and using what is thought of as archaic, savage, unstudied speech. He produces legends, it is believed, folklore, chants, and rituals, a kind of subliterature which has not taken a prominent place in the study of literature.

James Michener, in *Centennial* (1975), probably echoed the thoughts of most Americans concerning these traditional storytellers:

> Since no tribe could be at war constantly or hunt bison when there were no bison, and since there were no books, nor alphabet to print them in if there were, and since no one from Our People could converse with anyone from another tribe, and since there was no need of constant council meetings, Lame Beaver had days and weeks on end of idle time, with no great thoughts to occupy him and no one to share them with had they mysteriously arisen. He led a bleak, impoverished intellectual life, the highlight coming when younger warriors crowded into his tipi to hear him tell of his adventures of the past.

Surely, this vision is a far cry from the sophisticated, accomplished Indian writer of today. Yet it is from this perspective, however distorted, real, illusionary, or stereotypic it may be, that American readers must view the contemporary Indian short-story writer. Also, it may be that it benefits no one to insist that such precursors as Michener's Lame Beaver be taken seriously. In any case, the works which are included in the accompanying bibliography are materials of importance and are, very likely, informed through the process of Indian storytelling, surely an ancient and compelling tradition in Native American life and culture. More significantly, it is through the belief systems and collections of mythological and historical knowledge of the storytellers of the past, repositories of history, that contemporary writers are profoundly influenced.

The best of them, such as Leslie Silko, Acoma Pueblo, whose work began appearing in little magazines in the past decade, create the sense of environmental aesthetic particularly significant in Indian thought, in such pieces as "Storyteller," a comment upon the influence of the ancient precursors. In like manner, "Tony's Story," by the same author, seems to be created out of the sure knowledge and racial memory that a separate level of existence, whatever it is that is beyond the condition of the "other worldly" soul and the earthly body, matters. This idea, it seems to the discerning reader and to one who has read Alfonso Ortiz's *The Tewa World* (1969), is particularly appropriate to and characteristic of the Pueblo peoples.

A further example of this kind of influence is provided through the study of two recent short stories, "The Killing of a State Cop," by Simon Ortiz, Acoma Pueblo, and "Tony's Story," by Silko. These two stories fictionalize an actual historical event, and from the perspective of twenty years and from the perspective of Pueblo consciousness, they imagine the significance of the 1952 killing of a New Mexican state patrolman by two Acoma Pueblo brothers, Willie and Gabriel Felipe. The compelling themes of these two stories deal with the matter of evil as it exists in the Pueblo world, and the stories themselves function as communication tools which can bridge the gap between the isolated and submerged Pueblo thought concerning evil, and the broader American community's notion of evil. They assist others in accepting this Pueblo concept on its own merits. Although there is little criticism concerning these kinds of literary pieces, Lawrence J. Evers presented a scholarly paper in 1976 on the substantive historical imperatives included in these stories. The title of his unpublished paper is "The Killing of a New Mexican State Trooper: Ways of Telling a Historical Event," and it begins with a quotation from "The Man Made of Words" essay by the Kiowa novelist N. Scott Momaday:

> Do you see what happens when the imagination is superimposed upon the historical event? It becomes a story. The whole piece becomes more deeply invested with meaning.

These stories by contemporary Indian writers, then, draw upon religious and philosophic ideas which are, perhaps, the least understood and most misrepresented in America's pluralistic society. Because of this, and because the storyteller is able to "make others accept his version of things," as Saul Bellow tells us in the Introduction to *Great Jewish Short Stories* (1963), the contributions of Indian short-story writers are enormously important contributions to setting the record straight.

Bibliography of American Indian short fiction

Ballard, Charles L. (Oto). "Protection for Rosalie," in *Sun Tracks*. II, No. 2 (Spring, 1976), pp. 4-6.

Bates, Russell (Kiowa). "Rite of Encounter," in *The Remembered Earth*.

Burson, Fred (Ute). "Why Not? It's New Years!," in *Arrows Four: Prose and Poetry by Young American Indians*.

Campbell, Janet (Coeur d'Alene). "The Snow Keeps Falling," in *The Third Woman*.

Cohoe, Gray (Navajo). "Grandfather Tells the Cat Story," in *South Dakota Review*. VII, No. 2 (Summer, 1970), pp. 44-48.

_____ . "Great Spirit Protect Us," in *South Dakota Review*. IX, No. 2 (Summer, 1971), pp. 163-167.

_____ . "The Promised Visit," in *South Dakota Review*. VII, No. 2 (Summer, 1969), pp. 45-56.

Conley, Robert J. (Cherokee). "A Lone Oak in Kansas," in *Indian Voice*. II, No. 2 (March/April, 1972), pp. 30-31.

_____ . "The Night George Wolfe Died," in *Indian Voice*. II, No. 3 (May/June, 1972), p. 9.

Defender, Adelina (Sioux). "No Time for Tears," in *An American Indian Anthology*.

Downing, Linda (Cherokee). "Day of Confusion," in *Arrows Four: Prose and Poetry by Young American Indians*.

Eastman, Charles A. (Santee Sioux). "The Chief Soldier," in *Old Indian Days*.

───────── . "The Gray Chieftain," in *Harper's Monthly*. CVIII (May, 1904), pp. 882-887.

───────── . "She-Who-Has-A-Soul," in *Old Indian Days*.

───────── . "The Singing Spirit," in *Sunset*. XX (December, 1907), pp. 112-121.

───────── . "The Song of the Birch Canoe," in *Craftsman*. XXIII, No. 1 (October, 1912), pp. 3-11.

───────── . "War Maiden of the Sioux," in *The Ladies' Home Journal*. XXIII, No. 9 (August, 1904), p. 14.

Frederick, Judge White Bear (Hopi). "How BIA and Indian Joe Got to Heaven," in *Wassaja*. IV, No. 9 (September, 1976), pp. 6, 20.

Gerard, Mary Ann (Blackfeet). "It's My Rock," in *Arrows Four: Prose and Poetry by Young American Indians*.

Gorman, R. C. (Navajo). "Nowhere to Go," in *The Man to Send Rain Clouds: Contemporary Stories by American Indians*.

Green, Richard G. (Oneida). "Bronze My Skin, Dark My Eyes," in *Indian Voice*. (May, 1973) pp. 18-20, 30-31.

───────── . "The Coming," in *Indian Voice*. (April, 1973) pp. 26-29.

───────── . "Private Strangers," in *Indian Voice*. (April, 1973) pp. 34-35, 46-47.

───────── . "Sometimes a Lonely Business," in *Indian Voice*. I, No. 10 (December/January, 1971-1972), pp. 16, 26-27.

Hart, Hazel (Chippewa). "Ge Chi Maung Won," in *Arrows Four: Prose and Poetry by Young American Indians*.

Kelenaka-Henuok-Makhewe. "The Sick Child," in *Harper's Monthly*. XCVIII (February, 1899), pp. 446-448.

LaPointe, Frank (Sioux). "Millie's Gift," in *An American Indian Anthology*.

Lewis, Edward (Pima). "A Cowboy's Last Ride," in *Arrows Four: Prose and Poetry by Young American Indians*.

Link, Virgil Curtis (Apache/Navajo). "Remember Yesterday," in *Sun Tracks*. I, No. 2 (Fall, 1971), pp. 7-15.

───────── . "The Turquoise Beads," in *South Dakota Review*. VII, No. 2 (Summer, 1969), pp. 126-129.

Little, Joseph (Mescalero Apache). "Whispers from a Dead World," in *The Man to Send Rain Clouds: Contemporary Stories by American Indians*.

Lucero, Margaret (Santa Domingo Pueblo). "A Necklace for Jason," in *Arrows Four: Prose and Poetry by Young American Indians*.

Cook-Lynn, Elizabeth (Sioux). "A Child's Story," in *Pembroke Magazine*. VII (Bicentennial Issue, 1976), pp. 225-226.

───────── . "Three," in *Prairie Schooner*.

───────── . "LaDeaux," in *The Remembered Earth*.

_____ . "The Last Remarkable Man," in *Then Badger Said This*.

Mendoza, Durango (Creek). "Summer Water and Shirley," in *American Indian Authors*.

Momaday, N. Scott (Kiowa/Cherokee). "The Bear and the Colt," in *American Indian Authors*.

Montana, David (Papago). "Day Dawns on an Old Night," in *An American Indian Anthology*.

Ortiz, Simon J. (Acoma Pueblo). "The End of Old Horse," in *The Man to Send Rain Clouds: Contemporary Stories by American Indians*.

_____ . "Howbah Indians," in *Howbah Indians*.

_____ . "Kaiser and the War," in *The Man to Send Rain Clouds: Contemporary Stories by American Indians*.

_____ . "The Killing of a State Cop," in *The Man to Send Rain Clouds: Contemporary Stories by American Indians*.

_____ . "Men on the Moon," in *Howbah Indians*.

_____ . "The San Francisco Indians," in *The Man to Send Rain Clouds: Contemporary Stories by American Indians*.

_____ . "Something's Going On," in *Howbah Indians*.

_____ . "A Story of Rios and Juan Jesus," in *The Man to Send Rain Clouds: Contemporary Stories by American Indians*.

_____ . "Woman Singing," in *South Dakota Review*. VII, No. 2 (Summer, 1969), pp. 33-44.

Perea, Robert L. (Oglalla Sioux). "Dragon Mountain," in *The Remembered Earth*.

Platero, Juanita (Navajo) and Siyowin Miller. "Chee's Daughter," in *Literature of the American Indian*.

Popkes, Opal Lee (Choctaw). "Zuma Chow's Cave," in *The Man to Send Rain Clouds: Contemporary Stories by American Indians*.

Shoemake, Ben (Shawnee/Quapaw/Osage/Cherokee). "Dear Friends," in *An American Indian Anthology*.

Silko, Leslie (Laguna Pueblo). "Bravura," in *The Man to Send Rain Clouds: Contemporary Stories by American Indians*.

_____ . "Gallup, New Mexico—Indian Capital of the World," in *The Third Woman*.

_____ . "A Geronimo Story," in *The Man to Send Rain Clouds: Contemporary Stories by American Indians*.

_____ . "Lullaby," in *Best Short Stories of 1975*.

_____ . "The Man to Send Rain Clouds," in *The Man to Send Rain Clouds: Contemporary Stories by American Indians*.

_____ . "Storyteller," in *The Man to Send Rain Clouds: Contemporary Stories by American Indians*.

_____ . "Tony's Story," in *The Man to Send Rain Clouds: Contemporary Stories by American Indians*.

——————— . "Uncle Tony's Goat," in *The Man to Send Rain Clouds: Contemporary Stories by American Indians.*

——————— . "Yellow Woman," in *The Man to Send Rain Clouds: Contemporary Stories by American Indians.*

Sullivan, Elizabeth (Creek). "Legend of the Trail of Tears," in *Indian Legends of the Trail of Tears and Other Stories.*

Tapahanso, Luci (Navajo). "The Snakeman," in *Sun Tracks.* IV (1978), pp. 11-12.

Track, Soge (Sioux/Taos Pueblo). "The Clearing in the Valley," in *The American Indian Reader: Literature.*

Williams, Ted C. (Iroquois). "Bedbug," in *The Reservation.*

——————— . "Cassandra," in *The Reservation.*

——————— . "The Cucumber Tree," in *The Reservation.*

——————— . "Father," in *The Reservation.*

——————— . "The Feast," in *The Reservation.*

——————— . "Hogard," in *The Reservation.*

——————— . "The House That Song Built," in *The Reservation.*

——————— . "Many Lips and Lala La," in *The Reservation.*

——————— . "Mrs. Shoe's Gang," in *The Reservation.*

——————— . "Old Claudie and Bullet," in *The Reservation.*

——————— . "The Picnic Snake," in *The Reservation.*

——————— . "The Reservoir," in *The Reservation.*

——————— . "The Sultan," in *The Reservation.*

——————— . "The Tellers," in *The Reservation.*

——————— . "Thraangkie and You-swee(t)-dad," in *The Reservation.*

——————— . "The Trailers," in *The Reservation.*

——————— . "When I Was Little," in *The Reservation.*

Zitkala-Sä (Sioux). "The Soft Hearted Sioux," in *Harper's Monthly.* CII (March, 1901), pp. 505-508.

——————— . "The Tribal Path," in *Harper's Monthly.* CIII (October, 1901), pp. 741-744.

Elizabeth Cook-Lynn

BLACK SHORT FICTION

Black literature in America developed in the same generic order as white literature, beginning with didactic poetry and utilitarian prose (autobiographies such as slave narratives and diaries, sermons, and political prose) and followed by lyric poetry and fiction; successful drama developed last. Before the development of written fiction by black Americans, however, there was a strong oral fictive tradition, the most important stories being animal tales narrating the triumph of a weak but wily animal, usually a rabbit, over a strong, slower-thinking adversary, usually a fox. Although the folk tales had other ends—explanatory myths, for example—most common is this parable of eventual black success. Although claims can be made for the existence of the written black short story as early as the 1850's, when William Wells Brown's *Clotel*, the first novel by a black American, was published, it was not until the 1880's and the fiction of Charles Waddell Chesnutt (1858-1932) that black short fiction flourished.

Besides his talent, Chesnutt had two initial advantages: the friendly aid of William Dean Howells, who, in 1887, helped Chesnutt get his stories placed in the *Atlantic Monthly*, the first time that a black author had had access to a major national publication; and the 1880 appearance of Joel Chandler Harris' Uncle Remus stories. Although Harris' portrayal of Uncle Remus himself is patronizing and furthers the stereotyped view of blacks, the tales themselves are reported accurately. If Harris may himself have been unaware of the subversive nature of the stories' morals and the discrepancy between Remus' personality and his message, Chesnutt plainly was not, and with his greater artistry managed to use this now available tradition for the purpose for which the tales had originated.

Chesnutt's work is, at first glance, curiously divided between his conjure tales in the folk tradition and his highly polished tales of middle-class blacks. Indeed, black short fiction itself seems split between those authors who make full, conscious, comfortable use of the folk tradition—authors such as Langston Hughes, Zora Neale Hurston, and Ishmael Reed—and those who fit more easily into the mainstream of predominately white American literature. Yet just as careful examination of the fiction of, say, Ralph Ellison or James Baldwin, who would fall into the latter category, reveals an understanding and use of folk material, so too Chesnutt's conjure tales and his apparently more sophisticated tales have the same technical strengths and sharpness of tone.

The first collection of black short fiction in America is Chesnutt's *The Conjure Woman* (1899). In these seven tales, Uncle Julius, an old black man, narrates to two Northern whites stories of a conjure woman; each tale has a moral, which may or may not be made explicit, and each makes obvious comments about white-black relations and about human nature in general.

The white audience views the stories as entertainment, and the reader is left to surmise what morals they take away. Yet although, like Uncle Remus, Julius is wise and kind, he is, unlike Remus, manipulative, and the tales have also specific purposes that Uncle Julius wants accomplished. Thus, rather than discrepancy between tale and teller, there is a unity established by Chesnutt.

Chesnutt's second major group of stories is his satirical studies of the rising black middle class, the "blue-vein" society where the color line is as strictly enforced as in the larger society. More conventional than Chesnutt's conjure stories, these works are interesting for their early critical examination of black society and for their humor; they suffer, however, from a tidiness of structure which prevents them from being as rewarding as the conjure tales.

Probably Chesnutt's best single story is "The Sheriff's Children," a reworking of the conventional theme of a black who is about to be lynched, a good sheriff who tries to detain a mob, and the unruly mob which consists of men individually lacking in courage—all set in a backwater town. Chesnutt's inventional twist is that the good sheriff, who has throughout the story apparently only one child, discovers that he is the father of the prisoner; hence, the plurality of the title. Caught between versions of right, between his duty to the law and his duty to his child, the sheriff assumes mistakenly that he can honor them both, act morally in a corrupt situation, and triumph. At the end, however, the prisoner, having earlier been shot, rips off his bandages and allows himself to bleed to death, ending the sheriff's naïve illusions.

Chesnutt shows in his work a range of themes, techniques, and emotions, and he exemplifies, especially through his use of irony and layering, a control of his medium and its potential that is remarkable. Black short fiction thus finds in its first important writer a man who brings forth the form fully developed; although it would be another twenty years before a second black short-story writer of his equal, Chesnutt begins the genre forcefully.

One other writer of short stories of the early period merits mention: Paul Laurence Dunbar (1872-1906). Considerably more successful as a poet, Dunbar wrote a number of short stories, marked not only by technical proficiency and smoothness of telling, but also by a conservatism of attitude and a thinness of theme that make them finally unrewarding. "The Lynching of Jube Benson," for example, is Dunbar's version of the lynch story. Narrated by a white doctor in stilted, self-conscious language, the story depicts a faithful retainer who is unjustly accused of murdering the girl his master, a doctor, loves. Despite Jube's having once nursed the doctor back to health in scenes of unfortunately predictable behavior, the doctor turns on him and leads the lynching party. With Jube still hanging in view, men appear to say the mob has hanged the wrong man. "That was my last lynching," says the doctor. In its theme of the destructive powers of prejudice and in its briefly managed suspense, the story maintains some interest, but, and characteristically so for Dunbar, the stereotyped image of the black is offensive, the diction is inappropriate, and the ending is too hurried to seem other than contrived.

The second creative period in black short-story development was marked less by the efforts of one person than by those of several: the Harlem Renaissance, a decade-long spurt of creativity beginning around 1925, saw the rise of several black artists who left behind first-rate short stories. The setting was right: a concentrated area where many budding writers, most from out-of-the-way places, came to share their opinions and nurture one another's energies, and the time was right as well. Blacks were taking a new interest in their heritage, placing new value on their artistic traditions, while whites had also suddenly discovered black art. In this atmosphere, poetry and fiction flourished. Important short-story collections include Jean Toomer's *Cane* (1923), Eric Walrond's *Tropic Death* (1926), Claude McKay's *Gingertown* (1932), Langston Hughes's *Ways of White Folks* (1934), and Zora Neale Hurston's *Mules and Men* (1935). Rudolph Fisher, Jessie Fauset, Nella Larsen, and Sterling Brown were also writing short fiction, as was Arna Bontemps, a major figure of the time who did not collect his short stories until 1973 (*The Old South*).

Although the fiction of the Harlem Renaissance is widely varied, perhaps its major theme treats the relation between the rural and the urban, an examination of the longing to return to one's roots, be they African, West Indian, or Southern. For most fiction writers, however, the African experience seemed distant, and its presence is felt more strongly in the poetry of the time. The West Indian experience, while nearer, was held less in common; the Southern was the most problematical of all. Much of the fiction from this period is urban, but the South is usually there as background and counterpoint, a harsh reality left behind physically, but one which calls blacks back. In the short stories of *Cane* by Jean Toomer (1894-1967), for example, the protagonist goes North, but, discovering there the same prejudices and missing the natural strengths of the Southern environment, he returns South and makes what Dudley Randall calls the "desperate journey"—not in a simple search for roots, but in a complex effort to face his past, explore its feelings, and search for its support. The journey to the South is often compared to a trip to Hell, a literal and metaphoric descent; the climactic scene in *Cane* occurs in a cellar, a hellish setting in the novel, and the journey downward— to the South, to Hell, to the underground, or into one's self—becomes a major motif in black fiction.

Zora Neale Hurston (1903-1960), personally among the most urbane of the writers, sets most of her work in the small black Florida town from which she came. In her collection of black folklore, *Mules and Men*, a work which explores the means and purposes of taletelling both in the tales she reports and in the way she reports them, unobtrusively integrating into her commentary the fictive devices she discovers and thus blurring the line between the fictive and the nonfictive, she is the Northerner returned South, the outsider come home to view again her past culture.

Eric Walrond (1898-1966) was born in British Guiana, but lived in Harlem during the Renaissance. He looks backward to his home in "Tropic Death," the title story of his collection, a story also of descent in search of his past—in this case his father. He finds him a man dying of leprosy, and discovers the past to be one of ugliness, sin, and dissolution. In "Wharf Rats," set at the Panama Canal, young blacks entertain arriving white ship passengers by diving for money. One of them, Philip, dives too deep and, caught by tides, is unable to swim away from a shark. Maffi, a Trinidad servant girl, sings after his death, "Trinidad is a damn fine place/But obeah down dey. . . ." Her comment is justified; the descent is not simply dangerous; for Philip it was fatal.

Claude McKay (1890-1948), also a West Indian, set most of his fiction in Harlem. Although more talented as a poet, since the tightly controlled form intensified the impact of his anger, in his novel *Home to Harlem* (1928) and his collection of stories *Gingertown* he portrays an unglamorized vision of black corruption that upset a number of his contemporaries, including W. E. B. DuBois.

For Rudolph Fisher (1897-1934) the subject was also Harlem. When Miss Cynthie, the title character of a story, comes North to visit her grandson, she is shocked by his job and by Harlem life. Having wanted him to be respectable, an undertaker perhaps, she does not approve of his work as an entertainer. Yet at the end of the story, Fisher, whose vision is much gentler than McKay's, suggests what kind of community is possible within Harlem. As she listens to the music, Miss Cynthie is reminded of a hymn, and the last jazz number for her becomes a recessional. Fisher's story "Common Meter" has the same theme. During an intense and unfair ballroom battle of the bands, the cheese-colored Fess Baxter cuts the drumhead on his opponent's drummer's instrument; but the people supply the beat themselves with foottaps, and "the unfaltering common meter of blues" unites them, much as common meter in a hymn unites its singers.

Probably the most integrated expression of the rural-urban theme occurs in the work of Langston Hughes (1902-1967), who is the first black writer to use the rhythms and diction of black speech integrally in his work. His is not the simple dialect writing of, say, Dunbar, but the full use of black urban speech as a valid source of material, contemporary, urban, and rooted in the culture. In poetry, black verse had often in the past been modeled on older or contemporary white models; Hughes gives it a new sound. In fiction, his triumphant creation is Jesse B. Simple, the narrator of the Simple tales, who is a new incarnation of the black folk hero; put-upon and stepped-upon, he perseveres and gives voice with wit, humor, and intelligence, to the wiles of that hero.

The years between the Renaissance and the end of World War II are dominated in short fiction by one writer, Richard Wright (1908-1960). In both his long and short works, Wright powerfully develops the theme that is the hallmark of black fiction: the struggle of the black man to make himself free, knowing that only in complete freedom, with its complex and often tragic dimensions, can he be fully a man, fully human, with the potential for both great falls and great victories. Wright later criticized his own first collection of short fiction, *Uncle Tom's Children* (1938), saying, "I found that I had written a book which even bankers' daughters could read and weep over and feel good about," but the protagonists even in this early fiction are less victims than Wright's opinion suggests. In "Long Black Song" a black man returns home to find that his wife has slept with a white man. Although the black is present in the story only a short time, it is he in whom Wright is finally interested: he dies angry, fighting whites. He is the typical Wright figure, as exemplified by Wright himself in *Black Boy* (1945) and *American Hunger* (1977), in which the central metaphors of the protagonist's inner fire and hunger describe the man to whom Wright gives his allegiance. In "Bright and Morning Star," Aunt Sue, the protagonist, having made a mistake once in trusting one weaker than herself, gives up hymn-singing for gun-firing; she dies herself, but she dies vengeful.

In *Eight Men*, stories published posthumously in 1961, eight characters struggle to make themselves men, just as does Bigger Thomas in *Native Son* (1940). The central story is "The Man Who Lived Underground." At the Kafkaesque opening, Fred Daniels is fleeing from the police for an unnamed crime; he descends underground to hide. In his life there, with frequent encounters with the normal world, which now looks grotesque and unreal, he acquires the elements necessary for survival, learning that what is unnecessary, however valued aboveground, is worthless. Daniels, whose name we learn indirectly and only once, sees a watchman, who is about to be punished for a crime that Daniels has committed, shoot himself. Although he knows he could stop the watchman, Daniels realizes that everyone is guilty of something and that the man deserves punishment even if not for the crime of which he is accused. It is the same existential lesson that Bigger Thomas understands. He, too, learns that he must not allow himself to be treated as a victim and that in freely choosing responsibility, even if logically the guilt is not attached to the proper cause, he creates his own freedom. Fred Daniels then ascends again, goes to the police station, and confesses to the crime with which he is charged. By accepting responsibility he makes himself free. Two of the policemen think Daniels is simply crazy, but the third knows that this new free man is dangerous; they take him back to his hiding place and shoot him.

The story is in the mainstream of black short fiction in its depiction of the quest for personal freedom. Its distillation differs, however, from much black fiction in having little sociological or political base, preferring a more allegorical method of presenting the theme; in *Native Son*, the most important black novel, Wright unites the philosophy with the fictive reality. Here, too, the metaphor is the common one of descent; its corollary, ascent, is also a key in black fiction. The ascent is often in terms of flight, a punning reference that can mean simply to flee. Dave, in Wright's famous story "The Man Who Was Almos' a Man," having bought a gun, ties it loaded to his thigh. He later bungles his first attempt to shoot, killing a mule, but when the mule's owner, with the approval of Dave's parents, tries to make him surrender the gun and pay for the mule, he lies, hiding the gun. The next day he catches a train and flees. Dave is correct about the gun's power and about its identification with his manhood. If he is only almost a man, Wright leaves little doubt that with the next shot he will be more accurate, for Dave has learned and has acquired the power to be a man.

Wright is often thought of as a naturalist, but the philosophic bent of his fiction, a latent existentialism before the self-conscious existentialism of his less interesting later fiction, precludes naturalism. It is rather his tough refusal to sentimentalize his characters or their life that makes Wright similar to the naturalists. His influence is felt on three other writers of the period who fall into the realist tradition: Ann Petry (b. 1912), whose stories and novels depict life in grim urban settings; Willard Motley (1912-1965), whose tough-guy fiction resembles both social realism and hard-boiled detective fiction, and Chester Himes (b. 1909). The prolific romancer Frank Yerby (b. 1916), although he rarely wrote about blacks, also developed in this period. All four are better known for long fiction.

If Wright dominates black fiction before 1950, two authors stand out during the next fifteen years: Ralph Ellison (b. 1914) and James Baldwin (b. 1924). Ellison is, of course, best known for his novel *Invisible Man* (1952), but he also wrote a number of uncollected short stories. In "Flying Home," his first, he uses the second kind of flight—literal soaring. Todd, a World War II aviator, has flown too high, been startled by buzzards, and reacted too sharply, causing his plane to crash. "The closer I spin towards earth," he thinks, "the blacker I become," but he falls and finds himself surrounded by Southern blacks. He tells them of his childhood dreams of flying; as for Bigger Thomas, airplanes become a symbol of white freedom. One of the men tells Todd a cautionary tale about a black angel who flies so easily with one wing that Saint Peter threatens to put him in a straitjacket. In *Mules and Men*, Hurston quotes the folklore saying, "If a frog had wings, he wouldn't bump his rump so much." Soaring above experience is a consistent image in black short stories, but, as Todd discovers, it can be as dangerous in its consequences as descent.

In Ellison's "King of the Bingo Game," another black man has a moment of choice and power. Called up from the audience at a movie entertainment, he controls a button that stops the bingo wheel. Once holding the power in his hand, he refuses to use it, fearing that once he stops the wheel, his power will be gone. Flying too high, risking too much, he loses it anyway, when the impatient manager takes control.

If Ellison's short stories are ultimately less important than his novel, it is probably because the extraordinary control he exercises in his delicate structuring is in *Invisible Man* supplemented by a forceful accumulation of incident. James Baldwin, however, has had his greatest success in the short story. Like many black writers, such as Wright and William Demby, Baldwin expatriated. Baldwin differs, however, in that the urbanity of his tone owes as much to his homosexuality as to his blackness, and his images of marginal men and his portrayal of a specific milieu depend upon both blackness and homosexuality, thus becoming doubly complicated and sometimes doubly rich.

Much of Baldwin's short fiction explores his own past, suggesting a family setting with an often irrational, always threatening father. In "The Rockpile," an apparently inconsequential incident is turned by the belligerent father into a scene of intimidation. The story ends with the son bending down to pick up his angry father's lunch bucket, the father's shoe looming inches from the son's head. Whether the shoe strikes and the father's resentment and anger come out, one does not know; what one shares is the fear of being powerless.

In "This Morning, This Evening, So Soon," the European side of Baldwin's writing is presented; a black American singer, living in France with his Swedish wife and their son, is about to return home. Before that journey he muses on his last trip home, when he has been reminded of what he has been allowed to forget in Paris, of how difficult it can be for a black man in America and how very difficult it will soon be again. Later, out for an evening with his film director, he is joined by a group of black American students and then by Boona, an Algerian. Suddenly, there in Paris, famous and comfortable, the protagonist finds roles reversed. Boona is accused of stealing money from the purse of one girl. The narrator knows that Boona does steal and the act is witnessed, and yet he is reluctant to charge his friend, knowing that Boona may need the money to live and knowing what it is like to be disliked, accused, an outsider.

This story, too, ends without resolution. Baldwin shares with Ellison a preference for a balance of feeling, a holding of events in suspension. They differ markedly from the insistence of Wright and from many writers who follow them. Both are rather in the Emersonian tradition of acceptance of ambiguity and contradiction. In "Notes of a Native Son" Baldwin asserts that we must learn to accept life in all its complexity and reject its injustices at the same time; Ellison, for whom the acceptance of ambivalent feeling is a common theme, also indicates that one must accept potentialities while fighting many realities.

Other writers of the period include John Henrik Clarke (b. 1915), Albert Murray (b. 1916), John Oliver Killens (b. 1916), and John A. Williams (b. 1925).

By the mid-1960's, a new generation of short-story writers, most of them born in the 1930's, had appeared: among them were Hoyt Fuller (b. 1927), Lerone Bennett (b. 1928), Kristin Hunter (b. 1931), Conrad Kent Rivers (1933-1968), Woodie King, Jr. (b. 1937), Mike Thelwell (b. 1938), and Alice Walker (b. 1944). Imamu Amiri Baraka, also known as LeRoi Jones (b. 1934), and Ishmael Reed (b. 1938) are the most innovative, although their best work is done in other genres—the novel for Reed, poetry and drama for Baraka. More traditional are Paule Marshall (b. 1929), William Melvin Kelley (b. 1937), Ernest Gaines (b. 1933), and James Alan McPherson (b. 1943).

Marshall, like Walrond a West Indian, has said, "My work falls between two stools and is both West Indian and American." Typically her stories depend more on character development than plot; often a young black woman attempts to make sense of her life, the learning experience coming in an encounter with an older, supposedly more experienced, woman. In "To Daduh, In Memoriam," the title character is the narrator's grandmother; the narrator is a young girl coming from New York to visit her Barbadian relative. At first impressed and mystified by the forces of nature on the island and by her grandmother's relation to them, the young girl discovers that her grandmother is equally impressed by her and her urban world, by the girl's tales of buildings and conveniences. The story concludes after the grandmother's death, the narrator living in the shadow of her memory, but a shadow no longer than that cast by the Empire State Building in her grandmother's imaginings. Death—the setting is a wake—also forms the background for "Reena," a story in which the narrator listens to a more sophisticated young woman describe her life; the story also becomes one in which the narrator learns of incompleteness and learns that the life which she envies is more various and confused than she had thought.

Gaines's work is usually set in the Louisiana country in which he lived for fifteen years. His best story, "A Long Day in November," traces the breakup and reconciliation of a couple as perceived by their young son. Utilizing the hoodoo elements of the place, the husband comes to understand his faults and wins back his wife; the boy, who begins the story in uncontrollable fear, ends safe and happy, having watched his father regain pride.

In Kelley's most famous story, "The Only Man on Liberty Street," the subject is the same: a youth watching the relationship between parents. In Kelley's work, the pattern is reversed: a white man comes to Liberty Street to live with his black mistress and illegitimate daughter. Before his move, he has had friends and power; symbolically he wins a shooting contest. He cannot withstand the hatred and threats of his friends, however, and eventually moves back with his wife. Kelley's use of a narrator who cannot understand what is happening provides a distance that keeps the story from sentiment and melodrama.

Finally, James Alan McPherson treats delicately the isolated individual, white or black. His "On Trains" is a slight but careful portrayal of the neurotic fright of a Southern white lady contrasted with the world-weariness of the porters, barmen, and passengers on her train. "On Cabbages and Kings" also describes neurotic fear in the relationship between Howard, the narrator, and Claude Sheats, his roommate and the subject of the story. At first, with his rambling stories and prophecies and incriminations, Sheats is difficult to understand, but by the story's end the narrator and the reader have learned what powers Sheats has and the consequences of irrational intimidation.

Black short fiction from the mid-1960's to the present seems to be in a kind of second renaissance. In their concern with those whom society holds powerless, with the ways in which one comes to terms with himself and his society, and with the ways in which one transcends that society, achieves power for himself, and finds freedom, the current generation of black short-story writers continue to explore in a powerful way the concerns and images of the past.

Howard Faulkner

THE EFFECT OF COMMERCE ON
AMERICAN SHORT FICTION, 1850-1900

In the middle of the nineteenth century a number of social, political, and economic trends combined with technological advancements to create a thriving market for the American short story. As sophisticated printing processes made magazines both aesthetically pleasing and remunerative, the writing, distribution, and readership of the short story changed to conform to the new outlet. While these developments created the "magazinist," the writer who earned a living by providing weekly, sometimes daily, copy for a wide, general audience, they also influenced the belletristic writer to compress both language and plot to suit the demands of space. The readership grew and diversified; by the end of the century one can identify a magazine for every shade of opinion, from the elite conservatism of the *Atlantic Monthly* to the sensationalism of the Leslie publications. The rise in literacy is one reason for the growth of commerce, but the nationwide change in life-style must not be ignored. The financial crises were precipitated by Gilded Age investment practices, the Civil War and Reconstruction, the movement from an agrarian to an industrial economic base: these factors and others shaped the restless, inquisitive, and hardworking individual who, in the aggregate, subscribed to and avidly read a growing corpus of magazines.

The commercial climate, however, was not always temperate for the short story. Early in the century the custom of publishing anonymously discouraged all but underground recognition for the magazine author, while it allowed editors to disguise their reliance on a single author's works and to engage in indiscriminate blue-penciling. The *Atlantic Monthly* was reluctant to give up the custom for an added reason: it believed signatures to be a form of self-advertisement not needed by fine writing, which stood on its own merits. Another problem was the low rate of payment for short stories. Few authors could afford to support themselves on only two or three dollars per printed page. It was Robert Bonner, editor of the *New York Ledger* (1847) (dates in parentheses refer to the initial year of publication; the name of the first editor is given where pertinent), who scandalized his more moderate colleagues by offering the unheard-of sum of one hundred dollars per column to "Fannie Fern," a popular moralistic essayist. Bonner, whose unorthodox payments filled his wildly successful publication with sentimental fiction, is among those most responsible for changing the idea that writing is a genteel hobby for the wealthy.

Other developments, seemingly antithetical to good short fiction, sometimes encouraged it. In the absence of an international copyright agreement, trade courtesy was honored in the breach; pirated works were frequently inaccurate and almost never brought their authors monetary compensation. The lack of protection initially discouraged the growth of a native literature, for publishers gained higher circulations by pirating the works of well-known British authors than by promoting the efforts of little-known American ones. The editors of *Harper's Monthly* (1850), for example, began by reprinting installments of popular novels by Charles Dickens and Wilkie Collins; then, embarrassed by the outcry, they began to pay for "advance sheets" sent by the authors. Eventually, *Harper's Monthly* became known for its encouragement of native talent. On the other side of the Atlantic, some American authors took advantage of a more enlightened British law to obtain protection by establishing residency and then arranging for simultaneous publication in both countries. Many, however, engaged in bitter negotiations until 1891, when the United States Copyright law was finally passed.

While simultaneous publication and even pirating helped to gain a wide readership for many American authors, the financial crises of 1857 and 1873-1878 and the Civil War affected publishing adversely. When paper prices skyrocketed in 1857 and subscribers dwindled, many smaller and well-respected magazines, such as the *Knickerbocker*, did not survive. The war itself took a heavy toll among Southern publications, not only because of the high price of supplies but also because of the dependence of the South upon Northern shipments. Nevertheless, between 1840 and 1860 the number of magazines available almost tripled; by 1870 and the cessation of war, the number reached almost six thousand and at least doubled by 1880. The magazines that survived were strong, albeit different. While advertising rescued many from bankruptcy, it necessarily changed their complexion. The literary publications, such as *Harper's Monthly*, were reluctant to print anything but notices from the book trade, but others, such as the *Galaxy* and *Century*, weathered the 1870's by accepting miscellaneous advertising.

Such social and economic turmoil served to purge the market of foundering publications; with recovery came a new, thriving market for short fiction. On the one hand, there was an overweening public demand for sentimental tales, many supplied by women freed from household affairs by their families' newly gained industrial wealth. The Leslie publications, *Godey's Lady's Book* (1830, Louis A Godey), *Peterson's Magazine* (1842, Charles J. Peterson), and *Arthur's Home Magazine* (1852, T. S. Arthur), were all repositories for "pure literature" characterized by homilies and sentiment. Such tastes were certainly encouraged by the aftermath of the Civil War when, as most critics agree, anti-intellectualism swept the country. Not the least manifestation was the movement away from public lectures to public amusements and the rise of such entrepreneurs as P. T. Barnum; the taste in magazine fiction seemed to follow suit. The demand for such pieces, however, spurred circulation; it also created a critical movement which, following Edgar Allan Poe and his delineation of the short story as a viable form, called for intellectually satisfying magazine literature. Brander Matthews' distinction between the "short story" and fiction which is simply foreshortened is notable here; he and others like him provided the critical climate for such local colorists and humorists as Bret Harte, Mark Twain, and George Washington Cable, as well as for such realists as William Dean Howells, Henry James, and Hamlin Garland, all of whose work provided welcome relief from the generally popular emotion-laden fiction.

The single most important influence on commerce was the extraordinary technological developments in printing, developments which affected both form and content of the magazine. With inexpensive printing came an explosion of new publications; with wide circulation, a wide readership; with the readership, a demand for fiction. In short, the growth of the market contributed to the growth of the short story. What was essential to the new printing processes was, of course, Louis Daguerre's accidental discovery in 1839 that an image on an iodized silver plate could be developed by mercury fumes. One of the simplest applications that resulted was pasting the photograph directly on a wood block to facilitate accurate hand engraving, thereby saving many priceless drawings from being similarly treated. Another, more advanced application was developed by Walter Bently Woodbury in 1866. While woodburytype and analogous intaglio methods created fine photographic reproductions, none could be used in conjunction with ordinary press runs because the contours of the illustrations had to be inked in reverse to the contours of the type. It was Fox Talbot's 1852 "photoglyptic engraving" that prepared the way for the halftone, a revolutionary process which entailed breaking up a photographic image into dots or points and then bathing the plate in acid to produce a mechanically reproducible image. The popular press took immediate advantage of the discovery. According to some art historians, the New York *Daily Graphic* published the first such picture on March 4, 1880. Magazines seem to have been slower than newspapers to retool their presses; the 1884 *Century* was one of the first to print such an illustration.

With the new technology and consequent proliferation of magazines came a distinct shift in style, not only in illustration but also in writing. Not everyone approved of the changes; for example, R. W. Gilder, editor of the *Century*, complained that the new photo techniques made magazine illustration less creative. Few will now disagree, however, that some of the best illustrations were the result of improvements in the printing process, partly because the artist, no longer dependent on the engraver's skill, could have his work reproduced exactly as it appeared in the original. In short fiction, aesthetics and utility converged; writing, which became less discursive in accord with limitations of space, also became less ponderous, less aphoristic in the eighteenth century style. The new approach reflected the life-style of a readership which, caught up in the industrial revolution, exhibited great curiosity, but had little time.

Of the many thousands of magazines published during the latter half of the century, most were so ephemeral as to be all but forgotten today. Nevertheless, even some of the more durable political and humorous magazines may be cited as encouraging the rise of the short story, if only indirectly, by the numerous literary caricatures and parodies they carried, as is the case with *Puck* (1877, Sydney Rosenfeld), *Judge* (1881, J. A. Wales), and *Life* (1883, Edward Ames Mitchell). Moreover, reviews like the *Nation* (1865, Edwin Lawrence Godkin) should be noted for encouraging *belles-lettres* through perceptive literary criticism written by such men as Charles Eliot Norton. The conservative *Literary World* (1870, S. R. Crocker) offered scholarly commentary by Thomas Wentworth Higginson and others; the *Dial* (1880, Francis F. Browne), primarily a review in its early years, gave its approval to English writers in general and Oliver Wendell Holmes in particular. In addition, a handful of major periodicals are directly responsible for influencing the short-story form; these, along with their less popular and less well-funded contemporaries, illustrate the way in which commerce directly affected fiction.

The *Atlantic Monthly*, started in 1857, was blessed with a series of literary men as editors, among them James Russell Lowell (1857-1861), a Harvard professor noted for *The Biglow Papers* (1867) and as a foreign minister to England and Spain; the novelist William Dean Howells (1871-1881); and the poet Thomas Bailey Aldrich (1881-1890). Under a judicious editorial policy, the magazine became a formidable force against the popular taste for sentiment. Of its three famous nineteenth century editors, Howells was the most open to new writers outside the New England area, but all preferred realistic fiction, publishing such authors as Rose Terry Cooke, Constance Fenimore Woolson, Edward Everett Hale, Rebecca Harding Davis, and Henry James. The *Atlantic Monthly* also had one contributor who made another periodical famous in its own right. He was Bret Harte, editor of the San Francisco *Overland Monthly* from 1868 to 1870. While other contributors, notably Willa Cather, Gertrude Atherton, and Jack London, were in the *Overland Monthly*'s later pages, Harte made himself—and the West—famous with such stories as "The Luck of Roaring Camp" and "The Outcasts of Poker Flat." In 1871 Harte came under contract with the *Atlantic Monthly*, bringing a strong measure of local color to the Boston publication.

Somewhat less "literary" than the *Atlantic Monthly* were its two closest competitors. The *Galaxy*, founded and edited in 1866 by the brothers William Conant and Francis Pharcellus Church, attempted a broader geographical base than the New England publication. Before the *Galaxy* was sold to the *Atlantic Monthly* in 1878, it exemplified the divided personality of a periodical caught between the old sentimentalism and the new realism. To be sure, it published stories by Henry James, John William De Forest, Rebecca Harding Davis, and Constance Fenimore Woolson, but many of its files were devoted to serialized English novels and melodramatic wares peddled by popular and forgotten writers. Some leavening was provided by Mark Twain, who briefly served as editor of the humorous "Memoranda" column. *Lippincott's* enjoyed perhaps the same measure of popularity as the *Galaxy* and the *Atlantic Monthly*, all three somewhat eclipsed by their larger and wealthier contemporaries, *Harper's Monthly* and *Scribner's/Century*. The first editor of *Lippincott's* was John Foster Kirk (1868), who sought to attract contributors nationwide. Some, like Frank R. Stockton and Rose Terry Cooke, were shared with the *Galaxy*. Like the *Atlantic Monthly*, *Lippincott's* encouraged the development of the American short story by its initial determination to publish only native work. Its critical acumen helped as well: Brander Matthews' defense of the short story as a form was published here in 1885. Two years later the periodical began to publish a single long work of fiction in each issue, thereby losing the variety which had assured its popularity.

Perhaps the most well-known general magazines of their time, *Harper's Monthly* and *Harper's Weekly* boasted different editorial personalities. The weekly *Harper's* (1857) was intended to emphasize political news, but under George William Curtis (1863-1892) and later editors much good short fiction appeared. The monthly was devoted to belletristic matters, and while it was contemptuously treated by some of its contemporaries for its early penchant for sentimental tales, it provided an outlet for many new American authors in the 1870's and after, among them John William De Forest, Rose Terry Cooke, Elizabeth Stuart Phelps, Stephen Crane, Lafcadio Hearn, Henry James, Sarah Orne Jewett, and Owen Wister. Its early reputation for piracies and "English" tendencies sparked the establishment of *Putnam's Monthly* (1853), which, under Charles F. Briggs, was designed to compete through nationalism; Briggs encouraged the publication of Western and Southern literature as well as perceptive criticism.

Scribner's/Century, which competed so effectively for more than four decades, was one of the giants, a social and political force in its own right. Famous for its "Civil War Papers," *Scribner's/Century* encouraged purely American talent. It was here that Frank Stockton's popular conundrum tale "The Lady or the Tiger?" was published, and it was here that Henry James, George Washington Cable, Julian Hawthorne, Constance Fenimore Woolson, and others contributed both long and short fiction. Much of its stature can be attributed to its editors, the novelist Josiah Gilbert Holland (1870-1881) and his associate, the poet Richard Watson Gilder. In 1881 the magazine changed hands to become the *Century*, but continued its distinction in the short-story field with such noteworthies as Joel Chandler Harris. A new *Scribner's* appeared in 1887 under the editorship of Edward Livermore Burlingame; its immediate success showed the public's appetite for well-edited periodicals publishing fiction of high quality. All of the familiar names were represented, as well as Bret Harte, H. C. Bunner, and Edith Wharton.

Many of the "giants" described above continued through the twentieth century, but other post Civil War periodicals were also influential. Among them, the *American Magazine* (1876, Frank Leslie) provided an outlet for popular magazinists, as well as, on occasion, writers such as Bret Harte; the short-lived but well-staffed *Our Continent* (1882, Albion Winegar Tourgee) published work by Julian Hawthorne, Rebecca Harding Davis, and Sarah Orne Jewett. Other large, general audience magazines were established toward the end of the century. *Collier's* was one of these; set up by Nugent Robinson in 1888, the publication carried works by Julian Hawthorne and George Parsons Lathrop but eventually joined a growing trend by offering more news coverage and less fiction. Its initial persuasion that good literature was its strongest selling point became especially evident after 1900. A much larger magazine, eventually supported by Hearst money, was *Cosmopolitan* (1886, Frank P. Smith). It enjoyed the brief joint editorship of William Dean Howells, who increased the quality of contributions by attracting Hamlin Garland, Sarah Orne Jewett, and Frank Stockton. Later, Mark Twain, Jack London, and Edith Wharton joined its ranks. Another important general interest magazine was *McClure's*; begun in 1893, it featured some "unknowns" such as O. Henry. Finally, a family "institution," recently revived with much nostalgia, was the *Saturday Evening Post*. Tracing its genesis to 1821, the nineteenth century *Saturday Evening Post* published a healthy amount of sentimental and English work; not until George Horace Lorimer became editor in 1899 did the fiction improve, with both Frank Norris and Jack London contributing.

"Women's" magazines were benefactors as well in the development of the short story. The *Ladies' Home Journal* (1883, Louisa Knapp Curtis) is one; begun as a supplement to the *Tribune and Farmer*, it at first found it difficult to attract well-known writers, but eventually the "List of Famous Contributors" which formed part of its advertising included Rose Terry Cooke and Elizabeth Stuart Phelps. Under the editorship of Edward W. Bok (1889-1919), however, not only famous magazinists such as John Kendrick Bangs contributed, but Mark Twain, Bret Harte, Hamlin Garland, and Sarah Orne Jewett did so as well. Similarly, the *Woman's Home Companion* (1874, S. L. Thorpe) initially attracted practiced but now forgotten writers; under Arthur Vance, who assumed the editorship in 1900, the list grew to include Garland, Harte, Jewett, and London.

Taken as a whole, the foregoing magazines clearly provided a wide range of publishing opportunities for the short-fiction writer, who could place his contribution with the Brahminical *Atlantic Monthly* or the more populist Leslie or Hearst publications or anywhere in between. Magazines that were devoted entirely to fiction, such as the *Black Cat* (1895, Herman Daniel Umbstaetter) or the *Chap-Book* (1894, Herbert Stuart Stone) were other possibilities. One of the *Black Cat's* most famous contributors was Jack London, who immortalized the magazine in his novel *Martin Eden* (1909); he, like others, was attracted to the publication by the prizes offered, an idea perhaps copied by *Life*, which in June, 1898, offered cash awards and publication to the top three stories submitted.

Clearly, the effect of commerce on the development of the short story is not to be taken lightly. The very social, scientific, and political forces which signaled a changing life-style and fostered the growth of the magazine industry created a market for a new kind of fiction. The market allowed writers to get immediate (if not always well-paid) recognition for their work; and it provided them with a potential reading public which was much larger than that which they could expect through book publishing. Short stories, moreover, could be published singly, rather than collected over a period of years; magazine publication allowed many authors not only to support themselves while writing longer works but also to develop their skills in a form which is necessarily very precise. The movement from sentimental fiction to realistic fiction can be seen simply by analyzing the list of contributors to the periodicals in question, so that it may be said that commerce inevitably contributed to strengthening an important literary movement in the second half of the nineteenth century.

Patricia Marks

SHORT FICTION OF THE AMERICAN WEST

One early spring day in 1973 in the small mountain village of Skofja Loka, located in the Yugoslavian republic of Slovenia, two small children, participating in a kind of Slovene version of the "trick or treat" custom, knocked at the door of a house. One was dresssed as a cowboy, and the other as an Indian. These children had never seen nor probably ever would see a real cowboy or a real Indian in a real American setting; for that matter, there are many American children about whom the same could be said. The significant point is that this incident, occurring as it did almost two continents and an ocean away from the American West, underscores the almost incredible hold that that section of America has always had on the imaginations of people in nearly all parts of the world.

Another event, almost seven years later and of much more international import, occurred at Lake Placid, New York, at the Winter Olympics of 1980, when the American team marched in the opening ceremonies wearing Western-style winter coats and white cowboy hats. This costume choice may or may not have been coincident with the fact that America was having some problems on the international scene; in any case everyone knows that in the Western myth the white hat symbolizes the "good guy," the one who rides down from the mountains to solve the problems in the valley and then rides off again into the sunset. Indeed, an enormous number of such "good guys" have, in Western novels, stories, and films, ridden off into the sunset—only to show up again in another valley to solve other problems.

Although the two events mentioned above may seem to bear little relationship to each other, in a very real sense they throw into sharp relief the myth of the American West, which, like most myths, tends to overshadow reality. When the first colonists landed in America, they faced West, and the history of the nation was for a long time influenced by a westward movement. While the frontier was officially "closed" in 1890 and the great westward migrations were essentially over, the West has never loosened its hold on the imagination. Sal Paradise, the hero of Jack Kerouac's novel *On the Road* (1957), might say upon reaching San Francisco in the modern day, "Here I was at the end of America—no more land—and now there was nowhere to go but back," but that is the very condition which nourishes the myth in the minds of everyone—American or not—who yearns for some antidote for the mechanized and computerized world which now "fences" him in.

When the frontier hit the Western plains, it marked a new era and a new tradition in the pages of the American chronicle. Highlighting the tradition was Jean Jacques Rousseau's Natural Man, that romantic symbol of unbridled freedom who captivated the eighteenth century.

The real West at one time meant an opportunity for land and for new lives to many who joined in the movement there, but the mythical West provides limitless opportunities for the human imagination to venture beyond reality to a place not much different from fairyland. In the mythical West, the wicked witch is replaced by the outlaw or the land-grabber and the good fairy by the knight-errant cowboy who, in place of armor, wears a white hat, high-heeled boots, and batwing chaps and, in place of a lance, brandishes a six-gun. The land itself is wide, rugged, and picturesque—a dramatic land, fraught with dangers and many dragons to slay. It is, in the words of John Sisk, a violent land, "close to the fundamental issues of life and death . . . a world of sharp contrasts and clear-cut issues."

That most people—even present-day Westerners—identify the mythical West with the cowboy may on the one hand seem strange, since the years of the cattle kingdom numbered less than thirty. On the other hand, it is not so strange when one recognizes that the cowboy, even in reality, cut a rather romantic figure. To Theodore Roosevelt he was "the grim pioneer of our race" who "prepares the way for the civilization from before whose face he must disappear." To Bernard De Voto he was "a free man, an individualist, and equalitarian; his necessary clothes were romantic and his necessary behavior was daring." Thus, although his days of existence were short in number, the figure of the cowboy, with the help of fiction and film, has been indelibly stamped upon American tradition. One explanation, perhaps, is that the West turned out not to be another Eden, and something or someone was needed to assuage the disillusionment that resulted—a savior, as it were—and the cowboy was designated as such. In that respect it has been a clear case of America's creating a mythical background for itself where none existed.

Certainly nineteenth century America, much like modern America, was in need of a myth, a stabilizing factor to counteract the great social changes that were being brought about by industrialization and urbanization and the resulting circumscription of individual freedom. What could be more stabilizing than for a cowboy hero to shoot it out with a hired gunman on a dusty street of a Texas cowtown and thus make it safe again for its citizens? No one saw this more clearly than Erastus Beadle, the famous publisher of the dime novels during the latter part of the century. "A dollar book for a dime" was his motto, and he had a sizable stable of writers to produce such books with Western themes—including "Bruin" Adams, W. F. Cody, Edward S. Ellis, Prentiss Ingraham, Mayne Reid, Ann Stephens, Edward Wheeler, and Fred Whittaker. Other publishers followed Beadle's lead and established their own Western series. The heroes of these dime novels, with their morality, self-sacrifice, and honor beyond question, often took the law into their own hands and dispensed justice to villains without the restrictive and frustrating trappings of a legal system. Like Ingraham's hero Buck Taylor, they were, in the view of Marshall Fishwick, Nordics and racialists of the first order who carried the White Man's Burden around with them as they galloped over the plains and mountains.

If the dime novel brought the mythical cowboy to life for the reading public, the pulp magazines gave him constant sustenance. It was from these magazines that more talented writers were to pick up the cowboy and bring him to what David Lavender calls "middle-class respectability," or, more exactly, critical respectability. For one of the real problems in studying the Western is to cull from the plethora of titles those which are more than simply the work of a hack writer meeting the demands of the commercial market. Another problem in studying fiction of the West, just as it is in the study of the history of the West, is to identify the line between reality and myth. Vardis Fisher, a Western novelist and historian, says that if "a person wishing to know the history of the American West were to read a few hundred books and articles about it, chosen at random, he would come out of it with his head well crammed but there might be few historical facts in it."

Most critics agree, however, that there has as yet been no penetrating literary response to the Western experience. Despite the abundance of raw material out of which good fiction could be produced, what has appeared has for the most part been, according to De Voto,

> a stylized form of romantic fiction . . . conventionalized, formulized, and even ritualized. It is peopled by figures who do not become characters because they feel nothing that can rouse a responsive feeling in the reader. At its best it is expert narrative. But at its best it remains lifeless, implausible, and in fact essentially absurd. Emotionally and intellectually it is as naïve as fiction can be.

This is a harsh indictment indeed, but De Voto is not alone in his views. John Williams also feels that "the subject of the West has undergone a process of mindless stereotyping by a line of literary racketeers that extends from the hired hacks of a hundred years ago who composed Erastus Beadle's dime novels to such contemporary pulp writers as Nelson Nye and Luke Short." The result, Williams believes, is that Western subject matter was "exploited, cheapened, and sentimentalized before it had a chance to enrich itself naturally, through the accretion of history and change." The formula Western (novel or short story) focuses on action and romance, with clear-cut good and bad and characters who fit neatly into stereotypes. It is what John Cawelti calls a game in which the good man is pitted against the bad on a field of competition that is definable and predictable; the game is played under a set of rules clear to both the participants and the reader. Such a strategy is good for the mass production of stories, but it is hardly conducive to the production of serious literature.

In their above comments, De Voto and Williams are speaking primarily of the novel, and when the almost endless array of Western novel titles are surveyed, the reader is prone to agree with their conclusions. Owen Wister's *The Virginian* (1902), of course, stands out as an exception. Certainly this novel is held by many to be the one that fathered the genre. At its publication it went through six printings in as many weeks and over the years has sold more than 1,600,000 copies. Interestingly enough, however, *The Virginian* was put together from a number of short stories that Wister had published in *Harper's* during the 1890's with, as De Voto puts it, "the joints left visible." The point here is that the short story may well be the genre in which the Western reaches its best expression. In its compact structure, the short story is ideally suited for the simplicity of most Western themes. Among the more serious writers of the Western who have recognized this suitability are such well-known names as Bret Harte, Owen Wister, Conrad Richter, Stephen Crane, Eugene Manlove Rhodes, Willa Cather, and Walter Van Tilburg Clark. A brief look at these writers and some of their short fiction will show the advantages to which they have used that form in the handling of Western themes.

Any overview of the American Western may well start with Bret Harte. Such stories as "The Luck of Roaring Camp," "The Outcasts of Poker Flat," and "Tennessee's Partner"—read and reread the world over—literally opened up the West as a source of material for fiction writers. Not so dashingly romantic perhaps as the cowboy on horseback, Harte's miners (Argonauts as he called them) were just as strongly individualistic and pragmatic while they journeyed to the West to seek riches in the gold fields of California. The "faith, courage, vigor, youth, and capacity for adventure necessary to this migration," Harte once said, "produced a body of men as strongly distinctive as were the companions of Jason."

Although Harte had the highest regard for the pioneers of California, he was aware that, like most human beings, they could be bigoted and hypocritical as well as courageous and daring. In "The Outcasts of Poker Flat" he presents an ironic contrast between hypocrisy and true morality. The characters he chose for this story set the pattern for several of the stereotypes that have populated the Western over the years: John Oakhurst, the suave gambler who accepts whatever life brings with a philosophical coolness; Uncle Billy, a drunken reprobate who has no concern for anyone but himself; Mother Shipton and the Duchess, two prostitutes with hearts of gold; and Piney Woods and Tom Simson (the Innocent), two young people whose innocent love affects positively all of the others except Uncle Billy.

As the story opens, the residents of Poker Flat, in a burst of self-righteous indignation, have decided to run out all unsavory characters. Included among these are Oakhurst, Uncle Billy, Mother Shipton, and the Duchess. Heading over the mountain for Sandy Bar, the small group, against the advice of Oakhurst, stops for the night at a deserted shack. There they are joined by Tom and Piney, who are on their way to Sandy Bar to get married. During the night a heavy snow falls, and the group wakens to find not only that they are snowed in, but also that Uncle Billy has run off with the mules and most of their provisions. A week passes, and the snow builds up. Tom and Piney lift the group's spirits with songs and stories; the Duchess cares for Piney; and Mother Shipton fades and tells Oakhurst that she has secretly saved her ration of food for Piney. After she dies, Oakhurst sends Tom for help; but by the time he returns, all are dead—with Piney "pillowing the head of her soiled sister upon her virgin breast." Oakhurst, who was the strongest and yet the weakest of the outcasts of Poker Flat, is found a little way from the shack, shot through the heart.

In the eyes of the residents of Poker Flat, the outcasts serve as scapegoats for that community's own human weaknesses. While they may be seen by some as the lowest elements of society, the outcasts in their moment of need set up a community that is not based on hypocrisy or pseudomorality, but on compassion and respect. Products of the boiling surface of Western life, they are an integral part of the society of Poker Flat. That the community would expel them simply points to a paradoxical aspect of early Western culture: on the one hand a desire and need for gamblers, prostitutes, and the like, and on the other a periodic feeling of guilt for the rawness of the social milieu that condones such people. Harte, like the many Western writers who were to follow him, certainly relied on stock characters and sentimental plots for his stories, but he spiced them all with irony and humor.

Bret Harte was not a Westerner by birth, but neither was Owen Wister. Coming from an upper-middle-class Philadelphia background, Wister, too, wrote of the West as an outsider; perhaps it was because he was an outsider that the West held such a fascination for him. Visiting the West fifteen times between 1885 and 1914, he immersed himself in all aspects of Western culture and then recorded what he saw and experienced. As he sat one evening in 1891 in his club in Philadelphia, having recently returned from a trip to Wyoming, he carried on a conversation with a friend who was as much interested in the West as he was; both decried the fact that there was no "Kipling saving the sagebrush for America." Wister saw an epic "being lived at a gallop out in the sagebrush," and he decided at that very moment that he would begin to put it into fiction. Indeed, that night he wrote most of his first short story of the West, "Hank's Woman," which introduces the Virginian as a character.

A part of the local-color tradition so popular at the time, Wister attempted to do for the West what Sarah Orne Jewett and Mary Wilkins Freeman did for New England and George Washington Cable did for New Orleans. "No one," he said, "has touched anywhere near it. . . . Its rise, its hysterical and unreal prosperity, and its disenchanting downfall, all this and its influence on the various sorts of human character that have been subjected to it." And again, because he was an outsider, he took great pains to ensure accuracy in what he wrote. Wister was, however, caught between the reality of the West that he wanted to capture and the romance of it that his imagination demanded. He praised the physical beauty of the West and the self-reliant,

loyal, strong kind of man it produced, but he also recognized the physical
hostility and the cultural barrenness of the West. He wrote in 1891, "I begin
to conclude, after five seasons of observation, that life in this negligent,
irresponsible wilderness tends to turn people shiftless, incompetent, and
cruel." Although Wister's view of the West grew more skeptical as he grew
older, his earlier stories stress the self-reliant and manly cowboy hero, of
which the Virginian is the prototype.

"Hank's Woman" opens with a panoramic word picture of the setting, into
which Wister places the narrator and the Virginian. They are fishing, and the
Virginian is relating some recent events regarding an acquaintance named
Hank and his new Austrian wife, Willomene. A lady's maid, Willomene a
short time earlier had been abruptly dismissed from her position and left
stranded in the town of Cinnabar. It was at this point that both the Virginian
and Hank got to know her. While it is obvious that the Virginian has some
feeling for the girl, it was Hank who moved in first and married her. After
a short honeymoon Hank brought his new wife to the camp that the Virginian
and some other men had on Galena Creek. As the Virginian points out in
his tale, all of the men were shocked and angered at the way Hank treated
his woman, unused to life in the West as she was. He not only ridiculed her
cooking and her inability to ride a horse, but he also made fun of her crucifix.
"It will soon be a month since I left Galena Creek," muses the Virginian.
"But I cannot get the business out o' my head. I keep a studyin' over it."

Leaving Snake River, the narrator and the Virginian meet Lin McLean,
one of the men from the camp on Galena Creek. He reports that Hank and
Willomene are still at the camp and that not only has the camp been backing
her in her relationship with Hank, but also that she "has got the upper hand
of him herself. She has him beat." When asked how, McLean replies, "She
has downed him with her eye." Hank, at this particular moment, he says, is
on a drunk and has been forced by Willomene to sleep outside their cabin.
By the time they reach the cabin, it is empty. There is a bullet hole in
Willomene's crucifix and a bloody ax on the floor. Following some tracks,
they discover that Willomene has thrown the body of Hank over a cliff and
that she herself has jumped to her death. "Well . . . all this fuss just because
a woman believed in God," says McLean. "You have it wrong," replies the
Virginian. "It's just because a man didn't." The image the reader perceives
of the Virginian in this story is not that of the typical formula cowboy. Rather,
he appears as a kind of philosopher-cowboy, one whose concerns and feelings
run deep below the surface. Although seldom directly expressed, they nevertheless contribute significantly to making the Virginian an individualistic
character.

In "Little Big Horn Medicine," Wister shifts to a Crow Indian for his
protagonist. Cheschapah, the son of a chief, is a recalcitrant brave, a would-
be medicine man who wants war with the white man. He illustrates what

Lieutenant Stirbing of the First Cavalry, another character in the story, knows: "that the Indian is of a subtlety more ancient than the Sphinx. In his primal brain—nearer nature than our own—the directness of a child mingles with the profoundest cunning. He believes easily in powers of light and darkness, yet is a skeptic all the while." Cheschapah has succeeded in fooling the younger men of the Crow reservation into believing that he possesses big medicine, so much so that he even begins to believe it himself. His father, Pounded Meat, and the other chiefs, however, remain unconvinced and argue against any foolish war with the stronger white man.

A group of Sioux come from their reservation to visit the Crows and "to eat much meat together, and remember the day when war was good on the Little Horn, and our warriors killed Yellow Hair and all his soldiers." Cheschapah tries desperately to rouse them to join him and other young Crows in fighting the white man. Pounded Meat, however, scolds him and succeeds in driving him away from a confrontation with Stirbing and his soldiers, causing Stirbing to comment, "Bullets you get used to; but after the firing's done, you must justify it to important personages who live comfortably in Eastern towns and have never seen an Indian in their lives, and are rancid with philanthropy and ignorance." This view that the East can never understand nor appreciate life in the West is often expressed in the Western and perhaps has added considerably to the myth mentioned earlier.

Cheschapah continues in his efforts toward war until, with the help of some natural coincidents and a sly white trader, he convinces the majority of the Indians that he truly can make big medicine. Thinking himself invincible, he makes a suicide charge against the soldiers and is cut down. The Indians surrender and for a space of hours ride by the body of Cheschapah, "striking him with their whips." Only Pounded Meat mourns for his errant son. In this story Wister seems occasionally ambivalent toward his Indian protagonist. While he makes it obvious that Cheschapah is an egotistical young fool, he also focuses on his individuality and pride. The reader sympathizes more with Pounded Meat than with his son, because seen in the father is a depth of wisdom and understanding that surpasses the anger of the moment. Age, however, is perhaps as responsible for the father's wisdom as anything, since Pounded Meat apparently did have a hand in killing Yellow Hair and his soldiers. Because of the subtleties through which Wister approaches his tale, "Little Big Horn Medicine" is a cut above the usual cowboy-Indian story. Although he may have edged over into sentimentality and triteness on occasion, Wister nevertheless exhibits a strong sense of plot and incident and, for the most part, keeps his vision of the West true to what his inquiring mind observed over the years.

While Harte and Wister may both be seen as important figures in establishing the Western as a literary genre, probably no writer of the Western has produced stories of higher quality than Stephen Crane. Usually remembered for his naturalistic works such as *The Red Badge of Courage* (1895), he never-theless did find considerable Western materials to use in his short fiction. Interestingly enough, Crane not only was not a Westerner, but he also spent relatively little time there. Writing for Irving Bacheller's syndicate, he went to the West in 1895, spending a year in Nebraska, Texas, and Mexico, before returning to the East. Although his sojourn in the West was short, Crane's powers of observation, combined with some fascinating adventures, gave him an abundance of material for copy to send back to Bacheller. Of the many stories he wrote with Western settings (primarily Mexican), none is of the stature of "The Blue Hotel" or "The Bride Comes to Yellow Sky," both written in 1897. These two stories examine the West with an insight and penetration that are matched by few, if any, other Westerns.

Set in Nebraska, "The Blue Hotel" fits the pattern of Crane's intense stories of masculine adventure, action, tragedy, and irony. The story takes place primarily in Scully's Palace Hotel in the tiny town of Fort Romper. The hotel, painted a vivid light blue, "was always screaming and howling in a way that made the dazzling winter landscape of Nebraska seem only a grey swampish hush." Standing alone on the prairie, it is a stopping place for the passengers streaming through Romper on the railroad. To this hotel Scully leads three travelers one winter morning—a "shaky and quick-eyed Swede," a "tall bronzed cowboy," and a "little silent man from the East." Shortly after their arrival, a raging blizzard strikes Romper, isolating the hotel and those in it. Along with Johnnie, Scully's son, the three travelers play poker. The Swede, however, becomes convinced that he is to be killed by the other three. Scully tires to calm the frightened man with drink and talk, but to no avail. After beating up Johnnie, whom he accuses of cheating, the Swede swaggers out of the hotel to a nearby saloon, where he arrogantly picks another fight with a gambler and is stabbed to death. The story ends as, months later, the cowboy and the Easterner talk over the incident. The latter says that Johnnie had indeed been cheating and that he himself had "refused to stand up and be a man. I let the Swede fight it out alone. And you—you were simply puffing around the place and wanting to fight. And then old Scully himself. We are all in it. This poor gambler ain't even a noun. He is kind of an adverb. Every sin is the result of a collaboration. We, five of us, have collaborated in the murder of this Swede." The cowboy cries out against this theory with, "Well, I didn't do anythin', did I?"

Many critics agree that in "The Blue Hotel" Crane dramatizes what he sees as the pervasive influence of the dime novel in conditioning people's views of the "wild" West. Viewed in that sense, then, the Swede is a victim of his own mistaken notions of what the West is really like. Convinced that he is to be killed, he contributes in no small way to his own death. While what the Easterner says about their all being "in it" hints at a profound truth of human existence, it is the Swede's own unfounded fear and subsequent arrogance that causes his downfall. The cowboy's question at the end fits with an earlier comment he makes: "This ain't Wyoming, ner none of them places. This is Nebrasker." Taken together, these utterances seem to deny the prevalent romantic notion that there was a single West, a West described and presented so widely by so many writers of the Western—that one so feared by the Swede.

In many of the early pulp Westerns, the cowboy hero, after proving his bravery and independence, marries, settles down, and becomes a self-reliant man. This very neat formula permitted the cowboy to blend into the society for which he had paved the way. In "The Bride Comes to Yellow Sky," Crane gives this theme a striking variation as he juxtaposes the stable and the transient, the old and the new. The stable is represented in the institution of marriage as a rite of investiture, the transient in the old ways giving place to new in a "new" geography—the West. On a "Great Pullman" train sweeping Westward, a newly married pair sit painfully conscious and exposed in their new wedding attire. As if to compress profound change, the story of only eleven pages begins at 3:21 P. M.; the train arrives in Yellow Sky at 3:42 P. M., and the story ends a few minutes later.

Prominent among the rites, apparel, and vows of the transitional stages of existence—baptism, initiation, graduation, marriage, funerals, and swearing-in ceremonies—a wedding epitomizes profound psychological, physical, and social changes which Crane expresses in the phrase "the environment of their new estate." Such are the new stiff clothes, the rich furnishings of the Pullman car, and the condescending waiters, sophisticated persons who rejoice in the raw inexperience and awkwardness of Jack Potter and his bride. As the train approaches Yellow Sky at the apex of a triangle formed by the track and the Rio Grande, Jack Potter with trepidation and a heavy conscience feels the impact of his deed—bringing his bride "before an innocent and unsuspecting community."

The bride thus epitomizes the coming of social customs to an untrained community formerly regulated by the superior powers of the gun and the gunfighter. The train as it sweeps Westward leaves behind the social regulations of the East; but in its environment and in the newly wedded pair, it brings Eastern society to the untamed West. Several images mark a death to the familiar past: the crossing of the horizon as a "precipice," the "keening" Rio Grande. The "hour of Yellow Sky" Crane defines as "the hour of daylight" when no deeds and especially no new roles can be hidden from sight. Even the porter, as the train stops at the station, chuckles "fatuously": Western heroes traditionally took their women and remained single.

Meanwhile, as an example of the old ways, Part II reveals the habitual actions of saloon patrons—a drummer, three Texans, two Mexican sheep-herders—under attack from a notorious drunken gunfighter called Scratchy Wilson who routinely, when drunk, shoots up the saloon and terrorizes a dog.

The people wish that Jack Potter, their town marshal, would return to protect them. Part III shows exactly how trite Scratchy Wilson can be—and how vacuous. The dog recognizes Wilson's customary behavior but knows the danger as he performs the usual pantomime of fleeing from Wilson's gunfire; with mock heroics Scratchy fires at the saloon door but does not go in. This section amounts to a parody of thousands of television Westerns, as if Crane, writing in the late 1890's, had foreknowledge of later Western literature. Even Scratchy Wilson, however, senses a death to the old ways, for as he walks down Main Street looking for something to shoot at, it seems as if "the surrounding stillness formed the arch of a tomb over him."

Part IV reveals Potter and his bride attempting to reach their home without attracting attention, but, confronted by the drunken Scratchy Wilson challenging Potter to a gun battle, both man and bride experience the attitudes of death: Potter's mouth becomes "a grave for his tongue"; the bride's face goes yellow "as old cloth," and she becomes "a slave to hideous rites, gazing at the apparitional snake." Potter, without a gun, remembers "the environment of the new estate" and tells Wilson "You'll have to do all the shootin' yourself." Potter's revelation that he is married provides Wilson with a "glimpse of another world," and in the presence of this "foreign condition" he slinks away, "a simple child of the earlier plains." Several critics have commented on the closing image of the story: "His feet made funnel-shaped tracks in the heavy sand." With this hourglass image, time has run out for the old West and the likes of Scratchy Wilson.

Another Eastern writer who went West was Conrad Richter. A Pennsylvanian, he moved to New Mexico in 1928 for reasons of his wife's health. Edwin Gaston sees this enforced move as a fortunate one for Richter's career: "It brought about a searching re-examination of his purposes and led to the decision to write 'the best stories' of which he was capable." Nine of these stories Richter collected as *Early Americana* (1936), his first volume of Southwestern fiction. For these stories he did exhaustive research among old newspapers, rare books, manuscripts, and personal records—as well as interviewing various people who had settled the area. He was fortunate to meet Herbert and Lou Hardy, a couple who had experienced the early days when New Mexico was still a territory. From them he gained valuable insights into the Southwest. One result of all this research was his decision that historical fiction was to be his literary mode. "In short," says Gaston, "Richter may have realized that much contemporary historical fiction amounted to nothing more than escapism for readers desperately seeking relief from the complexities of industrial society and from the tribulations of economic reversals." Richter, however, was aiming at something more than that: he wanted "to bring frustrated contemporary man into closer contact with people of another age," according to Gaston, "people who also lived, loved, struggled, and died, but whose lives nevertheless reflected purpose, completeness, and serenity."

Thus, in *Early Americana* Richter sought to portray what he called the "small authenticities" of daily life, "without which life would not be life either then or today." Virtually all of his short stories, then, are simple episodes that deal with the kinds of incidents that were more or less common on the frontier—border raids, Indian troubles, arrivals of homesteaders, and feuds between ranchers and nesters. Perhaps none of Richter's stories better reflects his approach than "The Flood." Set in Texas, it illustrates the harsh demands made upon two people as they battle a flood and Indians in an effort to survive. Coe Elliott is a rancher who has been planning to join the Confederacy in its struggle for secession. Riding two days to reach town so that he can put his plan into operation, he wishes that he had "a woman to leave behind, somebody to think of him when he was away and to come back to when the war was over." Yet white women, as he knows, are scarce in the new Texas country. Almost before he realizes what is happening, he is being married to Bethia Todd, a young girl whose family has been killed by Indians. Feeling sorry for her, he proposes, saying, "The Mexican women will look after you till I get back from the wars. And if I don't come back, everything I got is yours as my widow." Bethia bitterly accepts, and they are married.

Most women in the stock Western are more ornamental than real and usually function to fill out the dramatic aspects of plot. Moreover, very seldom is there a real marriage between the cowboy and the woman. "The Flood," therefore, departs from the formula from the start. More than that, however, Bethia proves to be anything but shadowy or abstract. Following the marriage the couple sets out for Coe's ranch, some four days away by wagon. Because this is his wedding trip and the only time that he will be alone with his bride before he goes to war, Coe is in no hurry. Bethia, still bitter about the tragedy that has befallen her family, refuses to talk or to eat. At night she sleeps in the wagon and Coe sleeps under it. Rain plagues them throughout the trip, and they are soon caught in the overflow from the river they are following. As the overflow becomes a real flood, they see a nester's cabin floating down the river. Coe rides out on his horse to investigate and finds a baby still alive in the cabin. Reluctantly he carries the baby back to the wagon, worried that Bethia will be angry at having a "nameless orphan to tend, one that couldn't lift a finger to wait on itself and would likely die on her hands." Instead, he is surprised when, upon seeing the child, she cries, "Give it here to me!" and orders Coe to go to find a cow for milk. Somewhat baffffled at her sudden taking of command, he goes. He finally finds a cow and succeeds in getting milk, but on his way back his horse is shot from under him by two Indians. Hearing shots coming from the direction of the wagon, he tries to swim back before the Indians get Bethia and the baby. When he reaches the wagon much later, he discovers that Bethia has shot one Indian and scared the other off; moreover, she has prepared him a warm supper on a makeshift dutch oven.

When it is time for bed, she tells him that her bed on the platform they have constructed in the wagon is "wide enough for two."

While Coe Elliott may not be the formula cowboy and Bethia may not be typical of women in the Western, they nevertheless reflect in a dramatic way the kinds of people who made up the West of that period—people who needed a great deal of self-reliance in facing not only the disasters of nature, but also the dangers of hostile Indians. Coe, like Asa Putnam in "Early Marriage," another of Richter's Western stories, is a strong man whose strength has been tempered by frontier hardship; but he is also a man of feeling and compassion. Bethia, too, exhibits a strength that, when necessary, enables her to face without fear a life-or-death situation.

"The Flood" achieves a level of suspense without relying on the usual trite trappings of melodrama so common in the formula Western. The same may be said for Richter's "Early Americana," a story in which white settlers again face hostile Indians. His description of the setting prepares us for the drama to be enacted, as we are carried back to the early 1870's and the wind-swept loneliness of seemingly endless prairies. The story of Laban Oldham, an eighteen-year-old who is ready to strike out on his own, "Early Americana" has the dramatic element of an Indian uprising, the romantic element of a boy-meets-girl situation, and the initiation element of Laban's passage to manhood.

Planning to attend a wedding in the settlement before he strikes out, Laban discovers, upon his arrival, that neither the bride nor the groom has appeared. With concern that Indians may be responsible for their absence, Laban volunteers to go investigate. Not only does he find the bride and the groom, along with her entire family, murdered, but he also discovers that the Indians have attacked his own home, although his family apparently managed to escape. When he gets back with his news, the settlement prepares for an attack. Each of the men is assigned to a woman to make sure that if worse comes to worse no woman will be taken alive by the Indians. Laban is assigned to Catherine Minor, sixteen years old, who is smitten with him. The attack never materializes, and aid arrives with Laban's family and a group of buffalo hunters. Laban has become attracted to Catherine, but she says that she cannot wait for a single man who feels the need to follow the cattle herds. He responds, "The circuit rider isn't gone back to Dodge with the freighters yet. . . . You can make it that he didn't come to Carnuel for nothin', if you want to, Catherine." She agrees, and they are married. Laban has indeed passed into manhood.

Richter's stories present the Westering process with the drama of actuality and the power of simplicity. His characters are in direct contact with the land, and their motivations and actions stem from that contact; it is the source of their strength, the thing that gives them the ability to turn hardship into gain. It is this dimension that raises Richter's stories of the West above the typical formula Western.

We have seen that a number of Eastern writers were successful in exploiting Western materials for their fiction. Eugene Manlove Rhodes, however, was a real Westerner and a cowboy. During his sixty-five years, Rhodes not only wrote of life in the West; but he also lived it. Although he wrote eleven novels and hundreds of short stories and poems, he did not, according to his wife May Davison Rhodes, "think of himself foremost as a writer." On the contrary, he was more proud of his skill as a cowboy; but there is no question that he was a better writer of Westerns because of his firsthand knowledge of a cowboy's life. His stories, in De Voto's words, are "the only embodiment on the level of art of one segment of American experience. They are the only body of fiction devoted to the cattle kingdom which are both true to it and written by an artist in prose." De Voto may be stretching a point here, but the fact remains that Rhodes's stories do present a level of realism that the stock Westerns do not. In his stories, Rhodes, like Wister, tried to be as true to the actual situation as he could, often borrowing from his own experience for his plots.

His story "The Trouble Man," for example, is based on an actual incident. The theme is that of the cattleman against the sheepherder; but more than that, the story delineates the sense of fair play that Rhodes saw as a distinguishing characteristic of the true Westerner. Billy Beebe is a neophyte cowhand from the East. Turning his back on his college education and his rich family, he has decided to become a "rolling, bounding, riotous stone"; but because of his background, everyone shows deference to him—and that he resents. He envies Jeff Ballinger, a cowboy younger than himself, because Jeff's free and easy demeanor makes him fit in more. As the story progresses, Billy learns things, not only about Jeff, but also about range ethics.

As Billy and John Wesley Pringle are on their way to join the Rainbow herd, the latter says of the difference between Billy and Jeff, "You go into a project with a mental reservation not to do anything indecorous or improper; also to stop when you've taken a decent lickin'. But Jeff don't aim to stop while he can wiggle; and he makes up new rules as he goes along, to fit the situation." The proof of Jeff's talent comes later.

On their journey Billy and Pringle stop to visit with Jimmy, a cowboy who has been left to guard against encroachment by sheepherders onto the Three Rivers range. When some sheep are seen coming, Jimmy fires a couple of warning shots. One of them strikes a rock, sending a splinter into the leg of the man herding the sheep. Thinking he is shot, he fires back, killing Jimmy. Billy and Pringle argue that the herder is innocent, but the Three Rivers people want to hang him; and twenty of them have Billy and Pringle trapped in a small cabin. When Uncle Pete of Three Rivers pleads with them to give up the herder in order to save lives, Pringle replies, "I'm goin' to make my word good and do what's right." As the shooting is about to begin, Jeff, having learned of the situation, arrives and meets the Three Rivers men in front of the cabin. When he removes all the bullets from his gun but one, saying that he has picked one man at random to shoot if any of them try to take the cabin, Uncle Pete and his men turn around and head for home. Jeff explains to Billy what happened:

> Spose I'd made oration to shoot the first man through the gate. Every man Jack would have come 'a-snuffin'—each one tryin' to be the first. The way I put it up to 'em, to be first wasn't no graceful act—playin' safe at some one else's expense—and then they seen that some one else wouldn't be gettin' an equitable vibration. That's all there was to it.

Rhodes may well have based this story on an actual incident, but he no doubt added a twist or two of his own. While it goes beyond the formula Western in terms of realism, the ending seems a bit too contrived. It is obvious throughout this story and others by Rhodes that he presents a rather idealized view of the cowboy that occasionally betrays his otherwise realistic approach. This idealized view may come from the fact that Rhodes knew firsthand what he was writing about, in contrast to Wister, Crane, or Richter, who knew the West only as outsiders. As a result, they maintained an artistic distance that actually gives their stories a more realistic aura.

A character who often appears in the Western is the hired "gunny," a man who stands outside the law and is willing to use his gun in return for money. Rhodes presents such a character in "Beyond the Desert." In this story MacGregor, the hero, is being chased by a posse for a bank robbery he has committed. He manages to elude the posse and meets Clay Mundy, a rancher involved in a range war who prevails upon MacGregor to help him in his fight, agreeing to shelter the fugitive in return. In a variation of Romeo and Juliet, Mundy is in love with the daughter of one of his enemies and has been secretly meeting her. MacGregor learns of this liaison and hopes that a marriage between the two lovers will end the war. Mundy, however, puts his desire to hurt his adversaries before his love for the girl and arranges a mock marriage in order to strike at her family by dishonoring her. MacGregor discovers this plot and calls Mundy on it. The latter refuses to marry the girl, and a gunfight between the two takes the lives of both.

While MacGregor is a somewhat unbelievable character, he does represent a man caught between what he himself is—a hired gunman—and a moral code to which he holds. He chooses to honor that code. As James Folsom notes, however, the real irony of the story lies not in the conflict between MacGregor's divided loyalties, but "in the fact that MacGregor must think through the implications of the conventional code to which he, as many another Western hero, subscribes." As the two stories above indicate, Rhodes had considerable faith in the moralistic stance of the cowboy; he loved the West, and he loved the people who populated it. He had a fear that that West was passing, however, and with it happier times; his novel *Pasó por Aquí*

(1927), for example, may be seen as a lament for those happier times. The frontier, in terms of history, changed rapidly, and in one sense there was very little time for the "old times"; and perhaps that is why we mourn them as we do.

To assume, as perhaps most readers do, that the Western must always deal with cowboys and Indians disregards a number of writers whose stories treat other aspects of the West. In addition to Bret Harte, mentioned earlier, two such writers who come readily to mind are Willa Cather and Walter Van Tilburg Clark, both of whom drew on Western materials in a more modern sense than any of the writers discussed above.

A Virginian by birth, Willa Cather moved to Nebraska when she was a child. There, like Eugene Manlove Rhodes, she was witness to the passing of the last vestiges of the American frontier and to what she saw as a debilitating materialism replacing the heroic vitality and instincts of the early pioneers. In one sense an elegy to the loss of those qualities, her stories reflect the touch of the conscious literary artist, one more interested in the impact of frontier life on personality than on the physical aspects of that life. Her main theme is the contrast between civilization and the frontier; and no better illustration of this can be found than her classic story "Neighbor Rosicky."

Like Crane's "The Blue Hotel," this story is set in Nebraska. Focusing on the ephemeral quality of the frontier—ever receding before the advance of settlement and city—she not only presents the qualities and ideals of frontier life, but also notes the advent of the automobile; the fear that the agricultural life will be supplanted by the industrial life; the distrust of the cities; the vanity of upward striving; the problem of the immigrant "mixed" marriage; and the ever-recurring question of how parents can transmit their experience, values, and wisdom to the next generation.

That the frontier vanishes never to return dominates the story's first section, in which the elderly Neighbor Rosicky learns from his doctor that he must, in order to live five or six years more, refrain from most of his beloved outdoor activities; for example, the doctor warns that he may naver again ride a hayrake. Like the earth itself, however, a man's life turns through the cycles of nature; and on the way home Rosicky pauses to consider the vantage point of rest in his farmland's quiet cemetery, the first of two subtle death wishes as he watches the snow, "light, delicate, mysterious," which means "rest for vegetation and men and beast, for the ground itself." At home waits Mary, an earth mother for whom feeding creatures "was the natural expression of affection"; and "creatures" include "her chickens, her calves, her big hungry boys." She feels physical pleasure at the sight of people and "personal exultation in any good fortune that came to them," and she keeps geraniums blooming throughout the winter.

Following a eulogy to the ideal life of Mary and Rosicky, presented mainly through the doctor's breakfast-time visit, Cather returns to one of her favorite themes: the adjustment to frontier life through the mind of a person whose Bohemian and city background provides contrasts and clarifies values. Rosicky remembers with pain his two years in London after departing from his home country and his life in New York between the ages of twenty and thirty-five, when life was good but the city's effect of cementing a person "away from any contact with the ground" eventually drove him Westward. In his mind loomed the incomparable opportunity of the frontier: "Nobody in his family had ever owned any land." As a child he had lived temporarily in the country and learned to love it; the city made him realize that he wants what the frontier idealizes: "to see the sun rise and set and to plant things and watch them grow."

The adjustment to frontier life—to him a culmination rather than a condition—must still occur for his daughter-in-law Polly, an "American" girl who comes from the populous town and brings to the scattered peoples of the frontier a mixed-marriage problem: "A Czech should marry a Czech." Into the chilled atmosphere after a marital spat, then, Rosicky drops like a guardian angel with the car and a silver dollar to send Polly and his son Rudolph to the picture show for the evening. What he seeks to preserve for them is one half of his two current appreciations, for the second death wish occurs in the second half of his homeward view: "The kitchen with the shining windows was dear to him; but the sleeping fields and bright stars and the noble darkness were dearer still." What he seeks to preserve them from is symbolized in a story he tells of his life in London when, as a roomer living with a starving family, he had ravenously consumed by himself half a goose intended for a modest Christmas dinner; subsequently, he begged money for its replacement. His wife confirms his present philosophy of kindness and responsibility by relating an incident in which he arrived from the fields and called for a picnic, only afterward revealing that the hot wind had destroyed the corn crop. The neighbors, given to "getting ahead," consequently suffered in the midst of common losses; Rosicky and his family, amid those same losses, had enjoyed what little they had.

Polly's feeling for her father-in-law improves with these tales, but Rudolph still yearns for the security of paid wages at a packing house or railroad. Rosicky regards landlessness as a type of slavery, and in his son and his son's wife sees two problems: how to preserve their marriage and convert the transplanted towny to the frontier's values; and how to retain his son on the farm and protect him from the city's sorrows. After a fruitful life, Rosicky finds that his goals have shifted; in New York working as a tailor he had been "trying to find what he wanted in life for himself; now he was trying to find what he wanted for his boys." Mainly he wants them to appreciate the land. Hardships might come on the farm, but "there would be other years when everything came along right, and you caught up." His sons would not make more than a living on the farm, but, like him, they could live without ever taking a penny from anyone who needed it, and live close to the earth, away from the "foulness and misery and brutality" of human depravity. He has a deep fear of the cities, where people live "by grinding or cheating or poisoning their fellowman." He realizes also that, growing up in his own household, his sons have not been properly prepared for the evils of city life.

Almost as if consciously precipitating a decisive incident to implant his values, Rosicky chooses to rake the thistles from Rudolph's land in order to demonstrate his own care for the crops and oppose Rudolph's indifference that the thistles might "take the alfalfa." In keeping with the doctor's warning, the heart attack comes this summery day; Polly watches Rosicky's fall, supports him to the house, and nurses him back to consciousness. She thinks she derives a world of wisdom from holding his "gipsy-like" hand of cleverness and generosity, and admits to him the coming of a child. His problem of how to transmit his values has been solved in their clasped hands. That he has scored an ideological victory, however, does not occur to this simple man; but Rosicky lives long enough to reflect that he would not have discovered Polly's tender heart had he not followed his farmer's instincts.

The close of the story, like the beginning, belongs to Doctor Ed, who pauses by the beautiful graveyard to reflect on the open, free, undeathlike place where "a man who had helped to do the work of great cities" had got to at last. To this educated man, Rosicky's life seems to have been "complete and beautiful."

It may seem a long way from Crane's Scratchy Wilson to Cather's Rosicky, but in one sense they each are involved in the passing of a way of life— Scratchy Wilson, the end of the code duello that marked the early West; Rosicky, the loss of a true relationship with the land.

Even more modern in his view of the West than Willa Cather is Walter Van Tilburg Clark. His most famous work, *The Ox-Bow Incident* (1940), in Irwin Blacker's view, "shows the growth of the Western myth to the level of art." Calling it a morality tale in the medieval tradition, Blacker sees the novel probing "deeply into the entire concept of frontier law and justice." Certainly Clark does reflect a more realistic view of the West than do most other writers of the Western; and, like *The Ox-Bow Incident*, his short stories exhibit an authenticity that raises them well above the formula Western. One of the more interesting of these stories—and one that follows the same theme of a dying way of life as Cather's "Neighbor Rosicky"—is "The Wind and Snow of Winter," a story that in 1945 was awarded the O. Henry First Award.

In this story, Mike Braneen, an old prospector, is coming down from the mountains with his burro Annie to the town of Gold Rock. Disdaining the paved highway, whose automobile traffic makes him uneasy, he sticks to the rutted old wagon road—a throwback to the old Comstock days. As he walks, he is lost in memories and thoughts of the past. He knows that within the next few days winter will shut off the mountain with its snows; fifty-two years in this land have made him sure of such things. For the same number of years he has been coming down to spend the winter in Gold Rock; and those years now mingle in his mind so that time is no longer chronological for him. The burro Annie becomes Maria, a burro that he had years before. He tries to remember the winter he had stayed in the mountains, but he "would have to stop and try to bring back a whole string of memories about what had happened just before, in order to remember how old he had been, and it wasn't worth the trouble."

His home in Gold Rock over the years has been Mrs. Wright's rooming house, where he has always had the same room. It is to that place that his thoughts turn, and to the "meals in the dining room at the International House, and to the Lucky Boy, where he could talk to Tom Connover and his other friends, and play cards, or have a drink to hold in his hand while he sat and remembered." This particular journey seems somehow different, how- ever, from earlier ones. His rheumatism bothers him, and he feels that he is moving more slowly than usual. He feels clear and strong in his mind, and his memory seems sharp as it ranges back to a woman that he was with years ago.

Things, however, are not as they were in Gold Rock. When he comes to the summit of the old road, he looks down upon the town; but instead of the communal glow from rows of orange windows that he expects, he sees only a few scattered white needles of light. "You are getting to be an old fool," he tells himself. Gold Rock is changed, "but he loved it all the better. It was a place that grew old with a man, that was going to die sometime too. There could be an understanding with it." In that thought, however, Mike Braneen is wrong. The Lucky Boy is closed, and a man tells him that Tom Connover had died. He asks the man, who now recognizes him, where he should turn to get to Mrs. Wright's. The man says that she too is dead and that Mike must mean Mrs. Branley's, "where you stayed last winter." Mike finally agrees that that must be the place he wants. To his question as to when Mrs. Wright died, the man responds, "quite awhile ago, Mr. Braneen." And so the story ends.

In "The Wind and Snow of Winter" Clark catches the specific poignancy of a man whose life is nearing its end; but more than that, he focuses on an era that is coming to an end. When Mike Braneen sees the harsh white needles of light of the new Gold Rock instead of the softer and warmer orange ones of the past, he is coming face to face with reality. He may think that he can accept the change in Gold Rock and can even change himself, but he soon learns that he cannot. An offspring of Bret Harte's Argonauts, he has only his jumbled memories to hold on to. We know that when he passes from the scene, the West will indeed be a new place. Like the hunters and trappers before him who gave way to rutted roads and hospitable boom towns, he must give way to paved roads and towns that no longer cater to prospectors.

That this particular journey seems different to him is surely not strange, for it is his last, and he knows it.

In addition to the several writers examined here, there are, of course, many others—Mark Twain, Jack London, Zane Grey, Ernest Haycox, Dorothy Johnson, Clay Fisher, John Cunningham, to name but a few—who have written short stories dealing with the West. To label them simply Western writers wold be short-sighted, since a number of the better ones wrote stories with other than Western settings. To view as Western only those writers who limited themselves to such settings, however, would be equally inappropriate. C. L. Sonnichsen is correct when he says that "Southern writers speak for the South, Eastern writers speak for the East; but the West belongs to everybody, including the Swedes and the Italians, and speaks for everybody. It comes closer than the fiction of any other region to providing an index to America."

Certainly much of what makes up the Western genre, be it short or long fiction, is of inferior quality and could hardly be called serious literature. Sonnichsen is also correct, however, when he reminds us that "Gunfire has echoed even in the groves of Academe, and today it is respectable to have opinions about westerns, not as literature, but as popular culture." Whether the Western hero is a true representation of Nature's Nobleman or whether he is simply a product of man's need for a make-believe world, he has been portrayed broadly from the dime novels of Erastus Beadle to the screens of movie theaters and television sets. While the keepers of the American literary chronicle may give the Western little note, relegating it to fine print, and while they may wait expectantly for the great Western story to be written, no one can deny that in terms of its hold on the imagination of America and the world, the Western has had, and will continue to have, an impact matched by few other literary genres. For in a very real sense the Western is of all time and all places. Owen Wister perhaps phrases it best:

> What is become of the horseman, the cowpuncher, the last romantic figure upon our soil? For he was romantic. Whatever he did, he did with his might. The bread that he earned was earned hard,—half a year's pay sometimes gone in a night,—"blown in," as he expressed it, or "blowed in," to be perfectly accurate. Well, he will be here among us always, invisible, waiting his chance to live and play as he would like. His wild kind has been among us always, since the beginning: a young man with his temptations, a hero without wings.

Wilton Eckley

SHORT FICTION OF THE NINETEENTH CENTURY AMERICAN SOUTH

The Southern author aspiring to prominence in the antebellum South faced a number of obstacles perhaps unique in American letters. In addition to rejection from the North, which considered Southern literary productions *a priori* inferior, the Southern author had to contend with neglect from his own people. "An agricultural population," William Gilmore Simms wrote in 1867, "is rarely susceptible to the charms of art and literature." And so proved the South in the first half of the nineteenth century, when it was just beginning to emerge from its frontier phase into the first blooms of civilization. As a basically rural region committed to the land and income derived from agrarian pursuits, the South tended to view the artist's role in Southern society as a superfluous one. In one frequently quoted example of the Southern indifference to literature, a neighbor once said to the Virginia poet, Philip Pendleton Cooke, "I wouldn't waste time on a thing like poetry; you might make yourself, with all your sense and judgment, a useful man in neighborhood disputes." With the exception of the learned professions of law, medicine, and theology, "no pursuit which yielded income from personal effort and employment was respected." The noted historian Clement Eaton has commented on "the anti-intellectual nature of Southern society on the eve of the Civil War. . . . The literary man, the artist, and the teacher were not appreciated." Perhaps the most caustic condemnation, however, of the South's low regard for men of letters came from Henry Timrod, the most significant poet of the antebellum era, in his 1859 essay, "Literature in the South."

> We think that at no time, and in no country, has the position of an author been beset with such peculiar difficulties as the Southern writer is compelled to struggle with from the beginning to the end of this career. In no country in which literature has ever flourished has an author obtained so limited an audience. In no country, and at no period that we can recall, has an author been constrained by the indifference of the public amid which he lived, to publish with a people who were prejudiced against him. It would scarcely be too extravagant to entitle the Southern author the Pariah of modern literature.

In addition to prejudice and indifference from his own people, the Southern author also had to deal with limited publishing opportunities in the South. The South followed more than fifty years behind the North in the establishment of magazines. The North's two earliest magazines—Andrew Bradford's *American Magazine* and Benjamin Franklin's *General Magazine*—were published in Philadelphia in 1741; the South's first magazine, *The South Carolina Weekly Museum*, did not appear in Charleston until 1797. While the first half of the nineteenth century witnessed an incredible burst in the numbers of magazines and reviews being published in the South—Guy A. Cardwell, Jr., has figured that between 1795-1860 the city of Charleston alone produced seventy-five different magazines—the Southern public remained, however, largely indifferent, and many of the magazines, after hopeful and promising beginnings, folded within a year. Northern reading habits were deeply ingrained in the South, and most Southerners would not read a Southern magazine if a Northern one were available. In 1861, the Virginia editor and humorist, George W. Bagby, wrote:

> Southern patriotism never was proof against Northern newspapers and picture magazines. If the angel Gabriel had gone into the very heart of the South, if he had taken his seat on the top of the office of the *Charleston Mercury* and there proclaimed the immediate approach of the Day of Judgment, that would not have hindered the hottest secessionist, from buying the *New York Herald* and subscribing for *Harper's Magazine*.

The South also insisted upon implementing a restrictive code for the production and publication of a native author's works. It was essentially a principle of honor that Southern books were to be published in the South; yet if they were, the public promptly ignored them. As Henry Timrod states in "Literature in the South" of "the poor scribbler who has been so unfortunate as to be born South of the Potomac":

> He publishes a book. It is the settled opinion of the North that genius is indigenous there, and flourishes only in a Northern atmosphere. It is the equally firm conviction of the South that genius—literary genius, at least—is an exotic that will not flower on Southern soil. Probably the book is published by a Northern house. Straightway all the newspapers of the South are indignant that the author did not choose a Southern printer, and address himself more particularly to a Southern community. He heeds their criticism, and of his next book—published by a Southern printer—such is the secret though unacknowledged prejudice against Southern authors—he finds that more than one half of a small edition remains upon his hands.

The confluence of all of these factors induced *Russell's Magazine*, a Charleston periodical, to state in 1859 that "the South is as quietly ignored, as if an intellectual Sahara did, in reality, stretch from the Mason and Dixon's line to the waves of the gulf that washes the shores of Louisiana!"

Those Southern authors who did rise to any note did so by riding the great wave of romanticism which swept over the antebellum South and transformed it into "Walter Scott Land." Romanticism, as a clearly defined movement characterized by "a revolt of *sensibility* and *imagination* against a preceding age of *form, symmetry, precision, balance* and *reason*," swept through the North and the South in America during approximately the same period: between the War of 1812 and the Civil War. The manifest forms assumed by "American Romanticism" in the North and by Southern Romanticism were remarkably different. In the North, the themes associated with European Romanticism were

> . . . adapted to local environmental features and emerged as the notions of general

American romanticism . . . evident in the works of Longfellow, Cooper, and Irving, of Emerson, Melville, and Hawthorne, of Thoreau, Whitman, and Bancroft, of the Hudson River school of painters, of the Greek revival and Gothic revival architects . . . [and] are reflected in the humanitarian movements of New England and the religious revival meetings of the Western frontier.

Southern Romanticism developed along an entirely different path, one marked by a general interest in chivalry and chivalric ideals. By far, the writer to exert the greatest influence on the Old South was Sir Walter Scott; "few men ever had greater influence over the cotton planters than the beloved Scottish bard and novelist." The social and cultural atmosphere of the antebellum South was based upon the similarities the well-to-do Southern gentry perceived between plantation society and the feudal tradition. Scott confirmed the South in one of its most cherished illusions—the nobility of feudalism. In attempting to account for Scott's pervasive influence on the Old South, Rollin G. Osterweis has argued:

> A rural population is apt to like the ideas which make it comfortable and to resist any notions which threaten the status quo. Scott's brand of romanticism made the Southern planter feel like a chivalrous lord of the manor; it made the small farmer either ambitious to achieve this exalted position, or, in most cases, happy at sharing in its reflected glory. . . . That there existed a natural affinity in all this for the theme of medieval chivalry, emphasized by Scott's brand of romanticism, is perfectly obvious.

The effect of Sir Walter Scott's writings on the development of pre-Civil War Southern culture has generally been considered to be deleterious. Mark Twain has made the most caustic comment, stating that Scott "set the world in love with dreams and phantoms," with "decayed and swinish systems of government," with "silliness and emptiness, sham grandeurs, sham gauds, sham chivalries of brainless and worthless society long vanished." Twain even went so far as to perceive a direct link in the South between Scott's writings and the outbreak of the Civil War:

> Sir Walter had so large a hand in making Southern character as it existed before the war, that he is in great measure responsible for the war. It seems a little harsh toward a dead man to say that we never should have had any war but for Sir Walter; and yet something of a plausible argument might, perhaps, be made in support of that wild proposition.

The "dreams and phantoms" that Scott "set the world in love with" surfaced in Southern fiction of the antebellum period as a keen interest in making noble and heroic the particular distinctive character of the South. From English Romanticism, the Old South borrowed not only an interest in chivalry but a passion for adventurous tales, exotic settings, and idealizations of the "noble savage." The borrowings produced initially in the fiction of the Old South tales associated with the "local color" tradition. What was exotic, intriguing, or distinctive about particular areas of the South provided the basis for descriptions which focused upon capturing the "flavor" of an area through the use of dialect, stories from the oral tradition, including tall-tale humor, and elaborate, often sentimental, descriptions of natural settings. Chief among the writers of such sketches about the distinctive features of Southern life were Augustus Baldwin Longstreet and Joseph Glover Baldwin. Longstreet's *Georgia Scenes* (1835), composed of nineteen sketches of life in Georgia which were originally published in Milledgeville and Augusta newspapers in 1833 and 1834, and Baldwin's *The Flush Times of Alabama and Mississippi* (1853), a compilation of sketches originally published in the *Southern Literary Messenger* which describe life in the frontier towns during the flush times, were exceedingly popular books of the day for their interest in dialect, humorous tales, eccentric characters, and the customs and traditions of a given town or city. These fundamental elements are often identified as a major focus in Southern literature and can be seen in the works of writers as diverse yet thematically similar as Mark Twain, Joel Chandler Harris, William Faulkner, and Eudora Welty.

"Local color" sketches provided the roots of the short story in the nineteenth century South and presented relatively realistic, though often sentimental, images of life in the rural South. When the Old South sought more than realism and aspired to heroic depictions and adventure on a grand scale, it turned to the types of novels and short stories which best imitated admired English models and confirmed the South in its view that the South, too, possessed the elements of myth and legend. The rural atmosphere of the South lent itself easily and well to frontier romances and "noble savage" portrayals of Indians, blacks, and frontiersmen whose commonsense wisdom derived from years of experience and adventure. The South's history, from its first settlements through the Revolutionary period, also proved a suitable feast for scores of romantic works endeavoring to give epic sweep and depth to the South's emergence as a distinctive culture and region. The plantation tradition and its presumed association with chivalry and feudalism also became the topic of much high romance as plantation lords were magically transformed into regal barons and knights of the highest ideals of Neoplatonism. No other writer of this era captured the Old South's desire to be turned into romance and legend better or more fully than William Gilmore Simms, whose novels and short stories represent a compendium of the fundamental elements of Southern Romanticism. Simms was largely a writer for the popular imagination, and his stories, focusing primarily upon frontier life and tall-tale humor, are filled with melodrama, adventure, escapism, and triumphant moral endings. His stories, though interesting for developing such significant characters in the mythos of the South as the frontiersman, the plantation aristocrat, and the virtuous and devoted black slave, are essentially derivative and imitative, earning for Simms the sobriquet of "the Southern Cooper." It cannot be denied, however, that Simms was the Old South's central literary figure and that, more than any other artist of the period, he rendered a unique portrait of a developing South.

It is interesting and perhaps ironic to note that in its literary productions the nineteenth century South is best remembered for its authors who protested against the South's interpretation of the chivalric vision of Scott. Edgar Allan Poe, the near-mystic, absorbed in the pursuit of Beauty in the "Dream Land" of the imagination, could separate his poems and his short stories almost completely from the concerns of society, whereas Mark Twain, in *Life on the Mississippi* (1883) and *The Adventures of Huckleberry Finn* (1884), could see themes and settings in the passing of a civilization and the necessity of creating a new view of society.

Edgar Allan Poe is the least "Southern" of all the Old South writers. His themes, settings, and characters are not drawn from the Southern gestalt but bespeak a more universal framework. An atypical literary figure, Poe was interested more in the psychology of human motivations and reactions than in the Southern pull to regionalism and local-color writing. Bizarre, mysterious, exotic, and supernatural topics held his fancy, while surrealistic landscapes often became the locale of many of his poems and short stories. He was at his best in generating two types of stories, the "tale of effect," concerned with the arousal of intense emotion, and the "tale of ratiocination," from which he developed the first true examples of the detective story. In his Gothic tales of horror and supernatural happenings, his modernist and symbolic poetry, his extensive and insightful literary criticism, and his creation of the genre of the detective story, Poe stood *sui generis* in the nineteenth century South as the most original of all the writers of his day. Since he was born in Boston, lived in the South intermittently, and only occasionally made use of Southern settings in his writings, some critics contend that Poe should not be considered a Southern writer at all. Others, however, contend that he was the highest and most original expression of Romanticism in the South, even though he generally modeled his writings upon European sources.

Mark Twain is often considered a Western writer since he was born in Missouri, did not live in the South after his twenty-sixth year, and seldom in his later years referred to himself as a Southerner. Even a casual glance at Twain's literary output, however, reveals that his best writing is about the Old South, including the three books for which he is most remembered, *The Adventures of Tom Sawyer* (1876), *Life on the Mississippi*, and *The Adventures of Huckleberry Finn*. Twain was an avid reader of the Southern humorists and steeped himself in the *zeitgeist* of the antebellum era. When he came to write of the South, he adopted two positions, representing, roughly, the pre- and post-Civil War periods in Southern letters. In one pose, Twain wrote of the South much like his contemporaries, and his works are pervaded by a humorous and charming Romanticism and a focus upon unique and eccentric characters. Short stories such as "The Celebrated Jumping Frog of Calaveras County" contain all the elements of the local-color tradition, and sketches from *Life on the Mississippi* epitomize the Southern passion for Nature descriptions and capture the fundamental expansive spirit of the day. In another pose, Twain lived long enough to witness and to write about the destruction of the Old South by the Civil War. His portraits of the South in this phase of its destiny can be either empathetic for a lost dream and a vanquished civilization or bitter, satiric, and cynical in ridiculing the South for its self-deceptions and illusions of superiority. From this bitter perspective, Twain often worked to destroy the stereotypes the regionalists had endeavored to establish; thus, the destruction of the "local color" stereotype of the devoted, primitive, and largely ignorant black slave with the creation of the character of Jim in *The Adventures of Huckleberry Finn*. At a distance from the South in his later writings, Twain could readily see into the social corruptions of the day and reveal them for the injustices they were and for the suffering they generated. His most critical portrayal of all the self-deceptions the Old South lived by is the character of Tom Sawyer in *The Adventures of Huckleberry Finn* who cannot distinguish illusion from reality and thus inflicts needless suffering on Jim and others while enacting the role of the Southern aristocrat. Perhaps because he witnessed the demise of a culture and saw, too, that in the South, as well as in the North, materialism would soon invade the social fabric and corrupt the hearts of men, Twain grew cynical in a number of his later works and depicted humanity as a collection of fools easily duped by false promises and unable to distinguish good from the "fool's gold" of evil. In "The Man That Corrupted Hadleyburg" and *The Mysterious Stranger* (1916), Twain reveals that the disillusioned romantic is often the most biting and satiric of social critics.

In his short stories, Twain is recognized as the greatest humorist and satirist of the nineteenth century South. He is seen by many critics as a major figure in the development of the Southern tradition of humor that extends from the antebellum period into contemporary Southern literature in an almost unbroken line of similar depictions of the uniqueness of the South through charming, often exaggerated, portrayals of the delightful eccentricities of character, dialect, and folklore the South exhibits. It is not accidental or unusual that the Southern tradition of humor exists as a bond uniting the nineteenth and twentieth centuries, for it was by humorous portrayals of the South that post-Civil War Southern authors captured the imagination and interest of the North and established the foundation for the development of a truly respected tradition in Southern letters. The medium by which Southern authors most effected these changes and gained prominence and acceptance was the short story, particularly stories in the local-color tradition.

After the Civil War, when the South was no longer a threat to the culture of the North or the advancement of industrialization, the North became exceedingly interested in the South as a region which *Scribner's Monthly* in 1873 described as "almost as little known to the Northern states of the Union as it is to England." In the second half of the nineteenth century, America was becoming aware of itself as an amalgamation of disparate geographical regions with a variety of distinctive cultures, historical backgrounds, and folk traditions. A burgeoning interest developed in reading about these areas, an interest fed by the rapid growth of magazines during 1865-1900 as the middle classes discovered the joys of popular literature as a diversion for their leisure hours. As the popular literary magazines of the day sought to gratify the reading public's interest in the cultural and regional diversity of America, new markets developed for authors writing of the South and the West. As a result, the local-color style of writing began to blossom in the West and to develop into a cohesive tradition in the South, building from the early antebellum sketches of rural life in the South which had been popular in the South before the Civil War but largely ignored by the North. Regionalism flourished in Southern letters, as authors depicted for Northern audiences sentimental and nostalgic images of the South at its best.

The most significant writers in the heyday of the local-color era were George Washington Cable, Thomas Nelson Page, and Joel Chandler Harris. Cable's short stories, published in book form as *Old Creole Days* (1879), brought to popular attention romantic depictions of Creole life and life in exotic New Orleans. Thomas Nelson Page was the most significant writer of the day for establishing idealized images of the Old South and for glamorizing antebellum plantation life through exceedingly sentimentalized portrayals of plantation aristocrats and black slaves. Page's short stories were published as *In Ole Virginia* in 1887; a number of his stories, including his most famous work, *Marse Chan*, were written in black dialect, and Page is often credited with contributing to the popular interest in black characters as exemplifications of primitivism and pastoral themes. By far, the author most responsible for structuring fiction from black dialect and folklore was Joel Chandler Harris, whose sketches of Uncle Remus telling tales to a devoted little boy made Uncle Remus one of the most widely known and beloved characters in Southern fiction. The tales and anecdotes of Uncle Remus, collected in *Uncle Remus: His Songs and His Sayings* (1880), *Nights with Uncle Remus* (1883), *Uncle Remus and His Friends* (1892), *Told by Uncle Remus* (1905), and *Uncle Remus and the Little Boy* (1910), catapulted Harris to national fame and popularity and fixed the characters of Uncle Remus and Brer Rabbit in the popular folklore of the day.

While Southern literature advanced rapidly in acceptance between 1865-1900 and found a significant voice through the local-color tradition, a great deal of the literature produced during this period is of historical interest only and does not transcend to lasting quality in either style or theme. Much of the literature seems too much of one piece, with similar stock characters, similar sentimental portrayals of the South, and similar bland stances on moral or social issues. Since the main interest of the local-color tradition was in capturing the most apparent and distinctive qualities of a region and not in deep characterization, the fiction generated from this schema is often one-dimensional and sterotypical. Perhaps the most vigorous objection raised against the fiction of this era is its extreme glossing over of the moral issues, particularly of racial injustice, associated with life in the South, and the desire, instead, to present the South as a pastoral ideal where virtue reigned supreme and life was essentially an agrarian Garden of Eden. While there were exceptions to this trend, as, for example, George Washington Cable's probing of racial issues in the novel, *John March, Southerner* (1894), most of the Southern literature of the 1865-1900 period associated with the local-color tradition was not affected by the developing interests in realism and naturalism which dramatically altered the literature of the North in shattering facile optimism and emphasizing the bleakness of determinism in Nature and society.

To consider the short story in the South in the nineteenth century is to see a tapestry of Romanticism little interrupted by social issues or concerns of the day. By and large, Southern writers treated the South benignly in fiction and found little to criticize and much to idealize in the patterns of Southern life. From the tales and sketches of the early Southern humorists to the more finely wrought short stories of the best of the local-color writers at the end of the century, capturing the distinctive spirit of the South marked the parameters of the short story in the nineteenth century South. The period was largely an imitative and derivative one, producing many works of historical interest only. Its greatest significance lay in establishing so many of the elements of the Southern mythos and in setting the stage for the monumental accomplishments of Southern authors in the twentieth century.

Bibliography
Davis, Richard Beale, C. Hugh Holman and Louis D. Rubin, Jr., eds. *Southern Writing: 1585-1920*.
Dodd, William Edward. *The Cotton Kingdom*.
Eaton, Clement. *The Waning of the Old South Civilization: 1860-1880*.
Frazer, Charles. *My Reminiscence of Charleston*.
Hubbell, Jay B. "Literary Nationalism in the Old South," in *American Studies in Honor of William Kenneth Boyd*, edited by David Kelly Jackson.
_____ . *The South in American Literature: 1607-1900*.
_____ . "Southern Magazines," in *Culture in the South*, edited by W. T. Couch.
Landrum, Grace Warren. "Sir Walter Scott and His Literary Rivals in the Old South," in *American Literature*.
Osterweis, Rollin G. *Romanticism and Nationalism in the Old South*.

Ridgely, J. V. *William Gilmore Simms*.
Simms, William Gilmore. "The Late Henry Timrod," in *Southern Society*.
Timrod, Henry. "Literature in the South," in *The Essays of Henry Timrod*,
    edited by Edd Winfield Parks.
Twain, Mark. *Life on the Mississippi*.

Christina Murphy

619

SHORT FICTION OF THE TWENTIETH CENTURY AMERICAN SOUTH

The monuments are already beginning to accumulate: William Faulkner's *Collected Short Stories* in 1950, a book that A. Walton Litz has called "one of the richest volumes in the history of the American short story"; Katherine Anne Porter's *Collected Stories* in 1965; Peter Taylor's *Collected Stories* in 1970; Flannery O'Connor's posthumous *Complete Stories* in 1971; and the recent reissue of Eudora Welty's two classic collections, *A Curtain of Green* (1941) and *The Wide Net* (1943), in the Modern Library edition of *Selected Stories of Eudora Welty* (1954). When added to this list other later stories by these same writers—Eudora Welty and Peter Taylor in particular—and collections by writers such as Robert Penn Warren, Caroline Gordon, Carson McCullers, Truman Capote, John Barth, and Reynolds Price, there seems little need to argue that the modern short story, at least in the United States, has become a predominantly Southern genre.

It is always a risky business to try to account for the mysterious forces behind a sudden literary flowering, and the fact that the Southern story continues to thrive—in the works of Doris Betts, Andre Dubus, Eve Shelnutt, and Ernest J. Gaines, among others—makes the risk even keener. In looking back over the last several decades, the modern Southern story can be viewed as part of the general creative awakening of Southern literature that began with the poetry of the Fugitives and the novels of William Faulkner in the late 1920's and early 1930's. Unlike the poem or the novel, however, the Southern short story flourished later, in the late 1930's and 1940's and in the decades after World War II. It may eventually be determined that the modern Southern story, however much it shares with the original impulses of the Southern novel or poem, has sustained itself at such a high level of achievement simply because it is the most congenial form to the Southern literary mind. Certainly it is the genre most capable of fusing modern literary concerns and techniques with a native Southern idiom and oral storytelling tradition. Whatever explanation eventually proves to be the most convincing, the palpable fact is there: modern Southern writers excel most consistently in a single genre.

The South is a large and deceptively complex country, varied in its people and its climate and marked by strong differences of racial origins, social values, manners, temperaments, and landscapes. There are as many literary moods and contrasts in the modern and contemporary South as there are in its music—the ragtime guitar, the blues harp, the mountain banjo, the sacred song, the Cajun fiddle, and the honky-tonk piano; and in a domain like the modern short story, where the individual voice dominates all other matters, it is best to be wary of collective accents. Since most of the writers mentioned here will be treated separately—as they should be—elsewhere in this work,

this article avoids giving either a comprehensive survey of the modern Southern story or an analysis of representative Southern stories. The first approach
is simply too vast a project, and the second would inevitably tend to minimize
what is most important about an individual story by treating it as a type.
Instead, this article sketches out a few general suggestions about the common
heritage, fate, and concerns that Southern short-story writers do seem to
share, despite all their individual differences.

There are at least two general features of the Southern character that set
it distinctly apart from the rest of the United States and that continue to
inform its literature: its tragic history of slavery, war, defeat, guilt, and poverty, and its strong faith in certain traditional attitudes toward the power of
the spoken word. A preoccupation with history and the Southern past, what
Allen Tate has called the "backward glance," has been felt in every form of
Southern literature, the novel, the play, the poem, as well as in the short
story; but in the short story this backward glance has been felt not only in
terms of themes, but also in terms of narrative form. The special Southern
attitude toward language and the spoken word is again not limited to the
short story; but even more than the power of the past, the power of speech
has helped determine the choice and the shape of the short story as the most
Southern of the modern literary genres.

A third shared feature of the modern Southern short-story writer is perhaps
less evident, and certainly less spectacularly Southern. It involves his willingness to analyze his art, to judge his stories against the best work of other
writers and other countries, and finally, to speculate about how the short story
as a literary form best answers his dual needs as a modern artist and as a
Southerner with a still-vital native oral tradition.

Looking back, the broad outlines of Southern history are easily sketched
in. Since the Colonial period, Southern economy and society combined to
create a separate and distinctive culture. Even the few Southern cities, such
as Charleston, Savannah, and New Orleans, with their ornamented town-
houses, their festive café life, and their love of genteel manners, seemed more
European than American. The South was a predominantly agrarian society
dependent on a large mass of black slaves for its economic strength. With its
large, feudal plantations—first in the rich coastal lands of the Tidewater, and
later, as the cultivation of King Cotton spread, in the lush lowlands in and
around the Mississippi Delta—with its scattered, isolated small towns, and
with its rough-hewn, backcountry, upland farms, the South gradually assumed
an independence that finally asserted itself against the rest of the Union.

At first, the rebel States had every intention of remaining a separate nation.
After the first exuberant months of the Confederacy, however, when the
Southern army in its surprising victories seemed blessed by a reckless grace
that could do no wrong, there followed the series of devastating losses, the
final defeat, and the bitter aftermath of guilt, poverty, and a kind of permanent

religious fatalism. It is hard to realize the profound impact of slavery, war, and defeat on the Southern mind, not only during Reconstruction and the early days of the New South, but also today. The names of Southern leaders still seem names that are remembered rather than learned from history books. The predominant mood that remained after the war was a curious mixture of pride and guilt. There were those who locked themselves in the elegant myth of an idealized antebellum aristocracy and refused to live in the present; there were also those who zealously, often blindly, sought to remake the South after the model of the industrial North. Then there were those who, embittered with hate and heedless of their own responsibility, blamed everything on the blacks.

One good explanation of what is sometimes called the Southern Literary Renascence in the 1920's and 1930's is that it was a critical reaction to these extremes. For much of the nineteenth century, the writing that came out of the South was generally content to reflect a pleasing image of civilizing society, high ideals, and an amusingly eccentric population of contented folk. The Southern writer of the early twentieth century grew up in a time when the South he read about was largely denied by what he daily experienced.

Thus, what is perhaps most characteristic of the modern Southern writer is an urgent need to describe the actual world he knows and lives in, as immediately, as uncompromisingly, and as fully as he can. Since his world was a world of change and contradiction—the slowly embroidered, front-porch legends of the war suddenly juxtaposed with the hurried forward march of the new Chambers of Commerce, and all this under the deep shadow of racial discrimination—his art was complex, ironical, and unsentimental. He was as openly critical of the false images associated with the Old South as he was of the shamefaced imitations of the North. There were, however, important attachments to match his repudiations, a personal vision of the South to counter the public myths. If he attacked the illusions and failures of the South, he usually affirmed the traditional values of a rural, small-town community, where individual acts and individual words still counted and where large passions and large gestures were still recognized as such.

Indeed, most of the first generation of modern Southern writers—John Crowe Ransom, Allen Tate, Robert Penn Warren, William Faulkner, Thomas Wolfe, and Ellen Glasgow in her later novels—saw the danger for the South less in a debilitating dream of the past than in the empty, crude materialism of the future. Faulkner, for example, as his career advanced, became much more preoccupied with the irresistible rise of the acquisitive Snopeses than with the decayed aristocracy of the Compsons. Nowhere else in the United States was the intrusion of the twentieth century as late-coming and as brutal; and it is perhaps this conflict between the fatal flaws of the old order and the corrupt values of the new that accounts for the stress Southern art places on the tragic on one hand, and the satiric and the grotesque on the other. Some of the great Southern stories written before World War II—William Faulkner's "The Bear" and "Delta Autumn," Katherine Anne Porter's "Old Mortality," and Robert Penn Warren's "Blackberry Winter"—stem directly from the raw juxtaposition of Southern past and Southern present.

The post-World-War-II South—the period in which the short story asserted itself as the preeminent Southern genre—has done little to allay the fears of the 1920's and 1930's. The New South of commerce, speculation, and industrial growth has become a permanent reality. Naturally, none of the modern Southern writers would argue that the rapid development of the South in the twentieth century has been without its advantages. Southern universities have prospered, and Southern university journals have been a powerful force in giving encouragement and setting literary standards, particularly in the writing of the short story. Many of the negative legacies of the past—the oppressive poverty, the vicious exploitation of the sharecropping system, the rural isolation and illiteracy, the crimes of segregation—are gradually disappearing. The necessary changes have brought their modern plagues, however, and no Southern writer, no matter how enthusiastic he may be about the virtues of change, would deny that the face of his land has lost something of its old character. As Flannery O'Connor wrote in her essay, "The Fiction Writer & His Country," ". . . every day we are getting more and more like the rest of the country . . . we are being forced out not only of our many sins, but of our few virtues."

The last few decades generally have borne out Flannery O'Connor's complaint; the 1950's and 1960's brought more jobs and more money, but they also brought the interstate highway system, mass advertising, commercial television, the parasitic shopping center, rampant tourism, and the generally desolate urban-suburban sprawl. A modern Southern city begins to resemble anywhere and nowhere, a bleak uniformity of chain stores, parking lots, motels, pizza parlors, high-rise apartments, synthetic fabrics, and mobile homes. This is at least the South most visitors would see, bound as they are by the interstates and by their automobile windows. Certainly outside the commercial centers—and most of the stories of Flannery O'Connor, Eudora Welty, and Ernest J. Gaines are stubbornly rural and small-town—vestiges of a different South still persist. If the farms are larger and less populous, the farmlands continue to flourish. Almost any back road in North Carolina or Mississippi will eventually lead past a rotting cabin, an abandoned mansion, and perhaps an old flop-eared mule; but it will also lead past country stores, well-kept white wooden churches, and small towns full of large porches. Southern evenings continue to come alive with the dance of fireflies and the clamor of crickets, and along the country roads, the countryside, various, lush, and aggressively fertile, still overwhelms, still remains a supreme presence.

The South, however, has changed, perhaps more in the last thirty years than in its entire history, and it has changed toward the rest of the United States, toward a uniform existence of the same desires and the same tastes. For this reason, the contrasts and changes the Southern writers began to explore in the 1930's and 1940's continue to dominate the Southern short story, perhaps even more insistently as the old South withdraws into the backcountry and recedes into the past. More than ever, the art of the Southern writer requires a conscious act of memory, and more than ever the typical Southern short story takes the form of a personal remembrance.

Of course, most stories are accounts of events that have already taken place, but in the Southern story the act of memory that constantly seeks out meaning in the past is stressed almost as much as the remembered event. There is a sort of compulsive need to tell the same stories again and again, as if value lay in the telling, not the tale. In this sense the modern concern with individual style and multiple perspective meets the older, native oral tradition in the South through which the past is revealed never in a single telling, and never absolutely, but only in the telling and retelling by different voices living in the same place.

In order to judge better just how pervasive the theme of memory and change is in the modern Southern story, it might be useful to compare briefly three passages from three different stories whose publication dates span the entire modern period, from the beginning of the Southern Renascence to the present. Each passage is taken from the beginning of the story, and each shows a remembering mind defining itself and its values by measuring the past against the present. For the purposes of the point being made here, the thematic differences from passage to passage are less important than the fact that all three are in some way haunted by the past.

The first passage is taken from the beginning of William Faulkner's well-known story, "That Evening Sun," first published in 1931. Quentin Compson is looking back on a time when the threat of brutal violence to Nancy, his family's washing woman, stamped his young mind with questions of evil and fatality that continue to harry him. In his description of Jefferson fifteen years after the event, Quentin implies one of the few certitudes of Faulkner's world: evil is a permanent condition of the human race, but becomes even more so in the name of modern progress:

Monday is no different from any other weekday in Jefferson now. The streets are paved now, and the telephone and electric companies are cutting down more and more of the shade trees—the water oaks, the maples and locusts and elms—to make room for iron poles bearing clusters of bloated and ghostly and bloodless grapes, and we have a city laundry which makes the rounds on Monday morning, gathering the bundles of clothes into bright-colored, specially-made motor cars: the soiled wearing of a whole week now flees apparitionlike behind alert and irritable electric horns, with a long diminishing noise of rubber and asphalt like tearing silk, and even the Negro women who still take in white people's washing after the old custom, fetch and deliver it in automobiles.

The second passage is taken from Flannery O'Connor's story "A Good Man Is Hard to Find," first published in 1953, more than twenty years after Faulkner's "That Evening Sun." "A Good Man Is Hard to Find" is a richly ironic story in which no character escapes exposure, but it, too, turns the act of remembering, or misremembering, into a central theme. Unlike Quentin Compson, whose memory works on a highly self-conscious level, the grandmother's memory in O'Connor's story is superficial, predictable, and ridden with pat phrases. Still, it does distinguish her from the rest of her odd family. Her mistake in remembering the location of the plantation-house is responsible for the car accident and for the meeting with the Misfit; but despite her obvious failings, she is a recognizable human being and not a mere gadget like the other riders in the car. Along with her other qualities—willingness to speak, anticipation, storytelling, game-playing, sense of courtesy—her response toward the outside world as a place with a past, as a home, sets her apart from the passive aliens whose reality is confined to comic books and an occasional view from a moving window:

> She said she thought it was going to be a good day for driving, neither too hot nor too cold, and she cautioned Bailey that the speed limit was fifty-five miles an hour and that the patrolmen hid themselves behind billboards and small clumps of trees and sped out after you before you had a chance to slow down. She pointed out interesting details of the scenery: Stone Mountain; the blue granite that in some places came up to both sides of the highway; the brilliant red clay banks slightly streaked with purple; and the various crops that made rows of green lace-work on the ground. The trees were full of silver-white sunlight and the meanest of them sparkled. The children were reading comic magazines and their mother had gone back to sleep.
> "Let's go through Georgia fast so we won't have to look at it much," John Wesley said.
> "If I were a little boy," said the grandmother, "I wouldn't talk about my native state that way. Tennessee has the mountains and Georgia has the hills."
> "Tennessee is just a hillbilly dumping ground," John Wesley said, "and Georgia is a lousy state too."
> "You said it," June Star said.

The third passage, from Peter Taylor's "In the Miro District," resembles "A Good Man Is Hard to Find" only insofar as grandparents are used to weigh the past against the present. "In the Miro District" was first published more than twenty years after "A Good Man Is Hard to Find," and more than forty years after "That Evening Sun." In it, a grandson remembers an incident in his adolescence when his world and the world of his grandfather abruptly confront each other. It is a complex story of generations, although somehow the grandson and the grandfather are shown to have more in common with each other than either of them has with the grandson's parents. The opening paragraph of the story comes close to being an archetypal set piece of modern Southern fiction:

> What I most often think about when I am lying awake in the night, or when I am taking

a long automobile trip alone, is my two parents and my maternal grandfather. I used to suppose, after I had first got to be a grown man and had first managed to get away from Tennessee, that those two parents of mine thrusting my gradfather's company upon me as they did when I was growing up, and my company upon him when he was growing very old, and their asking the two of us to like it, though we possessed the very opposite natures, was but that couple's ruthless method of disposing of the two of us, child and aging parent, in one blow. But I can see now—from the vantage point of my own late middle age—that there was really no ruthlessness in it on their part. Because I realize that living their busy, genteel, contented life together in the 1920s they didn't have the slightest conception of what that old man my grandfather was like. Or of what that boy, their son, was like either. (Of what the one's past life had been or of what the other's would be like in the future.) They weren't people to speculate about what other people and other times were "like." They knew only that what they did was what everybody else still did about grandfathers and grandsons in or about the year 1925—in and around Nashville, Tennessee.

As suggested above, the same impulse in the modern Southern story that constantly refers the present to the past, that constantly seeks out some pattern of conflict or continuity in the changing times, also helps create a characteristically Southern form of story: the retrospective monologue. Peter Taylor's narrator in "In the Miro District" provides the best example in the examples above, but it is remarkable just how many Southern stories assume—in part or in whole—the same form. Faulkner's "The Bear," Katherine Anne Porter's "Holiday," and James Agee's "1928 Story" are all stories in which a narrator looks back on the past—either his own or his family's—in order to mine out a part of his own purpose or fate that had been up to then hidden to him. Robert Penn Warren's classic Southern story, "Blackberry Winter," adopts the same narrative strategy.

Not only is "Blackberry Winter" an exemplary Southern story in its rural setting, its insistence on the individual as a member of a family, its knowing distinctions between black and white behavior and belief, and its symbolic contrast between North and South—the evil-speaking stranger, the cold spell in mid-June, and the devastating flood all emerge out of the North—but it is also Southern in its special mode of narration. Once again, a middle-aged Southern narrator remembers in his own words a past event that somehow proves to be a living part of his present and future. As Faulkner remarked through one of his characters, in the South "the past is not dead. It is not even past."

In all these stories of retrospection, the language and narrative compulsion of the remembering character ring out convincingly with the sound of the spoken word and with the completeness of told stories. These qualities spring directly out of one of the few traditional convictions that remain general and largely unchallenged in the modern South: individual character is revealed most fully and most faithfully through individual speech. In this respect the modern South seems closer in spirit to a country such as Ireland than to any other region of the United States. Like the Irishman, the Southerner still tends to judge a man by his words and still has a certain faith in the power of speech to express not only information, but also value, belief, entertainment, and dream.

One good reason for the persistence of this conviction—and its strong influence on the written story—lies in the fact that the South continues to be nourished by strong folk traditions which today are alive almost exclusively in music and language. For if the visual community has changed, even disappeared, a certain communal identity remains, especially in the act of speech. The first difference that strikes a visitor to the South is the language, the accents, the tones, the vocabulary, and the rhythms. It is an English as distinctive as the English of Ireland. Unlike the stage Southern accent made popular by commercial television, the best of Southern speech is rooted in a rural society where the expressive power of language is highly prized. Characterized by concrete, sensual detail, sly humor, and vivid, dramatic images, the folk speech of both black and white is capable of a rich, evocative beauty.

The South has always sustained a strong verbal awareness with a conscious self-delight in creating new expressive forms. It is no accident that three of the most original forms of popular music in the twentieth century, jazz, blues, and bluegrass, had their beginnings in the American South. The two dominant folk cultures of the South, the black and the Scotch-Irish, brought with them already richly developed oral traditions in which those with special gifts for expression were praised and publicly encouraged. Black slaves, forced into a position where English had to be learned, breathed into it their own nature and their own experience and created an English as vital and as expressive as the Anglo-Irish speech of the white settler. The presence and creative forces of these two cultures, their intermingling and mutual influence primarily in the twentieth century, may help explain the special skills the South demonstrates in the modern story. This conjecture appears especially true at a time when traditional delight in words and story is about all the tradition that remains.

The short story originates in the told tale; the written story's concentration of plot, the literary skills needed to stimulate interest and to hold it without waste, all these are conversational skills as well. As William Faulkner remarked of the Southern writer in an introduction to *The Sound and the Fury* (1929): "we need to talk, to tell, since oratory is our heritage." Robert Penn Warren has recently made a similar observation in a little more detail:

> Among critics and historians the remark is not uncommon that tale-telling is (or was) a regional trait of the South—on the steps of the country store, where the whittlers gathered, at races, in taverns and saloons, while heel-sitting in the shade to get acquainted with a stranger, or in drawing rooms. Along with sermons, hellfire or doctrinal, and the arguments or rampaging satirical abuse of the hustings, such tale-telling lies behind Southern literature.

In the contemporary South, there are still exceptional storytellers in the oral tradition. Probably the best example of the existence and the importance of the told tale today is the series of recordings Theodore Rosengarten made in the early 1970's with a black sharecropper, Ned Cobb. Published in 1974, *All God's Dangers* testifies to the continuing power of the tradition. Ned Cobb's imaginative manipulation of language, his large and searching memory, and his natural impulse to make meaning out of each of his problems or successes by giving it dramatic form aligns him closely with the literary art of the modern Southern authors mentioned above. He is one of the master storytellers of his time.

The publication of Ned Cobb's stories in *All God's Dangers* should remind us that if the stories by modern Southern writers share a common history of the South and a common contemporary experience of great social change and contradiction, perhaps what unites them most strongly is the natural need for language—in both art and life—to delight, to explore, to give shape to experience, and to reveal meaning. Perhaps what is most Southern about this need lies in the communal foundations of language, a recognition by the artist that the reader shares the same need, and that the end of all art is a new communion. When Eudora Welty was asked in an interview about what made the Southern story distinctive, she responded:

> I think the Southerner is a talker by nature, but not only a talker—we are used to an audience. We are used to a listener and that does something to our narrative style. We like to entertain and please, and we also rejoice in response.

A strong oral tradition certainly accounts for some of the qualities in the modern Southern story, but it must be remembered that the modern story is a deliberately crafted work of art and that the Southern writer is fully conscious of belonging to the modern *literary* tradition as well as to a specific society. The South is a large country, and apart from the small group of intellectuals and poets who formed the Fugitive-Agrarian membership in Nashville, there was no well-defined literary movement such as in William Butler Yeats's Ireland, where diverse individuals were drawn into constant contact in a single city. What the modern South lacked in the way of a definite literary center, it compensated for by means of a different kind of literary community, one made of universities, textbooks, university-based journals, and private correspondence.

What was true of the first generation of modern Southern writers was even more true of the following generations. Not only did they benefit from the universities, but they also had the careers of Faulkner, Wolfe, Ransom, and Tate as encouraging examples; and they had the advantage of being close to some of the best literary criticism being written in the English-speaking world. Journals such as the *Southern Review*, founded in 1935 by Cleanth Brooks and Robert Penn Warren, were especially important to the great creative burst of Southern short stories in the 1930's and 1940's. These journals provided a place where Southern writers could publish their stories, and perhaps more important, in the long run, they provided a continuing forum where literary criticism, analysis, and speculation were made readily available. Southern textbook-anthologies were a direct result of this new critical activity, and the popular *Understanding Fiction* (1943) by Cleanth Brooks and Robert Penn Warren and *The House of Fiction* (1950) by Allen Tate and Caroline Gordon were influential through their judicious choice of stories and their high standards of critical commentary. Flannery O'Connor's letters mention both these books as having helped shape her own literary aims and judgment. Her letters also demonstrate, at least in her case, the importance of advice and encouragement from other writers. She developed many of her theories of the short story by corresponding with friends who asked her to read and criticize their stories; the letters she herself received from Caroline Gordon are models of clarity, precise detail, insight, and practical advice on the stories and novels O'Connor sent to her.

One of the important results of this lively interest in critical theory behind the short-story textbooks, the professional journals, and the examples of correspondence we do have is the fact that almost every major Southern writer has written original criticism on the short-story form. In a field that is notoriously meager—in France today, for example, there is not a single anthology of modern French stories, nor a single critical study of the modern short story—Southern writers have been particularly original and productive. Once more, the only comparable situation to the Southern one is modern Ireland, out of which two of the rare full-length studies of the short story have emerged: Frank O'Connor's *The Lonely Voice* (1963) and Seán O'Faoláin's *The Short Story* (1951).

Caroline Gordon, Katherine Anne Porter, Robert Penn Warren, Flannery O'Connor, and Eudora Welty have all been willing to discuss their own stories in as much instructive detail as they discuss those of others. Warren's account of his "Blackberry Winter" remains one of the best introductions to that story. Flannery O'Connor's various speeches and articles were collected posthumously in the volume *Mystery and Manners* (1969). Eudora Welty has recently published some of her wry, original critical essays in *The Eye of the Story* (1978). Both *Mystery and Manners* and *The Eye of the Story* contain valuable insights into the function and the form of the short story, and both demonstrate a wide and perceptive appreciation of all kinds of short-story writers, within and without the Southern tradition.

A more telling sign that the short story has natural roots in the Southern literary consciousness, however, is the curious fact that almost every writer in the South has an original theory about the form; there is something so general and so compulsive about the active speculation on the short story in the South that one is tempted to consider the genre almost a Southern mode of perception. The short story, of all literary genres, manages best to wed native Southern oral traditions with modern literary preoccupations, but there is something more to it than that. Consider the following passages from three contemporary Southern writers, Reynolds Price, Harry Crews, and Robert Penn Warren.

The first is taken from the introductory essay in Reynolds Price's *A Palpable God* (1978), a selection of stories he translated from the Bible; the essay is entitled "A Single Meaning: Notes on the Origins and Life of Narrative." In the midst of discussing the source and narrative form of some of the earliest biblical stories, Price makes the following statement:

> The oldest prose stories were set in virtually their present verbal form in about 950 B. C. by one of the greatest of epic writers, anonymous, known to us only as the Yahwist. There is considerable evidence of various sorts however—including the personal experience of anyone reared in a powerful oral-narrative tradition (contemporary American Southerners, for instance, or conservative Jews)—that the stories developed their present narrative armature and perhaps the greater part of their verbal form long before the Yahwist's editing.

The second passage is taken from Harry Crews's moving autobiographical portrait of his Bacon County, south Georgia home, *A Childhood: The Biography of a Place* (1978):

> It was always the women who scared me. The stories that women told and that men told were full of violence, sickness, and death. But it was the women whose stories were unrelieved by humor and filled with apocalyptic vision. No matter how awful the stories were that the men told they were always funny. The men's stories were stories of character, rather than of circumstances, and they always knew the people the stories were about. But the women would repeat stories about folks they did not know and had never seen, and consequently, without character counting for anything, the stories were as stark and cold as legend or myth.

The third passage, taken from a recent (1980) review article by Robert Penn Warren on Eudora Welty, offers an interesting contrast to the distinctions Crews makes above:

> There is another fact, a special kind of conversational flow among Southern women—or at least a remarkable plenty of them—that has provided another contribution to that literature. This was not ordinary gossip (although gossip no doubt thrived) but gossip providing the tale for its own sake, sad or humorous: the character sketch, the narrative, grotesque, comic or poetic description; gusts of feelings, delicate ironies and small, astute observations, bright as a needle point—all the things that characterize a "woman's talk," which is somehow so different from a man's tale, even when it is, itself, a tale.

These passages are placed together not to raise questions about their differences, but to demonstrate how vital the oral storytelling tradition remains in the South even today. Reynolds Price's parenthetical aside is part of a long, carefully argued thesis on biblical narration; Harry Crews's distinction appears undeveloped, almost offhandedly, in an autobiography that talks about much more than storytelling traditions; and Robert Penn Warren's remarks on gossip are just that, brief remarks in a short newspaper review. What is striking in these three passages is the natural use of a common experience of story to support each writer's different theory, and this seems unique in the history of modern letters. Writers from Russia, England, France, Ireland, and most recently several countries in South America have all contributed modern classics in the short story. In none of these countries, however, is the convergence of native traditions and individual speculation on the art of the story—O'Faoláin in Ireland and Jorge Luis Borges in Argentina, for example, are the exception, not the rule—as natural and as common as in the American South. Perhaps this is one reason why the modern Southern story continues to thrive and to breed new forms, and why it continues to reflect, more than any other region or country, the successful union of the communal, popular mind with an individual, original voice.

Ben Forkner

CANADIAN SHORT FICTION

In his Introduction to *Modern Canadian Stories* (1966), Giose Rimanelli says, "Art is tradition, even in its most experimental forms." A rich sense of tradition—that historical continuity of values, of culture, and of art—seems to be fertile ground for imaginative literature; a writer's knowledge that he belongs to a specific time and place gives his work its distinctive flavor. This sense of tradition informs the best work of most writers and, once it is established, it can be transcended to impart the universal truths of enduring literature. For many reasons, however, Canadian writers have always been uncertain about their identity. Indeed, the catalogue of comments by Canadian critics and writers throughout this century has focused almost exclusively on this problem. For both critic and writer, there is confusion about knowing where they came from, what they are, and where they are going. Consequently, since Confederation in 1867, Canadians have had a feeling that the important sense of spiritual and geographical identity has eluded them, and that in the end, they are victims in a land they have yet failed to understand or create. The Canadian short story reflects a great deal of both individual and collective skepticism, resulting in a literature of conflict and struggle against a vast, formidable, and intractable nature. Canadian writing, therefore, is perhaps the least definable of the world's literature.

The historical development of the short story in Canada is not well known. In fact, many native Canadians would say this apathetic attitude is typical. It is important, then, that the origins of the short story be traced to explore but not necessarily to perpetuate the myths of the Canadian personality. As late as 1960, Robert Weaver summarized the general feeling of Canadian critics. He says in his *Canadian Short Stories*, one of the few anthologies up to that year:

> What we do not have is much of that sophistication and intellectual intensity that distinguishes a good deal of contemporary fiction appearing in the old literary societies abroad. It seems that the Canadian writer still feels able to indulge a certain naiveté, and I suspect that some of the virtues and limitations of that outlook are pretty clearly reflected in this book.

As a criticism of what Canadian writers have accomplished with their short fiction, this statement is certainly true. One will not yet find a Guy de Maupassant, an Anton Chekhov, or a Nathaniel Hawthorne in Canadian literature. What one will find, though, are many writers of quality who convey the significant themes, influences, and patterns that persist as distinct cultural and personal values.

The history of the short story becomes very curious, especially for the foreign reader, when it is admitted that there has been very little criticism evaluating the progress of the Canadian writer. In *Essays on Canadian Writing 1979-1980*, David A. Kent regrets that this critical situation "has not as yet appreciably altered. . . . Perhaps the sheer variety of Canadian stories, with their different settings and concerns, makes them extremely difficult for criticism to assimilate effectively." He concludes, agreeing with most critics, that the regional and local nature of the short story, still much in evidence, has not given way to "a vision of the country as a whole."

Nor has the Canadian writer a substantial audience to give him the confidence to continue serious work. In Pre-Confederation days, writers had to rely on newspapers or periodicals such as the *Acadian Recorder*, the *Nova Scotian*, and the *Literary Garland* to publish their sketches and tales. After the *Literary Garland* collapsed in 1851, there were few magazines to fill the vacuum until after World War I. Even then, despite such efforts by the *Canadian Forum*, established in 1920, most outlets for short fiction were through popular magazines which encouraged the facile, sentimental, and romantic stories in vogue in the nineteenth century.

There was also what Robert Weaver calls "the fugitive existence" of the short story which prevented many writers from producing any substantial work. Good writers such as Raymond Knister and Morley Callaghan were forced to publish abroad in magazines such as *The Exile*, *Transition*, and *This Quarter*. Many other writers simply gave up the genre of the short story altogether. The complaint today is still that Canadian magazines of literary merit cannot compete with their more successful American counterparts. Some of the best stories by Mordecai Richler, Mavis Gallant, and Alice Munro are often seen first in the *Atlantic Monthly* and the *New Yorker*. In the 1970's there has been a noticeable but not a significant change in this process. In Canada there seems to be a rebirth of the short story; anthologies of many individual writers are coming forth that reflect regional, historical, and national concerns. To the credit of the editors, stories of considerable aesthetic worth are being presented, rather than the stories of dubious quality which were so prevalent in earlier Canadian fiction. With more tough-minded critical writing and a wider, more interested readership, Canadian writers can have a sense of intellectual recognition that encourages the commitment needed for first-rate work.

The concensus is that Canadian short fiction falls neatly, although arbitrarily, into three distinct phases based on political referents. They are: Pre-Confederation, Confederation to the end of World War I, and World War I to the present. There is a definite growth, especially in the formal quality of the work, but it would be premature to say that the Canadian short story has reached full development. Particularly striking is the similarity of theme throughout the years despite dramatic changes in cultural makeup and increasing urbanization of Canadian life. Canadian literature as a whole has been extremely depressing and bleak, and there is a keen sense of isolation, struggle, and hopelessness in the face of a vast geography and a merciless nature. Margaret Atwood, a Canadian novelist and poet, even contends that the main condition of Canadian life and letters is "survival." Because of the harshness of the land, Canada is noticeably different from Britain and the United States. Despite colonial settlement by the British and French, immigration from Europe and the East, and fear of assimilation by the culturally and economically powerful neighbor, the United States, Canada has grown separately, cautiously, retaining only some of the characteristics of the older societies. The land itself seems to have left its unique and indelible imprint on the Canadian mind. Even with the ever-present regionalism mirrored in the short story, the attitude toward the environment remains the same. In his article "The Canada of Myth and Reality," Robertson Davies says:

> The Canadian is the *coureur de bois* who must understand—understand, not tame—the savage land. And is it the savage land of rocks and forests only penetrable by the patient explorer? Only in the sense that this is a metaphor for the equally savage land of the spirit—.

The land, then, affects not merely the physical, but also the mental: the Canadian short story, at its best, describes this perilous but necessary journey into the inner depths of the mind.

It must be pointed out here that the Quebec short story, in French, has developed differently from the story in English, especially in technique, although many of the themes are substantially the same. The full treatment that analysis of French Canadian short fiction would demand is beyond the scope of this essay. The problem is that few Quebec authors have been translated into English, a fact that perhaps exaggerates their feeling of isolation within Canada. The ones who have been translated, such as Anne Hebert, Gabrielle Roy, Yves Theriault, and Jacques Ferron, have made significant contributions to Canadian literature. There is, unfortunately, little chance that English Canadians will become literate enough in the French language to feel the full impact of French-Canadian writing. Still, translation is at least the first step toward offering the reading public the special quality of mood and thought which distinguishes French-Canadian literature.

Philip Stratford made a start in 1974 with his book *Stories from Quebec*. In the Introduction he points out that the French are more precise in defining the short story:

> The *recit* is a small slice of life with a strong historical or autobiographical bias. The *conte* is more playful, a symbolic tale which stems, in Quebec, from folklore and a rich oral tradition. It is sometimes an intellectual conceit or a contemporary parable, often a fantastic fable. The *nouvelle* is generally longer, more concerned with character, more complex and more subtly structured.

Stratford goes on to outline the particular characteristics of Quebec writers.

Most stories have a strong and "joyful sense of the traditional tale teller," but even in the realistic ones "there is a stronger sense of person behind the narrative." They are more individual and personal, without the contrivance of aesthetic or moral detachment. Also, instead of a linear plot that proceeds to dramatic resolution there is "a cataloguing of effects" where similar incidents are repeated until the story reaches its sudden denouement. There is an incredible "speed and concentration of narration," a condensation of "a whole life into a few pages," which differs radically from British and American practice. Quebec writers are often noted for their morbidity, for their focus on oppression, incest, suicide, and violent death. As Stratford observes, however, there is also a "robust humour" that underlies even the blackest of Quebec stories. In this last point one can see a closer parallel to the stories of English Canada than has previously been thought. It can only be hoped that interest in the Quebec story will increase to add needed vitality to English Canadian literature and to dispel some of the uncertainty and discord that still exist between the two cultures.

Canadian stories, in general, have their origins in folktales of the oral tradition, especially Indian tales, but even the good translations of these tales have little literary interest. The quality of the folk story lies in its telling, the inventiveness of changing voice emphasis and physical gesture which cannot be captured in print. More important are the first narratives found in the early newspapers and magazines. A. J. M. Smith points out that the first efforts of Pre-Confederation writing served a utilitarian purpose, that the writers had no conscious intention of creating "literature." People such as Joseph Howe, primarily an orator and politician, and Thomas Chandler Haliburton, a journalist, provide interesting insight into the Canadian tradition although they were limited by the provincial interests of the time. David Arnason in his Introduction to *Nineteenth Century Canadian Stories* (1976) makes a stronger case for the importance of early letters to the editor, sketches, fables, and romantic tales. He says:

> Our forbears were not too busy struggling to survive to create a literature which captured the drama, the humour, the dreams, the expectations, and even the defeats of people of high enterprise in an exciting and challenging new land.

Although he recognizes the problems in this literature, the stern moral tone, the elevated artificial language, the sentimentality, and the contrived plot line, his point of view is a radical one. Except in certain isolated cases the stories are not very good and do not match the stature of stories in nations where short fiction was more developed. He does, however, make a welcome attempt to balance the opposing view that early Canadian literature is so barren that it is not deserving of attention.

Many Canadian themes have roots in this time period, and many bad habits which persisted until the twentieth century are found here. Many of the inhabitants were of English, Irish, and Scottish stock. There was considerable adjustment to be made, and the concerns of the writers were often consistent with popular British taste. In Canada there was the loss of the familiar class system, then largely unworkable, but there was still an antagonism towards egalitarian American democracy. There were melodramatic and romantic stories based on what many wanted Canada to be, an English village society with English justice and security. More subtle, though, was the underlying sense of exile and hardship that was to receive more explicit treatment in the late nineteenth and early twentieth centuries. A few significant authors do capture the realities of the age. John Richardson (1796-1852) is interesting for his energy and for his violent portrayal of frontier life. In "Jeremiah Desborough: Or, The Kentuckian," as David Arnason says, "It also demonstrates a fierce anti-Americanism which, though it appears in a number of stories of that day, is taken into little account by historians."

In a more positive way Thomas Chandler Haliburton (1796-1865) contributes to both the Canadian and American heritage of humor with his stories of the engaging Yankee clock pedlar, "Sam Slick." He has a distinct neoclassical bent, but he writes in credible dialect, both English and French, although he often sacrifices realism for his humor. His tales are filled with eccentric but well-drawn characters, and he has a good eye for local color and detail. Beneath the genial humorist, however, lay the Tory moralist, ready to use his satire to criticize the complacency and lack of individual industry in his colonial counterparts. Susanna Moodie (1803-1885) published sketches in the *Literary Garland* which were later revised and included in her influential book *Roughing It in the Bush* (1852). Born in Suffolk, England, and sister to author Catherine Parr Traill, she is, as Margaret Atwood says, the "reluctant immigrant" who goes from the city to the uncivilized wilderness where she suffers and documents the severe hardships of the Canadian reality. Her survival is dependent on her native British toughness and determination not to succumb to the forces of inexorable nature.

The achievement of Confederation in 1867 changed the attitudes of many writers, who, if not entirely comfortable with nationhood, were now at least conscious of it. With the new political status there was a more obvious transition from American rugged individualism to a greater feeling of community; this transition was, out of necessity, a convergence of British and American views of life, which is clearly evident up to this day. The perception of isolation, suffering, and victimization still existed, but the quality of life seemed more dependent on collective responsibility than on individual courage. Unfortunately, with commercial expansion and democratization from 1867 to the 1880's, much of the writing still reflected popular taste; it was entertainment without personal character and imitated the inferior romantic and sentimental models that were also popular abroad. With economic problems and the failure of many good literary magazines, readership dropped, and writers went to England or to the United States. In general, Canadian short-story writers lacked the technique and insight of their contemporaries abroad and did not engage in the exciting and successful experimentation of the age. There are, however, Canadian works of inventiveness and artistic merit which deserve special consideration.

Edward William Thompson (1849-1924), although born in Upper Canada (Ontario), was a Boston newspaperman and veteran of the American Civil War. He is well known for his *Old Man Savarin and Other Stories* (1895), which is in the heroic mode, often excessively sentimental and exaggerated. He is able to draw believable characters and place them in recognizable local settings. Often, as in stories such as "The Privilege of Limits," the honest values of the immigrant are rendered in a rural Canadian setting. There is no real dark side to his work, no firm ironic perspective, but his light touch is lively and is a forerunner of much twentieth century humor.

One of the most unusual forms of the Canadian short story is exemplified by Sir Charles G. D. Roberts (1860-1943), who writes "animal stories." These typical adventure stories are written from the animal's point of view and are often crude and artificial, produced for the most part according to formula. The human characterization is especially weak, although Roberts is able to capture the spirit of the wilderness and to describe accurately authentic qualities of animal behavior. In "The Watchers in the Swamp" and "When Twilight Falls on the Stump Lots," Roberts conveys imaginative sympathy for animals in situations where nature is just as much of a struggle for them as for people. In the latter story there is even a fine ironic attitude which contrasts the primitive violence of the animals and the refined slaughter of man. After a desperate struggle for survival a bear dies, defeated by a cow. The victory is futile, however, as the cow soon ends up on the "cool marble slabs of a city market."

The writer with the best technique of his time is Duncan Campbell Scott (1862-1947), whose first important collection of stories, *In the Village of Viger*, appeared in 1896. As a poet Scott is concerned with style and the special effects that form can bring to a work of art. His subject matter, like that of his contemporaries, is romantic, but he is more subtle, infusing his direct, simple, and controlled style with the symbolism of poetry. Adapting these techniques to prose he is able to present cogently and realistically the tragic existence of man on the early frontier.

The most well-known Canadian author, often called the Canadian Mark Twain, is Stephen Leacock (1869-1944), who moved from Swanmore, England, to Canada in 1876. Loved for his humorous depiction of small-town Canadian life, "Leacock," as Robertson Davies says, "spoke like a Canadian—simply, in sentences usually brief, avoiding slang but by no means unconscious of the flavour and impact of simple words used in unfamiliar contexts." Davies also suggests that Leacock grasps the essence of the Canadian mind—repressed, vigorous, and turbulent. Leacock, however, even in his most famous work, *Sunshine Sketches of a Little Town* (1912), often writes frivolously and carelessly; rarely does his work show the discipline of the accomplished stylist. His aversion to rigorous editing does not obscure his genius, which is evident in many of his stories, but it prevents him from being placed in the first rank of the world's humorists and satirists. Perhaps, too, Leacock fails to get at the darker side of human nature although there is an undercurrent of deeper criticism which is felt but is not developed or resolved. In his book *Moral Vision in the Canadian Novel* (1978), D. J. Dooley proposes that Leacock's materialistic view of life forces him into being only an "amiable humorist." Of course, we can make much of Leacock's inconsistencies and defects, but there is no doubt of his great achievement in bringing Canadians a lively, compassionate picture of themselves.

In the twentieth century, especially after World War I, the short story became an identifiable genre with a few notable practitioners. The market for stories was still small, but the writers, usually novelists, began to see writing the short story as a serious and demanding vocation, thus making it a more self-conscious, deliberate art form. Generally, both the French and English writers became more urbanized although this process was slow, and often there was a tension between depicting the struggle on the land and examining the life in the city. More obvious, however, was the sophistication of technique. The short story became more subjective and symbolic as emphasis was placed on character and psychology rather than on plot.

Frederick Philip Grove (1879?-1948) remains a very mysterious figure, whose early history was obscure before Douglas O. Spettigue's discoveries were published in 1973. Grove (real name Felix Paul Greve) was a German who taught and traveled in the Canadian West before settling in Ontario. His tragic vision of man is reinforced in realistic, sweeping narratives of the adversity of pioneer life. Most of his work follows the naturalism of Émile Zola and Theodore Dreiser; there is a great deal of power in his writing, but technically it shows signs of haste; it is sloppy and disconnected. In a story such as his justly famous "Snow" the writing is formal and harsh, but it forcefully portrays the unrelenting Canadian winter environment and man's courageous but futile efforts to overcome it. Man seems powerless to have even an illusion of hope when confronting inevitable death.

Mazo de la Roche (1879-1961) is internationally famous for her novels of the Whiteoak family of Jalna, but she was also prolific in her short-story output. Two collections, *A Boy in the House* and *Explorers of the Dawn*, show her as another in the line of the romantic storytellers, but her technique is more advanced. Her stories have good dialogue and an interesting use of symbolism. There is, however, little real depth of insight, and she lacked the ironic attitude that would give her stories bite. A South African by birth,

Ethel Wilson, born in 1890, is a superior writer who, perhaps because of her British background, uses language more carefully and ironically than de la Roche; her sense of urbanity and worldly knowledge which gives her characters, especially women, a social and psychological reality sets them apart from the types found in much humorous fiction.

The most important and influential Canadian short-story writer is Morley Callaghan, born in 1903, who writes with distinction in the short-story form. Giose Rimanelli says he is the most "American among Canadian writers," for he wrote in Paris in the 1920's with Gertrude Stein, F. Scott Fitzgerald, and Ernest Hemingway. His style is spare and direct, the simple language almost devoid of metaphor and symbolism. A serious moral and religious perspective, present in most of his work, arises out of character and situation, usually in an urban context, rather than out of artificial literary language. At times his writing appears banal and mannered, its point being obscured or lessened by lack of dramatic effect. The possibility of salvation in a world of increasing materialism, however, and the compassion for the suffering of ordinary people are often convincingly presented in this restrained, modulated style. The unaffected approach to the stories allows the reader to discover for himself the deeper significance and reality below the surface.

Raymond Knister (1900-1932) showed great potential, but drowned at a young age, becoming as much a victim of nature as the people in his stories. As a student at Iowa State University, Knister was influenced by the American Midwest and wrote perceptive but depressing stories of the adversity of rural life. Freedom from this tedious life seems impossible for his characters. In "Mist Green Oats" one of his characters rebels against this situation: "He began to descry the blind unwitting stupor of life, reaching for what it wanted, an ox setting foot on a kitten before its manger."

Sinclair Ross, born in 1908, a native of Saskatchewan, vividly dramatizes the strenuous life on the Canadian prairies, often in the depression years of the 1930's. Again, there is the theme of man versus nature and his seemingly impossible but still obsessive attempt to tame it. "The Lamp at Noon" best demonstrates Ross's approach to the short story: the struggle of coping with the dust and drought causes resentment within the family. Nature seems out to destroy human relationships, and for the individuals involved, all confidence in the future, faith in the land, and faith in themselves is illusory; finally, there is the reluctant recognition that the land has betrayed its people. The story, predictably, ends in the tragedy of death. This bleak view of life, reinforced by Ross's descriptive and psychological realism, is tempered only by his concern and understanding for people doomed to failure.

Historically, many writers that have contributed to Canadian literature have been immigrants. In the modern era, Malcolm Lowry (1909-1957), Brian Moore, born in 1921, and Clark Blaise, born in 1940, are three such writers who enrich the Canadian short story with their work. While living in British

Columbia from 1940 to 1954, Malcolm Lowry, an Englishman, completed his most significant work, *Under the Volcano* (1947). Both this novel and his collection of stories, *Hear Us O Lord from Heaven Thy Dwelling Place* (1962), illustrate the importance the Canadian environment played in his writing. As Greig Henderson says, however, "Lowry differs notably in that the Canadian environment functions symbolically in his works as a paradisal alternative to the subjective hells in which his characters have wilfully enmeshed themselves." Brian Moore, an Irishman, now a resident of California, still retains Canadian citizenship and continues to be influenced by Canadian personalities and attitudes although his concerns are much wider than merely the analysis of his adopted nation. Clark Blaise, born of Canadian parents in North Dakota, is now a permanent resident of Canada. As some critics have stated, Blaise's writing style and values are American, and he is important more for showing what is different about the Canadian experience than for examining traditional Canadian ways.

French-Canadian writing forms a vital part of the Canadian experience, but problems of language and politics have relegated it to second-class status in English-speaking provinces. In his novel *Two Solitudes* (1945), Hugh MacLennan dramatizes the conflict between English and French Canada; the tension seems to be a permanent aspect of aesthetic and political life, and in MacLennan's view Canada is essentially a nation segregated by two cultures. The concept of Canadian unity was most seriously challenged first during the "October Crisis" of 1970 when Prime Minister Pierre Trudeau invoked the *War Measures Act* to quell the violent outbreaks of Quebec "Separatists" and second, in the referendum of 1980 when Quebec voted to retain federal status within Canada. Despite the gravity of the problem, however, it may be more profitable to look at the situation as only another manifestation of Canada's regionalism.

Gabrielle Roy, born in 1909, is the central figure in French-Canadian literature, and the body of novels and short stories she has produced is impressive. Her themes are familiar ones. Phyllis Grosskurth says:

> In each of the books we have found variations on the theme of the illusion of individual freedom. The characters are frequently torn between a longing for a more expansive existence and the undeniable circumstances that restrain them.

Although Roy examines the struggle of existence, her characters "are never faced with agonizing moral problems." This inability to deal with the nature of evil, Grosskurth concludes, limits her effectiveness as a storyteller of great vision. Yves Theriault, born in 1916, gives us tales of Indian and Eskimo life and evocations of the primitive emotions of Quebec rural life. In the "Anguish of God" we see the prejudices and fears of the people in a small Quebec hamlet; the two main characters end in personal isolation and madness. Theriault has many stylistic faults, but Philip Stratford says, "The power of his tales lies in their sheer narrative drive and rugged authenticity."

Anne Hebert, born in 1916, continues the tradition of seeing people as victims of doubt and isolation; her creations are haunted by the rituals and deceptions of the past. As John Stevens suggests, Jacques Ferron, born in 1921, has much in common with the experimental, absurdist stories of younger English writers such as Ray Smith and Matt Cohen. Ferron, however, works within the older French tradition of the folktale; the narration is swift, the style almost point form. He places a strong emphasis on irony, fantasy, and fable as he satirizes and depicts the conventions of Quebec society. Michel Tremblay, born in 1944, is a very successful dramatist and storywriter whose work is winning much recognition outside Quebec. His stories are grotesque and fantastic, the precise, trenchant style communicating an almost tangible feeling of horror.

Much recent short fiction in English Canada is of high quality, with a more conscious exploration of urban values. Hugh Garner (1913-1980) brings a strong, sometimes overbearing moral and social conscience to his stories, the memories of the Depression being an especially significant focus. He sides with the common man who, for Garner, is obviously alienated in the modern materialistic city. Characteristically his sentimentality is balanced by the harsh criticism of those forces which conspire to overwhelm the ordinary citizen. Jack Ludwig, born in 1922, from Winnipeg, and Mordecai Richler, born in 1931, from Montreal, treat humorously and realistically Jewish life in the modern city. Both writers are adept at creating the character and values of an immigrant society confronted with the problems of social and cultural adjustment. There is a feeling of nostalgia for the past and compassion for the individuals who are isolated by poverty and worn-out traditions within their own restricted environments. Ludwig and Richler, however, can be seen as moralists; they give their stories a more universal appeal through ironic criticism of man as an individual as well as a member of a specific community.

Hugh Hood, born in 1928, often contrasts past and present, the rural and the urban, to establish the common bonds linking all people. He studies the psychology of his characters, implying that it is dangerous to escape from the weight of the past or from the reality of the physical environment. Mavis Gallant, born in 1922, is an expatriate writer who has experienced life in the United States and Europe as well as Canada. She employs a delicate, elegant style, but her method of characterization is tough and uncompromising. Alec Lucas says, "Mrs. Gallant normally takes a satiric view of her characters, largely middle class, dissecting their personalities with almost complete detachment, sometimes bordering on the pitiless."

Alice Munro, born in 1931, is another excellent stylist with the same kind of ironic detachment as Gallant. Her reputation continues to grow even though her writing is restricted to the precise description of small-town life. Of her collection of stories, *Lives of Girls and Women* (1972), Martin Knelman says, "The book creates a self-contained world as filled-in and persuasive as Faulkner's and Hardy's." It seems that if human nature is constant, it can still be examined successfully within a particular locality. In fact, for Munro, the frailties, obsessions, and passions of the individual personality can be more authentically revealed by being treated on a small scale. Margaret Laurence, born in 1926, spent seven years in West Africa and produced a collection of stories on African life. Since her return to Canada she has published stories set on the prairies of her birth. She is skillful in developing individualized characters who are true to their native culture and attitudes, but who also belong to the larger community of man. Again, the element of struggle, so much a part of Canadian fiction, is a salient point in her work, but her creations, especially women, have indomitable wills and rise to almost heroic stature.

Of the younger Canadian writers, Margaret Atwood, Dave Godfrey, John Metcalf, Ray Smith, Matt Cohen, and Margaret Gibson show much talent. Atwood is already internationally known as a novelist and poet and is able to create technically innovative, ironic studies of the crisis of personality in contemporary society. The other writers also demonstrate that the Canadian short story is not as provincial nor as facile as it once was; there is experimentation in theme and structure, and although not always successful, these efforts are refreshing indications that the short story is healthy and enduring.

In the *Canadian Forum*, 1926, Douglas Bush says, "In the literary way Canada is probably the most backward country, for its population, in the civilized world. . . ." This observation was probably not far wrong at the time, but it seems a spurious notion now. Traditional themes—the search for identity; the struggle against nature; the bleak view, tempered only by gritty humor, of man as victim; and the regional concerns—all have given the Canadian short story its particular quality. Short-fiction writers, however, are trying to avoid the innocent acceptance of these myths and stereotypes. Many of them see that fiction must be rooted in tradition, in a specific place and time, but they do not make this their only business. Within the Canadian experience the superior writers raise the local values to universal truths accessible to all people. As Margaret Atwood says, "A tradition doesn't necessarily exist to bury you: it can also be used as material for new departures."

James MacDonald

INDIAN SHORT FICTION IN ENGLISH

The first Indian novel in English—Bankim Chatterjee's *Rajmohan's Wife*—was published in 1864, twenty-nine years after the official introduction of English as a language in India. The first book of short stories in English—*Stories from Indian Christian Life* by Kamala Sathianandan—was brought out by a Madras publisher in 1898. Sathianandan's decision to become the first Indian to write short stories in English had at least three reasons behind it: the form was popular among readers; the language looked both exotic and sophisticated at that time; and he was able to portray India for the knowledge of those interested foreign readers who did not know any other "Indian" language. More than this, however, it was because he discovered that the ancient classics of his native land provided ready-made short stories in almost finished form.

The most important influences on the Indian short story in English came from the epics, the Puranas, and the popular tales, the most significant of these being the *Ramayana* (c. 350 B. C.), the *Mahabharata* (c. fifth century B. C.), the Vedas, the Upanishads, the *Bhagavadgita*, the *Kathasaritsagara* (eleventh century), the *Panchatantra* (fifth century), the *Dasakumaracarita* (c. sixth or seventh century), and the Buddhist Jatakas and Apadanas. All the important story writers have admitted their indebtedness to these ancient classics in matters of technique and content.

The Indian story writer has been always conscious of the glorification of domestic relations and family life that he found in the *Ramayana*; from the *Mahabharata* he has learned the value of nonviolence and the importance of self-realization through self-questioning. Indian stories have used the concepts of the ideal son (like a Rama of *Ramayana*), the ideal wife and Perfect Woman (like a Sita of *Ramayana*), the ideal upholder of moral virtues (like a Yudhisthira of *Mahabharata*), and the ideal hero (like Visma and Arjuna of *Mahabharata*). The Indian writer has received the "fabular" form of storytelling as much from Aesop's Fables of the West as from the highly concentrated *Panchatantra* of the East. Indian writers have been influenced by the typical Indian popular tale and folktale, and particularly by their loosely structured but imaginative rendering of the urges and aspirations of a people against a background of romance and fantasy. In the stories of R. K. Narayan and Manoj Das, the faintly satiric-didactic element of the fable has exquisitely merged into the imaginative, adventurous quality of the folktale.

The didactic fable and the popular tale have influenced the Indian writer in several ways. Their narration is racy and direct and full of the element of suspense; their language is simple and idiomatic, celebrating as it were the ancient virtues of order and harmony. Fables and tales are brilliant examples of the complete, well-told story, and the fascination they still hold for the modern writer is seen in their creative retelling of them, after incorporating into their basic structure contemporary Indian social problems. Mulk Raj Anand's "Five Short Fables," Raja Rao's "Kamakapala," R. K. Narayan's *Gods, Demons and Others* (1964), and Manoj Das's *Fables and Fantasies for Adults* (1978) are all set in the framework of either fable or the mythological tale. They are narrated in the manner of the traditional village storyteller who, like the tales that he retells, has been a vital part of the Indian literary tradition. The Indian short story in English being, therefore, a product of a living tradition of storytelling, the emphasis is always on the "voice." The "Talkative Man" of Narayan's stories, who displays a marvelous combination of witty humor and sympathy, is only a modernized and urbanized extension of that tradition.

Like the ancient classics, the two most important modern "events" that have influenced the Indian writer are the Nationalist movement and—something that is closely connected with it—Mahatma Gandhi. The Nationalist movement, as C. V. Venugopal explains, "made the Indian writer acutely aware of the unifying bonds of his country—her cultural tradition mainly—which he wished the others to know." It produced stories in which the emphasis was mainly on the problems of a society rather than on the private anguish of an individual. Mahatma Gandhi, with his philosophy of humanism and universal enlightenment ("sarvodaya"), his distrust of the machine, his faith in the sacred nature of the human body, his emphasis on the need for economic self-sufficiency, and his rejection of that literature which does not look continuously at life, exerted a considerable influence. His own prose, always simple, clear, and straightforward, became a model of good style. K. S. Venkataramani's collection of stories, *Jatadharan* (1937), as well as his longer works such as *Murugan the Tiller* (1927) and *Kundan the Patriot* (1932), bear ample witness to Gandhi's influence. If Murugan is an exponent of Gandhian economics with its celebration of rural self-sufficiency, then Kundan is an exponent of Gandhian politics with its celebration of "satyagraha."

The earliest short stories in English were passionately reformist in character. They attempted to draw the conscientious attention of those few Indians who were educated and sophisticated to the prevalent social evils, such as caste system, forced widowhood, child marriage, and untouchability. A. Madhaviah's *Kusika's Short Stories* (1916) portrays a traditional society that is in need of urgent, drastic change. A. S. P. Ayyar's *Sense in Sex and Other Stories* (1929) and *Finger of Destiny and Other Stories* (1932) also deal with contemporary social problems. What disappoints their reader, however, is their too obvious leaning towards didacticism, their almost obsessive desire to present a ready-made "message." Their dialogue sounds artificial; their characterization seems unconvincing and without depth; their endings are without much variety.

The 1930's and 1940's produced a better set of writers. The stories of K. S. Venkataramani record the reactions of a sensitive and intelligent individual to the fast-changing social and political circumstances in preindependent India. Although slow-moving and full of "thinking," they are made lively through mild touches of satire as when, for example, a story that criticizes overpopulation is kept side by side with another that deals with husband-wife "collisions." Venkataramani's stories have their basis in a social revolution that was begun by Raja Ramohan Roy, a contemporary of Lord Bentinck, and was then continued by Gandhi. His Jatadharan, after having had a brilliant academic career, chooses to become a pial teacher rather than a servant of the British government, in order that he will be able to educate the villagers. His other story, "The Bride Waits," is about the failure of Sastri to find a suitable match for his daughter despite all his most anxious efforts. Sastri must face the criticism of the extremely orthodox people of his caste for having kept his daughter so long in his house; he must also face the anger of his employers, in the form of a transfer to a god-forsaken place, for having availed of a leave at a time when he was not supposed to. Venkataramani's stories have their bright as well as their dark moments; his prose has glowing metaphors as well as poignant descriptions of poverty and sadness.

The two other writers who wrote at about the same time as Venkataramani are K. Nagarajan and Manjeri Isvaran. Nagarajan's *Cold Rice* (1945) offers interesting pictures of life in the South Indian districts on the Coromandel coast during the 1930's. Nagarajan, who in his novel *Athawar House* (1939) had introduced into fiction the concept of an interdistrict, interlanguage marriage between a Maratha girl and a Tamil boy, was the first writer to hold his stories up to the slow but steady erosion of traditional Indian values in the face of a gradual Westernization. He was also perhaps the first writer to deal effectively with the disillusionment, hypocrisy, corruption, and the opportunism that had become rampant during the last days of the British Raj and that undermined the general health of the Indian nation soon after the Independence. What his stories embody is *not* the conflict in the people serving the Raj between a loyalty to the British and a patriotic leaning toward national dreams, as was the case with A. V. Rao (*The Man in the Red Tie and Other Stories*, 1942); it is something simpler and more pathetic. Nagarajan, a lawyer by profession, has a lawyer's meticulous eye for detail and a talent for interpretation.

Manjeri Isvaran, at one time the Secretary of the National Book Trust of India and editor of a magazine called *The Short Story*, has approximately ten volumes of stories to his credit. He was also a poet, and his poetry certainly influenced the language of his stories, which is highly poetic. His stories display a remarkable tenderness and feeling for life. His themes, which are typically Indian, show a considerable variety: consequences of the World Wars and India's acquisition of freedom, the jealousy of one for another's "fruitful" lime tree, the intimate love affairs of a confirmed thief. He is critical of the typical Indian's blind faith in the Divine as well as of his superstitions. His story "At His Nativity" quietly mocks the belief that a male child born on the hour of Lord Krishna's birth will prove inauspicious to his uncle as Krishna did to his, the evil King Kamsa. His "Seashells" is the touching story of a young woman whose husband—following the belief that a bath in the sea wards off the evil effects of planets and stars—goes into the sea to take the "holy dip" but is finally sucked into it. Isvaran begins his stories leisurely with a scene in which he is present, then introduces the main story either through one of the other members of the group, or through an event that occurs and provides the group with their evening's gossip.

With Mulk Raj Anand and R. K. Narayan, one is brought into an entirely new phase in the history of the Indian short story in English. Anand wrote on such diverse subjects as Indian curry, Persian painting, and the Hindu view of art before turning to fiction. Although born into a high-caste Hindu family, as a child he loved to mix with the children of the "untouchables." These early friendships with "harijans" (Gandhi's term for the low-caste people which, translated, means "The People of God") were to produce the heroes and heroines of his first stories and novels. His stories, which have grown largely out of a deep-seated sympathy for the downtrodden and the neglected, were influenced as much by the Bengali writings of Sarat Chandra Chatterjee and the Hindi writings of Munshi Premchand as by those of Leo Tolstoy and Maxim Gorky. In his fiction he was, in his own words, rediscovering the vanities, the vapidities, the conceits and the perplexities with which [he] had grown up."

In Anand there is hardly anything like an exploration of an unknown. Perhaps with the single exception of the long story, "Lament on the Death of a Master of Arts," all of his best stories concern themselves with intensely dramatized proletarian realities. There is absolutely no mysticism involved in the kind of sympathy that these "realities" have produced in him. In stories such as "The Barber's Trade Union," "The Cobbler and the Machine," "Lajwanti," and "Torrents of Wrath," he writes with a reformer's anger about economically caused personal sufferings. People's sufferings are caused not only by economics; they also result from religious and social customs. "Mahadev and Parvati" is a straightforward satire against the lies and hypocrisies that reign at the "sacred" centers of India. The priests who harass the young couple—Mahadev and Parvati—symbolize the state of organized religion in the country as a whole. "Lajwanti" is the sad story of a beautiful village girl who, unable to withstand the amorous advances of her brother-in-law during her timid husband's absence, runs back to her father's house (she lost her mother when she was a child), only to be brought back by her father to her earlier fate. Her father, orthodox to the core, is more worried about preserving the honor of his family than about the well-being of his daughter. Lajwanti's story is a brilliantly fictionalized repetition of many such stories that occur every day in Anand's India but are hardly noticed. "The Priest and the Pigeons" is a mixture of mild satire and irony in which the priest vainly tries to scare away two amorous doves from the sanctum of the temple. He thinks that the birds defile the sanctity of the temple when, ironically, the temple itself is dedicated to the most loved romantic pair of the world of Indian legends—Radha and Krishna.

Anand creates what he describes as "a new kind of fable which extends the old Indian story form into a new age, without the overt moral lessons of the ancient Indian story, but embodying its verve and vitality and including the psychological understanding of the contemporary period." His understanding of his contemporary India meant an understanding of what he called "the dignity of weakness of others." His "Lament on the Death of a Master of Arts" is the product of a deep sense of compassion for the lonely and the weak. It is the tender story of Nur, a young and sensitive "Master of Arts" who has an angry father and an unsympathetic stepmother, and who is passing through the terminal hours of his consumptive life. Like Anand's novel *Untouchable* (1935), it is painfully moving and emotional. Yet the prose also has its other side, a rugged quality which is produced by Anand's incorporation of his native Punjabi words, phrases, and sentence structures into English. As a result, Anand has been criticized for "infelicities of style" and "strangeness of sounds," but one must keep in mind the fact that he rarely writes about people who have well-decorated drawing rooms and find rough sounds unpalatable; his stories are about smaller people who, as he says, "speak freely, unashamedly, expressively and may bring new metaphor to any written language."

Like Anand, R. K. Narayan has been a highly prolific writer whose stories successfully convey "the Indian quality of life." Unlike Anand's stories, however, which are full of scorn against the "old morality," Narayan's are a restatement of old values. By keeping himself close to the old morality, he has been able to evoke "the common rhythm of life" as it is lived in South India. In his stories, therefore, we do not find radical insights or deep-rooted emotional conflict. On the other hand, Narayan conveys that unique atmosphere of rural life or life in the small towns, where everything seems strangely colored by superstition. Narayan, who, like his brother, the cartoonist R. K. Laxman, enjoys a wide popularity, has employed the methods of a cartoonist very successfully in his stories. His forte is the comedy of manners; his career in journalism produced in him a faith in the value of understatement as well as exaggeration.

If we hear the echo of the Punjabi language in Anand, we also hear the echo of the Tamil in R. K. Narayan, although, as Anand says, "he seems very scrupulous in avoiding native turns of phrase in order to communicate with his large audiences." Narayan's language is very close to the journalistic; it is moderate and traditional with a limited vocabulary and a modest range of effect. It lacks the palpable, imagistic quality of much native English, but it has a limpid, translucent quality; it is a language that is meant to be seen through, and it is perfectly adapted to the author's fine comic sensibility. One is attracted to the affectionate Narayan's satire; his is that kind of humor in which even jokes are also a species of moral insight. In stories such as "Lawley Road," "The Artist's Turn," "A Night of Cyclone," "An Astrologer's Day," "Leele's Friend," "A Breath of Lucifer," "Seventh House," and "The Cobbler and the God," the comic voice of Narayan acquires a unique tone.

"The Cobbler and the God," for example, is the story of a chance meeting between a hippie who has given up the things of the world and a cobbler to whom "nothing seemed to belong." The cobbler sits between the "outer wall of the temple and the street" mending shoes and chappals. A margosa tree provides him the necessary shade and shakes down its flowers on his head. The hippie, observing him from the temple steps thinks, "Only the Gods in heaven can enjoy the good fortune of a rain of flowers." When he comes to the cobbler to get the straps of his sandals fixed, the cobbler glances up at him and reflects, "With those matted locks falling on his nape, he looks like God Shiva." By way of opening a conversation, the hippie says, "Flowers rain on you," and the cobbler, looking up, retorts, "Can I eat that flower? Can I take it home and give it to the woman to be put into the cooking pot? If the flowers fall on a well-fed stomach, it's different—the gods in Heaven can afford to have flowers on them, not one like me." The hippie asks him a question which can only surprise him: "Do you believe in God"? Can such a question be asked? Is there a need for such questions—such doubts? God will hear him when he is free, and until that time, he must bear. "'What, bear what?' asks the hippie. 'This existence. I beg him to take me away.' 'Why, aren't you happy to be alive?' the hippie asks again.'" The poor little man does not understand this question either; he is convinced that God is simply punishing him for deeds that he committed in his last birth. "What do you want to be in your next birth?" the hippie asks. The cobbler wonders whether he is talking to a god or his agent—does not that question contain the veiled promise of a gift? The hippie asks no more questions. By now a strange friendship has been quietly established between two lonely beings. The hippie does have something to offer—a little silver image of the goddess Durga which a yogi had given him in Nepal. The cobbler examines the figure and asks the hippie whether he stole it. The hippie appreciates the cobbler's question as indicating perfectly how he has ceased to look respectable. He replies, "Perhaps the man who gave it to me stole it." "Keep it, it will protect you," says the cobbler returning the figure. He reflects after the hippie is gone, "Even a god steals when he has a chance."

The story contains many things: the Indian's belief in the doctrine of karma, his deep faith in the Divine, his belief in rebirth, sin and hell, his total acceptance of life as it comes, and above all, an innocence which is so typical a quality of the rural folk. It is this innocence which is a recurrent theme of Narayan's works. Although his language does not possess the poetic dimension, he has been able to wield his "one-stringed instrument" to his best advantage, compensating for what he loses on the language front with a keen eye for the little details of Indian life and an intelligence that discovers significance among these details.

Raja Rao's language, like Narayan's, also springs from the Indian setting and the Indian manner of gesture and speech. His language does not suffer from the restricted vocabulary of Narayan. His stories, which are not many in number, and his novels are written in a fluent prose that almost trembles with symbolic suggestions; they have a quiet, meditative grace that reminds one of the ancient *rishis* of India. They rarely deal with personal relationships, although in his longer works, such as *Kanthapura* (1935) and *The Serpent and the Rope* (1962), he explores the nature of the man-woman relationship with a passion that reminds one of the best of D. H. Lawrence. His novels have a metaphysical abundance that his stories do not seem to have. The emphasis is not on character; it is rather on the quality of being human, or, more specifically, the quality of being Indian. The form he experiments with in his stories, therefore, is the folktale or popular legend, since that form offers, in the words of M. K. Naik, "simplicity and credulity . . . myth-making power . . . [and] the strong moralistic substratum on which it is, in its popular wisdom, often grounded."

Raja Rao mythicizes contemporary events in Indian history, viewing these against the saner background of Indian cultural heritage. In his "Javni," the inherited burden of superstition is made light through love. It is the story of the Untouchable Javni, who is widowed and hated by all. She is employed by a family in which, although she is treated with some affection, she is never allowed to forget that she is an Untouchable and that she must always stand on the threshold. The story moves on to the city-educated Ramu's encounter with Javni and her "long, long tale of misery," to Ramu's vain attempts to make his sister's family understand Javni's plight, and finally to the conclusion—Ramu's departure from his sister's home, leaving Javni to continue in her part mythic, part realistic role.

In another story, "The Cow of the Barricades," Rao offers an allegorical presentation of one aspect of India's struggle for independence: a confrontation between the "red men" and the Indian workers. The workers, against the advice of the "Master," have turned militant and erected barricades against the "red men." The "Master" of the story—an idealized figure who appears in several of Rao's stories, as the "Swami" does in Narayan's—may not be Mahatma Gandhi himself, but he certainly stands for all that Gandhi cherished most. The cow, Gauri, is a symbol of divine purity, goodness, and compassion (the cow is sacred for Hindus and is worshiped by them even today) whose sacrifice brings peace to an agitated land. After her death, Gauri—like everything else in an Indian village—becomes a part of the local legend. People now offer her statue "flowers and honey and perfumed sweetmeats and the first green grass of spring." The children of the village play between her legs, and putting their mouths to the hole in her breast, shout out resounding booms. The whole story is told with a poetic abundance that is rarely matched by anything in Anand or Narayan. If Narayan's emphasis is on the popular and dramatic, then Raja Rao's can be said to be on the philosophic and lyrical.

K. A. Abbas, who has been successfully writing scripts for and directing Bombay films, has written novels and stories in two languages—English and Urdu. His favorite form is the satire, and he performs his satiric task with an exaggerated voice which he seems to have learned from the world of films. His stories present him as a devout socialist impatient for revolution. The stories dramatize, for the most part, highly sentimental versions of subjective wishes and have for their themes the author's personal reactions to problems such as poverty, communalism, overpopulation, unemployment, government red tape, and refugee influx. "I am an Indian," he says with visible anger in *The Black Sun and Other Stories* (1963): "That means I am an idealist, an incorrigible optimist and a simpleton who lives on the vegetarian diet of illusions. Bring a wolf in sheepskin and we will give him a grand welcome with banners and flags and speeches." Although remaining an angry man like Anand, Abbas can also produce—again like Anand—extremely tender stories.

The story "Sparrows" is an example. It concerns Rahim Khan, who decides to avenge himself for the ambitions that he could not fulfill because of social pressures by being cruel to everybody, including his wife and children. The story, which looks like a more realistic, Indianized version of Oscar Wilde's "The Selfish Giant," is the sad account of a man who—like the Giant—has banished life itself from his "world." Everybody deserts him. He lies lonely, detested by all until one morning he discovers a nest of sparrows in his hut. The sparrows are the only creatures who are *with* him, and through them, he gradually learns to love again. One rainy evening, while trying to save his friends from the rain, he drenches himself completely; the next morning he wakes with a fever. Through a crack in the door of his hut, the villagers see him talking to himself, worrying about the possible fate of his dear birds after he is dead. "Poor fellow, he has gone mad," they say and send for his wife, who comes back the next morning with their sons, only to find the "large and gaunt frame of Rahim Khan lying in the brooding silence of the room, broken only by the flutterings of four sparrows."

Independent India has produced a considerable number of first-rate story writers, including Khushwant Singh, who has made significant contributions to the study of Sikh history and religion and who was for a long time the editor of *The Illustrated Weekly of India*. He holds an antiromantic stance and is intolerant of cant and hypocrisy, especially when they masquerade as wisdom and insight. One of his best as well as most familiar stories, "The Mark of Vishnu," is an attack on Hindu superstition; it tells the story of Ganga Ram, the snake-worshiping Vaishnavite Brahmin who meets his death when the "Kala Nag" which he has fed saucers of milk bites him. It digs its fangs right below the v-shaped smear on his forehead, the mark of the Preserver Vishnu.

"Karma" is the story of the Oxford-returned Sir Mohanlal, who is English in everything except the color of his skin. He detests everything Indian, including his wife. Then one day, while traveling on the train, he is forcibly thrown out of his reserved first-class compartment by two British privates, while his wife is sitting comfortably in another compartment among unsophisticated but loving Indians, chewing her favorite betel nuts. Khushwant Singh shows another side as well in stories such as "Black Jasmine," "The Portrait of a Lady," and "The Fawn," which are admirable exercises in tenderness and pity.

Manohar Malgonkar, a retired Colonel in the Indian Army who has the wit and elegance of Singh, has continued to offer refreshing instances of Indian life and character. Most of his stories are first-person reminiscences, comedies of everyday life, and vignettes of social and domestic follies. His "Bear on a Plate" is a highly interesting story about the hoodwinking of Elmer Finkenstein, a "Texan oil king" who is madly interested in hunting expeditions. On seeing an advertisement in a hunting magazine about an Indian man-eater, he decides to come to India. The "man-eater" is after all the "big cat" from the Parijat Circus who has now become old and small. "Pull-Push" is a story about the influence of ministers on every minor decision that is being taken in India including, as recorded in this story, a decision to transfer a high-ranking civil servant from one post to another merely because he reminds his ever-forgetful subordinates about their duties and responsiblities.

Like Singh and Malgonkar, Ruth Prawer Jhabvala is an extremely popular writer and certainly the best woman writer in India today. Born of Polish parents in Germany and educated in England, she has finally settled in India. Having had the experience of such diverse cultures and lacking a sentimental attachment to the Indian soil, she can be said to have brought a kind of objective, international outlook to the Indian problems. All of her stories in her first collection, *Like Birds, Like Fishes* (1956), are about the plight of such people in urban India as middle-class families with only one breadwinner, or an unemployed young graduate given to much introspection but very little action.

Jhabvala's second collection, *A Stronger Climate* (1968), is about the plight of Europeans in India. There is Richard, the British High Commission man in love with a beautiful, "mysterious" Indian girl whom he cannot take away from India because she "belongs here"—to this country of "ruins and gardens and fantastic moonlit nights." There is Cathy, who is married to an Indian and who finds herself in the orthodox cage of an Indian family. There is also the tender story of Dr. Ernst, "the Indian Citizen," who goes from place to place trying and failing to make friends. Perhaps he has stayed in India a little too long. Everything that was once fascinating and good has turned sour on him, making him experience the terrible state of being old in a country that no longer needs him. All of these Europeans look to India for something that Europe failed to offer them; they have been attracted by its stronger climate, stronger colors, and stronger personalities. Although her stories are sometimes inordinately long and her style is without anything remarkable about it, Jhabvala has her compensations. She conveys with sincerity what Angus Wilson, while awarding her the Booker Prize of 1975 for her novel *Heat and Dust*, called "the feeling of India—its squalor, its miseries, its excitements, the enticements of its Paradox."

Manoj Das, a marvelous storyteller, has achieved a perfect fusion of the narrative technique of the traditional Indian tale and themes from contemporary Indian life. His stories display a healthy, all-embracing humor and depict the innocence that lies behind the backward-looking and complacent attitudes of his country's people. The author's aim is to restore man to his original state of wholeness and health through a touch that tickles while it hurts. A look at the titles of his stories is sufficient to indicate their nature: "Mystery of the Missing Cap," "The Night the Tiger Came," "The Bull of Babulpur," "The Man Who Lifted the Mountain," "The Princess and the Storyteller," and "Sharma and the Wonderful Lamp." The relaxed, leisurely pace of his stories reminds one of the traditional Indian storyteller's enchanting gossip. His many stories about an aristocracy whose representatives even today try to find their own worth in a grace that they no longer possess are insistent pointers to the weaknesses of humanity in general.

Tenderness is abundantly present in the stories of Bhabani Bhattacharya. Like Narayan and Raja Rao, Bhattacharya is interested in life in rural India. Unlike theirs, however, his stories—especially "Glory at Twilight" and "A Moment of Eternity"—are superb examples of psychological fiction. "Glory at Twilight" raises important questions regarding man's responsibility to himself and to society. Satyajit's success in life was based on the detection of a fraud, but we now find him desperately trying to find his place in society after having lost his job. His instinctive need to return to his native village in a time of crisis underlines the security and strength that land can offer a man in a fundamentally agrarian society. The atmosphere of rural Bengal is evoked through the descriptions of customs and rituals.

"A Moment of Eternity"—certainly one of the finest stories written by any Indian—is an implicit satire on the Creator's judgment—namely, His infliction of poverty and death on those who do not deserve it and His failure to bring death to someone who devoutly wishes for it. It is the story of a poor woman's devotion to her family, her grief at the death of her husband amidst joblessness and consumption, her fatal administration of poison to her children, and her subsequent suicide attempt. She eagerly awaits a sentence of death for her murders so that she can join her husband and children, but it is denied to her; death cheats her again as it did when she had tried to commit suicide. Next she decides to destroy her sanity, for that would mean an escape from memory. With each drop of her heart's blood she prays for madness. Sanity however, remains, like a huge, burning light; it sharpens all that she hears, to the least undertone of her children's voices, "their crying and laughing, their sniffing from a touch of cold and their deep quiet breathing in sleep." The story has a sad, wet tone, and the voice that narrates it has forgotten to look into the future, or has even refused to look beyond itself. The reader, however, hears not only this voice, but also its echo resounding in many lonely and poor corners of paradoxical India.

The same seriousness of purpose as Bhattacharya in "A Moment of Eternity" can be found in the writing of Ruskin Bond. Apart from being a writer of short stories, his favorite medium, he is also a novelist, a biographer, an essayist, a poet, a writer of children's books, and an editor; his story "A Flight of Pigeons" has been filmed under the direction of the famous New Wave director, Shyam Benegal. His stories are magnificent evocations of the world of the child. They are imbued with a rare kind of poetry that receives its strength from the little ironies of common existence, from memory and nostalgia, from the natives and the tall green trees. His stories give the reader the feeling of being in intimate touch with the elemental world and the most enduring emotions.

Bond's "The Meeting Pool" is a tender evocation of boyhood. "It was Somi's idea that we should meet at the pool in ten year's time." That is how it begins. "When we are men . . . we must come back to this place . . . at midday on the fifth of April, 1964—we must return to the pool. No matter where we are, or what we are doing . . . we must meet at the pool." They shake hands and dive back into the water. The narrator does not remember how they finally broke up. Ten years later, he happens to be in that part of the country and decides to keep his part of the pledge; but instead of the pool, he finds only a dry bed of naked shingles. He waits for his friends for a long time and begins to feel foolish for having expected them to come. Maybe, he thinks, he is the only one who has not grown up. He turns away, disappointed.

Then suddenly from nowhere comes the sound of splashing water and shouting boys. Pushing his way through a thicket, he finds another stream and another pool, and several boys playing in the water. He watches them play without letting them see him. He does not really see them, however— instead he sees his old friends. He stands there for a long time, "a disembodied spirit, romping again in the shallows of our secret pool." The story powerfully conveys the sense of the passage of time and with it the gradual but irreparable loss of innocence. The new set of boys playing in the pool reminds the narrator of the continuity of life in the midst of all the discontinuities of individual existence. Bond's stories bring back to us our lost belief in the continuity of life in time and in space; they also speak of a creative continuity between man and the meanest of natural beings. They remind one of the best of Rabindranath Tagore, H. E. Bates, A. E. Coppard, and William Saroyan.

Two other writers—Arun Joshi and Kekki Daruwalla—have written stories in a serious vein. Joshi's stories, which are mostly about "the inner life of urban Indians," are all written in a low key. The common theme that runs through his stories is that of the "survivor." Joshi is equally concerned with the problem of expression and communication in a society that refuses to be sympathetic to certain kinds of relationships. His story "The Intruder in the Discotheque" is a surrealistic portrait of an old man, Shambu, who has fallen in love with a young girl in a discotheque. Shambu used to have dreams a long time ago when he was young and everything was fine. Now he begins to have dreams again. He tells his friend Vishwa that he wants that girl who moves "across the floor like a dream." "For that you must be made young once again, which is neither easy nor proper to do." Still Shambu must have his girl, so he and his friend go to "Mr. Gomes, Seller of Dreams," who gives Shambu color for his hair, pomades for his wrinkles, perfumes for his skin, and a suit of clothes that is like "skin upon skin." He can now go to his girl, but only on one condition—he must not touch her. How can one touch a dream? That night Shambu weeps in Vishwa's arms like a child.

Shambu spends many evenings with the girl, and like a good storyteller invents jokes that make her laugh. Then one evening he talks about the old man who borrowed the youth of his son and the girl laughs. Suddenly Shambu pleads, "I am an old man, I love you. I want you." At this time the girl's young lover enters the discotheque, his hair flying in the wind. Desperate now, Shambu clasps her by the wrist. The spell is broken; everybody knows who he is—a dirty old man with horrible wrinkles. "This is an intruder," a solemn voice declares, and the next moment the old man is lying on the floor, terribly lonely among all those people.

Keki Daruwalla's stories, like his poetry, are deeply rooted in the rural and tribal worlds; they are earthy and without signs of sophistication. His fifteen stories in the collection *Sword and Abyss* (1979) are full of the Northern hills, rivers, and deep forests where light plays so beautifully with the shadows. Most of his stories are steeped in a mystery whose best aspects are explored only within darkness and night. The believed transformation of a loving "stranger" into a tree with flowers, a *shaman*'s visionary enactment of his own future through a participation in the exuberance of a communal dance, the ending of long years of drought and disillusionment for a land and a people through a person of a beloved who has to be smuggled across the salt desert of a country's borders—these are some of Daruwalla's subjects. The stories themselves are a mixture of dreams, visions, and even nightmares, of flashbacks and flashforwards, so that it becomes difficult to find in them sure lines of narrative. There is a drifting, windborne quality about them—something that refuses to concentrate on any *single* object or person. In them the poet walks hand in hand with the storyteller. Daruwalla's best stories, particularly "The Tree," "Shaman," "Sword & Abyss," and "Love Across the Salt Desert," have the same magic of substance and tone as do some of Ambrose Bierce's stories.

Other writers such as Kewlian Sio, Jayanta Mahapatra, Sasthi Brata, Murli Das Melwani, Margaret Bhatty, Anita Desai, Bunny Reuben, G. D. Khosla, A. D. Gorwala, Dina Mehta, Shiv K. Kumar, and Nergis Dalal have made significant contributions to the world of the short story. Jayanta Mahapatra, one of India's finest poets in English, has used a poet's eye and ear in a fine way; both he and Kewlian Sio have demonstrated that short stories are not merely extended anecdotes or realistic portraits, but forms of writing that express rare moments of perception and illumination. Both authors have successfully dramatized the extremely indeterminate and incomplete nature of all relationships. Sio's "Let's Go Home," a touching story of a sensitive child who is closely attached to his widowed mother, and Mahapatra's "The Disappearance of Pratima Jena," about a young boy's infatuation with a woman, are wonderful instances of quiet observation and sympathetic understanding. In stories such as these one becomes secretly aware of a fine Indian sensibility living through its finest creative moments.

Bibhu Padhi

MODERN IRISH SHORT FICTION

In discussions of literature, there are only a few generalizations that matter, and those that usually matter the least are the ones eager to bracket national or regional characteristics. Especially in a genre such as the modern short story, a fully self-conscious art, it is best to remember that the individual voice always presides over the collective accent. Still, even with these reservations, the modern Irish story presents a special case. There is no arguing that in this century a remarkable number of major Irish writers have excelled in the short story, and that their stories are recognizably Irish.

As it happens, the modern Irish story does distinguish itself from other national or regional stories in two important ways. To begin with, it is closely bound up with a distinctly national movement: The Irish Literary Revival. This is especially true of the first generation of Irish short-story writers who drew on the resources of the Revival at the same time that they reacted against its limitations, but in varying degrees it is true also of each successive generation. When George Moore and James Joyce began writing their stories in the first decade of the twentieth century, they were able to measure their literary aims against a movement already openly devoted to expressing a national character. In this sense, the context of their stories is unique in modern letters. The only comparable situation—although there are more differences than similarities—might be the Fugitive and Agrarian movements in the American South in the 1920's and 1930's, followed in the 1940's, 1950's, and 1960's by a sort of golden age of the Southern short story.

The second reason is directly related to the first. Like the plays and poetry of the Literary Revival, the Irish short story is Irish not simply because of its subject matter, but because of its language. This is more than a question of faithfully recorded dialect, although certainly the vigorous Irish English heard in John Millington Synge's or Lady Gregory's plays strikes us immediately as something different from the standard comic stage-Irish brogue of the nineteenth century. One of the chief impulses behind the Literary Revival's attempt to develop a national literature was the search for a native Irish style. For the Irish writer, the dilemma was a peculiar one. On one hand, his mother tongue was usually English, an English associated with centuries of oppression, thus a kind of stepmother tongue. On the other hand, the native Irish language, Gaelic, had been gradually forced to the brink of extinction. Spoken only by a very small minority of Irishmen in isolated, scattered pockets primarily in the west of Ireland, it would always be an artificial language, an acquired tongue, for most modern Irish writers. The solution, of course, lay between the two in the ripe country speech of Irish English with its imaginative borrowings of syntax, metaphor, and rhythm from Gaelic. The use of Irish English became a way of asserting a national identity in a widely intelligible, and thus exportable, form. Rather than make the impossible choice between two opposed traditions, writers such as W. B. Yeats, Gregory, and Synge eventually learned to exploit them both in an English that even today—when many of the old distinctions have disappeared—helps distinguish Ireland from its British neighbors. Of course, since Irish English was primarily a *spoken* language before the Revival, it is discovered first, and more directly, in a genre such as the Abbey Theatre peasant play, where the spoken word predominates. The same impulse toward forging a native Irish English style in drama, however, helped determine the distinctive features of modern Irish prose fiction.

The beginning of the modern Irish story can be dated with something close to exactitude. In 1903, George Moore published a collection of stories entitled *The Untilled Field*. The following year the twenty-year-old James Joyce began publishing the first of his *Dubliners* (1914) stories in *The Irish Homestead*. In both cases these stories represented the first application of Continental literary realism to native Irish themes; and in keeping with one of the main tenets of literary realism, not only the dialogue but the impersonal narrative as well scrupulously adheres to a vocabulary and an imagery appropriate to the stories' themes and subjects. Moore and Joyce can legitimately be credited with transforming the Irish story into a modern art, but as with almost every other literary development in modern Ireland, W. B. Yeats was largely responsible for preparing the way.

From almost the beginning of his literary career—his first volume of poetry, *The Wandering of Oisin and Other Poems*, appeared in 1889—Yeats was fascinated with Ireland's rich oral culture. He remembered all his life stories he had heard as a young boy in the small port town of Sligo, and many of his own stories are literary versions of traditional Irish tales. Before he began writing stories himself, he edited several collections of Irish stories and folktales: *Fairy and Folk Tales of the Irish Peasantry* (1888), *Stories from Carleton* (1889), *Representative Irish Tales* (1891), and *Irish Fairy Tales* (1892). For the most part, these are stories written by nineteenth century Irish writers interested primarily in the quaint and eccentric aspects of native Irish life: superstitious beliefs, supernatural experiences, and the "world of faery." It was just such a world, bizarre and fantastic, that the modern Irish story writer would deliberately avoid, preferring instead the observable, but nevertheless distinctive, world of the ordinary Irishman. Still, Yeats's various collections, like the Revival's early fascination with Ireland's mythological and legendary Celtic past, do begin to give substance to the quest for a genuinely national literature.

A fifth collection by Yeats, *The Celtic Twilight*, deserves special mention. Published in 1893, it consists of literary reworkings of tales Yeats had heard himself, many, as he writes in the Preface, from Paddy Flynn, "a little bright-eyed old man, who lived in a leaky and one-roomed cabin in the village of Ballisodare." As the title suggests, *The Celtic Twilight* concentrates on the same sort of supernatural visitations Yeats's earlier collections had dealt with. Since they were his personal versions of traditional Irish folktales and regional legends, however, they moved him a step closer toward an original contribution to the Irish short story. In their descriptions of the Irish peasant and his surroundings, and particularly in their attempts to render accurately the Irish peasant's use of English, they reveal a shift away from what was merely strange and fantastic in the Irish countryside. Yeats did not always escape a tendency to portray the Irish peasant as he first wished him to be: poetic, mystical, and noble. In a few of his original stories, however, and in several of his plays, his characterizations are as convincing as those of any other writer of his generation.

Yeats's own stories, published in the 1890's and now collected in the single volume, *Mythologies* (1925), can be divided into two categories: those that deal with his esoteric theories and those that deal with the legendary past of native Irish culture. The former are elaborately designed stories filled with occult symbolism, mystical aesthetes, and wise-sounding absolutisms in the manner of the French symbolist Villiers de l'Isle-Adam. They are skillful and sonorous works of art—"Tables of the Law" and "The Adoration of the Magi" were favorites of the young James Joyce—but in the history of the central realist tradition of the modern Irish story, they are merely brilliant exceptions. In fact, there is nothing very *Irish* about either the subject or the *fin-de-siècle* Pateresque style of the stories, and they remain more representative of Yeats's private enthusiasms than of the general movement of the Literary Revival.

Yeats's Irish stories are found primarily in two groups, *The Secret Rose* and *Stories of Red Hanrahan* (1904), first published as one volume, *The Secret Rose*, in 1897. All these stories take place in earlier centuries, and all of them praise the spiritual virtues of solitary Irish types: the gleeman, the poet, the knight, the embattled aristocrat. Aside from their Irish subjects, however, there is little to distinguish these stories from Yeats's non-Irish stories. In both cases, the style owes much more to late nineteenth century English writers than it does to the Irish English that Yeats had begun to explore in *The Celtic Twilight*. The important change occurred in Yeats's revisions of the Hanrahan stories when he began to use his knowledge of Irish English speech to inform not only the dialogue in his stories, but their narrative prose as well.

Dialects of English in Ireland had been used before, of course, but almost exclusively for comic dialogue. Even a nineteenth century writer as knowledgeable of the Irish oral tradition as William Carleton all too often spoils the tone of his tales by surrounding his accurate dialogue with the stiff, artificial English of nineteenth century journalese. The false tones of this sort of awkward juxtaposition are not limited to nineteenth century fiction. Even the early and justifiably neglected stories of George Fitzmaurice and Sean

O'Casey, twentieth century masters of Irish English speech in their plays, commit the same mistake of trying to yoke unyokable styles. Yeats, on the other hand, after the false starts of the first Hanrahan stories, sought to give his revisions a unity of tone derived, dialogue and narrative alike, from the natural rhythms of Irish country speech.

In his search for a more appropriately Irish idiom, Yeats was greatly assisted by two other important figures in the Revival: Douglas Hyde and Lady Gregory. Hyde was the founder of the Gaelic League, and one of Ireland's best Gaelic scholars; in addition, he was thoroughly familiar with English dialects spoken by Irish peasants. In his book *Beside the Fire* (1890), he had translated into a strikingly convincing Irish English stories he had heard from native Gaelic storytellers. His translations were the first to demonstrate fully the deep resources of Irish peasant speech in forging a distinctly Irish narrative prose. Yeats, even before the appearance of *Beside the Fire*, had included Hyde in his collection of Irish fairy and folktales, and when he began reworking his Hanrahan stories, he clearly tried to give his own narrative the oral simplicity and force he had recognized in Hyde's translations.

Hyde was no doubt Yeats's original inspiration, but Lady Gregory helped him in a more direct and practical way: she shared with Hyde a gift for recreating the speech she had heard and remembered. In her trips with Yeats in the Irish countryside, and in her two collections of Irish legends, *Cuchulain of Muirthemne* (1902) and *Gods and Fighting Men* (1904)—written in the Kiltartan dialect of her region—she proved both a valuable adviser and an example. Yeats himself praised her contribution to the Hanrahan stories by writing how she helped change their style from "that artificial, elaborate English so many of us played with in the 'nineties' into that simple English she had learned from her Galway countrymen." On the title page of the revised collection he lists her name as a collaborator.

Yeats's revisions are not entirely successful, but the impulse behind them does mark a turning point in the history of Irish prose fiction. In many of the stories, Yeats's occult symbolism grates awkwardly against the natural, convincing flow of the dramatic narrative; but in at least one story, "The Twisting of the Rope," the reconciliation of style and subject places Yeats firmly within the realistic mode of the modern Irish story.

By the time *Stories of Red Hanrahan* was rewritten in 1907, the problem of an acceptable English for Irish literature had been largely solved. The Abbey Theatre and the early plays of John Synge had brought a new dimension to the literary uses of Irish English, informing it with a much greater sweep and depth of expression than previous writers had commanded. In addition, the success of the Abbey Theatre had helped bring the Literary Revival out of the backwaters of regionalism and into the mainstream of modern literature, and by doing so had given Irish writers new authority to express themselves in the English with which they had been reared. From then on, they were free to exploit the dual tradition of English literature and Irish English speech.

Once the question of language had been settled, a related question continued to be raised around the thorny and much disputed problem of *proper* Irish subjects. Obviously there could be no full, realistic expression of Irish life as long as abstract ideals kept fogging up what Joyce referred to as the "nicely-polished looking glass" of modern fiction. The early years of the Literary Revival had skirted the problem by concentrating on Ireland's mythological and legendary past. The varied spectrum of modern Irish life— from mountainy farmer to provincial priest and merchant to Dublin's middle classes—had been left largely unexplored. The kind of ironic, uncompromising realism that became the dominant mode of Irish fiction had to cope too with the understandably defensive passions of Ireland's struggle for national independence. In fact, the opposition between the individual Irish writer and the official version of Ireland provided by politicians, priests, and journalists helps determine, even today, the characteristic themes of Irish literature. In this context of rigid ideals and absolute passions, perhaps it is not too surprising that the aims and techniques of literary realism, at least in terms of the short story, were introduced by a native-born visitor, George Moore, on one hand, and a lifelong voluntary exile, James Joyce, on the other.

When George Moore moved to Dublin in 1901 to offer his services to the Literary Revival, the first phase of the Revival with its Celtic Twilight emphasis on Irish myth, legend, and supernatural affairs had begun to shift to a more realistic expression of Irish culture as it existed in the present. Since Irish culture, especially the native Irish culture of the West, conserved many archaic features of Gaelic manners and customs, the shift was not so much a reaction against Ireland's ancient past as it was a fresh interest in how much of that past still remained. With the arrival of Moore, however, a more abrupt shift occurred. Moore had already made a reputation for himself as a novelist and man of letters on the Continent, where he had been strongly influenced by the literary movements of realism and naturalism, particularly as they were defined in French fiction. During his stay in Dublin—he left Ireland for good after nine years—he contributed several important works to modern Irish literature, including the eccentric but brilliant autobiography, *Hail and Farewell* (1911-1914). By far his most influential book, however, was the collection of Irish stories he entitled *The Untilled Field* as an appreciative bow to Ivan Turgenev.

Moore claimed he wrote the stories "in the hope of furnishing the young Irish of the future with models," and the thirteen stories in the first edition do demonstrate an impressive display of narrative styles and Irish themes. In addition, they range through a variety of tones, perhaps implying a sly rebuttal to the nationalists' solemn claims that the only mode appropriate to Irish life was heroic tragedy. At any rate, the collection's variety was part of Moore's deliberate attempt to chart new directions in Ireland's literature. Several of the stories had appeared in a Gaelic translation in 1902. Moore, however, knowing no Gaelic himself although he was enthusiastic about the Gaelic language movement, was disappointed in the translation's reception, and published the rest of the stories in English. Moore once made the rather preposterous claim that *The Untilled Field* was the source for Synge's dramatic language. Given the fact that Synge's first play, *(In the Shadow of the Glen* (1903), was performed the same year *The Untilled Field* appeared, this claim, one of Moore's "little vanities" as he called them, should not be taken too seriously. The language of *The Untilled Field* does represent the different levels of Irish English accurately, but subject rather than expression is what stamps the collection as a new departure.

On the whole, the stories in *The Untilled Field* are credible portraits of ordinary Irish men and women in the throes of some typically Irish frustration or obsession, often religious. Many of the stories are loudly critical of the strong grip of Irish Catholic puritanism which Moore felt thwarted all impulse toward a creative culture. In the stories "Some Parishioners" and "Julia Cahil's Curse," for example, the priest is pictured as responding with a blind, negative fear when faced with a threat to his control over the community by an individual voice. Less directly an attack on the priesthood, but implying the oppressive weight of Catholic heritage, are the stories "In the Clay" and "The Way Back," bitter denunciations of Irish provincialism and its destructive hatred of art. These stories, and some of the others, are sometimes spoiled by rather strident attempts to make a point, but several are fully successful achievements of convincing characterization and dramatic action. "Julia Cahil's Curse," "The Window," "So On She Fares," and "A Letter to Rome" have all appeared in good anthologies of the modern short story. The latter story, "A Letter to Rome," is one of Moore's few sympathetic portraits of an Irish priest. Father McTurnan is a well-thinking, amiable, but entirely comical country priest who decides that the only way to save Ireland from the Protestants is to allow Irish priests to abandon their vows of chastity and beget large families.

The finest story in *The Untilled Field*, however, is unquestionably "Home Sickness." It was Frank O'Connor's favorite story by Moore, and it represents his realistic, ironic art at its most penetrating. Narrated in the third person, but written from the perspective of the protagonist, James Bryden, and in the quiet, natural tones of his own speech, "Home Sickness" concentrates in Bryden's dilemma—he has returned home to Ireland after thirteen years in the United States, but he hesitates between staying and leaving—most of the themes of *The Untilled Field*: exile, barren land, religious domination and interference, provincial boredom, and despair. In Bryden's struggle to make a choice between a quiet but monotonous life in rural Ireland and the noisy activity of his New York bar, Moore not only cuts through to one of the typical burdens of the modern Irishman, but also dramatizes the unresolved conflicts in his own mind.

In terms of modern literature, Moore's stories are not innovations, either in style or in structure. What makes them original in the history of the Irish short story is primarily their willingness to dismiss the romantic idealization of Irish rural society, and dramatize instead the poverty, fear, frustration, and provincialism that clearly did exist, despite all the heroic claims of the Irish nationalists.

James Joyce began writing his *Dubliners* in 1904, the year after the publication of *The Untilled Field*. Joyce's stories have often been described as a sort of urban counterpart to Moore's rural Ireland, and there are obviously similarities in their realistic exposures of Irish society. Joyce's stories, however, are not only far superior in stylistic precision and symbolic design, but they also reflect a bitter reaction to the dullness and despair that the twenty-two-year-old Joyce felt seeping into his own literary life. When George Russell generously invited Joyce to publish a few "simple stories" for *The Irish Homestead* magazine, Joyce saw an opportunity to offer his own candid antidote to the romantic excesses of the Literary Revival and to justify at the same time the necessity for exile. As Richard Ellmann explains in his study *James Joyce,*

> [Joyce's] short stories, with their grim exactitude and submerged lyricism, had broken away from the Irish literary movement in which, though he denied the fact, his poems fitted pretty well. As the author of these stories, he was free to attack his literary compatriots for dealing in milk and water which tasted no better for being Irish and spiritual.

Joyce published "The Sisters," his first story, in *The Irish Homestead* during the summer of 1904. Two other stories followed soon after, "Eveline" and "After the Race." By the time the latter story had appeared, Joyce had made the decisive step of his career; he had left Ireland for a lifelong exile, accompanied by Nora Barnacle, several unfinished manuscripts, and the hope of a job in Zurich that proved, like so many of his other hopes, a delusion. By December, 1905, he had completed twelve stories, and he sent them off to Grant Richards, a publisher in London. They were first accepted, then refused, and Joyce was subjected to nine bitter years of unreasonable demands, broken contracts, and futile correspondence before they were finally published in 1914.

In one of his many letters to Richards, Joyce clearly explained the motives behind the form and theme he had chosen:

> My intention was to write a chapter of the moral history of my country and I chose Dublin for the scene because that city seemed to me the centre of paralysis. I have tried to present

it to the indifferent public under four of its aspects: childhood, adolescence, maturity, and public life. I have written it for the most part in a style of scrupulous meanness. . . .

Most of the stories, from "The Sisters" to "Grace," are brilliant performances of an impersonal symbolic naturalism, describing in a precise ironic prose the futility of escape or change in a Dublin society paralyzed by debased dreams, corrupt religious authority, and blinding social convention. It cannot be overemphasized how Irish these stories are. Joyce's large and exact memory for local idioms, allusions, and places is evident in each story, and a familiar knowledge of Irish religion, Irish politics, and Irish English is as essential to a full understanding of *Dubliners* as it is to Joyce's other works. A quick glance at the notes in the standard Viking critical edition of *Dubliners* will bear out how deeply rooted Joyce's art is in a specific time and place. Stories such as "Ivy Day in the Committee Room" and "Grace," which the modern non-Irish reader *must* supplement with special information, perhaps foreshadow Joyce's deliberate demand in *Ulysses* (1922) and *Finnegans Wake* (1939) that the reader actively search out allusions and expressions for himself in order to make the books intelligible.

Joyce's finest and best-known story, "The Dead," differs from the other stories in a number of ways. As the final story in a book unified by the theme of Dublin paralysis, it does reverberate back to all the failed lives of the other stories. Its central character, Gabriel Conroy, however, is a much more complex figure. "The Dead" was written in 1907, two years after the other stories and three years after the beginning of Joyce's European exile. Richard Ellmann has suggested that three years of struggle on the Continent caused Joyce to look with a more sympathetic eye toward Ireland, but whatever the reason, the story does mark a distinct shift in his literary concerns and methods. Unlike the other characters in *Dubliners*, Gabriel Conroy is seen from within, and unlike the other characters, he does manage to redeem himself through at least a partial self-discovery.

The basic conflict of "The Dead" lies in the confrontation between Gabriel, a teacher, journalist, and sophisticated Anglo-Irishman, and the more primitive, vital Irish culture represented by the Irish nationalist, Miss Ivors, but more importantly by Gabriel's wife, Gretta. Gabriel is sensitive about his wife's origins—she comes from the West of Ireland—but his prejudice is reversed when his wife tells him about the boy who had loved her, Michael Furey. The native Irish past of which Gabriel had been so contemptuous early in the story becomes an image of living passion, and his own marriage is revealed to be weak-spirited and self-delusive, at least in Gabriel's inner vision of it.

The opposition that informs "The Dead"—between the country-bred Irishman and the Anglo-Irish journalist, between the primitive West and the sophisticated East, between simple passions and deliberate phrasemaking—is a type of conflict that has now become a standard theme in Irish fiction. Already present in the first Irish novel, Maria Edgeworth's *Castle Rackrent* (1800), the questions and problems raised by two distinct cultural traditions inhabiting the same small place have been treated by every major Irish writer up to the present. The conflict takes a variety of forms: the Irish Catholic versus the Anglo-Irish Protestant; the Irish tenant versus the English land-owner; and the Irish country folk close to an ancient Gaelic past versus the Anglo-Irish city-dweller much closer to London than to the Celts. In "The Dead," Joyce poses the opposition in terms of social and cultural attitudes without turning the story into a didactic battlefield. What interests him most is the effect of the conflict arising from Gabriel's judgment of himself. In this sense, Joyce is much closer to later Irish fiction, the kind that was written after the absolute divisions of the Rebellion eventually gave way to a more comprehensive view of Irish dualities. In the fiction of Seán O'Faoláin or Frank O'Connor, for example, the two traditions are treated in terms of character and culture rather than in terms of ideology. Contemporaries of Joyce were more likely to make a definitive choice. Somerville and Ross, authors of the hilarious stories in the *Irish R. M.* series, were entirely at ease with native Irish idiom and behavior, but they could never entirely escape the nineteenth century Anglo-Irish tendency of exaggerating certain Irish traits for comic aims. On the other hand, Daniel Corkery, whose first book of stories appeared in 1916—the year of the Easter Rising and two years after Joyce's *Dubliners*—tended to present all Anglo-Irish, no matter how long their families had been in Ireland, and no matter how deep their attachment was to their birthplace, as intruders.

Perhaps the feature of "The Dead" that best identifies the hand of the mature Joyce and prepares the way for the sophisticated narration of his successors in the short story is the way the language of the narrative is made to reflect the gradual movement of the story into Gabriel's inner thoughts. The easygoing, expectant, colloquial tones of the opening paragraphs as the two Miss Morkans welcome their guests progressively give way, especially after the false notes of Gabriel's dinner tribute, to the artificial, bookish vocabulary of Gabriel's inner speech, a late-Victorian romantic English as lifeless and as insubstantial as the conventional exchanges in the Morkans' music room.

Joyce's characterization of Gabriel's failure is masterly, and "The Dead" remains one of the great stories in the modern tradition. If Moore's stories in *The Untilled Field* were the first to adapt the methods of literary realism to specific Irish themes, Joyce's *Dubliners* gave the Irish short story a standard of artistic perfection that went far beyond national boundaries. With the stories of Moore and Joyce, it is not going too far to claim that the directions of the modern Irish short story were largely set. It was to be realistic and uncompromising, and it was to derive its dramatic form and ironic energies from the vigorous oral tradition of Irish English. Moore, the middle-aged convert, and Joyce, the rebellious young exile, in different ways and from different motives, proved together that the matter of Ireland was as distinctive and as varied as its speech.

In stating that the modern Irish story is predominantly a realistic genre, it is best to remember that "realism" in Ireland comprises a broader range of experience than modern conventional standards would ordinarily accept. The archaic Celtic beliefs in the local gods that fascinated Yeats in the folkways of the Irish peasant, and the easy coexistence of pagan and Christian worlds that Synge dramatized in his plays, to some extent represent permanent features of Ireland's collective memory. In particular, the strong oral tradition of Gaelic Ireland with its long fireside tales of ghosts and supernatural events pervades by necessity even the modern story insomuch as its subject is the actual speech and behavior of rural Ireland. A modern writer such as Daniel Corkery, for example, often uses realistic techniques to describe the strange effects of invisible forces because that is the sort of world he found in the West Cork hillsides. In general, what the modern Irish writers of realistic fiction reacted against was not the presence of mystery in the observable world, but the tendency of purely "literary" traditions to concentrate on the mysterious at the expense of the observable.

The Celtic Twilight infatuation with myth and legend, with the world of faery, and with all things spiritual seemed to writers like Joyce and Synge to exalt too often the disembodied spirit while neglecting material and social realities. Early in his career, the same year he began writing *Dubliners*, Joyce in his broadside "The Holy Office" contrasts his own fearless realism with the easy luxury of spiritual escapism. Later, in *Ulysses*, he makes Stephen mock the theosophical hermeticism of Æ (George William Russell) and his disciples: "Formless spiritual. Father, Word and Holy Breath. Allfather, the heavenly man. Hiesos Kristos, magician of the beautiful, the Logos who suffers in us at every moment. This verily is that. I am the fire upon the altar. I am the sacrificial butter." In much the same vein, and in the same decade as Joyce's "The Holy Office," Synge's poem on one of Æ's mystical paintings affirms the shifting attitudes of Irish fiction:

The Passing of the Shee
(After looking at one of Æ's pictures)

Adieu, sweet Angus, Maeve, and Fand,
Ye plumed yet skinny Shee,
That poets played with hand in hand
To learn their ecstasy.

We'll stretch in Red Dan Sally's ditch,
And drink in Tubber fair,

> Or poach with Red Dan Philly's bitch
> The badger and the hare.

Joyce's and Synge's reactions must be seen in the unique context of the Literary Revival. Their exasperation with inflated mysticism did not stop Joyce from weaving one novel around the mythic associations of a modern Ulysses and another around the mysteries of the collective unconsciousness, nor did it stop Synge from dramatizing the actual effects of an imaginary world on the material one. Their aim was to express *all* of human nature, and this meant a new look at the effable realities of Irish life.

Another literary tradition that is often associated with Irish fiction is that of fantasy. For the purposes of the modern Irish story, it is best to distinguish between the romantic, Gothic ghost stories of nineteenth century Irish writers such as Joseph Sheridan Le Fanu and Fitzjames, and the type of fantasy that represents a special Irish attitude toward language. The first tradition is not particulary Irish, although certainly some of its best practitioners were. In general, the nineteenth century fantasists were not concerned with accurate descriptions of Irish society; they were concerned, and rightly so, with the established conventions of the mystery tale and the ghost story. Oscar Wilde, for example, wrote several fine fairy tales, but Ireland is nowhere to be found within them. This "literary" tradition of fantasy fiction does continue up into the twentieth century where it assumes a more Irish aspect, notably in the works of James Stephens, Lord Dunsany, and George Fitzmaurice. In their works, fantastic though they might be, they share the contemporary concern with realistic detail and accurate Irish English speech. In James Stephens' celebrated *The Crock of Gold* (1912), the characters are recognizably Irish and speak a language as distinctively Irish as Synge's peasants or Joyce's Dubliners.

There is another tradition of Irish fantasy, however, more closely related to racial character than to literary convention, and that is the peculiarly Irish delight in the act of individual speech, especially when it involves verbal play, inventiveness, and parody. In his well-documented study *The Irish Comic Tradition* (1962), Vivien Mercier has shown how this delight goes back to even the earliest records of Celtic poetry and art and how it continues to be a major force in modern Irish literature. Unlike the literary tradition of fantasy, in which the strangeness of subject matter dominates, the element of fantasy in Irish speech accommodates itself perfectly to realistic techniques since it is part of the common Irish world the realist must attempt to express. In fact, in many modern Irish works, verbal extravagance is seen as such a typical Irish trait that it is treated with deliberate thematic emphasis. In the novels of Joyce, in the plays of Synge and Sean O'Casey, and in the short stories of Frank O'Connor and Seán O'Faoláin, very often the main themes revolve around characters whose intoxication with language has gotten the best of their grasp on the real world.

Another way the Irish love of the spoken word conditions the modern Irish story is revealed in what might almost be called a separate "subgenre"of the short story, the literary yarn. It differs from pure fantasy because it is based on the assumption that the story being told actually happened, but it differs from the orthodox realistic story because it tends to put more emphasis on the delight of spinning out an entertaining tale than on the contingencies of convincing action or description. The literary yarn is a written version of the oral yarn, and thus derives its form from the rhythms of the spoken word and from the running action and sudden digressions of comic anecdote.

The first masters of this Irish subgenre are the two Anglo-Irish cousins, E. Œ. Somerville and Martin Ross. Much of their best work humorously contrasts native Irish culture with the often bewildered Anglo-Irish gentry. Among numerous other works, they published three volumes of stories treating the adventures of the Englishman Major Sinclair Yeates, a Resident Magistrate (R. M.) in the West of Ireland: *Some Experiences of an Irish R. M.* (1899), *Further Experiences of an Irish R. M.* (1908), and *In Mr. Knox's Country* (1915). Frank O'Connor once observed that although George Moore has had the greatest influence on the direction of the Irish story, for every copy of *The Untilled Field* one can find a hundred copies of *Some Experiences of an Irish R. M.* Whatever their influence—or lack of it—Somerville and Ross have been followed by a small number of brilliant literary yarn-spinners. Some of James Stephens' stories, especially those from his collection *Here Are Ladies* (1913), are excellent examples of the combination of deliberate, self-conscious art and reckless, spendthrift speech that characterizes the literary yarn. The three great modern masters, however, are Flann O'Brien, Benedict Kiely, and Seán O'Faoláin, especially in his recent collection, *Foreign Affairs, and Other Stories* (1976).

O'Brien equals Joyce in his mastery of Dublin wit and Dublin speech, and although his best work is contained in such novels as *At-Swim-Two-Birds* (1939), *The Dalkey Archive* (1964), and *The Third Policeman* (1967), his rare short stories and abundant journalistic tales merit him a place in any survey of the modern Irish story. Kiely, like O'Brien, came to Dublin out of the North, but he has made Dublin as much his own literary province as his native Tyrone. All of Kiely's stories are marked by a keen ear for Irish absurdities and by an appreciation of imaginative digressions. His three finest literary yarns are "A Journey to the Seven Streams," "A Ball of Malt and Madame Butterfly," and "Down Then By Derry." Seán O'Faoláin's stories would normally be considered in the mainstream of the realist tradition, but in his latest collection, *Foreign Affairs, and Other Stories*, he proves himself one of the masters of the yarn. Actually, O'Faoláin has always experimented with the various tones of a dominant authorial voice, even in his early stories; but in *Foreign Affairs, and Other Stories* the narrative voices of stories such as

"Something, Everything, Anything, Nothing" and "Falling Rocks, Narrowing Road, Cul-de-Sac, Stop" are those of the type of self-delighting monologist who must be at the center of all literary yarns.

In order to shift from these obvious exceptions to conventional realism back to the beginnings of the modern Irish short story, two contemporaries of Moore and Joyce, Seumas O'Kelly and Daniel Corkery, best demonstrate the more subtle ways in which Irish realism extends conventional boundaries. As Frank O'Connor has remarked, Corkery and O'Kelly have one foot in Yeats's camp and the other in Moore's. By this he means simply that they maintain a vision of the Irish peasant as the privileged source of all that is most vital in native Irish culture, but that they apply to their vision the modern techniques of dramatic realism.

O'Kelly and Corkery shared a direct, lifelong contact with rural, peasant Ireland that set them apart from Moore and Joyce. O'Kelly was brought up in East Galway, and Corkery, whose influence was to assert itself so strongly in the early careers of Frank O'Connor and Seán O'Faoláin, possessed an intimate knowledge of the desolate West Cork hillsides and farms. Both depict the physical details of the Irish landscape and record the accents of Irish country speech with unerring accuracy; but both also accept the strange words and passionate gestures of a world where visionary experience is not limited to what Samuel Taylor Coleridge called the "despotism of the eye." O'Kelly and Corkery's stories are uneven in quality—the young Joyce strongly criticized O'Kelly's first volume, *By the Stream of Killmeen* (1906), as hopelessly idealistic—but each of them contributed at least one masterpiece to the modern Irish story: O'Kelly's "The Weaver's Grave" and Corkery's "Rock-of-the Mass."

O'Kelly's "The Weaver's Grave" was first published in 1919, a year after his death of a heart attack when a group of British soldiers staged a riot and vandalized the office of the nationalist Sinn Fein newspaper he edited. As its subtitle states, "The Weaver's Grave" is a story of old men. It is also a story of communal memory and the power of ritual taken to nearly grotesque extremes. The four men who dominate the story from the beginning—the dead weaver and his ancient contemporaries, the stone-breaker, the nailer, and the cooper—defy the modern world as fiercely as they defy one another. As the long search for the weaver's grave progresses, however, the center of the story shifts from the weaver to his widow. She is nameless at the beginning of the story, and her personality is obscured by the difficulties of deciding where to bury her husband; but slowly she awakens to the mysteries of her own individual youth as powerful as the old men's mysteries of their communal past. Finally, she combines wake and resurrection by choosing one of the gravediggers along with the site of her husband's grave. "The Weaver's Grave" is one of the great literary folktales of the twentieth century. The almost supernatural presence of the dead weaver and the exaggerated gestures and speech of the old men show a kinship with the old Gaelic arts of storytelling. The gradually mounting interest in individual character, however, especially in the specific thoughts and plausible reaction of the widow, places it securely within the modern tradition.

There is less exaggeration and less broad humor in Corkery's more modern story, "Rock-of-the-Mass," but the invisible forces assert their presence just as strongly. Corkery's story, published in the 1920's, eventually takes the form of a retrospective monologue, like so many modern Irish stories. An old farmer, Michael Hodnett, looks back on a life shaped by a single choice he has made between his old rocky farm in the hills and the new showplace farm in the lowlands which he has struggled, at great pains, to make prosper. He has lost three sons in the process, but the loss he regrets most is the holy place on his old farm, a pile of rock where Mass had been said in the days of penal laws. It is a compassionate portrait of a tragic conflict between spiritual and worldly realities. Like "The Weaver's Grave," it provides a typically Irish definition of the individual in terms of the collective community, although unlike the ending of "The Weaver's Grave," "Rock-of-the-Mass" concludes with the failure of the individual who finds a sort of comfort in the sympathetic support of his family. The fact that community enters so powerfully and yet so differently in the two stories shows that in Ireland, at least in the first decades of the twentieth century, the idea of community still remained a force to be reckoned with.

Corkery, like O'Kelly, affords the reader a good example of the continuity of the Irish story, of its filial links with old Gaelic Ireland. In many of his stories the spirit of declining native ways broods over his characters' lives as insistently as the abandoned rock pile broods over Michael Hodnett. More to our immediate purpose, however, Corkery with his long career of teaching and writing the short story—he was born in 1878, four years before Joyce, and he died in 1964—provides a sort of natural bridge between the first- and second-generation writers of the modern tradition. In his early volumes, he was responsible for introducing some of the major themes of the Irish story—religion, land, and nationality—and with his decision to devote an entire career to perfecting the art of the story, he helped determine the attitudes and aims of his two famous students, Frank O'Connor and Seán O'Faoláin.

By the 1920's, the first generation of Irish short-story writers could look back to an impressive achievement. If George Moore and James Joyce stand out as the most original, the first to wed successfully native themes with modern forms, their contemporaries, Somerville, Ross, Stephens, O'Kelly, and Corkery, each made permanent contributions to the genre. Yet even with these bright beginnings, if one period were to be singled out as the golden age of the modern Irish story, it would have to be that of the second generation, dominated by three names: Liam O'Flaherty, Frank O'Connor, and Seán O'Faoláin. Much of their best work was written in the late 1920's

(O'Flaherty) and the decades before and during World War II. There were other good writers, of course, but these three did more than anyone else to establish the Irish short story as an independent art form, a form as various and as demanding as the novel or the play. Unlike the period of Moore and Joyce, it was not a time of great experimentation or sudden new departures, but rather a deliberate ripening of the established realist tradition.

With the exception of Corkery, the first-generation writers did not think of their stories as the chief aim of their literary lives. Joyce, for example, wrote his last story when he was twenty-five. For the writers after Corkery, however, the art of the short story was one of conscious specialization. O'Flaherty is somewhat of an exception sinee his prolific career includes more novels than collections of stories, but he is admired primarily for a handful of powerful short-story portraits: "Red Barbara," "The Tramp," and "The Pedlar's Revenge," to list only a few. O'Connor and O'Faoláin did make a few infrequent forays into the novel, but they always considered themselves first and foremost professional craftsmen of the story. Largely because of Corkery, who instructed them in the great Continental masters when they were students in Cork, they were willing to judge their own work against the best stories of Russia, France, and the United States. Once again due to Corkery's influence and career, both of which they eventually left far behind, they both measured their artistic development in terms of each successive collection.

It is difficult to speak convincingly in general or collective terms when considering the main figures of the second generation. The individual voices of O'Flaherty, O'Connor, and O'Faoláin, as their stories never fail to demonstrate, are indelibly their own. For all their differences, however, they do share certain realities of a specific time, a common Irish fate reflected, however diversely, in their work. Like the majority of Irishmen reared in the first decades of the century, they all had firsthand experience of poverty, the Catholic Church, and nationalist fervor. They were young men at the time of Ireland's struggles for independence, and they all briefly fought for the defeated Republican forces. Most importantly, at least in terms of their art, they all suffered at the very outset of their careers from a society that tended to choke and suffocate its best creative energies. This was nothing new, of course—the work of Yeats, Synge, and Joyce stood out as particularly instructive examples—but the memory of war made the entrenchment of established authority even deeper. In trying in various ways to budge the fixed lines of official thought, O'Flaherty, O'Connor, and O'Faoláin all had stormy relations with Irish Church and state.

Long after the war and even in the 1960's almost ten thousand books, including most of the major writers of the century, had been officially forbidden. Such was the great extent of censorship power and hostility that both O'Connor and O'Faoláin at different times became focal points of national campaigns against their work. It is probably not so surprising then, that in so many of their stories, and in the stories of O'Flaherty, the drama centers on an individual in conflict with a social or religious order or in rebellion against official codes. If they reacted publicly as men of letters against cultural stagnation, censorship, and general authoritarianism, in their art they identified closely with the common man and with all his frustrations and humors. O'Connor and O'Faoláin may have dealt chiefly with the lower- and middle-class provincial Irish Catholic, and O'Flaherty with the more isolated figure of the Western peasant or the mountain farmer, but all three sided with the individual little man, however pigheaded, up against the powers of the world.

Liam O'Flaherty was born in 1897 on the main island of the Aran Islands. The harsh perspectives, immediacy and power of nature, and the tightly knit, determined island community of his birthplace have strongly marked his life and fiction. He once wrote of himself: "I was born on a storm-swept rock and hate the soft growth of sunbaked lands where there is no frost in men's bones. Swift thoughts, and the swift flight of ravenous birds, and the squeal of terror of hunted animals are to me a reality." He wrote his first book, a novel, *Thy Neighbor's Wife* (1923), in England after he had been forced to leave Ireland when the Republican forces were defeated. Later he returned to Ireland and has since published an impressive quantity of work, including novels, short stories, literary criticism, a tourist guide, a biography of Tim Healy, and several autobiographical pieces. Although he is probably best known for his novel *The Informer* (1925), he is admired primarily for such novels as *The House of Gold* (1929), *Skerret* (1932), *Famine* (1937), and for his short stories. *Spring Sowing* (1924) was his first volume of stories, followed by *Civil War* (1925), and, among others, *The Tent and Other Stories* (1926), *Red Barbara and Other Stories* (1928), and *The Mountain Tavern and Other Stories* (1929). Recently, in 1976, a good collection of his previously uncollected stories was published by Wolfhound Press: *The Pedlar's Revenge: Short Stories* (1977), edited by A. A. Kelly.

O'Flaherty has often been described as the most "naturalistic" of the Irish realists, but his brand of naturalism has very little in common with the self-satisfied certitudes of Continental writers. Always there prevails a deep sense of mystery in the face of uncontrollable passions, an attitude mindful of the primitive notion that the passions are the voices of the gods. Unfortunately, the willful intensity of his stories sometimes overwhelms his gift for characterization; characters such as Red Barbara, the tramp in "The Tramp," the tinker in "The Tent," and the cunning pedlar in "The Pedlar's Revenge" are so fully possessed by a single desire or force that they come perilously close to losing their credibility as human beings. When an O'Flaherty story does fail, however, it fails not so much because of the subject, but because of the style. He has often been criticized for cultivating an overblown, pretentious lyricism whose "literary" commonplaces seem entirely inappropriate to the fresh, wondrous awe an untamed nature inspires in him. Especially in those stories in which he attempts to glorify the Irish peasant, not as the Literary Revival did, but as a sort of unspoiled primitive, the awkward juxtaposition of strained phrasemaking with his characters' wild gestures turns his stories into melodrama. Despite these tendencies, O'Flaherty has written more successfully than any other Irish writer about the fierce, isolated world of the Irish outlands; and stories such as "Going into Exile," "Red Barbara," "The Tent," "The Mountain Tavern," and several others are legitimate classics of the genre.

Finally, just to mention one of the critical commonplaces concerning O'Flaherty's stories, he has often been described as a writer who writes more for the eye than the ear. This may be an accurate enough account of the luminous visual power of some of his best animal stories—"The Wounded Cormorant," "The Conger Eel," "The Rockfish," "The Cow's Death," "Wild Stallions"—but it misrepresents his keen ear for Irish speech in such stories as "The Post Office," "Lovers," and "The Pedlar's Revenge." This latter story is one of O'Flaherty's most successful stories, fuller and less melodramatic than many of his early "naturalistic" portraits. The harsh, shrewd voice of the pedlar is a variation on what has now become almost a standard Irish type, the wild old man.

There are few wild old men in O'Connor or O'Faoláin, although otherwise the gamut of Irish life their stories treat is much more varied than O'Flaherty's world. Unlike O'Flaherty, they discovered the Irish countryside and the Gaelic folkways from the perspectives of a large middle-class town, that of Cork City during the first decades of the century. For the most part, although they both knew poverty from firsthand experience, the Irish world they describe is much closer to the modern commercial world, provincial and rural, full of small towns and small shops, but usually within a short train ride to Dublin or Cork.

To a degree, it is fitting to discuss O'Connor and O'Faoláin together. They were born within three years of each other at the beginning of the century, and they grew up in Cork at a time when the Literary Revival was just beginning to penetrate the Ireland outside London and Dublin. Seán O'Faoláin has described in his autobiography, *Vive Moi* (1964), how his literary awakening came when he was fifteen and saw Lennox Robinson's Abbey Theatre play, *Patriots* (1912): "On the lighted stage I beheld, with an astonishment never before or since equalled for me by any theatrical spectacle, the parlour of a house in an Irish country town. . . ." O'Connor and O'Faoláin were both youthful enthusiasts of the Republican lost cause, and afterwards they became equally skeptical about all political ideologies. They were friends in Cork, and they were both strongly influenced by Daniel Corkery who taught them, lent them books, and encouraged them to write stories. They eventually played important roles in the cultural life of modern Ireland; and finally, they achieved international reputations as two of the best short-story writers in English of their generation. Despite all these links, however, there are far more differences than resemblances in their art.

Frank O'Connor was born Michael O'Donovan in 1903. His early life was marked by rock-bottom poverty and by his father's struggles with drink and work. He quit school before he was fourteen, but he eventually became a professional librarian, went to Dublin, and began publishing poems and translations in George Russell's *The Irish Statesman* and in Seumas O'Sullivan's *Dublin Magazine*. He published two novels and a number of translations, critical studies, and other works, but he concentrated primarily on the writing—and rewriting—of short stories. Among his original collections are *Guests of the Nation* (1931), *Bones of Contention and Other Stories* (1935), *Crab Apple Jelly: Stories and Tales* (1944), *The Common Chord: Stories and Tales* (1947), *Traveller's Samples: Stories and Tales* (1951), and *Domestic Relations* (1957).

O'Connor was concerned perhaps more than any other writer of his generation with the rhythms of speech and the various ways the spoken word reveals character. He once observed that he wrote about Ireland because he knew to a syllable how everything in Ireland could be said, and the great diversity of individual speech in his stories fully proves his claim. A good example of the important role of accurate speech in O'Connor's art is his story "In the Train," published in his collection *Bones of Contention*. "In the Train" is remarkable for the skill with which excerpts of dialogue as the speakers shift from one theme to another, and from one group to another, gradually fill in the story's background, exposing the characters' past and future in a few swift, dramatic exchanges. "In the Train" is also remarkable as a portrait of a small-town Irish community, tightly bound together in a collective refusal to "inform" on one of their own in the Dublin courts, but at the same time meting out a punishment in their private speech and behavior as severe and as cruel as that of any big-city judge. O'Connor thus combines two of his favorite subjects, public rebellion of native Irish values against the official system and the private rebellion of the outcast individual.

O'Connor is perhaps best known for his stories told from a child's perspective. "The Genius," "My Oedipus Complex," and "The Drunkard" all succeed in the difficult art of making a child's narrative voice convincing, probably because, at least in these stories, O'Connor is talking directly out of his own childhood experiences. Many of his stories are retold in his two fine autobiographies, *An Only Child* (1961) and *My Father's Son* (1969), both invaluable sources for his fiction. If O'Connor's child narratives are convincingly rendered, their plots are sometimes mechanical and predictable; they tend to revolve around illusions that are too easily deflatable. In his study of the short story, *The Lonely Voice* (1963), O'Connor distinguishes between the novel and the short story by describing the latter's gift for sudden, pervasive revelation: "The short story, which is always trying to differentiate itself from the novel and avoid being bogged down in the slow, chronological sequence of events where the novel is supreme seeks a point outside time from which past and future can be viewed simultaneously. . . ." O'Connor manages to meet his own aesthetic demands best, not in his child narratives, but in stories whose characters have enough experience to make of the revelation something definitive. In his more accomplished stories, "In the Train," "Bridal Night," "Uprooted," and "The Luceys," to mention only a few, the revelation illuminates entire lives, not merely makes an ironic, often sentimental point.

Seán O'Faoláin was born John Whelan in 1900 in Dublin, but he grew up in Cork. His father was a constable in the Royal Irish Constabulary and his mother took in lodgers. O'Faoláin in his autobiography describes his family as "shabby genteels at the lowest possible social level." After the Republican loss, he finished a B. A. and M. A. at University College, Cork, and went on to earn another M. A. at Harvard. After a short teaching career, he published in 1932 his first book, *Midsummer Night Madness and Other Stories*, a collection of stories partly based on his Civil War experiences. For six years in the 1940's he was editor of one of Ireland's major literary magazines, *The Bell*. Among O'Faoláin's collections of short stories are *A Purse of Coppers* (1937), *I Remember! I Remember!* (1962), *The Heat of the Sun* (1966), *The Talking Trees, and Other Stories* (1971), and *Foreign Affairs, and Other Stories* (1976). Recently, in 1979, he published his fourth novel, *And Again?* Since Frank O'Connor's death in 1966, Seán O'Faoláin is generally considered Ireland's leading man of letters. He continues to publish short stories regularly, and has announced a new novel and a new collection of stories to appear during 1980, his eightieth year.

Unlike many of his contemporaries who have generally chosen to have their characters narrate their own stories, O'Faoláin has experimented again and again with a single authorial voice. He has often been contrasted with O'Connor as a short-story writer who observes rather than embodies his characters, but such a comparison does an injustice to the wide range of tones his voice can cover. Moreover, he has written about a greater diversity of Irish character than any other Irish short-story writer. *Foreign Affairs, and Other Stories*, for example, his latest collection, includes some of the few successful treatments of those strange breeds, the Irish professional, doctor or diplomat, and the Irish intellectual. It is true, however, that O'Faoláin's stories are most convincing when the narrator's powers of invention most fully correspond to those of O'Faoláin himself, when the "literary" rhythms give way to the conversational, and when the narrator is a participant in the story he tells. In his Foreword to the collection, *The Finest Stories of Seán O'Faoláin* (1957), O'Faoláin has described the romantic failings of his early stories, but in so doing he touched on a characteristic of all his major stories:

I must, if only in self-defence, tell the reader of this volume that it opens with three stories from my first book of stories, *Midsummer Night Madness*, and that although I have chosen them because I like them very much they contain things that make me smile today—and, yet, I have been unwilling to rewrite them. I should like to explain why. They belong to a period, my twenties. They are very romantic, as their weighted style shows. I should have to change my nature if I were to change my style, which is full of romantic words, such as *dawn, dew, onwards, youth, world, adamant* or *dusk*; of metaphors and abstractions; of personalizations and sensations which belong to the author rather than to the characters.

Apparently his nature did change, for his style certainly does; but in most of his stories, even his most recent, the last statement in the above description remains as true now when applied to his mature art as it was when applied to his younger, romantic works. Some of O'Faoláin's best stories in his non-romantic mode would include "A Broken World," "The Old Master," "Unholy Living and Half Dying," "The Silence of the Valley," and "Lovers of the Lake," but the stories in which his narrative voice is most inventive, and yet completely natural and at ease, are the ones in his latest collection, *Foreign Affairs, and Other Stories*.

The tones of these stories range from the calm sophistication of "Murder at Cobbler's Hulk" to the lively, antic wit of "An Inside Outside Complex," but in each story the impression remains of a narrator who is telling his tale to a small, familiar, knowing audience, an audience who takes as much delight in the act of entertaining speech as in the tale itself. The best story in *Foreign Affairs, and Other Stories* is "Falling Rocks, Narrowing Road, Cul-de-Sac, Stop," a hilarious tale of middle-aged men in a small Irish town stumbling through their various sexual blind spots. This is O'Faoláin's special variation on the Irish short-story genre of the literary yarn, although perhaps a better term in O'Faoláin's case would be the intellectual yarn. The comic asides, the unembarrassed digressions, the ample description, the counterthrusts of learned allusion and earthy dialogue: this is the work of a master musician effortlessly showing off, enjoying the impromptu runs and brilliant variations, but all the time making sure, as all taletellers must, that the melody rings out clear and true and final.

No matter how conspicuously O'Flaherty, O'Connor, and O'Faoláin stand out during the middle years of the modern Irish story, the depth and diversity of the period might be best appreciated by reading the stories of their Irish contemporaries. Many of them are less well known simply because they wrote fewer stories.

Samuel Beckett, for example, although not especially recognized as a writer of stories or as a writer who draws on the particularities of Irish place and Irish speech, does both in his first published prose work, *More Pricks Than Kicks* (1934). The first story in the book, "Dante and the Lobster," is one of the masterpieces of Irish satire; its last line is a perfect fusion of Beckett philosophy and Irish diction. Elizabeth Bowen sets many of her stories in England, but she has written a small batch of Irish stories—now collected in the volume *The Irish Stories of Elizabeth Bowen* (1978)—wherein that strange, troubled world of Anglo-Irish aristocracy in the mid-twentieth century is probed in her characteristically impressionistic but penetrating style. Bryan MacMahon and Michael MacLaverty, both masters of regional dialects, have written in a variety of genres, including several well-received collections of stories. Two of their best are "Exile's Return" and "Six Weeks On and Two Ashore," both strong, ironic dramas of those typical Irish experiences, a return and a departure.

Mary Lavin deserves to be mentioned separately, but in the same breath as the three masters, since she is well on her way to becoming a fourth. She continues to publish a major collection every two years or so, and she has long proved herself to be one of the surest and most original stylists of the subject narrative. Her great themes are those intense states of anticipation or retrospection which frame the histories of intimate relationships. Her narrators always seem on the threshold or backstep of a definitive experience.

In turning to the contemporary scene of the Irish story, it is obviously misleading to speak too abruptly and too confidently of a new generation. Certainly there is no lack of new writers and new presses to publish them, but much of the best work is still being done by writers such as Benedict Kiely, Mary Lavin, and James Plunkett, whose careers stretch back to the 1940's. Even the old masters O'Connor and O'Faoláin can justifiably be claimed as contemporary figures. O'Connor wrote some of his best stories in the late 1950's and early 1960's, and Seán O'Faoláin continued to experiment with the genre in *Foreign Affairs*, a collection containing some of the freshest, most tonic stories of the last decade.

One recent development in the Irish short story has been the surprising ease with which young writers have published their first efforts. David Marcus, the literary editor for the *Irish Press*, is largely responsible for this new accessibility. He publishes a story each week in the Saturday issue of the *Irish Press*, and he also edits Poolbeg Press, a company that specializes almost exclusively in collections of short stories. Poolbeg not only reprints early out-of-print collections; it also publishes new collections of established writers, and most importantly, first collections of young Irish writers. Few of these latter collections have shown anything more than promising talents, and far too many of the younger writers seem ignorant of contemporary writing outside Ireland and England, but at least the possibility of publication and recognition now exists at a home press.

There is, however, a small group of younger writers who deserve to be included in any survey of the modern Irish story. Even though most of them began publishing in the 1960's, they have already established themselves firmly, perhaps permanently, in the modern tradition. In the stories by William

Trevor, Aidan Higgins, Edna O'Brien, John McGahern, and Eugene Mc-Gabe, the special virtues of the classic Irish story announced by Moore and Joyce—strong characterization, vivid, dramatic dialogue, and searching, ironic sightings on the failures and frustrations of Irish society—still seem predominant. If anything, the realism is more strident and closer to the subject. This new harshness obviously owes much to the daily jolts of violence and horror in Northern Ireland, but it may also owe something to the sudden changes Ireland shares with other traditional societies compelled to adapt pell-mell to the contemporary world. As the Dublin suburbs grow indistinguishable from their English counterparts, and as rural, provincial Ireland understandably yearns after those same suburbs' comfortable securities, there seems little to choose between Ireland's past and Ireland's future. What is perhaps most remarkable about these writers is their capacity to affirm voices all their own, and yet all unmistakably Irish, and to bring new vitality and new intelligence to a tradition that already loomed large, even before they began to make their own contributions, as one of the triumphant achievements of a national art in modern literature.

Bibliography
Ellmann, Richard. *James Joyce.*
Fallis, Richard. *The Irish Renaissance: An Introduction to Anglo-Irish Literature.*

Ben Forkner

This survey is a rewritten and expanded version of my Introduction written for the collection, *Modern Irish Short Stories* (New York: Viking-Penguin, 1980). I wish to thank Viking-Penguin for permission to reprint parts of the Introduction in this new form.—Ben Forkner

ITALIAN SHORT FICTION

The origin of short fiction is not an easy matter to settle; recent scholarship has come to the conclusion that the thought held by some authorities that such a genre originated from Oriental-Hindu literature is not as valid as was at first thought; at least, it is not considered a definite conclusion. In fact, all sorts of tales, anecdotes, and simple reports abound in all writings, including the Bible and other religious testaments of non-Christian faiths.

The European background of the short-fiction genre is perhaps less complex; without going into primary and extremely ancient sources one may point to the collection of the early *fabliaux* which blossomed in France from the end of the twelfth century to the beginning of the fourteenth century. These works, however, are brief, simple tales written in verse rather than prose; they are often monotonous in their rhyme schemes and most simplistic in their literary treatment.

It had also been thought that *The Arabian Nights' Entertainments* exerted a marked influence on the prose fiction that appeared in European countries in the first two centuries of our millennium, but such a possibility has also had many doubters, since it has not been clearly established when and how the work first appeared in Europe; there are only theories. From the view of literary importance, these Arabian tales cannot be deemed masterpieces in a true artistic sense. To be sure, all the antecedents of modern short fiction in thirteenth century Europe are important historically, since the various tales, anecdotes, and reports reveal the lives, customs, habits, and general culture of the peoples; but they were not as a rule true literature.

It was in Italy that, toward the end of the thirteenth century, a first collection of fuller tales and longer stories than those previously mentioned appeared under the title *Novellino* (1281-1300); they sprang from many sources and treated varied topics and peoples. This well-organized collection, even in its embryonic stage, gave rise to a new prose genre, the *novella*. A historically important collection, it contained many tales, anecdotes, and short stories of definite literary merit. For this reason, another historically important Italian collection of rather short medieval tales, the *Libro de' sette savi* (c. 1290, *The Book of the Seven Wisemen*), which antedates the *Novellino* by a quarter of a century, will be omitted from this discussion since the collection is composed mainly of remakings of old tales from Oriental or Indian provenance and lore, and thus lacks the unity or coherence of a literary work. The Italian *Novellino* was thus the first true gathering of such short literature and had an immense success and influence not only in Italy but in western European countries as well.

If both *The Book of the Seven Wisemen* and the *Novellino* (the first title of which was *Le cento novelle antiche* or *The One Hundred Old Short Stories*) have anonymous authors; some scholars have nevertheless believed that the author of the *Novellino* might have been Dante's teacher, the well-known writer Ser Brunetto Latini, or a Barberino, or a Lancia. It at least seems certain that there was a specific author (which was not always the case with other such collections in Italy and elsewhere) and that he must have been a cultured person. It was a work worthy of recognition, having a unity of style and diction, even if it had many sources. The work reveals a serious intent to write literature for the cultured persons of the courts in Italy rather than merely for the people in the streets, an intent which distinguishes it from similar previous anthologies.

The title of the work is significant. The term *novellino*, the diminutive of *novello* or *something new*, is perhaps in the masculine gender because the first writers of short stories had in mind a term such as *racconto novello*, that is a *new* or *different* kind of *story*. Later it became feminine (*novella*), perhaps because it was considered *una cosa novella* (a *new*, different *thing*); *cosa* is feminine in Italian as it is in French, a near source. Then, *cosa* was omitted as a shortcut, leaving *novella* standing alone. The term "novella" has remained intact in English as well as in other European languages, or it has been closely translated, even though in Spanish and in English, the terms *novela* and *novel*, respectively, acquired the meaning of a longer *novella*, hence a novel. In Italian, *romanzo* is used to designate a novel, as is the French term *roman*; in German the Italian term *novelle* is still being used. Thus, accidentally or not, the author must have had a high sense of esteem for his work, as one can read in his proud *proemio* or prologue to it, because he knew he was giving rise to something distinct, even *novel*, in this form of writing.

The paramount literary importance of the novella or short story, however, lies not so much in the etymological or semantic vicissitudes it went through as in the philological or aesthetic definition of such a literary concept. The definition of any genre (or the classification of any art) must take into account the characteristics of the country where the genre is being written and of the people who write it. Thus, aspects of the genre can differ somewhat from one country to another; in general, however, it can be said that the short fiction of many countries—including tales, anecdotes, reports, and the more popular or major classification which one calls short stories—is not only the prose progenitor of our modern novel, but is also akin to it in many facets. Indeed, many short stories have been developed into novels and into plays. If a novel or a play or a poem originating in a short story or tale becomes greater than its original matrix or vice versa, it is because of the literary artistry of an individual author. A short story is a prose narrative which can range from fantastic, realistic, naturalistic, sociological, psychological, or surrealistic to semihistorical; but it must have literary artistic merits, or it is merely a *notizia*, a *news item* typical of a gazette of yesterday or a newspaper of today. In view of this definition, the first true writer of our short-fiction literature was Giovanni Boccaccio.

Before studying Boccaccio's work, one should give a deserving note to what can be considered the first little novel or long short story dealing with the subject of love as a carnal and an idealist attraction (which makes this "little book," to quote its author, the real prototype of our modern, amorous novel): Dante's *Vita nuova* (c. 1292). This important work, which has been called a prelude to *The Divine Comedy* (c. 1320), is written in Vulgar Italian, a language that indeed comes closer to modern Italian than does Chaucer's *The Canterbury Tales* (1380-1390) to contemporary English, or the *Romance of the Rose* (c. 1230, 1275), or the Spanish *Jarchas*, perhaps even *El Cid* (c. 1140), to their respective present-day languages. (The *Vita nuova* does not need to be modernized or translated into the standard language to be understood today, whereas the other mentioned works do.) The *Vita nuova* cannot be evaluated at the level of Dante's supreme masterpiece, *The Divine Comedy*. Rather, it must be understood merely as the first *romanzo d'amore*, that is, (short) love novel; it is the first work of its kind: a long story (or short novel) dealing with love as its theme, written in a modern-language prose in the first person. Unwittingly, then, Dante created an original type with his *Vita nuova* which is both realistic and psychological, preceding not only Boccaccio but also several contemporary writers of short fiction or short novels. In the work, Dante tells the reader how he met his beloved Beatrice when they were both nine years old and met her again nine years later; the poet is tremendously in love with her but does not fail to pay attention to some other women, activities of which he repents as he returns to the primeval and ethereal love he has for Beatrice. He has dreams of witches and other "surrealistic" visions; finally, the "mirabile visione" ("the Wonderful Vision"), which gave rise to the symbolism and allegory which are to be fully developed in *The Divine Comedy*, came to him about eight to thirteen years later. In this vision Dante sees "things" which make him decide not to say any more "of this blessed woman" until he can write of her in a more worthy fashion; he kept this promise in *The Divine Comedy* and also provided an early example of a short story giving rise to a fuller work.

In addition to *The Book of the Seven Wisemen* and the *Novellino*, there were other collections of short prose which preceded *The Decameron* (1353). One example is the collection of popular tales known as the *Fioretti di San Francesco* (c. 1320-1330, *The Flowers of Saint Francis*), which has remained popular with the people of Italy because of its religious appeal. The tales are almost fables rather than miracle tales: the Poorman of Assisi speaks to the birds, and they listen and love him; he converts the bad wolves of Gubbio that ate children and becomes their friend. There are many similar stories. These tales have not really survived the proverbial test of time, however; Boccaccio's masterpiece alone has done so. If it is agreed that form as well as context make for a perfect artistic union in any creation, it follows that with *The Decameron* Italian prose has given to the world the first great prose masterpiece, which even today has not been surpassed and has only seldom been equalled as a consummate literary work in the short-fiction genre.

The author of *The Decameron* spent part of his younger years in Naples; his contact with that lively city, with its love for the exuberant and the hedonistic, influenced Boccaccio even though he hailed from the matronly, sedate city of Florence. There is no question that in the background of the Florentine life found in *The Decameron* there is furtively spread the clear Neapolitan sky and sea. Boccaccio's Florentine background, which was permeated with elegance, erudition, and linguistic knowledge, was complemented by the Neapolitan influence. The content of the one hundred short stories of *The Decameron* is varied, is always alive, and keeps the reader's interest; it runs the gamut of life itself. Yet the stories do not so much present a new way of life, as has been claimed, as they represent a new and daring procedure to portray life realistically and expose it with humor, sensuality, witticism, and also seriousness; to enjoy life and reveal its hypocrisy as practiced by monks, nuns, and others; and to elicit from everyday events the foibles, defects, and iniquities that befall everyone.

Other fine storytellers followed the Boccaccio school, authors such as Giovanni Fiorentino, Franco Sacchetti, Giovanni Sercambi, Poggio Bracciolini, Gentile Sermini, and Masuccio Salernitano, who deserves particular attention since he is generally acknowledged as the best *novelliere* (storyteller) of the fifteenth century. Masuccio's real name was Tommaso Guardati; he lived in the city of Salerno, not too distant from Naples, and hence earned the nickname *Salernitano*. He wrote his stories and tales mainly for his friends and addressed them to his protectors at the court of the Aragonese dynasty in Naples and later to persons at the court in Salerno. He titled his collection *Novellino*, published in 1476 but written some twenty-five years before; this title harks back to the earlier collection in Italian literature by the same name. It consists of fifty stories, and it is divided into five parts which tell of the vices of the clerics, women's betrayals, sexuality in women, macabre and violent incidents, comic events, good deeds performed by princes, and other subjects, clearly attempting to imitate the earlier Boccaccio.

Although his style is uncouth, Masuccio's writing is lively; his language is fresh and natural in that it approaches the spoken expression of the people (the Neapolitan dialect). His lack of knowledge of the elegant Florentine dialect confers on his prose a distinct, personal quality. The dialectal intonations of expression give a genuine feeling of the author's down-to-earth personality, and in this respect, Masuccio deviates from Boccaccesque prose; Benedetto Croce has maintained that our souls are dialectal, and it can be said that the dialect, not the standard tongue, is the first native language of all Europeans and other peoples in the world. Masuccio well proves that aesthetic axiom.

The sixteenth century produced not only Matteo Bandello, Il Lasca, Anton

Francesco Doni, and several other writers of lesser importance, but also Niccolò Machiavelli. Machiavelli was not a story writer in the usual sense, but he did write one short story which can stand in its own right among the best of its kind in world literature. The title is *Belfagor* (c. 1510-1520, *The Story of Belphagor the Arch Demon*), a pleasant, satirical, and witty story concerning the devil Belfagor who is sent to earth to experience married life; Belfagor, after having married a terrible woman, prefers to return to hell.

Matteo Bandello (1485-1561), by contrast, was a storyteller who strove to vie with Boccaccio himself, and indeed he was called at times the Lombard "Boccaccio of the *Cinquecento*." Although he failed to reach the artistry of the Florentine writer, he was nevertheless important for his stories that reveal the cultural customs and social habits of his time and people. Some of his stories are humorous although others are serious or even tragic, such as *Giulietta e Romeo*, a long novella. This story was Bandello's rendition of *Romeo and Juliet*, which inspired Arthur Brooke's poem, which in turn intrigued Shakespeare to the extent that he created the world-famous play based very carefully on the plot and even on some details of Bandello's story. To be sure, Bandello himself rewrote that tragedy from the short narrative first written by Luigi Da Porto, whose account of the two feuding Italian families and the resulting tragedy of the famous lovers was already popular among the people. Da Porto's story is better written than Bandello's version, as many Italian critics aver. Notwithstanding his imitation of Da Porto, in addition to some linguistic defects and stylistic weakness, it was Bandello who after Boccaccio influenced most other Italian writers, and also Shakespeare (*Much Ado About Nothing*, 1598-1599, and *Twelfth Night*, 1599-1600), Lope de Vega, Stendhal, Lord Byron, Alfred de Musset, and others.

To conclude a discussion of the short-fiction production of the sixteenth century, one ought to refer, however briefly, to two writers whose books cannot exactly be called collections of short stories, yet whose biographical sketches and etiquette vignettes were fascinating narratives of the lives of persons of their age: Giorgio Vasari who write about artists, and Baldassare Castiglione, who wrote about noble people attached to the princely courts of Milan, Urbino, and Mantova. Vasari's *Lives of the Artists* (1550) contains masterful as well as interesting sketches, stories, and tales of medieval and renaissance Italy which can be defined as biographical stories; they reveal indirectly the customs and intrigues behind the canvases of the age's supreme artists and describe the attitudes of the Church and her popes. The narrations are separate entities like *novelle*, yet a general background pervades the stories: the Italian Renaissance. The framework of *Lives of the Artists* is not entirely different from Boccaccio's original idea of a "cornice" to give a work unity, however varied the interior or content of the book may be.

To a lesser extent, *Il Cortegiano* (*The Courtier*), published in 1528, can be called a group of stories; the pieces are conversational topics and dialogues.

Nevertheless, a variety of subjects can be found in the author's witty, facetious, and semiserious anecdotes, revealing to the reader the habits and customs of the court and of an Italian society which, unquestionably, one would not have known as the great *Rinascimento* (Rebirth or Revival of Learning) had it not been for such a narrative. *The Courtier* is a compendium of behavior, manners, and customs which tells the history of a century not only in Italy but also as it was imitated in other European courts and in general society. To this day it has remained pleasant as well as profitable reading for those interested both in the life of courtiers and also in the rules of general social comportment.

If it were not for the fact that one of his short stories was chosen by Shakespeare for one of his greatest tragedies, one should probably not mention Giambattista Giraldi, called Cinthio. In 1565 he wrote the *Ecatommiti*, a collection of short stories, in which *Il moro di Venezia* (*The Moor of Venice*) is included; its latent dramatic possibilities attracted the English playwright's attention, and he wrote *Othello* (1604) based on it; thus Giraldi owes his "fame" to Shakespeare. Otherwise, it is agreed, he is not one of the important story writers of Italy.

As the spirit of the *Rinascimento* became a stereotype in Italian culture, the baroque era (1550-1750) slowly sprang up in European culture; its influence became noticeable most clearly first in the fine arts, and a little later in literature. In Italy, short fiction lost its luster, and the many and repetitious imitations of Boccaccio were not considered worthy of attention. Italy was under Spanish political domination, and the papacy did not encourage Italian unity; the appeals by Petrarch, Machiavelli, and other patriots fell on deaf ears. Still, within the arid culture of the seventeenth century, one writer of excellence, Giambattista Basile, wrote fables and tales. These tales were not in Tuscan (a regional adjective often used synonymously with Italian), but in the Doric dialect of Naples, a dialect that the ultra-Neapolitan writer, Ferdinando Galiani, of the eighteenth century considered superior to Italian (Tuscan) itself. Basile wrote the *Il Pentamerone* or *Lo cunto de li cunti overo lo trattenimento de piccerille* (1634-1636, *The Story of Stories*, published posthumously); the title reflects the purpose of the book: *fables and stories written in order to entertain children*. The book is a collection of fifty fables and tales narrated in five days by ten old, ugly women who plan to amuse a pregnant princess who has the "wish" to hear such stories (many Italians still believe that if an expectant woman does not have a strong wish or desire satisfied, something bad—a birthmark or worse—may mark the baby she is carrying).

Thus the princess hears tales such as the one about Antonio's donkey that excretes gems and gold, and about how, in spite of the good advice the ogre gives Antonio, the tavernkeeper incessantly fools and cheats him; she is also told a fable concerning two old sisters: one is jealous of the other because the latter is made young again by a fairy and succeeds in marrying a king; the jealous sister tries to duplicate her sister's luck but dies in her fantastic attempt.

These stories, with their popular folklore flavor, influenced writers beyond Italy, such as the Grimm brothers, Charles Perrault, and Ludwig Tieck, and attracted the attention of the great philosopher and critic Benedetto Croce, who edited and translated *The Pentamerone* from the Neapolitan dialect into Italian; Croce, moreover, considers it "the best work of its kind in world literature of popular fables."

Clearly it was not originality of themes and topics, which the tales lack, that made Croce and other critics praise the book, nor was it the baroque style, which often becomes heavy and monotonous; rather, it was the felicitous, artistic expression of each story that they found praiseworthy. Lastly, it should be noted that the framework of *The Pentamerone*—its division, its purpose, and other stylistic elements—follow the tradition of Boccaccio; notwithstanding this tradition, however, the spirit of the language, the style, and the multitude of these fantastic tales make the work vastly different from *The Decameron*.

There were a few writers of note who wrote in the following two centuries. These authors continued the style and purpose of the traditional short fiction, but in their content or thematic aim they were very different. In the eighteenth century, for example, Carlo Gozzi, a writer born in Venice into a noble family composed fablelike stories satirizing several persons in his city; he returned, in a sense, to the themes and purposes of the *commedia dell'arte*. His stories are long *novelle* or long stories, but not quite novels or short novels. He harks at times to themes from *The Arabian Nights' Entertainments* and also from Basile's *The Pentamerone*, but his scope is different. Gozzi polemicizes with other writers and especially with Carlo Goldoni, whom he opposes in the latter's attempt to destroy or change the glorious *commedia dell'arte*.

Gozzi wrote "scenic" stories such as *L'Amore delle tre melarance* (1761, *The Love of Three Oranges*), which was set to operatic music by Serge Prokofiev; *Turandot* (1762), which became an opera libretto for Giacomo Puccini's music; and *Il Re Cervo* (1762, *The Stag King*). These are all exotic, fantastic stories of an unreal world which delighted readers up to the turn of the twentieth century.

In the nineteenth century, Italian short-fiction production changed still further as its immediate purpose became politically tendentious at times; it should be remembered that this was the century of the beginning of the Italian *Risorgimento*, the political-nationalistic era during which Italians fought to redeem Italy from foreign control; it was the time of Giuseppe Garibaldi, Giuseppe Mazzini, Victor Emmanuel II, and Camillo Benso di Cavour. A great deal of patriotic literature was written, and some short stories, strangely enough, were written in verse as in the old French *fabliaux*. Other stories and novels, to be sure, were sentimental, romantic, and historical. There was Tommaso Grossi, for example, who in addition to writing a full-length novel with a historical, patriotic background, also wrote short stories in verse. There was also Silvio Pellico, whose *Le mie prigioni* (1832, *My Imprisonment*) is actually a group of short stories about his imprisonment; these vivid memoirs, written in simple and moving prose, are said to have cost Austria more than a lost battle. Other writers of patriotic, historical, and heterogeneous short stories are Cesare Balbo, Ippolito Nievo, and the popular Edmondo De Amicis. This last author wrote hundreds of mostly brief stories found in his *Vita militare* (1869, *Military Life*) and, above all, in his world-famous *Cuore* (1886, *Heart*).

In *Heart*, De Amicis is sentimental, realistic, patriotic, and poetic. His sympathy is always with the lower class and the poor people; in fact, politically, he was a Socialist and a follower of Mazzini's political thought, not that of the royal house. His oversweet style has been criticized by some critics, yet many people read his works with enjoyment today—including adults, even though De Amicis supposedly intended *Heart* to be merely for children. The book is written in the form of a diary by a schoolboy who tells of his experiences with his schoolmates and teacher. They are short pieces, some vignettes, others short stories. In one, the boy helps his father with his take-home work secretly during night hours to make the old man feel that he can still produce extra work and income even as he is becoming older. The father feels proud of himself until one night he discovers the beautiful deception; then he remembers that he has severely reproached his son many times for not doing good work at school anymore, because the teacher has complained that his son was sleeping in class.

Another story tells of a little drummer boy from Sardinia who helps a battalion of Italian soldiers win a battle against the Austrians in the war of 1848; the boy risks his life to bring an important message from the captain of a group of soldiers, totally besieged by the Austrians, to a nearby Italian post asking for help to break the siege. He brings the message, but is seen by the enemy and severely wounded in one leg. When the captain later meets the boy in a makeshift army hospital, he is glad that the boy is alive; he notices that the little drummer is very pale although clearly happy that he has done his duty. Then the boy reveals to the captain that he is pale because he has lost much blood, and quite proudly, as a proof, he lifts the bedsheet for the captain to see. The captain, a rough officer who has seen many soldiers die, is taken aback; he slowly takes off his kepi, pale like the boy, saying, "I am only a captain; you are a hero." The boy's left leg is amputated above the knee.

In contrast to the tearful and pathetic stories of *Heart*, at about the same time another book, also apparently meant for children only, appeared in Italy; today it is better known throughout the world than De Amicis' book: *The Adventures of Pinocchio* by Carlo Collodi of Florence. *The Adventures of Pinocchio* appeared first in separate serials and then in book form in 1883; like *Heart*, it has been translated into many languages. Collodi's book can be called a collection of stories since they are really tales and short stories on the same theme, episodes that, even if read independently of one another, can stand as separate happenings, like those found in *Heart*, can be read independently of one another. The overall story is well known, especially since Walt Disney adapted it for the screen in cartoon form. Disney, however, often betrayed Collodi's semiserious, semihumorous intent and made it strictly a fable for the amusement of children, and devoid of the true didactic purpose the author had intended.

The Adventures of Pinocchio is an allegory for all men and women; it is a childhood biography; it is a poetic yet realistic recounting of everyone's young and careless days. It is not a satirical representation, as some have claimed; it is a seriously humorous (or humorously serious) series of stories about childhood and a representation of life as beautiful, sincere, and simple.

If Italy influenced European *novelle* writers for a few centuries beginning with the *Novellino* in the latter part of the thirteenth century, equally, toward the very end of the nineteenth century (about 1880), it was the French school of realism of Honoré de Balzac, Gustave Flaubert, and Guy de Maupassant (and, a little later, Émile Zola) that began to influence Italian writers. It must be clearly understood that contrary to false interpretations, the Realist Movement did not arise in France, nor did such a school or movement change the format or purpose of the original *novelle* literature that had already assumed its true characteristics with the *Novellino* and *The Decameron*. What was new was the use of language that reflected more closely how the people spoke, and the use of a "slice of life" technique that presented the more sordid aspects of everyday living. The Realists shared the basic assumptions and intent of their novella-writing predecessors, but they were simply able to go further in the implementation of their goals. Thus, the difference between a story by Boccaccio and one by Balzac, Zola, or Giovanni Verga is merely a matter of style and degree. In Italy, literature dealing with the lower classes, which presented realistic portrayals of character in a language close to the people's own, came to be known as *verismo* because it was true to life, dispassionately objective, and impersonal so far as the storywriter was concerned. Of course, this objectivity was not maintained at all times, since the better authors, veristic or not, could not separate themselves totally from their work; this is fortunate, since art is always in the end personal.

If the Central and then the Northern regions of Italy produced the best Italian short fiction up to the twentieth century, it has since been Southern Italy—Campania, Calabria, Sardinia, and above all Sicily—that has led in the production of short stories, both in quantity and in literary achievement. It was Sicilian-born Luigi Capuana who first promoted French naturalism in Italian letters, and it was another Sicilian, Giovanni Verga, who brought *verismo* to high esteem in his country's literature. The versatile Capuana wrote fables such as *C'era una volta* (1882, *Once Upon a Time*) and many short stories in the veristic school that he was helping to develop in Italian literature, such as *Le appassionate* (1893, *The Passionate Women*) and *Le paesane* (1894, *The Country Women*), followed by *Nuove "paesane"* (1898, *New Country Women*). Interestingly, however, Capuana made his literary debut with stories other than veristic, more closely related to German fantastic and supernatural tales, as may be observed in the short story "Doctor Cymbalus," one of several similar stories found in his first collection, *Un bacio ed altri racconti*, published in 1881, where the propensity for the supernatural is evident. After his fashionable veristic output, it became evident that he was not naturalistic or veristic at heart, and he repudiated some of his former literary beliefs which he had acquired from French short fiction and novels.

A greater writer and perhaps the greatest of the Italian veristic school is Giovanni Verga, natural and expressive prose make him a consummate novelist and short-story writer. He began his career with a love for patriotic themes, having written for both political and literary journals, and he also wrote a novel with the Italian *Risorgimento* as its historical background. Soon, however, he embraced *verismo* and visited Florence—still the literary Mecca of most Italian writers—where he returned quite often. Like many other writers, Verga exhibited romantic traits in his early writings; it was not until later in life that he shed his youthful enthusiasm for the French and Italian postromantic writers (Alexandre Dumas, Eugène Sue, Francesco Domenico Guerrazzi, Caterina Percoto) and embraced Balzac, Zola, and Capuana, becoming veristic and positivistic (following Auguste Comte in this last regard).

By the time he was thirty-five, Verga had already written short stories which he published in book form, *Vita dei campi* (1880, *Life in the Fields*); these stories deal with rustic life and happenings in which Capuana's influence may be discerned. He then followed with novels and more short stories in which he describes the lives of people in small Sicilian towns often filled with crime, adultery, poverty, and revenge; these veristic stories were gathered in the collection entitled *Novelle rusticane* (1883, *Rustic Stories*). He also wrote the play *Cavalleria rusticana* (1884, *Rustic Chivalry*), which grew from an earlier short story and which began the veristic Italian theater; this play was then adapted into an operatic libretto for the composer Pietro Mascagni. Other short stories followed, such as *Pane nero* (1882, *Black Bread*), in which his islanders are again the protagonists and the victims.

There followed a long period of silence and literary inactivity, mainly between 1901 and 1919; only three years before his death in 1922, Verga wrote his last short story, "Una capanna e il tuo cuore" (1919, "A Hut and Your Heart"). It is a sad story about a company of singers who have met only with failure, and perhaps reflects Verga's mood in the last few years of his life; his style in this short story has been defined as aimless and disengaged. In the end Verga cannot be accurately classified as an impersonal writer, as it may be at first believed; he is strongly supportive of his poor and oppressed characters and shows love and compassion for them. His language is intense, terse, and temperate; it relates to the everyday language of Italians, not to classicism.

The Abruzzo region boasts as its regional veristic representative the great poet Gabriele D'Annunzio, whose large, versatile, and excellent-quality output in all literary genres is astounding. In his short stories, one can sense D'Annunzio's vibrant and dynamic personality; it was his exuberance that made him very popular with readers. His first stories, all dealing with his own experiences or with events told to him by others, include *Terra vergine* (1882, *Virgin Land*), *San Pantaleone* (1886, *Short Stories of Saint Pantaleone*), and a definitive edition, *Le Novelle della Pescara* (1886, *Short Stories from Pescara*). Although D'Annunzio was an eclectic writer who underwent extensive French and Russian influences (Maupassant, Count Leo Tolstoy, Fyodor Dostoevski), his exuberant, forceful personality nevertheless came through his works, becoming typically his own to the extent that an adjective was coined from his name: D'Annunzian. In fact, in a reverse action, the D'Annunzianism vogue eventually influenced other writers not only in Italy but also in all of Europe and even Latin America.

D'Annunzio's short stories deal with violent, sensual, criminal happenings, all written in an expressive style which can be called grandiloquent and decadent. In some of these stories, everyday life peers through with its weaknesses, problems, and its traditions. "La veglia funebre" ("The Funeral Wake") exposes the repressed sensual love of the recent widow and of the dead man's brother. Even in the presence of the dead body, which still lies in the bier in the center of a room as is the Italian custom, they embrace each other on the floor in love. "Gli Idolatri" ("The Idolaters") tells of two groups of villagers who in their pathological fanaticism for their patron saints really worship their own provincialism and folk pride. Some men of nearby towns, Mascalico and Ragusa, fight over their patron saints and town rivalries; the people of Ragusa carry their saint, San Pantaleone, on a cart to the rival church in Mascalico whose patron saint is San Gonselvo. Horrendous fights ensue and knives are wielded; the Ragusa people are beaten back and massacred while the statue of their Saint Pantaleone is thrown down from the cart, and the victorious rival saint, San Gonselvo, and his people step all over the dead bodies strewn in the church, a holy place.

Naples, capital of the Campania region, famous in Italian history and culture since Latin times (the setting for Petronius' *The Satyricon*, c. 60) and the capital of the Two Sicilies, also has its Neapolitan *verismo*, and three names among many stand out: Salvatore Di Giacomo, Matilde Serao, and Roberto Bracco. Di Giacomo's *Novelle napoletane* (1914, *Neapolitan Short Stories*) are possibly the best of this genre in describing Naples and its people who live in the so-called "bassi" (ground floor), low-income houses which often do not have a window. Thanks to Croce, these stories were brought to the attention of all Italy. While Di Giacomo's themes and language are not those of Verga or D'Annunzio, his topics deal equally with violence, adultery, revenge, but they are mitigated by a sense of poetical sympathy and human compassion in which the author himself becomes a sufferer. In one such story a father learns of his daughter's love affair with a man; his honor is hurt and he sends her out of his house at night. She is alone and afraid and does not know where to go; after roaming for a while she returns home and knocks on the door; her father answers and, crying, allows her to come in. Di Giacomo was primarily a poet, in his fiction as well as in his poetry; his language is not only soft and melodious, it is also a language that people really speak—a dialectal Italian.

If *verismo* in its strictly naturalistic confines carried the day with Capuana and Verga, it became mitigated, more Italianate, more personal and artistic, as it were, with D'Annunzio, Matilde Serao, and Di Giacomo because no literature is art without the human and personal appeal which must be reflected, not merely in the subject, but mainly in the language. In Sardinia there was a woman writer, like Serao of Naples, who, while relating Sardinian tales, tells of life's dilemmas, of people's passions as they happen on her native Italian island, which in reality does not differ from other peninsular regions of Italy; she was Grazia Deledda, who received the Nobel Prize in Literature in 1926.

Deledda began writing short stories when only seventeen years old; simple folk, farmers, and at times the middle or upper class are the principal characters of her tales, which are written in an easy, flowing, unassuming style. The belief that destiny is inescapable held by the lower class and ignorant plays a dominant role in both her short works and novels. Thus her superstitious Italian Southerners share a fatalism that has roots in ancient Greece and Roman Italy. Deledda does not portray psychological delineations in her early short stories; rather, she portrays realistically the outward violence and torment of a person. Her position has been defined as between *verismo* and decadentism; yet she wrote in a lyrical, enchanted style, and it is no small wonder that she is considered the greatest Italian woman writer by many critics.

At the turn of the twentieth century, there arose a large group of short-story writers; merely to mention the names of the most deserving ones would fill pages. These writers include Riccardo Bacchelli, Massimo Bontempelli, Corrado Alvaro, Dino Buzzati, Alberto Moravia, Elsa Morante, Giuseppe Marotta, Cesare Pavese, Italo Calvino, Indro Montanelli, and others who are still writing. Deserving special attention is one of the giants of contemporary world literature: Luigi Pirandello.

As a short-story writer, Pirandello is the same powerful, original, absurdist and dramatic writer that his plays reveal. Not since Boccaccio have readers had such an original writer of the short story. Just as he innovated and revolutionized the stage, he gave the novella a new dimension, creating an original concept with its own literary aesthetic; as one speaks of a Pirandellian drama, so also one might use the term "Pirandellian short story." The importance of his short fiction must also be recognized considering that it quite often afforded the thematic as well as stylistic background of his later plays, for which he received the Nobel Prize in 1934. The language of his stories is the same as that of his plays, except for some differences in intensity.

As for the *verismo* in Pirandello's work, it should be pointed out that the author's stories are not like those of his friends Capuana and Verga, also Sicilians, or similar to those of other regions of Italy; if it is a *verismo*, it is Pirandello's own brand. The plots and subject matter are not important; what is important is the psychological, pathological, neurotic approach as exhibited principally by the language, which is sober, incisive, semihumorous, and often pathetic. Like a magician, Pirandello can startle and amaze the reader; like a philosopher, he can also make the reader think; and as a narrator, whether it be in a Sicilian *novella* or in a universal play, he can move the reader and make him think. In his criticism, Croce is only partly correct: Pirandello does seem strange indeed at times, yet he is not purely intellectual. He also has a warm heart, as the author angrily stated in defending himself from the philosopher Croce. It is simply that his mode of expressing human qualities is different from what one is accustomed to; he originated a new kind of short story difficult to imitate because of the unique personal spirit that pervades his works. He fathoms the inner side of man's actions, his subconscious, his changing reality, which is an intimate, personal reality; in short, he fathoms man's loneliness and anguish.

Pirandello is by turns sarcastic and humorous; he is a sufferer in a world without solutions. When one reflects upon the world of most of his short stories, one begins to realize that he did not write short stories in the ordinary sense; it was the introspective reflections of the author with himself and his ability to build a narrative out of unconventional materials that make Pirandello a unique writer. Life wears a mask; man is alone; nothing is really true; one only thinks reality is definite; ideals become illusions; the absurd is part of life; one must escape into the metaphysics for relief—these are the tenets that make up Pirandello's world.

Twentieth century Italian writers attest to the fact that Italy even today continues its role of a leading, fertile, and literary land. Italy's long tradition of excellence in short stories has served as a source of inspiration for modern writers such as Basile, Gozzi, Verga, D'Annunzio, Di Giacomo, Deledda, and Pirandello, who have restored the etymological meaning of the word "novella" to the Italian short story by innovating and renewing it in content and form.

Ferdinando D. Maurino

THE STRUCTURE OF VIOLENCE IN
CONTEMPORARY SPANISH-AMERICAN SHORT FICTION

Since Edgar Allan Poe formulated his Aristotelian literary precepts for the short story, short fiction around the world has undergone a substantial transformation that the American master never conceived possible. In the past century, the short story has become an international art form and now treads a wayward path through contemporary letters, at times following the straight and narrow of Poe's critical norms, but often setting out in a direction all its own, unencumbered by the weight and strictures of normative conditions. This newfound independence has characterized English- and Spanish-speaking writers in particular, and indicates several commonalities in the development of short fiction in Hispanic and Anglo cultures.

The modern short story is a creation of an industrialized, urban society whose thirst for literary stimulation was first satisfied by popular journals and magazines of the nineteenth century. In order to conform the short-story form to current taste, writers of both traditions fashioned and firmly developed simple, unified plots which followed the ideas delineated in Aristotle's *Poetics*. If, as Poe concluded, a successful short story had a single, preconceived effect produced by one preestablished design, then critics and readers expected, at the very least, a semblance of wholeness in the unity of plot, as though each piece of prose fiction followed the guidelines that Aristotle had set down for classical tragedy.

Central to the question of plotting in the short story is the nature and placement of the climax. The word "climax" derives from the Greek term for "ladder," and as a literary term originally referred to a rhetorical "linking of utterances for a particular purpose, such as that of crescendo in poetry" (*Princeton Encyclopedia of Poetry and Poetics*, 1965) or to the sequence of elements of syllogisms. In modern literature, the climax is a "point of supreme interest or intensity of any series of events or ideas, most commonly the crisis or turning point of a story or play" (*Ibid.*).

As the most inherently "dramatic" of the prose genres, the short story "begins as near as possible to the end of an action, something like the final act of a play," as Thomas A. Gullason has claimed in his study, "The Short Story: An Underrated Art." To an extent, this dramatic quality of plot development in the short story, which typically features the climax at the end of the main action, is partly responsible for a denigration of the genre as a whole by some literary critics. Gullason claims the cause of the short story's underrating is the mechanically rigid conformity of the plot to standard devices in the placing of the climax, for example, as though by holding his readers in thrall until the story's final moments, the author were following a predictable formula for literary composition, which in some way necessarily demeaned his work. This study will examine recent developments in short-story lotting in Spanish America. By comparing techniques of depicting violence n short-story masterpieces over the past century, we will be able to observe ow the concept of short-story construction has changed. In particular, several writers from Spanish America are better able to maintain the "single effect or impression" so much a part of the short story by means of techniques in lot development and climax placement that are anything but preestablished or predictable. In a sense, contemporary writers best show their awareness of literary models and guidelines, such as those which Poe formulated, by their masterful avoidance of the precepts and molds.

The originator of the modern short story in Spanish America was the Argentine Esteban Echeverría (1809-1851), whose masterpiece "The Slaughterhouse" (c. 1837) vividly exploits the effects of violence within a classically dramatic plot, along the lines of Aristotle's *Poetics*. The principal climax falls predictably at the end of the main action. Although Echeverría was the first proponent of French Romanticism in Spanish America to foster a Hugoesque, conoclastic spirit with regard to the classical unities, "The Slaughterhouse" nevertheless approaches the neoclassic ideals of literary composition in its treatment of space, time, and plot development. Thus, Echeverría's work produces the "unique" or "single effect" which Poe deemed distinctive of the short story.

"The Slaughterhouse" presents a series of allegorical conflicts, such as Christianity versus Paganism and the Divine versus Demonic worlds, within the setting of political tyranny and violence of nineteenth century Buenos Aires. The time is Lent. The public consumption of meat has ceased, but its appetite has grown feverish during the Easter abstinence. Diluvial rains halt the even meager slaughter of beef for those who purchase indulgences, thus increasing the hunger for fresh meat. The principal conflict of Desire versus Denial is juxtaposed to another pair of forces, the people's sense of guilt brought on by the rains, and their need for a scapegoat who may be responsible for their suffering and fear of damnation. Led astray by superstition and a fanatical clergy, the masses imprecate against the Unitarians, an educated elite who represent the centralist minority in the Argentine political system. The resolution of all conflicts takes place in a violent confrontation within the slaughterhouse itself. Here the primitive drives of hunger and retribution for imagined sin are acted out by an enraged horde of butchers who mutilate all available livestock and then proceed to murder an innocent Unitarian with equal zeal. Echeverría summons up the images of conflict from his contemporary world to produce a horrifying metaphor of the modern world in his brutal climax.

Resembling a three-act drama, "The Slaughterhouse" ties and unties the plot to mirror Aristotle's concept of Tragedy. The first major division of the action or "act" in this morality play consists of the exposition which notifies the reader/audience of the allegorical significance of the piece. Echeverría

plays with the homonyms *historia/historia* denoting "history" and "story" as
he disclaims any biblical sources in his narrative. His narrator opens the story
and refuses to recite the entire history of the world from Noah's ark to the
present, even though this work is strictly "historical" and not fictitious. Despite
his disclaimer, the narrator immediately describes the new Deluge which
floods Buenos Aires during Lent, thus combining in this allegorical sweep of
history both Old and New Testament sources in a single stroke.

The second "act" of this melodrama focuses on the peak of public clamor
for meat. Fifty head of cattle are led to their deaths in the muddy corrals of
the slaughterhouse. The precise description of the castration and slaughter
of the last animal marks the high point of this part of the story and prepares
the reader for the climax in the third "act"—the murder of a Unitarian
gentleman, treated as a Christ figure, by the brutal butchers of the Federalist
regime, who are referred to as the executioners of Christ in the slaughterhouse

Although Echeverría scoffed at the artificial limitation of the classical unities
in his study of Romanticism and Classicism, "The Slaughterhouse" confines
action within Aristotelian norms. Echeverría controls all elements of his story
in order to anticipate and underscore the brutal denouement. The diluvial
rains that open the story foreshadow the numerous bloodbaths to follow—
for example, the slaughter of the forty-nine steers, that of a bystander who
is decapitated during the frenzied carnage, the death of the bull, and the
symbolic murder of the Unitarian who represents civilization and Christian
virtue. The motif of flowing liquids such as water, mud, and blood recurs in
and around the slaughterhouse, whose spatial arrangement embodies the
metaphor of a universal trap into which all nobly human impulses are fun
neled, and within which civilization is dissolved. Finally, Echeverría paces the
climax of the story, the death of the Unitarian, in neoclassic fashion. The
murder brings to a close the rapid flow of events at the slaughterhouse within
an hour of the opening of its gates.

Echeverría was not aware that "The Slaughterhouse" marked a point of
departure in the depiction of violence in Spanish-American short fiction; but
his masterpiece serves as a model for the study of social injustices and the
demand for violent reprisals against them in nineteenth century literature
The fiction of Spanish America through the mid-twentieth century document
society's suffering and its primitive, violent retribution. To portray the human
misery of the Hispanic world, the classical "fear" and "pity" of tragic plot
such as those developed in "The Slaughterhouse" were the primary mode of
expression. Writers of social protest literature relied primarily on the emotion
evoked by brutal violence. Such masters as Ricardo Palma (Peru, 1833-1919)
Ignacio Manuel Altamirano (Mexico, 1834-1893), Baldomero Lillo (Chile
1867-1923), and Ricardo Jaimes Freyre (Bolivia, 1872-1933) reinforce the
tradition of violence established by Echeverría within a classically dramatic
plot.

During the twentieth century, the depiction of violence receives a new treatment which transforms the plot structure of the short story and radically alters the once mechanical placement of the climax. Ariel Dorfman, an authority regarding violence in contemporary Spanish-American fiction, discusses the abandonment of naturalist documentation of violence in the contemporary novel. Rather than an external force which brings suffering upon a passive fictional character, violence now has become a problematical force. In contemporary fiction the character actively combats violence in a highly individualistic way. Furthermore, the reader observes this process of struggle from differing points of view, occasionally from that of an omniscient narrator, but more often from that of a participant in the struggle. To translate Dorfman's claim in *Imaginación y violencia en América* (1970):

> . . . in order to free themselves from the weight of Naturalism, writers investigate violence in the recesses of consciousness, seeing personal dilemmas from within, and enveloping the reader in that fiction. It is a matter of creating a panorama of various possible attitudes, the parallel solutions to our immediate and inescapable problems. But denunciation of misery and of those who cause it has not been abandoned; rather, we now describe the consequences which that exploitation has had and continues to have on the delineation of personality, and of conduct that we can recognize as our own. We assume that the environment in which the character moves has been documented already. Now it is important to outline the character within which the environment operates. How can I survive in this world? How can I maintain my human dignity? How can I free myself? How can I use this violence instead of allowing it to use me? How can I communicate with others? What shall I do with my unavoidable, concrete dilemmas?

Dorfman underscores here the sense of alienation inherent in the modern fictional character's response to violence, an alienation brought into sharp focus by psychological realism and the exploration of thought processes in contemporary fiction. To be sure, the conclusions which Dorfman draws reflect the treatment of violence in the novel, but these same trends also characterize the short story in Spanish America as well.

Ironically, one of Poe's closest adherents in Spanish America, the Uruguayan Horacio Quiroga (1878-1937), began the new paths in the treatment of violence which surpassed the standards Poe established. Quiroga's view of modern, alienated man affects the very structure of the short story in ways that go beyond the treatment of character to experiment with the placement of the climax. He communicates to the reader his interpretation of the effects of violence on the character and the reader himself. In his technical achievements, Quiroga anticipates the accomplishments of later twentieth century writers who view violence in a new way, now from within the character as Dorfman noted above.

For the contemporary writer of short fiction, the climax which accompanies violent events must not necessarily be placed at the very end of the story. Contemporary writers maintain tension and suspense by subverting the traditional development of plot. The climax is now a flexible entity which each author utilizes for his own desired effects. William Carlos Williams considers the new uses of fictional climax when he discusses violence in *A Beginning on the Short Story* (1950):

> They all have a frame—like a picture. There *is* a punch, if you like. But what *is* that punch? What kind of punch do you want: philosophic, as Plato's *The Republic* and—what in a woman shooting her husband's head off with an elephant gun? What in the *Gold Bug*? Murder is nothing at all but death—and what's new about death? Violence is the mood today. Now it's something if a son cuts his mother's throat, as in the *Agamemnon*. Maybe Plato was a bit fed up on the Sophocles. His endings are arguments, but he did give Socrates the hemlock (and a rip for a wife who could even outtalk him) finally.
> What today will be the punch paragraph? or maybe today we'll shift the emphasis and get a punch from having no punch. Maybe the buildup and the documentation will be merely hinted.

In his discussion of fictional "punch" or climax, Williams unwittingly describes some of the developments in twentieth century Spanish-American fiction, particularly with respect to the flexibility of the climax and its relationship to violent themes. The remaining portion of this study will explore some of the new directions in plot structure in short stories depicting violence included in the works of Quiroga, Enrique López Albújar (Peru, 1872-1966), and Gabriel García Márquez (Colombia, 1928). For example, Quiroga's "The Dead Man" and "Drifting" begin with the climax. (Citations in English from the works of Quiroga refer to the following edition: *The Decapitated Chicken and Other Stories*, translated by Margaret Sayers Peden, 1976.) His "The Decapitated Chicken" conceals the violent event in a veiled moment of fictional climax. Here, the effect of the climax is both muted and intensified by the absence of explicit detail in the description of the horrible denouement. López Albújar and García Márquez also find that the use of a flexible climax best conveys to the reader the horror of violent events in their fiction. López Albújar carefully inserts several false climaxes throughout "Ushanan-Jampi." (All citations from López Albújar's story refer to Harriet de Onís' translation in *An Anthology of Latin American Folklore in Literature*, 1948.) This multiplies the number of possible "punches," as Williams terms them. García Márquez, the foremost short-story writer in Spanish America today, purposely removes the climax from the story and "builds up the documentation" to hint at the extent of a violent climax yet to occur in "One of These Days."

An examination of these short stories will show how the treatment of violence and the variable placement of the climax is associated with a new concept of the intimate relationship between narrator and reader in Spanish-American literature. (Subsequent references to "One of These Days" pertain to J. S. Bernstein's translation contained in *No One Writes to the Colonel and Other Stories*, 1968.) No longer a passive initiate as in the nineteenth century, the modern reader is now an active participant in the tying and untying of the plot. The reader now reacts in unforeseen ways in accord with the changing rules of the fictional game. These rules, in harmony with the aesthetic requirements of the work of art, much as the Romantics advocated, operate in a unique way for each author, fictional composition, and even each new reading of the literary text.

Horacio Quiroga often heightens the full horror of fictional violence by placing the climax at the beginning of his stories such as in "The Dead Man." A field worker accidentally disembowels himself with his machete while he crosses a fence. The event is treated with a matter-of-fact tone which underscores the absurdity of the accident, and sums up the author's sense of tragic existence.

> With his machete the man had just finished clearing the fifth lane of the banana grove. Two lanes remained, but, since only chirca trees and jungle mallow were flourishing there, the task still before him was relatively minor. Consequently the man cast a satisfied glance at the brush he had cleared out and started to cross the wire fence so he could stretch out for a while in the grama grass.
>
> But as he lowered the barbed wire to cross through, his foot slipped on a strip of bark hanging loose from the fence post, and in the same instant he dropped his machete. As he was falling, the man had a dim, distant impression that his machete was not lying flat on the ground.
>
> Now he was stretched out on the grass, resting on his right side just the way he liked. His mouth, which had flown open, had closed again. He was as he had wanted to be, his knees doubled and his left arm over his breast. Except that behind his forearm, immediately below his belt, the handle and half the blade of his machete protruded from his shirt; the remainder was not visible.

The main theme of the story is the death of the protagonist's world consisting of all of his richly detailed mental impressions of the land and his family in contrast to the mundane indifference of the external world to his personal tragedy. By placing the climax at the onset of the action, Quiroga notifies the reader that this is a world in which events are running out of control, and that humankind, represented by the protagonist, is a victim, rather than an overlord, of nature.

Quiroga sounds his skepticism regarding the nature of human progress in this story in a way which has escaped translation. The Spanish original begins, "El hombre y su machete acababan de limpiar la quinta calle del bananal." Here we note the presence of a dual subject: the man and his machete "had just finished clearing the fifth lane of the banana grove." Both individuals are the agents of banana cultivation, rather than the man alone as the translation originally suggested. Quiroga presents a harsh irony here, as the machete, the cohort of the worker, his faithful companion and aide, subverts the order of things and turns upon its master. Thus, the tools of progress are double-edged swords. They can provide for man's well-being, but, if taken for granted, they can undercut his future. Quiroga concludes that man is sensitive, imperfect, and hence vulnerable to the forces of nature, much as the Naturalists claimed. However, his presentation of a naturalist world, a world of nature reclaiming its pound of flesh from rapacious man, in this case the field worker, astounds the reader with the novel treatment of the climax and plot development. The entire story is an anticlimax during which the pitiful protagonist evokes a life which rapidly fades from consciousness.

A deathly climax also begins Quiroga's "Drifting" when a man steps on a snake. As in "The Dead Man," an innocuous tone belies the significance of the transcendental event as the snake mortally wounds the protagonist: "The man stepped on something soft and yielding and immediately felt the bite on his foot." Unlike the protagonist of "The Dead Man," the victim struggles against pain to seek aid as he floats downstream in his canoe. As the day wears on, the man drifts through primeval jungle and slowly reviews the passage of his life. His physical sensations gradually abandon him, and he takes refuge from solitude in his fantasies and memories. He dies during the process of reliving a moment from the past:

> Suddenly he felt freezing cold up to his chest. What could it be? And his breathing, too. . . .

> He had met the man who bought Mister Dougald's timber, Lorenzo Cubilla, in Puerto Esperanza on a Good Friday. . . .
> Friday? Yes, or Thursday. . . .

> The man slowly stretched the fingers of his hand.

> "A Thursday. . . ."

> And he stopped breathing.

In this story, Quiroga exploits the long anticlimax for effects other than those he achieved in "The Dead Man." Here, the victim of a violent encounter with nature creates a relationship between himself and another in his mind to build a measure of well-being to last him through his dying moments. Although his body is cast adrift on the river, his mind has arrived at a goal, a memory or fantasy of solace to counteract the finality of death. Various Spanish American authors experiment with time during a protagonist's death throes. Carlos Fuentes in *The Death of Artemio Cruz* (1964), Jorge Luis Borges in "The Secret Miracle" from *Ficciones* (1962), and Julio Cortázar in "The Night Face Up" (1967) show how dying men can evoke real or imaginary events in order to escape from the inevitability of death. In a sense, Quiroga must be considered a forerunner of these modern masters in this technique as demonstrated in "Drifting."

As we have seen, Quiroga reverses the traditional order of plot development as prescribed by Poe and others. The turning point occurs at the very moment that the plot begins to develop, rather than at the end. The author unties the action in the manner of slow-motion cinema and forces the reader to find meaning in his protagonists' lives, which are apparently drained of significance as they drift into oblivion.

Quiroga's story which best explores violence and the artful placement of the climax is "The Decapitated Chicken." John Englekirk, in *Edgar Allan Poe in Hispanic Literature* (1972), has said that Quiroga "tries to outdo Poe in the depiction of madness and of foul horror" in this tale, perhaps the Uruguayan's most brutally animalistic short story. Here, Quiroga also demonstrates the creative use of the climax which again serves to place the author at the forefront of experimental fiction in Spanish America. The narrator prepares the reader for a violent denouement, but masks the bloody climax in order to stimulate feelings of repulsion in the reader who can only imagine the full dimensions of the violent act.

The story deals with the universal drives of hunger and love which have become confused in the family of the protagonists. Mazzini and Berta are parents of five children—four idiot sons and a normal daughter. The boys, long since neglected by their parents who favor their Bertita, are unable to communicate their envy. Nevertheless, after witnessing the servant's slaughter of a chicken for their supper, the brothers silently perform the identical operation on their sister. Finally, the parents are overcome by self-loathing and grief as they contemplate the destruction of their marriage in the person of their beheaded daughter.

In many ways, this tale is a demonstration of traditional short-story technique, as Poe set forth in his 1842 review of *Twice-Told Tales* (1837). From the outset of the story, the reader senses that the boys' overwhelming appetite will resolve their lethargy and mental stagnation. In the manner of a behavioral psychologist, Quiroga prepares the ground for an experiment in conditioned responses to the animal drive for food. From the first paragraphs of the story, the narrator reveals the response to the world of the idiot sons in terms of food:

All day long the four idiot sons of the couple Mazzini-Ferraz sat on a bench in the patio. Their tongues protruded from between their lips; their eyes were dull; their mouths hung open as they turned their heads.

The patio had an earthen floor and was closed to the west by a brick wall. The bench was five feet from the wall, parallel to it, and there they sat, motionless, their gaze fastened on the bricks. As the sun went down, disappearing behind the wall, the idiots rejoiced. The blinding light was always what first gained their attention; little by little their eyes lighted up; finally, they would laugh uproariously, each infected by the same uneasy hilarity, staring at the sun with bestial joy, as if it were something to eat.

As in "Drifting" and "The Dead Man," nature, or in this case human nature, is out of control as seen in the small boys. Unable to groom themselves or to control their body processes, these children offer the reader a glimpse of a parody of Jean-Jacques Rousseau's state of nature in which man's innate goodness and *bons sens* are but a distant, mad illusion. This preparation Quiroga offers his reader, moreover, is essential to the violent denouement which predictably follows the main action.

Quiroga provides a study of causes of familial violence within the story itself. The children have inherited a family trait for "madness" from their paternal grandfather. Nurture, as well as nature, also explains their condition. Berta and Mazzini have brutalized their sons and are, in part, responsible for their degeneration to an animal level of existence. They insult and assault each other out of feelings of guilt for their abnormal offspring. They suffer from the sin of pride as well, longing for a normal child as a symbol of redemption from the degeneracy they feel has been visited upon them. Finally, their feelings of guilt and reactions of pride lead them to dote upon their daughter and to withhold love from their damaged sons. Berta and Mazzini never refer to their boys by name, leave their care to a servant, and provide for their physical necessities alone.

Motivated entirely by food now, the brothers utilize the drive of hunger to express their every need in gestures symbolic of their appetite. They stare at brightly colored objects and drool for something to eat all day long. Quiroga includes these actions of the boys as elements of a behaviorist equation involving the stimulus of food as a substitute for love, and the reaction of eating as the children's ritualistic way of expressing their relationship with the rest of the family. The author moves this equation to a rapid conclusion when little Bertita peers over the wall of the patio to view the sunset better. Putting in motion a fatal sequence of mental and physical responses, Bertita's silhouette resembles that of the chicken's head the boys have just seen the servant sever from its body:

> The idiots' gaze became animated; the same insistent light fixed in all their pupils. Their eyes were fixed on their sister, as the growing sensation of bestial gluttony changed every line of their faces. Slowly they advanced toward the wall. The little girl, having succeeded in finding a toe hold and about to straddle the wall and surely fall off the other side, felt herself seized by one leg. Below her, eight eyes staring into hers frightened her.
> . . . One of the boys squeezed her neck, parting her curls as if they were feathers, and the other three dragged her by one leg toward the kitchen where that morning the chicken had been bled, holding her tightly, drawing the life out of her second by second.

This buildup toward a climax ends here as the narrator withholds the climactic slaughter of the little girl. Quiroga forces the reader to see the murder from differing points of view, rather than from that of an omniscient narrator, as in Echeverría's "The Slaughterhouse" in which the murder of the Unitarian parallels that of the bull in every detail. Here, the reader first interprets the killing from the father's point of view. Mazzini enters the house and hears no one. Then, "he ran frantically toward the back of the house. But as he passed by the kitchen he saw a sea of blood on the floor. He violently pushed open the half-closed door and uttered a cry of horror." Quiroga avoids describing more than the blood in order for the reader to form a personal image of the mayhem.

When Mazzini's wife enters the kitchen, her husband restrains her so that she will not see the carnage. Throughout the conclusion of "The Decapitated Chicken," the reader conjures mental images of the boys' secret ceremony of bloodletting. The reader sees the event, in a way, from their perspective as well as from that of the other characters in the story. The narrator indirectly provides a glimpse of the murder in its mirror image, the slaughter of the chicken earlier in the story:

> The brilliant day had drawn the idiots from their bench. So while the servant was cutting off the head of the chicken in the kitchen, bleeding it parsimoniously (Berta had learned from her mother this effective method of conserving the freshness of meat), she thought she sensed something like breathing behind her. She turned and saw the four idiots, standing shoulder to shoulder, watching the operation with stupefaction. Red . . . Red. . . .

Now, at the end of the story, the reader superimposes the sight of the slaughtered fowl upon the scene in which the climax should occur. The result is a vision of two decapitated chickens. These, at least in the metaphoric reasoning of the brothers, are one and the same.

In the techniques of depicting violence, contemporary writers, led by Quiroga's example, have utilized a flexible concept of dramatic climax in the short story. "The Dead Man," "Drifting," and "The Decapitated Chicken" each explore the quality of violence in daily life from various perspectives along the lines discussed in Ariel Dorfman's article. These stories maintain suspense and tension in their fresh treatments of an ancient theme.

The Peruvian Enrique López Albújar paints detailed portraits of the Andean Indian in *Cuentos andinos* (1920), which includes "Ushanan-Jampi." In this short story, an Indian village expels Cunce Maille in punishment for the crime of theft. The wise men of the village, his judges, warn him that if he returns home, he will suffer "Ushanan-Jampi," a ritualized form of capital punishment. On the surface, then, the theme of violence deals with a conflict of Romantic proportions, that of the pursuit of freedom in contrast with society's restriction of personal liberty. In this case, society attempts to cleanse itself of an undesirable whom it has condemned. The violent climax of the story is worthy of Echeverría's scenes of butchery in "The Slaughterhouse" as the community slaughters Cunce Maille in the "Ushanan-Jampi":

> A horrible scene, a cannibal-like orgy, followed. When the knives were weary of stabbing

they began to slice, cut, dismember. As one hand tore out the heart, another gouged out the eyes, another slashed out the tongue, another ripped out the bowels. And all this accompanied by shouts, peals of laughter, insults, maledictions, and the fierce barking of the dogs, which, through the legs of the assassins, snatched mouthfuls of flesh from the corpse and buried their sharp muzzles in the pool of blood.

The "final solution" described above is the preestablished denouement which the reader expects will occur from the start of the story. Even the title of the work indicates that a bloody execution will mark the tale's climax. The story is further unified by a simple progression of events leading from Cunce Maille's trial, sentence of ostracism, return, and execution.

Such a classically constructed plot suffers from the potential weakness of predictability. López Albújar, however, rescues the plot from the reader's facile foreshadowing of the conclusion by means of several false climaxes which view the progression of violent events from various perspectives, as in Quiroga's "The Decapitated Chicken." López Albújar disarms the reader by bringing a number of possible turning points into the action which ambiguously indicate the protagonist's triumph or defeat. Therefore, when the true climax arrives, the violent moment retains its intended power to affect the reader's sense of fear and pity. The true climax also leaves the reader exhausted from the intense anxiety produced by identifying with the protagonist during the sequence of false and true climaxes as well.

Constructed around two indigenous rituals, the *jitarishum*, or expulsion of Cunce Maille and the *ushanan-jampi*, or execution, the story contains four "false climaxes" which move the plot toward its peak moment of violence in crescendo. All of these false climaxes occur during the second part of the tale which narrates Cunce Maille's return home. The protagonist's personality and the nature of the crime lead the reader to suspect that he will succeed in his quest and avoid execution as he risks his life to visit his mother's shack. He has been sentenced for stealing the cow of another villager who Cunce claims stole his bull. Cunce condemns the hypocrisy of a town in which all people steal but only he is found guilty during his trial. Just as Cunce's ostracism flies in the face of a Western concept of decency, sympathy for the protagonist is generated by the characterization of the Indian. López Albújar casts his protagonist as the very image of the noble savage, "features . . . so well cut, his body so lithe, his glance so uncringing, his bearing so proud, that, in spite of his bloodshot eyes, he radiated attention, the attraction aroused by those men who possess beauty and strength." As in the writer's other stories from this collection, Cunce is a "man of great tenacity who unwaveringly pursues a single course, although this trait may be disguised by his ability to dissimulate his motives before his own people."

Cunce is a free-thinking individualist who threatens society's mass mentality and blind conformism. Bound by his guards and bloodied by the ever-present dogs, the protagonist, rather than being a malefactor brought to justice, inspires outrage in the reader who sees how society demeans its most noble member.

The narrator highlights the severity of the sentence, further arousing the reader's sympathy for the convicted Cunce:

> If to any man expulsion is an affront, to an Indian, and an Indian like Cunce Maille, expulsion from the community is all possible affronts, the sum of all suffering and the loss of everything worth while: cabin, land, gods, and family. Above all, the cabin.

In the second part of the story, López Albújar summons up a series of suspenseful cues which capture the protagonist's overriding fear and anticipation of violence. The first of these cues or false climaxes occurs as Cunce crosses the river, the outer limit of the village:

> . . . as Maille set foot on the forbidden land, he felt as though a cold hand had clutched his heart, and a shiver of fear ran through him. Fear? of what? Of death? But what did death matter to him who was accustomed to risk his life at the drop of a hat? Besides, didn't he have his rifle and his hundred bullets? Enough to fight the whole village and make his escape whenever he wanted to.

This moment of anxiety prepares the reader for the series of tension-packed incidents which rapidly follow. A veil of mystery surrounds the village at night from Cunce's point of view. A magical, animistic world greets him on his return one month after the ostracism. The air of terra incognita sets the scene for the betrayal and deception Cunce will suffer as the narrator refers to Cunce's ancestral home merely as "a cabin" for the second false climax when "the door opened, and two arms twined about the exile's neck as a voice murmured: 'Come in, my son, come in.' "

The respite from Cunce's wanderings, however, is short-lived. When the townspeople learn of his presence, they silently gather around the cabin to apprehend him. Nevertheless, the protagonist, "too astute and suspicious to trust this silence," barely escapes as a volley of gunfire perforates the cabin's door. Cunce takes refuge in the church and keeps his pursuers at bay as he shoots down from the bell tower. Lacking the accuracy or firepower to overcome Cunce, the elders select one of the sniper's friends to lure him out. José Facundo gains Maille's confidence and falsely promises release from *ushanan-jampi* if Cunce will embrace him. He relents and embraces the traitorous José. "Instead of the brief, warm embrace he expected, what Maille felt were two sinewy arms fastening about his neck, almost strangling him." The last false climax arises in the reversal Cunce achieves over José. "As swift as a tiger, he clasped his adversary still more tightly, lifted him off his feet, and attempted to climb back up the stairs with him." This struggle culminates with an ironic execution of José Facundo by Cunce Maille. Cunce, displaying his sense of betrayal through the words of Facundo, cuts out José's tongue.

Briefly vindicated, Cunce now contends with the anonymous mob which prepares to finish him off. Throughout this last false climax, Cunce's bravery and stoicism promise to save him once again:

> A blow over the head from a club dazed him; a knife thrust in the back made him reel; a stone hit him in the breast, and he dropped his knife and put his hand to his wound. Yet he had strength enough to clear a path for himself through the crowd with his fists and his feet and, fighting a rear-guard action, he managed to reach his house.

Cunce's pride and impudence, however, are reduced to failure as he is outnumbered: ". . . the villagers who were on his heels swarmed in after him just as he fell into his mother's arms. Ten knives buried themselves in his body."

Several generalizations emerge from this examination of violence in the contemporary Spanish-American short story. First, the motif of violence, which appeared in the opening chapters of Spanish-American literature, is in full vigor today and continues to form a thematic basis for the contemporary narrative. Aside from an interest in violence for its own sake, however, twentieth century writers such as Quiroga and López Albújar depict terror and bloodshed in startlingly fresh ways. They depart from the standard, dramatic climax which characterized nineteenth century plot development in order to maintain suspense and to keep the reader at a distance from the denouement. Techniques such as false climaxes, veiled or masked climax, and shocking openings to the short story in the examples noted above serve to maintain a high level of reader interest and "complicity" in the development of plot, as some writers would term their readers' involvement. All of these techniques create a text and characters which develop in unpredictable ways as they depart from the preestablished plan of Poe's idealized short story.

One of the most painstaking craftsmen of the contemporary short story is Gabriel García Márquez. Reared during a period of social, political, and economic upheaval in Colombia, García Márquez uses violence as the foundation of all his literary production. In his novels and short stories, the nightmare of violence is most effectively portrayed as the author accurately depicts the effects of violence on contemporary man. The story "One of These Days" shows in miniature García Márquez's interpretation of violence in daily life and recapitulates the techniques earlier writers such as Quiroga and López Albújar used in its portrayal.

The scenario of Spanish-American political and civil violence that has plagued the continent down through the years is played out in the simple office of an unlicensed dentist in "One of These Days." In this unlikely place, the town Mayor and Dentist will do battle as the Mayor, an unwilling patient, comes for an extraction of his abscessed tooth. While the physical pain of the Mayor is the focus of the story and the *raison d'être* of his visit, the description of the extraction, which should be the moment of peak interest for the reader, receives scant, violent impact:

> The Mayor felt the crunch of bones in his jaw, and his eyes filled with tears. But he didn't breathe until he felt the tooth come out. Then he saw it through his tears. It seemed so foreign to his pain that he failed to understand his torture of five previous nights.

The climax or climaxes of the story lie entirely outside the main action of the piece, such as in the chronological order of events which prepare the reader for the main action but which occur before it, in other events occurring outside the dentist's office, and in apparently insignificant details of life within the office, details which seem to be irrelevant to the main action but which reinforce the system of violence underlying the structure of the story.

In the form of a multilayered structure whose visible surface serves to conceal deeper levels of meaning which recede from view down to an invisible core of violence, "One of These Days" is disquieting to the reader in its evocation of a violence which is absent from the main action. A thread of imminent violence runs through the story beginning with its title. The peak of violence, however, never arrives in print, but remains dormant, ready to erupt at the story's close as the reader establishes the necessary links with violent events preceding and following the action.

García Márquez writes in the mainstream of the violent tradition of Quiroga and López Albújar. Violence charges the exposition when the Dentist informs the Mayor that he intends to avenge the deaths of twenty men executed by order of his patient. As in "Ushanan-Jampi," "One of These Days" contains several opportunities for violent climaxes which are never realized. For example, when the Mayor enters the office, the Dentist's son introduces the possibility of a bloody denouement with his strident announcement of the patient's arrival:

> The shrill voice of his eleven-year-old son interrupted his concentration.
> "Papá."
> "What?"
> "The mayor wants to know if you'll pull his tooth."
> "Tell him I'm not here."
>
> . . .
> "He says you are, too, because he can hear you."
>
> . . .
> "So much the better."
>
> . . .
> "Papá."
> "What?"
>
> . . .
> "He says if you don't take out his tooth, he'll shoot you." Without hurrying, with an extremely tranquil movement, he stopped pedaling the drill, pushed it away from the

chair, and pulled the lower drawer of the table all the way out. There was a revolver.
"O.K.," he said. "Tell him to come and shoot me."

The suggestion of gunplay, however, remains only a potential threat.

The key to García Márquez's use of violence is the juxtaposition of potential and real violent struggles occurring in the story, all of which combine during the reading to produce an atmosphere of incessant malevolence. Framing the confrontation between Dentist and patient are two other fields of combat outside and inside the office. The Dentist sets up his day's work while contemplating "two pensive buzzards . . . on the ridgepole of the house next door." These birds of prey, omnipresent in the works of García Márquez and symbolic of the presence of death, prepare the reader for carnage as they patiently await their prey. A mirror image of this imminent violence appears in the description of a dusty corner of the office. After the painful extraction, the Mayor sees "the crumbling ceiling and a dusty spider web with spider's eggs and dead insects." García Márquez builds a structure of animalistic violence in and around the Dentist's office by utilizing three levels of violent experience in parallel. Juxtaposed against the microcosm of the spider's web is the macrocosm of the buzzards. Between the two extremes García Márquez situates his exemplary tale of life's struggle.

Much in the way Horacio Quiroga denoted the horror of the decapitated daughter, García Márquez suggests the magnitude of violence on three distinct levels: the spider and the dead insects, the Dentist and the Mayor, and the buzzards avid for prey. The three levels reinforce one another, but serve to dehumanize the human arena of the Dentist and the Mayor. As parallel incidents of violence, the various struggles for life are indicative of the instinctual drives that motivate nature and life itself. This is Charles Darwin's amoral, naturalistic world in which strong and weak engage in perpetual conflict. García Márquez underlines the dubious value of the Dentist's momentary victory at the end of the story when the Mayor arranges payment for the Dentist's services:

"Send the bill," he said.
"To you or the town?"
The Mayor didn't look at him. He closed the door and said through the screen:
"It's the same damn thing."

The Mayor reasserts his primacy as the town's power broker in this parting salvo against the Dentist. His obscene "Es la misma vaina" demonstrates that while the Dentist has won the battle, the war rages on. In keeping with the natural images of violence the author has juxtaposed in the story, the ending suggests more skirmishes to come between the two factions headed by the Mayor and Dentist, as human nature acts in harmony with the system of natural, instinctive animal violence abroad in the world.

From a comparison of these masters of violence in the contemporary Spanish-American short story, several conclusions emerge. Quiroga, López Albújar, and García Márquez select violent events from the simple, even insignificant moments of daily life. They build dramatic structures in fiction and magnify the impact of these violent moments by means of a variety of techniques affecting the nature and placement of the climax, as we have seen. Through their experimentation with false climaxes, veiled climax, and elimination of climactic moments in their short stories, these writers infuse the genre with renewed vigor. Their stories accomplish what the form was designed to do: they provide incisive commentary on life; entertain while producing tension in a reader anxious to discover an intense denouement; and leave a lasting impression or "single effect" after the reading is over. While these goals for short fiction agree with Edgar Allan Poe's assessment of the directions fiction should take, Spanish-American writers have realized them with new techniques. They see the short story as an opening on reality rather than a photographic description of life. The imminence of violence in these stories serves to disquiet the reader, insecure about himself upon discovering the problematical world of fiction. Perhaps the best description of the quality of violence in the contemporary Spanish-American short story is that supplied by Julio Cortázar, one of the most creative writers on today's literary scene. To Cortázar, the contemporary short story is like a "seed within which the gigantic tree is sleeping." The same metaphor can well describe violence in the short story, waiting to erupt and grow during its unpredictable moment of truth.

Bibliography
Aldrich, Earl M., Jr. *The Modern Short Story in Peru.*
Englekirk, John. *Edgar Allan Poe in Hispanic Literature.*
McMurray, George R. *Gabriel García Márquez.*
May, Charles E., ed. *Short Story Theories.*
Monegal, Emir Rodriguez, ed. "Introduction," in *The Borzoi Anthology of Latin American Literature from the time of Columbus to the Twentieth Century.*
Reid, Ian. *The Short Story.* Vol. 37 of *The Critical Idiom* series.

Howard M. Fraser

THEMES OF WOMEN'S SHORT FICTION

In contemplating women's short fiction, one would like to reach for some familiar, comforting theory or formula so that one could proceed in at least an orderly fashion. One would like to be able to fill in the blanks: The themes of women's short fiction are _____ , _____ , and _____ . There are, however, few theories, fewer formulas. The most perceptive critics take roles as historians and seers when speaking of women's fiction. That is, they describe the poverty of the past and they predict the richness of the future: sometimes they suggest how to obtain that richness.

In examining the conditions under which women write in *A Room of One's Own* (1929), Virginia Woolf, the most brilliant of these critics, noted women's limited experiences, their habitation of rooms and houses rather than worlds, their poverty, the restrictions of childbearing and rearing, the lack of a tradition upon which to build, and the paucity of women's education. Woolf observed that those few women who did write, created heroines who are always viewed in relation to men. All of these limitations, Woolf declared, could be remedied if aspiring women writers had rooms of their own and a stipend of five hundred pounds a year upon which to live independently.

Moreover, continued Woolf, the task of a woman writer is not to ape the male tradition, but rather to depict those aspects of life from which men have been excluded. She suggested that women describe their domestic world, the world of rooms and houses whose walls vibrate with the unexpressed souls of generations of women who have lived in them; that they describe themselves from their own point of view—not only in relation to men—and that they describe men. Woolf cautions that these tasks should not be bitterly completed, should not be executed from the perspective that the oppressed has of her oppressor, should not be written from the female aspect of the psyche alone, but from the point of view of the "androgynous" sensibility freed from sexual bias, able to see "things in themselves."

Have women writers taken Woolf's advice? Certainly there are more women writers taken seriously than in the past. In most recent short-story anthologies, although they do not have equal representation with male writers, women have more than token representation. Woolf's observation that women portray themselves only in relation to men, however, seems correct especially for writers whose careers began before the mid-twentieth century and even for a great many that began later. Indeed, in a recently published anthology of women's short fiction, the central issue of fourteen of the twenty-six stories concerns the relationship between a woman and a man. The heroine may be victim or victor; she may be temptress, torturer, suffocating mother, bitch-goddess, or innocent; she may be free or enslaved. Whatever her condition and identity, she is defined in relation to a man. This acknowledgment of traditional roles, however, does not always mean acceptance or acquiescence.

Although women still portray themselves as having submerged or incomplete egos, they sometimes regard their condition from radical perspectives—at times astonishingly rebellious, frequently upsetting patterns, mocking expectations, indeed saying the unsayable.

Kate Chopin, a late nineteenth century artist, wrote stories expressing a rage that still commands attention. In "The Story of an Hour," the heroine's joy springs perversely from the information that her husband, a not unkind and a not bad man, died in a train accident. She begins to see her now unfettered future. She becomes ready truly to live. When her husband turns up at the front door alive, the heroine's fatal heart attack is thought by her friends to have been motivated by a "joy that kills." The reader knows, however, that the heroine has died of disappointment. Although the heroine is still viewed in relation to a man, she has redefined this relationship, and she has said the unsayable: "I'm glad my husband is dead so that I can be free."

Perhaps even more startling is the idea that children may be a mother's enemies. In the stunning story "The Children," by Joyce Carol Oates, just this is said. Ginny, the central character, willingly gives up a career in chemical research to marry and enter the suburban life of placid housewife and anxious mother. At first Ginny accepts this life; indeed she never awakens to her own dissatisfaction, although the unacknowledged demons in the end possess her. When her beautiful daughter is able to roam the neighborhood on her own, to have a will of her own, Ginny resents her daughter's independence. When her daughter invents a secret language that she uses with her friends and that she refuses to teach to her mother, Ginny becomes suspicious. Her suspicions become increasingly pronounced. When her daughter teases her new baby brother in the usual spirit of sibling rivalry, the now crazed Ginny is sure that her daughter is evil, that she presents danger. The story ends with a shocking scene: the husband comes home from work to see his wife beating his daughter with a now bloodied spoon. Although Ginny is mad, it is surely a madness borne of despair.

Women writers not only portray the malevolent or tragic possibilities in traditional roles, but they also have enjoyed portraying ironic reversals of these roles for their comic effect. In Edith Wharton's delightful "The Other Two," Mr. Waythorn learns to accommodate himself to the fact that his wife occasionally slips and puts cognac in his coffee as a previous husband liked it. He accepts the fact that there were two other husbands who preceded him, and their habits, indeed their presences, sometimes impinge on his marriage. He painfully and slowly learns to accept the fact that he is part of a "syndicate" and not the sole possessor of his wife.

Colette's "The Secret Woman" is an urbane, witty, fantasy-fulfilling tale. The story opens with a husband telling his wife that he will be unable to attend the masked ball to which they have been invited because of a pressing meeting. He urges his wife, Irene, to attend alone; she says she could not possibly do so. The scene shifts to the ball. The rest of the story is told through the husband's point of view. We learn that he has come to the ball by himself as he had hypocritically intended, hoping that under the cover of his costume he can engage in prurient amusements. As he wanders through the masqueraders, he hears a familiar laugh coming from a woman possessing a familiar gold case. She is, of course, his wife. He follows her, fearful that she is meeting a lover. Anxiously, he watches her dance passionately with several men, shamelessly kiss another, erotically place her gloved hand on the breast of another woman, and finally sit down. In an epiphanal moment, he realizes that he need not fear betrayal, for Irene is merely enjoying a temporary hour as "the unknown woman, eternally solitary and shameless. . . ." In a reversal of the usual dilemma, it is the husband who learns to tolerate the extramarital flirtations of the wife.

Doris Lessing, our age's most acute and perceptive painter of women, explores the modern relationship between men and women with great subtlety and psychological insight. Her stories engage the reader because they are so deeply convincing; because they provide such a clear mirror of our vanities, our self-imposed barriers, and our fragmented souls. In "A Woman on a Roof," three construction workers notice a woman nearly nude in a very brief bikini, sunbathing on a roof below the one on which they are working. Although they whistle and shout, she remains cool and remote, ignoring them, refusing to be interrupted. Day after day the same exchange occurs. Yet as she persists in her indifference, they grow increasingly furious, their collective manhood assaulted and threatened. One of the workers, Tom, begins to dream nightly of her. In his dreams she is loving, warm, and understanding. When the construction work is completed, Tom finally gathers the courage to visit her on her roof, sure that she will welcome him as she does in his dreams. Of course, at the sight of this stranger, she demands that he leave; she makes him feel foolish; she turns her back to him, reiterating her indifference.

Although the story speaks on several levels, on a political level the story tells of a woman's refusal to become man's object; it speaks of her stubborn insistence on maintaining a separate selfhood, of remaining on her roof in her near-nudity despite the efforts of the workers to define her in terms of their lust or, in the case of Tom, their dreams.

Woolf's idea that women should describe their experiences in the rooms and houses in which they live out their lives has proved less a suggestion than a prediction concerning women's fiction. It is often observed of Lessing that much of her fiction is set in rooms, that she is a writer concerned with small spaces. The dramas in women's short stories do unfold in rooms and houses with persistent regularity. A "room" means safety, security, a controllable space. The heroine of Lessing's "To Room Nineteen," for example, commits suicide when her private room is invaded by the outside world. In Tillie Olsen's story "I Stand Here Ironing," the space has shrunk to an ironing board, where the heroine attempts to "iron" out her relationship with her daughter. In Olsen's story "Tell Me a Riddle," a dying woman's last wish is to return to her house. Hortense Calisher's "The Scream on Fifty-Seventh Street" concerns a lonely widow, Mrs. Hazlitt, who lives in a small apartment and who at the end begins to talk to the possessions of the apartment's previous occupant, another widow. Alice Munro's "The Office" and Sherry Sonnett's "Dreamy" both speak of a saving room of one's own, where there is refuge, peace, and freedom, although as in Lessing's "To Room Nineteen," these goals are not always achieved.

A room is not only a metaphor for the small proportions of a woman's living space; it is in "Dreamy" also a metaphor for the small proportions of her dreams. Compared to male fictional dreamers, the central character in Sonnett's story dreams very small dreams indeed: she dreams of a room whose key does not stick, of a car that does not stall, of time to read the newspaper from beginning to end, of a neatly made bed and clean sheets, of a comfortable chair and the time to read a book in it, of a job as a ticket collector in a movie house. Indeed, much of women's fiction is devoted to mastering the smaller routines of life and to becoming comfortable in the self and in the world.

Certainly contemporary women writers are less reticent about their biological processes than were previous generations of women. Pregnancy, childbirth, and menstruation are almost common images in female fiction. As a matter of fact, the female experience of life as depicted in fiction has in some ways changed our understanding of our world.

For example, as an image, blood has traditionally been associated with violence and gore. It is usually a male image. As an image related to menstruation, however, its associations are quite altered. It becomes a symbol of life and of natural processes. Joyce Carol Oates uses menstruation as a symbol of nature in all its irreverance and implacability in her story "At the Seminary." The Downeys—a family that includes an indifferent father, a nagging mother, and an overweight, belligerent daughter, Sally—visit Peter, the son, at the seminary where he is studying for the priesthood. Peter is in the throes of an identity crisis and his family has been requested to visit him. Sally, dressed in a too-small dress the color of the sun, contrasts sharply with the cold, modern blue and white marble and glass structure that is the seminary. This contrast is developed and deepened in the story. Sally's noisy, irritating, yet vivid presence is at war with the icy silence and asceticism of the seminary. The climactic battle of this war occurs in the chapel through which the Downeys are being escorted. Sally suddenly realizes that she is menstruating. For a moment she contemplates excusing herself to use the bathroom. Perversely, obdurately, she decides against convention; and in retribution against the seminary and its arrogant exclusion of the sloppy, unpredictable nature she represents, she allows the blood to flow unimpeded; she allows it to become visible, indeed to stain the seminary. The story's point that nature has final authority despite the impressive barriers man creates to ignore and exclude it, is not new. The fact that the menstrual cycle is used to make this point, however, is quite novel and effective.

It is a curious phenomenon that most women writers, in examining the lives of themselves and their sisters, find few strong women to portray realistically—that is, with the exception of the archetypes of the earth mother and the emasculating female. The stronghold, for the most part, of the dominant "good" woman is in fantasy literature or in science fiction. Although some younger, more politically minded writers are impatient with indecisive, oppressed victim-heroines, their portraits of strong women are restricted mainly to fantasy or science fiction. It is curious to note, however, that the victory of their heroines often relies on the oppression or submission or, in more than one case, the imprisonment of the male, especially the husband. In Julia O'Faolain's "Man in the Cellar," for example, the wife imprisons her domineering and physically abusive husband in the cellar. We are invited to hear her plot to execute this plan, and, after listening to her account of his cruelty, we are not sorry that she succeeds.

M. Pabst Battin's "The Sisters" is a modern fable employing many of the elements of this genre, including method of characterization and cadence of the prose. The story begins, "In their sorrow, they became sisters. One was tall, and very fair. . . ; the second was small and frail, dark-eyed and hurt. . . . And the third stood between. . . ." The story relates how these three women, sisters in that they live without their men, create a happy existence. They keep a "shrine room" to house "the things of their husbands": bags of silver to represent the rich husband; trophies to represent the brave husband; and books to represent the scholarly husband. These we learn are reminders of the tools with which their husbands had imprisoned them. Eventually, the husbands return, promising not to repeat their old, selfish ways. In time, however, they become competitive and begin to pursue their old goals. Seeing this, the sisters lead them into the shrine room, seducing them with the goods inside. Once they enter, the sisters lock them in, stating, "We will keep them as they have kept us . . . prisoners of the things that are in the shrine. . . . We cannot let them go free. So that we will not be their prisoners, they must be ours." Of course, neither O'Faolain's story nor Battin's is realistic. They express feminist fantasies, but it is perhaps instructive how angry these fantasies are.

Finally, there is little that is, in Woolf's term, "androgynous" about women's short fiction. It seems to express with great variety and force a uniquely female view of life. Perhaps the one weakness in Woolf's otherwise brilliant advice to women writers is her suggestion that they write out of an androgynous sensibility. Indeed, Elain Showalter argues that Woolf's theory of an ideal androgynous sensibility expresses Woolf's refusal to confront her own femaleness. Androgyny is a rejection of and a retreat from the self. Androgyny, Showalter asserts, is a self-denying, egoless state, a version, in fact, of the traditional subordinate female role. Women's short fiction, although it honors the harsh realities by being faithful to them, is rarely finally self-denying or egoless or retreating. It is almost without exception willing, indeed eager, to confront bravely the nature of being female.

Ellen G. Friedman

THE GROTESQUE IN SHORT FICTION

Any attempt to discuss the term *grotesque* entails the necessity of distinguishing between the adjective and noun forms of the word. Adjectival use is common, as a reference to anything which is freakish, bizarre, or fantastic. It is, however, much more difficult to assign a meaning to the noun form. Usage is often restricted to painting and sculpture and to the plural, as in "Hieronymous Bosch is a medieval painter of grotesques." Literary critics often show a strange ambiguity in attitude: on one hand, there is general reference to writers such as Charles Dickens, William Faulkner, Nathanael West, and Flannery O'Connor as depicting grotesque characters, settings, and situations; on the other hand, there is often a refusal to accept *the* grotesque as a basic aesthetic category. At the same time, the phrase *the grotesque* (and the article here is important) is rather carelessly tossed about: "Sherwood Anderson is a writer of the grotesque." Such a reference, of course, demonstrates at least an implicit recognition that there must exist such a literary category, and further, that there must be elements which constitute this concept. A very small number of critics have thoughtfully explored the subject in an attempt to define the term and to isolate the elements which distinguish it from related terms and modes.

Art historian Wolfgang Kayser has traced the development of the grotesque in art and literature from the Middle Ages to modern times. While it is neither tragedy nor comedy, he says, the grotesque combines elements of both to arrive at a form which yields a tension between the ridiculous and the horrifying. Kayser isolates three essential elements in the nature of the grotesque structure: "The estranged world," in which a character is alienated from himself, others, and the world (which is seen as abysmal and threatening); "A play with the absurd," situations and characterizations which are ludicrous but frightening or embarrassing at the same time; and "An attempt to invoke and subdue the demonic aspects of the world."

Kayser's work is by far the most thorough analysis of a very difficult but artistically fruitful mode. More recently, Philip Thomson, in the Critical Idiom series, has explored the term as it has evolved into modern usage. He defines the grotesque broadly as "the unresolved clash of incompatibles in work and response," with a secondary definition as "the ambivalently abnormal." Both of these critics stress the equal importance of the work of art and the reader's response to it as necessary considerations in distinguishing the grotesque. The reader's reaction itself is ambivalent: he does not know whether to laugh or to scream; thus the response might be a sense of hysteria covered by embarrassed laughter, followed by a thoughtful attempt to understand this reaction. The various elements of the grotesque, in turn, merge to form a composite for the reader: the author's vision as conveyed through this shocking but thought-provoking means.

William Van O'Connor classifies the grotesque as a genre and, in fact, refers to it as "an American genre" most appropriate to express modern man's alienation from the universe. O'Connor classifies it as a "new genre, merging tragedy and comedy, and seeking, seemingly in perverse ways, the sublime." Thomas Mann, whose short novel *Death in Venice* (1913) utilizes major elements of the grotesque, recognizes the potential of the grotesque to depict man's condition:

> . . . the striking feature of modern art is that it has ceased to recognize the categories of tragic and comic, or the dramatic classification, tragedy and comedy. It sees life as tragicomedy, with the result that the grotesque is its most genuine style—to the extent, indeed, that today that is the only guise in which the sublime may appear. For, if I may say so, the grotesque is the genuine anti-bourgeois style.

Modern man no longer accepts the meaningful, moral universe of tragedy; he derides the rational social order inherent in comedy. The logical blend, then, yields a meaningless, chaotic existence abounding in the incongruous, often irrational actions and devices of comedy. Man, however, attempts to cope with the diverse alien forces which confront him, and, despite his absurdity, he may attain a measure of nobility.

Despite its popularity in modern (and particularly contemporary) literature, the grotesque, of course, is not a new form, nor is it the exclusive domain of American writers. German writers such as E. T. A. Hoffmann and Thomas Mann, the great Russian storyteller Nikolai Gogol, and French writers Charles Baudelaire and Samuel Beckett utilize the grotesque to express their concerns.

The term appears as early as the fifteenth century in descriptions of decorative figures in painting, sculpture, and architecture; human and animal figures characteristically distorted, incongruous, and fantastic. Italians used the word *grottesco* to refer to forms fantastic and playful but at the same time somehow ominous in suggesting an unfamiliar world in which man, plant, and animal are inextricably intertwined and the laws of nature are violated or suspended. In art as in literature, of course, the grotesque form functions only in relation to the normal; the unreal must be grounded in reality. Thus, Hieronymous Bosch, in his painting of Christ carrying his cross, depicts a handful of hideously grinning, incredibly ugly characters in direct contrast to the serene, patient face of Christ. The viewer, in turn, perceives the discrepancy and is led to seek the symbolic associations inherent in the exaggerations of caricature. The term, by extension, was applied to misshapen and ludicrous figures in literature, a usage which still prevails. Many writers, of course, utilize grotesque figures and devices in the adjectival sense; writers of *the grotesque*, however, are those who create an entire work—a poem, a short story, a novel—which can be seen as grotesque, encompassing the major elements and metaphysical functions of a literary category.

The grotesque assumes special significance for writers of short fiction because of its ability to suggest meanings beyond the surface. It becomes a tool for compacting character, setting, and action: the motifs which are a logical outgrowth of grotesque elements serve as figurative devices to convey additional meanings. John Ruskin, in *Modern Painters* (1843-1860), traces Edmund Spenser's use of the grotesque in his poetry:

> A fine grotesque is the expression, in a moment, by a series of symbols thrown together in bold and fearless connection, of truths which it would have taken a long time to express in verbal way, and of which the connection is left for the beholder to work out for himself; the gaps left or overleaped by the haste of imagination, forming the grotesque character.

Thus a simple description of a character as a puppet triggers the usual associations: we see him as someone readily manipulated, incapable of individual action, absurd in his jerky, uncoordinated movements. In addition, there is the underlying sense of alienation—the character depicted as an inanimate object loses his humanity. There is, too, the impact on the reader, characterized by G. K. Chesterton in *Robert Browning* (1903):

> It is the supreme function of the philosopher of the grotesque to make the world stand on its head that people may look at it. If we say "a man is a man" we awaken no sense of the fantastic, however much we ought to, but if we say, in the language of the old satirist, that "man is a two-legged bird, without feathers," the phrase does, for a moment, make us look at the man from the outside and gives us a thrill in his presence.

The world of E. T. A. Hoffmann in *The Tales of Hoffmann* (1817) is full of characters who perceive an estranged world; sinister forces threaten their sanity and very existence; ambiguous demonic figures confront those who demonstrate imagination and pursue artistic endeavors. Hoffmann's stories resemble fairy tales in their use of transformations and apparently supernatural elements. Fairy tales, historically, abound in grotesque elements— dwarfs, dragons, monsters, and freaks threaten the average characters—but these forces are invariably subdued or at least transformed through the influence of heroic characters. Whereas fairy tales assert the victory of goodness and always restore social order, Hoffmann's tales grant supremacy to the malevolent forces and necessitate the defeat of a leading character.

In "The Sandman," for example, the protagonist Nathanael is a student and poet who is brought face to face with evil as a child. He combines his mother's innocent remark about impending sleep—"the Sandman is coming"—with the nursemaid's superstitious description of the Sandman as a merciless ogre who steals children's eyes in order to feed its own brood. This sinister figure is further associated in the child's mind with the frightening character of Coppelius, a mysterious night-visitor who performs experiments in alchemy with Nathanael's father. Coppelius is clearly a grotesque character:

his physical characteristics—"an immensely big head, a face the color of yellow ocher . . . piercing, greenish, catlike eyes . . . distorted mouth" from which strange hissing noises are emitted—are matched by the obvious pleasure he takes in tormenting the children of the household. After an explosion takes the father's life, Coppelius escapes unharmed and disappears mysteriously. Years later, he reappears at Nathanael's university as Coppola, a hawker of glass wares and eye instruments. Or is Coppola the same man? It is characteristic of works of the grotesque that we are left in doubt about sinister characters: the association, as the prior one with the Sandman, may simply exist in Nathanael's imagination. The young man is obsessed by fear of this ominous man, but his fears are somewhat allayed by the calm, reasoning voice of Clara, a childhood friend to whom he is engaged. To prove his new confidence, he purchases from Coppola a small telescope, an instrument which progressively leads Nathanael to an estrangement from society, to insanity, and to the ultimate alienation—death.

A key aspect of alienation explored by works of the grotesque is the failure to distinguish between reality and illusion; it is this tendency which is exhibited by Nathanael and magnified through the telescope. He glimpses and "falls in love" with a beautiful automaton named Olivia. The mechanical movements and responses of Olivia are perceived by the other students; Nathanael, however, blindly ignores the flaws of his "beloved," until he is shocked into reality upon witnessing the destruction of the puppet in a tug of war between Coppola and Olivia's "father," a professor at the university. The figure loses its lifelike qualities and is seen as a mere doll, whose eyes have fallen on the ground.

The recurrent image of the eyes in this story is a motif which appears frequently in stories of the grotesque. Kayser emphasizes the importance of the eyes "as an expression of the soul, as a link with the world; the eyes as the actual seat of life." The alienation of the grotesque character serves this link and the eyes become lifeless or blind. Throughout "The Sandman" Nathanael is obsessed with eyes and vision, his own and those around him. His figurative loss of vision (aided by the distortions of Coppola's telescope) leads to the loss of true vision evidenced by the insane. In the climactic scene, an apparently recovered Nathanael strolls atop a tower balcony with Clara and looks at her through his pocket telescope. Hoffmann offers a complete reversal of the prior scene with Olivia: Clara, who is real, is perceived by Nathanael as a puppet, and he attempts to destroy her. Instead, he plunges to his own death, thereby completing his alienation from the rational world. Hoffmann conveys *his* vision through the extended metaphor of vision: the obstacles which must be surmounted by the artist in controlling his imagination to present the truth. Ironically, Nathanael, the student-poet-artist whose function as seer is archetypal, allows alien forces to distort his vision; he not only fails to lead others to a purer vision, but destroys himself through his blindness.

Hoffmann's is a grim tale, and the only relief from oppression is offered by his sense of the absurd. Nathanael dancing amorously with an automaton, Olivia mechanically murmuring "Ach, Ach" to the young man's revelations of his innermost thoughts, must strike the reader as ludicrous at the same time that we perceive the meaninglessness of a "relationship" in which one member cannot respond. Yet we are prevented from pure laughter because the frightening near-reality of the puppet suggests the inverse of actual persons who think, act, and react in a mechanical manner. It is a discordant world in which puppets seem human and humans seem puppetlike; a world in which dreams assume the appearance of reality and the actual becomes a nightmare.

One cannot, however, dismiss these abysmal visions as dreams from which the sufferer will awaken. Again and again, writers of the grotesque insist explicitly that we accept the reality of our shocking or incongruous nightmare world. Thus when Franz Kafka's Gregor Samsa awakes to find himself changed into a giant bug in "Metamorphosis," he is immediately forced to face the truth: "What has happened to me? he thought. It was no dream." Similarly, Nikolai Gogol in *The Nose* (1836) refuses to allow Kovalyov to indulge in wishful thinking. Discovering one morning that his nose has disappeared, Kovalyov rationalizes that he is still asleep or that his imagination has betrayed him: ". . . it's incredible that a nose should be lost. It must be a dream or an illusion."

Just as the line between sleep and wakefulness is very fine, the distinction between dream and reality is extremely delicate: it is significant that many grotesque characters find themselves in a nightmare situation immediately upon awaking. The false sense of security offered in the state of slumber is shattered rudely as we awaken and must adapt to the real world. Literal wakening becomes an awakening in the figurative sense; while the fictional character is forced to confront a world which, because of his changed state, no longer seems secure, the reader is impelled to search for analogies and metaphorical meanings.

In Gogol's story, Kovalyov leads the seemingly secure and bland existence of a lower-level government official. His nonsensual, nonvital condition is objectified by Gogol through the literal disappearance of Kovalyov's nose. Suddenly made different and grotesque, and not perceiving that he has been a spiritual grotesque all along, Kovalyov encounters threatening forces everywhere. Except for the lack of a nose, he is the same man, yet acquaintances and institutions upon which he had relied become hostile and cruel forces. Even his own nose, which Kovalyov recognizes masquerading as a civil councillor in full-dress uniform, is an alien entity. It is, of course, however disjointed, still a vital part of Kovalyov, a member that somehow assumes more vitality than its owner—the nose, after all, attempts to escape the restrictions of convention and the soul-deadening rituals of an insignificant life. Shocked out of his complacency, Kovalyov is thus offered a glimpse of the real state of things, a glimpse which he joyfully rejects when his nose miraculously reappears in its accustomed position. The conclusion appears to be a happy ending, culminating in the restoration of normalcy, yet such a reading is rendered impossible by the implications of the grotesque.

Gogol's short story, through the devices of the grotesque, offers a miniature of the Russian world, a world explored more fully, but not necessarily more effectively, in the great Russian novels. He is able to suggest the paralyzing effect of a highly structured class system as he depicts this grotesque world: a ritualistic, bureaucratic society in which people are not individuals but "ranks," readily identified by the uniforms corresponding to their status. Kovalyov certainly is grotesque; his deeper deformity is reflected by his disfigurement, and he is seen as an alienated, absurd figure who must cope with supernatural forces. The witchcraft, real or imagined, is nevertheless less ominous than the life-draining ritual he cheerfully faces every day.

Inextricably intertwined in this, as in all grotesque works, are the intent of the author, the reality of the work itself, and our ambiguous reaction to the work. The narrator, at the end of *The Nose*, grapples with this aspect:

> Only now, on thinking it over, we perceive that there is a great deal that is improbable in it. Apart from the fact that it certainly is strange for a nose supernaturally to leave its place and to appear in various places in the guise of a civil councillor . . . what is more uncomprehensible than anything is that authors can choose such subjects. I confess that is quite beyond my grasp, it really is . . .—and yet, when you think it over, there really is something in it. Whatever any one may say, such things do happen—not often, but they do happen.

Here, as in grotesque fiction in general, there are no clear-cut villains—the powers which assail the protagonist are, as Kayser states, "incomprehensible, inexplicable, and impersonal"—and we cannot identify the forces of the abyss. If one were able to find a rational explanation for these invisible antagonists, the basic quality of the grotesque would be lost.

Just as there are no absolute villains, there are few heroic characters in works of the grotesque. In fact, one of the reasons the grotesque seems modern even when written centuries ago is the presence of the antihero. The characters resemble one another as common, ordinary, insignificant men— not beautiful, not terribly intelligent, not powerful, not idealistic—often engaged as obscure clerks, salesmen, and farmers. To a great degree, they are victims of an impersonal, bureaucratic society—victims, however, who are not romanticized but presented in all their dreariness as contributing toward their own victimization. In this, they conform to the assessment of Thomas Mann and others who see the grotesque as antibourgeois. Thus Gogol's tale presents us with a protagonist who is a collegiate assessor, a government official of the eighth rank, struggling to maintain the status symbols of a borderline gentleman, nevertheless impressed by and cowing to authority, titles, and appearances. Almost one hundred years later, Franz Kafka chooses as his protagonist a traveling salesman, Gregor Samsa, bullied by his superiors and taken advantage of by his family, whose insignificant life in many ways parallels that of his fictional predecessor.

Kafka's "Metamorphosis" opens on a prosaic, matter-of-fact note which reveals a distinctly unrealistic occurrence: "As Gregor Samsa awoke one morning from uneasy dreams he found himself transformed into a gigantic insect." Yet as the tale unfolds, the transformation is extremely logical, conforming to our tendency to see man figuratively through association with animalistic qualities. A brave and courageous ruler reveals the courage associated with a majestic beast, and we call him Richard the Lion-Hearted; an average young man blends in with his surroundings, struggles to maintain his position in the face of hostile superior beings, and we call him an insignificant insect. The difference, of course, is that Gregor Samsa is not *like* an insect, he *is* an insect, at least in external appearance. Once we accept this premise, the events which follow proceed with unassailable logic. What better image of the antihero than the many-legged, uncoordinated insect which leaves a trail of slime in its wake?

This insect, however, maintains his human consciousness and all of the accompanying anguish necessary for a sense of alienation. In his hybrid state, Gregor Samsa is the complete grotesque, neither insect nor man, cut off from intercourse with either species. He hears and understands all that transpires around him, yet he cannot communicate with his family. Nevertheless, after the initial shock and the father's cruel attempts to beat him with a stick, the family reluctantly accepts him as a cross to be borne, an embarrassment that refuses to go away. Samsa's former, seemingly secure world crumbles as he is exposed to his manager's unjust harangue about the quality of his work and sales performance; as he discovers the duplicity of his father, for whose sake Samsa had devoted years of mind-deadening labor; as he sees his sister's devotion turn to disgust; and as he finds his mother's love become a sense of duty.

The grotesque is an ideal vehicle to objectify the impersonal, hostile environment perceived by an existential twentieth century. Samsa's environment attains grotesque stature; familiar pieces of furnishings become obstacles to movement; his room is a prison from which he is seldom permitted to move and which finally becomes a filthy repository for the family's unwanted objects and garbage containers. In this aspect, too, our nightmare visions become reality as surroundings and landscapes attain hideous quality. The grotesque world, whether remote or immediate, is not ordered and safe but chaotic and threatening; the Romantic's vision of a benevolent nature is inverted to present us with landscapes which are repulsive and ominous. This vision serves to emphasize the character's alienation: he is estranged from family, society, and finally the universe.

It is, then, hardly surprising that death becomes the only means of escape for characters of the grotesque. Alienated and absurd, lacking dignity and redeeming human characteristics, confronted by destructive forces, the grotesque character often embraces the release of death: fear of life surpasses the fear of death. Thus Hoffmann's Nathanael plunges from a high tower toward the beckoning death figure of Coppola; Kafka's man-insect willingly accepts the approach of his death:

> The rotting apple in his back and the inflamed area around it, all covered with soft dust, already hardly troubled him. He thought of his family with tenderness and love. The decision that he must disappear was one that he held to even more strongly than his sister, if that were possible. In this state of vacant and peaceful meditation he remained until the tower clock struck three in the morning. The first broadening of light in the world outside the window entered his consciousness once more. Then his head sank to the floor of its own accord and from his nostrils came the last faint flicker of his breath.

Samsa's disintegration, after the metamorphosis, is complete as he moves inevitably towards death: he finds his appetite diminishing, his body is uncared for and weakened, and even the family ceases to think of him as a member. The sister's change of pronouns signals complete rejection; the early statement, "Well, he liked his dinner today," contrasts with the callous "We must try to get rid of it," at the end. In fact, his death brings relief and new vigor to the family: the body is unceremoniously dumped by the charwoman and the family members take an excursion to the country. Life goes on as a son, a brother, a traveling salesman—truly insignificant, truly an insect—passes from the scene.

Kafka's story is not a depiction of utter despair, however, and, again, it is the elements of the grotesque which negate such an evaluation. Kafka lends greater absurdity to the original premise of transformation through his sense of irony and matter-of-fact tone. Samsa sees his shattering transformation as "an indisposition," "a slight illness," or a "mishap," and considers himself merely "temporarily incapacitated." His family's efforts to secure help in releasing him from his locked room trigger an absurdly ironic response: "He felt himself drawn once more into the human circle and hoped for great and remarkable results from both the doctor and the locksmith, without really distinguishing precisely between them."

The humor relieves our sense of oppression, while grotesque motifs suggest some redeeming aspects of life. The imagery of vision, so extended in Hoffmann's "The Sandman," also assumes importance in "Metamorphosis." While Samsa's literal vision decreases with his disintegration, his ability to perceive things more clearly increases. His nightly observations of the family permit him to see them as they are, not as he wished them to be. Despite his own sense of loneliness, and despite their unaffectionate treatment of him, Samsa is able, at the end, to view them with compassion.

Several of the characters in the story are grotesque to a greater or lesser degree, including the father, whose pathetic porter's uniform grows greasier and dirtier every day; the Amazon charwoman with the ostrich feather in her hat; and the three puppetlike boarders who move and speak in unison. It is, of course, ironic that the insect shows more feeling and insight than the surrounding humans. Samsa observes: "I'm hungry enough, but not for that kind of food. How these lodgers are stuffing themselves, and here am I dying of starvation!" It is finally his sister's violin-playing which offers some beauty and meaning to his life: "Was he an animal that music had such an effect upon him? He felt as if the way were opening before him to the unknown nourishment that he craved." In this aspect, Kafka resembles the other writers considered: Gogol in extolling the imagination of the artist, Hoffmann in his depiction of the function of the artist. The artist as seer is able to rid himself of illusions and to accept the reality of suffering and death; in the process he offers—to counter the chaotic and grotesque world—the redeeming power of his art, a theme which becomes literally the plot of Kafka's "A Hunger Artist."

The grotesque, through its paradoxical nature which necessitates inversions, is thus able to depict despair and offer hope, to reveal indifference and hate, to suggest compassion, and to stress death and imply the forces of life. Chesterton, in tracing strains of the grotesque in Browning's poetry, notes this effect: ". . . in a cosmos where incompleteness implies completeness, life implies immortality. This then was the first of the doctrines or opinions of Browning: the hope that lies in the imperfection of man."

Chesterton's assessment, of course, is shaded by his strong religious beliefs, but it demonstrates the power of the grotesque in transcending ideology. While the overwhelming majority of modern writers utilize grotesque motifs to express a sense of atheism in a meaningless world, a few dissonant voices revert to the earlier function of the grotesque: an effort to demonstrate the grotesqueness of characters who refuse to believe in a meaningful existence, an existence shaped by a caring Being. Outstanding among these writers is Flannery O'Connor, whose novels and short stories invariably rely on the grotesque.

O'Connor's *The Complete Stories* (1971), which received the National Book Award in 1972, offers a parade of grotesque characters, placed in grotesque settings and situations, behaving grotesquely. It is interesting to note that O'Connor's artistry is critically acclaimed mainly for her short fiction; her novels, *Wise Blood* (1952) and *The Violent Bear It Away* (1960), which attempt extended characterization, are not always successful in maintaining unity while sustaining a grotesque tenor for the entire work. The short stories are peopled by a stock assembly of farmwives (usually strong-willed widows), farmhands, and, increasingly in the later stories, proud pseudointellectuals. Despite this recurrence of types and some obvious caricature, the characters do acquire personality, mainly through the suggestive powers of grotesque motifs. There is no need for complete, individualized characterization because, as in most short fiction, the nameless quality of the characters universalizes their condition. Thus, while we recognize the particular Southern tensions of O'Connor's characters and the spirit of their culture, we resist the tendency to explain away their eccentricity as simply "Southern."

O'Connor's later stories become more subtle, and thus often more horrifying, in depicting the grotesque, but an early story, "Good Country People," perhaps most clearly demonstrates O'Connor's particular application of the grotesque in order to depict man's fallen nature. The protagonist, Joy Hopewell, a Ph.D. with an artificial leg, is the most obviously grotesque of O'Connor's intellectual characters. Through all of her protagonists, O'Connor speaks negatively; that is, she conveys her vision of what man ought not to be, rather than what man ought to be. She often achieves the effect of alienation through caricature: she relies on physical deformities and name symbolism, as well as on more subtle techniques, to suggest spiritual deformity. Name symbolism, a simple form of caricature used in the grotesque for emphasis, reinforces characteristics established through other techniques, suggests an opposing image through irony, or serves to imply the character's function.

O'Connor suggests the absence of qualities in naming her protagonist in "Good Country People." Joy Hopewell demonstrates neither joy nor hope; she is also not well, either physically or spiritually. In addition to the artificial leg, for which she cares "as someone else would his soul," her "weak heart" implies a more basic deformity—the absence of emotion and the ability to care for others—and her blurred vision is not corrected by her glasses. Moreover, Joy Hopewell consciously rejects the qualities implied by her name: she chooses her new name, Hulga, precisely because it is ugly; and she rejects hope because she claims to have no illusions.

This thirty-two-year-old virgin, who lives on an isolated farm with her mother, becomes fascinated by the idea of seducing a simple young Bible salesman who visits their home. Her attempt to seduce is guided by intellectual motives, not sensual; she wishes to destroy the boy's illusions. Manley Pointer (another name rich in symbolism), characterized by Hulga's mother as "good country people" (O'Connor is fond of having her characters voice absurd clichés as if they were profound thoughts), turns out to be less innocent than he appeared. Ironically, he emerges as the one without illusions. He appears at their picnic date with his Bible, which contains a flask of whiskey, a pack of obscene cards, and a box of contraceptives, and he reveals his nihilism: "You ain't so smart. I been believing in nothing ever since I was born!" In a shattering climax, he leaves Hulga sitting in a loft and departs with her wooden leg and glasses. It is Hulga whose illusions are destroyed, as she murmurs: "Aren't you just good country people?"

While there are few explicit religious applications, for O'Connor, these moments of awakening constitute an offering of Christian grace. The grotesque figure, through the means of an equally grotesque, satanic character, is given the opportunity to face reality—a reality which must admit the existence of a sense of mystery which O'Connor equates with God. Her characters are alienated through their own ignorance or pride, and they see a chaotic, meaningless universe, but they are given the opportunity to search for meaning.

In O'Connor's fiction all of the grotesque elements converge and offer a structural basis for her stories. Her alienated characters emerge as ludicrous and absurd and are faced with demonic forces. These ominous characters or events serve an important function in plot, and O'Connor insists that the devil figures be seen as "real"—not some vague symbolic shapes of evil. Paradoxically, the devil-figure is often the harbinger of truth and goodness: as Chesterton implies, we acknowledge the good through our perception of its opposite.

Present, too, in O'Connor's short stories are all of the themes, motifs, and devices of the grotesque. Her landscapes are invariably grotesque—"the sky was a dying violet and the houses stood out darkly against it, bulbous liver-colored monstrosities of a uniform ugliness though no two were alike"—and the elements of nature are never benevolent: the sky is "chill-gray," the sun is "startling" or "glaring," the woods are "black" and "like a solid wall." Animal and puppet imagery abounds, suggesting the corresponding loss of human characteristics; the dichotomy of illusion and reality repeatedly stresses her figures' estrangement; the absurd is reinforced by her strong sense of irony and the devices of caricature, name symbolism, and overblown rhetoric (itself a form of verbal grotesqueness—the failure to communicate meaningfully). The motifs of eating and gluttony, of vision and blindness (and the variation of distorting mirror images), of paralysis of spirit—motifs which recur individually in all grotesque fiction—contribute to the sense of tension which is so characteristic of the grotesque.

It is tension, finally, that lends the basic flavor to short fiction which is grotesque. The combination of the realistic and fantastic, of the comic and the terrible, yields a corresponding set of contrasts, very delicately balanced, which contribute to our sense of ambiguity. In these works, there is but a fine line between the beauty and the beast, hope and despair, sanity and insanity, freedom and imprisonment, the sublime and the satanic, life and death. There are no happy endings as the balance invariably tips toward the negative side and the shadowy forces succeed. As evident in Kafka and Hoffmann, and in many of O'Connor's stories, death often presents the final resolution—and the ultimate alienation. This stress on death is characteristic of most writers of the grotesque, in novels as well as in short fiction. William Faulkner in *Sanctuary* (1931), *The Sound and the Fury* (1929), and *As I Lay Dying* (1930), Nathanael West in *Day of the Locust* (1939) and *Miss Lone-*

lyhearts (1933), and Norman Mailer in *The Naked and the Dead* (1948) and *An American Dream* (1965), works which exemplify a more extended structure of the grotesque, utilize the shock value of deaths which are often ironic or brutal. Yet somehow these deaths seem less than tragic; they impress us as a form of liberation, expressed by the uncle in D. H. Lawrence's "The Rocking-Horse Winner," upon the death of his nephew: "But, poor devil, poor devil, he's best gone out of a life where he rides his rocking-horse to find a winner."

No discussion of the grotesque in short fiction would be complete without a consideration of two writers who are often associated with the mode—Sherwood Anderson and Edgar Allan Poe. The association, of course, is made explicit by the titles of their works—Anderson's *Winesburg, Ohio: The Book of the Grotesque* (1919) and Poe's *Tales of the Grotesque and Arabesque* (1840). Anderson's self-alignment with the grotesque is somewhat tenuous: while many of his characters can be described as grotesque in appearance or action, and many are indeed alienated in that they are emotional cripples, the most basic elements of the grotesque are conspicuously absent. Thus, while Wing Biddlebaum in "Hands," for example, is certainly estranged and at times seems ludicrous, we finally see him as a rather sad and pathetic character, a victim of the town's prejudices. There is nothing ambivalent about the reader's reaction to the story; Anderson's tendency to sentimentalize negates such a response.

Poe's tales, on the other hand, abound in motifs and imagery of the grotesque. In a fantasy world peopled with mysterious doubles, dwarfs, and assorted strange creatures; in a world where death figures stroll familiarly and inanimate objects or animals have strange powers, we are overwhelmed by a sense of terror. As Kayser points out, Poe offers a comprehensive "definition" of the grotesque in "The Masque of the Red Death." The prince in the story has gathered around him a select group of friends, aristocratic characters who withdraw into the safety of an abbey to escape the threat of plague but who cannot forego entertainment. The narrator describes the masked ball:

> Be sure they were grotesque. There were much glare and glitter and piquancy and phantasm—much of what has been since seen in Hernani. There were arabesque figures with unsuited limbs and appointments. There were delicious fancies such as the madman fashions. There was much of the beautiful, much of the wanton, much of the bizarre, something of the terrible, and not a little of that which might have excited disgust. To and fro in the seven chambers were stalked, in fact, a multitude of dreams. And these—the dreams—writhed in and about, taking hue from the rooms, and causing the wild music of the orchestra to seem as the echo of their steps.

Poe's description reflects the classic tension of the grotesque: the blend of beautiful and ugly, the fantastic and bizarre, the disgusting and terrifying, made more exotic through the interplay of the different colors in each of the rooms. The verbs Poe chooses reinforce the terror: "stalked" carries the connotation of pursuit and threat; "writhed" associates the action with the scrolls and snakelike movements of the decorative grotesque. Suffusing it all is the dreamlike quality of the scene, an expression of our nightmare visions.

Missing in this scene, and in most of Poe's work, is the *combination* of horror and humor so vital to the grotesque; we are finally left with a terror unmitigated by a sense of the absurd or ludicrous. Hoffmann, Kafka, Gogol, and O'Connor offer this aspect through the actions, words, or perceptions of the characters, or through the ironic tone of the narration. Poe offers us the terror of the Gothic rather than the ambiguity of the grotesque. The dancer in red who appears in "The Masque of the Red Death" certainly is ominous, but he is identifiable; unlike Coppola in "The Sandman," we know the figure must represent death. Similarly, the cat in "The Black Cat" can finally be seen as a constant reminder of the evil self, whereas the double in "William Wilson" is, at the end, clearly a representation of the protagonist's conscience, or good self. The emphasis, as in most Gothic fiction, is on a depiction of our subconscious fears. Elizabeth MacAndrew, in *The Gothic Tradition in Fiction* (1979), describes the function of the monsters and hostile forces in the Gothic tale:

> They are the shapes into which our fears are projected and so can be used in literature to explore the subterranean landscape of the mind. Terror is evoked when the ghost, the double, or the lurking assassin corresponds to something that is actually feared, known or unknown. The fictional beings of Gothic fiction, whether they be human or animal, or manifestations of from the "Beyond," whether they be universal archetypes or the pettiest of childhood bogies, symbolize real but vague fears that the reader recognizes as his own and all men's. Beneath the surface fiction there is a probing of humanity's basic psychological forces, an exploration of the misty realm of the subconscious, and the symbols correspond to psychological phenomena that yield to literary analysis.

Gothic fiction, while it utilizes features of the grotesque to show the confusion of the mind, looks inward into man's psyche, whereas the grotesque looks outward to show the external forces which alienate and threaten man. The Gothic demonstrates the delicate balance within the self; the grotesque demonstrates the delicate balance of the self with the universe. This difference in domain can be perceived in the function of these two forms: the Gothic must, finally, concern itself with the moral nature of man, whereas the grotesque, as we have seen, can be utilized by writers at opposite philosophical poles—the deeply religious as well as the existential atheist.

Twentieth century man, of course, is seen as existential man: alienated, set adrift in a meaningless chaotic universe. He is absurd; the universe is absurd. Nevertheless, certain writers—Franz Kafka, Jean-Paul Sartre, and Albert Camus, for example, in some of their fiction—can depict the existential condition and suggest, often through the tensions of the grotesque, the hope implicit in man's noble endurance. Other absurdist playwrights and fiction writers—such as Eugene Ionesco, John Barth, and Donald Barthelme—clearly utilize grotesque elements in their absurdist works, but the final effect again differs from the grotesque. As the Gothic fiction is finally dominated by terror, fiction of the absurd is usually characterized by humor, albeit a black kind of humor. The characters are ludicrous and absurd, but since their actions are meaningless, our only reaction can be laughter. There is a sense of lethargy, a frozen quality which emerges from such works: man has no options when his world is totally alien, when the laws of space and time are suspended, when hostile chance reigns.

Although there is an element of discomfort to our laughter, a discomfort caused by the obvious relationship of these unrealistic characters to our real world, the balanced tension of the grotesque is often lacking. Donald Barthelme, for example, chronicles the hanging of a man in "Some of Us Had Been Threatening Our Friend Colby." Irony prevails as a group of "friends" plans the "event" as though it were a party or wedding. The group must hang Colby because he has "gone too far"—although we are never told what he has done. The "June hanging" is handled with delicate taste, from the wording of the invitations to the music which is to be played. Classic grotesque elements exist—Colby has alienated himself from his friends (but not completely; they consult him about his preferences), the actions are absurd, the story culminates in death—yet the tenor of the story is such that it cannot be grotesque. Despite the terribleness of the deed, we must laugh, as we do in reaction to satire.

Finally, the grotesque, by its nature ambiguous, is a most suitable vehicle to express the concerns of the twentieth century. Modern man is fascinated by machinery; he relies on it yet is repulsed by it. He sensationalizes the bizarre and freakish, yet he repels that which is different. He seeks a meaning for life and joins exotic cults, yet he rejects organized religion. The grotesque reflects his bewilderment; the grotesque in short fiction universalizes his condition. The grotesque defies categorization: nothing is black *or* white; everything is black *and* white.

Bibliography
Kayser, Wolfgang. *The Grotesque in Art and Literature.*
MacAndrew, Elizabeth. *The Gothic Tradition in Fiction.*
Muller, Gilbert H. *Nightmares and Visions.*
O'Connor, William Van. *The Grotesque: An American Genre and Other Essays.*
Thomson, Philip. *The Grotesque* (The Critical Idiom, 24).

Zita M. McShane

HORROR SHORT FICTION

The Basis of the Horror Short Story

The tale of terror and the supernatural is one of the oldest forms of literature in existence, dating back to a tradition of oral storytelling which precedes written literature. Modern anthropologists and psychologists suggest that tales of terror arose so early in human history because they spring from two central human needs. The more obvious of these is the need to conceive of mysterious and frightening phenomena in terms of a supernatural world which, although radically different from the physical world and sometimes inimical to it, has an order of its own.

Accordingly, the horror short stories of the eighteenth, nineteenth, and twentieth centuries impose their own order and explanation on apparently meaningless and potentially overwhelming events. In doing this, horror stories differ from scientific or pseudoscientific accounts of psychic or supernatural phenomena. Most claims of actual "sightings" of ghosts or spirits, or of contacts with the other world in any form, are characterized by their apparent lack of pattern or meaning. In horror fiction, however, representatives of the other world are almost always motivated in their behavior by the actions of some human being. Because horror stories do impose this kind of order and cause-and-effect rationality on their material, they induce a kind of catharsis, or an enjoyment of bearable terror at one remove, which is a major factor in their popularity. Readers experience a *frisson*, a thrill of fear, which contrasts with, and is compensated by, the ordinary circumstances of their lives.

The second human need reflected in stories of horror and the supernatural is the need to externalize, in the form of allegory or analogy, the innate and universal patterns of thought and imagery which make up the unconscious level of mind. Clichés such as "I don't know what came over me" and "I wasn't myself" *are* clichés precisely because they express a very common state of mind: the feeling of being directed or even possessed by compulsions which the individual, at least in terms of his conscious mind, cannot control and does not even recognize as his own. This sense of being devoured, drained, overpowered, transformed, invaded, pursued, or deceived by alien forces underlies all the major themes of the horror story.

The horror story is a particularly appropriate literary form for the reflection of this type of psychological experience or sensation because it is by definition removed from the limitations of the ordinary physical world, and can therefore express a sense of the uncanny in terms of tangibly anomalous externalizations. For example, an author of horror stories can express the sense of being psychologically fragmented by depicting an actual double figure, as Edgar Allan Poe does in "Willliam Wilson." Similarly, an author can depict the sensation of psychological compulsion in terms of an alien force which invades the victim's consciousness in some form: the hypnotic figure of the Judge in

Bram Stoker's "The Judge's House" is an example. Stories like these evoke a thrill of horror from their readers because they are at once strange and frighteningly familiar.

Because the appeal of the horror story is affective rather than intellectual— because it relies on a holistic impression which includes intuitive identification and a strong emotional response—the horror story is most effective when it is short. Thus the horror story, more than any other type of tale, is suited to and associated with the short-story form. The best-known statement of this idea is Edgar Allan Poe's dictum in "The Philosophy of Composition" (first published in *Graham's Magazine*, April, 1849):

> If any literary work is too long to be read at one sitting, we must be content to dispense with the immensely important effect derivable from unity of impression—for, if two sittings be required, the affairs of the world interfere, and everything like totality is at once destroyed.

Poe did not limit the applicability of that premise to horror stories, but it is to such stories that he and other writers have most faithfully applied it.

Because the horror story was one of the earliest and most persistently popular forms of entertainment, and because it is so well suited to the short-story form, it is not surprising that the horror tale was one of the earliest forms of short story written, and one of the most prolific. The horror genre has also contributed to the development of several other types of short stories. For example, it was the first form of the short story to employ fantasy as a mode of entertainment and communication of ideas, and this technique of creating an unreal world or introducing alien elements into a common environment became the basis for the nonhorror fantasy story and for science fiction. Many of the same authors wrote in more than one of these short-story forms, and the forms themselves sometimes overlap in a single story. H. G. Wells, for example, wrote tales in which the traditional horror story blends into the emerging science-fiction genre. In one of them, "A Dream of Armageddon" (1920), Wells uses the traditional horror story devices of a recurrent dream, a mysterious alter ego, and the fear of madness to depict a futuristic hell of technological warfare. More recently, Ray Bradbury, now firmly established as a writer of first-class fantasy and science-fiction short stories, began his career by producing horror stories for pulp magazines such as *Weird Tales*, *Amazing Stories*, and *Famous Fantastic Mysteries*.

Just as the otherworld element of the horror short story contributed to the development of the fantasy and science-fiction genres, its elements of mystery, fear, and general goriness and mayhem contributed to the emergence of mystery and detective stories. The detective story itself was introduced by one of the greatest writers of horror short stories: Edgar Allan Poe. In the world's first detective story, "The Murders in the Rue Morgue" (1841), Poe included such horror-story elements as a body stuffed up a chimney, apparently supernatural events which turn out to have a rational explanation, and bloodcurdling descriptions of violence which produce the *frisson* associated with the horror genre. Other detective short-story writers, such as Sir Arthur Conan Doyle, combined a taste for the occult with their skill at composing rationally oriented mysteries. Several of the Sherlock Holmes stories, notably "The Adventure of the Musgrave Ritual," contain elements which are decidedly "spooky"; and Doyle also wrote a number of purely occult tales. A more recent example of this connection between the horror story and the detective story is the work of the American author John Dickson Carr. His short detective novel *The Burning Court* (1937), for example, has a highly ambiguous ending which does not exclude the possibility of witchcraft and reincarnation.

Another type of short story which has roots in the horror genre is the psychological tale. From its inception, the horror story has lent itself to the expression of psychological experience; and as the genre developed, the parallels between the otherworld and the human unconscious became more deliberate and more pronounced. A classic example of this psychological element in the horror short story is Joseph Sheridan Le Fanu's "Green Tea" (1872). The central character of the story is an unmarried Anglican clergyman who is painstakingly described as shy, repressed, fearful of emotion, and reluctant to share any of his feelings with even his closest friends. This clergyman embarks upon a study of pagan beliefs, using as a stimulus frequent drinks of green tea. Presently he finds himself attended by a familiar in the form of a shaggy black spectral monkey with glowing red eyes. This monkey haunts the clergyman, distracts him from prayer, and finally introduces into the clergyman's mind thoughts which are lewd and blasphemous. The unfortunate clergyman seeks the help first of the famous Dr. Harley and then of Dr. Hesselius, the medical philosopher from whose point of view the story is told. The clergyman attributes the haunting to his guilt over spending so much time and attention on pagan studies. Dr. Hesselius believes that the use of green tea, combined with long hours of study, has opened an inward eye which allows the clergyman to see into a dimension usually concealed from men. Most readers infer that the hallucination of the hairy black beast is an externalization of the clergyman's repressed energies, evoked by his study of a sexually oriented pagan religious system.

This type of allegorical or hallucinatory representation of an inner state gradually developed into a short-story genre in its own right. Authors such as Henry James picked up horror-story themes and images—for example, the double figure—and transferred them to such tales as "The Private Life" and "The Jolly Corner." The horror element became less central to these stories, while the issue of psychological exploration became correspondingly more important.

The Antecedents of the Horror Short Story

The major themes and images of the horror story originated in a preliterary religious tradition which postulated the existence of a spiritual world which complemented the material world perceptible to the senses. These themes and images are evident in the earliest examples of written literature. Ghosts walk in the Babylonian tale *The Epic of Gilgamesh* (c. 2000 B. C.) and the Greek epic hero Odysseus provides a pit full of sheep's blood so that the spirit of the dead prophet Tiresias, refreshed by the blood, has strength to speak. The earliest examples of deliberate attempts to structure coherent horror stories for the purpose of evoking a thrill of fear occur in the later stages of Roman literature. For example, a character in *The Satyricon* tells an after-dinner tale featuring a werewolf in order to frighten the other guests.

The rise of Christianity lent new directions to tales of terror because of the popularity of sermons regarding the devil, evil spirits in general, original sin, and the souls of the dead who wait in pain in Purgatory for final redemption. Educated Christians who understood the import of these doctrines were not likely to believe in such horrors as werewolves, vampires, and ghouls. The uneducated majority, however, frequently confused the Church's teaching on Purgatory, for example, with the idea of restless dead—or undead—whose unredeemed state and inner suffering might cause them to prey upon the living.

During the Middle Ages there were a number of religious tales of supernatural or preternatural punishments visited upon sinners by evil beings whom God permitted to victimize the wicked; and there were also tales such as romances or beast fables which included horror elements from paganism and folklore. Writers of the Renaissance combined these horror themes with newly rediscovered Roman themes to produce such bloodcurdling literature as the Senecan revenge tragedies. One of these, Thomas Kyd's *The Spanish Tragedy* (1586), includes one ghost, one preternatural spirit, five murders, two suicides, one execution, two cases of madness, one kidnaping, and one biting out of a tongue.

Despite this long-standing fascination with horror themes and images, it was not until the eighteenth century that these themes and images were used as the center of works intended to be horror stories as such. During the eighteenth century the emphasis which was placed on reason, materialism, and order paradoxically generated a rise of interest in the spiritual world, which culminated in the beginnings of the Romantic movement. Meanwhile, the work of such writers as Daniel Defoe and Jonathan Swift laid the groundwork for the immense developments in fiction which took place during the eighteenth century. These factors of interest and technique combined to produce the horror short story.

Defoe himself wrote what is probably the world's first ghost short story: "A True Relation of the Apparition of One Mrs. Veal" (1706). It was supposed at one time that this story was pure fiction, written to help promote a religious tract, "Drelincourt upon Death," which is mentioned twice in the narrative. Facts, however, have come to light which indicate that Defoe actually did travel to Canterbury to interview one Mrs. Bargrave, who claimed to have seen the apparition of a deceased friend. Defoe's fictionalization of Mrs. Bargrave's account set a precedent for later ghost short stories: he provided the rather fragmentary, meaningless episode with order and motivation.

The real development of horror fiction began later in the eighteenth century, after the rise of the novel form at the hands of such writers as Henry Fielding, Samuel Richardson, and Tobias Smollett. In 1764, Horace Walpole published the first Gothic novel, *The Castle of Otranto*. Although it influenced a number of later horror tales, this multivolume work is not by any means a pure horror story in itself. It is a variation of the sentimental novel, involving a number of separate episodes, each with its own climax. The same is true of Mrs. Ann Radcliffe's immensely popular *The Mysteries of Udolpho* (1794), and of other examples of the early Gothic novel. Mrs. Radcliffe and her followers also undermined the horror elements which do exist in their novels by providing rational and/or mechanical explanations for apparently preternatural phenomena.

Two years after the publication of *The Mysteries of Udolpho*, Matthew Gregory Lewis published *Ambrosio: Or, The Monk*, which is by far the most violent, terrifying, and haunting of the eighteenth century Gothic novels. It is also the forerunner of a great deal of Romantic literature, and the source for a number of horror short stories. The protagonist of the story, Father Ambrosio, is a cold and passionless priest who hands over a young nun to torture when he learns of her love affair and expected child. He himself then falls in love with Matilda, a seductress who has gained entrance to his monastery by disguising herself as a man and becoming a novice. Matilda turns out to be a tool of the Devil, who has tempted the proud priest into sin; and even after Ambrosio has ceased to love her, she provides the means for him to satisfy his aroused lusts by drugging and raping a young girl, Antonia. In the course of his assault on Antonia, Ambrosio murders her mother, Elvira. He later murders Antonia herself, and he and Matilda are eventually arrested by the Inquisition. Matilda is condemned to death, but is freed by the Devil to tempt Antonio into selling his soul in return for release from prison. As he hears the footsteps of men approaching his cell to take him, as he thinks, to torture, Ambrosio concludes the bargain. The Devil takes Ambrosio to the edge of a high cliff, where he tells the monk that Antonia was actually Ambrosio's sister, and Elvira his mother. Then the demon reveals to Ambrosio that the footsteps he heard just before he sold his soul were not those of torturers, but of men who would have released him. Finally, the Devil lifts Ambrosio high into the air and drops him to a lingering and horrible death on the rocks below, to be followed by an eternity of hell. The novel aroused a great deal of protest because of its intense horror, violence, and overt sexuality; and Lewis himself never wrote anything like it again. *The Monk*, however, remains a landmark in horror fiction because of its own power, and because its atmosphere, language, situations, and characters have served as a source for many of the horror stories which followed it.

The last major Gothic novel, and the best, is Charles Robert Maturin's *Melmoth the Wanderer* (1820). As the title suggests, the story is based on the traditional horror theme of the cursed wanderer who, like the Flying Dutchman and the Wandering Jew, cannot die and cannot rest. A great deal of *Melmoth the Wanderer* is actually a series of separate episodes, held together by the narrative frame. The most important episode is one in which an illegitimate young member of a noble Spanish family, doomed against his will to monastic vows for the sake of his family's convenience, attempts to escape from the convent. The violence and cruelty of this section of the story, together with the gloomy cloistral settings and the brooding presence of the Inquisition, are reminiscent of Lewis' *The Monk*. *Melmoth the Wanderer* is by far the best written of the Gothic novels, and it made a deep impression on several later writers of horror stories, notably Honoré de Balzac and Poe.

Chapbooks, Penny Bloods, and Penny Dreadfuls

By the turn of the nineteenth century, the immense popularity of the major Gothic novels and their many imitators made it obvious that there was a large and eager audience for this type of literature. Further, the movement toward mass literacy had already begun, and many members of the working classes were now able to read. This fact, combined with the invention early in the nineteenth century of the rotary steam printing press and of a machine for making cheap paper, produced both the means and the market for selling large quantities of cheaply printed horror fiction. The earliest examples of this kind of fiction are found in the Gothic chapbooks, sometimes called "Shilling Shockers." These were designed for partially educated readers who could neither afford nor understand the multivolume Gothic novels, but who were enthusiastic about the chapbooks' condensed, simplified versions. Another attraction of the chapbooks was the lurid drawings which illustrated each five-page story or installment of a story. The most popular source for chapbook material was Lewis' *The Monk*, followed by Maturin's *Melmoth the Wanderer*. These two works were plagiarized, compressed, extracted, pirated, and imitated unmercifully for almost a century in the chapbooks and their successors.

Hard on the heels of the chapbooks came the eight-page Penny Bloods, which were able to maintain their low price through the use of plagiarism, sweated labor, and underpaid writers. Each issue, set up in double columns of tightly packed small print, began without any attempt to fill the reader in on previous episodes, and the narrative ended abruptly at the bottom of the eighth page, often in the middle of a sentence. The best-known—and the most notorious—publisher of Penny Bloods was Edward Lloyd. His stable of original authors (as opposed to those who simply borrowed from the works of other writers) included Thomas Peckett Prest and James Malcolm Rymer. Prest was the author of the favorite story of the period, *Sweeney Todd*, which appeared in serial form starting in 1846. Sweeney Todd, the Demon Barber of Fleet Street, had in his shop a barber's chair which rested on a trap door set on a pivot. When Todd drew back a bolt in the next room, the trap door would rotate, dumping the occupant of the chair onto a stone floor twenty feet below. If the fall failed to kill the victim, it would at least stun him long enough to allow the barber to finish him off without trouble. The bodies of the victims were then dismembered, and the chunks of meat delivered through a secret underground tunnel to a baker's shop. There Sweeney Todd's accomplice, Mrs. Lovett, baked what appeared to be veal or pork pies with a great deal of succulent gravy. These she sold to the clerks in the nearby law offices, who enjoyed them hot or cold depending upon the hour of the day. The story was probably based on the Scottish legend of the cannibal family of Sawney Bean, which was also reprinted in the Penny Bloods.

Besides tales of crime and horror, the Penny Bloods printed stories which drew upon folklore concerning the occult. The most popular of these was James Malcolm Rymer's *Varney the Vampire* (1845-1847). This rambling and episodic tale exploits the legend of the bloodthirsty "undead" which Bram Stoker would later employ in his novel *Dracula* (1897). A representative episode of *Varney the Vampire* is "The Resuscitation of a Vampire," in which Varney is summoned to be part of a group of five vampires who must attend the awakening of a newly dead man who is to become one of them. The man is condemned to vampirism because of his sins; although outwardly a religious man, he has been guilty of great cowardice and cruelty. The five vampires exhume the coffin and open its lid to allow the cold rays of the moon to touch the dead man. Then, when he stands on level ground and has been told of his state, they leave him. He rushes through the streets of the town, trailing his graveclothes, in helpless terror.

Although *Varney the Vampire* was the most popular of the occult Penny Blood stories, it was closely followed by the works of George W. M. Reynolds, another of Edward Lloyd's writers. Reynolds produced three major works with preternatural themes: *Faust* (1845-1846), a popularization of the famous legend; *Wagner the Were-Wolf* (1846-1847), which is probably the first story in English to exploit the werewolf legend in fictional form; and *The Necromancer* (1852), concerning a pact with the Devil, extended life, and human sacrifice.

Around the middle of the nineteenth century, the Penny Bloods began to shift their emphasis to a younger audience. The heroes and heroines of the stories themselves became younger, and the situations were contrived to suit the taste of juvenile readers. At this point the publications began to be known as Penny Dreadfuls. Surprisingly, the general level of their content and style improved with this change in emphasis. Parents and other authority figures, however, disapproved of the Penny Dreadfuls, and blamed them for juvenile violence in much the same way as such persons now blame television and film.

Chapbooks, Penny Bloods, and Penny Dreadfuls, although they contained for the most part a very inferior grade of writing, contributed to the mainstream of the horror short story by demonstrating the popularity of horror fiction. This induced the editors and publishers of better periodicals to include horror short stories in their own journals. Further, several better writers, notably Robert Louis Stevenson, were fascinated by the horror stories they read in these cheap publications and went on to write some of the classic short stories of the horror genre.

The Horror Short Story in the Nineteenth Century: Great Britain
From the eighteenth century ownard, interest in horror fiction was by no means limited to the working classes. Many of those who read the original versions of the Gothic novels developed a keen appetite for the spine-chilling events and the emotional impact of such stories. The authors of the Gothic novels themselves wrote a few horror short stories, but their major contribution to the genre was the interest their longer works aroused in other writers, such as Sir Walter Scott, Charles Dickens, William (Wilkie) Collins, and Edgar Allan Poe. Scott was one of the first major writers to produce horror short stories. For example, he inserted a coherent and thematically complete short story called "Wandering Willie's Tale" into his novel *Redgauntlet* (1824). "Wandering Willie's Tale" concerns a poor farmer, Steenie, who is forced to go to hell in order to collect a receipt for a rent payment he had made to his landlord. The landlord had died before he could supply the receipt, and his heir refused to believe that Steenie had in fact paid his rent. This story is an example of the combination of horror elements, humor, and humanity which would become a popular style of horror-story writing in the later nineteenth century. Scott also wrote several other ghost stories, including "The Tapestried Chamber" and "My Aunt Margaret's Mirror," both published in *The Keepsake* for 1828.

Like those two stories of Scott's, most horror short stories of the nineteenth century appeared for the first time in periodical form. Apart from the inexpensive and often poorly written Gothic chapbooks and Penny Bloods, there were a number of highly literate magazines, intended for the middle and upper classes, which frequently carried horror stories written by first-class authors. These authors had already realized that the most effective form for horror fiction is the short story, and editors welcomed their contributions as single-issue complements to the serials which occupied much of the space in nineteenth century periodicals. Charles Dickens, as editor of *Household Words* and later of *All the Year Round*, did more than anyone else to encourage the writing and dissemination of horror short stories. He made a point of including ghost stories in his magazines, particularly in the Christmas issues; and he commissioned such stories as William (Wilkie) Collins' "The Dream Woman" (1855) and Edward Bulwer-Lytton's "The Haunters and the Haunted" (1859). (The solution of this story, which involves both occult science and the topical scientific issue of magnetism, is an example of the inclusion of pre-science fiction elements in early horror short stories.)

In addition to the contributions he made to the horror short story in his role as editor, Dickens wrote a number of such stories himself. These stories often included the elements of humor and humanity which were present in some earlier ghost stories, such as Scott's "Wandering Willie's Tale." Dickens' earliest ghost stories were episodes inset into *The Pickwick Papers* (1837); of these, the most commonly reprinted tale is "The Story of the Bagman's Uncle." The best known of Dickens' ghost stories are *A Christmas Carol* (1843) and his other contributions to Christmas literature, such as *The Chimes* (1844) and *The Cricket on the Hearth* (1845). He also wrote stories which exploited the belief in the occult, in spiritism, and in psychic phenomena which was on the rise during the mid-nineteenth century. His story "No. 1 Branch Line: The Signalman" (1866), for example, centers around a railroad signalman's uncomprehended premonition of disaster and, at last, of his own death.

Although *Household Words* and *All the Year Round*, under the editorship of Dickens, published large numbers of horror stories, these were not the only journals in which such stories appeared. The single best source of nineteenth century horror short stories is *The Romancist and Novelist's Library* (1839-1842). These volumes contain not only works by the best British authors of horror fiction—including Horace Walpole, Ann Radcliffe, Matthew Gregory Lewis, Charles Robert Maturin, and Mary Shelley—but also translations from French and German authors. A number of other periodicals of the time, including *Blackwood's Magazine*, *The Strand Magazine*, and the *Dublin University Magazine*, also published these immensely popular tales.

One of the editors of the *Dublin University Magazine*, Joseph Sheridan Le Fanu, was in his own way as important to the development of the horror short story as Charles Dickens was. As a contributor to the *Dublin University Magazine*, later as its editor, and finally as its proprietor, Le Fanu encouraged the dissemination of horror short stories. More importantly, his own work played a leading role in the development of the horror short story from the Gothic novels and the chapbook stories. Le Fanu's strong point, which was evident even in his earliest story ("The Ghost and the Bone-Setter," 1838), was his ability to shape the rather chaotic tale of terror into a coherent short story with clearly delineated characters, definite narrative structure, and thematic unity. Further, his stories bring to a high level of sophistication one of the primary functions of the horror short story: the depiction of a state of mind, or a type of universal psychological experience, in terms of allegory or analogy. He was particularly adept at suggesting the salient points of his protagonists' personalities very briefly and yet with great clarity, so that the reader is able to draw comparisons between the external manifestations in the story and the state of the protagonist's mind. In addition to his best-known work, "Green Tea," Le Fanu wrote a number of horror short stories dealing in an original way with the activities of his protagonists' lower selves or of their consciences. These stories include "A Drunkard's Dream" (1838), "Sir Dominick's Bargain" (1872), and "The Familiar" (1872).

Although a number of different horror-story themes were used in nineteenth century short stories, many of them of topical interest (such as mesmerism, magnetism, and mediumism), the two which were most popular and became most closely associated with the genre were the man-made monster and the vampire. The motif of the man-made monster was exploited most effectively in 1818 by a nineteen-year-old girl writing in competition with Percy Bysshe Shelley, Lord Byron, and Dr. John Polidori. The four writers entered into a contest in order to beguile their time during a prolonged period of rain, and, incidentally, in order to provide a distraction from the quarreling which had begun to take place among them. The object of the contest was to produce a horror tale modeled after the German works in *Fantasmagoriana*, which they had been reading. Mary Shelley's *Frankenstein: Or, The Modern Prometheus* was the only important work produced on that occasion, and it had such an impact on the public when it was published the following year that the entire man-made monster motif has come to be known by its name. Short stories which are based on the man-made monster motif include Ambrose Bierce's "Moxon's Master" and Jerome K. Jerome's "The Dancing Partner." In a broader sense, the themes and motifs of *Frankenstein* are the forerunners of the technologically oriented horror stories which gradually merged into the science-fiction genre. This is particularly evident in the idea of man, in his pride and incomplete state of knowledge, creating for himself the entities which destroy his own happiness.

Like the motif of the man-made horror, the idea of the vampire is central to a large number of horror short stories. It is undoubtedly the most popular of the occult themes which appear in the horror genre. The figure of the vampire itself goes back to the preliterary period and appears in some of the earliest works of written literature. The vampire figures who are most closely related to those in nineteenth and twentieth century horror stories, however, arose during the Middle Ages and the Renaissance from a combination of traditional vampire themes and legends arising from actual events which took place in Eastern Europe. The two major figures around whom these legends arose were Vlad Dracula, who ruled Wallachia from 1456 to 1462 and again, briefly, in 1475-1476; and his relative the Countess Elizabeth Báthory of Hungary, who died in 1614. Vlad Dracula was a strong ruler whose maintenance of domestic law and order and fierce repulsion of foreign invaders have led some historians to regard him as a national hero. His methods of dealing with criminals, traitors, and enemies, however, were somewhat harsh. His favorite form of punishment was impalement, or spitting his enemies on sharply pointed upright stakes which operated like spindles. He once had a large number of captured enemy troops impaled in this manner along a highway which would be used by other troops coming to invade his capital, reasoning that the sight of these mutilated bodies hanging on stakes would discourage the invaders from coming any farther. It did. Not unnaturally, Vlad's enemies pursued him with every intention of turning the tables by impaling him, and there is some evidence that after his death his body was dug up and treated in this fashion. Remnants of this desire to impale Dracula can be seen in the notion that the best way to deal with a vampire is to drive a stake through his heart.

A little more than a century after Dracula's death, his relative, the Countess Elizabeth Báthory of Hungary, added to the vampire legend by her habit of bathing in the blood of virgins, and sometimes drinking it, in order to preserve her own youth. The connection between this practice and the idea of the vampire preying upon the blood of innocent women for the sake of preserving his existence and renewing his youth is obvious. Elizabeth also took excessive sexual delight in the torture of these girls, which contributed to the element of perverted eroticism which characterizes modern vampire stories. Le Fanu's novelette "Carmilla" (1871) is one of the closest literary approximations to the actual sadistic/lesbian atmosphere which surrounded the horrors in the castle of Elizabeth Báthory.

Although several vampire stories preceded *Dracula*, it is Stoker's sinister Count who captured the popular imagination and became the prototype of the vampire in twentieth century fiction and film. Stoker took from the historical Dracula his description of a tall, dark, rather tragic figure who possessed a great deal of courage and the promise of greatness, but whose unexplained perversion led him into a hellish existence of suffering and evil. He took from Eastern European folklore the details which, in combination with the figure described, produce many of the thrills associated with the character: the failure to cast a reflection or a shadow, the inability to cross water unaided, the dread of religious materials, the need to sleep by day in his own earth, and the ability to fly and to assume animal shape. The total effect is of a paradoxical being who is at once repelling and hauntingly attractive, powerful and yet limited by the laws of his own existence, which prevent him from overcoming humankind entirely.

Stoker himself used Dracula as the basis for a few short stories, some of them published in his collection *Dracula's Guest* (1914); but his real contribution is one of influence. Twentieth century writers of horror short stories in both England and America, fascinated with Stoker's themes and impressed by the popularity of his vampire count, have produced countless stories derived from *Dracula*. Many of these are the work of hack writers and have appeared in pulp magazines and cheap paperbacks; but even these are significant by virtue of the attraction they exercise over the crowds of people who read and enjoy them. A few of the twentieth century stories which owe something of their characterization and theme to *Dracula*—including M. R. James's "Count Magnus" and Lafcadio Hearn's "Haceldama"—are first-rate stories in their own right.

The Horror Story in the Nineteenth Century: The United States

Although American writers were influenced by the British Gothic novels and by the horror short stories which followed, they also derived some of their material from a newer but rapidly strengthening American tradition of horror fiction. For example, eighteenth and nineteenth century American horror stories were often set in the thick, dark forests which had for centuries been inhabited only by beasts and savages. American writers often combined with the physical properties of these settings—darkness, impenetrability, a sense of brooding presences—a suggestion of heathen Indian rites. This has much the same effect on the reader as the whisper of long forgotten Druidical sacrifices in a British wood. Further, from the Colonial period onward, the wild aspect of North American nature was the background for various kinds of "hellfire and damnation" religious beliefs. Storms, floods, Indian raids, and epidemics were seen as the just and inescapable punishments of an angry God; and the Devil was no abstraction, but a very real force waiting to drag the unwary into unbearable torments. Because of the relatively undeveloped state of the country and the isolation of small hamlets and individual farms, there were very few distractions from the sense of terror which was induced by the combination of a dangerous and often violent natural setting, and a preoccupation with sin, demons, and hell.

The leading American writer of Gothic novels, Charles Brockden Brown, exploits both gloomy wooded settings and religious fanaticism in his best-known work, *Wieland: Or, The Transformation* (1798). This story centers around a fanatically religious Pennsylvanian who, convinced that he has heard supernatural voices commanding the act, sacrifices his wife and children. His sister barely escapes with her life, and it is she who narrates the story. Like Ann Radcliffe, Brown undercuts the preternatural elements of his story by providing a rational explanation (in this case, a ventriloquist); but his striking portrayal of guilt-ridden psychopathology remains unaltered.

With the advent of American Romanticism in the nineteenth century, a number of writers turned the elements of the American horror short story to the portrayal of characters whose most intimate fears and desires are reproduced allegorically in the external world. Nathaniel Hawthorne, for example, often used the forest and the town as antithetical images for the dream world of the unconscious and the daylight world of external reality. In one of his stories, "Young Goodman Brown" (1835), the protagonist is a young man who, leaving his wife Faith in the town, goes out alone into the forest. There he meets with the Devil in the shape of Goodman Brown's grandfather. The Devil tells Brown that Brown's father and grandfather, whom Brown had believed to be above any suspicion of sin, were in fact servants of the Devil's who had inflicted cruel suffering in the name of righteousness and religion. Brown later accompanies the Devil deeper into the forest in order to attend a midnight coven. There he finds all the most respected people of his town, including the minister, the deacon, and the catechist. Even Brown's young wife Faith seems about to join the unholy group. Brown himself rejects the Devil at the last moment and awakens the next morning alone in the forest. He returns to the town a transformed man: sour, suspicious, and sure that he is the only virtuous human being there. Brown lives to an embittered old age and dies in gloom. The story is delicately balanced with regard to an explanation for its events. Brown might have dreamed the entire episode; or it might have happened; or it might be an allegorical representation of the state of Brown's unconscious mind which, because of Brown's own sinfulness, projects the assumption of sin onto everyone else. What is certain in the story is that Brown lives and dies in pain because his belief in his own righteousness isolates him from the community of his fellows.

This theme of a soul destroyed by pride, by intolerance of human imperfection, and by self-isolation from the human community is the most common idea expressed in Hawthorne's horror short stories. "The Birthmark" (1846), whose use of a "mad scientist" protagonist, an innocent victim, and an Igorlike laboratory assistant anticipates the later development of the horror short story into science fiction, shows another facet of the same themes. Its plot concerns an alchemist, Aylmer, who is unable to rest in the enjoyment of his beautiful young wife because she has on her cheek a small blemish: a tiny hand which shows pink against her skin. Aylmer insists on removing the hand through the use of a quasimagical potion, and in doing so destroys his wife because of his impious desire to possess perfection. Still another aspect of Hawthorne's master theme appears in "Ethan Brand" (1851), a tale of a man who sets out to seek the Unpardonable Sin in the souls of his fellow men. Finally he discovers that the Unpardonable Sin exists nowhere but in himself because in his pride he has placed intellect above compassion and has looked on as an observer where he should have offered sympathy. In the climactic scene of the story, Ethan Brand stands in the flame and heat of a lime-kiln, declares himself to be damned and cast out from heaven and from earth, and throws himself into the fire. In the morning only his bones remain, together with a heart too hard to burn.

A contemporary of Hawthorne, and an admirer of some of Hawthorne's stories, was the master of the horror short story: Edgar Allan Poe. The variety, imaginativeness, and sheer power of Poe's stories have never been surpassed. His first horror short story, "Metzengerstein" (1832), was Gothic in setting, format, and conception; but after that Poe wrote in a style that was his alone. He observed, "I maintain that terror is not of Germany, but of the soul." He portrayed the terror of the soul in a long succession of stories which chill the blood not only because of their grisly and gory external events, but also because they reflect with such unmerciful accuracy the dark places of the human psyche. Poe removed from the horror short story the last traces of didacticism, artificiality, diffuseness, and moralizing; and he concentrated on a single effect which represented without amelioration the kinds of feelings which are really involved in evil and terror.

One of Poe's best horror short stories is "William Wilson" (1839). It tells of a headstrong young boy who, as he grows older, grows more and more corrupt. Accompanying him through life is a spectral figure which appears whenever Wilson is about to do something particularly evil. The climax of the story occurs at a masquerade ball at which Wilson plans to seduce a young married woman. Frustrated beyond endurance by the specter's interference, Wilson stabs it. He then realizes that what he has killed is his own double, and that he has, in a sense, killed himself.

The double figure in "William Wilson" has been interpreted by a number of readers as Wilson's conscience. The situations in which it appears, its whispering voice, and its dying declaration that Wilson has doomed himself to be "dead to the World, to Heaven, and to Hope" support this reading. This interpretation is also supported by the epigraph of the story, "What say of it? what say CONSCIENCE grim,/That spectre in my path?" Poe's manner of presenting the double figure, however, is a masterpiece of psychological horror. He does not simply impose the figure upon the story; he allows it to grow, to develop, from Wilson's own behavior and perceptions. Gradually it becomes clear that this haunting is not something which is happening to Wilson, even as a punishment for his sins; it is something which he himself is doing. In Poe's world, man is himself the source of his own hell and generates his own horrors.

Even when Poe capitalized on topical concerns of the nineteenth century, such as polar exploration (for example, *The Narrative of Arthur Gordon Pym* (1838) or air travel ("The Balloon Hoax"), he combined those issues with themes of universal interest. For example, one of his last stories, "The Facts in the Case of M. Valdemar" (1845), exploits the popular topic of mesmerism or hypnotism. This story is a chilling account of a man who, hypnotized shortly before death, remains capable of speech even after he has died. "The Facts in the Case of M. Valdemar" illustrates the intense desire of the living to reverse, or at least to gain some control over, the finality of death. The futility of such attempts is made clear in the final paragraphs of the story, when the mesmerist finally breaks the hypnotic spell. Thinking that he has overcome death, the hypnotist expects to see M. Valdemar awaken; but what actually remains on the bed after the spell is broken is "a nearly liquid mass of loathsome—of detestable putrescence."

Not all of Poe's horror stories are as grim as these. He wrote a few stories which include genuine, if dark, humor; among these are "The Unparalleled Adventure of One Hans Pfaall," "The System of Dr. Tarr and Prof. Fether," and "Never Bet the Devil Your Head." The American writer who is most closely associated with the inclusion of black humor in horror short stories, however, is Ambrose Bierce, a misanthropic journalist known as "Bitter Bierce." His best-known humorous horror short story is "My Favorite Murder" (1891). The narrator of the story seeks out his uncle, explaining:

> One morning I shouldered my Winchester rifle, and going over to my uncle's house, near Nigger Road, asked my Aunt Mary, his wife, if he were at home, adding that I had come to kill him. My aunt replied with her peculiar smile that so many gentlemen called on that errand and were afterwards carried away without having performed it that I must excuse her for doubting my good faith in the matter.

The narrator greets his uncle pleasantly, knocks him cold with a rifle butt, hamstrings him, and carries him off in a sack in order to avoid exciting remark among the neighbors. A rope swinging from a tree suggests a method of murder; so the narrator hangs up the sack containing his uncle and goes off to get a large ram which he describes as being "in a state of chronic constitutional indignation." He sets the sack containing his uncle swinging from the tree, and watches with great amusement as the ram butts the sack to and fro. Finally the ram hits the sack so hard that all the clocks for miles around stop running because of the shock, and the narrator concludes his tale on a note of great satisfaction.

In some respects, "My Favorite Murder" is a parody of Bierce's more serious horror stories. He was particularly interested in the idea of getting inside the mind of the criminal, not often in a sympathetic manner but for the sake of observation and analysis. Such stories—"The Middle Toe of the Right Foot" is a good example—act as a link between the horror short story and the psychologically oriented detective stories which became popular around the time of World War I.

The psychological horror story itself reached its peak with the publication of Henry James's ghost stories, beginning with "The Romance of Certain Old Clothes" in 1868. James includes in his ghost stories a number of elements which were present in earlier horror fiction; but he organizes them differently, and he adds a more detailed and deliberate level of psychological themes and imagery. For example, "The Jolly Corner" (1908) resembles Poe's "William Wilson" in centering around a protagonist who is haunted by a figure which at first he does not recognize, but which turns out to be his own alter ego. In James's story, however, the double represents a more complex psychological construct than conscience or a fragmented personality. Conversely, the emotional elements which play such a large part in Poe's story are muted here.

One sign of this transition from the pure horror story to the psychological short story is that James, who unlike Poe was not striving for striking effects, is much more likely to work with the vagaries of normal psychology rather than seeking the more sensational plots which arise from psychopathological states. For example, the protagonist of "The Jolly Corner," Spencer Brydon, is not corrupt in the sense that William Wilson is. He is simply a weak and selfish man whose blindness to those very qualities in himself deprives him of any chance of overcoming them. The ghostly element enters the story when Brydon begins to spend his evenings alone in his old family home and develops a sense of being watched, of being haunted, by some entity which lives in the house. Brydon begins a nightly search of the house and is finally confronted with a spectral form which holds its hands over its face. The posture of the figure suggests Brydon's own inability to face the truth about himself and to deal effectively with it. When the specter shows himself more clearly, its thick eyeglasses and maimed right hand support that interpretation. In all other respects the specter is identical to Brydon. It is, in fact, the external embodiment of Brydon as he actually is. Brydon faints, and when he recovers he denies all kinship with the specter, thus condemning himself to continued blindness and inactivity. "The Jolly Corner" does carry an emotional impact, but that impact springs not from the language and imagery of the story— which are quite restrained—but from the frightening portrayal of a deeply troubling aspect of "normal" psychology: a wasted life.

While writers such as Henry James were entertaining educated readers during the late nineteenth and early twentieth centuries, descendants of the Penny Blood writers were publishing cheaper versions of the horror short story in the pulp magazines. Like the Gothic chapbooks and the Penny Bloods, the pulp magazines presented sensational fiction printed on cheap paper and accompanied by lurid illustrations. Most of the pulp magazines published some horror fiction, but a few were devoted exclusively to horror, fantasy, and science fiction stories. These included *Strange Tales*, *Terror Tales*, *Horror Stories*, and *Weird Tales*.

Although the pulp magazines often published the work of hack writers who are deservedly forgotten, they also carried stories by a number of first-rate horror-story writers, including Algernon Blackwood and H. G. Wells. The magazine which consistently maintained the highest level of excellence was the legendary *Weird Tales*. This magazine, which was the world's first periodical devoted exclusively to any form of fantasy, began in March, 1923, and continued for thirty-two years. Its authors and comparatively small but devoted body of readers were exceptionally loyal to the magazine. The *Weird Tales* authors included some of the best horror short-story writers of the time; H. P. Lovecraft, August Derleth, Clark Ashton Smith, and Robert Bloch were regular contributors.

The pulp magazines survived until 1953, when a major distributor refused to handle anything except the more profitable "slick" magazines and a few digest-sized fiction magazines. This, combined with the general climate of postwar affluence and sophistication and with the rise of cheap paperback books, meant the end of the pulps. In 1973, Leo Margulies made an attempt to revive the horror magazine by purchasing the rights and title to the defunct *Weird Tales* and putting it back in business. The resurrected magazine contained a number of reprints, including many stories which are of interest to horror short-story fans because of their rarity and historical significance. The new *Weird Tales*, however, was not of interest to the general public, and it ceased publication after four issues.

The Horror Short Story in the Twentieth Century

By the turn of the twentieth century, the line of distinction between British and American horror short stories was beginning to blur. Frequent international reprintings and trips abroad by the authors themselves to lecture or to gather material led to a pooling of resources and interests. Most of the better horror stories which have been written on either side of the Atlantic during the twentieth century show the influence of earlier writers such as Poe, Le Fanu, and James in dealing with the more alarming aspects of the human condition rather than depicting purely external horrors. Also, an increasing number of stories fall into the gray area between horror literature and fantasy and science fiction.

One of the most representative horror short-story writers of the twentieth century is Algernon Blackwood, whose interest in extrasensory phenomena led him to investigate various kinds of extensions of the human senses. Like James, Blackwood usually wrote about normal protagonists caught in an unusual situation or faced with some type of externalization or personification of drives which are ordinarily hidden. "The Occupant of the Room," for example, concerns a traveler who is given the hotel room of an Englishwoman who has never checked out of the hotel, but who has been missing for some time. The protagonist, Minturn, suffers a sense of uneasiness which centers around a locked cupboard in the bedroom. By the middle of the night, he finds himself in a state of despair bordering on suicide. Finally he awakens the hotel staff and insists on having the cupboard unlocked. When the door is opened, the body of the missing Englishwoman is found hanging from a hook. A suicide note explaining the woman's depression contains the words of despair which had been echoing in Minturn's mind.

In contrast to Blackwood's deliberately "spooky" style of writing, his contemporary Montague Rhodes James produced horror short stories which are conversationally matter-of-fact in tone. James often used actual ghosts rather than the suggestions, sensations, or atmospheres which had become popular by the turn of the century. Further, James's ghosts have nothing of the ethereal quality of Victorian spirit-photography; they are usually squat, dark, ugly, and either brutal or stupid. One of James's best stories, and his own favorite, is "Count Magnus" (1904). This is the terrifying story of an intelligent but over-inquisitive writer named Wraxall, who in the course of his researches in Sweden finds a record of an evil seventeenth century figure, Count Magnus. Wraxall learns that the peasants who lived under the Count's rule feared and hated him because of the cruel punishments he inflicted for trifling offenses and because he visited the birthplace of the Antichrist and brought back a squat, dark, brutal companion. In the time of Wraxall's adventure, local superstition claims that the Count and his dark familiar still haunt the castle grounds. Wraxall finds that the Count's tomb, sealed with three heavy padlocks, is decorated with images of a tall cloaked figure directing an ugly squat form in pursuing terrified victims. Each time Wraxall, secure in his skepticism, wishes that he could meet the Count, one of the padlocks falls from the tomb. When the last padlock falls, Wraxall finally recognizes the folly of his attitude toward the mystery of the Count and flees for his life. On the ship back to England, he notes that two travelers—a tall cloaked figure and his squat companion—never dine with the other passengers. Once he has landed in England, Wraxall attempts to shake off his pursuers. The state of Wraxall's body after his sudden death, however, suggests that he failed.

At the opposite end of the horror short-story spectrum from M. R. James is Edward John Moreton Drax Plunkett, eighteenth Baron Dunsany. His Biblical prose, his use of folklore elements, and his tone of long-ago-and-far-away Romanticism give a mystic touch to Dunsany's stories. Dunsany is particularly important as a transitional figure between the horror short story and the fantasy genre. He is often given credit for having been the first to develop a complete fantasy world within the short-story form. One of his best combinations of fantasy and horror was written as a result of a dream Dunsany had in the trenches in France during World War I: "The Bureau d'Echange de Maux." As the title suggests, the story centers around an agency which offers to its clients the opportunity to exchange evils or misfortunes with one another. When a pair of clients have agreed upon an exchange, the sinister old man who runs the agency ratifies the signed document and each client finds himself with a new set of ills. The narrator visits the shop repeatedly, and finally exchanges fears with another client. The narrator has been told that no one ever rescinds one of these bargains; and when, after his own exchange has been made, he walks down the well-known streets to the shop he has visited so often, there is no trace of it.

Although Dunsany's prewar stories have a light-hearted touch of humor, he was embittered by his experiences in France and for several years wrote less imaginative and more pessimistic stories. The effect of World War I on Dunsany's writing, both in theme and in mood, reflects the tremendous impact that the war had on the horror short story in general. In fact, World War I is in many respects the dividing line between the world of the old-fashioned ghost story, and a science fiction world in which the traditional horror story is somewhat anachronistic. It was during World War I that most people realized for the first time the truly hellish potential of the technological revolution. Traditional horror stories such as Poe's, Le Fanu's, and James's, which depict the sufferings, however horrible, of single individuals, seemed inadequate expressions of the state of danger which now threatened the entire world. Readers continued to enjoy the thrill of ghost stories which had already been written; and some established authors, such as M. R. James and Algernon Blackwood, continued to produce traditional horror stories. Very few of the serious writers who emerged after World War I, however, were interested in carrying on the old-fashioned horror-story tradition.

One of the few postwar writers who did continue to use the horror short story not only for sensational entertainment but also for serious social and psychological commentary was Howard Phillips Lovecraft. Lovecraft wrote a large number of horror short stories for the magazine *Weird Tales* and won for himself an enthusiastic audience of readers. Lovecraft himself was intensely misanthropic, and his isolation from the human race was aggravated by his many physical ailments. These included nervous disorders, nephritis, and poikilothermism, a rare disease which prevents the body from regulating its temperature in the way that warm-blooded mammals normally do. Because Lovecraft's body temperature fluctuated like a reptile's according to the temperature around him, he was severely limited in his ability to leave his own home. Lovecraft also had a pathological hatred of tobacco, liquor, seafood, salt water, cities, dogs, films, and much of the human race.

Lovecraft's antisocial attitudes are evident in his horror short stories. Like Stevenson and Wells, although to a greater degree, Lovecraft was obsessed with the idea of the semibestial nature of man. Therefore, he tended to center his stories around miscegenation between men and beasts, or sometimes between men and horrors from another dimension. He was also fascinated by the idea of a human personality being dispossessed and replaced by an alien intelligence. In many of Lovecraft's stories, these themes are acted out in a totally original setting, and/or by completely imaginary beings that usually have a multitude of antennae, suction cups, and amorphous protuberances. As a result, Lovecraft is a transitional figure between the horror short-story and the fantasy and science-fiction genres.

One of Lovecraft's stories which clearly illustrates his view of the human condition is the chilling tale "The Rats in the Walls." The protagonist of this story, de la Poer, is a wealthy American who is the sole surviving member of an ancient British noble family. The ancestor who had moved to the American colonies had first murdered his entire family, with the heartfelt approval of the civil and religious authorities. The secret of his reason for doing so, passed down in a sealed envelope from one generation to the next, had been lost in a fire during the American Civil War. Returning to England in ignorance of his family's evil, de la Poer sets about restoring the long-neglected family castle. He is puzzled by the hostility that the local villagers display toward him and toward his project, but he eventually completes the restoration. Once he has moved into the castle, de la Poer is disturbed by the noise of rats in the walls. Finally he and a guest hunt the rats down to the pre-Christian foundations of the castle, which had been the scene of savage sacrificial ceremonies. Below this level they discover a long-hidden lower crypt which apparently leads into the bowels of the earth. Moreover, the tunnel has been dug from beneath—upward from below the earth. In this lower crypt they find gnawed skeletons of all the stages of man, back through prehistoric evolutionary levels. There is also evidence that the de la Poers had, for centuries, bred and herded men in these crypts and used them as their staple food. As de la Poer enters the subterranean passage, picking his way over the piles of gnawed bones, he finds himself possessed by the ancestral spirit present in the cave. His speech degenerates through eighteenth century, Renaissance, and medieval English, then through Latin and Saxon to primitive grunts. He is finally overpowered, some hours later, while feeding on the body of his companion.

The point of this story is, of course, the innate bestial and cannibalistic savagery of so-called civilized man. The castle itself serves as the image of the human soul. It is newly covered over with wainscot and tapestry, as the essential de la Poer himself is covered with his few generations of harmless American progenitors. Underneath the new covering, however, the old walls remain, full of vermin and evil memories. Further, below the level that is open to the daylight and to the public view—sinister as even that may be— is an endless series of basements and crypts going back to a period before recorded history. There de la Poer succumbs to the urges of that part of his own soul which parallels these primeval surroundings: the indescribably bestial portion of him which, like the crypt itself, has been shaped by even darker forces emanating from as yet older and lower levels of existence. Lovecraft, who admired and was influenced by Poe, shared something of Poe's sense that real evil and real terror are not outside but inside the human soul. His conception of the nature of that soul, however, is even blacker than Poe's. In most of Poe's stories, the sufferer has earned his pain by personal evil; but in Lovecraft's world, humanity is its own damnation.

Despite Lovecraft's popularity with the comparatively elite reading audience of *Weird Tales*, it is probable that he would have fallen into obscurity had it not been for the efforts of August Derleth. Derleth admired Lovecraft's work immensely, and after Lovecraft's death in 1937, Derleth collected a number of his stories and offered them to several publishers. No one was interested. So Derleth and another writer of horror short stories, Donald Wandrei, founded Arkam House for the purpose of publishing Lovecraft's work, Derleth's and Wandrei's own stories, and the tales of writers such as Robert Bloch, Carl Jacobi, and H. Russell Wakefield. Because of his own interest in the genre, and because he provided serious authors of horror short stories with a place to publish their work, August Derleth was largely responsible for keeping the horror short story alive at all during the latter part of the twentieth century. In addition to his work with horror stories, Derleth continued the Cthulhu Mythos which Lovecraft had originated and wrote and published other forms of the fantasy short story.

Despite the efforts of Derleth and his associates, the number and the general quality of horror short stories is steadily declining. One reason for this is the increased interest in mystery, fantasy, and science fiction—all of which derive, to some extent, from the horror short story—on the part of those who might once have been the audience for horror short stories as such. Another reason for the decline of horror short stories is the fact that the periodicals which once carried them have been replaced as a vehicle of popular entertainment by television, films, radio, and paperback novels. The horror literature which is popular today tends to be sensational rather than reflective in nature; and the same is true of contemporary horror films and television programs. Even within the circle of those who enjoy traditional horror short stories, there is a feeling that very little unexplored ground is left; and writers tend to branch off into related but less worked-over genres. Many of the issues which underlay serious horror short stories in the nineteenth and early twentieth centuries, such as religious skepticism, materialism, personality fragmentation, and evolution, are now too well known and too widely accepted to carry the impact they once did. Finally, the highly symbolic nature of horror short stories, combined with the psychological nature of the subject matter they often treat, has made them the target of Freudian criticism which goes beyond explicating the story to psychoanalyzing the writer. Some of the images in Henry James's ghost stories, for example, have led several of his critics to speculate about the probability of his sexual impotence; and Le Fanu's "Green Tea" has led to interpretations which question his own emotional balance. It is not surprising, therefore, that current writers of horror short stories are reluctant to "let themselves go" in ways that might produce striking horror stories but embarrassing interpretations.

Bibliography
Ashley, Mike. *Who's Who in Horror and Fantasy Fiction.*

Barclay, Glen St. John. *Anatomy of Horror: The Masters of Occult Fiction.*
Briggs, Julia. *Night Visitors: The Rise and Fall of the English Ghost Story.*
Haining, Peter, ed. *The Penny Dreadful; Or, Strange, Horrid and Sensational Tales.*
_____ . *Terror! A History of Horror Illustrations from the Pulp Magazines.*
Lovecraft, Howard Phillips. *Supernatural Horror in Literature.*

Joan DelFattore

DETECTIVE SHORT FICTION

Detective Elements in Pre-Nineteenth Century Literature

In the broadest sense, the idea of detecting crime and criminals has appeared in literature since ancient times. The Book of Daniel, for example, includes an episode in which the prophet saves a young woman from unjust execution by exposing two perjured witnesses; and in Book VIII of Vergil's *Aeneid*, the hero Hercules encounters the first recorded set of forged footprints. The detective element in ancient tales such as these, however, plays a small and relatively unimportant part in the plot. The same is true of the detective element which appears in a few medieval legends and in some examples of Renaissance prose.

A reasonably close approach to the detective story did, however, appear in London in 1776 with the publication of *The Annals of Newgate: Or, Malefactor's Register* (4 volumes) by the Reverend John Villette, chaplain of Newgate Prison. The chaplains of Newgate had for many years published the confessions and/or the last words of condemned criminals; these were usually sold in the form of broadsheets to the crowds which attended the public executions of these criminals. The Reverend Villette, however, included in *The Annals of Newgate* a detailed description of the way in which each criminal discussed in the book was caught. For example, Villette explains that the notorious highwayman Dick Turpin escaped detection for several years by living quietly at York under the name of John Palmer. One day, he became drunk, shot his landlord's rooster, and threatened to shoot the neighbor who tried to interfere. The neighbor complained to the magistrates, who had Turpin/Palmer arrested and jailed. Turpin wrote to his brother in Essex for money to buy his way out of prison, but the brother did not claim the letter for several days. Meanwhile, Turpin's former schoolmaster saw the unclaimed letter, recognized the handwriting, and confirmed his suspicion by comparing the writing on the envelope with some old school exercise books Turpin had written while he was a student. The schoolmaster reported his finding, and Turpin was located, tried for highway robbery, and executed.

The Annals of Newgate and its successors, especially the various issues of *The Newgate Calendar* and *The New Newgate Calendar*, became the source for a number of "Newgate novels" which centered around the exploits of these criminals. A romanticized version of Turpin, for example, is the hero of several such works, including *Rookwood* (3 volumes, 1834) and *Jack Sheppard* (3 volumes, 1839), published anonymously by William Harrison Ainsworth. These "Newgate novels" were, however, picaresque or rogue tales rather than true detective stories. In spite of the attention given to the detection of crime in these and other early works, the idea of writing a story which featured a detector of crime as the hero and detection as the central point of the story, would have been unthinkable before the nineteenth century.

Police and friends of police had traditionally been associated in the minds of most people with the oppressive secret police forces of totalitarian states; and in the struggle between the individual and organized authority, public sympathy was usually with the individual.

Because of this attitude, citizens of countries which regarded themselves as democracies, including England and the United States, looked with suspicion on proposals to form any sort of organized police force because they feared the loss of individual liberty. By the late 1820's, however, growing industrialization and large-scale immigration were beginning to lead to overcrowded cities where frequent riots were becoming a serious problem and where the crime rates were rising very quickly. As a result, many citizens, especially members of the upper and middle classes who were concerned about protecting their property, were willing to risk the formation of an organized police force to control these disturbances. The Sûreté was founded in Paris in 1810, and London had its first official police force in 1829. In 1842, the Detective Department was established in London for the exclusive purpose of crime detection. New York established its Police Department in 1845, and other American cities soon followed. Most important, the attitude of many people was veering toward sympathy with the idea of the detective who could, without infringing on the liberty of the individual, protect the social order and help to keep the peace by uncovering crimes and identifying criminals.

One of the most direct connections between the rise of the detective police and the detective story was the influence of the *Memoires* of François Eugène Vidocq, published in 1828-1829. Vidocq was a reformed criminal who became the first head of the Sûreté and later founded the first modern detective agency, Le Bureau des Renseignements. Vidocq's autobiography is not entirely reliable—in fact, it has been suggested that so much of the book is untrue that Vidocq should be considered the father of detective fiction. In any case, the *Memoires* introduce a number of elements which are important in early detective fiction, including the idea of contempt for routine police methods and glorification of the detective genius who can solve a case by drawing inferences from apparently unimportant clues. Vidocq also prepared the way for the detective story by providing the inspiration for a number of early detective characters and plots, and by creating an audience for such stories by stirring up popular interest in the detection of crime.

The Beginning of the Detective Story

The world's first true detective story—that is, the first story which centered exclusively on the process of solving a crime—was Edgar Allan Poe's "The Murders in the Rue Morgue," which appeared in *Graham's Magazine* in April, 1841. "The Murders in the Rue Morgue" is a locked-room mystery in which a murder takes place in a room which is apparently closed in such a way that no one could enter or leave it. The protagonist of the story, the Chevalier C. Auguste Dupin, solves the mystery by drawing logical conclusions—or, to use Poe's term, by "ratiocination"—thus representing the beginning of the analytical school of detection. Dupin, like many of his successors, is highly eccentric; for example, he refuses to come out of his house in the daylight, and he is completely passionless. His companion, the narrator of the Dupin stories, is the prototype of the admiring but slightly dense friend who records and publishes the detective's exploits; this type of character later became known as a "Watson" figure, after Sherlock Holmes's famous companion.

Poe's second detective story, "The Mystery of Marie Rogêt," appeared as a serial in *Snowden's Ladies' Companion* for November and December, 1842, and February, 1843. The story is based on an actual crime—the murder of Mary Cecilia Rogers in New York City in July, 1841. Dupin solves the mystery entirely on the basis of evidence which he gleans from newspaper cuttings about the crime, which are virtual copies of actual newspaper articles on the fate of Mary Cecilia Rogers. Since Dupin does no investigating at all, but solves the problem by applying reason to the facts which are brought to him, "The Mystery of Marie Rogêt" is the first example of "armchair" detection. It is also the first story in which a writer of detective fiction undertakes to solve an actual case.

Poe's third and last detective story, "The Purloined Letter," appeared in *The Gift* for 1845 (published at the end of 1844). As the title indicates, Dupin locates a stolen letter, thus solving the first of a long line of detective stories based on that idea. The letter is hidden by not being hidden; that is, it has been placed in such an obvious location that the police have overlooked it entirely. This idea of hiding something in the open has also become a convention of detective stories. Dupin's method of solving the problem anticipates the advent of the psychological detective: Dupin reasons that since the thief knew that his house would be searched thoroughly, and since he was both intelligent and bold, he would attempt to hide the letter in just the way he did.

Poe's contribution of a new story form to literature was not immediately recognized in America. A collection of his detective stories was published as *Tales* in 1845; the volume includes "The Gold Bug," which many modern writers do not consider a true detective story, as well as the three Dupin stories. No other book containing a detective story by an American was published until 1862, when Thomas Bailey Aldrich's *Out of His Head* appeared. Chapters XI through XIV constitute a detective short story in themselves, featuring a detective, Paul Lynde, who exaggerates Dupin's eccentricity to the point of madness. The plot is a variation of the locked-room device used in "The Murders in the Rue Morgue," but Aldrich contributes the original idea of making the detective responsible for the fact that the murder takes place.

The Early Detective Story in England

Although Edgar Allan Poe's work had an indirect influence on the British detective story, its direct antecedents were stories of police work which either were, or purported to be, true. For example, a number of Bow Street Runners, members of a loosely knit group of law officers who recovered stolen goods or captured criminals in order to collect rewards, published their reminiscences during the 1820's, 1830's, and 1840's. The best known of these works is *Richmond: Or, Scenes in the Life of a Bow Street Officer: Drawn up from His Private Memoranda* (1827; written anonymous but attributed to Thomas Gaspey). In 1850, Charles Dickens published four articles based on the work of some plainclothes police friends, and this in turn sparked a new series of more or less fictional accounts supposedly based on real-life police experiences. The most important of these were *Recollections of a Detective Police-Officer* (1856) and a number of later volumes of short stories by William Russell, who wrote under the pen name of "Waters." "Waters," who wrote his stories in the first person, claimed to be a member of London's Metropolitan Police Force with two assistants, one of whom was an expert ventriloquist. The success that "Waters" enjoyed attracted a number of imitators, who wrote for the inexpensive British "yellowbacks."

In addition to his articles on police work, Charles Dickens wrote several detective short stories, including "Hunted Down" (1859), based on the story of Thomas Griffiths Wainewright, a notorious poisoner. (William) Wilkie Collins also wrote a number of early detective short stories, although he is better known for his novel *The Moonstone* (1868). The most significant of the early British detectives, and one of the most important fictional detectives in the world, is of course Sir Arthur Conan Doyle's Sherlock Holmes. Doyle was an unsuccessful medical doctor whose lack of patients left him with a great deal of free time and the need to make a living in some other way. After writing some rather unsuccessful minor pieces, Doyle had the idea of modeling a detective character on Dr. Joseph Bell, a tall, hawk-nosed man whose insistence on minute observation and logical deduction had impressed Doyle when he was Bell's pupil in medical school. The first Sherlock Holmes story, *A Study in Scarlet*, appeared in November, 1887, in the twenty-eighth issue of *Beeton's Christmas Annual*. Holmes became popular when the editor of *Lippincott's Magazine* read *A Study in Scarlet* and offered to pay Doyle handsomely for another Holmes story. In February, 1890, *The Sign of Four* appeared in that magazine, and from then on there was a market for as many Holmes stories as Doyle could produce. Most of Doyle's short stories appeared in *The Strand Magazine*, beginning with "The Adventure of a Scandal in Bohemia" (1891). In this story, Holmes meets Irene Adler, the only woman—and one of the few people—who ever outsmarted him. Thereafter, Holmes always refers to her admiringly as "*the* woman." Other popular Holmes stories include "The Adventure of the Blue Carbuncle," a Christmas-time adventure centering around a stolen gem hidden inside a live Christmas goose; "The Adventure of the Speckled Band," a locked-room mystery in which a scheming stepfather employs a trained swamp adder as a murder weapon; and "The Red-Headed League," which begins with an advertisement which clogs one of London's streets with red-headed men looking for an easy way to make money.

Holmes's eccentricities—his deerstalker cap, his violin, his shag tobacco kept in the toe of a Persian slipper, his habit of shooting patterns of bullets into the sitting room wall, his use of cocaine—have become part of one of the most popular characterizations in fiction. Holmes's ability to draw conclusions from apparently meaningless data, such as the spacing of a dog's toothmarks on a walking stick or the discoloration of a man's thumb, is reminiscent of both Vidocq and Dupin; but Doyle added to his character a furious nervous energy expended in intensive searches for clues. Doyle also placed Sherlock Holmes against a vividly drawn background of gaslight, hansom cabs, London fogs, and misty moors. In fact, the Sherlock Holmes stories give such an impression of reality that many people have written letters of appeal to the fictitious address at 221B Baker Street. There are also several organizations devoted to Sherlockiana, including the Baker Street Irregulars, an American group whose members are forbidden to refer to Sir Arthur Conan Doyle except as "Dr. Watson's literary agent."

The Rise of the *Scientific Detective*

Both Dupin and Holmes relied heavily on the use of logic to determine the real significance of physical evidence. A number of their successors in the period before World War I relied on the same combination—logic and physical evidence—but some emphasized the process of thought and became known as "thinking machine" detectives, while others emphasized the collection and analysis of physical evidence and became known as "scientific" detectives.

The first American after Poe to publish a book devoted exclusively to detective short stories was Jacques Futrelle, whose Professor Augustus S. F. X. Van Dusen was known as "The Thinking Machine." Van Dusen uses his powers of reasoning to solve cases brought to him by a reporter, Hutchinson Hatch. The Professor's most famous adventure is "The Problem of Cell 13," in which he wins a bet by using logic to escape from a cell on death row. This story appeared in *The Thinking Machine* (1907; reissued as *The Problem of Cell 13* in 1917). This was followed by *The Thinking Machine on the Case* (1908; British title, *The Professor on the Case*). Other stories appeared in volumes of short stories not devoted exclusively to Professor Van Dusen, in *Ellery Queen's Mystery Magazine*, and in newspapers during 1905 and 1906.

A British version of the thinking machine detective appeared at approximately the same time in the person of Baroness Emmuska Orczy's Old Man in the Corner, who sits at a corner table of an ABC tea shop, eating cheesecake and tying intricate knots in a piece of string, as he uses logic to solve cases brought to him by a young female reporter, Polly Burton. (This type of detective, who solves cases by analyzing the information brought to him by someone else, is also known as the "armchair" detective.) When Baroness Orczy grew tired of her character, she conceived a highly original way of getting rid of him: the last case that Polly Burton describes to the Old Man in the Corner hinges on the clue of some intricate knots tied in a window cord. As the reporter raises her eyes in sudden suspicion when she thinks of the Old Man's constantly busy fingers, she sees that he has gone; and he is never heard from again. Books about the Old Man in the Corner are *The Case of Miss Elliott* (1905), *The Old Man in the Corner* (1909; United States title, *The Man in the Corner*), and *Unravelled Knots* (1925).

As the twentieth century began and the technological revolution gathered momentum, a number of detective-story writers turned their attention to the process of collecting and analyzing scientific data. The most famous of these post-Holmesian scientific detectives was R. Austin Freeman's Dr. John Thorndyke, an expert in forensic medicine. Like Doyle, Freeman was a medical doctor who turned to writing detective fiction; and like Doyle, Freeman modeled his character to some extent on a former professor from medical school, in this case Dr. Alfred Swaine Taylor, a forensic scientist. The Thorndyke stories are now appreciated chiefly for the painstaking precision of their plots, although some experts in the field of detective literature regard them as classics. Freeman was also responsible for the invention of the "inverted" detective story in *The Singing Bone* (1912). The stories in this volume begin with a discussion of who committed the crime, how, and why, and the reader then watches the detective unraveling clues and moving toward a solution. This technique anticipates the psychological detective tale by allowing the reader access to the mind and motives of the criminal throughout the story. Volumes of short stories about Dr. Thorndyke include *John Thorndyke's Cases* (1909; United States title, *Dr. Thorndyke's Cases*); *The Singing Bone* (1912); *Dr. Thorndyke's Case Book* (1923; United States title, *The Blue Scarab*); *The Puzzle Lock* (1925); and *The Magic Casket* (1927).

The rise of psychology as an accepted field of scientific study led to a number of stories in which the detective solves a case through understanding the psychology of the criminal and/or of the victim. The first story of this type was "The Man in the Room" by Edwin Balmer and William MacHarg, in which their detective, Luther Trant, solves a case by measuring the lapsed time in a psychological association test. Luther Trant never became very popular, but one of his imitators, Arthur B. Reeve's Craig Kennedy, did. Kennedy, a professor of chemistry at Columbia University, uses psychoanalysis in solving cases. He is also the first fictional detective to rely heavily on machines such as the lie detector, the gyroscope, and the seismograph, which were all novel and rather mysterious gadgets in the early years of the twentieth century. The long series of Kennedy short stories began with *The Silent Bullet* (1912) and ended with *Craig Kennedy on the Farm* (1925). Arthur B. Reeve also served as editorial consultant for the magazine *Scientific Detective Monthly*. The publisher of this magazine also published an early radio and popular science magazine, *Electrical Experimenter* (later *Science and Invention*), which occasionally carried scientific detective stories. Many of these stories feature Joe Fenner, who solves technologically oriented problems such as the case of "The Educated Harpoon" (April, 1920), in which a radio-controlled model airplane stabs a man to death on the sixteenth floor of a skyscraper.

The Intuitive Detective

Not all the early fictional detectives are masters of logic and/or science. Some, like G. K. Chesterton's Father Brown, solve cases by using common sense and a type of intuition which is based on an understanding of human nature. Father Brown, a dumpy little man whose rather blank round face suggests a grown-up Charlie Brown, solves mysteries whose fantastic or paradoxical nature contrasts with Brown's own prosaic appearance and behavior. The Father Brown stories are often poetic variations on detective story techniques developed by earlier writers: for example, "The Miracle of Moon Crescent" is a locked-room mystery in which a man is removed from an apparently sealed chamber and hanged by the neck from a tree in a nearby park; "The Flying Stars" features a jewel thief who uses the idea of hiding something in the most obvious place by including stolen gems among the paste stones of his masquerade costume; and in "The Secret Garden," Father Brown accuses a Vidocq-like criminal/police officer of beheading a man in his own garden and then hiding the crime by substituting the head of a guillotined convict for the head of the victim. The Father Brown stories are collected in *The Innocence of Father Brown* (1911); *The Wisdom of Father Brown* (1914); *The Incredulity of Father Brown* (1926); *The Secret of Father Brown* (1927); and *The Scandal of Father Brown* (1935). All the Father Brown stories are also collected in *The Father Brown Omnibus* (1951).

Melville Davisson Post's Uncle Abner is another early example of the intuitive detective. Post actually started out writing stories about a clever but unscrupulous lawyer named Randolph Mason, who cleared his clients, innocent or guilty, by exploiting legal technicalities and loopholes. In the last book of Mason stories, however, Post was moved by conscience and/or by public opinion to have his character reform and begin to use his skill to fight for justice. By the time he began to publish Uncle Abner stories ten years later, Post had moved to the opposite extreme from the earlier Randolph Mason stories. Uncle Abner regards himself as the instrument of divine justice, ordained by God to prevent malefactors from escaping the punishment they deserve. Uncle Abner is a Virginia squire of Lincolnesque appearance who carries a Bible in his pocket, and is often compared in the stories with such religious leaders as Oliver Cromwell. One of the best-known Uncle Abner stories is "An Act of God," in which Uncle Abner clears a deaf man accused of a crime by pointing out that a note the man is supposed to have written contains a phonetic misspelling. There are only two collections of Uncle Abner stories in book form: *Uncle Abner: Master of Mysteries* (1918) and *The Methods of Uncle Abner* (1974; this is a compilation of stories which had not been published previously in book form). Uncle Abner influenced the characterization of Uncle Gavin, the protagonist of William Faulkner's collection of detective stories, *Knight's Gambit* (1949).

The Golden Age of the Detective Story

The period between World War I and World War II is generally considered to have been the Golden Age of detective fiction. By that time, large numbers of people were literate, and had a certain amount of leisure time to spend on books. Rental libraries and public libraries were fairly widespread, and cheap editions of paperback books were available. Some of the detectives who appeared during this period are still popular today, but other fictional detectives who were widely read during the Golden Age represent both social and literary conventions which do not appeal to many modern readers.

One of the most popular detectives of the Golden Age was Henry Christopher Bailey's Reggie Fortune. Bailey began writing detective stories during World War I, when he was a war reporter trying to forget the fear and strain involved in his frequent visits to the front. The first collection of Reggie Fortune stories was published as *Call Mr. Fortune* in 1920; this was followed by *Mr. Fortune's Practice* (1923); *Mr. Fortune's Trials* (1925); *Mr. Fortune, Please* (1927); *Mr. Fortune Speaking* (1929); *Mr. Fortune Explains* (1930); *Case for Mr. Fortune* (1932); *Mr. Fortune Wonders* (1933); *Mr. Fortune Objects* (1935); *A Clue for Mr. Fortune* (1936); *This Is Mr. Fortune* (1938); and *Mr. Fortune Here* (1940). Reggie Fortune loves children and helps the persecuted; he is sympathetic toward suffering but can be hard when the occasion demands it. He is blond, blue-eyed, and youthful in appearance; a gourmet, an epicure, an upper-class Englishman who uses fashionable slang and seldom pronounces the last consonant of words ending in "ing." Fortune gets involved in mysteries because he is an adviser to Scotland Yard on medical matters, but his real interest is moral. The Reggie Fortune stories were written at a time when society had just been seriously disrupted by war, and when most people were looking forward to the reestablishment of an ordered way of life with firm standards and with effective sanctions against anyone who threatened that order. Therefore, much of the emphasis in the Reggie Fortune stories is on the protection and preservation of the moral and social standards which were prevalent at the time the stories were written, and, for this reason, they are not generally popular with modern audiences.

The rigid moral and social standards which prevailed in many Golden Age detective stories were paralleled by equally rigid literary standards. A number of the writers who flourished during this period believed that the detective story is first and foremost a puzzle or riddle which must be presented according to very specific rules and conventions; and that the detective writer's major responsibilities are to play fair with the reader by providing all relevant information, to avoid tricks and clichés, and to provide a logical but unexpected solution to the mystery. All other considerations, including depth of characterization and theme, were subordinated to these requirements of plot construction. Several writers formulated lists of rules governing such puzzle-oriented stories: Monsignor Ronald Knox, for example, wrote a "Detective Decalogue" or set of ten commandments forbidding the use of such tricks as sinister Chinamen, late-appearing criminals, supernatural solutions, concealed clues, or suppressed thoughts on the part of the Watson figure. Members of the prestigious Detection Club also had to swear upon admission that they would not conceal clues from the reader, or solve mysteries by means of "Divine Revelation, Feminine Intuition, Mumbo-Jumbo, Jiggery-Pokery, Coincidence or the Act of God." The most popular and the most influential of this school of detective-story writers was S. S. Van Dine (pen name of Willard Huntington Wright). Van Dine created the character of the brilliant but effete Philo Vance, whose trademark is the imported Regie cigarettes with rose petal tips which he smokes in a platinum-rimmed ivory cigarette holder. Unfortunately, Van Dine did not write any short stories; but he exercised a great deal of influence over those who did.

Of course, the fact that it was writers of the period known as the Golden Age who were largely responsible for formulating and popularizing many of these rules for detective fiction does not mean that the practice of writing puzzle-oriented stories began with them. Many of the early armchair and scientific detective stories, including some of the Holmes adventures, are designed as puzzles which provide the reader with the clues necessary to unravel the case before the solution is revealed on the last page. Although many Golden Age writers believed in strict adherence to the rules of presenting a puzzle or riddle story, there were a few rebels. For example, although Agatha Christie followed the rules closely in several of her early works, she soon began to deviate from them for the sake of surprise endings or more interesting plots. In her most famous work, a novel entitled *The Murder of Roger Ackroyd* (1926), Christie committed the technical "fault" of concealing the thoughts of the Watson figure in order to allow him to be the murderer. Purists, including S. S. Van Dine, did not consider this solution of the mystery to be acceptable practice in detective-story writing; but some detective-fiction writers, notably Dorothy L. Sayers, defended it. Most importantly, the public loved it, and Agatha Christie became one of the most popular detective-story writers of the period. She has since violated most of the rules in the Detection Club's oath at one time or another, to the intense annoyance of those who enjoy identifying the criminal for themselves, and who therefore feel cheated by Christie's occasional failure to provide them with all the pertinent information. Because of her zest and her emphasis on making her plots interesting and exciting, however, Christie's books have remained extremely popular.

Agatha Christie's two most important characters are variations of the armchair detective. Miss Marple, an elderly spinster who knits with soft pink wool and loves gossip, resembles both the intuitive and the psychological detectives as she solves crimes by seeing parallels between the behavior of people involved in a crime and the behavior of people with similar personalities who live in her little village, St. Mary Mead. Hercule Poirot, the little Belgian detective with the great mustaches and the pointed patent leather shoes, solves crimes by employing his "little gray cells" on the problems which are brought to him. He relies heavily on information gathered by interviewing suspects, and has little patience with the type of physical evidence—cigar ash, footprints, and so forth—associated with Sherlock Holmes and the scientific detectives. In one adventure he says to a friend who has suggested searching for footprints, "Am I the dog, Hastings, that I should cry 'Woof, woof' and sniff along the ground?" Poirot is modeled to some extent on Robert Barr's Eugene Valmont, one of the first important humorous detectives in English literature. Valmont, who appears in book form only in *The Triumphs of Eugene Valmont* (1906), is fooled much more easily than the shrewd Poirot, but they share a humorous pomposity and a tendency toward bombast which amuse English and American audiences. This element of humor is another factor which makes Christie's books so popular. Christie occasionally uses other detective characters, such as Parker Pyne, Harley Quin, and Tuppence and Tommy Beresford, but she is best known for Poirot and Miss Marple. Agatha Christie's short stories are collected in *Poirot Investigations* (1924); *Partners in Crime* (1929; Tuppence and Tommy Beresford solve a series of cases, each of which is a pastiche of a well-known fictional detective character such as Dr. Thorndyke, Sherlock Holmes, Father Brown, the Old Man in the Corner, Reggie Fortune, and Hercule Poirot); *The Mysterious Mr. Quin* (1930); *The Thirteen Problems* (1932; United States title, *The Tuesday Club Murders*); *The Hound of Death and Other Stories* (1933); *The Listerdale Mystery* (1934); *Parker Pyne Investigates* (1934; United States title, *Mr. Parker Pyne—Detective*); *Murder in the Mews and Other Stories* (1937; United States title, *Dead Man's Mirror*); *The Regatta Mystery and Other Stories* (1939); *The Labours of Hercules* (1947); *The Witness for the Prosecution and Other Stories* (1948); *Three Blind Mice and Other Stories* (1950); *The Under Dog and Other Mysteries* (1951); *The Adventure of the Christmas Pudding* (1960); *Double Sin and Other Stories* (1961); and *The Golden Ball and Other Stories* (1971).

Another writer of the Golden Age whose works are still read today is Dorothy Leigh Sayers. Like Agatha Christie, Sayers sometimes violated the strict rules of detective fiction in order to make her stories more interesting. She did try at first to keep romance and emotional entanglements out of her stories because she felt that these would interfere with the detective element; however, she also attempted to join the detective story with the novel of manners in order to bring it closer to more standard or "serious" literature, and this eventually led to the inclusion of emotional interplay among the characters in her stories. Further, Sayers apparently had an intense emotional attachment of her own to her detective, Lord Peter Wimsey; she tended, therefore, to describe and discuss him in highly personal terms.

Lord Peter Wimsey belongs to the school of aristocratic dilettantes which includes Reggie Fortune, and like him Lord Peter uses fashionable slang, pronounces "ing" "in'," and has assorted personality quirks and small eccentricities which some readers find maddening. Many of Lord Peter's mannerisms, however, are represented as being his defense against the effects of an unhappy love affair and of a case of "shell shock" following World War I; and as Wimsey ages, his eccentricities tend to decrease. Further, Wimsey is essentially down-to-earth and tolerant of other people's quirks and inadequacies. Wimsey, with the help of his Jeeves-like servant Bunter, solves problems which usually have some element of the bizarre or the fantastic about them. In "The Abominable History of the Man with the Copper Fingers," for example, a murdered woman has been silver-plated and made into a modernistic sofa. Lord Peter pushes the murderer into his own electro-plating vat, purchases the sofa at an auction of the dead villain's belongings, and gives it a decent burial. In another popular story, "In the Teeth of the Evidence," a dentist fakes his own suicide by murdering another man, changing the corpse's dental work to correspond to the murderer's own dental record, and then burning the body.

Sayers wrote a few detective stories about Montague Egg, a wine salesman, but most of her detective fiction centered around Lord Peter. Her short stories are collected in *Lord Peter Views the Body* (1928); *Hangman's Holiday* (1933); and *In the Teeth of the Evidence* (1939). *Lord Peter* (1972; edited by James Sandoe) contains all the Lord Peter stories, including "The Haunted Policeman" and "Striding Folly," which had appeared previously only in magazine form, and "Talboys," which had been written in 1942 but never previously published. In her later years, Dorothy L. Sayers turned from detective fiction to writing critical or religious material. During these years she sometimes spoke slightingly of her detective stories; but, like Sir Arthur Conan Doyle, she is remembered chiefly for these and not for her more "serious" writing.

Detective Short Fiction in Magazine Form

One of the factors which contributed to the popularity of the detective short story from its inception through the Golden Age was its availability in magazine form. The early landmark tales, such as Poe's Dupin stories and Doyle's Sherlock Holmes stories, appeared in this form before they were collected between hard covers. Besides the better detective stories which appeared in reasonably prestigious magazines, however, there were a number of detective stories written expressly for inexpensive magazines which specialized in sensational fiction. In Britain, Penny Bloods and Penny Dreadfuls provided the nineteenth century reader with inexpensive—and often poorly written—sensational literature, including crime and detective stories. In the United States, Dime Novels, originally called Beadle's Dime Novels, were published in paperback between 1860 and 1874 by Irwin Pedro Beadle. The word "novel" is used loosely, since these were sometimes collections of short stories; and the whole phrase is now used to refer to any paperback sensational fiction published in the United States between 1860 and 1915. The Dime Novels originally featured frontier heroes, but as more people began to move to the cities, the Dime Novels centered around city heroes, often detectives. The first Dime Novel weekly which published only detective stories was the *Old Cap. Collier Library*, published from April 9, 1883, until September 9, 1889.

Some weekly magazines were devoted exclusively to the exploits of one detective hero. In the United States, the most popular of these was Street and Smith's *Nick Carter Library* (August 8, 1891, to December 26, 1896), which was succeeded by the *Nick Carter Weekly* (January 2, 1897, to September 7, 1912) and *Nick Carter Stories* (September 14, 1912, to October 2, 1915). This in turn became the pulp magazine *Detective Story* (October 5, 1915, to Summer, 1949). Nick Carter stories were written by a number of authors, notably Frederick Van Rensselaer Dey, who wrote more Nick Carter stories than any other single author—more than one thousand. Nick Carter was originally a dashing, handsome all-American boy who was physically and intellectually keen, a master of disguise, and a defender of virtue and of the moral order. He never smoked, drank, swore, or fornicated. Nick Carter stories are still being written and published in paperback form, but the ageless Carter—who should be approximately 108 years old—is now a spy operating more or less in the tradition of James Bond.

In Britain, the most popular of these weekly magazines devoted to one character was *Union Jack*, featuring stories about Sexton Blake, and later *The Sexton Blake Magazine*. Sexton Blake lives on Baker Street and has a boy-Watson named Tinker, a landlady named Mrs. Bardell, and a bloodhound named Pedro. The first Sexton Blake story, "The Missing Millionaire," appeared on December 20, 1893, in a boys' paper called *The Halfpenny Marvel*. Blake stories are still being written, and he has now solved more cases than any other fictional detective, with Nick Carter a close second. Like the Carter stories, the Sexton Blake stories are written by several different authors.

A number of inexpensive magazines published during the period between the wars were known as pulp magazines because of their untrimmed wood pulp paper. These magazines carried various kinds of sensational stories, including detective fiction; Street and Smith's *Detective Story*, which succeeded the Nick Carter magazines in 1915, was the first of these pulp magazines to be devoted exclusively to crime fiction. Later crime-oriented pulp magazines included *Black Mask*, *Dime Detective*, and *Detective Fiction Weekly*. Several of the people who worked for these pulp magazines were hack writers whose stories are deservedly forgotten; but one set of writers not only became part of the mainstream of detective fiction, but also introduced a major innovation into the genre: the hardboiled school.

The Hardboiled School

On June 1, 1923, a story entitled "Knights of the Open Palm," by Carroll John Daly, was published in *Black Mask*. Its protagonist, Race Williams, introduced himself in this way: "I'm what you might call a middleman—just a half-way house between the cops and the crooks. . . . I do a little honest shooting once in awhile—just in the way of business—but I never bumped off a guy that didn't need it." With those words, the hardboiled detective story was born.

The hardboiled detective was a reaction against the effete dilettantes epitomized in Philo Vance. Stories featuring hardboiled detectives challenged what Julian Symons called "The fairy tale land of the Golden Age . . . in which murder was committed over and over again without anybody getting hurt." The writers of the hardboiled school took murder out of the country house atmosphere of traditional detective stories and put it out on the streets; and violent action took the place of intricate plots and academic murder puzzles. The sordid sex, poverty, and police brutality which accompany many real crimes appeared for the first time in detective fiction. This movement, of course, paralleled the social changes following World War I, and the growing tendency toward realism and naturalism in nondetective literature. Americans were disgusted with increasing political corruption, with the acceptance of gangsters into socially and financially powerful circles, and with the growing crime rate; and these concerns were reflected in the stories of the hardboiled school. These stories reversed the right-wing tendencies of earlier detective fiction, which usually involved the middle and upper classes and in which the main concern was often the preservation or restoration of the social order. The new stories involved all classes and included a rough sort of social commentary which was often unflattering to the propertied and politically powerful classes.

A number of authors produced hardboiled stories for the pulp magazines; among the better writers were Carroll John Daly, Cornell Hopley-Woolrich (who also wrote as Cornell Woolrich, William Irish, and George Hopley), and Erle Stanley Gardner (pre-Perry Mason; he also wrote as Charles M. Green, Robert Parr, Kyle Corning, Les Tillray, Carleton Kendrake, and Charles Kenny). The two leaders of this subgenre, however, were Samuel Dashiell Hammett and Raymond Chandler.

Dashiell Hammett's detective fiction was based to some extent on his own experiences and on the experiences of acquaintances at the Baltimore office of the Pinkerton National Detective Agency. Hammett's work took him to a number of other cities, including San Francisco, which later became the scene of many of his fictional cases. Hammett, like his contemporaries in the hardboiled school, was reacting against both the literary conventions of traditional detective fiction and the absence of social reality in such stories. In fact, Hammett's own socialist views got him into trouble with Senator Joseph McCarthy's subcommittee in 1953, and he and his stories went through a period of unpopularity as a result; but much of it had cleared away before his death in 1961. Hammett was an extremely talented writer whose clear, incisive prose style is believed to have influenced writers of "serious" fiction, including Ernest Hemingway; and some of Hammett's heroes resemble Hemingway's in the sense that, although they live in a hard and sordid world and sometimes come to terms with that world through hard and sordid acts of their own, they have an unconventional code of courage and integrity to which they adhere religiously.

Hammett's most famous short story detectives are Sam Spade and the Continental Op. Sam Spade is described as having the face of a fair Satan, with his jaw, chin, mouth, nostrils, eyebrows, and widow's peak forming a series of V's. Spade recognizes the unlovely realities of his own life and of other people's lives, but he remains idealistic in his search for justice. The Continental Op, an unnamed operative for a large detective agency, is a chubby man whose toughness and cynicism, like Spade's, accompany a real desire for justice. Hammett's stories appeared in magazine form, particularly in *Black Mask*, throughout the 1920's, 1930's, and 1940's. Many of his stories were later collected in book form in *The Adventures of Sam Spade and Other Stories* (1944); *The Continental Op* (1945); *The Return of the Continental Op* (1945); *Hammett Homicides* (1946); *Dead Yellow Women* (1947); *Nightmare Town* (1948); *The Creeping Siamese* (1950); *Woman in the Dark* (1952); *A Man Named Thin and Other Stories* (1962); and *The Big Knockover and Other Stories* (1966).

The other major early writer of hardboiled detective fiction was Raymond Chandler, a Quaker whose passion for justice became a leading characteristic of his detectives. Chandler worked in the oil industry until he lost his position in 1929, when he turned to writing fiction. He used several different names for the detectives in his early stories, but he was writing about the same character in all of them, and he finally gave that character the name of Philip Marlowe. (Many of the early stories have since been reissued with the name of the detective changed to Marlowe.) Like Hammett, Chandler was a very talented writer, and his style—particularly his descriptions and his use of metaphor—is far superior to that of some writers of more standard fiction. His collections of short stories include *Five Murderers* (1944); *Five Sinister Characters* (1945); *Finger Man and Other Stories* (1946); and *The Simple Art of Murder* (1950). *Killer in the Rain* (1964), which was published after Chandler's death, includes several stories which Chandler had used as sources for novels and which he had, therefore, refused to publish in book form.

Chandler wrote an explanation of his own beliefs and goals in writing detective fiction in an often-quoted essay entitled "The Simple Art of Murder," which summarizes the world of Chandler's stories and contrasts it with the drawing-room atmosphere of traditional detective fiction. In part, it says:

> The realist in murder writes of a world in which gangsters can rule nations and almost rule cities . . . where the mayor of your town may have condoned murder as an instrument of money-making, where no man can walk down a dark street in safety because law and order are things we talk about but refrain from practicing. . . . But down these mean streets a man must go who is not himself mean, who is neither tarnished nor afraid. The detective in this kind of story must be such a man. He is the hero; he is everything.

In its own way, hardboiled detective fiction of the kind that Hammett and Chandler wrote is more romantic than traditional detective fiction because of its emphasis on a simple, common man who seeks justice in a corrupt and sordid world; and its primary influence on detective fiction as a whole stems from its emphasis on character and on realistic emotions rather than on murder as an intellectual puzzle.

The Modern Detective Story

The detective story following World War II is highly diversified: there are some puzzle stories, some hardboiled stories, some character-oriented stories, and all sorts of hybrids. Unfortunately, with the fading of the pulp magazines and the tendency of their successors to publish serialized novels rather than short stories, the detective short-story writer has lost one of his main sources of publication; and book publishers usually prefer novels to collections of short stories. There are a few detective story magazines still in existence, however, notably *Ellery Queen's Mystery Magazine*, which encourages the writing of detective short stories not only by providing a place for their publication but also by offering prizes for various kinds of stories: for example, best first story, best Sherlockiana, or best riddle story. Among the best-known of the modern writers who have published detective short stories in *Ellery Queen's Mystery Magazine* are Margery Allingham, Stanley Ellin, Hugh Pentecost, Roy Vickers, Georges Simenon, and Julian Symons. Ellery Queen has also edited several anthologies of detective short stories, including a series of volumes which contains in book form the best of the short stories which appeared originally in *Ellery Queen's Mystery Magazine*.

Ellery Queen himself has written a prodigious number of detective stories. Ellery Queen was originally the pen name of Frederick Dannay (Daniel Nathan) and his cousin Manfred B. Lee (Manford Lepofsky); but since the latter's death in 1971, it has been the pen name of Frederick Dannay alone. Ellery Queen is also the name of the detective in most of these stories. Ellery Queen solves unusual crimes through a combination of psychology, logic, and erudition. For example, in "Trojan Horse" he determines the identity of a jewel thief by recalling the story of the Trojan horse and by recognizing the significance of the fact that a man who is normally indifferent to football is vitally concerned about the outcome of a particular game. The Ellery Queen stories have tended to move from the puzzle story solved by a learned, rather eccentric, detective toward the more personal or character-oriented approach of the later mystery writers. The Queen stories are notable for their scrupulous attention to fairness; in fact, in his earlier novels Queen issued a "Challenge to the Reader" when all the clues had been revealed, suggesting that the reader pause to consider the identity of the criminal. Ellery Queen's short-story collections include *The Adventures of Ellery Queen* (1934); *The New Adventures of Ellery Queen* (1940); *The Case Book of Ellery Queen* (1945); *Calendar of Crime* (1952); *Q. B. I.: Queen's Bureau of Investigation* (1955); *Queens Full* (1965); and *Q. E. D.: Queen's Experiments in Detection* (1968).

John Dickson Carr is another modern writer whose short stories contain a number of puzzle elements. Carr, who also writes as Carter Dickson, specializes in locked-room mysteries and in crimes which appear to have a supernatural origin but which are, of course, the work of human villains. Carr's major detectives are Dr. Gideon Fell, a two-hundred-fifty-pound detective modeled on G. K. Chesterton; Sir Henry Merrivale, who appears almost exclusively in novels; and Colonel March, whose Department of Queer Complaints investigates any reports made to Scotland Yard which are notably unusual or bizarre. In "The New Invisible Man," for example, Colonel March investigates a report brought to Scotland Yard by a thoroughly sober and respectable middle-aged gentleman in a bowler hat, who claims to have watched a pair of gloves with no hands inside them shoot an old man who did not exist, and put a bullet through a window without leaving a hole in the glass. Carr's short story collections include *The Department of Queer Complaints* (1940); *Dr. Fell, Detective* (1947); *The Third Bullet and Other Stories* (1954); and *The Men Who Explained Miracles* (1963).

Although a number of modern detective-story writers have achieved a great deal of success with the classic puzzle-oriented techniques, other modern writers of detective fiction have carried on and adapted the image of the hardboiled detective. Most of these authors produce novels rather than short stories, but a few use both forms. The best-known writer of modern hardboiled detective short stories is Ross Macdonald (pen name of Kenneth Millar, whose wife Margaret has written several successful mystery novels). Macdonald's character, Lew Archer, resembles Raymond Chandler's Philip Marlowe because he is essentially a lonely, gentle, sensitive man who can fight when he has to and shoot when he has to, but who does not enjoy violence. Archer, who works out of an office on Sunset Strip, is appalled and depressed by the injustice he witnesses; and he brings to his gilded and corrupt environment a sense of old-fashioned conscience and dedication and a genuine compassion for the pain that surrounds him. Archer's cases seldom have tidy or happy endings; for example, in "Find the Woman" Archer surmises, but cannot prove, that a jealous mother has brought about the death of her daughter in an attempt to get even with the girl for marrying a man whom the mother had intended to keep as her own lover. Macdonald also uses the medium of his mystery stories to express his views on political, racial, and environmental topics.

A few modern detective-story writers have succeeded in using both a traditional armchair detective and a type of hardboiled detective in the same stories. By far the most popular of these is Rex Stout, with his beer-drinking, orchid-loving, massive genius Nero Wolfe and Wolfe's brash assistant, Archie Goodwin. Wolfe belongs to the school of armchair detectives; in fact, he has a specially designed armchair which is the only comfortable depository for his seventh of a ton. Wolfe, who seldom leaves his house on business, solves cases by extensive interviewing and by analyzing the evidence brought to him by Goodwin and, on occasion, by other operatives headed by Saul Panzer. Archie Goodwin is a milder form of the hardboiled detective: he is a professional investigator, tough, dedicated to his work, and loyal to his employer and to their clients; but he is less violent and less cynical than most of the earlier hardboiled detectives. Rex Stout's stories are memorable for their vivid descriptions of the "regular" characters, for their ingenious plots, and perhaps most of all for Archie Goodwin's incomparable narrative style. Collections of Nero Wolfe stories—actually novelettes—are *Trouble in Triplicate* (1949); *Three Doors to Death* (1950); *Curtains for Three* (1950); *Triple Jeopardy* (1952); *Three Men Out* (1954); *Three Witnesses* (1956); *Three for the Chair* (1957); *And Four to Go* (1958); *Three at Wolfe's Door* (1960); *Homicide Trinity* (1962); and *Trio for Blunt Instruments* (1964).

The Future of the Detective Story

Because of the postwar decrease in magazines which publish detective short stories, the tendency of publishers to prefer novels to short-story collections, and the preference of many detective writers for the additional space which the novel form gives them, comparatively little modern detective fiction appears in short-story form. Further, not only the form but also the content of suspense stories, which have always been responsive to public moods and concerns, has undergone a change. Leslie Charteris, author of the Simon Templar (the Saint) stories, observed that when World War II began, he felt that his earlier plots, which were based on conflicts with individual villains, were inadequate for a world faced with impending atomic warfare and widespread threats against human freedom and dignity. Since the war, a number of other writers have come to feel that same sense of inadequacy, with the result that many recent adventure stories have as their heroes not detectives but spies, who ferret out and destroy plots which would affect millions of people rather than a few murder victims. Some of these stories are written by the same authors who wrote individual-oriented mystery stories earlier in their careers, and in some cases these spy stories feature the same characters who appeared in the earlier detective stories: Nick Carter is a prime example. At the same time, new popular heroes such as James Bond and his many imitators continue to appear. Some of these spy figures share many of the characteristics of the hardboiled detective: they are tough, ruthless, cynical, and often libidinous; but they are also loyal, courageous, and passionately devoted to justice. Although the puzzle element of detective fiction is sometimes missing from spy stories, some of the other conventions of the detective story do carry over: for example, spies often find that the least likely person is a double agent, as detectives discover that the least likely person is a murderer; and spies, like detectives, must frequently rely on logic, experience, and luck to help them locate vital clues. Most spy stories, however, like most new detective stories, are written as novels rather than as short stories.

All of this does not mean, of course, that the death of the detective short story is imminent. Classic detective stories have risen to the top, as the best stories do in any genre, and are frequently anthologized and reprinted. In fact, the best detective stories have begun to take their rightful place among the short stories taught in high school and college courses, and to be discussed seriously by academics who had previously tended to regard them as inconsequential literature. New stories do continue to appear in book form, in magazines such as *Ellery Queen's Mystery Magazine*, and in a few nondetective magazines.

Bibliography

Barzun, Jacques and Wendell Hertig Taylor. *A Catalogue of Crime.*
Haycraft, Howard. *The Art of the Mystery Story.*
——————. *Murder for Pleasure: The Life and Times of the Detective Story.*
la Cour, Tage and Harald Mogensen. *The Murder Book: An Illustrated History of the Detective Story.*
Queen, Ellery. *The Detective Short Story: A Bibliography.*
——————. *Queen's Quorum: A History of the Detective-Crime Short Story as Revealed by the 106 Most Important Books Published in this Field Since 1845.*

Steinbrunner, Chris and Otto Penzler, eds. *Encyclopedia of Mystery and Detection.*
Symons, Julian. *Mortal Consequences: A History—From the Detective Story to the Crime Novel.*

Joan DelFattore

THE HISTORY AND PRACTICE OF SCIENCE FICTION

Science fiction makes more use of the short-story form than any other popular genre. Kingsley Amis, in *New Maps of Hell* (1960), his study of the science-fiction genre, observed that:

> An idea that will comfortably fill out a few thousand words will not do for a novel, or rather there will be an attempt to make it do by various kinds of padding. . . . One hopes that as the audience for science fiction increases, and with it the authors' remunerations, there will be less of this forced expansion, but I cannot foresee any change in the basic fact that this is a short-story or at any rate a long-story mode, with hundreds of successes in these forms as against a bare couple of dozen in the novel.

The argument which Amis uses to support his case is that science fiction characteristically makes use of "idea as hero"—which is to say that the focus of interest in a science-fiction story is usually the central hypothesis rather than the characters and their motives. He claims that it is the ingenuity of the writer in discovering notions which are both new and interesting, and then developing the notions in a rational manner to show unexpected consequences implicit in them, which makes science-fiction stories rewarding. Good science-fiction stories, he notes, frequently sound good in paraphrase because their effect is largely independent of style.

Since 1960 the economics of the science-fiction marketplace have dramatically transformed the relative demand for novels and short stories. Paperbacks have become much more important and magazines much less. The science-fiction short story, however, continues to thrive. Not only have the major magazines of the 1950's—*Analog* (formerly *Astounding Science Fiction*), *Galaxy*, and *The Magazine of Fantasy & Science Fiction*—survived to the present day, but two recently founded magazines—*Isaac Asimov's Science Fiction Magazine* and *Galileo*—have proved very successful. In addition, there has been considerable activity in the production of anthologies featuring original material; some are anthologies on particular themes, while others are annual collections of high-quality material. Robert Silverberg's *New Dimensions* and Terry Carr's *Universe* are perhaps the most prestigious. Although these original anthologies are frequently unsuccessful as commercial ventures they are stubbornly persistent; both editors and writers apparently feel that they have an important contribution to make.

Amis' explanation of the unusual dependence of science fiction on the short-story form is undoubtedly correct. One of the most consistent features of reader demand is for novelty and for the widening of imaginative horizons. The audience has always been willing to forgive literary incompetence provided that it is compensated by an appeal to the "sense of wonder." The preoccupation with ideas at the expense of characterization represents, however, more than the expression of a preference. It is true that much science fiction is poorer than it need be in terms of its literary quality, but it would be a mistake to assume that it could ever compare to mainstream short fiction in terms of its delicacy of characterization. Characterization is the art of making characters seem "real"—complete and convincing. A writer builds a character by demonstrating how he thinks and acts in relation to others, making use of what the reader already knows about the correlation of behavior and character. When a writer must show a character who is a product of a different culture, acting in a social environment different from anything the reader can have known, characterization becomes very difficult. When some characters are not even human, it becomes well-nigh impossible.

It is possible for science-fiction writers to create whole cultures with the same degree of detail that the best writers of historical novels bring to their re-creations of the past, but there is no history of the future to help them, and the feat of imagination required is tremendous. No science-fiction novel could ever offer an account of future society as coherent and comprehensible as the accounts of present and past society offered in mainstream fiction. In the short-story form, in which description has to be cut back to the essential minimum, the advantage possessed by mainstream fiction in being able to use the reader's intimate acquaintance with his own social milieu is immense. To expect science-fiction stories to emulate the qualities of the mainstream short story would be to set an impossible standard, or at least to restrict the range of the medium very greatly.

Science-fiction stories, therefore, tend to have more in common with the "wonder tales" of oral tradition than with the polished literary gems which the invention of print made possible. They gain their effect more by the strategic violation of expectancies than by any attempt to fit in with and make use of what the reader already knows. Where their implications extend back into the mundane world, they operate as fables, and a certain stylized naïveté is often an asset.

These observations are highly relevant to the emergence and evolution of science fiction as a genre. The nineteenth century origins of science fiction can be seen most clearly in the work of short-story writers, and the genre thrived only when circumstances made available markets which put a heavy emphasis on short fiction.

An examination of the history of science and the imaginative speculation encouraged by the emergence of new scientific theories can easily lead one to wonder why there was not much more "science fiction" written in the eighteenth and early nineteenth centuries. The principal reason for this is to be found in the limitations of the literary forms that were readily available. The form most amenable to the incorporation of speculative material was the imaginary voyage, which became gradually less important as the eighteenth century progressed, and which was set firmly in the present. The novel, as it evolved, was essentially concerned with simulating actual experience and was for the most part determinedly mundane. Its fantastic counterpart, the Gothic novel, *could* incorporate speculative material, but characteristically operated within an ideative framework entirely at odds with the world view of science.

As the nineteenth century progressed, however, the short story became gradually more important as a literary form in both Europe and America. It was perhaps of most vital importance in France, where the art was extensively practiced by writers of such quality as Honoré de Balzac, Prosper Mérimée, Théophile Gautier, Erckmann-Chatrian, and Léon Daudet. America, in the same period, produced Washington Irving, Edgar Allan Poe, Nathaniel Hawthorne, and Ambrose Bierce. Another strong tradition was formed in Germany by E. T. A. Hoffmann, Johann Zschokke, Ludwig Tieck, and the Brothers Grimm. In Britain, although such writers as Charles Dickens and William Makepeace Thackeray produced some excellent short work, the emphasis remained very much on novel-length work until the final decade of the century, and the American tradition was by far the more important before 1890.

Much of the short fiction produced in America and Europe during the nineteenth century is fantastic in kind; indeed, many of the writers named above were active in giving literary expression to regional folklore. For the writers of original wonder tales, the wealth of supernatural anecdotes collected by anthologists such as Stefano Guazzo and Joseph Glanvil during the seventeenth century witch-hunts provided a ready resource, and the Romantics in particular took considerable advantage of it. In Europe, the supernatural imagination remained dominant; the European landscape provided an abundance of scenarios redolent with antiquarian fascination—the natural haunts of revenants and folk devils of all kinds. The American Romantic tradition, by contrast, suffered from the lack of a distant past. Irving and Hawthorne were able to produce a certain amount of authentic Americana, but compared to France or Germany, America's imaginative heritage was poverty-stricken. This is perhaps the most important reason for the fact that American writers began to look more and more to the scientific imagination for inspiration in shaping their fantastic stories. The transitional phase from the supernatural vocabulary of symbols to science-fictional apparatus can be most clearly seen in the work of Hawthorne and Poe.

Hawthorne's science-fiction stories are moral fables in which the work of the scientist attempting to "improve" nature is seen as a kind of hubris and is appropriately cheated by ironies of fate. His best works in this vein are "The Birthmark" (1843), "The Artist of the Beautiful" (1844), and "Rappaccini's Daughter" (1844).

Poe's work, by contrast, is much more interested in the fantastic for its own sake. In his supernatural fantasies, guilt is often externalized as hallucination or haunting, but many of his works are straightforward grotesques. "The Unparallelled Adventure of One Hans Pfaall" (1835) is turned by its frame narrative into an ironic farce, although the account of Pfaall's preparations for his lunar voyage involves a halfhearted attempt at speculative realism. "The Conversation of Eiros and Charmion" (1838) is a bizarre meditative dialogue involving a cosmic disaster. "The Thousand-and-second Tale of Scheherezade" (1848) is an uneasy parody of a traditional wonder tale in which the marvels of science replace the miracles of the supernatural. The most rigorously rationalistic of Poe's tales are the detective stories, and his more imaginative science-fiction stories, by contrast, are inclined to value intuition rather too highly. This is especially true of the visionary essays "A Mesmeric Revelation" (1844) and *Eureka* (1848). "The Facts in the Case of M. Valdemar" (1845) has been devalued as a *science*-fiction story by the decline in the respectability of mesmerism.

Because the scientific imagination is used in early American science fiction largely as a replacement for the supernatural imagination, rather than as a subject of interest in its own right, most early science-fiction stories are little more than bizarre anecdotes. One finds them much more frequently in anthologies of horror stories than in science-fiction anthologies, and those which are not horrific are mostly humorous, after the fashion of Edward Everett Hale's "The Brick Moon" (1869), a farce describing the construction of an artificial satellite. The other writer of the mid-century period frequently quoted as an important proto-science-fiction writer, Fitz-James O'Brien, is no exception to this generalization. His story "The Diamond Lens" (1858) is perhaps the archetypal example of "supernatural science" employed as apparatus in Romantic tragedy.

In the 1860's the imaginary voyage was given a new lease on life by the production of the earliest works of Jules Verne, and it did not take long for this new kind of science fiction, with its emphasis on imaginary inventions and careful technological realism, to be reflected in the short story. Earlier writers had made little attempt to cultivate an illusion of plausibility by representing their stories as records of events which might actually happen in the near future (the major exception being the newspaper hoaxes perpetrated by Richard Adams Locke and Poe in the New York *Sun*). Now, however, the attempt to develop imaginative premises in a careful and rational manner came to the fore as priorities to be observed in the writing of fantastic stories. An interesting early collection of such stories is *Caxton's Book* (1876) by the little-known writer W. H. Rhodes, and a number of stories written for newspapers by Edward Page Mitchell have recently been exhumed by Sam Moskowitz in a collection entitled *The Crystal Man* (1973). It was at this point, however, that science fiction began to be divorced from the main tradition of American short fiction, as an idiosyncratic endeavor practiced mainly by specialist writers. The last major American writer who wrote any significant amount of science fiction as part of a much broader output was Jack London. His first effort in the medium was the Hawthornian moral fable "A Thousand Deaths" (1899), but he later went on to write stories of a more modern aspect, including "The Shadow and the Flash" (1903), "The Enemy of All the World" (1908), and the novelettes "The Scarlet Plague" (1912) and "The Red One" (1918). By this time, however, America had lost its primacy as the home of the science-fiction story.

A more elaborate account of nineteenth century American science fiction, including an anthology of the most interesting examples, is H. Bruce Franklin's *Future Perfect* (revised ed. 1978).

In the last decade of the nineteenth century there was a rapid expansion of the short-fiction market in Britain. New papermaking processes made it cheaper to produce magazines, and several new titles appeared to fill the price gap between "highbrow" literary journals like the *Cornhill* and the cheap ephemera ("penny dreadfuls" and twopenny novelettes) mass-produced for the newly literate working class. The most successful of the new publications was *The Strand Magazine*, first published in January, 1891. Its imitators included *Pearson's Magazine*, *The Windsor Magazine*, and *The Idler*. Most of these magazines had American editions, but there were relatively few American publications of a similar nature, the most important being *Cosmopolitan*. These magazines thrived in Britain between 1891 and 1914, when they became casualties of World War I, and they created market opportunities for British short-story writers which had not previously existed. Several writers made considerable reputations for themselves writing serials and short stories for publications of this kind, and many wrote science fiction, among them Arthur Conan Doyle, George Griffith, Grant Allen, and—most important of all—H. G. Wells.

By this time the fascination of new inventions was well-established, as Britons became acclimatized to the rapid march of technology. The prospect of a European war was much-discussed, and there was a flourishing subspecies of futuristic fiction concerned with the next war. The publication and popularization of Darwin's theory of natural selection had also encouraged much speculation about man's place in the universe and his evolutionary prospects. All these influences made themselves obvious in the work of Wells, who moved quickly from popular scientific journalism to the writing of fiction. His earliest stories, collected in *The Stolen Bacillus and Other Incidents* (1895), are mostly biological whimsies, but his novella *The Time Machine* (1895) is an imaginative masterpiece which opened up vast new territories for imaginative exploration. His second collection, *The Plattner Story and Others* (1897), contains some imaginatively adventurous stories, but it was his third, *Tales of Space and Time* (1899), which really shows his range and brilliance. "The Crystal Egg" is a vision of life on Mars; "The Star" is a classic story of cosmic disaster; "A Story of the Stone Age" is an anthropological fantasy about the remote origins of civilization; "A Story of the Days to Come" is a futuristic novella about a class-divided, high-technological society; and "The Man Who Could Work Miracles" is a brief fantasy reflecting ironically on the vanity of human wishes. (The same year, incidentally, saw publication of another short-story collection entirely devoted to scientific romance: George Griffith's *Gambles with Destiny*.)

From 1900 to 1914, speculative fiction drawing on the scientific imagination for its inspiration accounted for a considerable fraction of the short fiction produced in Britain. Wells went on to produce "The Land Ironclads" (1903), "The Country of the Blind" (1904), and "The Empire of the Ants" (1905). Doyle's science-fiction pieces include "The Horror of the Heights" (1913) and the war-anticipation story "Danger!" (1914) as well as the Professor Challenger stories. Rudyard Kipling wrote two fine stories about a future dominated by the Aerial Board of Control, "With the Night Mail" (1905) and "As Easy as A.B.C." (1912). E. M. Forster produced his definitive attack on the logic of technological Utopianism in "The Machine Stops" (1909).

No writer of this period devoted himself entirely to the writing of science fiction, although Wells, Griffith, and (in a slightly different way) Doyle all built their reputations on the novelty and cleverness of the *ideas* which they put into their fiction rather than on their purely literary merits. The only writer of the day still regarded as having made a notable contribution to the genre whose output was almost entirely fantastic is William Hope Hodgson, but his work is very much on the margin separating science fiction from fantasy. (There were, of course, several specialist fantasy writers, most notably M. R. James).

It was in this period that it first became necessary (or, at any rate, convenient) to invent a category label that would group together all stories of this type and oppose them to stories of different types—the term "scientific romance" was widely used, especially in connection with the work of Wells. Despite the prestige enjoyed by Wells, however, the production of "scientific romances," like the production of "detective stories," came to be seen as an endeavor distinct from the mainstream of literary art. Wells felt the need to build himself a new career as an authentic novelist, and Doyle always bitterly regretted the relative popularity enjoyed by Sherlock Holmes and Professor Challenger at the expense of his attempts to win a reputation with "serious" historical fiction. Partly, this disreputability is associated with the great popularity enjoyed by *The Strand Magazine* and its imitators, on the supposition that what is popular is thereby disqualified from being the reserved property of the cultural elite. What must also be taken into consideration, however, is that a marked difference in priorities had now become apparent between scientific romance and the main literary tradition. The new scientific romances very obviously featured "the idea as hero," and although frequently replete with moral rhetoric, scientific romance seemed crucially divorced from the moral dilemmas of everyday life.

In America, the new generation of magazines which appeared in the 1890's made somewhat less impact on the domestic production of short fiction. The abundance of material imported from Britain restricted the size of the market somewhat. In addition, the newly literate reading public in America—the target audience of these publications—was perhaps a little less extensive and a little less sophisticated. Consequently, magazines such as *Cosmopolitan* and the American *The Strand Magazine* soon found themselves in competition with cheap all-fiction magazines printed on pulp paper which were more ephemeral but also more appealing. Even though World War I affected American publishing far less than British publishing, the character of the popular-fiction media nevertheless underwent dramatic changes in the early twentieth century. The pulps underwent a remarkable proliferation in the 1920's in search of new specialist brands of fiction.

The general-fiction pulps such as *Argosy* and *The Cavalier* thrived on serials rather than on short fiction, and the peculiar kind of scientific romance which emerged within them—with much more emphasis on exotic landscapes and spectacular disasters—is virtually always of novel length. Writers such as Edgar Rice Burroughs, A. Merritt, and George Allan England wrote very little in shorter lengths, although Burroughs pioneered a stratagem popular among pulp writers which was later to be conspicuously in evidence in the work of some science-fiction writers: the writing of series of connected novelettes which could later be reprinted as "fixed-up" novels. Largely because of this priority on novel-length stories, most early-pulp fiction which warrants consideration as scientific romance consists of odysseys of adventure set in exotic environments—other worlds or postdisaster scenarios. Hypothetical fantasies of the kind written by Wells and others for the British magazines never featured significantly in the general-fiction pulps. The main exception to this rule is a curious subspecies of detective fiction in which new inventions become the means of committing innovative crimes or the means of trapping orthodox criminals. Examples of this kind of story include the "Craig Kennedy" stories of Arthur B. Reeve and several early stories by Murray Leinster.

When pulp publishers began to experiment lavishly with new specialist titles, they produced such bizarre subgenres as *Zeppelin Adventures* and "yellow peril" pulps, and such strange hybrids as *Phantom Detective* and *Spicy Detective*. It was inevitable that specialist imaginative-fiction pulps should appear, and they did. *The Thrill Book* had a brief existence in 1919, and *Weird Tales* appeared in 1923. The latter title eventually concentrated on supernatural fiction, but in its early days it featured a good deal of interplanetary romance and also put a greater priority on short fiction than was standard. The first pure science-fiction pulp, however, was *Amazing Stories*, subtitled "The Magazine of Scientifiction." This was a large-sized pulp, more impressive than the usual pulp-fiction magazines, and was regarded by its publisher, Hugo Gernsback, as being a vehicle for the popularization of science. In its early years it relied heavily on reprinted material, especially works by Verne and Wells, but much of its short fiction was new. Other pulp publishers quickly moved into the newly delineated area—most notably the Clayton chain, with *Astounding Stories of Super-Science*. Gernsback lost control of *Amazing Stories* in 1929 and started a new magazine—*Wonder Stories*—in competition. It was in connection with this group of magazines that the term "science fiction" came into common usage and eventually became established as the definitive category label.

Because Gernsback considered science fiction to be an essentially didactic medium, his first and most urgent priority was to present stories containing exciting ideas. He also expected science fiction to be prophetic, but he was not a good judge of the competence of many of the ideas which appeared in the stories he published. Literary quality was afforded a low priority among his criteria of judgment, and his magazines were aimed primarily at young readers. The writers he recruited to the field, in consequence, tended to be fascinated by ideas but painfully unsophisticated as writers. The most notable short-story writers to emerge in the science-fiction pulps during their first decade were David H. Keller, whose best work is collected in *Tales from Underwood* (1952), and Stanley G. Weinbaum, whose output is assembled in *A Martian Odyssey & Other Tales* (1974). A notable anthology of the period is *Before the Golden Age* (1974), edited by Isaac Asimov.

The other pulp publishers who dabbled in science fiction were primarily concerned with presenting standardized pulp adventure fiction set in science-fictional milieux—a kind of futuristic costume drama. It quickly became apparent, however, that science fiction had built up during the late 1920's and early 1930's an extremely loyal and devoted audience who were fascinated by the medium itself, and especially by its ideas. All the magazines began to pander to the idiosyncratic demands of this audience, the editors placing a heavy emphasis on originality of ideas. By 1935 there was a noticeable divergence of priorities from those pertaining to the other pulps, and by 1938 this difference was exaggerated by the fact that members of the science-fiction fan community were being recruited to edit the magazines with the aid of their intimate knowledge of the community's idiosyncrasies. The most important of these editorial recruits was John W. Campbell, Jr., who had already cultivated a reputation as a short-story writer with pieces published under the pseudonym Don A. Stuart.

Campbell wrote a new "manifesto" for science fiction, whereby the work of the science-fiction writer was to put forward some kind of hypothesis consistent with the present state of scientific knowledge, and then to explore by careful ratiocination the consequences of that premise in the repertoire of human action and social organization. Although he called for human interest as an essential ingredient of his stories, his prospectus nevertheless enshrined the "idea as hero" as a central feature of the methodology of science fiction. It is notable that the magazine which he took over—*Astounding Stories* (later *Astounding Science Fiction* and eventually *Analog*)—devoted much more space to short fiction than was usual in a pulp magazine. Within two years of taking over his editorial chair he had recruited to his cause a number of writers who were to become the leading figures in the genre, and virtually all of them built their early reputations with short fiction: Lester del Rey, L. Sprague de Camp, Isaac Asimov, Robert Heinlein, Clifford Simak, A. E. van Vogt, and Theodore Sturgeon.

Astounding Science Fiction was at its best during the years 1940-1942, during which it set the pattern for magazine science fiction. The stories which may be taken as the archetypal examples of the attempt to marry imaginative extravagance with realistic and rational development were written during those years. There were two classic stories about the future uses of atomic power, Robert Heinlein's "Blowups Happen" (1940) and Lester del Rey's *Nerves* (1942). On a related theme, there was Alfred Bester's grim post holocaust story "Adam and No Eve" (1941). Isaac Asimov wrote his most popular story "Nightfall" in 1941, the same year that he published the first of his classic exercises in robot psychology, "Reason." The following year he wrote the first novelette in his "Foundation" series. Asimov was one of two writers who were ideal practitioners of the kind of science fiction Campbell was promoting, the other being Heinlein, who was astonishingly prolific in this period, using several pseudonyms as well as his own name. Heinlein's best stories of the period included an account of a future industrial dispute, "The Roads Must Roll" (1940); a vignette about the human significance of the conquest of space, "Requiem" (1940); and a grim story about the politics of colonizing other worlds, "Logic of Empire" (1941).

Astounding Science Fiction was the one science-fiction magazine that held a regular monthly schedule throughout World War II, becoming a digest-size publication in order to save paper while conserving wordage. The war did, however, interfere with its development by taking away several of its most important contributors, including Heinlein. Although Campbell managed to recruit some new blood and persuaded several established writers to produce better work than they had ever done before, the drain on the available talent still showed. Quality material continued to appear through the war years and after, but the dramatic flourish of the prewar years could not be repeated.

The best fiction from the science-fiction magazines of the 1940's (almost all of it from *Astounding Science Fiction*) is displayed in numerous anthologies and collections. The first big anthologies, which had the pick of the available material, appeared in 1946: *Adventures in Time and Space*, edited by Raymond Healy and J. Francis McComas, and *The Best of Science Fiction*, edited by Groff Conklin. Collections exemplifying the work of individual authors include George O. Smith's *Venus Equilateral* (1947), Lester del Rey's *And Some*

Were Human (1948), Theodore Sturgeon's *Without Sorcery* (1948), Isaac Asimov's *I, Robot* (1950), Clifford Simak's *City* (1952), A. E. van Vogt's *Away and Beyond* (1952), and Henry Kuttner and C. L. Moore's *No Boundaries* (1955).

By the time the 1940's drew to a close, the market situation in America had changed dramatically. The pulp magazines were on the verge of dying out because of higher production costs, but there was nevertheless a vast proliferation of magazine science fiction. *Astounding Science Fiction* retained its market position, but its primacy came to be shared with two other digest magazines, *The Magazine of Fantasy & Science Fiction* and *Galaxy*. Both these magazines put their priority on short fiction rather than novels, and each promoted a particular kind of short fiction. *The Magazine of Fantasy & Science Fiction* put more emphasis on style than on technological hardware, and although it published its fair share of grim stories, it presented far more pieces that were slick, lightweight, and amusing. *Galaxy*, under the editorship first of H. L. Gold and later of Frederik Pohl, seemed more assured of its identity. It promoted a rather more cynical and satirical view of the future than its rivals, and its writers imported into the Campbellian story of ideas an essential *irony* that set their endeavors apart from the intently serious didactic works that Campbell himself preferred. Campbell did not lack a sense of humor, and one of the writers he had discovered—Sprague de Camp—had a particularly fine sense of irony, but *Astounding Science Fiction* had carried the banner for science fiction for many years, and Campbell had had to work hard to advance his claim to intellectual seriousness against the skepticism of a literary establishment which regarded pulp fiction as cheap trash. It was not until the 1950's that writers working for the magazines were able to relax into the luxury of taking themselves less seriously. Many of Campbell's stable—again, Heinlein and Asimov are the archetypal examples—never lost the spirit of revolutionary zeal which made them propagandists for science fiction as a unique and important species of fiction.

Both *The Magazine of Fantasy & Science Fiction* and *Galaxy* began reprinting stories in series of annual anthologies, and these annuals adequately display the spirit and range of the two magazines. *Galaxy's* most popular writers, however, were abundantly represented by collections of their best stories. The best of these provide an excellent showcase of 1950's science fiction: Frederik Pohl's *Alternating Currents* (1956) and *The Case Against Tomorrow* (1957); Robert Sheckley's *Untouched by Human Hands* (1954) and *Citizen in Space* (1955); William Tenn's *Of All Possible Worlds* (1955) and *The Human Angle* (1956); Cyril Kornbluth's *A Mile Beyond the Moon* (1958); James Blish's *Galactic Cluster* (1959); Algis Budrys' *The Unexpected Dimension* (1960); and Damon Knight's *Far Out* (1961).

A great many of these collections were published by Ballantine Books, and they heralded another dramatic change in the market situation of science fiction. Before World War II, labeled science fiction had been confined to magazines. Hardcover science-fiction books began to appear in the late 1940's, but most were published by small specialist publishing houses established by science-fiction fans. Major hardcover publishers produced large anthologies and the occasional novel, but were relatively uninterested in producing collections of magazine stories, or in stimulating the production of more novels than the magazines could conveniently handle as serials. From 1960 onward, however, paperback publishing houses became the principal economic forces operating within the category. Although they made the production of novels a much more attractive proposition, they also encouraged the continued production of short fiction by leading writers by virtually guaranteeing double payment for the best work. Practically everything of merit that appeared in the magazines in the postwar period (and a considerable fraction of the material that was not particularly meritorious) was reprinted in book form, usually quite rapidly.

While the other popular genres which had established themselves in the pulps as publishing categories became totally dominated by novels as a result of the transfer to the paperback medium, science fiction did not. The magazines proved to be resilient even in competition with paperback books that were frequently cheaper and had a longer "shelf life," and book publishers found that science fiction short-story collections did not suffer in the marketplace by comparison with novels (as they did in virtually every other enclave of category-publishing).

Very little American speculative fiction appeared outside the pulp magazines in the period between the two world wars. Why this should be true is not entirely clear, but the fact that futuristic fiction was regarded as a species of pulp adventure fiction and hence unfit for the attention of serious writers may have been partially responsible. In Britain the situation was markedly different, with several writers active before World War II continuing to write at least some speculative works, and numerous new writers emerging: S. Fowler Wright, Olaf Stapledon, John Gloag, E. C. Large, Aldous Huxley, and C. S. Lewis all wrote notable works of speculative fiction in this period. What is striking about the work of this period, however, is the fact that so little short fiction appeared. World War I had drastically reduced the British magazine market, and the gap created in the market had been filled by cheap books. There was no British equivalent of the pulp magazines.

For this reason, few of the writers who were active in Britain in this field between the wars produced any significant amount of short fiction. Wells wrote several science-fiction novels after 1918, but no significant short fiction unless one counts two novellas which appeared as books: *The Croquet Player* (1936) and *The Camford Visitation* (1937). Neither, in any case, can compare to his earlier works. The only writer who published a collection of stories devoted entirely to science fiction in this period was S. Fowler Wright, the collection being *The New Gods Lead* (1932; issued in the United States with two extra stories as *The Throne of Saturn*, 1949), although John Beresford's *Signs and Wonders* (1921) is mostly science fiction, and John Gloag wrote a few science-fiction stories that are scattered through his various collections.

The situation began to change on both sides of the Atlantic after World War II. In America, science fiction began to expand out of the specialist magazines to invade some general fiction publications, while Britain acquired specialist magazines of its own.

The first science-fiction writer to move outside the pulps was Heinlein, who began selling near-future stories to the *Saturday Evening Post*; that magazine continued to use a certain amount of science fiction throughout the 1950's, and in 1964 there appeared a *Saturday Evening Post Reader of Fantasy and Science Fiction*. The style and manner of the stories therein are similar to those characteristic of *The Magazine of Fantasy & Science Fiction*, although perhaps less adventurous in their inventions. The other nonspecialist publication which found itself able to release such an anthology in the 1960's was—perhaps curiously—*Playboy*, whose *Playboy Book of Science Fiction and Fantasy* (1966) proved to be the first of a series of science-fiction anthologies issued by the Playboy Press. It is worth noting that other "men's magazines" provided an important market in the early 1960's for Harlan Ellison, perhaps the only postwar writer of science fiction who has made his reputation entirely on the strength of his short fiction. Why this affinity should exist is not immediately obvious, although Kurt Vonnegut once had one of his characters suggest that science fiction and pornography have much in common because each presents visions of "an impossibly hospitable universe."

The first science-fiction writer who contrived to make the transition from being regarded as a pulp writer to hollow out his own niche in the annals of modern American literature was Ray Bradbury, who achieved considerable success with his collection *The Martian Chronicles* (1951). Bradbury was already exceptional among science-fiction writers because his use of science-fictional themes was antipathetic to Campbell's prospectus, being antitechnological, nostalgic, and frequently mock-naïve and moralistic. His main connection with the genre was his affinity with the more exotic writers of interplanetary romance, and, following Edgar Rice Burroughs and Leigh Brackett, he built up a kind of "Martian mythology" representing the red planet as an arena of derelict dreams, a replacement for the Land of Faerie as an imaginary space where all manner of wonders may happen. His fiction ranges from alarmist near-future horror stories like "The Pedestrian" (1952) to sentimental tales of childhood, but the accent is very much on whimsy. Bradbury places a high priority on the power of the imagination to effect escapes from reality, and he was one of the first genre writers to use its vocabulary of symbols as a straightforward replacement for the apparatus of traditional fantasy. He also has affinities, however, with a literary tradition which, in a sense, runs parallel to that of scientific romance/science fiction—the tradition of surrealist fiction, in which notions derived from the scientific imagination have frequently been called upon to effect a crucial dislocation of the narrative from mundaneness.

Some surrealist writers made use of images drawn from scientific theory even in the nineteenth century, the most notable examples being found in the work of Alfred Jarry. More recent writers who have had a considerable influence on modern speculative fiction include Jorge Luis Borges and Italo Calvino. Writers outside the publishing category who make prolific use of science-fictional ideas and images have been dubbed "fabulators" by Robert Scholes, and the most important English-language short-story writers who invite that description are perhaps Gerald Kersh and Donald Barthelme. Although such writers are frequently fascinated by scientific discoveries—see, for instance, Calvino's collection *Cosmicomics* (1965)—their view of science is almost always ambivalent. They tend to see scientific ideas as forces threatening alienation, always disturbing, and perhaps posing a threat to the spirit of community. Fabulators are, in general, much less interested in technology than are genre science-fiction writers, and they are certainly not apologists for material progress. Rather, they are concerned with the human reaction to a new set of mysteries, which are not any the more comforting for being scientific than were the mysteries of old, and perhaps rather the reverse.

One of the most significant changes within labeled science fiction in the postwar period has been the gradual importation into it of this kind of outlook. In Ray Bradbury's wake there have followed several other writers of surrealist science fiction. Several American writers did significant work in this vein, notably David R. Bunch, whose stories are collected in *Moderan* (1971), but for reasons already noted, the suspicious attitude of such writing toward technology, and even scientific knowledge itself, went against the grain of the American magazine tradition, and it was in Britain that the trend received more encouragement.

The British science-fiction magazines were initially founded to cater to an audience who had become converts to the emergent genre by courtesy of American pulps shipped over the Atlantic in a rather haphazard fashion before World War II. They were, at least to begin with, pale imitations of their American kin. There were some readers, however, who were aware of the rather different tradition of British speculative fiction and who saw potential in the genre beyond the range characteristically emphasized by American writers. Two of the most important native writers who began to supply *New Worlds*, the principal British science-fiction magazine, with material during the 1960's were Brian Aldiss and J. G. Ballard. Both were writers of great ability, surrealistically inclined, who found Campbell's version of "the idea as hero" rather too materialistic. Like Scholes's fabulators, they were more interested in the psychological implications of the products of the science-fictional imagination than with technological hardware. Aldiss' early stories were collected in *Space, Time and Nathaniel* (1957) and *The Canopy of Time* (1959), and his best subsequent collection is probably *The Moment of Eclipse* (1970). Ballard's best work is in the collections *The Four-Dimensional Nightmare* (1963) and *The Terminal Beach* (1964). Although both are occasionally nostalgic, their work rarely recalls Bradbury, largely because they lack his sentimentality. Ballard, in particular, is a determinedly antiromantic writer.

In 1964, *New Worlds* was sold by its publisher and reappeared in a new format, edited by Michael Moorcock. Moorcock's *New Worlds* became the focal point of a "new wave" which was experimental in terms of narrative technique and ironically iconoclastic in attitude. It was dominated by the imagery of a world that technology had already transformed rather than by images of remote worlds yet to be found or made, and it was for the most part unenthusiastic about the newly transformed, technologically sophisticated twentieth century. Moorcock promoted both British and American writers, including Ballard, John Sladek, Thomas M. Disch, M. John Harrison, Keith Roberts, and Barrington J. Bayley. Of these, the most important is Disch, an extremely stylish writer of striking black comedies and tragedies of alienation and demoralization. His best works are collected in *Fun with Your New Head* (1968) and *Getting into Death and Other Stories* (revised ed. 1976). Although all have written novels, Sladek and Roberts have worked primarily in shorter lengths, and the best work of Harrison and Bayley is their short fiction. Exemplary collections are Sladek's *The Steam-Driven Boy and Other Strangers* (1973), Roberts' *The Grain Kings* (1976), Harrison's *The Machine in Shaft Ten* (1975), and Bayley's *The Knights of the Limits* (1978).

The chief propagandist for the British new wave in America was Judith Merril, once a writer of sensitive science-fiction stories herself, but by this time devoting her time chiefly to the compilation of a series of excellent "Best of the Year" anthologies. A rather different new wave was sparked in America by the ebullient Harlan Ellison, whose brilliant and emotionally intense stories won him several awards during the late 1960's. His own best collections are *I Have No Mouth and I Must Scream* (1967) and *Deathbird Stories* (1975), but he also played a crucial role in editing the series of anthologies begun with *Dangerous Visions* (1967), which declared war on editorial taboos. Although the stories presented in this book and its sequel, *Again Dangerous Visions* (1972), did not quite live up to Ellison's claims on their behalf, the loud blast of the trumpets thus sounded did indeed result in the demolition of the taboos concerned, allowing American science-fiction writers much greater scope in exploring the implications of their ideas. Sex, religion, and pessimism have become much more common in recent science fiction in consequence. This change has allowed the forging of somewhat closer links with the mainstream, where fiction has always been dominated by these preoccupations.

Another editor active in promoting a new approach to the writing of science fiction has been Damon Knight, editor of the *Orbit* series of anthologies. Here, too, the emphasis has been on intense psychological dramas, with much surrealism and some very fine writing. The series has been a showcase for the works of such writers as Gene Wolfe and Gardner R. Dozois, both of whom are long overdue for a collection of their short stories, and also for Kate Wilhelm, whose best short fiction appears in *The Infinity Box* (1975).

Two other leading figures in the American science-fiction community, active both as writers and as anthologists, who invite association with the new trends of the 1960's and 1970's are Robert Silverberg and Barry Malzberg. Both have been highly prolific, but their best collections are respectively *Sundance and Other Stories* (1974) and *Down Here in the Dream Quarter* (1976). They also testify to a kind of crisis of identity that has come to the genre during the period of its conspicuous success. Both writers "retired" temporarily from writing during the 1970's, and along with Harlan Ellison have ceased to identify themselves with the genre. The main reason for this decision is that they feel that the label, with its implications of pulp heritage, has become burdensome. The name, of course, matters little insofar as it functions as a descriptive term for the content of their fiction, but it has also become the emblem of a curious subculture of writers, fans, and editors. This community, like any other, has its moral conflicts and pressures, and Silverberg, Malzberg, and Ellison are not the only ones to feel that their particular literary ambitions and purposes are crucially at odds with the weight of the genre's traditions. Their dissatisfaction reflects the fact that as a brand name the term "science fiction" no longer forms any useful function in marking a boundary between one species of imaginative fiction and the several others existing parallel to it.

Science fiction owing allegiance to the Campbellian prospectus still thrives today, most notably in the pages of *Analog*, and new writers still emerge to carry that particular banner—recent recruits being Charles Sheffield and Orson Scott Card. At the opposite end of the spectrum, however, are writers like R. A. Lafferty, whose work all appears under the genre label although it is surreal metaphysical fantasy in character. In between the two extremes there are rich imaginative territories, and perhaps the most striking thing about the best new writers who have recently started working in the genre is their versatility. There seemed at the end of the 1960's to be a real possibility that the ideative extravagance of the genre might decline, and that future science fiction might be more concerned with stylistic experimentation and with the elaboration of more subtle implications of known ideas, but in fact the genre has not lost its innovative thrust. This is amply demonstrated by the collections of the best work of the most successful new writers: *Ten Thousand Light Years from Home* (1973) by James Tiptree, Jr. (Alice Sheldon) and *The Persistence of Vision* (1978) by John Varley. Tiptree is particularly interesting in that she is the leading representative of a growing community of female science-fiction writers who emerged in the wake of the American women's movement. Their fiction is often polemical, using the imaginative devices of science fiction to conduct thought-experiments in sexual politics.

It would be misleading to suggest that contemporary science fiction has rather less to say about science than it once had, although possible technologies play a smaller part than they once did. The point is that writers within the genre have realized that the differences between our reality and the infinite range of imaginable alternatives (including possible futures) are not simply matters of increased environmental control and technical ability. While science-fiction writers were slowly coming to realize the full implications of this observation, however, writers outside it were slowly coming to the complementary realization that the rapid increase in scientific knowledge and technological capability was opening up new horizons and posing new moral choices that threatened the more insular and traditional forms of contemporary fiction with instant fossilization. The two trends engendered by these realizations had to meet, and the last decade has been the time of that meeting.

It seems probable that in the next decade the label "science fiction" will be employed in a more or less arbitrary way, for the convenience of the marketing strategies of publishers. Wherever the label settles or refuses to settle, however, it is very likely that more and more contemporary fiction will absorb aspects of the science-fictional vocabulary of symbols and images. This will apply particularly to short fiction, because the short story has advantages for the deployment of such material which the novel does not. The science-fiction novel poses would-be writers an extremely difficult problem in creativity: the construction of an imaginary world whose technology, sociology, economics, and politics all knit together into a coherent whole; and the construction of characters whose individual psychologies, reflecting that whole, must be distinct from the psychology of the reader, alienated from immediate understanding. Of course, no one has ever done this job properly, and perhaps no one can. The great science-fictional novels remain heroic failures or colossal frauds. The short story, however, can be much more impressionistic in *suggesting* all that the novel must display. It is not too difficult for a skillful science-fiction writer to offer brief glimpses of alternative modes of being.

The other advantage which short stories have over novels is that in short fiction it is possible to tackle one idea at a time, whereas novels require several notions to be coordinated. Thus, again the crucial problem of *integration* frequently defeats the technique of the novelist while the short-story writer finds it easy to contrast one focal point (the idea as hero) with a background where other, complementary innovations may be allowed to lurk undeveloped. It is for this reason that we find the story series playing such an important role in science fiction at all stages in its history, at least since the economic priority began encouraging writers to aim for book publication as an eventual end. The fashion was set by A. E. van Vogt, who knitted together virtually all his shorter pieces to form "fix-up" novels, beginning with *The Voyage of the Space Beagle* (1950). Some of the most successful works in the genre are connected short-story sequences of a less intricately interwoven kind, notably *A Canticle for Leibowitz* (1960) by Walter M. Miller, *Pavane* (1968) by Keith Roberts, and *334* (1977) by Thomas M. Disch. A further advantage enjoyed by such works as these is that they can spread out both in time and in space (this advantage they enjoy, of course, by virtue of being *series* rather than series of *short stories*). The ideas used by science-fiction writers do characteristically spread out in this way, affecting individuals and societies differently through their different aspects and their progressive stages of development. Similarly, there is no other species of fiction more suited than science fiction to the display of "variations on a theme," whereby a single premise can be developed by a dozen different writers to display different sets of hypothetical corollaries. This potential is currently being exploited to the full by "theme anthologies," usually using original material. A collection of short stories— where it is *not* a series—can show off the many facets of a particular premise.

In view of all this, it is not surprising that publishers are continually experimenting in the hope of finding the best way to market short science fiction. Original anthologies seem to have demonstrated their inability to displace the magazines, although they will probably survive in parallel with them. Perhaps the attempt of Ace Books to combine the two in the paperback-format magazine *Destinies* will successfully take over the market advantages of both. In the meantime, the science-fiction short story continues to increase its influence in most areas of general fiction publishing, whether it is recognized as such or not.

Brian Stableford

SHORT FICTION ON FILM

The motion picture as an art form is more closely related to narrative fiction than to any other genre or medium, even more than to photography and drama, which, like motion pictures, depend on visual representation or acting out. For movies communicate primarily as narrative fiction does; they tell stories by means of the linear structuring of specific detailed events.

The development of the film as a storytelling medium owes much to D. W. Griffith's pioneering adaptation of fictional techniques to the new medium just after the turn of the century. Griffith has mentioned Charles Dickens in particular as an important source of many of these storytelling devices, and Sergei Eisenstein has analyzed that influence in more detail in his well-known 1940's essay. Using examples from *Oliver Twist*, Eisenstein illustrates how Griffith developed the technique of montage from Dickens' use of parallel action, the device of intercutting from Dickens' technique of moving from crowd scenes to details and character close-ups, as well as other film devices such as the dissolve and the pan.

The debt movies owe to fiction is also indicated by the large number of films which are literary adaptations, variously estimated to range between twenty-five to fifty percent of all films. In fact, the important movement of film out of the nickelodeons and into the theaters was made possible by the realization of early filmmakers that "high class" audiences who turned up their noses at slapstick and melodrama would pay to see film versions of literary classics. This snob appeal, combined with Griffith's insistence that good films depended on good stories, led to early film versions of the works of Edgar Allan Poe, Dickens, Guy de Maupassant, Robert Louis Stevenson, O. Henry, and others.

The most basic differences between fiction and film spring from their treatment of *time* and *point of view*. It has often been noted by film theorists that film has only one time frame—now—and only one point of view—the camera eye. Short of using camera tricks such as altering the focus or the light, film cannot make distinctions between present, past, and future. This is not to say that film cannot make use of flashbacks or even flashforwards; rather it is simply to point out that if one were to walk into a movie theater after the film had begun, there would be no way of knowing whether the event being depicted was taking place in the past, in the present, or in the future. Whereas a still photograph always depicts a past event, it is a psychological fact that a picture in motion can only be perceived as present.

Because of the radically mimetic nature of film, it cannot be as subjective as fiction; that is, whereas fiction can be filtered through various points of view, film has no equivalent flexibility. As Russian film theorist Siegfried Kracauer sums up this difference, film captures life as a "material continuum," whereas the world of fiction is a "mental continuum." Most literary critics agree that the most important tension in fiction is, in fact, between the teller and the tale. The most important tension in film is between the tale and the objective nature of the visual image. This is not to say that film can only present brute physical thereness; quite the contrary, film, to use Kracauer's phrase, attempts to "redeem reality," to give us a heightened perception of reality—reality patterned and arranged by means of how the director calls our attention to it. Film is more limited than fiction, however, in escaping the materiality of the physical world.

If we assume that a film adaptation strives to preserve the theme and tone of the original work, then it seems clear that it is more difficult to adapt a short story to film than a novel. Short stories have always been less mimetic than novels; they often do not present individualized characters, nor do they always depend on the similitude of a real physical or social context. Moreover, some of the best short stories in literature do not depend on a linearly structured plot in which a character development takes place in an obvious way.

Thus, for these reasons, film versions of short stories, especially full-length film versions, often flatten out the meaning of the story, add new material to supply more obvious character motivation, and fail to capture the often visionary and mythical significance of the original. The demands of the popular audience who view theatrical films, the economic necessities of those who make such films, and the intrinsic demands of the real time involved in a 90- to 120-minute film have resulted in some significant distortions when short stories have been made into full-length films.

One well-known such distortion is *My Foolish Heart*—the 1950 film version of J. D. Salinger's "Uncle Wiggily in Connecticut." The movie was so loosely based on the story and so sentimentalized that Salinger has rejected all film offers since then. Whereas the story itself is in many ways a satire of the soap opera mentality, the film is pure Hollywood soap. Similar in treatment is the 1954 version of F. Scott Fitzgerald's "Babylon Revisited," entitled *The Last Time I Saw Paris*. Fitzgerald's subtle story of a father's relationship with his daughter takes a back seat to the love story of Van Johnson and Elizabeth Taylor. Ernest Hemingway's stories have also come under the Hollywood romanticizing treatment in films based on "The Snows of Kilimanjaro" and "The Short Happy Life of Francis Macomber," both starring Gregory Peck. *The Macomber Affair* (1947), perhaps because of its dramatic story line, fares better on film than "The Snows of Kilimanjaro," which depends more on strictly fictional techniques of impressionistic memory.

A typical example of how full-length films use the original story as climax for which additional invented motivation and background must be supplied is the 1946 version of Hemingway's compact and cryptic little story, "The Killers." The story of Nick Adams' initiation into inevitability becomes a detective tale in which Edmond O'Brien digs up the reasons for Burt Lancaster's murder. True to Hollywood fashion, the reasons involve a woman,

Ava Gardner. As a well-constructed and engaging suspense film in the Hollywood manner, the movie cannot be faulted, but it is not a translation of the Hemingway story. The story was adapted again in 1964 as a made-for-television movie which was distributed to theaters instead. This time John Cassavetes plays Ole Anderson and Angie Dickinson is the love interest, but the focus is on tough guy Lee Marvin, who plays one of the gunmen looking for Ole.

By no means are all full-length films adapted from short stories flawed by romance and invented motivation. Two British films manage to remain quite faithful to their original stories without excessive additions. *The Rocking Horse Winner* (1950), directed by Anthony Pelissier from D. H. Lawrence's short story, and *The Fallen Idol* (1949), directed by Carol Reed from Graham Greene's "The Basement Room" both involve the interrelationship of the fantasy world of children with the real world of adults. Although Pelissier chooses not to include any of the possible masturbatory or mythic elements of Lawrence's story, he does create an ominously atmospheric parable of adult greed and a young boy's effort to ride his fantasy to fulfill his mother's needs. In *The Fallen Idol*, Carol Reed gives us a tightly structured story about a young boy's romanticizing of a male servant (played by Ralph Richardson) and his confusing of fantasy with reality. Although, with the exception of introducing a small garden snake the boy plays with, Reed chooses not to deal with the Garden of Eden echoes in the original story, the film is a successful treatment of a child's fantasy world and its effect on the adults who encourage it.

Other films that face the problem of expanding on short stories but manage it successfully are Frank Perry's film version of John Cheever's "The Swimmer" and Michelangelo Antonioni's highly successful film treatment of Julio Cortázar's "Blow-Up." Perry manages quite well to present what is basically a parabolic story and to make it believable. Burt Lancaster plays the lead in this 1968 film of a man who, wishing to escape his suburban life-style, symbolizes his effort by swimming home from a party through the many pools in his neighbor's yards. Because Cortázar's story is based on the premise of the illusory nature of reality and uses the visual vehicle of a photograph to symbolize this philosophic notion, Antonioni's film version was able to make use of the camera to emphasize the point. Although the film focuses more on the hedonistic life-style of the photographer than Cortázar's story does, the ambiguous relationship between reality and fantasy is still effectively portrayed.

Some full-length theatrical releases have dealt with short stories by presenting them as omnibus films, anthologies of three or four stories with no interrelationships. Well-made stories such as those by W. Somerset Maugham, Guy de Maupassant, and O. Henry seem particularly adaptable to such treatment. British filmmaker Ken Annakin directed two such anthologies of

Maugham stories—one in 1949 entitled *Quartet* which featured "The Alien Corn," "The Colonel's Lady," "The Kite," and "The Facts of Life"; and another the following year entitled *Trio*, which featured "The Verger," "Mr. Knowall," and "Sanitorium." In 1952, director Pat Johnson put together another British film of Maugham stories entitled *Encore* which included "The Ant and the Grasshopper," "Winter Cruise," and "Gigolo and Gigolette." The secret of the success of these films is that Maugham is a popular storyteller who exploits the ironic potential of the short-story form. Adaptation of simple plot or character ironies to short film is easy enough.

Hollywood found the same ironic potential in the stories of O. Henry and released a film in 1952 entitled *O. Henry's Full House*, which featured five stories, each by a different director. The stories are "Last Leaf," "Gift of the Magi," "The Ransom of Red Chief," "Clarion Call," and "Cop and the Anthem." The all-star cast of Charles Laughton, Anne Baxter, Jeanne Crain, David Wayne, and Marilyn Monroe helped contribute to this film's success. European filmmakers have also found these omnibus collections successful. Two such films are Jean-Luc Godard's *Masculine-Feminine* (1966), based on "Paul's Mistress" and "The Signal" by Maupassant; and *Spirits of the Dead*, based on three stories by Poe and directed by three famous European directors. "Metzengerstein," starring Jane and Peter Fonda, was directed by Roger Vadim; "Toby Dammit" ("Never Bet the Devil Your Head"), a minor but delightful Poe fantasy, was directed by Federico Fellini; and "William Wilson" was directed by Louis Malle.

Such omnibus films are tacit recognition of the fact that the most appropriate film length for the short story is the short film of fifteen to thirty minutes; and indeed the most successful adaptations of short stories are short films that seldom, if ever, reach the local theaters. The remainder of this discussion will focus on selected short films in an effort to illustrate some of the basic problems of short-story/short-film adaptation and to point out some of the variety of ways filmmakers attempt to deal with these problems.

One of the most basic characteristics of the short story is its lyrical quality—a subjectivism and impressionism that places it closer to the poem than to the novel. An adaptation that illustrates the difficulty of translating such quality to film is Gene Kearney's 1966 short based on Conrad Aiken's "Silent Snow, Secret Snow." The plot of the story focuses on a young boy drifting farther and farther away from the real world into fantasy; the central metaphor is the slowly encroaching snow. The point of view of the story, that is, the telling voice, however, suggests that this is not a simple case history of schizophrenia, but rather a metaphoric story about the beauty of the imagination and the philosophic implications of man's preference for the world of self-creation over the world of brute reality. The story is filled with references to the exploration of a new world, to the difference between metaphor and external reality, and to the art work itself as an attempt to regress back to ultimate origins. Gene Kearney has capitulated to the visual immediateness of film with a vengeance, however, by choosing to make the presentation simply about a little boy retreating from reality. This simplified interpretation of the film is emphasized by Kearney's giving the film a docudrama effect; the filming is in grainy black and white and the acting is amateurish. The young Paul is played as a rather slack-jawed child distracted by visions that the film does not even try to present. The beautiful, indescribable snow is seen as simply real, dirty snow complete with footsteps and tire tracks in it. Because of Kearney's quite literal visual treatment, the voice-over which reads portions of Aiken's alliterative and highly assonant story seems out of tone with the images. The voice gives us a story of beauty of the imagination; the visuals give us a poor confused child becoming more and more autistic.

A quite different attempt to present a dreamlike parabolic story can be seen in Donald Fox's 1973 version of Nathaniel Hawthorne's "Young Goodman Brown." Whereas Kearney stubbornly sticks to hard reality, Fox makes use of various camera tricks to suggest the dream vision of Brown in the forest. When Faith's ribbon drops from an infinite sky, Brown declares "My Faith is gone" and runs through a multicolored filtered landscape to a background of discordant music. The camera tilts precariously, the convex lens distorts Brown's features, and the running is unnaturally speeded up. When Brown reaches the site of the witches' gathering in the forest, Hollywood special effects are brought into play to present a ball of light streaming out of the sky which explodes and materializes into a hooded man ringed with fire. When the devil's hand dips into a fiery liquid and glowingly comes close to Brown, another explosion fades out to day, running water, the sound of birds, and Brown's hand dangling in a clear stream. Thus, the film indeed emphasizes the ambiguity of Hawthorne's story: did it really happen or was it all a dream? The complex metaphysical and moral issues of the story, however, are ignored to focus instead on social questions of scapegoating and witch-hunting.

Literal translations of fiction into film seem most successful when the original vehicle is a purely realistic story with no suggestions of symbolic significance. Such a success with a rather limited story can be seen in Robert Stitzel's short-film version of "To Build a Fire." Jack London's story is a simple plot story of a man who freezes to death in the Yukon because he is unable to build a fire. The story has no metaphysical significance; the snow and cold are simply real snow and cold. Stitzel's fifteen-minute film version easily captures the helplessness of the man in face of the severe cold; the camera watches impassively as he fumbles with the matches and drops them, moving in for close-ups of his panic and final despair, and moving back for a long shot of the body lying in the frozen waste. The story is a purely physical story about a physical man in a physical world. The director captures this realm of reality perfectly because it is what film captures best.

The success of film versions of other "simple" stories in which the conflict is clear and easily externalized can be similarly accounted for. The film *A Time Out of War*, which won an Academy Award for best short live-action film in 1954 for its two young filmmakers, Dennis and Terry Sanders, is a faithful version of Robert Chambers 1895 story, "Pickets." The characters are few (one Confederate soldier and two Union soldiers); the setting is physically and symbolically simple (they are on two sides of a river); the situation is unambiguous (they call a time-out from the shooting to swap tobacco for hardtack and take a rest); and the climax is inevitable (they discover a dead Union cavalryman in the river and the idyll ends). A plot summary of the story is sufficient to explicate its meaning. The film version is faithful to the original because the piece has no significance beyond its surface. The tone of the film, from the opening background music of "Shenandoah" and the peaceful shots of the river to the final silhouette at dusk, is consistent with the bucolic tone of the story. The banter of the soldiers during the opening gunfire suggests, as does the story, boys at play rather than men at war. It is a sweetly sad story, more than a little sentimental and completely predictable. The film captures this simplicity perfectly.

A more intense confrontation with death is presented in Stephen Crane's very brief story entitled "The Upturned Face." Edward Folger's 1972 short-film version of the story manages to capture this intensity. Again the major figures are three—two soldiers who must bury a fallen comrade on the battlefield while the bullets whiz over their heads. The story is about the problem of how to face the face of death. The army and the war are mythical, out of time and place. The issue in the story is sounded in the first line spoken by one of the soldiers: "What will we do now?" The situation here, however, is not simply the external conflict of how to bury a man during a battle, but rather how to deal with the upturned face of the dead man at the bottom of the shallow grave. Folger captures this by focusing on the faces of the surviving two soldiers as they cope with this situation, as they look first at each other and then at the dead face. It is the simple external situation itself that carries psychological and philosophic significance; all Folger has to do is remain faithful to it. This he does, with the exception of one minor event which, however, has major importance. In the Crane story, as the first shovelful of earth is thrown over the dead man's face, Crane's last line is: "Lean swung back the shovel. It went forward in a pendulum curve. When the earth landed it made a sound—plop." This line suggests a typical Crane ambiguous tone—between seriousness and absurdity. We wince from it even as we sense the incongruity of the sound and the event. For whatever reason, Folger decided to avoid this final tone—perhaps because of its being too risky to attempt—and instead we have a final close-up shot of the face as the shovel slowly slides the dirt onto it. The camera then holds on the covering dirt for a few seconds until the fade-out. We can only feel the seriousness of the event with such a shot, not the ambiguous absurdity which Crane's story suggests.

A film version of a story does not have to follow the original story faithfully to communicate the original's basic theme and tone. For example, one such film, which changes time and place and thus social milieu of the original, which makes no use of camera trickery, which sticks closely to physical detail and character, but which still manages to communicate much of the subtlety and significance of the original, is Jack Sholder's 1973 production of Katherine Mansfield's "The Garden Party." Instead of England in the 1920's, the setting is America in the 1940's; instead of English gentility, we are concerned with American *nouveau riche*. Young Laura's discovery of death and her ambiguous reaction to that discovery, however, are admirably captured. Much of this is due to the delicate performance of Maia Danziger, who plays Laura; but it is also due to the adaptation, which consists of sparse but significant dialogue, and to the direction, which contrasts the world of the garden party with the world down in the hollow where the workman died in such a way as to indicate there is ugliness up the hill as well as beauty, just as there is beauty down the hill as well as ugliness. The scene in which Laura goes down to offer leftover sandwiches to the bereaved family is particularly effective. The beauty of the grief-stricken widow's face is inextricable from its tear-streaked ugliness. When Laura is taken unwillingly into the dead man's room the camera cuts from a full-length shot of the prone man's peacefulness to Laura standing with her head down; she slowly raises her head until the light strikes her eyes under her broad-brimmed hat, and we know she has seen a new vision of reality. We are left, however, with the ambiguity of not knowing whether Laura has left the fantasy beauty of the garden party for the real ugliness of death or whether she has perceived in death a higher kind of beauty than she has known before. There is no way to articulate this discovery, and Laura is left with stammering to her brother, "Isn't life. . . . Isn't life. . . ." The film is a model of how film can maintain a dogged adherence to physical reality, and yet still communicate a meaning that is complex and ambiguous. It is an exception to the usual rule that the better the story the more difficult and problematical the adaptation.

Before moving on to a discussion of some special film series that deserve special consideration for their technique and ambition, it might be well to mention briefly a few short films that present animated versions of short stories. Two animated versions of Edgar Allan Poe stories are especially interesting. Columbia Pictures released an eight-minute animated film version of Poe's "The Tell-Tale Heart" in 1969 as a theatrical short subject. Directed by Ted Parmalee and narrated by James Mason, the film represents a departure from American animation in being a "cartoon" short which dealt with a serious rather than silly subject. It is a remarkable piece of work in capturing not only the madness of the Poe story but also in suggesting the complex philosophic nature of the madness.

In the story, the narrator tells of his uncontrollable desire to kill the old man he lives with for no other reason except that he cannot bear the old man's eye. The story's focus on time (the only tale that the heart can tell) and on the eye itself both suggest that this is a story of a man's desire to stop time through the destruction of self; this need to destroy the "I" is projected in dream-pun fashion on the "eye" of the old man. The film, which is done in highly surrealistic images, emphasizes this identification of the narrator with the old man.

The film opens with the voice of Mason denying his madness while we see the shadow of the narrator inside a cell. A moth flies by and a white, heavily veined hand clasps it only to unfold showing nothing. The film then dissolves to an extended flashback which depicts the events leading up to the imprisonment. We are given close-ups of the eye of the old man which dissolve into superimpositions of the moon and the white face of a freestanding clock. As the voice describes the slowness of time, we see images of a light ascending the stairs to the old man's room over which is superimposed the previous image of clock gears. The trope is that of moving within the mechanism of time itself. The *mise-en-scène* is made up of geometrical lines contrasted with white circular objects which suggest the obsessive eye. For example, the camera holds on a white pitcher sitting on a table before a mirror. An image of the old man's eye shattering is echoed by the shattering of the pitcher and the mirror. Both the "eye" of the old man, which the narrator sees all around him, and the "I" he sees in the mirror are the same.

When the "I" finally dashes into the old man's room to kill him, the scene is stylistically imaged in the whirl of a geometrically patterned coverlet until we see the old man's death as one white hand extended outside the coverlet. The geometrical pattern of the hole in the floor where the narrator buries the old man is picked up in the wallpaper, in the shapes of tables, and in freestanding objects throughout the film. When the police arrive and inquire about the scream, the narrator, quite appropriately given the identification the narrator has made with the old man, replies that it was only his own in a dream. The sound of the old man's beating heart which forces the narrator to confess is, of course, his own heart. The final shot of the narrator's white hand against the prison door as he once more declares he is not mad visually echoes the hand that clasps the moth in the beginning as well as the old man's almost identical hand in the climactic death scene. The moth is a directorial invention, but metaphorically it works perfectly with the ambiguity of the narrator's intention. The paradox of the moth drawn irresistibly to that which will destroy him parallels the narrator's situation.

This animated film can so clearly capture the irrationality and symbolism of the Poe story precisely because animation is not limited to physical reality as is live-action film; on the contrary, the forte of animation is its ability to create a world of its own physical laws and realities which run counter to the real world.

Another excellent film version of a Poe story is the 1970 production of "The Masque of the Red Death" by the Zagreb School of animation in Yugoslavia. Directed by Pavao Statler, this ten-minute film involved approximately eighty oil paintings in which the paintings of the figures were changed for each movement, the new movement being painted over the old one. Statler has said that the job took him two years with occasional breaks. Although one major story change is made by Statler—the embodiment of the Red Death in the figure of a beautiful woman—the theme and tone of the film capture Poe's story faultlessly.

Poe's story is quite obviously a parable. Prince Prospero and his followers are not so much real people as they are embodiments of the desire to escape death. The highly stylized, minimal movements of the painted figures suggest this allegorical intent. There is no voice-over narrator and no dialogue. The premise of the story is so emphatic that the visual scenes of the Red Death's effect on the countryside, the cut to the castle being closed up, and the scenes of party or masque inside are clearly communicated. The meaning of the Poe story is not simply Prospero's effort to escape death, but rather his effort to create a hermetically sealed world of illusion, song, dance, mime, and art that shuts out life. The fact that the death's sign is the redness of blood suggests this. Blood itself is not a sign of death, but rather of life; but for Poe, inescapably, the sign of life *is* the sign of death. Statler's use of oil paintings suggests indeed that Prospero's life in the castle is an effort to live inside the art work itself. Statler's echoing of several famous art works such as "The Last Supper," "The Giaconda," and "The Naked Maja" further suggests this alternate art world. The choice of a seductive woman as the Red Death furthers this interpretation. The woman enters the ball as an embodiment of physical life: sexual and alluring. Prospero pursues her through the castle until he catches her and they embrace. When the woman rises from the embrace, she quickly changes first into hag, then into putrid corpse and death's-head, and finally into the cowled blackness of the Red Death itself. Seduced by physical life, Prospero pays the price of death. Again, as in "The Tell-Tale Heart," the irrational, representative nature of the story seems easily adaptable to the stylized and metaphoric nature of animation. Whereas live action can only awkwardly present tropes that make such a story posssible, animation finds such tropes its forte.

In the remainder of this survey, three series of films which are probably the best-known short-story adaptations will be discussed: the three films that French filmmaker, Robert Enrico, adapted from Ambrose Bierce stories and released under the title *In the Midst of Life* in 1963; the eight films in the *Short Story Showcase* series adapted and directed by Larry Yust for Encyclopedia Britannica; and the magnificent seventeen-film series, The American Short Story, produced in 1977 and 1980 by Robert Geller's Learning in Focus,

Inc., for the Public Broadcasting System.

The Enrico films have been released separately in 16mm as "Chickamauga," "The Mockingbird," and "Occurrence at Owl Creek Bridge." The best-known of the three is the latter, which won an Academy Award in 1964. The stories of Ambrose Bierce are frequently filmed, with films having been made of "Coup de Grace," "The Man and the Snake," "The Boarded Window," "One of the Missing," and others. Bierce's stories involve simple plot lines and are often quite scenic in their structure. The opening paragraphs of "The Mockingbird" and "Occurrence at Owl Creek Bridge" read as though they were film treatments.

"Chickamauga" is about a small boy who wanders away from home during the Civil War and stumbles into the middle of a disastrous retreat. Not knowing what the situation means, he thinks it is a game and tries to play with the wounded soldiers, finally leading them in a mock crawl-march with his wooden sword held aloft. The irony of men playing war "games" with horrible consequences into which a child wanders with his own games is well presented in the film. The weakest scenes are those in which Enrico attempts to translate simple Bierce tropes too simplistically. For example, a Bierce line about the clumsy multitude dragging itself down a slope "like a swarm of great black beetles" is imaged by cutting from a shot of the men to a close-up insert of actual beetles. Similarly, the boy's "seeing" a man as a bear or a pig is shown as quick cuts from man to bear-insert to man to pig-insert. That the blood-streaked faces of the men remind the boy of clowns prompts Enrico to cut to an insert of a clown who smiles at the boy before he collapses. The boy's innocent unawareness of the seriousness of the event is sufficiently communicated by his trying to play leapfrog with a dying man, stepping on the upturned stomach of another, and beating the drum of the dead "clown." The somewhat forced tropes only prove distracting. Our knowledge of the little boy's deafness comes to us only gradually, rather than abruptly, as in the conclusion of the Bierce story; we simply sense throughout the film the boy's more than ordinary detachment from the events in which he participates. The climax of the film when the boy returns home to find his house afire and his mother dead is not as violent and graphic as the Bierce story, but is more poignant. The antiwar message is clearly presented.

"The Mockingbird" is interesting primarily for its use of dream/flashback sequence. The story is about a Union soldier at watch who shoots a man in the dark. Not finding the body, he goes back later searching for him. During the search he falls asleep by a tree and dreams of himself as a boy, of having a twin brother, and of the mockingbird they own. When the children's mother dies, William (the narrator) is sent to the "Realm of Conjecture" while John is sent with the mockingbird to the "Enchanted Land." When the narrator awakes, he moves on and finds the dead man; it is the image of himself—his twin, John Grayrock. The ambiguity of the story and also of the film is whether we are reading/watching a realistic story with an inserted dream piece or whether we are reading/watching an allegory. The "Realm of Conjecture" is obviously the North; the "Enchanted Land" is the South; and the twins embody the war of "brother against brother." The mockingbird serves as a mocking echo of this grotesque situation. The film underlines this theme with shots of the mirror-image twin boys, with mock repetition of several actions, and with the constant refrain of the bird's song. The conclusion of the story when William Grayrock faces his dead brother and therefore faces himself is made more emphatic in the film than in the story since the actor playing both roles is the same. Thus the effect is that Grayrock does indeed face himself in visual literal terms.

"Occurrence at Owl Creek Bridge" has always been a favorite short-story anthology piece. Its striking surprise ending when we "discover" that the escape which takes up half the story has taken place only for the span of time required for Peyton Farquar to "reach the end of his rope" (Bierce was not beyond such morbid puns) never fails to fascinate. The story itself is not a complex story either metaphorically or thematically; it is almost purely a story of manipulative fictional technique. It appeals to us because of the powerful human urge to live, which allows us to read it over and over again, each time cheering Farquar on, irrationally hoping that this time when we read it he will escape. The film captures this feeling admirably. In fact, in many ways, the film is better than the story in achieving this purpose—first of all, because Farquar is seen as a real man, not an imaginative and abstract construct of our imagination, and second, because the dangers of his escape and the superhuman power of his efforts are vividly protrayed.

The film is divided into three separate parts: the scenes leading up to the hanging, the escape, and the painfully short snap (again the implied Bierce pun) at the end when we are abruptly brought back to the bridge and see Farquar hanging there. The first part of the film is characterized by a static frozen quality; the only thing that seems to move is the camera as it slowly tracks and pans the lines of geometrically placed soldiers. Enrico has said that he designed these scenes after studying old Mathew Brady daguerreotypes, and indeed the gray and grainy filming makes us feel that we are watching such photographs haltingly come to life. Ironically, the second half of the film, Farquar's imaginary escape, seems more alive than the early scenes in which he is indeed alive. This reversal seems appropriate for a story about the power of the imagination to triumph, at least momentarily, over death. The film is richly textured and tightly constructed; the escape scenes are so believable (even though they are so fantastic) that when the final inevitable snap of the rope occurs, the viewer is shocked again no matter how many times he has seen the film.

Among the best-known short films based on short stories is the *Short Story Showcase* series made for Encyclopedia Britannica by Larry Yust. Widely available on 16mm film, the films have probably been seen by more high school and college students than any others. We shall examine briefly the film versions of Herman Melville's *Bartleby the Scrivener*, Joseph Conrad's "The Secret Sharer," and Shirley Jackson's "The Lottery." The other five films in the series are listed in the filmography at the end of this essay.

Conrad's "The Secret Sharer," long recognized as a subtle symbolic masterpiece, is one of the most praised and popular stories in British literature. The genius of the story is that it communicates several different yet corresponding meanings at once: it is a story about the responsibilities of command, a story of moral conflict between loyalty to the community and loyalty to the individual, a story about a split within the self, and a story about the initiation into adult responsibility. Yust's short film manages to suggest all these levels. The young Captain (played by David Soul) is facing his first command when the mysterious Leggatt comes out of the sea asking for asylum. Having been accused of a murderous act on his own vessel, Leggatt seeks only someone to believe in his innocence. The obvious conflict the Captain faces is between his allegiance to his crew and his allegiance to the mysterious stranger he hides below decks; the more subtle conflict exists within the divided self of the young Captain and his secret sharer. Yust presents several suspenseful scenes in which the Captain must adroitly hide Leggatt from the crew; the voice-over thoughts of the Captain make us aware of the constant split between his command and his secret. The most difficult thematic aspect of the story for film to present is the suggestion that Leggatt and the Captain are indeed a single self—that Leggatt is a *doppelgänger* of the Captain himself. Yust makes use of lighting and cuts to suggest this identification.

In the first part of the film, there are several quick cuts from Leggatt to reaction shots of the Captain in which the lighting makes it look as if Leggatt has a beard as the Captain does. Below decks, where the overhead lighting seems quite natural, there are several shots in which we see the bent heads of the two, in which their blond hair makes them look like doubles. The fact that Leggatt and the Captain are both dressed at first in the Captain's sleeping suits furthers the identification and suggests that Leggatt is indeed a figure from the realm of sleep or dream—the realm of the unconscious. There are also several silent scenes in which the Captain and Leggatt are seen together—one particularly in the bathroom as Leggatt stands impassively while the Captain shaves—that communicate an intimacy so complete as to suggest one person rather than two. Thus, the film, like the story, can be read on several levels at once; Yust does not give in to the temptation to simplify and focus on one level only.

Yust tackles a much simpler story structure in Shirley Jackson's famous shocker, "The Lottery." Although the plot line of the story is simple and the characters even simpler, the story involves a rather carefully balanced literary trick which caused a great deal of controversy when the story was first published and has continued to "catch" readers ever since. The basic success of the story is that while the matter-of-fact tone suggests that the event is happening in the real world, as the events unfold the reader gradually begins to realize that what he is reading is a parable about human scapegoating. Because the story is presented both as parable and "as-if-it-were-really-happening," the reader gets drawn into the as-if-actual events so strongly that the parabolic ending comes as an unprepared-for shock. The filmmaker faces the choice of these two possible presentations: he can present a basically realistic story or he can stylize the story to suggest its fabulistic nature. The reader of the story can, after finishing it, look back again and see how Jackson has carefully stylized the telling from the beginning. Thus, although he has been tricked, he can see the careful blending of the realistic and the fabulistic. The filmmaker must make a choice as to his interpretation—either real event or fable—and stick to it throughout.

Larry Yust chooses the realistic presentation. His town is not a parabolic "once upon a time" world nor are his characters one-dimensional figures of fable. Rather, his town is a real town peopled with real, everyday people. In fact, Yust made use of the townspeople of Taft, California, to play the extras in the film, and he situated his story in what looks like a real town square. The realism of the presentation is so radical that the final shocking death by stoning comes as a hard-to-accept "fact." Anticipating this problem, the Encyclopedia Britannica company had the line—"The following is fiction"— inserted on the screen at its opening. Indeed, the problem of the story itself is its ambiguous situation between fiction obviously ascertained and fiction concealed by verisimilitude. Film, because of its own radically realistic nature, reduces the ambiguity. Yust's decision to use "real people" in the film as well as actors, however, creates an unsettling feeling in the viewer in spite of the film's realism. If we pull back away from the events of the film story and consider the making of it, we realize that Yust has taken his film crew and a small group of professional actors into a small California town and created a fictional world there. He has invited the townspeople to take part in this world. As we watch the film it is easy to determine which of the characters are actors, that is "pretend people," and which are the nonactors, that is, "real people." The irony of this realization results from our perception that the "real people" are the ones who do not seem to belong, the ones that stand out as uncomfortable in the fictional world they participate in. This uncomfortable position between fiction and reality is precisely what makes Jackson's story the successful trick that it is. Yust's choice of locale and casting, whether intentional or not, captures this uneasiness in the film.

Yust's production of Herman Melville's classic short story, *Bartleby the Scrivener*, is perhaps the best film in the Short Story Showcase series. Like "The Secret Sharer," *Bartleby the Scrivener* is a symbolic masterpiece of nineteenth century short fiction. It marks a transition point between the tale form practiced by Hawthorne and Poe and the realistic short story predominant in the latter part of the century. Rather than being simply a story in which characters are representational figures, as in the tale form, or purely realistic characters, as in later stories, *Bartleby the Scrivener* involves a "realistic" character— the narrator—confronting a parabolic figure—Bartleby— about whom there is "nothing ordinarily human." Bartleby "prefers not to" do anything because of the "wall" that he faces outside the office window on Wall Street. Bartleby responds to the wall "as if" it were an objectification of all that isolates him and frustrates him. There is nothing personal about Bartleby's malady; it is metaphysical. Bartleby's obsession with the wall transforms him into a symbolic figure who becomes an embodiment of a "wall" for the narrator. The conflict between Bartleby and the narrator is the conflict between a man who operates on "assumptions" and an idealization who operates on "preferences." None of the narrator's assumptions apply to Bartleby. Bartleby's need—to be accepted on his own terms, terms deemed perverse in relation to what is "ordinarily human"—cannot be fulfilled. Thus the story is an experience in frustration for the narrator, who attempts to relate to a character who has transcended the human realm of assumptions.

Yust's film captures this impasse excellently. The contrast between the implacable, stonelike mildness of Bartleby (played by Patrick Campbell) and the animated, expressive face of the narrator (played by James Westerfield) is the central focus of the film. The relationship between the two characters is presented primarily by close-ups of the two contrasting faces and by the spatial relationships between the two in the lawyer's office. For example, close-ups of the narrator's face as he expresses amazement, anger, puzzlement, determination, wheedling, and resignation in reaction to Bartleby's repeated "I prefer not to" are all contrasted with shots of Bartleby's unchanging expression. Profile two-shots of the narrator trying to reason with Bartleby further emphasize that Bartleby's situation goes beyond reason. Various shots of the narrator sitting comfortably behind his desk with Bartleby barely visible behind a screen suggest the closeness yet separation of the two figures. This sense of separation is further suggested by scenes in which the narrator gives Bartleby notice, but in which Bartleby is offscreen and the narrator appears to be talking to no one. Several long shots of the narrator alone at his desk or high angle shots of him standing in the office emphasize the emptiness around him; we are aware of the irony of the narrator thinking how lonely Bartleby is when in fact he himself is walled off and yet unaware of his isolated situation.

The film strikes a tone between whimsy and moral seriousness. This tone is created not only by the extreme contrast between narrator and Bartleby, but also by the caricatured figures of the others in the office—Turkey, Nippers, and Ginger Nut—and by the whimsical musical background and the separation of the segments of the story by printed time-frames of "The Second Day,"

"Several Days Later," "A Week Later," and so on. That the absurdity of Bartleby's stance can lead only to pathos at the end is emphasized by the final shots of Bartleby's "walled-in" situation in the prison yard. The film is an excellent example of the camera's ability to make use of close-ups and spatial situations to emphasize a dramatic conflict, and in this case, a dramatic conflict created by a symbolic metaphysical impasse. It is little wonder that Yust himself has called this the best of the Short Story Showcase series.

The most ambitious attempt to bring the short story to the screen is the seventeen-film series, The American Short Story, produced in 1977 and 1980 by Robert Geller's Learning in Focus, Inc., for the Public Broadcasting System and supported in part by grants from the National Endowment for the Humanities. Nine films aired on PBS stations in 1977; a second round of eight films aired in early 1980. Featuring top directors, writers, and actors (often willing to work for scale), the films offer a wide spectrum of film techniques and talents. Rather than comment extensively on two or three of the films, a few comments will be made about several of the most successful. (Full information is included in the filmography at the end of this essay.)

Probably the two most interesting films in the first series are the treatments of Flannery O'Connor's "The Displaced Person" and John Updike's "The Music School." The dramatic situation in O'Connor's story is similar to that in *Bartleby the Scrivener*, in that the displaced person, Mr. Guizac, is less a real character than a representative figure who confronts Mrs. McIntyre with a moral dilemma. The magic of O'Connor's story is that while on one level it embodies a social/moral conflict, on a symbolic level it is an exploration of Catholic metaphysics. Screenwriter Horton Foote and director Glen Jordan do not try to avoid the subtle and difficult symbolic and metaphysical ironies of the story, yet neither do they force these ironies. For example, when Mrs. McIntyre says that Mr. Guizac is her salvation (meaning economic salvation) at the end of the film, we realize that he has been her spiritual salvation instead. When Mrs. McIntyre faces the priest (solemnly played by John Houseman), and the priest says of the outspread tail of the peacock, "Christ will come like that," Mrs. McIntyre, still talking about Guizac, says "He didn't have to come in the first place." The priest says, "He came to redeem us." Indeed, Guizac, who must be sacrificed, serves as the Christlike figure who redeems Mrs. McIntyre (symbolically, "makes her entire"); thus at the end of the story, we leave the priest talking to the withdrawn Mrs. McIntyre about purgatory. The story is a difficult one which necessitates an acceptance of the harshness of purgatory as a prerequisite for salvation; the film stays remarkably true to the grotesque world of Flannery O'Connor and to her insistence on the hard road to salvation.

John Updike's "The Music School," also a difficult story, is about the narrator Alfred Schweigen's attempts to understand the abstract relationship between his reading of the murder of an acquaintance, his hearing a young priest talk about the church's adoption of a Eucharistic wafer that must be chewed rather than dissolved, and his feeling about taking his daughter to her music lesson. The story is almost a textbook example of the modern short story's movement away from linear plot lines toward more spatial poetic metaphors. It is also an example of the modern short story's tendency to be more and more self-reflexive, that is, less about the external world and more and more about its own means of communication. Alfred Schweigen is a writer who writes the story we read and, who, in the very process of writing the story, comes to some resolution about the nature of the artistic process and its relation to the religious experience.

John Korty, who both wrote the screenplay and directed the film, makes his presentation as elliptical and fragmented as the original story. The mystery of the transubstantiation which obsesses Schweigen is also the mystery of how the materials of life become transformed into the spiritual nature of art itself. The paradox of the spirit becoming embodied is the central paradox that preoccupies the story. Korty chooses to allow the actor playing Schweigen to communicate the language of the story as a voice-over; thus there is no dialogue in the story to distract from the various images of the wafer, the murder, the music school, and so forth. The tension between the material and the spiritual, the translucent and the opaque, and what must be chewed and what must be dissolved makes up the central tension in the story. In the film, Korty sets against the hard, chewable physical images of the world of reality various images of translucence such as lace curtains blowing in the breeze, Schweigen's bare feet in early morning grass, the song of an invisible bird in the trees, a windowpane sprayed by water—all presented against the background mystery of how art—music in this particular case—makes the mysterious movement from vision to percussion to music to emotion and back to vision again.

Also interesting but perhaps less successful attempts to translate basically metaphysical issues to film are the verions of Stephen Crane's "The Blue Hotel" and Henry James's "The Jolly Corner." The situation of the Swede in Crane's story is somewhat similar to that of Bartleby and O'Connor's displaced person—a "stranger in a strange land" who makes a tragic error in perception. Jan Kadar's direction of the story makes the card game the central metaphor and the central dramatic action. The story, as a result of this focus, becomes somewhat slow and static. The most significant tension in the story, a tension which Kadar communicates in the film primarily through Harry Petrakis' dialogue, is between the game played "for fun" and the game taken dead seriously. The major issue is one in which the Swede, whose view of the "West" is conditioned by reading dime novels, arrives expecting violence and threats. When he is told that such a view is only fiction, that he is safe and can "make himself at home," he takes this invitation too far and mimics the natives. The result is the Swede's death. The story is Crane's attempt to create a classical tragic structure reminiscent of Greek tragedy. Jan Kadar's film only fitfully fulfills this intention.

The basic problem with Arthur Barron's version of Henry James's famous ghost story is that the James dialogue and characterization constitute a risky stylization to attempt to translate the film. Although Fritz Weaver (as Spencer Brydon) and Salome Jens (as Alice Staverton) try valiantly to make the reticent James style believable, the story becomes intolerably slow and static. The complex story of Spencer Brydon coming home to America to confront the spectral image of a self he might have been is simplified in the film by suggesting that that self is simply a sexual being or a corrupted robber-baron. Even the image of the other self that Brydon finally corners and confronts in his childhood home looks like a character out of the old Spencer Tracy film version of *Dr. Jekyll and Mr. Hyde* (1941). Furthermore, Barron's use of a dream sequence by Alice Staverton in which she is a dance hall girl and Brydon is a lecher further emphasizes Barron's basically sexual interpretation of the story.

The film versions of Sherwood Anderson's "I'm a Fool," Ernest Hemingway's "Soldier's Home," and Richard Wright's "Almos' a Man" are rather straightforward treatments of classic American initiation stories. Joan Micklin Silver's version of F. Scott Fitzgerald's "Bernice Bobs Her Hair" is a stylishly whimsical version of a basically simple story. Silver's focus on the comic world of youth in the 1920's, caught somewhere between childhood and adulthood, makes the film even more interesting than the original. Silver uses various images such as the girls putting on "lipstick" with red jellybeans and the boys alternately playing prep-school sophisticates and "horsing around" to suggest this transition. The film becomes a study in male/female stereotypes more interesting than the simple plot line of Bernice's transformation from wallflower to *femme fatale*.

Of the eight films presented in the second series in 1980, the most interesting are the adaptations of Willa Cather's "Paul's Case," directed by Lamont Johnson, and Katherine Anne Porter's "The Jilting of Granny Weatherall," directed by Randa Haines. Much of the success of "Paul's Case" is due to the performance of Eric Roberts, who plays the art-bedazzled Paul with just the right blend of naïveté and sophistication. In contrast to the fantasy world of the young boy in Conrad Aiken's "Silent Snow, Secret Snow," the alternate realm of reality which Cather's Paul aspires to is objectified in drama, music, painting, and literature. Moreover, the story is less about the ineffable art world than it is about the contrast between Paul's dreams and his social reality. As such, it is an easier theme to present on film than the theme of the origin and essence of art with which Aiken's story deals. The difficult task in portraying Cather's story on the screen is to walk the fine line between presenting Paul's desire as a genuine artistic obsession or presenting it as a spurious dilettantish ideal. For the most part, Lamont Johnson creates a tone and Eric

Roberts presents a personality which allows the audience to waver between these two views; the final suicide scene is thus appropriately both tragic and pathetic at once.

Katherine Anne Porter's elegiac story, "The Jilting of Granny Weatherall," because it is so filled with Granny's impressionistic memories of the past, is not an easy story to adapt. Corrine Jacker's screenplay deals with the problem by changing the time frame from that of Granny lying on her deathbed to the last full day of her life as she, prescient of the end, prepares for the inevitable. The change works well; although it provides a more realistic framework for the story, it still allows for Granny Weatherall to experience those hallucinatory scenes from the past that make Porter's story so memorable. The tone of the film is a combination of gritty reality, as Granny goes about the kind of work that has indeed allowed her to "weather all," and poetic beauty, as she remembers lost hopes and dreams. Geraldine Fitzgerald plays the title role superbly; her face as she lies on her deathbed is both illuminated and lined, rugged and beautiful at the same time. The theme of the story is a complex one that provides no easy answer to the question of whether love can be earned or can only be freely given. Similarly, the film version, although the viewer can sympathetically identify with Granny's final agony, does not offer false hope that Granny has not been jilted again, this time ultimately.

Perhaps the most disappointing of the films in this second series is the adaptation of Nathaniel Hawthorne's "Rappaccini's Daughter," one of the most complex and morally ambiguous short fictions in nineteenth century American literature and surely the most metaphysically subtle of all of Hawthorne's short stories. Hawthorne's parable is about a latter-day Adam who finds his Eve in a "poisoned" garden and destroys her by attempting to bring her into his own mundane world. Dezso Magyar's film is primarily a love story—a haunting and magical love story, but a love story nevertheless. Hawthorne's story is much more than that; yet as we lament that Magyar did not try to go beyond this surface plot, we sympathize with the difficulty of presenting the complex mythic symbolism of the original. Kathleen Beller is indeed beautiful as Rappaccini's daughter, but she is too much the beautiful girl and too little the magical creature of Hawthorne's imagination.

The considerably lighter comic and satiric stories of Ring Lardner, James Thurber, and Mark Twain are also the subjects of adaptation in this second series. Lardner's "The Golden Honeymoon" is a delightful monologue in the Lardner idiom. The film version, unable to capture the sustained voice of Charley Tate, is amusing and charming, but must content itself with simply dramatically presenting the story of the two elder couples. The story itself depends almost solely on the voice of the narrator. Thurber's "The Greatest Man in the World" is a broad and easy satire about the habit Americans have of making heroes out of the most unlikely candidates; it translates easily to film. Twain's "The Man That Corrupted Hadleyburg" is also a simple satire which is presented on film in broad, caricatured strokes; the problem with the adaptation is that the humor and stereotyping are played so broadly that the film misses much of the bitterness and bite of Twain's story.

William Faulkner's "Barn Burning" receives a faithful treatment in an adaptation written by Horton Foote and directed by Peter Werner. The essence of the story—the difficult tension between a boy's idealization of his father and his equally questionable idealization of a social reality beyond his reach—is clearly communicated in the film. The ambience of Faulkner's world is finely captured; the dogged desperation and pride of the Snopes family, the agony of young Sarty's decision, and his final desperate act are all translated to film convincingly.

The American Short Story series is a magnificent testament to the excellence of the short story as a fictional genre and to its adaptability to short film. One can only hope that the series will continue; it is probably the most important revitalization effort the short story has received in the twentieth century.

Filmography

Agee, James. *A Mother's Tale*. Rex Goff, dir. Learning Corp. of America, 1977. Live action with voices of Maureen Stapleton and Orson Welles, 18 min.

Aiken, Conrad. *Silent Snow, Secret Snow*. Gene Kearney, dir. Audio Brandon, 1966. A second version of this film was shown on the Rod Serling television series, *Night Gallery*, in 1971 with Orson Welles narrating, 17 min.

Akutagawa, Ryunosuke. *Roshomon*. Akira Kurosawa, dir. 1951, 83 min. In 1964, Martin Ritt made an American Western version of this story entitled *The Outrage*, with Paul Newman, Claire Bloom, Laurence Harvey, and Edward G. Robinson, 97 min.

Aleichem, Sholom. *The Fiddler on the Roof*. Norman Jewison, dir. With Topol. 1972. A Musical based on several Aleichem stories, 180 min.

Anderson, Sherwood. *I'm a Fool*. Noel Black, dir. Learning in Focus, Inc., 1977. The American Short Story Series. With Ron Howard, 38 min.

Balzac, Honoré de. *La Grande Breteche*. Britannica, 1975. Part of Orson Welles's Great Mysteries Series, 24 min.

―――――――― . *The Maid of Thilouse*. Nathan Zucker, dir. Audio Brandon, 1953. On Stage Series, 15 min.

Benét, Stephen Vincent. *The Devil and Daniel Webster*. William Dietrle, dir. *All That Money Can Buy* was the original title of the film. With Walter Houston, 1941, 109 min.

Bierce, Ambrose. *The Boarded Window*. Alan W. Beattie, dir. McGraw-Hill, 1978, 18 min.

―――――――― . *Chickamauga*. Robert Enrico, dir. McGraw-Hill, 1963, 33 min.

_____ . *Coup de Grace*. Barr Films, 1978, 19 min.

_____ . *The Man and the Snake*. Pyramid Films, 1976, 26 min.

_____ . *The Mockingbird*. Robert Enrico, dir. McGraw-Hill, 1963, 39 min.

_____ . *Occurrence at Owl Creek Bridge*. Robert Enrico, dir. Mc-Graw-Hill, 1963, 39 min. A 1931 short film adaptation, directed by Charles Vidor, entitled *The Bridge*, is distributed by Audio Brandon, 11 min.

_____ . *One of the Missing*. Audio Brandon, 1971, 56 min.

_____ . *Parker Adderson, Philosopher*. Arthur Barron, dir. Learning in Focus, Inc., 1977. The American Short Story Series. With Harris Yulin, 38 min.

Böll, Heinrich. *Dr. Murke's Collected Silences*. Per Berglund, dir. McGraw-Hill, 1971. Swedish film with subtitles, 23 min.

Capote, Truman. *Trilogy*. Frank Perry, dir. Hurlock Cine World, 1969. Adaptations of "Among the Paths to Eden," "A Christmas Memory," and "Miriam," 110 min.

Cather, Willa. *Paul's Case*. Lamont Johnson, dir. Learning in Focus, Inc., 1980. The American Short Story Series. With Eric Roberts, 60 min.

Cheever, John. *The Swimmer*. Frank Perry, dir. Columbia, 1968. With Burt Lancaster, Janice Rule, Kim Hunter, 94 min.

Chambers, Robert W. *Pickets*. Dennis Sanders and Terry Sanders, dirs. Pyramid, 1954. Based on "A Time Out of War," 22 min.

Chesterton, G. K. *The Detective*. Robert Hamer, dir. Based on the Father Brown stories. With Alec Guinness, 1954, 100 min.

Chekhov, Anton. *The Bass Fiddle*. M. Fasquel, dir. McGraw-Hill, 1962, 28 min.

_____ . *The Bet*. Ron Waller, dir. Pyramid, 1969, 24 min.

_____ . *Black Sabbath*. Mario Bava, dir. Audio Brandon, 1964. Adaptations of "The Telephone Call," "A Drop of Water," and "The Wurdalak." With Boris Karloff, 99 min.

_____ . *The Boarding House*. Macmillan, 1977. Narrated by John Gielgud, 27 min.

_____ . *The Boor*. Nathan Zucker, dir. Audio Brandon, 1955. On Stage Series, 15 min.

_____ . *Desire to Sleep*. Macmillan, 1977. Narrated by John Gielgud. 14 min.

_____ . *An Event*. Vatroslav Mimica, dir. Walter Reader, 1970, 93 min.

_____ . *The Fugitive*. Macmillan, 1977. Narrated by John Gielgud, 15 min.

_____ . *Grief*. Mark Fine, dir. New Line Cinema. With Burgess Meredith, 28 min.

_____ . *The Lady with the Dog*. Joseph Heifitz, dir. Audio Brandon,

1960. Russian with subtitles, 86 min.

——————— . *Revenge*. Macmillan, 1977. Narrated by John Gielgud, 26 min.

——————— . *Rothchild's Violin*. Macmillan, 1977. Narrated by John Gielgud, 23 min.

——————— . *Volodya*. Macmillan, 1977. Narrated by John Gielgud, 25 min.

——————— . *A Work of Art*. M. Kovalyvov, dir. Macmillan, 1960, 10 min.

Clark, Walter Van Tilburg. *The Portable Phonograph*. Britannica, 1972, 24 min.

Connell, Richard. *The Most Dangerous Game*. RKO, 1932. With Leslie Banks, Joel McCrea, and Fay Wray, 78 min.

Conrad, Joseph. *The Secret Sharer*. Larry Yust, dir. Britannica, 1973. Short Story Showcase Series, 30 min. A 1952 version of this story was directed by John Brahm—half of a film entitled *Face to Face*; the other half was Stephen Crane's "The Bride Comes to Yellow Sky." With James Mason, 45 min.

Cortázar, Julio. *Blow-Up*. Michelangelo Antonioni, dir. With David Hemmings and Vanessa Redgrave, 1966, 111 min.

Crane, Stephen. *The Blue Hotel*. Jan Kadar, dir. Learning in Focus, Inc., 1977. With David Warner and James Keach, 54 min.

——————— . *The Bride Comes to Yellow Sky*. Bretaigne Windust, dir. 1952. Half of *Face to Face*; see Conrad above. With Robert Preston and Marjorie Steele, 45 min.

——————— . *Face of Fire*. Albert Band, dir. Based on "The Monster." With Cameron Mitchell and James Whitmore, 1959, 83 min.

——————— . *Stephen Crane's Three Miraculous Soldiers*. BFA Educational Media, 1976, 18 min.

——————— . *The Upturned Face*. Edward Folger, dir. Pyramid, 1973, 10 min.

Dickens, Charles. *The Signalman*. Nathan Zucker, dir. Audio Brandon, 1955. On Stage Series, 15 min.

Dinesen, Isak. *The Immortal Story*. Orson Welles, dir. Audio Brandon, 1963. With Orson Welles and Jeanne Moreau, 63 min.

Dostoevski, Fyodor. *The Crocodile*. Larry Yust, dir. Britannica, 1973. Short Story Showcase Series, 29 min.

Dreiser, Theodore. *The Lost Phoebe*. Mel Damski, dir. Perspective Films, 1978, 30 min.

Faulkner, William. *Barn Burning*. Peter Werner, dir. Learning in Focus, Inc., 1980. The American Short Story Series. With Tommy Lee Jones, 38 min.

——————— . *The Long Hot Summer*. Martin Ritt, dir. Includes "Barn Burning" and "The Spotted Horses." With Paul Newman, Joanne Woodward, Orson Welles, Lee Remick, Anthony Franciosa, and Angela Lansbury. 1958, 117 min.

Fitzgerald, F. Scott. *The Last Time I Saw Paris*. Richard Brooks, dir. Based on "Babylon Revisited." With Elizabeth Taylor, Van Johnson, Walter Pidgeon, and Donna Reed, 1954, 116 min.

_____ . *Bernice Bobs Her Hair*. Joan Micklin Silver, dir. Learning in Focus, Inc., 1977. The American Short Story Series. With Shelley Duvall, Bud Cort, and Veronica Cartwright, 47 min.

_____ . *F. Scott Fitzgerald and the Last of the Belles*. George Schaeffer, dir. Intercuts the adaptation of the story with dramatizations of Fitzgerald's life. With Richard Chamberlain, Blythe Danner, Susan Sarandon, and David Huffman, 1974, 98 min.

Gaines, Ernest. *The Sky Is Gray*. Stan Lathan, dir. Learning in Focus, Inc., 1980. The American Short Story Series. With Olivia Cole, James Bond III, and Cleavon Little, 60 min.

Gogol, Nikolai. *Diary of a Madman*. Robert Carlisle, dir. 1967, 87 min.

_____ . *The Nose*. Contemporary Films, 1963. A pin-board animated film, 16 min.

Greene, Graham. *Across the Bridge*. Ken Annakin, dir. 1957. With Rod Steiger, 103 min.

_____ . *The Fallen Idol*. Carol Reed, dir. Based on "The Basement Room." With Ralph Richardson, 1949, 94 min.

Gorky, Maxim. *Twenty-Six Men and a Girl*. Michael Weiskopf, dir. Viewfinders, 24 min.

Hale, Edward Everett. *Man Without a Country*. McGraw-Hill, 1953, 25 min. Warner Bros. made a 21-minute short of this story in 1938.

Harte, Bret. *Luck of Roaring Camp*. Film Classics Exchange, 1937, 60 min.

_____ . *Outcasts of Poker Flat*. Joseph M. Newman, dir. Twentieth-Century Fox, 1952. With Anne Baxter, Dale Robertson, Cameron Mitchell, 81 min. Warner Bros. released an adaptation of this story in 1931; RKO released another version in 1937.

_____ . *Tennessee's Partner*. Allan Dwan, dir. With John Payne, Ronald Reagan, and Rhonda Fleming, 1955, 87 min.

Hawthorne, Nathaniel. *Dr. Heidegger's Experiment*. Larry Yust, dir. Britannica, 1969. Short Story Showcase Series, 22 min. Another version of this story was directed by Nathan Zucker for the On Stage Series in 1954, 15 min.

_____ . *Rappaccini's Daughter*. Dezso Magyar, dir. Learning in Focus, Inc., 1980. The American Short Story Series. With Kristoffer Tabori and Kathleen Beller, 60 min.

_____ . *Young Goodman Brown*. Donald Fox, dir. Pyramid, 1973, 30 min.

Hemingway, Ernest. *Adventures of a Young Man*. Martin Ritt, dir. Based on the Nick Adams stories in *In Our Time*. With Richard Beymer, Paul Newman, Dan Dailey, Arthur Kennedy, and Susan Strasberg, 1962, 145 min.

——————— . *The Killers*. Robert Siodmak, dir. With Burt Lancaster, Ava Gardner, Edmond O'Brien, 1946, 105 min. Another adaptation, directed by Don Siegel, was released in 1964, with Lee Marvin, John Cassavetes, Ronald Reagan, and Angie Dickinson, 95 min.

——————— . *My Old Man*. Larry Yust, dir. Britannica, 1969. Short Story Showcase Series, 27 min. A full-length film version, directed by Jean Negulesco and starring John Garfield, was released in 1949 with the title *Under My Skin*, 86 min.

——————— . *The Macomber Affair*. Zoltan Korda, dir. Based on "The Short Happy Life of Frances Macomber." With Gregory Peck, Joan Bennett, and Robert Preston, 1947, 89 min.

——————— . *Soldier's Home*. Robert Young, dir. Learning in Focus, Inc., 1977. The American Short Story Series. With Richard Backus, 41 min.

——————— . *Snows of Kilimanjaro*. Henry King, dir. With Gregory Peck, Susan Hayward, Ava Gardner, and Hildegarde Neff, 1953, 117 min.

Henry, O. *O. Henry's Full House*. An omnibus film of five adaptations directed by five different directors. The stories are: "Last Leaf," "Gift of the Magi," "The Ransom of Red Chief," "Clarion Call," and "The Cop and the Anthem." An all-star cast including Charles Laughton, David Wayne, Marilyn Monroe, Anne Baxter, Jeanne Crain, 1952, 117 min.

Huxley, Aldous. *A Woman's Vengeance*. Zoltan Korda, dir. Adaptation by Huxley of his story "The Gioconda Smile." With Charles Boyer, Ann Blyth, and Jessica Tandy, 1948, 96 min.

——————— . *Prelude to Fame*. An adaptation of "Young Archimedes," 1950, 77 min.

Irving, Washington. *The Legend of Sleepy Hollow*. Stephen Bosustow, Producer. Pyramid, 1972. Animated, 13 min. The Walt Disney Studio version of this story was released in 1949 as *The Adventures of Ichabod and Mr. Toad*. Will Rogers played Ichabod in a 1922 film entitled *The Headless Horseman and Will Rogers*.

Jackson, Shirley. *The Lottery*. Larry Yust, dir. Britannica, 1969. Short Story Showcase Series, 18 min.

Jacobs, W. W. *The Monkey's Paw*. BFA Educational Media, 1979, 19 min. A 1932 version of the story was directed by Wesly Ruggles, 56 min.; in 1942, Norman Dee directed another adaptation, 64 min.

James, Henry. *The Jolly Corner*. Arthur Barron, dir. Learning in Focus, Inc., 1977. The American Short Story Series. With Fritz Weaver and Salome Jens, 43 min.

Kafka, Franz. *The Hunger Artist*. Paramount Communications, 1976, 10 min.

Kipling, Rudyard. *The Man Who Would Be King*. John Huston, dir. With Michael Caine, Sean Connery, and Christopher Plummer, 1975, 127 min.

London, Jack. *To Build a Fire*. Robert Stitzel, dir. BFA Communication

Media, 1975, 15 min. David Cobham directed an adaptation in 1969, narrated by Orson Welles, 56 min.

Lardner, Ring. *The Champion*. Stanley Kramer, dir. With Kirk Douglas, Arthur Kennedy, and Ruth Roman, 1949, 99 min.

—————— . *The Golden Honeymoon*. Noel Black, dir. Learning in Focus, Inc. 1980. The American Short Story Series. With James Whitmore, Teresa Wright, Stephen Eliot, and Nan Martin, 60 min.

Lawrence, D. H. *The Rocking Horse Winner*. Anthony Pelissier, dir. With Valerie Hobson, John Howard Davies, and John Mills, 1949, 91 min.

Malamud, Bernard. *Angel Levine*. Jan Kadar, dir. With Zero Mostel and Harry Belafonte, 1970, 104 min.

Mansfield, Katherine. *A Doll's House*. S-L Film Productions, 1969, 17 min.

—————— . *The Garden Party*. Jack Sholder, dir. ACI Films, 1974, 24 min.

Maugham, W. Somerset. *Rain*. Lewis Milestone, dir. With Joan Crawford, Walter Huston, and Guy Kibbee, 77 min. *Miss Sadie Thompson*, directed by Curtis Bernhardt, and starring Rita Hayworth, Jose Ferrer, and Aldo Ray, 1953, is also based on this story, 91 min.

—————— . *Encore*. Pat Jackson, dir. An omnibus film with adaptations of "The Ant and the Grasshopper," "Winter Cruise," and "Gigolo and Gigolette." With Glynis Johns, Kay Walsh, and Nigel Patrick, 1952, 90 min.

—————— . *Quartet*. Ken Annakin, dir. Another omnibus film with adaptations of "The Alien Corn," "The Colonel's Lady," "The Kite," and "The Facts of Life." With Cecil Parker, Mai Zetterling, and George Cole, 1948, 120 min.

—————— . *Trio*. Ken Annakin and Harold French, dirs. Still another omnibus film with adaptations of "The Verger," "Mr. Knowall," and "Sanitorium." With Jean Simmons and Nigel Patrick, 1950, 91 min.

Maupasssant, Guy de. *Angel and Sinner*. Film Classic Exchange, 1946. A French film based on *"Boule de Suif,"* 1946, 90 min.

—————— . *A Day in the Country*. Jean Renoir, dir. Contemporary Films, 1937. French title is *La Partie de Campagne*, 37 min.

—————— . *Diary of a Madman*. Reginald Le Borg, dir. Based on "La Horla." With Vincent Price and Nancy Kovack, 1963, 96 min.

—————— . *Mademoiselle Fifi*. Robert Wise, dir. With Simone Simon and Jason Robards, Sr., 1944, 68 min.

—————— . *Masculine-Feminine*. Jean-Luc Godard, dir. Adaptations of "Paul's Mistress" and "The Signal," 1966, 103 min.

—————— . *The Necklace*. Filmfair Communications, 1979, 24 min.

—————— . *Le Plaisir*. Max Ophuls, dir. Adaptations of "The Mask," "The Model," and "The House of Madame Tellier," 1953, 95 min.

Melville, Herman. *Bartleby*. Larry Yust, dir. Britannica, 1969. Short Story

Showcase Series, 28 min. Other film versions of *Bartleby the Scrivener* include a 1970 British version directed by Anthony Friedman, with Paul Scofield and John McEnery, 79 min.; and a 1964 adaptation by George Bluestone for the University of Washington, 29 min.

——————— . *The Happy Failure*. Nathan Zucker, dir. Audio Brandon, 1954. On Stage Series, 15 min.

——————— . *The Lightening Rod Man*. Pyramid, 1975, 16 min.

Mishima, Yukio. *Rite of Love and Death*. Yukio Mishima, dir. Grove, 1968. An adaptation of "Patriotism," in which Mishima plays the lead, 21 min.

Oates, Joyce Carol. *In the Region of Ice*. American Film Institute, 1977, 38 min.

O'Connor, Flannery. *A Circle in the Fire*. Victor Nunez, dir. Perspective Films, 1976, 49 min.

——————— . *Comforts of Home*. Jerome Shore, dir. Phoenix Films, 1974, 40 min.

——————— . *The Displaced Person*. Glen Jordan, dir. Learning in Focus, Inc., 1977. The American Short Story Series. With Irene Worth and John Houseman, 57 min.

——————— . *Good Country People*. Jeff Jackson, dir. 1975, 32 min.

Poe, Edgar Allan, *The Assignation*. Curtis Harrington, dir. Audio Brandon, 1953, 8 min.

——————— . *The Black Cat*. Edgar G. Ulmer, dir. With Boris Karloff and Bela Lugosi, 1934, 65 min. Other adaptations of this story include a 1941 version directed by Albert Rogell, with Bela Lugosi, Basil Rathbone, and Broderick Crawford, 70 min.; and a 1966 version directed by Harold Hoffman, 77 min. All three are only loosely based on the story.

——————— . *The Cask of Amontillado*. Nathan Zucker, dir. BFA Educational Media, 1955. On Stage Series, 15 min.

——————— . *The Fall of the House of Usher*. Larry Yust, dir. Britannica, 1969. Short Story Showcase, 30 min. Other adaptations of this story include Jean Epstein's 1928 version entitled *La Chute de la Maison Usher*, which combines the story with "The Oval Portrait," 55 min.; James Sibley Watson's 1928 version, which is distributed by the Museum of Modern Art, 12 min.; and a Roger Corman adaptation entitled *The House of Usher*, with Vincent Price and Mark Damon, 1960, 85 min.

——————— . *The Masque of the Red Death*. Pavao Statler, dir. McGraw-Hill, 1970. A production of the Zagreb school of animation in Yugoslavia, 10 min. There is also a Roger Corman version of this story which combines "The Masque of the Red Death" with "Hop-Frog." With Vincent Price and Hazel Court, 1961, 89 min.

——————— . *Murders in the Rue Morgue*. Gordon Hessler, dir. Swank, 1973. With Jason Robards, Jr., Herbert Lom, and Christine Kaufmann, 86 min. Other adaptations include a 1932 version directed by Robert Florey, with Bela Lugosi and Sidney Fox, 62 min.; and a 1953 version directed by Roy Del Ruth, with Karl Malden, 84 min., entitled *The Phantom of the Rue Morgue.*

_____ . *The Mystery of Marie Roget.* Phil Rosen, dir. With Maria Montez and Maria Ouspenskaya, 1942, 91 min.

_____ . *The Oblong Box.* Gordon Hessler, dir. With Vincent Price and Christopher Lee, 1969, 95 min.

_____ . *The Pit and the Pendulum.* Roger Corman, dir. With Vincent Price and John Kerr, 1961, 80 min.

_____ . *The Premature Burial.* Roger Corman, dir. With Ray Milland and Hazel Court, 1962, 81 min. A 1935 version directed by John H. Auer is entitled *The Crime of Doctor Crespi*, 63 min.

_____ . *Spirits of the Dead.* Audio Brandon, 1969. An omnibus film of three adaptations directed by different directors: *Metzengerstein*, directed by Roger Vadim; *Toby Damnit* ("Never Bet the Devil Your Head"), directed by Federico Fellini; and *William Wilson*, directed by Louis Malle, 118 min.

_____ . *Tales of Terror.* Roger Corman, dir. An omnibus film with adaptations of "Morella," "Facts in the Case of M. Valdemar," "The Black Cat," and "The Cask of Amontillado." With Vincent Price, Peter Lorre, Basil Rathbone, and Debra Paget, 1962, 90 min.

_____ . *The Tell-Tale Heart.* Stephen Bosustow, producer. Learning Corp. of America, 1969, animated, 8 min. Other adaptations include *The Avenging Conscience*, D. W. Griffith, dir., 1914, 70 min.; *Bucket of Blood.* Brian Desmond Hurst, dir., 1934, 49 min.; as well as versions directed by Ernest Morris, 1961, 81 min.; and Steve Carver, 1973, 26 min.

_____ . *The Tomb of Ligeia.* Roger Corman, dir. With Vincent Price and Elizabeth Shepherd, 1965, 79 min.

_____ . *War Gods of the Deep.* Jacques Tourneur, dir. Based on "A Descent into the Maelstrom." With Vincent Price and Tab Hunter, 1965, 85 min.

Porter, Katherine Anne. *The Jilting of Granny Weatherall.* Randa Haines, dir. Learning in Focus, Inc., 1980. The American Short Story Series. With Geraldine Fitzgerald, 60 min.

Pushkin, Alexander. *Queen of Spades.* Thorold Dickinson, dir. 1949. With Dame Edith Evans, 95 min. Nathan Zucker directed an adaptation for his On Stage Series in 1957, 15 min.

Saki. *The Open Window.* Richard Patterson, dir. Pyramid, 1972, 11 min.

Salinger, J. D. *My Foolish Heart.* Mark Robson, dir. Based on "Uncle Wiggily in Connecticut." With Susan Hayward and Dana Andrews, 1950, 98 min.

Sillitoe, Alan. *The Loneliness of the Long Distance Runner.* Tony Richardson, dir. With Tom Courtnay and Michael Redgrave, 1962, 103 min.

Steinbeck, John. *Flight*. Barnaby Conrad, dir. San Francisco Films, 1961, 54 min.

——————— . *Leader of the People*. BFA Educational Media, 1979, 23 min.

Stevenson, Robert Louis. *The Strange Door*. Joseph Pevney, dir. Based on "The Sire de Maletroit's Door." With Boris Karloff and Charles Laughton, 1951, 80 min.

Stockton, Frank. *The Lady or the Tiger*. Larry Yust, dir. Britannica, 1969. Short Story Showcase Series, 16 min.

Thurber, James. *Battle of the Sexes*. Charles Crichton, dir. Based on "The Catbird Seat." With Peter Sellers, 1960, 88 min.

——————— . *The Greatest Man in the World*. Ralph Rosenblum, dir. Learning in Focus Inc., 1980. The American Short Story Series. With Brad Davis and Carol Kane, 60 min.

——————— . *The Night the Ghost Got In*. Robert Stitzel, dir. BFA Educational Media, 1976, 16 min.

——————— . *The Secret Life of Walter Mitty*. Norman Z. McLeod. With Danny Kaye and Virginia Mayo, 1947, 105 min.

——————— . *The Unicorn in the Garden*. Stephen Bosustow, producer. Learning Corp. of America, 1962. An animated version, 9 min.

Turgenev, Ivan. *Bezhin Meadow*. Sergei Eisenstein, dir. Audio Brandon, 1935, 30 min.

Twain, Mark. *The Best Man Wins*. Based on "The Celebrated Jumping Frog of Calaveras County," 1948, 75 min.

——————— . *The Man Who Corrupted Hadleyburg*. Ralph Rosenblum, dir. Learning in Focus, Inc., 1980. The American Short Story Series. With Robert Preston, 38 min.

Updike, John. *The Music School*. John Korty, dir. Learning in Focus, Inc., 1977. The American Short Story Series. With Ron Weyland, 30 min.

Wells, H. G. *The Man Who Could Work Miracles*. Lothar Mendes, dir. With Roland Young, Joan Gardner, and Ralph Richardson, 1936, 90 min.

Williams, Gene. *Sticky My Fingers, Fleet My Feet*. John Hancock, dir. Time-Life, 1970, 23 min.

Wright, Richard. *Almos' a Man*. Stan Latham, dir. Learning in Focus, Inc., 1977. The American Short Story Series. With Levar Burton, 39 min.

Charles E. May

FICTION WRITERS ON WRITING SHORT FICTION

If one considers the amount of scholarly work devoted to an attempt to establish a theoretical base for the short story, one may be tempted to conclude that the short story is the most underrated and least understood of literary genres. Indeed, although there have been sporadic attempts to define the short story, and although critics have noted certain apparent changes in the form, there is no consensus among critics as to just what a short story is beyond what short-story writers have themselves said about the genre. What the writers themselves have said, however, is considerable and may be, when we get right down to it, the base upon which critics need to work if further refinement of definition or new definition is to be forthcoming.

In his famous review of Nathaniel Hawthorne's *Twice-Told Tales* (1842, 2nd ed.), Edgar Allan Poe set down what many people believe was the first theoretical statement about the form of the short story:

> A skilful literary artist has constructed a tale. If wise, he has not fashioned his thoughts to accomodate his incidents; but having conceived, with deliberated care, a certain unique or single effect to be wrought out, he then invents such incidents—he then combines such events as may best aid him in establishing this preconceived effect. If his very initial sentence tend not to the outbringing of this effect, then he has failed in his first step. In the whole composition there should be no word written, of which the tendency, direct or indirect, is not to the one pre-established design. And by such means, with such skill and care, a picture is at length pointed which leaves in the mind of him who contemplates it with a kindred art, a sense of the fullest satisfaction.

The short prose narrative, Poe believed, was "unquestionably the fairest field for the exercise of the loftiest talent, which can be afforded by the wide domains of mere prose." Next to the poem, the short story takes the most talent to write and, because of its length, affords the reader the opportunity to grasp in the time of a single sitting "the immense force" derivable from totality of effect. Poe's insistence that a reader read with an art kindred to that of the author makes of readers cocreators in the literary process; otherwise "obvious meaning" can smother "insinuated" meaning and undercurrents of suggestion will go unnoticed.

Poe's review unquestionably gives to the short story the status of an art form, and his insistence on the reader's shared participation in the story makes the very important point that meaning emerges from a story through indirect rather than direct means. Poe's review was originally published in *Graham's Lady's and Gentleman's Magazine* in 1842. In an article first appearing in the *Saturday Review of London* in the summer of 1884, Brander Matthews, another American and a writer of short stories, actually asserted that the short story was a distinct genre, a separate kind, a genus by itself. Poe's insistence that the short prose narrative must be devised with a single effect in mind was the basis for Matthews' differentiation of the short story from other prose forms. The short story, Matthews maintained, has a unity of impression which the sketch or tale does not have and which the novel cannot have. With this distinction of kind as a base, Matthews went on to formulate the now generally accepted conditions of the genre. The short story, he said, deals with a single character, a single event, a single emotion, or the series of emotions called forth by a single situation.

In the study of the short story Matthews' work is of great historical importance. Following the publication of his article (later expanded and published in 1901 as *The Philosophy of the Short Story*), commentators who approached the short story as a distinct genre took their critical approach from him. Although they acknowledged Poe as the first theorizer upon the form, they discussed the short story in the terms that Matthews set forth. Nevertheless, it is clear that Poe's review had profound effect on Matthews as well as on those students of the form who came after him. The short story, it is commonly agreed, has unity of effect with its concomitant firmly knit plot, brevity, and freedom from excrescence. Poe's influence on such a description is obvious. What is missing, however, is Poe's suggestion, not stated overtly but clearly implied, that the short story radiates a whole that is not described but suggested, that story becomes metaphor.

Although Poe does not make the statement overtly, Hawthorne does, and it must be remembered, after all, that Poe's review was in response to a collection of Nathaniel Hawthorne's stories. Hawthorne's avowed purpose was to get beyond the surface level of impressions, beyond ephemeral facts, to something lasting, eternal. His artistic credo is announced in the famous definition of the Romance, which he set down in the Preface to *The House of the Seven Gables* (1851). Unlike the novel, which aims at "minute fidelity, not merely to the possible, but to the probable and ordinary course of man's experience," the Romance, Hawthorne wrote, "has fairly a right to present that truth under circumstances, to a great extent, of the writer's own choosing or creation," so long as it presents "the truth of the human heart." The necessity that Hawthorne felt to get beyond the facts, to penetrate them, so to speak, in an effort to locate "the truth of the human heart" is the philosophic basis for the structure his successful stories take. There is always a surface level, what might be called a manifest content, which embodies symbols that must be understood before the meaning of the stories emerges. Everything in the stories functions to guide the reader to an understanding of the latent content, the realm of truth.

For many years Hawthorne was considered to have had a rather naïve approach to the craft of fiction, if, indeed, he had one at all. In his book *Hawthorne* (1879), Henry James wrote, for example, that Hawthorne "was not a man with a literary theory; he was guiltless of a system, and I am not sure that he had ever heard of realism." Hawthorne was a highly conscious literary artist, however, knowledgeable in the techniques he used to create his fiction; and although his comments, found in prefaces, essays, and sketches, are not related by him specifically to the realm of short fiction, they are applicable not only to his short stories but also to the short stories of many masters of the form who came after him.

The basis of Hawthorne's aesthetic is his attempt to evaluate the art object and to fix its ontological status in the real world. Fiction, thus, is a means of approaching that which is unchanging and real, as distinct from the ever-shifting matters of fact of the ordinary world of experience. The ordinary world is, according to Hawthorne, not the fictional world. What the artist creates is an illusion of the real world, and what the artist needs is a means not only to see beyond the facts himself, but also a means to seduce the reader into accepting the illusion for the real. In "The Custom House" essay prefacing *The Scarlet Letter* (1850), Hawthorne speaks of moonlight, a kind of half-light, which glimmers over matters of fact, half obscuring them, enabling him to see beyond the facts and allowing him to penetrate through them to a deeper reality. In the Preface to *Twice-Told Tales*, Hawthorne identifies the half-light that helps the reader accept the illusion for the real. "The book," he says, "if you would see anything in it, requires to be read in the clear, brown, twilight atmosphere in which it was written; if opened in the sunshine, it is apt to look exceedingly like a volume of blank pages."

As important as any of Hawthorne's essays or prefaces to an understanding of his basic aesthetics is the sketch called "Main Street," which consists of interaction between a showman and a critic. The showman is attempting to set a scene but is constantly interrupted by the critic who sits in the front row. The showman answers: "But, sir, you have not the proper point of view . . . you sit altogether too near to get the best effect. . . . Pray, oblige me by removing to this other bench, and I venture to assure the proper light and shadow will transform the spectacle into quite another thing." The critic objects to unreal settings, pasteboard figures that stand for characters, and the showman's lack of attention to the probability of the action and to historical fact. The showman is concerned to get at a deeper reality than that which is manifested in the material objects of the world. Truth, for the showman and for Hawthorne, is not synonymous with detail. The showman's purpose and Hawthorne's is to signify the truth, rather than to profess it, to question the reality of appearances, and by questioning at once to cast doubt on that which is immediately apparent and to signify the timeless universals beyond the ordinary world of appearances.

A remarkable similarity exists between Hawthorne's literary theory and that of a representative group of modern short-story writers, although, again, it must be noted that many authors who write both long and short prose narratives make no distinction between the two in their general statements about the nature of fiction. In the discussion that follows, only Sherwood

Anderson, Katherine Mansfield, and Eudora Welty are clearly speaking of the short story as a distinct genre, although all of the comments are relevant to the form.

In the famous essay "The Condition of Art," which was published as a Preface to *The Nigger of the "Narcissus"* (1897), Joseph Conrad set down elements of a philosophy of literature which show that he, like Hawthorne, was concerned with lasting truths:

> . . . art itself may be defined as a single-minded attempt to render the highest kind of justice to the visible universe, by bringing to light the truth, manifold and one, underlying its every aspect. It is an attempt to find in its forms, in its colors, in its light, in its shadows, in the aspects of matter and in the facts of life, what of each is fundamental, what is enduring and essential—their one illuminating and convincing quality—the very truth of their existence.

In a letter (printed in *The Indispensable Conrad*, 1951) Conrad reveals his cognizance that events must be treated as only illustrative of "human sensation,—as the outward sign of human feelings." "Imagination should be used," he states, "to create human souls: to disclose human hearts." The similarity of Conrad's aesthetic to Hawthorne's is again manifest in a statement concerning the meaning of an art object. Conrad says: "I wish at first to put before you a general proposition that a work of art is very seldom limited to one exclusive meaning and not necessarily tending to definite conclusion. And this for the reason that the nearer it approaches art, the more it acquires a symbolic character."

D. H. Lawrence makes similar kinds of statements. In *Studies in Classic American Literature* (1923), he writes that "art-speech is the only truth." He continues:

> The curious thing about art-speech is that it prevaricates so terribly, I mean it tells such lies. . . . And out of a pattern of lies art weaves truth. . . . The artist sets out to point a moral and adorn a tale. The tale, however, points the other way, as a rule, two blankly opposing morals, the artist's and the tale's. Never trust the artist, trust the tale.

For Lawrence, truth is expressed through art, but not through what the author does convey. The exterior events of a story are subterfuge; what lies under the exterior events is truth.

In the much quoted Nobel Prize Speech (1950), William Faulkner speaks also to the problems of the "human heart in conflict with itself" and to "the old universal truths lacking which any story is ephemeral and doomed." Perhaps his entire method is summed up in a statement Faulkner made in the interviews at Nagano: "It's best to take the gesture, the shadow of the branch, and let the mind create the tree" (*Faulkner at Nagano*, 1956).

This statement by Faulkner is, of course, remarkably similar to one made by Ernest Hemingway in *Death in the Afternoon* (1932): "The dignity of movement of an ice-berg is due to only one-eighth of it being above water." Hemingway's emphasis in his writing is in presenting *what really happened* as opposed to *what happened*. *What happened* is an account of the facts, whereas *what really happened* is an account of the truth beneath the facts. In this way the artist can tell truth "truer . . . than anything factual can be."

Throughout her writing career, Katherine Mansfield was concerned with understanding principles of composition of the short story and with setting down what, for her, was the essence of the form. "Lord," she says in her *Journal* (1927), "make me crystal clear for the light to shine through." The writer, she believed, must escape from surface impressions, penetrating through them to reveal a deeper truth. Through the great complex of events and surface data the writer seeks new forms "in which to express something more subtle, more complex, 'nearer' the truth." In one of her reviews (published in *Novels and Novelists*, 1930), she makes the point that the facts of reality are binding. "The citizens of Reality are 'tied to town' and very content to be so tied, very thankful to look out of the window on to a good substantive wall, plastered over with useful facts and topped with a generous sprinkle of broken glass bottles." However, truth lies outside these walls, and the writer must not be content with the "timid flight just half-way to somewhere, just so far that Reality and its wall is out of sight, for such a journey distracts, but does not disturb." Yet disturb it must, for great writers have not been mere entertainers. They have been seekers and explorers, aiming to reveal the mystery of life. Thus Mansfield rejected "plotty stories" that skim surfaces, stories in which the presentation of event as event constitutes the whole of the creative act.

Sherwood Anderson also rejects what he calls "poison plot" stories. There are no "plot stories" in life, he says, in his autobiographical *A Story Teller's Story* (1924). The magazines were, however, filled with plot stories: "'The Poison Plot,' I called it in conversation with my friends as the plot notion did seem to me to poison all story-telling." What Anderson wanted "was form, not plot, an altogether more elusive and different thing to come by." Facts are not important, Anderson writes in his *Memoirs* (1942): "Facts elude me; I cannot remember dates. When I deal in facts, at once I begin to lie. . . . Besides men do not exist in fact. They exist in dreams." The artist, Anderson says, must know that "the unreal is more real than the real, that there is no real other than the unreal." The artist who treats only surfaces is untrue to his craft and does violence to the imaginative world.

Eudora Welty set down some of her thinking on the form and craft of the short story in two related articles in the *Atlantic* (February and March, 1949) titled "The Reading and Writing of Short Stories." The purpose of the art she takes to be communication; the end, the creation of beauty, passion, and truth. In discussing such authors as Lawrence, Hemingway, Faulkner, Mansfield, Anderson, and Virginia Woolf, Welty emphasizes the point that the solid outlines of their stories seem to be obscured. The story, she says, "seems bathed in something of its own. It is wrapped in atmosphere. This is what initially obscures its plain, real shape." Of Hemingway, Welty comments that his stories are not in the open. "The arena functions like an ambush. Meaning comes not from the front, but from the side." Such stories, though, are not formless. "Form is what is connected with recognition; it is what makes us know, in a story, what we are looking at." Welty believes that a plot is not in the way if it becomes the "outward manifestation of the very germ of the story." A plot can reveal secrets of "hidden (that is, 'real') life." Plots, Welty says, can be what we see with, but "what's seen is what we're interested in." Welty points out that in "Miss Brill," for example, Mansfield presents a story in which drama is slight. "There is no collision." There is something more significant, however: "this is because, although there is one small situation going on, a very large and complex one is implied—the outside world, in fact."

All of the writers discussed here seem to speak with one voice on the nature of fiction and their craft together with its relation to the outside world. Changes, however, in ways of looking at the world do occur, and when they occur in some dramatic way, fiction seems to change; and the way that authors talk about their fiction changes, too. Such a change has recently taken place. In his *The Death of the Novel and Other Stories* (1969), Ronald Sukenick makes the point:

> Fiction constitutes a way of looking at the world. . . . Realistic fiction presupposed chronological time as the medium of a plotted narrative, an irreducible individual psyche as the subject of its characterization, and, above all, the ultimate, concrete reality of things as the object and rationale of its description. In the world of post-realism, however, all of these absolutes have become absolutely problematic.
>
> The Contemporary writer—the writer who is acutely in touch with the life of which he is a part—is forced to start from scratch: Reality doesn't exist, time doesn't exist, personality doesn't exist.

In line with what they take to be the findings of modern physics, many writers today look around them and find no guarantee as to the authenticity of a "real" world, absolute in its bounds. Fiction, then, can no longer be seen as something more real than the real, since writers no longer know what any "real" is. Susan Sontag comments: "And there aren't, really, any 'facts.' Or if there are facts, they are so primitive they're hardly worth mentioning; they're the things everybody agrees on." If there are no longer any facts, if there is not "reality," then fiction can no longer be seen as "an illusion of the real." Sukenick says: "Nobody is willing to suspend disbelief in that particular way anymore. Including me." Fiction must be recognized as what it is: artifice. Sukenick continues: "Here I am a writer writing on a blank page, and there's really no division between if I write a dream and if I write what happened yesterday—it's all what I'm writing. . . . it's all make-believe."

Writing, however, is a way of knowing; it is a normal epistemological experience; it is a creation of experience; it is, for many contemporary writers, not an imitation of reality but the creation of reality; for it is only through language that meaning exists. This is why so many contemporary writers call attention to their stories as artifice. Their attempt is to authenticate the epistemological act. Other contemporary writers abandon so-called reality altogether and in their fiction move to fantasy, games, and parody or they merge "reality" and illusion in such a way that the everyday world and the dream world cease to be separate realms. Susan Sontag makes the point: "I am most interested in kinds of fiction which are in the very broadest sense 'science fiction' which moves back and forth between imaginary or fantastic worlds and the so-called real world." In this kind of fiction, writers avoid linearity and seek simultaneity often by making use of the apparently disconnected and incongruous. A limiting factor, Kurt Vonnegut, Jr., says, is the reader, who must learn to respond to the effect of simultaneity in the same way that the writer must find different techniques to create it. (The quotations above from Sontag, Sukenick, and Vonnegut are taken from David Bellamy's book of interviews with writers entitled *The New Fiction*, 1975.)

Deriving from such masters as Jorge Luis Borges, Franz Kafka, and Vladimir Nabokov, writers in the "new fiction" mode are too numerous to be discounted and too skillful and influential to be considered part of a passing fad. Even a partial listing makes the point: John Barth, Joyce Carol Oates, William Gass, Donald Barthelme, Ronald Sukenick, Kurt Vonnegut, John Reed, Susan Sontag, Robert Coover, Sidney Michaels, Richard Brautigan, Imamu Baraka, Gabriel García Márquez, Nathalie Sarraute, Alain Robbe-Grillet, Robert Creeley, Thomas Pynchon, and John Hawkes.

Although short-story writers are talking about their work in different ways, a question remains as to whether the work itself is so different that new definition must be sought. One could, for example, argue that although surfaces have changed, short stories remain alike in their essence. One could maintain that symbolic substructures in stories by Poe, Hawthorne, Mansfield, and the like belie surface linearity and provide the same kind of effect of simultaneity that contemporary writers demand. Perhaps, to use the cliché, the problem is that the "new fiction" is so new that scholars and short-story writers cannot see the forest for the trees. Whatever the case, however, given the continuing vitality of the short story and the writers' continuing interest in the form itself, one can be sure that short-story writers will continue to theorize about what it is they write. Perhaps, scholars will come anew to what the writers have already said, using that as a base for either new definition or renewed and vigorous discussion.

Mary Rohrberger